WOMEN
AND THE
ECONOMY

FAMILY, WORK, AND PAY

The Addison-Wesley Series in Economics

Abel/Bernanke
Macroeconomics

Bade/Parkin
Foundations of Economics

Bierman/Fernandez
Game Theory with Economic Applications

Binger/Hoffman
Microeconomics with Calculus

Boyer
Principles of Transportation Economics

Branson
Macroeconomic Theory and Policy

Bruce
Public Finance and the American Economy

Byrns/Stone
Economics

Carlton/Perloff
Modern Industrial Organization

Caves/Frankel/Jones
World Trade and Payments: An Introduction

Chapman
Environmental Economics: Theory, Application, and Policy

Cooter/Ulen
Law and Economics

Downs
An Economic Theory of Democracy

Ehrenberg/Smith
Modern Labor Economics

Ekelund/Tollison
Economics

Fusfeld
The Age of the Economist

Gerber
International Economics

Ghiara
Learning Economics

Gordon
Macroeconomics

Gregory
Essentials of Economics

Gregory/Stuart
Russian and Soviet Economic Performance and Structure

Hartwick/Olewiler
The Economics of Natural Resource Use

Hoffman/Averett
Women and the Economy: Family, Work, and Pay

Hubbard
Money, the Financial System, and the Economy

Hughes/Cain
American Economic History

Husted/Melvin
International Economics

Jehle/Reny
Advanced Microeconomic Theory

Klein
Mathematical Methods for Economics

Krugman/Obstfeld
International Economics

Laidler
The Demand for Money

Leeds/von Allmen
The Economics of Sports

Lipsey/Courant/Ragan
Economics

Melvin
International Money and Finance

Miller
Economics Today

Miller
Understanding Modern Economics

Miller/Benjamin/North
The Economics of Public Issues

Miller/Benjamin
The Economics of Macro Issues

Mills/Hamilton
Urban Economics

Mishkin
The Economics of Money, Banking, and Financial Markets

Parkin
Economics

Perloff
Microeconomics

Phelps
Health Economics

Riddell/Shackelford/Stamos/ Schneider
Economics: A Tool for Critically Understanding Society

Ritter/Silber/Udell
Principles of Money, Banking, and Financial Markets

Rohlf
Introduction to Economic Reasoning

Ruffin/Gregory
Principles of Economics

Sargent
Rational Expectations and Inflation

Scherer
Industry Structure, Strategy, and Public Policy

Schotter
Microeconomics

Stock/Watson
Introduction to Econometrics

Studenmund
Using Econometrics

Tietenberg
Environmental and Natural Resource Economics

Tietenberg
Environmental Economics and Policy

Todaro/Smith
Economic Development

Waldman
Microeconomics

Waldman/Jensen
Industrial Organization: Theory and Practice

Weil
Economic Growth

Williamson
Macroeconomics

WOMEN
AND THE
ECONOMY

FAMILY, WORK, AND PAY

SAUL D. HOFFMAN UNIVERSITY OF DELAWARE
SUSAN L. AVERETT LAFAYETTE COLLEGE

PEARSON
Addison
Wesley

Boston San Francisco New York
London Toronto Sydney Tokyo Singapore Madrid
Mexico City Munich Paris Cape Town Hong Kong Montreal

Editor-in-Chief: Denise Clinton
Editorial Assistant: Catherine Bernstock
Production Supervisor: Meredith Gertz
Production Services: Nesbitt Graphics, Inc.
Design Manager: Regina Hagen Kolenda
Cover Designer: Leslie Haimes
Text Designer: Leslie Haimes
Senior Media Producer: Melissa Honig
Marketing Manager: Deb Meredith
Senior Manufacturing Buyer: Hugh Crawford
Cover Imagery: © 2005 Getty/PhotoDisc. Original art
Women in the Workplace by Robin Jareaux.

Library of Congress Cataloging-in-Publication Data

Hoffman, Saul D., 1949–
      Women and the economy: family, work, and pay / Saul D. Hoffman, Susan L.
Averett.
           p.   cm.
      Includes index.
      ISBN 0-201-74559-3
      1. Women—Economic conditions. 2. Sex role—Economic aspects. 3.
Women—Employment. 4. Sex discrimination against women. I. Averett,
Susan. II. Title

      HQ1381.H64 2004
      306.33'615—dc22   2004006567

1 2 3 4 5 6 7 8 9 10 PHT 08 07 06 05 04

To the memory of our friend and colleague,
Leslie Whittington, and to our families — Susan, Jake,
and Nate; Albert, Rebecca, and Natalie.

Contents

CHAPTER 1 Women and the Economy—Introduction 1

Introduction 1

Economic Analysis 5

Overview of the Book 7

Learning More 8

BOX 1.1 Women and the Nobel Prize in Economics 9

BOX 1.2 Women's Lives Back in the Day . . . But Not So Long Ago 12

Final Words 16

CHAPTER 2 Economics Tools and Economic Thinking 17

Introduction 17

Microeconomics—The Basic Approach 17

Microeconomics—Basic Tools and Concepts 26

Microeconomics—Supply and Demand Analysis 32

Empirical Methods in Economics—An Introduction 36

Regression Analysis 38

BOX 2.1 Using Models in Economic Analysis 24

BOX 2.2 Difference-in-Differences—A Natural Experiment Example 46

Summary 48

Key Terms 49

CHAPTER 3 Marriage and the Family—An Economic Approach . . . 51

Introduction 51

Marriage and Family Structure—An Overview 53

The Economics of Marriage—An Overview 61

Production, Specialization, and the Gains to Marriage 63

Other Economics Approaches to the Benefits of Marriage 75

A Supply and Demand Model of Marriage 80

Changes in Supply and Demand—What Happens to the Marriage Market? 88

BOX 3.1 Divorce, Specialization, and the Gains to Marriage 76

BOX 3.2 Does Marriage Matter? 81

BOX 3.3 Marriage Then and Now . . . One Economist's Personal and
Professional Perspective 94

Summary 97

Key Terms 98

**CHAPTER 4 Marriage and the Family—Economic Issues
            and Applications** **101**

   Introduction 101

   Race and Family Structure—An Economic Analysis 101

   Marriage and the Earnings of Men 117

   Divorce and Its Consequences 123

   BOX 4.1 Did Changes in Divorce Laws in the 1970s Cause More Divorces? ... 132

   Summary 136

   Key Terms 137

CHAPTER 5 The Economics of Fertility **139**

   Introduction 139

   Fertility Facts and Trends 140

   Fertility—The Modern Economic Approach 148

   Making New Choices—The Comparative Statics of the
      Demand for Child Services 157

   Going Further—The Interaction of Quality and Quantity 165

   What Actually Happened—Why Did Family Size Decline? 167

   BOX 5.1 The Easterlin Hypothesis 170

   BOX 5.2 "The Pill": A Tiny Tablet with a Mighty Impact 172

   Summary 171

   Key Terms 174

   APPENDIX: Fertility—Malthusian Style 176

CHAPTER 6 Nonmarital and Teen Fertility **181**

   Introduction 181

   Nonmarital and Teen Childbearing—Facts and Trends 181

   Causes and Explanations 189

   The Consequences of Teen Childbearing 202

   Summary 210

   Key Terms 211

CHAPTER 7 Women at Work **213**

   Introduction 213

   Women's Labor Force Participation 214

   An Economic Model of Women's Labor Force Participation 222

   Explaining the Increase in Women's U.S. Labor Force Participation—
      The Effect of Changes In Wages, Income, and Household Productivity 238

   BOX 7.1 Family and Work Among College-Educated Women—
      A 20th Century History 223

Summary 249

Key Terms 250

APPENDIX: Labor Supply Analysis—An Alternative Approach 251

CHAPTER 8 Earnings, Occupation, and the Labor Market—An Overview **275**

Introduction 275

The Gender Gap in Earning 276

Occupational Segregation 285

How Labor Markets Work—An Overview of Wage Determination 295

Summary 305

Key Terms 307

CHAPTER 9 The Gender Gap in Earnings: Explanations **309**

Introduction 309

Human Capital—The Supply of Skills to the Labor Market 309

Gender Differences in Human Capital 315

Labor Market Discrimination and Women's Earnings 328

Alternative Explanations 340

BOX 9.1 The Return for a College Degree During the Baby Boom 318

BOX 9.2 Discrimination in Professional Sports 337

Summary 346

Key Terms 347

APPENDIX: Present Value Analysis and the Return to Human Capital Investment 349

BOX A9.1 What's It Worth? 356

CHAPTER 10 The Gender Gap in Earnings: Methods and Evidence **361**

Introduction 361

The Statistical Analysis of The Gender Gap 362

The Evidence—Do Women Deserve to Earn Less Than Men? 370

Specialized Studies of Women's Earnings 387

Summary 396

Key Terms 398

CHAPTER 11 Women's Employment and Earnings: Policy **399**

Introduction 399

Government Programs to Combat Discrimination 401

Comparable Worth: An Alternative Approach 422

BOX 11.1 Sandra Day O'Connor—Economic Inefficiency in Practice 403

BOX 11.2 On the Passage of the 1964 Civil Rights Act 406

BOX 11.3 Regression Analysis in the Courtroom 409

BOX 11.4 Discrimination on Wall Street 411

BOX 11.5 Affirmative Action in Action 418

BOX 11.6 Efforts to Diversify the Faculty at Virginia Tech 423

BOX 11.7 The Status of Comparable Worth Legislation in the United States . . 432

BOX 11.8 Do Women Face Discrimination Based Upon Their Marital Status? 433

Summary 432

Key Terms 434

CHAPTER 12   Poverty, Welfare, and Women **437**

Introduction 437

Poverty in the United States 438

Welfare Programs in the United States 455

The Earned Income Tax Credit 474

BOX 12.1 One Woman's Lasting Contribution to the Measurement
of Poverty 439

BOX 12.2 Child Support 452

BOX 12.3 Welfare to Work: California's Success 468

Summary 483

Key Terms 483

APPENDIX: AFDC and Labor Supply—An Indifference
Curve and Budget Constraint Analysis 485

CHAPTER 13   Women, Taxes, and Social Security **491**

Introduction 491

Income Taxes 492

Social Security 514

BOX 13.1 The Potential Tax Consequences of Legalizing
Same Sex Marriage 500

BOX 13.2 Widows Waiting to Wed 522

Summary 528

Key Terms 529

CHAPTER 14   Family Policy **531**

Introduction 531

Labor Force Participation Rates of Women with Children 531

Explaining the Family Gap in Earnings 535

Family Leave Policies 539

Child Care Policy and Issues 559

BOX 14.1 Family and Career: A Balancing Act for the Modern Woman 540

BOX 14.2 The Executive Woman's Maternity Leave 558

BOX 14.3 My Daddy Takes Care of Me 563

BOX 14.4 Summer Child Care for School-Age Children 564

BOX 14.5 The Universal Unified Child Credit 569

BOX 14.6 Employer-Provided Child Care Assistance 571

Summary 583

Key Terms 584

CHAPTER 15   Family Structure and Children's Well-Being 587

Introduction 587

The Family Structure Revolution 587

The Effect of Family Structure on Child Well-Being 593

The Distribution of Resources Within the Family 610

Who Is Responsible for Children? 616

BOX 15.1 Women's Employment and Children's Obesity 611

Summary 618

Key Terms 620

Index **621**

Preface

Welcome to our new textbook on women and the economy. In this text, we take the tools of economics and use them to examine women's lives, from the family to the labor market. We examine not only women's work and pay, the traditional topics of most economics courses on women's issues, but also marriage, divorce, fertility, and family policy, just to name a few. We blend economic theory with discussions of cutting-edge empirical research and contemporary policy issues to offer a different and fascinating perspective on women's lives in the 21st century. Women and economics—what could be more interesting?

Our experience as teachers of courses on women and the economy has taught us that students truly enjoy thinking about these personal issues from an economics perspective, and that they find it rewarding and insightful. We hope the material will make students think like an economist about some of the most personal aspects of their own lives, and the lives of their sisters, mothers, aunts, grandmothers, and great-grandmothers. We hope that occasionally they will be moved to pause and say, "Hey . . . I didn't know that economics could help explain . . . [fill in the blank]. That makes sense . . . it's kind of [insert appropriate adjective]." That's certainly how we feel about many of the ideas in this book. Frankly, it was economic analyses like the ones in this book that made lifetime economists and economics professors out of the authors. When you get that feeling—and we're sure many of you will—you are well on your way to thinking like an economist. We hope to contribute to that.

Distinctive Features

There are a number of features in this book that distinguish it from other textbooks about women and their economic lives. One is its emphasis on issues outside of the core of work and pay that dominate other textbooks. In all, six chapters address family issues—Chapters 3 and 4 on marriage, Chapters 5 and 6 on fertility, Chapter 14 on family policy, and Chapter 15 on family structure and its effects on children. In other texts, family issues are mostly used to explain labor force trends. In this book, these issues receive the direct attention they deserve. Indeed, we begin the book with the analysis of family issues, because it sets the stage for what follows.

Another distinctive feature is our treatment of labor supply issues. Most other textbooks primarily examine the labor-leisure choice with an emphasis on hours of labor supplied to the market. But that approach makes much more sense for men's labor supply than for women's. Our approach is quite different: We emphasize labor force participation within a labor-leisure-household production model. The virtue of this is that it emphasizes the dimension of labor supply that has changed the most—labor force participation—and integrates changes in the household and in the technology of household activities into the analysis. At the same time, this approach is easier for students, since the theoretical and graphical complexity of income and substitution effects can be avoided. An instructor who prefers the traditional labor-leisure model will find it in the appendix, along with the more elaborate labor-leisure-household production model, as developed by Gronau.

Every chapter includes something special. Here are just a few of the highlights:

- A section on women in the economics profession as part of a discussion of when a woman will win the Nobel Prize in Economics (Chapter 1).

- An introduction to natural experiments in economics and, more generally, to the difficulties of making causal inferences (Chapter 2). Examples of this appear throughout the book.

- Becker's supply and demand approach to marriage market equilibrium (Chapter 3). Applications of that approach include a numbers mismatch, the effect of rising wages for women, and a change in attitudes about sexual activity outside marriage.

- A discussion of the economic impact of divorce on women and men that points out a famous and widely-cited error made by a well-known scholar (Chapter 4). Students can appreciate the idea that social scientists are fallible and do sometimes make errors.

- A full and careful discussion of the child quantity-quality distinction and its implications for fertility (Chapter 5). This is sophisticated and fascinating material that is presented in no other textbook of this kind.

- A careful discussion of Claudia Goldin's research on the life-cycle pattern of women's labor force participation (Chapter 7 and Chapter 9) and also her work, with Cordelia Reimers, on sex discrimination in hiring in symphony orchestras (another example of a natural experiment) (Chapter 10).

- Detailed discussion of the Earned Income Tax Credit, in addition to the traditional discussion of welfare (Chapter 12 and 13). We examine how the

Earned Income Tax Credit might affect labor supply and how it might reduce poverty.

- Detailed examples and explanation of the marriage tax and marriage subsidies in the Federal tax system, Social Security, and the Earned Income Tax Credit (Chapters 12 and 13).

- A thorough discussion of the child care market, including a careful accounting of the various child care subsidies and issues related to quality and affordability (Chapter 14).

- Over 30 boxes, ranging from Barbara Bergman's classic description of "occupation housewife" to Belle Sawhill's remembrance of college life when she was a student to changes in child support laws that have been a part of welfare reform to the power of the birth control pill. This material is designed to stimulate student interest and point out interesting or unusual applications of economic theory or new empirical findings.

- The companion Web site, www.aw.com/hoffman-averett, includes features that enhance the book's content.

The book also has important pedagogical features. The theory chapters (Chapters 3–10) have a common structure. Each begins with an introduction that motivates the material and then turns to the basic empirical magnitudes and trends of, for example, marriage or fertility, in the process emphasizing the broad issues or puzzles that any theory would need to explain. For example, the marriage chapter emphasizes the decline in the proportion of adults who are married and the fertility chapter stresses the decline in fertility rates. After presenting the facts, each chapter then introduces the relevant economic theory, which is developed with an eye toward explaining the facts—exactly what theory should do! Finally, comparative static analysis is used to explain the key changes and trends that the first section introduced.

The pedagogical goal is to have students first appreciate the facts to be explained, then see an economic analysis designed to explain the facts, and finally see how well the models perform. By the end of the text, students will not only have seen a great deal of interesting economic analysis, but they will have begun to absorb and appreciate the underlying economic approach and distinctive economic way of thinking.

We have pitched the presentation of economic theory to a level consistent with the preparation of students who have completed a standard one-semester course in microeconomics. A basic understanding of supply and demand, opportunity cost, and the idea of maximization is all that is necessary to understand the analyses we present. Students without that background can use the review material in Chapter 2 to get up to speed. There is one requirement, however, whatever the background—the ability to think abstractly and out-of-the-box.

As a practical matter, the text includes no indifference curves, no isoquants, and no budget lines. These tools appear only in the appendices to Chapter 7 (basic labor supply and labor supply with household production) and Chapter 12 (labor supply in the context of a welfare program). Students with a more advanced background in economics may find those appendices quite helpful. Very sophisticated economic concepts and economic thinking are used in many places, but not highly technical and graph-intensive expositions. We have worked very hard to make explanations simpler, while still doing justice to the analysis. The analyses of fertility and labor force participation are particularly good examples of this approach.

Using this Book

There are many different paths through this text, as well as different potential audiences. Chapters 2, 3, 5, 7, and 8–10 are the core analysis chapters, and we strongly recommend using as many of them as your course schedule allows. They cover economic thinking and methods (Chapter 2), marriage (Chapter 3), fertility (Chapter 5), labor force participation (Chapter 7), and earnings (Chapters 8–10). Chapters 4 and 6 are extensions of the basic theory. Chapter 4 addresses three marriage-related issues—the male marriage premium, the low rate of marriage among black men and women, and divorce. The three sections are entirely free-standing; an instructor could teach any or all of them. Similarly, Chapter 6 is an application of the analysis of fertility, focusing on teen and nonmarital fertility, both causes and consequences. It, too, is free-standing and could be included or not as your course allows. Students do like thinking about those issues, because the issues concern young adults like themselves.

Chapters 11–15 present public policy applications. Chapter 11 explores the various policy options for addressing the gender wage gap. Chapter 12 asks why women are more likely than men to be poor and explores the two main antipoverty programs in the U.S.—TANF and the EITC. Chapter 13 focuses on taxes and Social Security, Chapter 14 on family policy, especially parental leave and child care, and Chapter 15 on the consequences of changes in family structure on children.

Wherever possible, we have linked these policy chapters back to the relevant theory in the core chapters. Each chapter is free-standing. They can be taught in almost any order or integrated into the core chapters. For example, the policy chapters on family policy and family structure could be taught right after the theory chapters on marriage and fertility. Chapter 11, which deals with policies related to closing the gender wage gap, is a natural to follow Chapters 8, 9 and 10, which explore women's earnings. Furthermore, our four-chapter series on women's earnings and policy (Chapter 8–11) could be taught on its own or before the marriage and fertility chapters.

This text can readily be adapted for courses in economics of the family or in basic economic demography. Courses like that might use Chapters 2–7, some of Chapters 8–10, and Chapters 13–15. The material here ought to be accessible to students from disciplines outside economics, for example, advanced undergraduates and graduate students in demography, sociology, public policy, or urban affairs, who want a taste of the economic approach to these issues.

Acknowledgments

When this textbook was first conceived and planned, the authors were Saul Hoffman and Leslie Whittington. Leslie was a very accomplished professor of economics at the Georgetown University Institute of Public Policy. She was an acknowledged expert in tax policy, especially as it affected women and influenced decisions about marriage, cohabitation, and fertility. She even wrote a fascinating paper on the tax implications of legalizing same-sex marriages which we discuss in Chapter 13. Leslie died tragically on September 11, 2001 as a passenger on American Airlines Flight 77, which was hijacked and crashed into the Pentagon. She and her husband, Charles Falkenberg, and their two daughters, Zoe (age 8) and Dana (age 3) were heading to Australia where she was to be a visiting fellow at Australia National University and where she had planned to work on this book.

Leslie made valuable contributions to the planning of the textbook. As a mother and a professor, she lived firsthand many of the topics in this book. A favorite area of inquiry for Leslie was how to balance work and family, something that she and her husband were experts at. In addition to supporting each other's career endeavors, they even rotated who put the kids to bed each night!

The trip to Australia was for Leslie's work; previously, the family had spent two summers in Alaska supporting Charlie's work as a computer programmer.

Susan Averett joined the textbook project in early 2002. Susan was a good friend and co-author of Leslie Whittington. Susan and Leslie met in 1986 when they were students in the Ph.D. program in the Department of Economics at the University of Colorado. Leslie was two years ahead of Susan in the program and her successes in the job market and in her research were a source of inspiration for Susan. Professionally and personally, Susan and Leslie were quite close and they published two papers together that are discussed in this textbook. Both papers explore issues that women in the labor market face.

Leslie's many contributions to economics were remembered in a special session of the 2003 annual meetings of the American Economic Association, in a special issue of *The Review of Economics of the Household,* which will be published in her honor, and also in a memorial lecture given annually in her honor at Georgetown University. Leslie was known for her quick wit, charismatic personality, and loyalty to her friends. She is sorely missed, both personally and professionally.

We are deeply grateful to the many scholars and students who made important contributions to this book. Saul Hoffman first began teaching a course on women and the economy in 1998 at the invitation of the Women's Studies Program at the University of Delaware and with the support of a course development grant from the university's Center for Teaching Effectiveness. Without the invitation and support, the course, let alone this book, would never have gotten off the ground. His students read and reacted to early drafts of many of these chapters. They made many contributions to this text, probably without realizing it. UD students, Emily Burek and Patty Cordes, made special contributions as proofreaders.

Marissa Moore worked as Susan Averett's research assistant and sounding board on many of the chapters in this book. Lafayette College generously provided funding for Marissa Moore's time. Her enthusiasm and painstaking research are greatly appreciated and immensely strengthened this book. Susan Averett would also like to thank the students at Lafayette College who enrolled in this course in the fall and spring of 2003 and the students at Moravian College who took the course in the spring of 2004. Their excitement about the subject matter and willingness to work with drafts of chapters is greatly appreciated.

We received tremendously helpful ideas from the scholars who reviewed early drafts of this manuscript: Sandy Baum, Andrea Beller, Carole Biewener, Colleen Fahy, Hilarie Lieb, Evelyn Lehrer, Manouchehr Mokhtari, David Molina, Kim Marie McGoldrick, Michael Robinson, Elaina Rose, and Elizabeth Dunne Schmitt. We literally reorganized four chapters based on their suggestions. We gratefully acknowledge their contributions. Jean Kimmel of Western Michigan University and John Graham of Rutgers University-Newark taught from our early drafts and shared their experience with us. We are indebted to them for their willingness to try us out and the encouragement and comments they provided. Jean also made extensive comments on the child care section of the book. Laura Argys provided important information on child support issues for which we are grateful.

Victoria Warneck, Economics Editor at Addison-Wesley, initiated this project by following up a throw-away comment by Saul Hoffman about possible textbook plans. Her immediate enthusiasm for the project caused him to think seriously about actually writing the book and for that he is grateful. She also offered moral support at key moments. Victoria left the project for one of her own—her first child, who was born in the summer of 2003. We are also grateful to the many professionals at Addison-Wesley, all of whom do their job wonderfully. Among the individuals who helped in this project were Denise Clinton, Editor-in-Chief, who took over supervision of our book when Victoria departed; Catherine Bernstock, who helped often and effectively with all sorts of logistical matters; Regina Kolenda, art designer; and Meredith Gertz, production supervisor. Maria McColligan of Nesbitt Graphics was the project manager who pulled the manuscript together; she took great care of us and treated us with unusual patience and understanding, even when we were neither patient nor understanding. We thank them all, and hope that we have not overlooked anyone.

We would love to hear from the professors and students who use this book. Please write, call, or e-mail with your reactions and suggestions. We can be reached via e-mail at Averetts@lafayette.edu or hoffmans@lerner.udel.edu. We look forward to hearing from you.

CHAPTER 1

Women and the Economy—Introduction

Introduction

There's no better way to introduce this book than to turn directly to its main subject—women and their economic lives. It's certainly no secret that women's lives have changed enormously in the past several decades, not to mention over the course of the twentieth century. This change is especially obvious in the economic sphere, where the word "economic" is understood broadly. Anyone—female or male—who pays the least bit of attention to what's going on in the world certainly has a sense that things have changed but may not know exactly what has changed and by how much.

Figure 1.1 shows some of the major changes that occurred between 1960 and 2000 in the United States in terms of marriage, fertility, education, work, and pay.

In 1960, women's choices and opportunities concerning fertility, marriage, education, and occupation were very different from what they are today. Women were still underrepresented at colleges and universities. Early marriage was the norm, and fertility was very high. Most births were to married women. The married-couple family was by far the dominant adult family structure. Not surprisingly, a married women's place was in the home, and that's where she spent most of her adult life. Many older women had never worked for pay since their wedding day or shortly thereafter. As a group, women earned considerably less than men, even when they worked full time.

By 2000, things had changed. Men are now underrepresented at colleges and universities. Later marriage is now the norm. Fertility has fallen sharply to about half its level just forty years before. The link between marriage and fertility has been greatly weakened. Births to single women—once a relatively rare event that families hid—have grown and are now one third of all births; consequently the proportion of families with children that are headed by a single mother has also increased. Married

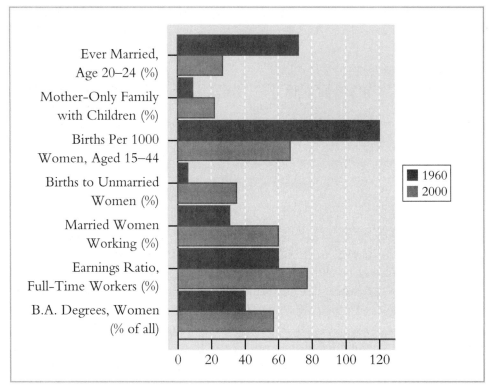

Figure 1.1 Then and Now—Changes in Women's Lives Since 1960

women have joined the workforce in record numbers. Many younger women have worked nearly every year since their wedding day, barely leaving the labor force even to give birth. The gender gap in earnings remains, although it has been considerably diminished.

This book is about changes like these and the many public policy issues that have resulted. Public policy refers to the intersection between economics and politics—in some sense, how economics gets translated into policies. These public policy issues include familiar debates, such as the controversy over the future of Social Security and whether or not there should be paid parental leave in the United States, as well as conflicts that are less familiar, such as the marriage tax and what can and ought to be done about it.

Why Study Women?

Why is there a separate economics course on women in the first place? After all, most universities don't offer an economics course on men. There are actually quite a few good reasons for a special economics course focused on women's issues. First, most courses in economics are male-oriented, even when they don't explicitly say so. For example, some of the topics discussed in this book are parts of standard nongendered courses in economics. Labor supply analysis, the welfare system, and poverty are important parts of courses in labor economics. Federal income taxes and the Social Security system are part of courses in public sector economics. But when a typical labor economics course considers labor supply issues, it almost always examines a model of behavior that fits men's choices well enough yet all but ignores women's choices—often without ever saying that this is so. As is explained more thoroughly in Chapter 7, the standard model of labor supply considers an individual who chooses between market work and leisure, thereby excluding from the analysis the activity that has occupied much of women's time for generations—namely, family responsibilities. By incorporating this extra dimension, the analysis in this book provides a much richer framework. In the process, it enables us to make sense of the incredible increase in women's labor force activity over the course of the last century, something that is impossible to do using the standard (male) labor supply model. Similarly, when courses in public sector economics talk about tax and Social Security issues, they rarely focus on their impact on women. This book does. It shows how the federal income tax system puts women at a disadvantage in terms of their work and earnings and how the Social Security benefit schedule penalizes working wives at the expense of nonworking wives. In much of the economics curriculum, women are invisible. In this book, they are very visible.

Second, women are often much more interesting from an economic standpoint than men are. As Figure 1.1 illustrates, so much has changed over time in so many parts of women's economic lives that a great deal of explanation is necessary. In contrast, men's economic lives haven't changed nearly as much. Women's economic behavior, especially in their participation in the labor force, is still more varied than that among men, so again, additional explanation is vital. Additionally, many timely public policy issues are closely related to women's issues. Many of them can be boiled down to family and work, from family leave policy and the marriage tax to welfare reform and the problems of children in single-parent families. Studying women's economic behavior provides a natural tie-in to many interesting public policy issues. A consistent focus on women helps tie many interesting issues together.

Third, focusing on women is an excellent way to learn some interesting economics. The major topics in this book provide a great opportunity to learn economics thoroughly, precisely because they seem so far afield from traditional economics. At first glance, many of the items shown in Figure 1.1, especially marriage and fertility, are more like the topics traditionally studied in sociology. They sound less rigorous than the usual fare in economics courses. Make no mistake, though—this is a course in economics. The approach taken to examining these topics is utterly different than the approach that would be taken in another discipline. You will soon appreciate that economic analysis has a great deal to contribute to the understanding of these topics. Why have marriage rates fallen? Why did fertility fall? Why are more married women working? Why have earnings for women increased relative to men, but yet remain stubbornly lower? What economic forces were at work in all these changes? What kind of economic impact did these changes have? The process of thinking about these questions will surely provide a broader understanding of just what economics is.

Fourth, the issues discussed in this book are personal in a way that economics often is not. This book isn't "X-rated," but it does include discussions of marriage, children, and, yes, even sex. The major topics of this book—family and work—are central features of virtually every adult's life. They affect most of us more immediately and more directly than do some of the traditional topics of economics—monopoly versus competition, the benefits of international trade, and the economics of pollution to name just a few. Those topics are tremendously important, but they are more abstract and often not part of an individual's daily life in the tangible way that family life is. Thinking analytically—thinking like an economist—about personal issues is fun in a crazy kind of way. In fact, most students learn more about economics when they are personally engaged in the topics.

An Example

To understand the kind of analysis that lies ahead, let's think about one of these topics a bit further: Why did fertility fall? Why do women throughout the world have roughly half as many births as forty to fifty years ago—in some cases resulting in fertility rates so low that, if sustained long enough, the total population would actually fall? The full analysis is the subject of Chapter 5, but we can catch a glimpse of the answer here. The decline in fertility is a particularly good example of economic analysis because it seems like the kind of behavior that is so personal that economics would have little or nothing to contribute.

An economist would point out that children are expensive, and one of the primary components of their cost is the human time devoted to their upbringing. Later on in Chapter 5, we will say, more formally, that children are a *time-intensive household-produced commodity*. Historically, of course, the time spent in child care has been primarily women's time. The cost of time is best measured by the earnings that are given up when a woman spends her time in household production—caring for a family full-time—rather than working in the labor market. This can be thought of as an opportunity cost (i.e., by staying home and raising children, women incur an opportunity cost equal to the wages they give up). Over the course of the twentieth century, women's wages have risen by a factor of about 10 to 15, even after accounting for inflation, thereby making children a "good" whose price has risen particularly sharply. Of course, family incomes have risen, too, because both women's and men's earnings have increased. In response to all of these changes, many families have reduced the number of children they choose to have but increased the amount they spend on each child, primarily in the form of spending on goods rather than time. Fertility fell, but total spending on children has probably increased: Families have substituted more spending per child for more children. The smaller family is probably here to stay.

Economic Analysis

The economics used in this book is *microeconomics*, which focuses on the behavior of individuals and firms, as compared to *macroeconomics*, which focuses on the performance of the economy as a whole. Roughly speaking, supply and demand analysis is microeconomics, while unemployment and inflation are major topics in macroeconomics. Microeconomic analysis is about how individuals and firms and other economic agents make the best choices they can, given the constraints they face, and about the market conditions in which they make those choices. Microeconomics is, according to one of the common definitions of economics, "the science of rational choice."

Prices and incomes are usually the most important parts of the constraints that influence choices. Prices play a particularly central role, so much so that microeconomics is sometimes called *price theory*. Prices are the glue that binds all the separate pieces of the economy together. The price system summarizes and conveys vital information about the value of resources to all market participants, allowing each to make decisions on the basis of common information. The prices themselves are determined in markets, which might be competitive, monopolistic, or oligopolistic. In this book, a particularly important price will be the price of time, measured by the wage rate that an individual can earn. Indeed, the change in the price of time is a key element of almost every chapter in this book. We have just seen that the price of time was a key part of the economic explanation for declining fertility.

This kind of microeconomic analysis, with its emphasis on choices and constraints, is characteristic of the approach of *mainstream* or *neoclassical* economics. Mainstream economics is the economics practiced by most economists and taught in most economics classes, which is why it is called "mainstream."

It is not the only approach to economic analysis, although it is certainly the dominant one by a very substantial margin.[1] It is easy to caricature and exaggerate the rational choice approach. Rationality does not imply that individuals are robots who do nothing but calculate all day. Rather it means that individuals know their available options and the constraints they face reasonably well and then make the best choices they can. That can apply to shopping at the mall, picking a career, or choosing a spouse. In the next chapter, we will discuss the rational choice approach and how economists use it much more thoroughly.

Positive and Normative Economics

Economic analysis attempts to explain the way things are—not the way things should be. In other words, economics focuses on what is termed *positive economics* rather than *normative economics*—explaining with economic theory what is observed in the real world rather than arguing for or against a particular position or policy. Economists, as individuals, certainly have opinions about what is good and bad, but those opinions are not and ought not to be part of economic analysis.

To understand this approach, consider the many trends shown in Figure 1.1. All of them are "facts" (i.e., events/trends that are actually documented with U.S. data). In this book, economic theory is used to explain these trends. Thus, the rise in the labor force participation of women, the gender gap in earnings, the falling marriage rate, the rising rate of out-of-wedlock childbearing, and the high teenage pregnancy rate can all be examined using the tools of economics. The goal is explanation. That is what is meant by "positive economic analysis."

When we discuss these issues, we strive to stay within the realm of positive economics and try not to offer an opinion about whether or not the rise in women's labor force participation, the bias in the Social Security system in favor of nonworking women, or the falling marriage rate is good or bad for society. That would involve making value judgments, something mainstream economic analysis is not well equipped to do. However, as a citizen and voter,

---

[1]One new alternative approach particularly relevant to this course is feminist economics. Like feminist thought in other scholarly disciplines, feminist economics argues that the values and orientation of mainstream economics reflect the values and orientation of its predominant practitioners—males. Julie Nelson, a leading contributor to feminist economics, has written that "masculine-gendered perspectives on subject, model, method, and pedagogy" have dominated work in economics. "Traditionally," she writes, "male activities have taken center stage as subject matter, while models and methods have reflected a . . . masculine pattern" (Nelson, "Feminism and Economics," *Journal of Economic Perspectives,* p.132, 1995). There is now a well-respected scholarly journal, *Feminist Economics,* that publishes research in this area.

you will have to make value judgments about many of the issues we discuss in this book. The analysis in this book should help you to understand the issues better and make you a more informed voter—whichever way you vote.

Overview of the Book

This book is organized into two major parts. Chapters 2–10 present the basic economic analysis that guide our analysis. Chapter 2 introduces the tools and techniques used in economics, including both theoretical and empirical or applied work. Chapters on marriage and fertility follow. Beginning with these chapters is important for two reasons. First, most students are not familiar with the idea that economic analysis can enlighten our understanding of these very personal decisions. Thus, it is fun to begin with what is novel. Second, these decisions are actually central to women's lives and their economic well-being. In fact, as you will see, decisions that women make about marriage and fertility can sometimes determine their economic well-being to a larger extent than do labor force decisions. Each of these chapters begins by setting out the facts and then presenting the economic theory that offers an explanation for the facts. In other words, theoretical models are used to explain the trends in marriage and fertility that have been observed over the past 100 years or so.

The focus then shifts from the family to the labor market. Chapter 7 focuses on a transitional topic, namely a discussion of the time allocation decision: How do women decide whether or not to work for pay in the labor market? The goal there is to explain the incredible increase in women's labor force activity over the past century, a change that has reshaped not only the labor market but family life as well. Finally, Chapters 8–10 focus squarely on women's wages, the price of time that is so important in all the analyses. These chapters examine the basis for the gender gap in earnings and consider competing explanations for women's lower earnings. These explanations focus on differences in human capital (e.g., the education and experience that women and men bring to the labor market) and on labor market discrimination in the form of unequal pay or unequal access to certain jobs based on sex and not on productivity differences. Chapter 10 includes a discussion of how economists measure the extent of wage discrimination and what the many empirical studies of the gender gap in pay tell us about why the gap exists and why it has changed over time.

The last five chapters present applications of the theory to different public policy issues. Public policy is where economics and politics intersect. These chapters focus on understanding when and how the government and/or businesses might intervene in the workings of the market. A government might want to intervene in the market for two general reasons. The first is an equity or fairness argument. If women (or any other group) are treated unfairly in the labor market, corrective government action might be justified. Furthermore, discrimination in the labor market may lead to an inefficient allocation of resources, thereby making society as a whole worse off. That is the second basis for government intervention.

These policy chapters focus on a wide range of issues. They use an economic perspective to examine such issues as the feminization of poverty, the costs and benefits associated with offering family leave, the costs and benefits of implementing comparable worth as a means of reducing sex-based pay differentials, the reform of the welfare system and the development of the Earned Income Tax Credit, why President Bush has been promoting initiatives aimed at increasing marriage rates among low-income women, the effects of family structure on family and child well-being, and many, many more.

Although the primary focus of the book is on women's lives in the United States, an international perspective is often helpful to see whether behaviors and trends are particular to the United States or are broadly experienced. Thus, international statistics and evidence are introduced whenever possible. Also, because the experiences of women are diverse and often differ along broad racial and ethnic lines, information on differences by race and ethnicity is presented wherever the data allow. Following the Census Bureau, we use the term "Black" to refer to African-Americans and "Hispanic" to refer to persons of Spanish or Latin ancestry.

Learning More

It is inevitable that statistics change after a book goes to print. All the facts, figures, and numbers included in this book about marriage, fertility, work, and earnings were the latest available as of the fall of 2003, usually for 2001 and occasionally for 2002. However, by the time this book is published, newer figures will have been released and the numbers will have changed.

More often than not, change over a period of a year or two or three is gradual, so that the figures presented will rarely be truly off the mark. At the same time, more current numbers are always better than slightly older ones. Fortunately, official government web sites make updating the figures easy. In the process, a few other interesting facts will probably surface. A truly amazing amount of very useful statistical information about women's issues is readily available. Here are the web site addresses for the most important data presented in this book:

- Marriage—U.S. Census Bureau at www.census.gov. Annual data on marriage is presented in the P-20 Series, now called "America's Families and Living Arrangements." Much of the data is available as Excel spreadsheets.

- Fertility—Vital Statistics Division of the National Center for Health Statistics at www.cdc.gov/nchs/. Annual information is available in the National Vital Statistics Reports.

- Labor Force Participation—U.S. Bureau of Labor Statistics at www.bls.gov. Annual information is available. Information on this web site is not as easy to locate as it ought to be.

- Earnings—U.S. Census Bureau at www.census.gov. Annual information on earnings and on poverty status is available in the P-60 Series, "Money Income in the United States" and "Poverty in the United States."

- Welfare Use and Welfare Policy—U.S. Department of Health and Human Services at www.acf.dhhs.gov/news/welfare/index.htm.

If you can't find what you are looking for, try the alphabetical index available on most web sites. Sometimes simply locating the entries for "Women," for example, can help you find what you want.

To end this chapter, here is some information on where women stand in the economics profession, on what one U.S. president from not so long ago thought about women in government, and on two views of the essential skills of that totally female occupation—the housewife.

Box 1.1   Women and the Nobel Prize in Economics

Which will come first—a woman elected president of the United States or a woman awarded the Nobel Prize in Economics?

The Nobel Prize in Economics has been awarded annually since 1969. Through 2002, it has been won by fifty one men, including such pioneers of modern economics as Paul Samuelson, Kenneth Arrow, Gunnar Myrdal, and Milton Friedman. Several men have won the award for work related to women's issues, most prominently Gary Becker, who won the award in 1992 and who will figure prominently in this book, and James Heckman, a labor economist and statistician who developed ground-breaking statistical methods that are widely used in analyzing women's work choices. He won the award in 2000. So far, no woman has won the award.

In this respect, economics is rather like the hard sciences, where women have traditionally been underrepresented at the highest ranks of the profession. Are there women who could have won the Nobel Prize in Economics? The most obvious overlooked nonwinner is Joan Robinson, an English economist who was part of John Maynard Keynes' academic circle. She was famous not only for her contributions to macroeconomics and growth theory but also for developing the theory of imperfect competition (now often called monopolistic competition). For many years, she was on the short list of plausible candidates; many economists thought she was a shoo-in in 1975, which had been proclaimed as International Women's Year. Instead, the award that year went to Leonid Kantorovich (USSR) and Tjalling Koopmans (United States), two men who had made important mathematical contributions to the theory of optimal resource allocation. Still, with no offense to Professor Robinson, her nonaward probably wasn't a gross injustice; much of her work was controversial, and many men with arguably stronger credentials haven't won it yet. She died in 1983 and, thus, is no longer eligible.

There probably aren't any other historical candidates who have risen to the same level of achievement as the Nobel Prize winners. Anna Schwartz, who collaborated with Milton Friedman on his most important (Nobel Prize–winning) work in macroeconomics, and Margaret Reid, who made important contributions to the analysis of consumer economics, are two other well-known and influential women economists. But most economists (mostly men, to be sure) would agree that neither one merited a prize.

What about the future? Who are some prospective candidates to be the first woman to receive the Nobel Prize in Economics? Handicapping the future is perilous. There are many well-known women economists, although whether any has made the kind of major contribution to the field that merits the Nobel is hard to say. A hard-nosed economist might well argue that the prospective first woman Nobel Prize winner is still just a bit below the current horizon.[2] Here's a selective list of well-known women economists, perhaps not laureates-to-be, but important and influential nevertheless:

- Laura Tyson was the first woman to head the prestigious Council of Economic Advisors, serving under President Clinton.

- Janet Yellen followed Tyson as head of the Council of Economic Advisors. She has also made important contributions to the analysis of labor market contracts and coauthored an interesting and provocative article on the effect of abortion on nonmarital births, which we discuss in Chapter 6. Her coauthor was her husband, the economist George Akerlof, who won the Nobel Prize in 2001.

- June O'Neill was the first women to head the Congressional Budget Office, an extremely important office that prepares all budget forecasts and analyses of the economic impact of legislation. She has contributed important analyses of the gender gap in wages, which we discuss in Chapter 10.

- Rebecca Blank is a leading scholar in the area of poverty and public policy. She is the author of the book, *It Takes a Nation,* and is currently the Dean of the Gerald R. Ford School of Public Policy at the University of Michigan.

- Isabel Sawhill is an expert on issues involving the family, poverty, the welfare system, and teen childbearing. Currently she is Vice President and Director of Economic Studies at The Brookings Institution, a Washington, D.C., think tank, where she directs the Roundtable on Children and codirects the Welfare Reform and Beyond Initiative. Previously she served as Associate Director at the Office of Management and Budget during the Clinton administration (1993–1994) and helped found the National Campaign to Prevent Teen Pregnancy, an organization that she continues to serve as President.

- Anne Krueger is a well-known scholar of international economics who was one of the first women to become a full professor at a top Economics Department (MIT). She was also the first woman to serve as Chief Economist at the World Bank.

---

[2]The American Economics Association awards the John Bates Clark Prize every two years to an American economist under the age of 40 credited with having made a significant contribution to economic thought and knowledge. The Clark Prize is widely thought to be a good, if imperfect, predictor of a possible future Nobel Prize, although, of course, some economists do make unusually important contributions after age 40. Through 2003, the Clark Award has been awarded to twenty-eight men and no women.

- Claudia Goldin has made path-breaking contributions to our understanding of women's economic history, particularly in her book, *Understanding the Gender Gap*. She also recently became the first woman to become a tenured full professor in the Economics Department at Harvard. You will read a lot about her work in this course.

Women continue to be underrepresented in the economics profession, although change is afoot. In 1972, the first year that statistics on the status of women in the economics profession were collected, only 6% of all faculty in economics departments were women and only 3% of full professors were women. Representation at the top PhD-granting universities was even lower. Only 12% of graduate students were women. In 1998, the percentage of women graduate students in economics is up to about one third, and women are 44% of all assistant professors. They continue to be greatly underrepresented as full professors, although the proportion is now up to about 15%.

A woman winning the Nobel Prize? It's just a matter of time. But if we were betting, we'd bet on a woman as President of the United States first.

Although women haven't won a prize yet, the Nobel Prize has raised one interesting women's issue. In 1995, Robert E. Lucas, a University of Chicago economist, won the award for his contributions to macroeconomics. He had long been on the short list of candidates, so much so that when he and his wife divorced some years earlier, their legal agreement called for him to share the award money with her if the award was received within ten years. Indeed, he won the award, just as the deadline was expiring, and his ex-wife received her share—$500,000. Lucas, incidentally, appeared to be a good sport about it. More broadly, their arrangement raises the question about the not-so-uncommon case of a wife who sacrifices her own career to aid her husband. If they subsequently divorce, is she entitled to some portion of the gains she has made possible?

Box 1.2   Women's Lives Back in the Day . . . But Not So Long Ago

Presidential Views

As you may know, President Richard Nixon was forced from office in August 1974, as a result of the Watergate burglary and subsequent cover-up. He resigned rather than face certain impeachment and conviction by the

Congress. The key source of incriminating evidence against him was his White House tapes that provided the "smoking gun" of his involvement in the cover-up. You may not know, however, that the tapes also included some choice comments that reveal President Nixon's opinion of the suitability of women in important government positions.

In September 1971, Nixon was faced with filling two vacancies in the Supreme Court. According to the tapes, he first considered the possibility of nominating a woman, who would have been the first woman on the Court. In a taped conversation with his Attorney General, Nixon said, "To play an awful long shot, is there a woman yet? That would be a hell of a thing if we could do it." Two days later, he discussed the issue with another aide and revealed a rather different opinion. He said, "I'm not for women in any job. I don't want any of them around. Thank God we don't have any in the cabinet."

A few weeks later, he again considered the possibility, thinking that it might get him an extra one or two percentage points in the upcoming 1972 election. He was apparently willing to nominate a woman to the Supreme Court, despite his deep misgivings. He told the Attorney General: "I don't think a woman should be in any government job whatever. I mean, I really don't. The reason why I do is mainly because they are erratic. And emotional. Men are erratic and emotional, but the point is a woman is more likely to be."

In the end, Nixon did informally consider a woman, but the American Bar Association found her unqualified, and Nixon dropped the idea. In 1981, Sandra Day O'Connor was nominated by President Ronald Reagan, becoming the first woman—after 101 men—to serve on the Supreme Court. She was joined twelve years later by Ruth Bader Ginsberg, nominated by President Bill Clinton in 1993.

A Perfect Wife . . . According to the Textbooks

In the twenty-first century, a clear majority of married women combine family and work responsibilities. But this was much less common in the 1950s. And, indeed, being a wife was a sort of occupation! School courses in home economics often served the function of training women in the domestic arts—sewing, cooking, and so on. They also provided some useful tips on how to be a successful wife. The following excerpts come from a home economics textbook published in 1950 and used in a Lincoln, Nebraska, public school.

- "Have dinner ready: Plan ahead, even the night before, to have a delicious meal . . . on time. This is a way to let him know that you have been thinking about him and about his needs."

- "Prepare the children: take a few minutes to wash the children's hands and faces . . . comb their hair, and, if necessary, change their clothes. They are little treasures and he would like to see them playing the part."

- "Some don'ts: Don't greet him with complaints or problems. Don't complain if he is late for dinner; count this as minor compared with what he might have gone through that day."

- "Make the evening his: Never complain if he does not take you out to dinner or to other places of entertainment. Instead try to understand his world of strain and pressure, his need to be home and relax."

- "The goal: Try to make your home a place of peace and order, where your husband can renew in body and spirit."

Occupation Housewife?

Being a housewife isn't traditionally considered an occupation. Household output isn't included in the National Income accounts and women don't receive credit toward Social Security benefits for their household work (see Chapter 13 for more on women and Social Security). But, as Barbara Bergmann, a well-known and early feminist economist, noted in an article in 1981, being a housewife certainly met the dictionary definition of an occupation as "an activity that serves as one's regular source of livelihood." Indeed, as she pointed out, it was undoubtedly the largest single occupation in the United States at that time!

Upon thinking of a housewife as an occupation, it's natural to describe it and compare it to other occupations. Here is what Prof. Bergmann had to say about it:

> The housewife's occupational duties . . . usually include cooking, dishwashing, housecleaning, laundry work, child care, and a "personal relations" component, which includes sexual relations. . . . The nonsexual component of housewives' duties are broadly the same as the duties of paid domestic servants, although the housewife usually has more discretion than the servant, and a more responsible role with respect to the children and the finances. A housewife whose "job" ends, either at her own discretion or that of her husband, will probably have to enter some other occupation at least for a time. She will be faced with the

fact that the alternative occupation most like the one she has left, and the one for which she has the most fitting recent experience, is one with both low pay and low status. . . . They will be at a disadvantage in the job market. . . . Because of the failure to build up, during their services as housewives, that part of their human capital thought to be most serviceable on non-domestic jobs.

. . . Like the airline stewardess, part of the housewife's job is being attractive. Unlike the stewardess, however, the housewife's duties clearly include cohabitation. . . . Of course, sexual cohabitation in this context forms a perhaps vital part of the intimacy of the marriage relationship, with its presumption of caring, consideration, and long-run commitment. It is usually, at the outset at least, considered a highly valued fringe benefit rather than an onerous duty. However, the sex component of the housewife's duties, and the children who may appear as a result of it, make it difficult to go from one "job" to another within the occupation.

The housewife's attractiveness to her husband can be thought of as a component of the human capital needed for her job, and she may be in the position of seeing this part of her portfolio of assets wane in value either gradually or suddenly. Her husband's attractiveness to her may also suddenly or gradually diminish, reducing the value of the intimacy fringe benefit. These possibilities obviously make for high risk both with respect to "working conditions" and tenure.

Another component of a housewife's human capital which contributes to the value of her work is her identity as the mother of the husband's children, and thus as the person usually assumed to be most fitted to give them attentive and loving care. As the number of children born to marriages has . . . diminished and as the number of years in which a married couple has preschool children in the home has diminished, this component of a wife's human capital disappears faster, leaving her more open to the threat of displacement from her "job."

. . . The decline in the value of a wife's services in the home occurs at a time when her husband's earnings and status are usually growing. The discrepancy in economic position and in the social opportunities of a housewife and the man to whom she is married typically grows as they go through their forties.

From Barbara Bergmann, "The Economic Risks of Being a Housewife," *American Economic Review,* Vol. 71, No. 2, May 1981, pp. 81–85. Copyright © 1981 by the American Economic Association.

Final Words

Although this book is about women, many, if not most, of the topics considered also involve men. Certainly that is true for marriage and for fertility. There is a groom for every bride. A birth still usually requires both a man and a woman, and decisions by married couples about the number of children they will have are usually made together. Both men and women make decisions about working in the labor market. Even if women are from Venus and men are from Mars, their economic lives intersect regularly and in ways that are often of great importance to both of them. So even though the subject of this book is women, it definitely ought to be of interest to both women and men.

Finally, the economics in this book is not the economics that your mother or father may have learned when they were in school. Many of the analyses presented here are on the cutting edge of economics. Topics like the economics of marriage, fertility, and household production, are relative newcomers to economics. Analyses of why marriage rates have fallen so much for young Black men and women, why married men earn more than single men but not as much more as in the past, how changes in women's wages might affect how well they are treated by their husbands, and how the legalization of abortion may have affected the incidence of shotgun marriages are also current issues that you will learn about in this book. These topics pushed and stretched economic analysis into previously uncharted territory. Not every analysis is fully formed and widely accepted, and you may well find a few quarrels to pick. That's as it should be. You don't have to agree with everything; we don't agree with absolutely everything either, although we think all of it is interesting and provocative, if nothing else. We urge you to think critically and carefully in this course and elsewhere.

CHAPTER 2

Economics Tools and Economic Thinking

Introduction

The goal in this chapter is to explore the distinctive way of thinking that characterizes the economic approach to a problem. Microeconomics can sometimes be difficult for students to understand. Because it has many graphs and also numerous concepts and definitions, it is certainly possible to lose sight of the forest with all those trees in the way. But, as all microeconomists understand, the core of microeconomics is relatively simple; even better, the core is relatively constant from problem to problem and chapter to chapter. Microeconomics, much more so than macroeconomics, has a distinctive way of thinking. If you can grasp the shape of the forest, you will have much less trouble finding your way through the trees.

We begin by focusing on the core ideas in microeconomics—choice, constraints, maximization, and comparative statics. Then we define some specific terms and relationships and review supply and demand analysis. The last section is an introduction to empirical methods widely used in economics. It is important to understand these methods in order to appreciate and evaluate the extensive body of empirical research on women's economic issues.

Microeconomics—The Basic Approach

Choices

Microeconomics is about choosing. One popular definition of microeconomics is that it is the "science of choice." Individuals or firms or workers or whoever else may be the focus of a particular problem make choices about something. For the most part, things don't just happen. Somebody chooses to make them happen.

These choices have some common, though not inevitable and unchangeable, characteristics. First, the choices are usually purposeful and goal-directed. Often, economists assume that the chooser is trying to maximize the value of something. Second, the chooser is assumed to be reasonably well informed so that the actions taken are consistent with the desired goals. And third, the choice is usually made in a context that involves some limits or constraints. Without limits, there isn't much difficulty in choosing—we can have everything!

Now, thinking of objections to this choice-based approach is easy enough. First, sometimes the constraints are so severe that there really isn't much of a choice—certainly no good choices. Sociologists are fond of quoting James Duesenberry, a famous economist, who once wrote that "Economics is all about how people make choices; sociology is all about how they don't really have any choices to make." In a case of extreme poverty, choosing between food and clothing and shelter and health care, knowing that choosing one means sacrificing the others, is clearly not an attractive proposition. It may be tempting to think that there is no choice here, but it's much better social science to think of someone choosing even in that setting. Understand that the decision to analyze choices doesn't presume that the choices are themselves particularly attractive. Second, sometimes individuals aren't sufficiently informed; this scenario is certainly the case in some of the issues we'll examine. At what developmental stage do individuals clearly see the implications of their actions so that we might regard them as acting purposefully? When we talk about teen childbearing and try to apply a choice model, the issue of purposefulness is genuine. Let's agree to act like economists and approach problems via this choice apparatus but be sensitive to the possibility that it may not fit every possible situation.

The shorthand economics jargon for the choice situation described in the preceding paragraph—maximization, reasonably complete information, and a constraint—is **constrained maximization.** The concept of constrained maximization lies at the heart of microeconomic analysis. Let's write this idea out in a very general way.

Many, if not most, microeconomics problems have the following general structure:

> Some economic actor (a person or a firm, for example) chooses the
> value of some economic variable to maximize something that depends

on that variable, subject to a constraint that involves the variable being chosen and usually some other variables as well.

To put this in a yet more compact way, let X stand for the variable to be chosen, and let V stand for whatever it is that will be maximized. For example, X could be the amount of output a firm produces and V could be its profits. The link between V and X can be written as $V(X)$, which is read "V of X" and which means that for every value of X there is a corresponding value of V. Mathematically speaking, we say that V is a function of X or that V depends on X. Finally, let Z stand for all the other variables in the constraint. Then the constrained maximization problem can be written this way:

Choose X to maximize $V(X)$ subject to a constraint involving X and Z   (1)

Two more pieces of jargon will be useful. In a problem like this one, the variable X is called the **endogenous variable,** which means it is chosen inside the model ("endo" = inside). The variables that are "givens" and are not chosen, like Z, are the **exogenous variables,** which means they are determined outside the model ("exo" = outside). The exogenous variables are particularly important, as you will see shortly. Simply keeping track of what's endogenous and what's exogenous is very valuable.

That's it. Most microeconomics problems involve not much more than a clever adaption of equation (1) to fit the basic characteristics of a particular problem. We'll look at an example after we examine a few more pieces of the economics approach.

Solutions

Choice problems like those defined by equation (1) usually have a unique solution. That is, there is some value of X that "solves the problem" and yields the maximum value of V given the relationship between V and X and the particulars of the constraint. Call that best choice X^*. We will use the asterisk (*) often, almost always to indicate the solution to a maximization problem.

The solution to a choice problem can be usefully represented in two related ways. First, it is almost always possible to write out a rule or a condition that must hold at the value of X that solves the problem. Typically, this rule involves finding the value of X that causes two different expressions to be equal to one another. A firm choosing its output where marginal revenue equals marginal cost is an example of a rule of this kind. These rules are usually called **marginal conditions** because they virtually always involve focusing on the value of the last or "marginal" unit of X. The marginal conditions are particularly useful for understanding the economic logic behind a solution to a choice problem.

The solution to the problem can also be written in terms of X^* and the exogenous variables in the problem. Generally, it looks something like this:

$$X^* = F(Z) \tag{2}$$

which means that the best choice of X depends on (is a function of) all the exogenous variables in the problem (Z). In equation (2), F stands for an unspecified function that links the variables in Z to X^*. This solution is derived from the marginal condition; the X^* in equation (2) is exactly the value of X that solves the problem, given the particular values of the variables in Z. The relationship between the best choice and the exogenous variables is emphasized in this form.

Expressing the solution in the form of equation (2) can often be very useful. Sometimes it is too difficult (at least for most students) to find and understand the marginal conditions of a problem. In that case, however, we can often write the solution as in equation (2) if we can express the problem as a constrained maximization problem using equation (1) and correctly identify the endogenous and exogenous variables.

Changing Choices—Comparative Static Analysis

Finally, economists often are interested in how the best choice of X will change when the exogenous variables change. This is called **comparative static analysis.** The name is not as helpful as might be hoped: "Comparative" refers to a comparison of the before-and-after choices, and "static" means that we are looking at the choices themselves rather than the dynamic process of getting from "before" to "after." A good theory will usually be able to offer a specific prediction about how X^* will change when Z changes.

To analyze this, we use the solution in the form of equation (2), in which X^* is a function of the exogenous variables in Z. (The equation is useful already!) The theory might, for example, hypothesize that a positive relationship exists between X^* and one of the variables in Z. Let's call that variable Z_1. Then the predicted relationship can be written as

$$\Delta X^*/\Delta Z_1 > 0 \tag{3}$$

In equation (3), Δ, the Greek letter delta, stands for "change in." The positive relationship means that X^* increases when Z_1 increases (ΔX^* and ΔZ_1 are both positive) and that X^* decreases when Z_1 decreases (ΔX^* and ΔZ_1 are both negative).

The theory might also suggest a negative relationship between X^* and Z_2, which would be written like this:

$$\Delta X^*/\Delta Z_2 < 0 \qquad (4)$$

The negative relationship means that X^* increases when Z_2 decreases (ΔX^* is positive, and ΔZ_2 is negative) and that X^* decreases when Z_2 increases (ΔX^* is negative and ΔZ_2 is positive).

The comparative static predictions of a theory are absolutely its most important feature. This is true for two reasons. First, it is often exactly what we want to know. For example, we might want to know how an increase in the earnings of women in the twentieth century has affected choices about work, marriage, and family size. Second, it is the way we can tell whether a theory is useful and valid. If a theory predicts a positive relationship between X^* and Z_1, but testing establishes that the relationship is negative or zero, then the theory is rejected. If testing indicates that the relationship is positive, as the theory hypothesized, then the theory is tentatively accepted, pending further testing and possible future rejection. When a theory has been confirmed often enough, it often gains the status of a "law," like the Law of Demand.

The **Law of Demand** is, in fact, a perfect example of precisely how this whole choice apparatus works. In consumer demand analysis, economists attempt to explain consumer demand choices; for example, they would explain the demand for some goods X and Y. (Economists often use just two goods in a case like this because it substantially simplifies the problem, without distorting it.) Economists assume that individuals choose the amount of the goods they consume to maximize something called **utility,** which means pleasure or satisfaction. The amount of utility an individual receives depends on the amount of goods he/she consumes; we can write this relationship as $U(X, Y)$, which is referred to as a **utility function.** We discuss the idea of a utility function more fully a little later, but for the moment it should be clear enough that it expresses the idea that the amounts of X and Y affect the value of U.

In choosing the amounts of goods X and Y, individuals are constrained by their income (I) and the prices of the goods (P_x, P_y). This constraint, which is referred to as the **budget constraint,** limits the amounts of the goods they can afford in a pretty obvious way. They can't, for example, buy goods that cost more than their income. (We're abstracting here from credit cards.)

So the constrained maximization consumer demand problem could be written formally this way: *An individual chooses the amounts of goods X and Y to maximize U(X, Y) subject to a budget constraint that involves X, Y, P_x, P_y, and I.*

A unique best solution to this consumer demand problem can be written in terms of a marginal condition, in this case, in terms of something called **marginal utility** and prices or, in a more sophisticated version, the **marginal rate of substitution** and relative prices. The details don't matter; it's enough to know that there is *some* best answer. The solution indicates the best amounts of goods X and Y to consume to maximize utility.

Let's focus on the demand for good X. In this choice problem, X is the endogenous variable and prices, income, and preferences are the exogenous variables. The relationship between the endogenous variable and the exogenous variables, written in the form of equation (2), is

$$X^* = D(P_x, P_y, I, \text{Preferences}) \tag{5}$$

This is the individual's demand function, which is why D is used to represent the function. The demand function indicates that the utility-maximizing choice of the amount of X depends on its own price, the price of the other good, the individual's income, and preferences.

Finally, the most important comparative static relationship is $\Delta X^*/\Delta P_x$, which is the response of X^* to a change in its own price, holding constant I, P_y, and preferences. The model predicts that $\Delta X^*/\Delta P_x < 0$, which is simply the famous Law of Demand.[1] When the price goes up, the amount demanded falls (and vice versa), when the goal is to maximize utility. Other important comparative static results examine the effect of changes in other prices or income on the demand for X.

When economists are doing comparative static analysis, they invariably emphasize changes in prices and/or incomes rather than changes in preferences. Economists do not believe that preferences never change. Clearly preferences do change—just think about clothing or hairstyles or music, for example. Then why do economists tend to downplay changes in preferences? For one thing, preferences tend to change slowly, so it's often reasonable to think of

---

[1]More precisely, the model predicts that the Law of Demand holds for *normal goods*, which are goods that an individual buys more of as his/her income increases. For *inferior goods*—goods that an individual buys less of at a higher income—the Law of Demand almost always holds, but that is not a direct prediction of the theory.

preferences being constant as prices or incomes change. More importantly, though, resorting to changes in preferences as an explanation for changing behavior is a bit too easy and almost impossible to verify. It's probably prudent to think of preferences as a last explanation, after examining and exhausting observable changes in prices and/or incomes.

In a nutshell, microeconomics is simply economic actors choosing endogenous variables to maximize something. That choice depends on some exogenous variables that are part of the constraint. The details depend on the particular problem being analyzed. The best solution can be described by both a marginal condition and the corresponding function that relates the best choice to the exogenous variables. The theory predicts how that best choice will change when the exogenous variables change, and those predictions are the comparative static results. If the predictions are wrong, the theory goes into the trash can or at least back to the blackboard or the laboratory for re-working. This is the basic workings of microeconomics.

Theories and Models in Economics

Like most social and natural sciences, economic analysis relies on theories to explain things observed in the real world. To make a theory easy enough to understand, economists virtually always construct a *model* of the real-world situation they want to analyze. In doing that, they invariably simplify the problem to be studied by making assumptions that eliminate some real-world factors. A good model in economics or any other subject successfully manages the delicate task of retaining the essence of a problem while simultaneously stripping away all the complicating factors that make the underlying relationships difficult to see.[2] For example, a model of the labor market might assume the absence of government laws (e.g., the minimum wage) and market institutions (e.g., labor unions). It might also assume that all workers are identically productive. The goal is to see how the labor market might work in such

---

[2]You may have heard the joke about the physicist, the architect, and the economist marooned on a desert island with a can of beans. Each proposes a plan to open the can. The physicist suggests placing the can on the fire. Eventually the heating of the can will create so much pressure that the can will explode and the beans can be retrieved. The architect thinks that this will be a rather messy solution to the problem and suggests building a small enclosure around the fire. Then, when the can explodes, the beans will splatter on the walls of the enclosure, from which they can then be scraped. The economist has a better solution: "Assume that we have a can opener . . ." Like most jokes, this one has a kernel of truth in it. Some models do assume so much that they determine the result, rather like the magician putting a rabbit in a hat before proudly pulling it out later. These are bad models.

Box 2.1   Using Models in Economic Analysis

The economic analysis of labor market discrimination nicely illustrates the way in which economists use models. Economists typically begin their analysis of discrimination where sociologists, anthropologists, and psychologists stop theirs. Researchers in these fields might investigate such topics as how and why feelings of discrimination develop, how those feelings persist, strengthen, or erode, the forms that discrimination takes, the functions it serves, and its psychological and sociological effects on all parties. They do not, however, usually inquire into how these feelings are translated into the economic realm: how they influence economic behavior and economic outcomes. Those are precisely the topics emphasized by economists in analyzing discrimination, because those are the areas where economic theory can be most usefully applied.

Economists tend to ignore the development of discriminatory attitudes not because that topic is unimportant, but because economic theory has relatively little to contribute. Instead, as you will see in Chapter 9, the economic approach to discrimination is to pose the problem this way. Suppose that feelings of discrimination take the specific form that employers prefer one type of worker over another, even if the workers were equally skilled and if their wages were the same. How will this affect labor market equilibrium? Note the important assumption that workers are equally skilled. This is not intended to be realistic. Economists surely know that not all workers are equally skilled. Rather, the purpose of that assumption is to isolate discrimination as the sole source of any wage differences.

The analysis of discrimination also shows the potential value of economic theory. Consider the following two assertions, both of which have their advocates: (1) "Labor market discrimination is a natural outgrowth of the actions of profit-maximizing firms operating in an unregulated, competitive economy;" (2) "Competitive markets tend to eliminate the effects of discrimination. Discrimination can thrive only when competition is weak." Clearly, only one of the two statements can be correct. The difference is not just academic. The design of effective government policy to eliminate discrimination in the labor market depends critically on which view is correct. Should government restrict competitive behavior, as the first view suggests, or should it encourage competition and seek to strengthen it,

following the second? How can we determine which of the two statements is correct?

That is exactly where economic theory comes in. We can save the details for later (Chapter 9), but the basic idea is this. First, economists do not have to start from scratch in analyzing discrimination. There already exists a well-developed model—the competitive model—which has proven useful for analyzing the behavior of profit-maximizing competitive firms in the absence of discrimination. The analytical task, then, is to modify that model by incorporating discrimination and then seeing what difference it makes in the outcomes predicted by the model. How do the results with and without discrimination differ? For example, are discriminating firms more or less profitable than firms that do not practice discrimination? If the model suggested that discriminating firms were more profitable, this would lend support to the first assertion. But suppose that discrimination turned out to require a sacrificing of profits. That would certainly suggest that in competitive markets, where the profit motive is strong, discrimination might be weak. A good theoretical model of how discrimination affects the behavior of competitive firms should help us to find the answer.

a setting. What determines labor demand? What influences labor supply? What will the wage rate be? Will there be unemployment? When these questions are answered, an economist might then incorporate minimum wage regulations, labor unions, and productivity differences into the model. This procedure makes seeing the basic economic forces that operate in the labor market possible. It also helps identify exactly how minimum wage laws or labor unions or individual productivity affect the outcome. Another very good example of using models to analyze a very complicated problem is the analysis of the economic impact of labor market discrimination. See Box 2.1.

The purpose of a model is to explain behavior and outcomes in the real world. Thus, after a model is constructed, it is tested against real-world data to see how well it predicts. Those models that don't predict or explain real-world behavior reasonably well are quickly discarded. A model that repeatedly performs well is accepted. Fortunately, in the area of women's economic behavior, a very substantial amount of data is collected by both the government and private entities. As a result, economists working in this area have ample access to data, which allows them to test their theories. Be aware, however, that the data are seldom perfect, so it is always prudent to be cautious in drawing conclusions. There is a great deal of interesting thinking in economics research right now about how best to carry out economic analysis in the face of imperfect data. Some of the new methods are discussed later in this chapter.

Microeconomics—Basic Tools and Concepts

Not only is there a basic economic approach to many problems, but there are also basic relationships and tools that are common across many analyses. If you learn them, you can get a lot of mileage out of them. In this section, we introduce some basic tools and concepts that we will use repeatedly.

Functions

We actually introduced the idea of a function in the previous section where we talked first about the function $V(X)$ and then later the functions $X^* = F(Z)$, $U(X, Y)$, and $X^* = D(P_x, P_y, I, \text{Preferences})$. But let's spend a few minutes to understand the ideas and then to examine two particular functions that appear throughout this book.

Functions are very convenient shorthand ways to show what depends on what. In the function $X^* = F(Z)$, the variable on the left-hand side of the equality (X^*) is postulated to depend on the variables in the parentheses on the right-hand side (Z). If we knew exactly how the variables were related, we might write that explicitly. For example, perhaps $X^* = 3Z_1 + 2.5Z_2$ or $X^* = Z_1 \times Z_2$. But usually, we don't know the exact relationship; instead, we know only that the variables are related and sometimes also whether the expected effect is positive or negative. When we don't know the exact relationship, we often use a letter like F (for "function") to stand for some unspecified relationship between X^* and Z. The letter F doesn't mean anything in particular. In fact, sometimes, it's convenient to substitute another letter, such as D for the demand function or S for the supply function.

In the functions $V(X)$ and $U(X, Y)$, there is no equals sign, but the general idea is the same. The value of V depends on X and the value of U depends on X and Y. We could have written $V = V(X)$ or $U = U(X, Y)$, but that is usually not done in some circumstances (e.g., a maximization problem). In the $V = V(X)$ form, the V on the left-hand side is the *value* of the function and the V on the right-hand side is the *function* itself.

So the general rule with functional relationships is that whatever is in parentheses affects the other variable, whether that variable is on the other side of the equation or is just a function where the other side of the equation is implicit. The variables inside the parentheses are called the **arguments of the function.** In many economics problems, identifying the arguments of the function is an important first step in the analysis.

Two Special Functions

We will regularly use two special functions—a **utility function** and a **household production function.**

In microeconomics, whenever an individual is doing something that provides some direct benefit to herself or himself, we use a utility function to analyze the behavior. Economists assume that individuals do whatever they do to make themselves as happy, as satisfied, as well-off as possible, given their own subjective evaluation of what they like. This doesn't imply that they are totally selfish; an individual might well gain happiness from the happiness of others (e.g., family members). As a measure of well-being, economists use the word "utility," a concept that comes from the nineteenth century economists and means happiness, satisfaction, pleasure, and the like.

A utility function is a way of specifying the things that provide utility, that is, the things that individuals like. These things, which are called the arguments of the utility function, will vary, depending on the particular problem being analyzed. The simplest, most general way to write a utility function is

$$U = U(X, Y) \tag{6}$$

In equation (6), the U on the left-hand side stands for the amount of utility, X and Y are consumption goods, and $U(X, Y)$ is the utility function itself. A utility function gives the utility associated with a particular amount of X and Y. In general, there is a positive relationship between the amount of X or Y and the amount of utility. We discuss that in more detail later.

Utility isn't directly measurable. It doesn't really make any sense to say that a particular meal gave you 11 utility units (sometimes called **utils**) or 27 utility units or any other number. The numbers themselves don't mean anything, but that doesn't matter. The only numerical comparison that matters in utility analysis is that more utility is better than less, so a bigger number is better than a smaller number. This is an *ordinal comparison.* We will sometimes use numbers to represent utility, but they are just illustrative. The only important feature of one particular number is whether it is bigger or smaller or equal to another number. If individuals want to maximize their utility, they will always prefer more utility to less.

Utility functions are a central element in the economic theory of choice. Suppose an individual is comparing two mutually exclusive situations that we will call A and B. Either an individual will do A or B. A and B could be literally anything—going to graduate school versus not going, getting married versus not getting married, and so on. Let's refer to the utility of these situations as $U(A)$ and $U(B)$; $U(A)$ is the utility the individual would receive if she makes choice A and $U(B)$ is the corresponding utility if she makes choice B. If $U(A) > U(B)$, we expect that she will choose A instead of B; however, if $U(B) > U(A)$, we expect that she will choose B. This simple bit of logic is referred to as a **rational choice model.** It will turn out to be very important reasoning later on. In fact, sometimes we might even work backwards. If an individual is observed to choose A when B was available, then it must be true that $U(A) > U(B)$. This idea is referred to as **revealed preference.** The name says it all—the preferences are revealed by the choice.

A *production function* is used to describe the production process. Originally, it was applied to firms to summarize the relationship between the amount of inputs used and the amount of output produced. In its most general form, it can be written as Amount of Output = F(Amount of Inputs) or $Q = F(L, K)$, where Q is the amount of output and L and K stand for labor and capital. In the 1960s, Gary Becker proposed a new approach to consumer theory that used production functions to analyze consumer behavior.[3] In his new approach, consumers were producers of what he called "household commodities." These household commodities, and not market goods and services, were the ultimate source of utility. For example, the food in my refrigerator and my kitchen cabinets doesn't provide me utility until I use it, along with some of my own time, to first produce and then consume a meal. My utility comes from the household-produced good—a meal—rather than the raw materials—the food itself.

The point is much broader and not confined to food preparation. In Becker's view, households produced a wide range of very basic goods for themselves—nutrition, health, entertainment, even children—by combining market goods with their own time. The market goods that were previously considered the

---

[3]These ideas were originally presented in Becker, "A Theory of the Allocation of Time," *Economic Journal,* Vol. 75, 1965. A somewhat more accessible, though still difficult, version is Michael and Becker, "On the New Theory of Consumer Behavior," *Swedish Journal of Economics,* Vol. 75, #4, 1973.

direct sources of utility are now viewed instead as inputs into the production process. He called the production functions in this process "household production functions."

A household production function is exactly the same idea as a conventional production function. It shows the maximum amount of output associated with any particular set of inputs. The only difference is that a household production function refers to the household and a conventional production function to a firm. It will often be useful to write out a household production function in the following way:

$$G = G(T, Z) \tag{7}$$

In equation (7), the G on the left-hand side stands for the amount of household goods produced, T stands for the amount of time, Z stands for the amount of all other inputs, and the G on the right-hand side stands for the production function that links the amounts of T and Z to the amount of G produced. Just as in the traditional production function, there is a positive relationship between the amounts of T and Z used and the amount of G produced.

This idea of household production will be an important concept throughout much of the book. Much of women's lives in the twentieth century has taken place in the household, rather than in the market, and household production is the way to describe what they were and are doing. We use the idea of household-produced goods to describe and explain marriage in Chapter 3, to explain fertility in Chapter 5, and then to analyze labor force participation in Chapter 7.

Totals and Marginals

When economists work with functions, they are usually interested both in the total amount of utility or total amount of output and in the change in the total amount when one of the arguments of the function is increased. This latter idea involves looking at what are called **marginal changes.** For example, if we were working with the utility function, $U = U(X, Y)$, we would want to know about the change in utility if X or Y increased by a little bit. If we were analyzing household production with the household production function, $G = G(T, Z)$, we might want to know about the change in output if T or Z increased by a little bit. We might write these changes as

$$\Delta U/\Delta X \text{ or } \Delta G/\Delta T \tag{8}$$

where, again, Δ stands for "change in."

It turns out that totals and marginals are related in a very specific way that will be useful and important to us. In Figure 2.1(A) and (B), a particular possible relationship exists between U and X. Figure 2.1(A) describes the total function; that is, it gives the total value of U for every value of X. In the case drawn in Figure 2.1(A), the total function is a straight line with a constant slope. That slope, like all slopes, is just the change in the vertical-axis variable divided by the change in the horizontal-axis variable (the rise over the run). So the slope equals $\Delta U/\Delta X$, which is the marginal change. This important idea bears repeating: *For any total function, the associated marginal function equals the slope of the total curve at the particular point at which the change is occurring.* Since the slope in Figure 2.1(A) is constant, the marginal change is constant. It is just a horizontal line, whose height is equal to the slope of the total function, as shown in Figure 2.1(B).

The particular relationship shown in Figure 2.1(A) and (B) with a linear total curve and a horizontal marginal curve is actually not very common in economic analysis. It implies, not very realistically, that if more X is added, the same additional amount of additional U is received. It's more likely that the change in U will diminish as the amount of X increases. Think of eating slices of pizza. The first slice tastes best and provides the most utility. Each successive piece is enjoyable, but it is a bit less so than the preceding ones. Eventually, the marginal value is so low that eating another slice of pizza would not be enjoyable. If the pizza were free, we would eat it until its marginal utility was zero. The same idea holds for most goods that are consumed—the marginal value usually declines as you have more and more of them.

This kind of relationship is shown in Figure 2.1(C) and (D). In Figure 2.1(C), the shape of the total function is curved. It gets flatter and flatter as X increases, which means that U rises more and more slowly as X increases. This is exactly equivalent to saying that the change in U gets smaller and smaller as X increases. But that means that the marginal curve in Figure 2.1(D) falls steadily. Each unit of X adds less and less to U. The height of the curve at each value of X in Figure 2.1(D) is exactly equal to the slope of the total curve at that same value of X in Figure 2.1(C). When the total curve is at its maximum in Figure 2.1(C), the marginal curve equals zero. The vertical dotted line in Figure 2.1(C) and (D) shows this relationship.

Do not confuse a fall in the marginal curve with a fall in the total curve. When the marginal curve is positive, even if it is falling, the total curve is still rising. If the total curve were falling, the marginal curve would actually be negative.

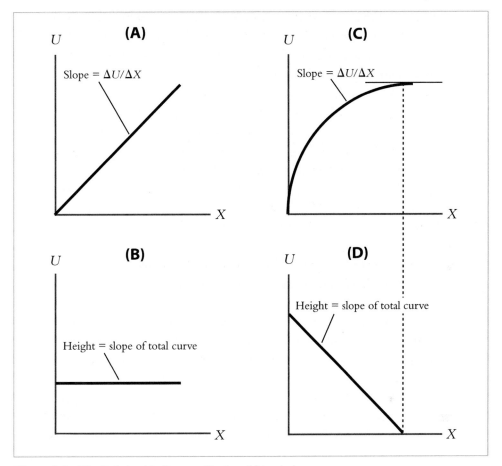

Figure 2.1   The Relationship Between Totals and Marginals

The increase in utility when the amount of one good increases is called *marginal utility.* We write this as $MU(X) \equiv \Delta U/\Delta X$, where the $\equiv$ means that the expression is an identity, true for all values of X and U by definition. The idea that marginal utility falls as the amount of X increases is called **diminishing marginal utility.** This concept will be important later.

When we work with a production function, the increase in output when one of the inputs increases, with all other inputs held constant, is called the **marginal product.** For the household production function $G = G(T, Z)$, the marginal products are $MP_T \equiv \Delta G/\Delta T$ (Z constant) and $MP_Z \equiv \Delta G/\Delta Z$ (T constant). Here, the idea is that each additional unit of input provides less and less additional output. The marginal product is typically positive—adding more input does increase the amount of output—but declining. This relationship is described in one of the most famous laws in economics, the **Law of Diminishing Marginal Returns.** We will use it later.

The economic details behind diminishing marginal utility and marginal product will be explained later when we use those ideas. For now, it is important to realize that a function can be described in two related ways, by looking at either the total function or its associated marginal function. Both provide the same information, but they highlight different features. Most functions used in economics will look like Figure 2.1(C) and (D) rather than Figure 2.1(A) and (B).

Microeconomics—Supply and Demand Analysis

Supply and demand analysis is such an important idea in microeconomics that it is worth reviewing here. It is the fundamental, though not exclusive, model for explaining how prices are set in a market economy.

Supply, Demand, and Equilibrium

Briefly, a demand function summarizes the relationship between the quantity demanded of a particular good and the various factors that influence that amount. The market demand function is $Q_D{}^* = D(P, P', I, \text{Preferences})$, where P is the price of the good, P' stands for all other prices, and I is income. Holding P', I, and Preferences constant and allowing P to vary traces out the demand curve. The Law of Demand tells us that the price and the quantity demanded vary inversely or negatively. When price goes up, the quantity demanded goes down. When price goes down, the quantity demanded goes up.

When the price of a product changes, two things happen at once, and both changes usually operate to cause the negative relationship between price and quantity demanded. First, the **relative price** of the product changes. The relative price is the price of the product compared to the price of other goods that a consumer could buy instead. Second, a change in the price of the product causes a change in consumers' real income, that is, in what they can buy with their income. When the price of a good increases, consumers' real income goes down, because they can no longer buy as much of everything as before. Similarly, when the price of a good decreases, real income goes up—it is as if consumers were a bit richer than before the price decrease.

Suppose, for example, the price of a good goes up. Because the relative price of the good is now higher than before, consumers will typically substitute away from that good and toward goods that are now relatively less expensive than before. This is called the **substitution effect.** In addition, because the price increase reduces real income, consumers typically compensate and buy less of that good and other goods as well. This effect is called the **income effect.** When the price of a good falls, these two effects work in reverse. Consumers substitute toward the now-cheaper good (the substitution effect), and because the lower price makes them richer by increasing their real income, they buy a bit more than before (the income effect).[4]

The supply curve functions in exactly the same way to summarize the amount supplied to the market by competitive firms. The major influences of supply are the price of the good, the prices of the inputs used in the production process, and the state of the available technology, which affects productivity and hence production costs. The market supply function can be written as $Q_S^* = S(P, W, Z)$, where W stands for all the input prices and Z stands for the available technology. Holding W and Z constant and allowing P to vary traces out the firm's supply function. The supply function is just the set of profit-maximizing outputs for each possible price. In general, the relationship between price and quantity supplied is positive. When price increases, so does the quantity supplied. When price falls, quantity supplied falls, too.

A competitive market is one in which there are many demanders and many suppliers, none of whom has any meaningful influence over the price of the product. In such a setting, the competitive market equilibrium is the price at which supply and demand just balance. It is a price P^* such that $D(P^*; P', I, \text{Preferences}) = S(P^*; W, Z)$; in words, it is the price at which the amount demanded just equals the amount supplied. This price is the price that is likely to emerge from a competitive market left to its own devices, that is, unregulated by government. Figure 2.2 illustrates the familiar supply and demand diagram. The price is on the vertical axis, and the amount demanded or supplied is on the horizontal axis. The demand curve is negatively sloped, while the supply curve is positively sloped. The two curves intersect at P^*, which is the equilibrium price. There—and only there—does the quantity demanded exactly equal the quantity supplied. The associated equilibrium quantity bought and sold is Q^*.

---

[4]The income effects described here are for normal goods. For inferior goods, the effect is just the opposite.

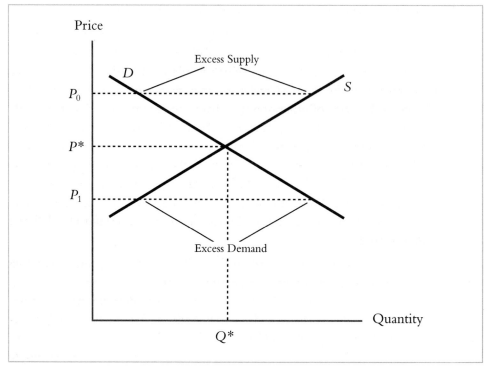

Figure 2.2   Supply, Demand, and Market Equilibrium

At the other two prices shown in Figure 2.2, the market is not in equilibrium because the quantity supplied and the quantity demanded are unequal. At a price above equilibrium like P_0, the amount supplied is quite large, but the amount demanded is much less. The excess supply is the horizontal distance between the two curves. Usually, price will fall in this situation, thereby increasing the amount demanded, decreasing the amount supplied, and moving price and quantity back toward the equilibrium at P^* and Q^*. Similarly, at a low price like P_1, the amount supplied is much less, the amount demanded is much more, and a shortage exists, again measured by the horizontal distance between the curves. Now, there is likely to be upward pressure on price, moving price back up to the equilibrium. When the market equilibrium is reached at price P^* and quantity Q^*, there is no reason for any further change unless either the supply curve or the demand curve changes.

Comparative Statics of Supply and Demand

Supply and demand analysis is particularly useful for predicting how the equilibrium price and quantity will change if there is a change in one of the two curves. Suppose demand changes, which would occur if there were a change in a variable in the demand function other than the price of the good—a change in the price of other goods, a change in income, or a change in preferences. These are the exogenous demand variables in a supply/demand model. An increase in demand means that more is demanded at every price or, equivalently, that consumers are willing to pay more for any given quantity. Thought of the first way, the demand curve shifts out to the right; thought of the other way, the demand curve shifts up. The impact is exactly the same in either case. A decrease in demand would be a shift to the left or a shift downward.

Figure 2.3 shows how a demand change affects price and quantity. The two arrows indicate the two ways to represent an increase in demand, either as an outward or upward shift of the demand curve. When demand increases from D_0 to D_1, equilibrium price and quantity both increase to P_1^* and Q_1^*, respectively. At the original equilibrium price P_0^*, there is excess demand with demand curve D_1, so price rises. The new equilibrium moves up the supply curve.

When demand falls from D_1 to D_0, thereby reversing the process, price and quantity fall. Now there is excess supply at price P_1^* with demand curve D_0, which causes price and quantity to fall. In summary: when demand increases, equilibrium price and quantity both rise; when demand decreases, equilibrium price and quantity both fall.

The effect of a change in supply can be analyzed in the same way. You need to be careful in thinking about what an increase in supply means and how it is represented. Here, an increase means either that the supply curve shifts out (more supplied at the same price, just as for an increase in demand) or that the supply curve shifts down, meaning that any amount will now be supplied at a lower price than before. Figure 2.4 shows the effect of an increase in supply. Again, the two arrows show the two ways to represent an increase in supply. Here, as supply increases, equilibrium price falls from P_0^* to P_1^*, and equilibrium quantity increases from Q_0^* to Q_1^*. The price change occurs because, at the original equilibrium price and with the new supply curve, there is excess supply (the horizontal distance between the original market equilibrium

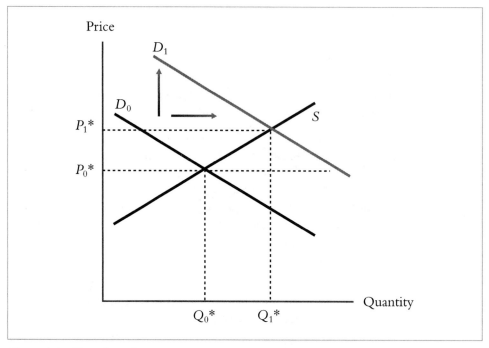

Figure 2.3   The Effect of an Increase in Demand on Equilibrium Price and Quantity

and the new supply curve). So price falls, reducing the amount supplied, increasing the amount demanded, and creating a new market equilibrium at P_1^* and Q_1^*.

If supply decreased, the supply curve would shift to the left (less supplied at any price) or up (any amount now supplied at a higher price). In Figure 2.4, a decrease in supply would be the movement from supply curve S_1 to supply curve S_0. Equilibrium price would increase, and equilibrium quantity would decrease. In summary, when supply increases, price falls and quantity increases; when supply decreases, price increases and quantity falls.

Empirical Methods in Economics—An Introduction

Economic theory—indeed, theory of any kind—usually makes a prediction about the relationship between two variables. For example, the Law of Demand predicts that price and quantity demanded are negatively related; the Law of Diminishing Marginal Returns predicts that the amount of an input

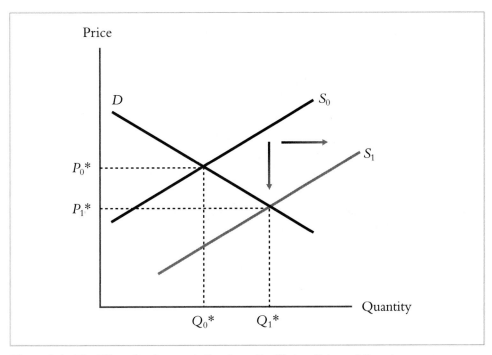

Figure 2.4 The Effect of an Increase in Supply on Equilibrium Price and Quantity

and its marginal product are negatively related. A theory that doesn't make a prediction that can be tested isn't a theory in any scientific sense because it can't be proved or disproved. A **qualitative prediction** involves the *sign* of the relationship–positive or negative—while a **quantitative prediction** involves the *size* of the relationship. Most theories in economics make a qualitative prediction about the relationship between the two variables; the theories are rarely precise enough to make a quantitative prediction. Thus, for example, the Law of Demand does not say how much quantity demanded will fall when price rises; it only predicts that quantity demanded will fall.

For many purposes, however, it is essential to estimate the quantitative relationship between two variables. There are two distinct reasons to do this. First, it tests the qualitative prediction of the model. If we can determine the actual relationship between the variables, we can test whether the prediction of the model is correct or not. Second, even if the qualitative predictions of the model are supported, it often makes a huge difference whether the relationship is weak or strong. A model may be correct in the sense that its qualitative predictions are borne out, but it may be unimportant if its quantitative effect is small. Economic policy will usually be guided by quantitative estimates.

To estimate quantitative relationships between variables, economists and other social scientists turn to real-world, *empirical data* and then use statistical methods to estimate the relationship between variables. Two main techniques are currently used in economics research. One is **regression analysis,** which is a statistical technique for estimating the relationship between two or more variables. It is by far the most widely used statistical technique in economics and most other social sciences. The other is quite new and quite popular. It is called **natural experiments,** and it attempts to imitate what laboratory and medical scientists do when they run controlled experiments. When done well, it is both very easy to use and very reliable. We will briefly examine both techniques, which are important elements of the economics tool kit.

Regression Analysis

Suppose a theory hypothesizes a causal relationship between some outcome Y and some variable X. For example, X could be price and Y could be quantity demanded or X could be years of education and Y could be annual earnings. We've already seen that we can write the relationship between the variables as a function $Y = F(X)$ and that the theory will usually specify the sign of $\Delta Y / \Delta X$.[5] The goal of regression analysis is to estimate the sign and size of $\Delta Y / \Delta X$.

To do that, we first write the function as a regression equation:

$$Y_i = \alpha + \beta X_i + \mu_i \qquad (9)$$

In equation (9), Y is called the **dependent variable,** X is the **independent (or causal) variable,** and the Greek letter μ (pronounced "mew") represents all other factors that affect Y but are unobserved. The term μ is called the **error term** of the equation, and we assume that it is uncorrelated with X, has a mean of 0, and is normally distributed. A normal distribution is the familiar symmetric bell curve; in this case, it is centered on a value of zero, and thus equally likely to be positive or negative. Note the i subscripts on Y, X, and μ.

---

[5]Note the change in notation here. In statistical analysis, Y always stands for the outcome variable, and X stands for the causal variable. In contrast, when we discussed economics choice problems, X was the outcome variable, and Y was one of the determinants of X.

We use subscripts because regression involves using a sample of many persons or many firms or whoever or whatever it is whose behavior is being examined. The subscript means that each person or firm has his/her/its own value of Y, X, and μ.

Finally, α and β, the Greek letters alpha and beta, are the **regression coefficients.** β shows the sign and size of the relationship between X and Y. If X increases by 1 unit, then Y will change by β units. More generally, $\Delta Y = \beta \Delta X$ or, rearranging, $\beta = \Delta Y / \Delta X$, which is precisely what we want to know. α is called the *constant term* of the equation, just like the Y-intercept in the familiar equation for the slope of a line. It is not multiplied by X, rather it just adds on to create the total value of Y. You can think of it as the value of Y when $X = 0$, exactly like a Y-intercept.

Regression analysis is a statistical technique that provides an estimate of the best values of α and β, given the actual values of Y and X. The estimated values are written $\hat{\alpha}$ and $\hat{\beta}$, pronounced "alpha hat" and "beta hat." The hat or carat indicates that it is an estimated value. Here, the best values are those that make the predicted value of Y as close as possible to the actual value of Y.

The various terms and relationships are shown in Figure 2.5. This diagram is called a **scattergram.** The dots represent actual data observations, showing the relationship between X (on the horizontal axis) and Y (on the vertical axis).[6] The straight line through the scatter of points shows the relationship between X and Y. Its slope is β—note that in this case the slope is negative—and α is where the line intersects the vertical axis. Notice that there isn't a perfect relationship between X and Y—there almost never is in social science research. The vertical difference between the predicted value shown by the regression line and the actual value shown by the dots shows the influence of the error term.

In most real problems, the dependent variable Y is affected by more than one variable. In that case, we can write the regression equation as

$$Y_i = \alpha + \beta_1 X_{i1} + \beta_2 X_{i2} + \beta_3 X_{i3} + \cdots + \mu_i \qquad (10)$$

This kind of analysis is called **multiple regression,** where "multiple" refers to the many explanatory variables. In this case, the βs represent the effect of the corresponding variable, holding constant or "controlling for" the value of all

---

[6]The relationship represented here is between the teen birth rate on the vertical axis and welfare benefits on the horizontal axis. Each dot represents a state.

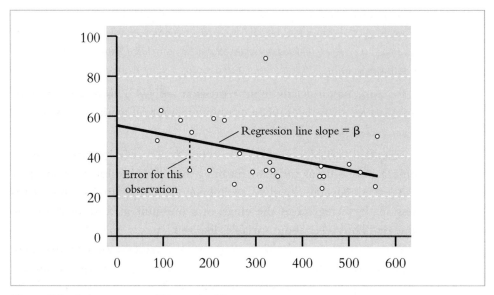

Figure 2.5   A Scattergram and Regression Line

the other Xs. This corresponds exactly to the idea of *ceteris paribus* in economics models—all else held constant. Other than the fact that there are more X variables, the interpretation of multiple regression is exactly the same as the simpler one-variable regression discussed earlier. Note, however, that multiple regression cannot be readily represented by a diagram like that in Figure 2.5.

In practice, the hardest thing about regression analysis is including all the relevant explanatory variables in a multiple regression equation like equation (10). In most problems that social scientists examine, a researcher might be particularly interested in measuring the impact of one specific independent variable on some outcome. In order to do that, however, he must control for all the other influences of that outcome by including them in the equation. Often that is difficult to do—it is hard to measure many of the factors that influence people's behaviors. When important variables are omitted, the estimated coefficients on the included variables will often be *biased*, which means that they are not equal to the true effect of that variable on Y. In layman's terms, a biased coefficient is a poor estimate. There is a lengthy statistical literature about this kind of bias, but it can be easily summarized: *If variables that affect the dependent variable are omitted from a regression equation, they bias estimates of all variables with which they are correlated.* In this case, the included variable spuriously (incorrectly) captures some of the explanatory power of the omitted variables with which it is correlated. This idea is very important. The corollary is also true: *Omitted variables that are uncorrelated with the variable of interest do not bias estimated coefficients.* That is also a very important idea.

Here are some useful details about regression analysis. This material may be valuable as a reference later when examining empirical work or reading supplementary articles.

1. Independent variables come in two types. Some variables, like age or income, are continuous variables, meaning that all numerical values are possible (except possibly negative or extremely high ones). In that case, the regression coefficient gives the effect of a one-unit increase in X on the value of Y. But what about variables like gender, race, and ethnicity, which are not numeric and only have a few possible "values"? Variables like these can be included in a regression by using a **dummy variable.** A dummy variable for gender would work this way: Let $X = 0$ if a person is male; let $X = 1$ if a person is female. Now, the regression coefficient for the gender dummy variable would measure the impact of being female rather than male on the value of Y. For example, if the estimated regression coefficient on a female dummy variable is negative, it means that women have a lower value of Y than men, with all else being equal. Dummy variables are commonly used in statistical research.

2. Dependent variables also come in two types. Some are continuous variables, like a person's wage rate, but others have yes/no values, such as whether an individual is employed, had a teen birth, or is officially poor. Yes/no values are treated much like dummy variables. If we let $Y = 1$ represent an individual who is a yes (i.e., employed, had a teen birth, officially poor) and $Y = 0$ an individual who is a no, then the regression coefficient measures the effect of X on the *probability* of being a yes.

3. In some studies, the dependent variable is a continuous variable but is represented in logarithms, usually natural log units. This is commonly done for regressions involving wages or income. The natural log of Y is written $\ln(Y)$. When the dependent variable is in logarithm units, the regression coefficient shows the *percentage* change in Y that is caused by a one-unit change in X. For example, if Y is $\ln(\text{Earnings})$ and X is Years of Education, the estimated coefficient might be close to .10, meaning that a year of education increases earnings by an average of 10%.

4. Because the regression coefficient is estimated from a sample rather than the entire population, it is subject to sampling error. It is possible that the estimate differs from the true regression coefficient. Consequently, researchers compute a standard error of the estimated coefficient. The ratio of the estimated coefficient to its standard error is called a **t-statistic.** The smaller is the standard error relative to the coefficient, the greater is the t-statistic and the more reliable is the estimated coefficient. If the t-statistic is greater than 1.65 (in absolute value), then there is only a 10% chance that the true coefficient is zero; if the t-statistic is greater than 1.96 (in absolute value), there is only a 5% chance that the true value is zero. In these two cases, we say that the estimated coefficient is statistically significant at the 10% or 5% level. Significance levels bigger than 10% are considered too imprecise, and researchers will usually report that "the estimated coefficient is not statistically different from zero."

5. R^2 is a measure of how well the independent variables explain the variation in the dependent variable. If the points in the scattergram of Figure 2.5 were very close to the regression line, then the independent variable would explain most of the variation in the dependent variable. The more scattered the points in the scattergram are, the less variation in Y is explained by the independent variables. R^2 goes from a minimum of 0 when the independent variables explain none of the variation in Y to a maximum of 1 where all the points lie right on the regression line. A typical R^2 in microeconomic studies might be in the .25 to .35 range, which means that the independent variables explain 25 or 35% of the variation in the dependent variable. Don't get too hung up by a low R^2. A low R^2 means that unmeasured factors or unknown factors are important, not that the included independent variables are unimportant or unreliable or that the coefficient estimates are biased.

Natural Experiments in Economics

When medical researchers want to examine the effect of a new drug, they use an experimental method called **random assignment.** The basic idea of random assignment is illustrated in Figure 2.6. A sample of subjects is chosen and then randomly assigned to one of two groups—the experimental or treatment group that receives the drug or the control group that gets either nothing or a placebo. In many experiments, neither the participants nor the re-

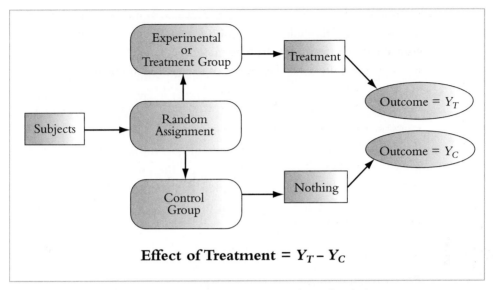

Figure 2.6   Schematic View of a Controlled Experiment with Random Assignment

searchers know which group is which. This is called a *double-blind random as-signment experiment.*

To determine the effectiveness of the drug, the researchers need only compare the outcomes for the two groups. The effect of the treatment is Y_T (the outcome for the treatment group) $-Y_C$ (the outcome for the control group). There is no need to do multiple regression even though other factors beside the drug may affect the outcome. The researchers don't need to worry about these other factors because the random assignment guarantees that these variables are unrelated to (uncorrelated with) the outcome. We noted earlier that the exclusion of these uncorrelated variables does not bias coefficient estimates.

Random assignment, where feasible, is a perfect technique. To see this, consider the relationship between smoking and lung cancer. The available evidence is based on individuals who choose to smoke and who, in addition to smoking, have lifestyles that may differ in some important ways from nonsmokers. It is always possible that some of the apparent effect of smoking on lung cancer is actually the result of these other differences. Technically, this would mean that the estimated effect of smoking on the probability of developing lung cancer is biased. Cigarette manufacturers made an argument like that for many years, although it is not clear that they actually believed their own argument. Researchers try as well as they can to measure and control for these other factors via multiple regression, but it is, as a practical matter, impossible to control for every possible difference.[7]

Imagine, instead, that a large sample was chosen; some individuals were randomly assigned to smoke one pack of cigarettes a day, while others were assigned to smoke no cigarettes. Then the other lifestyle differences would be irrelevant because they would be uncorrelated with the smoking "treatment." The difference in cancer rates for the two groups would provide an accurate estimate of the effect of cigarette smoking on the probability of developing lung cancer. Of course, no experiment like this could ever be done for ethical reasons, but the difference between this approach and the statistical approach that is actually used is obvious.

Economists now sometimes do experiments with random assignment. In the 1990s, states were allowed substantial freedom to reform their welfare systems, but the reforms had to be scientifically evaluated using a random assignment procedure. In these cases, one group of welfare recipients might receive special services or be held to special rules, while another group, randomly assigned, did not receive the services or was not held to the new rule. In this case, the reform was the treatment, and the difference between the treatment group and the control group was a measure of the effectiveness of the reform. New Jersey did this when they implemented a "family cap" provision that denied additional benefits to women on welfare who had another child. Some women were randomly assigned to receive this treatment, while others were randomly assigned to the control group and did not face this penalty.

Natural experiments are like random assignment experiments but with one important difference—they are "natural" in the sense that the researcher doesn't plan and control the experiment. Rather, the experiment occurs inadvertently, created by a particular policy or by some event. A famous example of a natural experiment in economics was the Mariel boatlift in which 125,000 Cubans were allowed to emigrate to Miami between May and September of 1980, creating a large and unexpected increase in labor supply in Miami. This influx of workers was analyzed to assess the impact of immigration on labor market outcomes.[8] Earlier research was suspect because immi-

---

[7]We certainly don't want to suggest that the effect of cigarette smoking on lung cancer is not causal. The research evidence on this relationship is clear and compelling.

[8]See David Card, "The Impact of the Mariel Boatlift on the Miami Labor Market," *Industrial and Labor Relations Review,* January 1990.

gration was often greatest in those cities with booming labor markets: the booming labor market attracted the immigrants. That problem did not occur in this case, however, because the immigration occurred for reasons quite unrelated to the economic climate in Miami.

Figure 2.7, which is very similar to Figure 2.6, shows the basic idea of a natural experiment. For example, suppose a government policy affects the wages of low- to moderate-income women with children but not the wages of low- to moderate-income women without children. (This result is, in fact, a common outcome of several current government policies, including welfare and the Earned Income Tax Credit.) This is a natural experiment in which one group is given a treatment (a new wage) and the other group is given nothing. Then if we want to measure the effect of this policy on some outcome, such as work or marriage, we can simply measure the difference in outcomes between the two groups. Because there may be initial differences between the groups, researchers usually go one step further and compare the *change* in the outcome for the treatment group with the *change* in the outcome for the control group. This is called a **difference-in-difference approach.** The difference-in-difference estimate equals $[(Y_{T1} - Y_{T0}) - (Y_{C1} - Y_{C0})]$. This is shown at the bottom of Figure 2.7. For an interesting example of a natural experiment that examines a recent change in government policy, see Box 2.2.

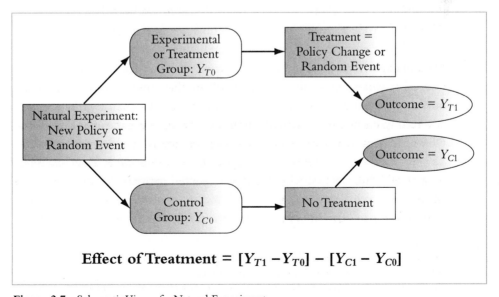

Effect of Treatment $= [Y_{T1} - Y_{T0}] - [Y_{C1} - Y_{C0}]$

Figure 2.7   Schematic View of a Natural Experiment

Box 2.2   Difference-in-Differences—A Natural Experiment Example

In a very interesting paper, Nada Eissa and Jeffrey Liebman used a natural experiment approach to examine the impact of the Earned Income Tax Credit (or EITC) on the labor force participation of single women with children. We discuss the EITC in Chapters 12 and 13—it is a particularly important government program which provides income assistance to low- and moderate-income families.

In 1986, the EITC was expanded and made more generous in a way that could reasonably be expected to increase labor force participation. Only women with children benefited from this new provision. Thus, Eissa and Liebman compared the labor force participation of single women with children before and after the EITC change with the labor force participation of single women without children before and after the EITC change. They wrote, "We use single women with children as our . . . treatment group [and] . . . single women without children as our control group." They also examined subgroups, especially single women with children and low levels of education who would be likely to have earnings low enough that they would benefit from the EITC. In this case, the control group was single women without children and with low levels of education.

Their findings are summarized in Table 2.1. The numbers in the table are the proportion of women in each group who worked during the year, before and after the policy change in the EITC. The first rows of the table show the participation rates for all unmarried women with and without children; the second two rows show the same information for unmarried women with and without children and with less than a high school education. As you can see in the first two rows, the participation rate for unmarried women with children rose 2.4 percentage points, while the participation rate for unmarried women without children remained constant. The underlying assumption is that only the EITC accounts for the difference; otherwise, the two rates would move together. Thus, the difference-in-difference estimate for this group is $2.4\% - 0\% = 2.4\%$. In the second two rows, the participation rate for less-educated single women with children rose by 1.8 percentage points while the corresponding rate for women without children fell by 2.3 percentage points. Thus, the difference-in-difference estimate for this group

is 1.8% − (−2.3%) = 4.1%. Again, the underlying assumption is that in the absence of the change in the EITC, the participation rate for the women with children would actually have fallen by 2.3 percentage points, just like the women without children. It is, of course, important to verify that assumption; otherwise, the procedure may attribute too much to the policy change.

When natural experiments can be identified, they are very simple to analyze—simply subtract after the numbers are in place.

Group	Before (%)	After (%)	Difference (%)	Difference-in-Difference (%)
Unmarried women with children	72.9	75.3	2.4	2.4
Unmarried women without children	95.2	95.2	0	
Unmarried women with children, education <12 years	47.9	49.7	1.8	4.1
Unmarried women without children, education <12 years	78.4	76.1	−2.3	

Table 2.1 Labor Force Participation Rates of Unmarried Women Before and After 1986 Policy Change in Earned Income Tax Credit

Source: Nada Eissa and Jeffrey Liebman, "Labor Supply Response to the Earned Income Tax Credit," *Quarterly Journal of Economics*, Vol. CXI, No. 2, pp. 575–604, 1996. Copyright © 1996 by the President and Fellows of Harvard College & The Massachusetts Institute of Technology.

The general point is this: Sometimes it is possible to identify real-world situations that are very much like random assignment experiments. They aren't literally experiments, but they amount to almost the same thing. The key characteristic of a natural experiment is that individuals are either treated or not treated randomly; they cannot choose their treatment status themselves. Natural experiments, when they can be identified, provide a very simple and very reliable estimate of quantitative effects. In the absence of valid natural experiments, we must use regression analysis and other more sophisticated and complex statistical procedures.

Summary

In this chapter, we reviewed and surveyed the basic approach of microeconomics and the research methods that economists use to test their theories and to provide quantitative estimates of effects. We looked at the core concept of constrained maximization with its emphasis on choice, maximization, and constraints. We will use these concepts repeatedly. Economics is not so much difficult as it is relentless. It really is not too much more than the repeated and clever application of constrained maximization to an enormously wide variety of problems. Anyone who can master this approach and apply it naturally in answer to a personal problem is well on the way to becoming an economist.

Most of the economics problems that we will encounter have a four-step structure.

Step 1: Write down the constrained maximization problem in general form, at least indicating what is being chosen, what is being maximized, and what variables are in the constraint. Be certain to distinguish exogenous from endogenous variables.

Step 2: Solve the problem, either for the marginal conditions if possible or for the associated expression in which the endogenous variable is a function of the exogenous variables. Try to understand how the exogenous variables affect the choice.

Step 3: Examine the comparative statics. What happens to the chosen value of the endogenous variable when the exogenous variables change?

Step 4: Test the predictions of the theory, either using statistical analysis or a natural experiment. Only when the predictions have been supported can we have real confidence in the analysis.

We also developed several useful tools and concepts. Functions express the relationship between variables. A utility function expresses the relationship between the amounts of particular goods or services and the amount of utility that an individual receives. A household production function expresses the relationship between the amounts of particular inputs and the amount of household goods that an individual produces. By using the ideas of household production functions and household goods, economists can apply standard ideas of production economics to the household sector. Economists and other social scientists use regression analysis and natural experiments to test their theories and produce quantitative estimates of causal effects. With such an array of tools at our disposal, we are well prepared to analyze the economic circumstances of women's lives. We begin with marriage.

Key Terms

arguments of the function   27

budget constraint   21

comparative static analysis   20

constrained maximization   18

dependent variable   38

difference-in-difference approach   45

diminishing marginal utility   31

dummy variable   41

endogenous variable   19

error term   38

exogenous variables   19

household production function   27

income effect   33

independent (or causal) variable   38

Law of Demand   21

Law of Diminishing Marginal Returns   32

marginal changes   29

marginal conditions   19

marginal product   31

marginal rate of substitution   22

marginal utility   22

multiple regression   39

natural experiments   38

qualitative prediction   37

quantitative prediction   37

random assignment   42

rational choice model   28

regression analysis   38

regression coefficients   39

relative price   32

revealed preference   28

scattergram   39

substitution effect   33

t-statistic   42

utility   21

utility function   21

utils   27

Marriage and the Family—An Economic Approach

Introduction

Why do we start a book on women and the economy with marriage? There are several very good reasons. First, marriage has certainly been a central feature in women's lives for a very long time. It's true that in a monogamous society with roughly equal numbers of men and women, marriage is, at least arithmetically, an equally central feature in men's lives. But, of course, marriage has traditionally meant something different for women. For a woman, it has provided not only a husband but also often an occupation—mother and housewife—and a change in identity, as the woman usually takes on a new surname. A man's occupational status and, of course, surname has usually remained distinct despite a change in marital status.

Second, the family is an important economic institution. Family structure makes an enormous difference in the economic well-being of adults and children. This observation may sound obvious, but economists didn't fully appreciate the fact until the mid-1970s when a series of important studies of family income, poverty, and welfare receipt were published. A famous survey called the Panel Study of Income Dynamics followed a representative national sample of 5000 households year after year to chart their economic ups and downs. This type of study had never been done before. Its goal was to find out what mattered most during those ups and downs. Over and over again, the researchers found something they hadn't expected to find: *Changes in family structure dominated changes in the labor market in terms of the impact on income dynamics, especially poverty and welfare receipt.* Getting married, getting divorced, and having a nonmarital birth made a bigger difference in more people's lives than getting a better job or losing a current one. Since then, the importance of family structure for economic well-being has been confirmed repeatedly.

Third, marriage is economic behavior in the broad sense of "economics as choice," which we mentioned in the last chapter. With very few exceptions, women and men choose whether to marry, who to marry, when to marry, and so on. Presumably they do so with an eye (and a heart) on their well-being, broadly defined. Some constraints, however, limit their choices. In this sense, marriage is a great example of how the core ideas in economics can be used and applied to nontraditional topics.

This approach to the economics of marriage was introduced into economics by Gary Becker, a Nobel Prize–winning economist. Becker is famous—some would say notorious—for expanding the conventional boundaries of economic analysis.[1] In a well-known and controversial article published in 1973, he applied economic tools to marriage for the first time.[2] He wrote at the very beginning of that article:

> In recent years, economists have used economic theory more boldly to explain behavior outside the monetary sector. . . . Yet, one type of behavior has been almost completely ignored by economists, although scarce resources are used and it has been followed in some form by practically all adults in every recorded society. I refer to marriage. (p. 813)

On the next page, he outlined his approach:

> Two simple principles form the heart of the analysis. The first is that, since marriage is practically always voluntary. . . . the theory of preferences can be readily applied, and persons marrying can be assumed to expect to raise their utility level above what it would be were they to remain single. The second is that, since many men and many women compete as they seek mates, a *market* can be presumed to exist. Each person tries to find the best mate, subject to . . . market conditions. (p. 814)

Even though the idea of applying economic analysis to the institution of marriage may be unsettling, the language that Becker uses ought to sound familiar—it is all about choices with constraints.

Fourth, a family is in many ways a miniature economy. Like any economy, it makes decisions about consumption and investment, about work and leisure, about the allocation of resources. It solves economic problems of allocation and distribution of resources

---

[1]A recent article referred to him as an economic imperialist, always trying to wrest away subject areas from other disciplines, especially sociology. See the very readable and interesting article by Edward Lazear, "Economic Imperialism," *Quarterly Journal of Economics*, Vol. CXV, pp. 99–146, 2000.

[2]Gary S. Becker, "A Theory of Marriage, Part 1," *Journal of Political Economy*, Vol. 81, No. 4, 1973. Copyright © 1973. Reprinted with permission of The University of Chicago Press.

daily. Economic analysis provides real insight about many family issues. A relatively new area in economics research and teaching, called the economics of the household, focuses on these kinds of issues and supports a new journal called *The Review of Economics of the Household*.

Finally, marriage and the family are interesting subjects and far too important to leave to the sociologists and demographers. Marriage eventually is a part of the lives of most adults—over 90%. The ideas we explore in this chapter may well resonate with many readers in very personal ways. In contemporary American life, the institution of marriage remains terribly important. It is also controversial—witness the many discussions about the disappearance of the traditional family, about "family values," about the potential legalization of gay marriage, and about the problems of children in single-parent families, just to name a few.

We begin with an overview of marriage and family structure in the United States and how they have changed over time. This overview will provide us with some insight that will be helpful later.

Marriage and Family Structure—An Overview

There are many different ways to describe marriage and family life and the ways it has changed over time. One way is to describe the *current* marital status of men or women and then to compare it over time. However, because a person's marital status typically changes over time—indeed, sometimes it changes many times!—it is also useful to describe marriage in terms of a marital history. For example, we can compute the proportion of men or women ever married by a given age. This measure may give a clearer and cleaner picture of the role and importance of the institution of marriage in adult life. The same approach may be taken with divorce: A relatively small proportion of persons may be currently divorced compared to the proportion who are ever divorced.

To make things more complicated, the marital status categories themselves have changed. Cohabitation of unmarried persons of the opposite sex accounted for a minuscule proportion of households in the 1950s and 1960s; it was even scandalous in some places. Now, it is very nearly a demographic norm for many young adults, often serving as a kind of transition to marriage. Some demographers have stopped talking about "marriage" and now talk about "unions," a term that included both marriage and cohabitation. Yet another change is the rise in same-sex households and same-sex unions.

We cannot here do justice to the full complexity of adult domestic relations. Our goal is to identify the basic trends and tendencies, particularly those that speak to economic issues. For a more detailed discussion of family issues, see *Marriage, Divorce and Remarriage* by Andrew Cherlin or *The New American Reality* by Reynolds Farley or take a basic course in demography or the sociology of the family.

Marital Status

Let's start by considering women's current marital status in the United States and how it has changed over time. In 2002, there were about 115 million women aged 15 and older. Of these, about 58 million, or just over half, were married with spouse present. (The broader category "married" includes both married with spouse present and married with spouse absent; this latter group is mostly individuals who are separated, but not yet divorced.) Almost exactly one quarter of these 115 million women were never married, and about 13% (15 million women) were currently either divorced or separated. Widows made up the remainder, just about 10%.

Table 3.1 shows these figures for selected years between 1950 and 2002. To make the table clearer and to focus on the major issues, the proportion widowed is omitted. The trends are quite clear. The proportion currently married with spouse present has fallen steadily and quite sharply, from two thirds in 1950 to its current figure of just over half. Some of this drop is the result of an increase in the proportion of those who never married, which increased by about 6 percentage points. The increase in the proportion of those who are divorced or separated, 11 percentage points, is responsible for an even larger portion of this drop.

Even more dramatic than the change in the proportion of women who are currently married is the change in the age at which women first marry. These changes are shown in Figure 3.1, which presents the proportion of women ever married by age for 2000, 1980, and 1960. In 2000, relatively few young women have been married—only about 5% at ages 18–19 and about 27% at ages 20–24. The peak age for first marriage is now the late 20s and mid 30s, when nearly half of women first marry. But as the figure reveals, most women eventually do marry: at ages 45–54, only 8.5% of women are never married.

The marriage profiles shift up, showing earlier marriage in earlier years. In 1980, almost 20% of 18- and 19-year-old women were married, and 50% of women between ages 20 and 24 were already married. In 1960, almost one

	Married, Spouse Present (%)	Never Married (%)	Divorced/ Separated (%)
2002	50.5	24.7	13.2
1990	53.3	22.8	11.8
1980	55.4	22.4	9.4
1970	58.4	22.1	5.7
1960*	63.0	17.8	5.0
1950*	66.8	18.8	2.4

Table 3.1   Current Marital Status of U.S. Women, Age 15 and Older, 1950–2002

*1950 and 1960 figures have been adjusted slightly to account for the fact that 14 year olds are included in the population base. The 1950 numbers for married include married, spouse absent; separated women are not included in the divorced/separated column. Because divorce and separation were relatively uncommon in 1950, this makes little difference.

Sources: Current Population Reports, Series P-20: #547, Table A1 (2002); #450, Table 1 (1990); #365, Table 1 (1980); #212, Table 1 (1970); Series PC(2)-4B, Table 2 (1960, 1950).

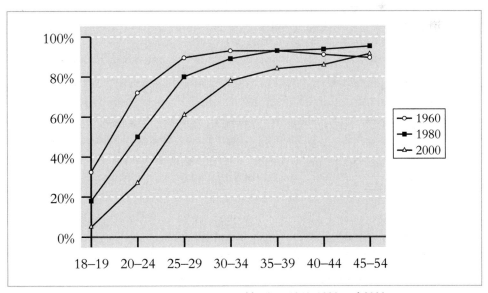

Figure 3.1   U.S. Women, Percentage Ever Married by Age, 1960, 1980, and 2000

Source: Current Population Report, Series P-20: #514, Table B (2000); #450, Table B (1980, 1960)

third of 18- and 19-year-old women were already married, and more than 70% were married by ages 20–24. In 1960, the median age at first marriage for women was 20.3; by 2000, it had increased by nearly five years to age 25. Despite this very obvious trend toward later marriage, there is very little difference across the years in the proportion who ever marry. At ages 45–54, about 91–95% of women have ever been married in each of the three years shown in Figure 3.1.

As already seen in Table 3.1, the proportion of women who are divorced or separated rose very sharply in the years since 1950. The *divorce rate,* measured as the annual number of divorces divided by the number of existing marriages, rose as well. In the 1950s, less than 1% of all marriages ended via divorce in any given year. But, starting in the early 1960s, the divorce rate began to rise, increasing 14 years in a row, and finally leveling off in the early 1980s at about 2.1% per year. This means that for every 1000 existing marriages, 21(2.1%) were ended by divorce each year. In 1998, the divorce rate was approximately 1.8%.[3] That may not sound like a lot, but a marriage is at risk of divorce year after year. Using life-table methods,[4] which are based on the divorce rate for each particular year of a marriage, demographers can compute the expected proportion of new marriages that will end in divorce. With a divorce rate of 1% per year, about one quarter of all marriages would end in divorce within 30 years; with a divorce rate of 2% per year, the proportion ending in divorce within 30 years jumps to 45%. Using current divorce rates for each specific year of marriage, the proportion of marriages that will likely end in divorce is well over half and perhaps as high as two thirds.[5] In the first half of the twentieth century, the corresponding proportion was between 15 and 20%.

The basic message thus far is twofold and a bit contradictory. Clearly, marriage as an institution is still strong. Most women and most men, for that matter, marry—eventually. But because women marry much later than in the past and marriages are now more likely to end in divorce, a falling proportion of women are married at a particular point in time. While the institution of marriage may be relatively strong, particular marriages are not nearly so strong.

---

[3]Official divorce rates were issued by the vital statistics system of the federal government through the early 1990s, but they are no longer available. In 1999, there were approximately 1 million divorces—actually 920,000 without counting divorces from California, Indiana, and Louisiana, which did not report divorces. With 55 million married women in 1998, the divorce rate is 1.8%.

[4]Demographers use life-table methods to compute the proportion of the population that survives to any given age on the basis of age-specific death rates.

[5]Teresa Martin and Larry Bumpass, "Recent Trends in Marital Disruption," *Demography,* Vol. 26, No. 1, pp. 37–52, 1989.

Let's return to the analysis of current marital status that we began in Table 3.1. The broad changes shown there have not, in fact, been uniform across different groups of women. Look at Table 3.2, which presents information on the change in the proportions currently married and never married by age and education for the time period 1970–1995. The sample here is women age 25–64, so the overall percentages married are higher than in Table 3.1. The figures in Table 3.2 show the percentage point change in the proportions currently married and never married between 1970 and 1995.

For all women aged 25–64, the proportion married fell 12.5 percentage points between 1970 and 1995, from 77.7% to 65.2%, a decline that is quite similar to the pattern seen in Table 3.1. That is certainly a substantial decline. As shown in the last column, the proportion never married increased by 7.3 percentage points, thus accounting for about 60% (7.3%/12.5%) of the decline. For women aged 25–34, the decline in marriage has been enormous—nearly double the decrease for all women. About 18 percentage points of the decrease for the young women is caused by an increase in the proportion never married, which nearly tripled from about 9% to almost 27%. This is consistent with the trend toward later marriage shown in Figure 3.1. The rest of the change is an increase in divorce and separation; this is so, despite the fact that so many more young women are still never married. Women who have less than a high school education also exhibit a larger-than-average decrease in marriage. For them, the proportion married fell 17.5 percentage points, and they are now considerably less likely to be married than the average woman. Again, the

Year	Married, Spouse Present	Never Married
All women	−12.5	+7.3
Age 25–34	−23.0	+18.0
Education <12 years	−17.5	+10.0
Education 16+ years	−6.9	+3.5

Table 3.2   Percentage Point Changes in the Percentages of Women Married and Never Married by Selected Characteristics, 1970–1995, for Women, Age 25–64

Figures in table are the percentage point change between 1970 and 1995 in the proportion of women who are married, spouse present or never married.

Source: Adapted from Francine Blau, "The Well-Being of American Women," *Journal of Economic Literature,* Vol. XXXVI, March, 1998, Table 8. Copyright © 1988 by the American Economic Association. Reprinted with the permission of the author and publisher.

increase in the proportion never married is important, rising 10 percentage points over this time span. Finally, college-educated women had a smaller-than-average decline in the proportion married, just about 7 percentage points. In 1970, these women were less likely to be married than less-educated women. By 1995, this trend turned around, and there is now a big gap favoring the more-educated women.

For most of the groups, the biggest changes occurred in the 1970s. Since then, the rates have stabilized a bit. One exception is women with less than a high school education, for whom the changes have been quite steady through the mid-1990s.

Lastly, new marriage-like institutions have appeared on the scene. The largest is cohabiting couples or **POSSLQs** for Persons of Opposite Sex Sharing Living Quarters (pronounced as "poss-el-ques") in the Census Bureau jargon. According to the 1960 and 1970 Censuses, there were about a half million such couples in those years, although they were not yet called POSSLQs. That was just barely over 1% of the number of married couples. The Census Bureau began collecting annual information about these couples in 1977. Since then, the numbers have increased every year, nearly quadrupling in the process. Currently about 4.2 million heterosexual couples are cohabiting, which amounts to 7.5% of the number of married couples. Well over 10% of young adults, age 25–29, are currently cohabiting.[6]

Cohabitation has also increased among same-sex couples. The Census Bureau does not provide direct information about the number of these households, but information in the 1990 and 2000 Census does enable researchers to identify same-sex individuals living together in a marriage-like relationship. A recent analysis of this data suggests that the number of these households ranged between 120,000 and 360,000, roughly equally divided between gay and lesbian couples.[7] This means that the number of same-sex cohabiting couples is between 3 and 10% of the number of heterosexual cohabiting couples.

------

[6]In April, 2003, the North Dakota State Senate voted against repealing an anticohabitation law that says that a man and woman cannot live together "openly and notoriously" as if they were married. Violations carry a maximum 30 days in jail and a $1000 fine. According to a newspaper account (*The News Journal,* April 4, 2003), Census data show that North Dakota has more than 11,000 unmarried couples living together.

[7]For details and related analyses, see Black et al., "Demographics of the Gay and Lesbian Population in the United States," *Demography,* Vol. 32, No. 2, pp. 139–154, 2000.

Family Structure

These changes in marriage have deeply affected household and family structure as well as the lives of children. A bit of Census Bureau nomenclature is needed here. A household contains one or more persons; everyone living in a housing unit makes up a household. There are two kinds of households—family and non-family. A **family household** contains two or more persons who are sharing living quarters and who are related by blood, marriage, or adoption; a **non-family household** can be composed of a person living alone or of unrelated individuals, like college students and young adults, who live together. Finally, when there is a single adult in a household, that adult is called the **householder.** Naturally, there are male and female householders.[8]

In 2002, there were 109 million households in the United States, containing among them about 285 million people. Of these households, 74 million were family households; the other 35 million were non-family households. Let's focus on the family households, whose distribution by marital status in 2002 and 1960 is shown in Figure 3.2. In 2002, a bit more than three quarters (76.3%) of these family households were married-couple households, about 18% had a single female householder, and the remaining 6% had a single male householder. Back in 1960, married-coupled families were far more prevalent, and male and female householder families were much less common. In that year, more than 87% of family households were married-couple households, about 10% were female-householder families, and less than 3% were male-householder families. Thus, the proportion of families headed by single women or single men has more than doubled in the years since 1960, while the proportion that are married-couple families has fallen.

These changes are even more dramatic if we focus just on families with children under age 18 (see Figure 3.3). In 2002, 72% of these families were two-parent families, with the other 28% living with only a single parent. In 22% of all households, that single parent was a woman. Back in 1960, more than nine out of ten families with children had two parents and just one twelfth (about 8%) were headed by a single female. Single males heading families with children were barely noticeable at less than 1%.

---

[8]This language is deliberately neutral. In a famous and otherwise wonderful study of families called the Panel Study of Income Dynamics (PSID), the husband in a married couple was arbitrarily identified as the "head of household." The PSID was begun in 1967, so it has a bit of an excuse for its sexist leanings.

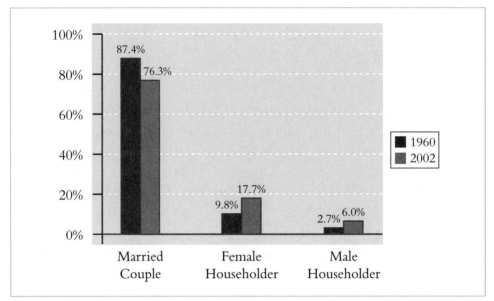

Figure 3.2   U.S. Families by Type, 1960 and 2002

Source: Current Population Reports, Series P-20: various years.

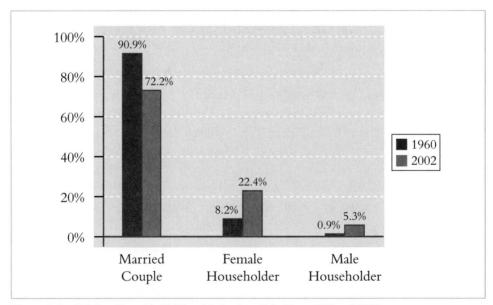

Figure 3.3   U.S. Families with Children Under Age 18 by Type, 1960 and 2002

Thus, especially from the standpoint of children, family structure has changed enormously. In 2002, about two thirds of all children under age 18 lived with two parents and 28% lived in a single-parent family. In 1970, 85% of children lived with two parents, and 12% lived with a single parent. Even further back, in 1960, 88% lived with two parents, and just 9% lived with a single parent.

We've covered a great deal of ground. Let's summarize briefly:

- The institution of marriage remains popular, but is no longer an imperative. Over 90% of women marry eventually, but they marry at much older ages than 20 and 40 years ago. Because of later marriage and more frequent divorce, the proportion of adult women who are married at any particular point in time has declined substantially. Cohabitation is on the rise as a kind of substitute or test marriage.

- The decline in marriage is not uniform across subgroups. The decline is greater for younger women and less-educated women.

- The change in family structure has followed the change in marital status. Among families with children under age 18, the proportion of two-parent families has shrunk from more than 90% in 1960 to about two thirds. The proportion of female-headed single-parent families has increased from less than 10% to more than 25% of families with children.

The primary task of any theory of marriage is to explain both the underlying strength of the institution as well as the general decline in the importance of marriage in the lives of today's women.

The Economics of Marriage—An Overview

Let's begin by thinking about what we might mean by the phrase "the economics of marriage." We've seen in the facts and trends that marriage is a durable social institution, but that its importance and primacy have been eroded. Clearly broad trends and differences among groups merit examination and explanation.

In fact, there are many different economic approaches to marriage and the family. One economist noted in a review article that different kinds of economists saw the family in quite different ways.[9] From the perspective of labor

---

[9]Theodore Bergstrom, "A Survey of Theories of the Family" in *Handbook of Population and Family Economics,* Vol. 1a, edited by Oded Stark and Mark R. Rosenzweig, Elsevier: Amsterdam, 1997.

economics or industrial organization, a family looked like "a little factory" dealing primarily with issues of efficient production. From the standpoint of public economics or urban economics, it looked like "a little city or little club" with issues of public production and public goods. From the perspective of game theory, it looked more like two persons bargaining over outcomes and the distribution of goods and services.

The starting point for an economic analysis is the benefits of or gains to marriage. Because marriage is almost always voluntary, an economist, applying the idea of **rational choice,**[10] would note that individuals marry only when they expect to be better off married than single. This must be true for both parties to a marriage, not just for the husband or for the wife. The demographic fact that marriage is widespread suggests that this condition typically holds, although perhaps less so than in the past and with some substantial differences among subgroups. The first task of an economic theory of marriage, then, is to think about the nature of the gains to marriage. What are they and what is their source?

In the next section, we examine the oldest economic approach to the gains to marriage. This analysis is part of the little factory approach because it emphasizes production. It draws on one of the most important ideas from the economic analysis of international trade—the role of specialization and trade. This approach is particularly useful for analyzing the benefits of marriage in a time and place when men and women were very different from one another in terms of skills and expectations. It does a great job illuminating the benefits of the traditional male breadwinner–female homemaker marriage. It clearly has somewhat less relevance now than in the past—a point well made by the model itself.

After we consider this approach, we look more briefly at other sources of gains to marriage, including some of the other approaches mentioned earlier. Then we shift our focus a bit. Instead of thinking about the gains to marriage, we will consider how the marriage market works and how well off men and women are in a marriage. For example, we consider how differences in sex ratios and changes in women's wages affect marriage outcomes, using a supply and demand approach derived from the work of Gary Becker.

---

[10]Recall that rational choice means that when individuals choose among mutually exclusive alternatives, they choose the one that appears to provide the highest utility, that is, makes them as well off as possible, where "well off" is interpreted broadly.

Production, Specialization, and the Gains to Marriage

In this section, we lay out a model of a traditional marriage, based on underlying gender differences in productivity. In these circumstances, marriage, thought of as a union of two people with different productivity, is a valuable economic institution, quite apart from any particular feelings of love and pleasure that might exist between the parties. Our goal here is to explain the logic of the model and how it leads to gains that make both parties potentially better off. We also investigate why these traditional gains might now be much more modest than in the past, leaving marriages much more dependent on emotional ties.

In this model, we focus on the choices of a representative man and a representative woman, whom we call Mr. M and Ms. F. It makes sense here to think of all women being exactly like Ms. F and of all men being exactly like Mr. M. They have a choice of being single or getting married to each other. We focus on the material standard of living they are able to achieve, leaving old-fashioned sentiments such as love to the side.

Living the Single Life

Let's begin by considering how Mr. M and Ms. F fare as single individuals. Let's assume that our representative individuals get utility from just two kinds of things—market goods (called C) and household-produced goods (called G). Thus, they have a utility function $U = U(C, G)$. They have only two ways to get these goods—working in the labor market to earn income and working in the household sector to produce household goods and services.

In the labor market, each has some wage rate, $\$w$. They use their earned income to purchase market goods and services. To keep things simple, we'll let the price of goods be $\$1$, so that they can buy w units of goods with $\$w$. In the household sector, the amount of output they can produce depends on both their underlying ability and the amount of time (T_H) they spend in production. We can represent that by a household production function $G = G(T_H)$. Still keeping things simple, we will assume that each hour spent working at home yields h units of household output; this means that $G = h \times T_H$. This assumption is a bit unusual,[11] but it simplifies things without affecting the important predictions of this model.

---

[11]This assumption implies a constant marginal product of time spent in household production, which is not very likely. In a more realistic model, the marginal product would fall—each additional hour spent would yield a smaller amount of output. The results here do not depend on that assumption.

The resulting production and consumption opportunities as single-person households are shown in Figure 3.4. The two graphs show the amount of market goods [Figure 3.4(A)] that can be purchased and the amount of household goods [Figure 3.4(B)] that can be produced on the vertical axis and the number of hours spent at each activity on the horizontal axis. Since we assumed that each hour of market work provides w of goods, the production possibilities line for market goods is a straight line with slope equal to w. The production possibilities line for household goods is also a straight line (Slope $= h$) because we assumed that each hour spent there was equally productive. The horizontal dotted line shows the maximum of either good that Mr. M or Ms. F could have if he or she spent all T hours in that activity—not a very probable choice, of course, but possible.

We can use Figure 3.4 to draw a single graph that summarizes Mr. M's or Ms. F's production possibilities. Figure 3.5 illustrates the **production-possibilities curve** or **production-possibilities frontier.** It shows all feasible combinations of market goods (on the vertical axis) and household goods (on the horizontal axis) that Mr. M or Ms. F could produce, given the total time available and their productivity in the market and household sectors. For example, if all available time (T hours) were spent in the market sector, it would yield a total of $w \times T$ units of market goods; of course, since no time would be available for household production, G would be zero. That point is the endpoint

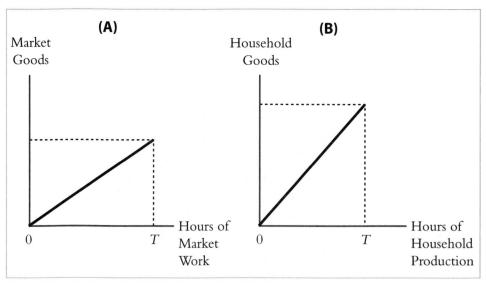

Figure 3.4   Production Possibilities for Mr. M and Ms. F

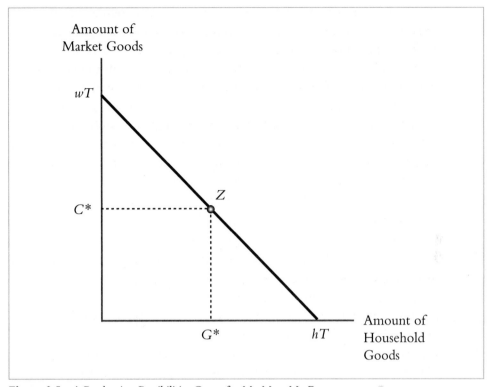

Figure 3.5 A Production Possibilities Curve for Mr. M or Ms. F

of the production-possibilities curve on the vertical axis. Similarly, if all time were spent in the household sector it would yield $h \times T$ units of household goods, but no market goods could be produced. That point is the endpoint on the horizontal axis. The straight line connecting the two endpoints shows all combinations of market goods and household-produced goods that are just possible given the wage (w) and household productivity (h).

All the points on the straight line come directly from the two separate graphs in Figure 3.4. Points to the northeast of the production-possibilities curve are unattainable, while points inside the line toward the origin are feasible but inefficient in the sense that they could have more of both goods or more of one without sacrificing the other. The slope of the production possibilities curve shows the rate at which Mr. M or Ms. F can "trade" one kind of good for the other by "trading" time across sectors. For example, he or she could give up wT units of market goods and get hT units of household goods by transferring all T hours from the market to the household sector. The slope of the line is, therefore, $-(wT/hT)$ or simplifying, $-w/h$; this tells us that the slope depends on the wage rate and household productivity. If w is very large relative to h, then the production-possibilities curve will be very steep. In that case, a person would have to give up a lot of market goods to obtain household goods, and we would say that they face a high "price" for household goods. If h were large relative to w, the production possibilities curve would be flat, and the "price" of producing household goods would be low. These prices are not the usual kind but rather reflect what must be given up to acquire household goods. They are **opportunity costs,** the cost of something measured in terms of what you must give up to get it.

Mr. M or Ms. F will choose some point along the production possibilities curve that maximizes his or her utility. We could write this out as a complex choice problem, involving decisions about how much time to spend working the market and how much time to spend working in the household sector. We will do exactly that in Chapter 7 when we analyze women's labor force participation. For our purposes here, however, the exact choice does not matter. Almost certainly, if Mr. M and Ms. F were single, each would choose to spend time working in both sectors because almost everyone wants both some household goods and some market goods. Point Z is a possible candidate; the exact details would depend on their preferences for market versus household goods and on the slope of the production-possibilities curve.[12] At Z, consumption of the two goods is indicated by the dotted lines to the horizontal and vertical axis. Total consumption is G^* and C^*.

Marriage Between "Economic Identicals"

Now consider a possible marriage between Mr. M and Ms. F and how that would affect their production-possibilities curve. Suppose, first, that Mr. M and Ms. F are identical in the sense that they have exactly the same household and market productivity as each other and, therefore, exactly the same production possibilities curve; that is, $w_M = w_F$ and $h_M = h_F$. If they were to marry, what would their joint production possibilities curve look like? The two endpoints are easy to compute. If they both spend all their time at home, they could now produce $2hT$ units of household goods, and if both spent all their time in the market, they could have $2wT$ units of market goods.

---

[12]If we were using indifference curve analysis, the chosen point (like point Z) would be where an indifference curve was tangent to the production possibilities curve, which here functions as a budget line.

Figure 3.6 shows a production-possibilities curve (PPC) for them individually and for their joint output. To make the analysis more concrete, we have used numbers, but the analysis is perfectly general. Suppose that by themselves, each could produce 10 units of market goods and 10 units of household goods. Their joint curve is based on these two curves. All the points on the joint curve are exactly double every point on the individual production possibilities curves. The joint curve runs from 20 on the vertical axis (if both spent all their time in market production) to 20 on the horizontal axis (if both spent all their time in producing household goods). Similarly, if each produced 5 units of market goods and 5 units of household goods (point *B*), collectively they would have 10 units of market goods and 10 units of household goods (point *A*).

In this situation, Mr. M and Ms. F have absolutely no reason to specialize in production on the basis of gender. For example, point *A* on the joint production-possibilities curve could be produced in many very different ways. First, our newlyweds could specialize completely on the basis of gender, one

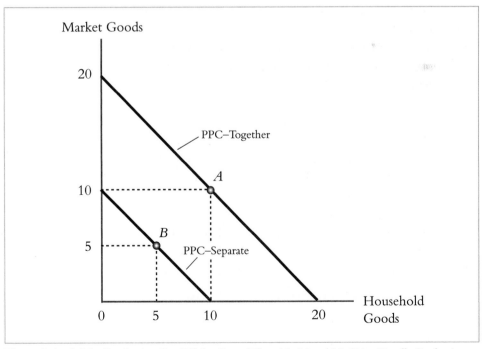

Figure 3.6   A Joint Production-Possibilities Curve When Mr. M and Ms. F Are Equally Productive

working full-time at home and one full-time in the market. If Mr. M worked full-time at home, he would produce 10 units of household output, and Ms. F could contribute her 10 units of market output. Conversely, Ms. F could produce 10 units of household output, and Mr. M could contribute 10 units of market output. But combination *A* could also be produced by each one combining market and household work. For example, if each chose a point like *B* on the lower production-possibility curve, the sum of their outputs would yield point *A*. Point *A* could also be produced with a large range of choices between complete specialization and complete equality. What is true of *A* is true of every other point. Given the underlying productivity of Ms. F and Mr. M, any desired combination can be constructed in any number of different ways, none of which require specialization of task on the basis of gender.

But there is more. Suppose our newlyweds chose a point like *A*, and then shared the resulting goods between themselves equally. That would leave each one consuming a bundle of goods at point *B* along their own individual production-possibilities curves. Note that they are no better off—materially, that is—by linking their production skills via marriage and then sharing what they produce. They end up at a point that they could achieve on their own. And, unless they share equally, one of them will actually be worse off than if he or she were single! The same thing is true of every other point on the joint production-possibilities curve—dividing the outputs equally leaves each on their original production-possibilities curve.

Actually, they could possibly be better off, but in a subtle way. If Mr. M preferred market work and Ms. F preferred household work—or just the opposite—then specialization would leave them no better off materially, but happier because they get to do what they like doing.

Mr. M and Ms. F may dearly love each other. And let's hope they do because the basis for marriage for them must be love. It isn't the ability to produce and make each other materially better off. And note carefully why: The reason they can't join forces and improve their material lot is that they are identical to one another.

Marriage When Productivity Differs

Now consider a rather different and stereotypical situation. Suppose Mr. M is a whiz in the market and has a high wage but is not very productive around the house. Ms. F is just the opposite; she can make a household purr but doesn't have much luck in the market. Formally, we have $w_M > w_F$ (his wage is higher) and $h_F > h_M$ (she is more productive at home). It doesn't matter just yet why these differences might exist or whether the differences are fair or innate. Ms. F may well be the victim of sex discrimination that lowers her wage rate. For the moment, let's just see what these differences imply.

The particular case described here is called **absolute advantage** in which each partner is more productive than the other in one sector—Mr. M in the market and Ms. F in the household sector. But the same analysis that we are about to develop would also hold in the case of **comparative advantage,** in which, for example, Mr. M is better than Ms. F in both the market and the household sector (or vice versa) but is relatively better in one of them. In that case, Mr. M (or Ms. F) has an absolute advantage in both sectors but a comparative advantage in the sector in which he or she is relatively better. Unless someone has an equal absolute advantage in both sectors, he or she must always have a comparative advantage in one sector, while the other party will then have a comparative advantage in the other sector. The theory of comparative advantage is the cornerstone of the economic theory of international trade, and it is one of the most famous ideas in economics.

First look at Figure 3.7, which shows the production-possibilities curves for Mr. M and Ms. F under these circumstances. The two curves are drawn for the case in which Mr. M's wage is two times Ms. F's, and she is twice as productive as he in the household sector. Specifically, Mr. M can produce a maximum of 20 units of market output and 10 units of household output, while Ms. F can produce just the opposite. Mr. M's production possibilities curve is therefore quite steep. This means that, for him, the price of household goods, measured by the amount of market goods he must give up to get them, is very high. The price of household goods would be equal to w_m/h_m (i.e., the amount of income he would give up per hour divided by the amount of goods he could produce in one hour). In this case, that price equals 2 because he gives up 2 units of market goods for every unit of household output he produces.

Ms. F's production-possibilities curve is quite flat because she can produce relatively few market goods but a great deal of household goods. For her, the price of household goods is w_f/h_f, which is much lower than the corresponding price for Mr. M. To be precise, the price of household goods to her equals $^1/_2$ because she gives up 1 unit of market goods and gets 2 units of household goods in return. On the other hand, market goods are expensive for her—they cost h_f/w_f—while market goods are less expensive to Mr. M.

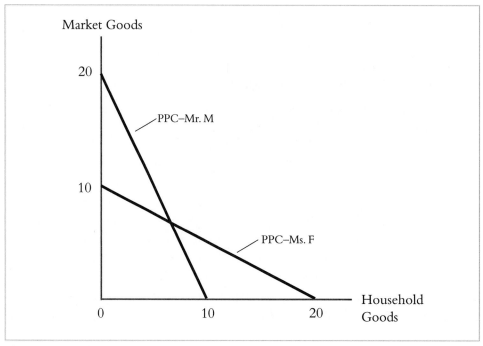

Figure 3.7   Production-Possibility Curves for Mr. M and Ms. F when Productivity Differs

Again, because Mr. M is skilled at market production, but less adept at household production, he faces a high price for household goods but a low price for market goods, where both prices are measured in terms of the amount of the other good that is given up to get it. And Ms. F is in exactly the opposite situation. Household goods are cheap for her, but market goods are expensive. Thought of this way—in terms of how much of one good they must give up to get a unit of the other—one of them must always have a lower price for one good than the other.

Figure 3.8 reproduces the two separate production-possibilities curves for Mr. M and Ms. F but adds their joint production-possibilities curve. (Ignore the lower kinked curve for the moment.) The joint curve is a tricky one to construct, but it is important, so let's go over it carefully. The two endpoints are easy enough; they are just the sum of the outputs that could be produced if they both devoted full-time to either household or market work. In this case, this yields a maximum total market output of 30 (20 from Mr. M and 10 from Ms. F) and a maximum total household output of 30 (10 from Mr. M

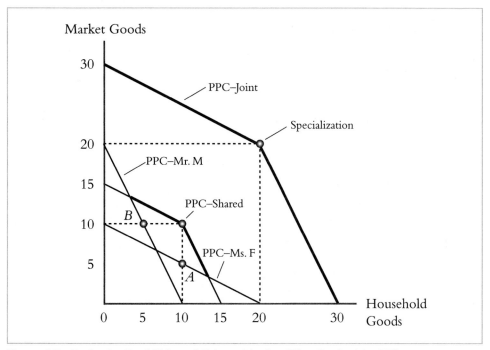

Figure 3.8   Production Possibilities and Gains to Marriage When Productivity Differs

and 20 from Ms. F). The kink point is where each one specializes in the domain in which he or she is more productive. Notice that it is exactly the combination corresponding to full-time market work by Mr. M and full-time household work by Ms. F. It is the bundle (20, 20).

Now look at the slope of the joint production-possibility curve. Starting from the vertical axis, it is first very flat, meaning that relatively few market goods are being given up as household goods are being produced. That part corresponds to Ms. F switching her time from the market to the household, from where she is not very productive to where she is more productive. The slope of this part of the line is exactly the same as the slope of her production-possibilities curve. Every time she reduces her market output by 1 unit, she can increase their joint household output by 2 units. At the "kink point" she has transferred all of her market time to household time.

To the right of the kink point, the curve is very steep. Why? Because for Mr. M and Ms. F to produce yet more household goods, Mr. M must now transfer his time from the market to the household. In so doing, the amount of market goods falls sharply (because Mr. M is productive there) and the amount of household goods increases slowly (because he is not very productive here). Now, to increase their household goods by 1 unit, they must give up 2 units of market goods.

The bold kinked curve represents their joint total production opportunities as a married couple, taking account of the differences in their productivity. What point will our newlyweds choose? There are many possibilities.[13] The kink is an obvious candidate, in which case there would be complete specialization along gender lines. Mr. M would work only in the market, and Ms. F would work only in the household sector; each would specialize in the particular area where they are more productive. But if Mr. M and Ms. F have a strong preference for market goods, they might choose a point to the left of the kink, along the flat portion of the curve. In that case, Mr. M would work only in the market, but Ms. F would combine market and household work. On the other hand, if they strongly prefer household goods, they might choose a point like the steep portion of their budget constraint. In that case, Mr. M would work in both sectors, but Ms. F would specialize in household work.

For our purposes, it does not matter which choice the happy couple makes. Let's see what they can consume, if they share what they have equally. To find that, we take half of each point on the joint curve to get the points on the lower kinked curve. Notice that the kink point is (10, 10), exactly half of the (20, 20) kink point on the total production curve. And the endpoints are exactly half of the corresponding points as well—(0, 15) and (15, 0). Each point is constructed in that way, showing the individual consumption of Mr. M and Ms. F if they join forces and then share equally what they have.

Now here is the key point. Notice that much of the shared PPC curve—the parts that are on the darkened portion of the shared production line—lies above the single-person production-possibility curves available to both Mr. M and Ms. F. For example, look at the kink point on the shared PPC curve. Here Ms. M gets 10 units of market goods and 10 units of household goods, whereas on her own, she could get only 5 units of market goods to go with 10 units of household goods. (This is point *A* on her production-possibilities curve, directly below the kink point.) Similarly, Mr. M gets 10 units of market goods and 10 units of household goods at the kink point, but he can produce

---

[13]Again, the actual choices here can be shown precisely by using indifference curves that represent their joint preferences.

only 10 market units and 5 household units on his own. (This is point *B* on his production-possibilities curve directly to the left of the kink.)

In other words, our newlyweds can join forces, produce, and share, and in the process increase the material standard of living of each of them. Both Mr. M and Ms. F can end up consuming a bundle of goods that exceeds what they could consume if they were single. *They can both be better off by joining forces, specializing, and sharing.*[14]

If they enjoy each other's company, that's even better. But as long as they can tolerate each other, they have something to gain—they can make themselves a material life that they cannot achieve if they are single. And both stand to gain.

What is the source of the gains? The gains derive from the relative differences in market and household or nonmarket productivity, that is from the comparative advantages of Mr. M and Ms. F. Precisely because they are different, they benefit from specializing and then "trading" with one another. Think of it this way. Mr. M can "buy" household goods from Ms. F who can produce them at a much lower market goods price than he can. And Ms. F can "buy" market goods from Mr. M who can get them at a much lower household goods price than she can. So each benefits by getting access to a lower cost producer. These differences in relative prices are determined by the differences in relative productivity, which are the basis for the gains to marriage in this case.

The shared curve shown in Figure 3.8 is based on a 50–50 split of the total family output. In fact, one party could possibly take more than his or her share, still leaving the other one better off than if he or she were single. That doesn't change the basic point of this analysis—the existence of gains to marriage on the basis of comparative advantage—but it opens up another set of possibilities. Maybe the more powerful party in the marriage is able to appropriate most of the gains, leaving the other one little or no better off than if he or she were single.

Getting More Alike—The Gains to Marriage with Smaller Productivity Differences

Figure 3.9 shows the same kind of problem, but now the differences in the underlying productivity of Mr. M and Ms. F are smaller. Mr. M is only 33% more productive in the market (a maximum output of 20 compared to 15 for

---

[14]This exact point is made in the analysis of international trade. Contrary to much popular opinion, both parties in international trade gain by taking advantage of underlying differences in productivity.

Ms. F), while Ms. F is only 33% more productive in the household sector. The joint production-possibilities curve is constructed in exactly the same way as before. The endpoints are at 35 and 35. The kink point is still (20, 20), but the curve is much less kinked—the slope doesn't change as much precisely because their relative productivities are more similar. The shared curve is still kinked, and there is still a region for both to be better off—the lower darkened kinked line. (To simplify the figure, the rest of the shared curve is omitted.) Notice that—and this is the key point—the gains are much smaller now. Compare the parallelogram-shaped areas of "both better off" in Figures 3.8 and 3.9. You can see immediately how they differ.

If we were to redraw Figure 3.9 with even smaller differences, the joint production-possibilities curve would be yet less kinked, and the shared curve would now yield yet smaller gains. This demonstration brings us back to a key point—as Mr. M and Ms. F become more and more like each other, the traditional gains to marriage, based on specialization of task and within-marriage trade, become increasingly smaller. In fact, redrawing with even smaller differences would bring us closer to Figure 3.6, where there are no differences in market and household productivity—and no material gains to marriage.

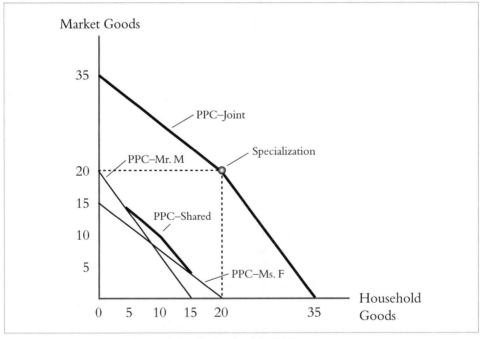

Figure 3.9   Gains to Marriage with Smaller Productivity Differences

As the material gains to marriage become increasingly more modest, the marriage must rest on other grounds. Perhaps that is one reason why contemporary marriages have become more fragile. They can't rely on sheer increases in the material standard of living to see them through.

Other Economics Approaches to the Benefits of Marriage

There are, of course, other kinds of economic benefits to marriage. Let's take stock.

Principal–Agent Issues

Marriage, and especially love, may reduce principal–agent problems. This is a rather subtle idea, so let's develop it carefully.

First, what do we mean by a principal and an agent? A principal–agent relationship exists whenever someone, referred to as the **principal,** hires someone else, referred to as the **agent,** to do something. For example, an employer typically is a principal, hiring an employee (the agent). Anyone who visits a doctor, an attorney, or an auto mechanic is the principal, and the doctor, attorney, or auto mechanic is the agent who is being engaged for his/her expertise. In the same vein, a stockholder is the principal, and the managers of the company are the agents. In each of these situations, the principal wants the agent to act in the principal's best interest. For example, the employer wants the employee to work hard and efficiently, while you want the doctor, attorney, and auto mechanic to solve your problem at least cost to you and the managers to run the company so that you make money. Principal–agent relationships are a common feature of economic life and an important part of contemporary economic analysis.

A **principal-agent problem** exists when the agent doesn't fully do what the principal wants him/her to do. The interests of the principal and the agent are generally very different. The agent may not fully share the principal's interests and may act instead in a way that is most beneficial to the agent rather than the principal. Thus, for example, the employee may not want to work particularly hard if he/she can get away with it; after all, it's not the agent's profits that are being diminished, and hard work is often less enjoyable than goofing off. A doctor may want to order too many medical tests or too few, depending on the

Box 3.1   Divorce, Specialization, and the Gains to Marriage

We focus directly on divorce later, but, for the moment, let's consider how the possibility of divorce might affect specialization and the gains to marriage.

Here's a natural and quite correct objection to specialization on the basis of gender. "This is all well and good, as long as Mr. M and Ms. F live happily ever after. But suppose Mr. M has a wandering eye and, out of the blue, dumps Ms. F. What is she going to do? Having specialized in household production, her market skills have deteriorated. Poor Ms. F. She is utterly vulnerable." Or, equivalently: "Suppose Ms. F has a wandering eye and, out of the blue, dumps Mr. M. What is he going to do? Having specialized in market work, his household production skills have deteriorated. He can't even boil water. Poor Mr. M. He is utterly vulnerable."

In a world in which divorce is extremely rare, these considerations might not arise. Mr. M and Ms. F could imagine themselves in a kind of binding long-term contract (i.e., a marriage contract) that lasts "in sickness and in health, till death do you part." In those circumstances, Mr. M and Ms. F might willingly agree to specialization of task, knowing that it implied relatively little risk. The material gains to marriage, which derive from this specialization, would therefore be large, and, as a consequence, neither Mr. M or Ms. F might be tempted to stray.

In a world in which divorce is more common, however, these concerns will naturally arise. Mr. M and Ms. F, no matter how much they are in love, must allow for the possibility that at some future date the marriage contract could be unilaterally broken. In these circumstances, Mr. M and Ms. F might be a great deal less willing to adopt the extreme specialization of task that maximizes the material gains to marriage, precisely because of the risk it entails. The material gains to their marriage would therefore be smaller than in a world of certain long-term marriage. (In terms of our analysis, they would be operating inside their joint production-possibilities curve.) The smaller gains to marriage then, in turn, make divorce more attractive because each party now has less to lose.

Thus, the possibility of divorce reduces the gains to marriage, which raises the probability of divorce. Can anyone say "chicken and egg?"

particular financial incentives he/she faces.[15] A mechanic may replace parts that were working perfectly well, an attorney may run up hourly bills doing all sorts of things that aren't particularly useful, and the management of a company may be more concerned with maximizing their own income rather than yours (see, for example, Enron, Worldcom, and Tyco, just to name a few).

The common source of the problem is knowledge, or actually the lack thereof. If you knew as much as the agent and could fully monitor what he/she is doing, the agent would have no opportunity to take advantage of you. But where the agent knows much more than you do—like the doctor or the mechanic—or where it is impossible or impractical to observe and monitor the agent's activity—like the employee and the management of the firm whose stock you own—the agent has the opportunity to advance his or her own interests, rather than yours. That, in a nutshell, is the principal–agent problem.

What does all this have to do with marriage? One feature of married life is that the two partners provide goods to one another as nonmarket transactions. One partner doesn't literally pay the other to clean the house, provide meals, bear and care for children, or earn the income to provide the necessary market goods. The transactions are implicit rather than explicit.

Family life could be organized quite differently than it typically is. For example, instead of marrying one another, single men and single women could contract with one another for all the many outputs of household production, from preparing food to doing housework to bearing and caring for children to, well, even sex. If a woman wanted to have a child, she could contract for a sperm provider; similarly, a man could contract for someone to bear his child. (These arrangements are, in fact, not unheard of. Lesbian couples sometimes do have a child in precisely that way.) If you use your imagination, you can probably think of all sorts of market arrangements that could be made to substitute for the non-market intrafamily arrangements that currently prevail.

Of course, this market provision of household goods is not the common arrangement, and principal–agent issues are part of the explanation. In each of these examples of market arrangements, a principal–agent relationship exists in which a principal (a single male or single female) engages an agent to cook

---

[15]Who hasn't heard the complaints that HMOs provide too little care? In the old fee-for-service insurance arrangement, the common complaint was that doctors often provided too much service because they often benefited financially from the additional tests.

his/her food, clean his/her house, bear his/her child, care for his/her child, and so on. The obvious question that arises in each and every case is whether the agent will do the job well, that is, do it as the principal would want it done. Or will the agent cut corners, take it a bit easy, and suit him- or herself where it is feasible?

It certainly is possible, perhaps likely, that a principal–agent problem will arise in many of these cases. Consider the specific case of hiring an agent to bear a child. It is impossible to monitor the agent's behavior 24 hours a day. Because it is the principal's child, not the agent's, the agent might not be as motivated to do the many little and not always so pleasant things that contribute to the health and well-being of the child—eating carefully, not drinking alcohol or coffee, and so on. The same kind of issues arise across the board—it isn't the agent's house or food or child. The agent may be a perfectly decent person, but even so, in most cases, the agent might simply and naturally care less about the outcome than the principal. So we might well expect outcomes that are not nearly as desirable as the principal would want and that could potentially be achieved.

The institution of marriage, especially a marriage based on love and mutual respect and shared goals and values, is a kind of solution to this principal–agent dilemma. In a marriage, there is no principal hiring an agent. Even in the kind of old-fashioned division-of-labor marriage analyzed earlier, the husband no more hires the wife to bear his children and care for his house than the wife hires the husband to provide her food and shelter. Rather, they are both principals. What they jointly produce, they jointly consume. She is just as interested in the well-being of the children as he is because the children are theirs, not his or hers. Each cares about the utility of the other.

This does not mean that there are no problems, of course. Each partner may wish that the other would pick up a larger share of the work load. They might disagree about whether their children should take piano lessons or join the soccer team and a million other such decisions. But the core principal–agent problems ought to be far less because theirs is not a market relationship.

Economies of Scale

Marriage allows individuals to achieve economies of scale in household production. **Economies of scale** exist when the average cost of producing a good falls as more of the goods is produced. It is quite clear that economies of scale do exist in many areas of household production. Two-person households don't need twice as many refrigerators, stoves, sinks, toilets, rooms, and so on as a one-person household to reach the same level of household production. It doesn't take twice as long to cook for two as for one. As a result, a two-person household with the same per capita income as a single-person household will typically have a higher standard of living.

Household economies of scale like these are built into the official poverty standards used in the United States to measure the number of persons who are poor. To be officially poor in the United States, a household must have income that falls below a specified income level called the **poverty threshold.** These poverty thresholds are adjusted for family size; the idea is that for each family size, the corresponding poverty threshold provides an equivalent (low) standard of living. For example, in 2001, the official poverty threshold for a non-elderly (less than age 65) single adult was $9214. Any non-elderly single adult with an income less than that was considered poor, and any with an income greater than that was considered non-poor. For a non-elderly two-adult family, the poverty threshold was $11,920, just 28.7% more rather than twice as much, as it would have been in the absence of economies of scale. Similarly, the poverty threshold increases by about 50%, rather than 100%, when family size increases from two to four. Clearly, these figures suggest the existence of very substantial economies of scale as family size increases from one to two and important, but smaller economies of scale when family size increases from two to four persons.

Formal marriage, however, is not essential to capturing these economies of scale. Any two persons who are sharing living quarters and facilities are able to capture these economies. They need not be married, nor even of the opposite sex. So this cannot be a primary benefit of marriage.

Risk Sharing

In most marriages, economic resources are pooled; that is not the case, however, for most roommates. Pooling of resources reduces the risk of income loss, in the event that one partner loses his or her job and becomes unemployed—unless they are work partners, too. In general, this reduction of the risk of income loss enables a married couple to see their way through what would be a severe problem for a single-person household.

Risk sharing and economies of scale together are compelling reasons why marriage is particularly important in poor countries and for poor persons in the United States. Individually, a low income provides a very poor standard of living, and there is the risk of substantial declines in the standard of living if the individual becomes unemployed. Together, two low incomes provide a much better standard of living because of the existence of economies of scale as well as insurance against a complete loss of income.

A Supply and Demand Model of Marriage

Supply and demand analysis is the workhorse of microeconomics. It is the oldest and still most useful economic model for understanding how markets work to set equilibrium prices and the associated quantities demanded and supplied. Can we apply it to marriage and the marriage market? It's a bit of a stretch—what, for example, is the price in a marriage market—and a bit of work, but it does lead to some interesting insights and predictions.

This approach, which is based on Becker's original article on the economics of marriage, emphasizes the decision to marry or remain single and, especially, the way the gains to marriage are divided between husband and wife. We skirted that latter issue in the previous analysis. Our goal there was to show that there *were* gains to marriage, and we focused on the case where the marital output was equally divided. Here, we'll examine how the marriage market might work and how it determines the way marital output is distributed. We'll think about how well off women (and men) are within marriage, and what things might determine that or cause it to change.

Basic Concepts and Notation

To implement the model, we need to introduce some basic concepts and notation. Becker assumed that the utility of single men and single women depended on their ability to produce market and non-market goods for themselves, which depends, in turn, on their wage rate and their productivity in the household sector. The production-possibility curve for Mr. M and Ms. F as single individuals, which we looked at in Figure 3.4, captures this idea. It is, however, also possible to think about the utility as reflecting more broadly life as a single person, and that interpretation will be useful later on. In most of the analysis that follows, however, we will follow Becker and refer to the *output* produced by households rather than their *utility*. An individual's utility depends on the amount of output he/she consumes, so when output is larger, utility is larger as well—and more utility is a good thing.

Becker assumes in this model that there is only a single household-produced good called Z. The output of single-person households is Z_M for men and Z_F

Box 3.2   Does Marriage Matter?

We've talked repeatedly about the idea of the gains to marriage. But what exactly are the gains to marriage? Are the benefits large or small?

Sociologist Linda Waite attempted to answer the question: Does marriage matter? in her presidential address to the Population Association of America in 1995 and in her book *The Case for Marriage: Why Married People Are Happier, Healthier, and Better Off Financially,* coauthored with Maggie Gallagher. She gave her address in the wake of an acrimonious public debate about "family values." Her goal was to document some of the ways that married individuals benefited from marriage. Her concern was that individuals really didn't appreciate the benefits of marriage, especially those that had been established by solid social science research. Here are some interesting conclusions from her study:

- Married men and married women have lower levels of negative health behaviors than the unmarried. They report a lower incidence of problem drinking than divorced or widowed men and women. Perhaps not surprisingly, men report far more problems than women regardless of marital status. Married men and women are also less likely to be risk-takers, measured by accidents caused by being careless, driving too fast, and having serious arguments or fights at home or at work. On these measures, men and women are relatively similar, but married men and women exhibit far fewer risky behaviors than divorced men and women.

- Both married men and women are more likely to survive to age 65; they do better not only than the never marrieds but also than those who are divorced or widowed. Why? Waite speculates that "marriage appears to reduce risky and unhealthy behaviors," "increases material well-being," and "provides individuals . . . with others who rely on them and on whom they can rely" (p. 489).

- Married couples are wealthier. Even on a per capita basis, they have 50% more wealth on average than those who are widowed and twice as much as individuals who divorced or never married.

- Children fare better in married-couple families. Research by McLanahan and Sandefur[16] shows that children from one-parent families are more

---

[16]Sara S. McLanahan and Gary Sandefur, *Growing Up With a Single Parent,* Harvard University Press: Cambridge, MA, 1994.

likely to fail to complete high school, more likely to have a teen birth, and more likely to be jobless as young adults. We talk more about that in Chapter 15.

The big question is whether these benefits of marriage are causal in the sense that a random single person who became married could expect to reap the benefits. It is possible, instead, that the apparent benefits of marriage simply reflect the kind of men and women who become and remain married, rather than the impact of marriage per se. After all, the marital status in which we observe men and women is not the result of a random assignment experiment or a natural experiment. (Try to visualize the random experiment—you two marry, you two remain single, etc.) Rather, men and women choose whether to marry, who to marry, and whether to remain married on the basis of the benefits they receive. So there is a real possibility that the apparent benefits cannot be attributed to the impact of marriage. They could just reflect the particular characteristics of the men and women who are married.

Waite, however, offers some evidence to suggest that the effects are real and causal. Researchers can attempt to control for **selection bias,** which is the bias that is introduced because individuals select the status (here, married versus divorced) in which we observe them. Such selection bias can be handled to some degree through a statistical technique that pays special attention to the underlying selection of marital status (married versus unmarried). She argues that the benefits remain in most studies, even after control for selection bias.

What causes the benefits of marriage? Waite identifies four factors, some of which ought to sound very familiar:

- *Specialization.* The long-term nature of the marriage contract "allows the partners to make choices that carry immediate costs but eventually bring benefits." The long time period "makes it sensible—rational choice is at work here—for individuals to develop *some* skills and to neglect others because they count on their spouse to fill in where they are weak."

- *Risk sharing.* In Waite's words, "Spouses act as a sort of small insurance pool against life's uncertainties, reducing their need to protect themselves *by themselves* from unexpected events."

- *Economies of scale.*

- *Social obligation.* "Marriage connects people to other individuals, to other social groups, and to other social institutions."

One of the most interesting things about Waite's research is how "economic" it is, even though she is a sociologist and demographer. For more on Waite's argument, see her article and book.

Sources: Linda J. Waite, "Does Marriage Matter?" *Demography*, Vol. 32, No. 14, pp. 438–508, Nov. 1995. Reprinted with the permission of the author and the Population Association of America. Linda J. Waite and Maggie Gallagher, *The Case for Marriage: Why Married People Are Happier, Healthier, and Better Off Financially*, New York: Doubleday, 2000.

for women. The corresponding output of a married-couple household is written Z_{MF}. (The outputs of same-sex households would be Z_{MM} and Z_{FF}. Virtually everything in this analysis could apply to same-sex or cohabiting households.) Finally, the total marital output Z_{MF} is divided between M and F. We will use S_M to stand for the amount of Z_{MF} that goes to M (the husband) and S_F to stand for the amount that goes to F (the wife). We are not assuming that $S_M = S_F$, as we did when we analyzed the gains to marriage. It will be important later on to recognize that $S_M + S_F \equiv Z_{MF}$, which simply means that all the marital output goes to either the husband or the wife. Again, the greater is Z_M or Z_F, the better off a single man or single woman is. Similarly, the greater is S_M or S_F, the better off a married man or married woman is.

If marriage is voluntary, then individuals are willing to marry if and only if they expect to be better off. (In everything that follows, we should always preface it with "expect" as an acknowledgment that it is difficult, if not impossible, to know exactly how things will turn out in matters like this. We won't always say it, however, and wherever the "expect" is omitted, add it in.) Thus, a man is willing to marry only if $S_M > Z_M$, and a woman is willing to marry only if $S_F > Z_F$. From these two inequalities, it follows that for a married couple, $S_M + S_F > Z_M + Z_F$; both terms on the left-hand side of the inequality are greater than the corresponding terms on the right-hand side. Further, since $S_M + S_F \equiv Z_{MF}$ and since most individuals are married, it must be true that typically $Z_{MF} > Z_M + Z_F$. That's a formal way of stating that there are gains to marriage for most individuals. In effect, Becker is suggesting that the very fact that most men and women are willing to marry means that there must be gains to marriage. If there weren't, marriage couldn't make them both better off. Of course, we already know something about those gains to marriage, and their source.

Supply and Demand Curves for Marriage

A supply and demand model requires four things—a price and a quantity plus supply and demand curves. In this case, the quantity term is easy to determine; it is the number of men and the number of women in the marriage market. They are the prospective "buyers" and "sellers." The price is far less obvious because there is no literal monetary exchange.[17] As a price term, we will use what a woman must receive to be willing to marry and what a man is willing to pay to be married. We measure this by S_F, the marital output that a woman receives, and S_M, the marital output that a man receives.

To derive a supply curve of women to marriage, we need to find the number of women willing to marry at each possible value of S_F. To do that, we use the idea that marriage is voluntary and depends on a comparison of expected utility if married versus expected utility if single (i.e., a comparison of S_F with Z_F.) Suppose that Z_F varies across women, ranging from quite low to much higher. These differences could reflect differences in wages or differences in preferences or anything that causes a woman's well-being as a single woman to vary.

To construct the supply curve, we let the value of S_F range from very low to very high, each time thinking about how many women would be willing to marry at that particular "price." Because a women is willing to marry only if $S_F > Z_F$, then, when S_F is very low, very few women will be willing to marry—only those with the very lowest values of Z_F. If S_F were a bit higher, a few more women would now join the supply curve; they are the women with values of Z_F just a bit higher. If S_F were yet a bit higher, yet a few more women would join the supply curve, and so on and so on, with more women added to the supply curve each time as S_F rises. Finally, at some high value of S_F, all women, even those with the best prospects as single women, will be willing to marry. At that point, the supply curve becomes vertical, because there are simply no more women. The result is a supply curve of women to marriage that is upward-sloping and then vertical. There is a positive relationship between the number of women willing to marry and S_F, what they get in marriage.

---

[17]We are ignoring dowries (payments from a bride's family to a groom) and brideprices (payments from the groom's family to a bride's family). They are no longer very common.

We could do exactly the same thing for men, substituting S_M for S_F and proceeding in exactly the same way to find a supply curve for men to marriage. But we don't want two supply curves. Instead, we need a demand curve of men for wives to go with our supply curve of women willing to marry.[18] This demand curve must depend on S_F so that we can then put the supply and demand curves together on the same graph. To do that, note that as S_F increases, S_M falls; this follows because $S_M + S_F \equiv Z_{MF}$, so $S_M \equiv Z_{MF} - S_F$. This shows us that when S_F is very high, S_M is very low, and when S_F is lower, S_M is higher.

Thus, when S_F is very high, S_M is very low, and relatively few men will be willing to marry. Most men will be better off staying single rather than marrying and giving such a large S_F to their wife. However, as S_F gets smaller, more men will find that what they get in marriage after "paying" S_F exceeds what they would get if they remained single (Z_M). Consequently, the demand curve of men for marriage is downward-sloping. The higher the price men must pay, the smaller is the number of wives demanded. As the price falls, the quantity demanded increases. This demand curve obeys the Law of Demand. Finally, when all potential husbands are accounted for, the demand curve becomes vertical.

We illustrate these supply and demand curves in Figure 3.10. Figure 3.10 (A) is the supply curve of women to marriage; Figure 3.10 (B) shows the demand curve of men for marriage. Like any supply and demand diagram, the quantity is on the horizontal axis, and the price is on the vertical axis. The horizontal axis shows the number of women or men willing to marry. The price is S_F, which is what a woman gets and what a man pays. The husband then gets what is left over. Note that, as discussed previously, both curves become vertical when we reach a price at which all men or all women are accounted for. Note also that we could easily have reversed the roles of the men and the women by using S_M as the price. Then the men would be represented by the supply curve, and the women, by the demand curve. Absolutely nothing would change in the analysis or the results. Using S_F as the price is actually more convenient because we can see directly from the analysis how well off women are in different supply and demand situations by looking at changes in the equilibrium value of S_F.

---

[18]It may be natural to think of the demanders as being in charge. Nothing of the sort is implied here.

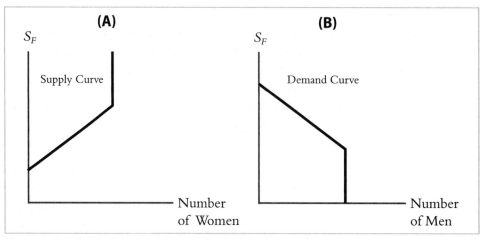

Figure 3.10   Supply and Demand Curves for the Marriage Market

Marriage Market Equilibrium

Now let's put the supply and demand diagrams together. Our goal is to find the equilibrium price. This is a tricky idea. Instead of thinking of each couple as negotiating individually over who gets what, imagine instead that the general terms are set by the market. Those terms are the equilibrium values for S_M and S_F, which we'll refer to as $S_M{}^*$ and $S_F{}^*$. Think of them as widely understood social norms for how men and women fare within a marriage. They are something like "this is what married life is like for men and women."

It is important to appreciate that, in the analysis that follows, we are not trying to explain who marries whom. In fact, it is probably useful to think of the men and women in the model as having absolutely no preference for one person over another. Of course, even economists know that's not true, but our goal here is to analyze general forces determining how men and women are treated within marriage, rather than who marries whom.[19] Simplifying in this way is, therefore, acceptable—and, indeed, necessary—to make progress on this particular issue.

Figure 3.11 puts the supply and demand curves together to find the equilibrium. When S_F is very high, as at S_{FH}, marriage is a great deal for women, but

---

[19]There is a substantial literature in economics about who marries whom that focuses on whether likes marry likes or unlikes.

not so good for men. The price is too high for equilibrium, and you can see
that there is excess supply—more women looking for a husband than men
looking for a wife. The excess supply is shown as the horizontal distance between the supply curve and the demand curve at that price. In the same fashion, when S_F is very low, as at S_{FL}, marriage is a great deal for men but not so
good for women. Now the price is too low for equilibrium, and there is excess demand—more men looking for a wife than women looking for a husband.

The **marriage market equilibrium** is at S_F^*, the only price where supply and
demand just balance. It's interesting to think about how the equilibrium
might get established. At a low price like S_{FL}, there are more men looking for
wives than women willing to marry. So a man might figure that if he offered
a somewhat better deal by raising S_F, he would improve his chances. The men
who don't do that end up without a wife. Eventually, all the men get the message, and S_F rises. As S_F increases, more women are willing to marry, but now

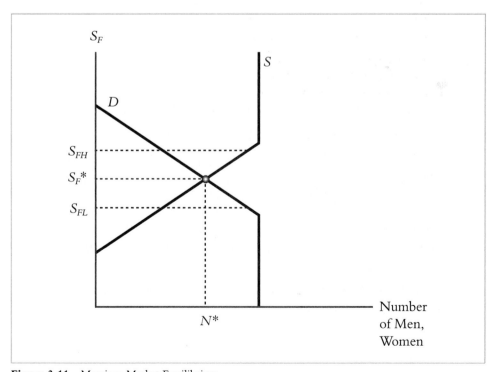

Figure 3.11   Marriage Market Equilibrium

fewer men are willing to marry, so the surplus of men starts to shrink. Finally, when S_F has increased all the way up to $S_F{}^*$, the market is in balance.

Exactly, the same kind of logic works starting at a high price like S_{FH}. Now, marriage is great for women but not for men. Women would reason that they could find a husband if they got a bit less for themselves. S_F would fall, bringing more men into the market, reducing the number of willing women, and eventually reaching an equilibrium at $S_F{}^*$.

In the marriage market equilibrium, there are N^* married men and N^* married women. But not everyone is married. The horizontal distance from N^* to the vertical portion of the demand curve represents the number of unmarried men. They are the men who would marry if they got a better deal, but at the marriage market equilibrium price, they prefer to remain single. Similarly, the horizontal distance from N^* to the vertical portion of the supply curve represents the number of unmarried women. They are the women who would marry if they got a better deal, but at the marriage market equilibrium price, they prefer to remain single.

Changes in Supply and Demand—What Happens to the Marriage Market?

The most important and valuable part of a model like this is considering what happens if the supply curve or demand curve changes. Here's where it really starts to get interesting. What factors make $S_F{}^*$ big or small? Under what circumstances do women fare better or worse in marriage? This kind of analysis is called **comparative static analysis;** see Chapter 2 for more about this kind of analysis. The goal is to see how actual changes in the conditions that underlie the supply and demand curves of the marriage market will affect marriage market equilibrium.

It's interesting to think about a few obvious changes that would affect the supply and/or demand curve. One is the relative numbers of men and women. What happens when the sex ratio is way out of balance? Another is the effect of women's improved labor market opportunities on the marriage market. How does that affect the marriage position of women? Still another is the effect of birth control pills, abortion, and AIDS.

To brush up on the comparative statics of supply and demand analysis, review Chapter 2. The most important point to remember is that comparative static analysis takes a few steps. The changes we examine affect the outcome indirectly by first affecting either the supply curve or the demand curve. That change, in turn, will affect the outcome that we are interested in.

The Sex Ratio and the Marriage Market

Differences in sex ratios can arise in marriage markets from many different causes. A major war would typically cause a shortage of men, certainly temporarily, possibly for a longer time. Changes in birth rates can do the same, if men typically marry women who are a few years younger than they are. Suppose birth rates are rising, as they did during the baby boom of the mid-1950s (see Chapter 5). Then the older birth cohorts will be a bit smaller than the younger ones, or, equivalently, there will be fewer men in the older cohort than women in the younger ones. When birth rates fall, as they did in the mid-1970s, the imbalance will work just the opposite. Now there will be more older men than slightly younger women. College campuses are another site of sex ratio imbalances. When many traditionally all-male colleges first admitted women, there were often 10 or more men for every woman on campus. Currently, women substantially outnumber men on most college campuses as the result of a gender gap in higher education favoring women over men. In 2000, men received only 43% of bachelor's degrees, down from more than three quarters in 1950.

Finally, there are also differences in the general population, especially in the Black and Hispanic populations.[20] Table 3.3 shows the sex ratio among the civilian non-institutional population for Whites, Blacks, and Hispanics in 2002 by five-year age brackets from age 20 to age 39. The numbers shown are the number of women per 100 men. For Whites, the figures range from 96 to 99, so there is rough balance, and if anything men are in excess supply. For Blacks, the numbers are far from equal, and women are in surplus at all prime marriage age groups. Between age 25 and age 39, there are 25% more Black women than Black men.[21] Women are also in surplus in the Hispanic population, with a high of 120 Hispanic women age 25–29 for every 100 Hispanic men. The overall sex ratio is in balance, but if marriage is largely within race and ethnic groups, then the imbalance could be an important factor.

---

[20]Women, of course, outlive men, so there are large differences at older ages. Those differences are not particularly relevant for the issues we are considering.

[21]The imbalance in the sex ratio among the Black population reflects a number of factors, including differences by gender in mortality, incarceration, and military service. Currently, at age 15–17 there are equal numbers of men and women.

Age	All	White	Black	Hispanic
20–24	99	98	117	116
25–29	100	96	125	120
30–34	98	98	125	108
35–39	98	99	125	117

Table 3.3 Female-to-Male Ratio by Age, Race, and Ethnicity, 2002*

*Entries are the number of women per 100 men.

Source: U.S. Bureau of the Census, P20:#547, Table A1.

Let's see how a change in the sex ratio might affect the outcome of the marriage market. To be specific, let's focus on an increase in the number of women with no increase in the number of men. Clearly, a change like that will affect the supply curve. A parallel analysis could be based on a decrease in the number of men with no change in the number of women. In that case, the demand curve would be affected.

Exactly how an increase in the number of women affects the supply curve depends on who the additional women are in terms of their own personal Z_F. The case that seems most sensible is if the additional women are very much like those already in the supply curve. Let's call that a *balanced increase in supply,* which is intended to suggest that the increase is similar in percentage terms at all values of Z_F. In that case, the supply curve would shift out to the right proportionately—say 10 or 20% at all values of S_F.

This change is shown in Figure 3.12, which includes the original supply curve from Figure 3.11, now labeled S_1, and adds a new supply curve labeled S_2. Note that the two supply curves are not parallel. Rather each point on S_2 represents the same percentage increase in the number of women willing to marry. That's a smaller absolute increase at low values of S_F and a larger absolute increase as S_F increases. The new curve is flatter than the original one.

What happens to the marriage market? At the old equilibrium price ($S_{F1}*$), there is now excess supply—more women looking for husbands than men looking for wives. As a result, the equilibrium price will fall to $S_{F2}*$ where the new supply curve and the original demand curve are now in balance. The absolute number of married men and women increases from N_1* to N_2*. The equilibrium price falls, so that married women are worse off than before,

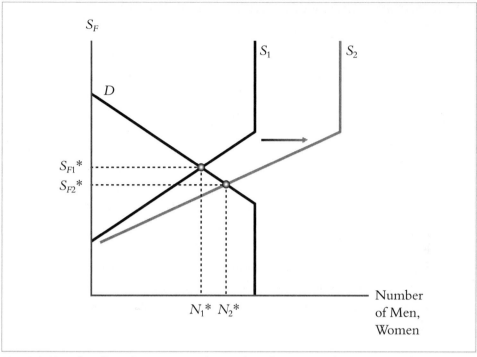

Figure 3.12   The Effect of an Increase in the Number of Women on the Marriage Market

while married men are better off. So the change in the sex ratio has an immediate impact on the marriage market.

If there were a decrease in the number of women relative to men, the situation would be just the opposite. Now the supply curve would shift to the left—fewer women willing to marry at every price. The equilibrium price would rise. Men would be worse off, and women would be better off.

We began this section by referring to sex ratios at college campuses, where the ratios are often quite skewed. Suppose we reinterpret the model in terms of dating behavior. Does it make any sense to you? Would the women be "wined[22] and dined" better when the sex ratio was in their favor than when it favored the men? That's roughly the equivalent of a high value of S_F in our model. There probably isn't any good data, but anecdotal evidence is roughly consistent with that.

---

[22]Only if over the legal drinking age, of course.

Women's Wages and the Marriage Market

How do women's wages affect the marriage market? If women's wages increase, is that good or bad for the marital prospects of women?

Figure 3.13 shows how we might analyze that. An increase in women's wages will increase Z_F, their well-being as single women. Because they earn more, they can support themselves better. Again, let's think of this as a balanced change, with the wage for all women increasing proportionately. Then this kind of change will shift the supply curve up or in. It is probably easier to think of shifting the curve up, so that each woman is now willing to marry at a value of S_F that is proportionately higher than before. Or you can think of fewer women being willing to marry at any value of S_F, so the supply curve shifts in. This is exactly the opposite of the change in supply we analyzed in Figure 3.12.

In Figure 3.13, S_1 is the original supply curve, and S_2 is the new supply curve with the higher (balanced) wages for women. Because the number of women doesn't change, the two supply curves eventually join up where all women are accounted for on the new supply curve. The original equilibrium is at $S_{F1}*$

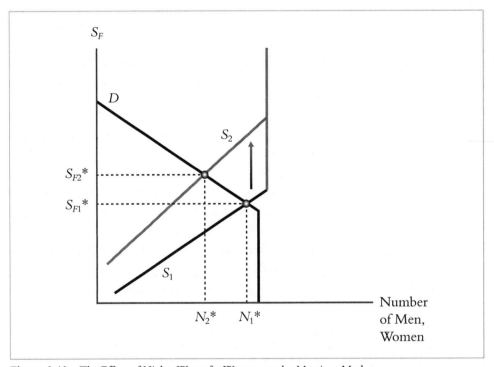

Figure 3.13   The Effect of Higher Wages for Women on the Marriage Market

and $N_1{}^*$. When the supply curve shifts, the equilibrium moves up along the demand curve. The new equilibrium price rises to $S_{F2}{}^*$ and the number of married men and women falls to $N_2{}^*$. How do these changes occur? At the old equilibrium price, fewer of the now better-off single women are willing to marry, so there is excess demand by men for wives. So, just as we saw in Figure 3.11, the price must rise. Women gain within marriage precisely because they are better off outside of marriage. Men must treat them better—in our terms, the women get a larger share of marital output—because otherwise the women are better off single and will be unwilling to marry.[23] This is an important conclusion and one that is far from obvious.

Instead of wages increasing, try to picture the supply curve for women a century or even two centuries ago. Their labor market opportunities were, with rare exceptions, virtually nonexistent. Their supply curve was therefore positioned very low, and the corresponding equilibrium price was very low. The marriage market equilibrium gave women a relatively small share of marital output, again precisely because their nonmarriage opportunities were so limited.

Changes in Single Life—The Sexual Revolution and All That

Single life has changed in many other ways as well. Not too long ago—say, in the 1950s—sexual activity prior to marriage was relatively uncommon, certainly by today's standards. This was not just a matter of different moral standards. Contraception, both for men and women, was far less available than it is today. The birth control pill was not yet available. Condoms were "behind the counter" in the drugstore, not on shelves in broad daylight.[24] In Connecticut, it was illegal even for married couples to buy contraceptives, a provision that was not struck down by the U.S. Supreme Court until 1965.[25] And, of course, abortion was illegal and, even where available, often not very safe. As a result, sexual activity, outside of marriage, carried real risks for both men and, especially, women. Can we incorporate these facts into our supply and demand model?

It is reasonable to think of these things as lowering Z_M and Z_F, which we are using as measures of the well-being of single men and women. Single men and women didn't have it quite so good. (This is a broad generalization, of

---

[23]There is an additional impact that might make the analysis yet more complicated. An increase in women's wages, holding men's wages constant, reduces the gains to marriage via specialization and exchange.
[24]Some things haven't changed. Advertisements for condoms are still incredibly rare, except on MTV.
[25]The case is *Griswold v Connecticut,* 381, U.S. 479 (1965).

Box 3.3   MARRIAGE THEN AND NOW . . . ONE ECONOMIST'S PERSONAL AND PROFESSIONAL PERSPECTIVE

Isabel Sawhill is a very well-known and influential economist who has written for many years on issues involving the family, poverty, the welfare system, and teen childbearing. Currently she is Vice President and Director of Economic Studies at The Brookings Institution, a Washington, D.C., think tank, where she directs the Roundtable on Children and codirects the Welfare Reform and Beyond Initiative. Previously she served as a Senior Fellow at the Urban Institute and an Associate Director at the U.S. Office of Management and Budget from 1993 to 1995 and helped to found the National Campaign to Prevent Teen Pregnancy, an organization that she continues to serve as President.

The following excerpt comes from a recent article by Sawhill about marriage and single parenting.

> When I was growing up, marriage was something one took for granted. Its desirability was unquestioned. Especially if one were a girl, it was at the center of one's dreams and aspirations. This was at a time when women had few roles or opportunities beyond being a wife and mother. We even joked in college[26] that you should have a ring by spring or get your money back.
>
> Needless to say, a lot has changed—and changed, in many respects, for the better. Marriage is no longer the principal source of economic and social status for women. No one need feel trapped inside an abusive or neglectful relationship because there are so few other options. And as a result of widening opportunities, women have gained considerable leverage with which to bargain for more equal treatment and respect within marriage. In my first book, *Time of Transition: The Growth of Families Headed by Women* (coauthored with Heather Ross and published by the Urban Institute in 1975), we argued that rising divorce rates were one consequence of women's no longer being tied to a single life script.
>
> A weapon like divorce doesn't have to be used to be effective. The mere threat or availability of the option may be enough to change be-

---

[26]Sawhill graduated from Wellesley College.

havior. Our research, and that of others, provided lots of empirical support for the idea that women's expanding opportunities were simultaneously responsible for rising divorce rates on the one hand and for better—including more egalitarian—marriages on the other. We also predicted that once the wider culture had adapted to women's new roles, and men in particular had adjusted their expectations and behaviors, the divorce rate would level off, but at a new and higher level. That, of course, is exactly what happened in the early 1980s. And I, for one, would most certainly not want to turn back the clock. It is less clear to me how all of this has affected men. The politically correct position is to argue that it has made their lives better as well. I would like to think that this is true, but it may not be, and a part of me will always be just a tiny bit suspicious that advocates of marriage are people who want to return to a world in which men resume their "rightful place" as patriarchs within the family. In short, there are some good reasons why feminists are wary of the new emphasis on revitalizing marriage as an institution.

That said, the research suggests that two married parents with a lifelong commitment to each other is the best environment for raising children. In addition, the much greater social acceptability of divorce has increased the likelihood that couples will split up over relatively minor differences. And the spread of no-fault divorce in the wake of this more permissive environment has made women who choose to invest in homemaking or child rearing vulnerable to being left in the lurch. Finally, higher divorce rates have made the younger generation wary of marriage and eroded the social support that young married couples once received from family and friends.

course, and we don't mean to offend anyone.) In terms of our analysis, this would increase the supply of women willing to marry. Because life as a single person was less attractive, women would be willing to marry at lower marital shares than otherwise or, equivalently, more women would be willing to marry at any value of S_F. This would shift the supply curve down or out. What about the men? Probably, in a world like this, the demand curve would increase. Since their well-being as single men is now lower, they'd be willing to marry even if they ended up with a smaller share of the marital output. Thus, they'd be willing to pay more. The demand curve would shift up. It seems reasonable to suggest that the supply curve would shift by more than the demand curve since women inevitably bear greater costs in the event of pregnancy.

Figure 3.14 illustrates how this might work out. The demand curve shifts up from D_1 to D_2, while the supply curve shifts down from S_1 to S_2. In this case, the big change in the equilibrium is in the number of marriages, which jumps from N_1^* to N_2^*. The change in the share of marital output for men and women doesn't change nearly as much. Taken by itself, the increase in the supply curve would have made women worse off, but the increase in the demand curve compensates for that. In the case depicted in Figure 3.14, women end up just a bit worse off, because, as argued previously, the shift in the demand curve was less than the shift in the supply curve.

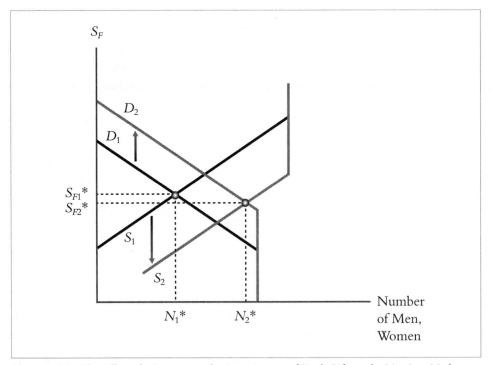

Figure 3.14   The Effect of a Decrease in the Attractiveness of Single Life on the Marriage Market

Reversing all the arrows and subscripts in Figure 3.14 lets time flow as it really did. The "sexual revolution" of the 1960s and 1970s likely increased the attractiveness of being single relative to marriage. This shift decreased the supply of and demand for marriage and thus reduced equilibrium marriage rates. In fact, the median age at first marriage jumped for both men and women by four to five years during this time period. In the mid-1990s and in the 2000s, the fear of AIDS and a somewhat more conservative social order may have shifted the curves again, this time increasing both the supply of and demand for marriage. It will be interesting to see whether age at first marriage falls as a result.

Summary

We have covered an enormous amount of ground in this chapter. We began with the demographic facts. The institution of marriage remains strong, although weaker than in the past. Women marry at much older ages than in the recent past, and divorce rates are high enough that more than half of all marriages are dissolved. Family structure and the family relationships of children have been substantially altered by these changes.

The basic economic approach to marriage emphasizes the gains to marriage, the existence of which can be inferred by the fact that most men and women still do marry. When men and women have different underlying abilities with respect to market wages and household productivity, marriage enables them to both end up better off than if they were single. They can do this by specializing in either the market or household sector, taking advantage of the better skills of their partner in the other sector, and sharing what they can produce. This explanation fits very nicely into the traditional husband-breadwinner, wife-homemaker marriage model that was so common a century ago and persisted quite strongly through the 1950s and beyond. But as underlying differences between the sexes diminish, this source of gains to marriage diminishes as well. That puts contemporary marriages on a very different footing than marriages in prior generations.

There are other sources of gains to marriage. Marriage as an institutional solution to difficult principal–agent problems is a very interesting explanation. Economies of scale and risk sharing are other sources of gains.

The supply and demand approach to marriage works out quite a bit better than might be expected. It is based on some important simplifying assumptions, but it nevertheless manages to capture some interesting and even realistic features about how men and women behave about marriage. It weds (as it were) two strands of economics—the idea of household production (i.e., what a marriage produces) and the idea of utility maximization.

We derived conventional-looking supply and demand curves, although they are, in fact, anything but conventional. We also found an equilibrium in the marriage market that describes both the proportion of the eligible population of men and women who are actually married and, more importantly, the relative well-being of husbands and wives within marriage.

The comparative statics are the most important part of the analysis because with them we can ask how the results would change if the underlying supply and demand curves changed. What happens if sex ratios are out of balance or if women's wages and work opportunities are either very good or very bad or if the noneconomic features of single life versus married life change? All of these changes could be sensibly represented in the supply and demand curves. Each change leads to clear predictions about corresponding changes in the nature of the marriage market equilibrium. Talking to your mothers, grandmothers, or great grandmothers about these ideas would be particularly interesting.

Key Terms

absolute advantage   69

agent   75

comparative advantage   69

comparative static analysis   88

differences in sex ratios   89

economies of scale   78

family household   59

householder   59

marriage market equilibrium   87

non-family household   59

opportunity costs   66

POSSLQs 58

poverty threshold 79

principal 75

principal–agent problem 75

production-possibilities curve 64

production-possibilities frontier 64

rational choice 62

risk sharing 79

selection bias 82

CHAPTER 4

Marriage and the Family—Economic Issues and Applications

Introduction

In this chapter, we continue our discussion of marriage and the family, focusing on three important issues. First, we examine race differences in marriage and family structure. The analysis of race and family structure is very complex and highly controversial. It has been so since at least the mid-1960s, when a government report, written by then U.S. Department of Labor analyst and later United Nations Ambassador and U.S. Senator Daniel Moynihan, drew a link between family structure and poverty. We first sort through the facts and then examine possible economic causes, using the framework of the marriage models we discussed in the previous chapter and focusing especially on the work of William Julius Wilson. We also examine the possible impact of the welfare system and of women's wages on marriage rates among Black men and women.

Then we examine an interesting feature of men's earnings that sheds some light on the analysis of the gains to marriage that we discussed in the previous chapter. This feature is the male marriage premium, the common finding that married men earn more than otherwise similar single men. Our goal is to figure out why it might exist and, interestingly, why it appears to be declining.

Finally, we look at marriage in reverse—that is, divorce. We discuss both the economic analysis of divorce and the economic consequences of divorce.

Race and Family Structure—An Economic Analysis

Overview

In the last chapter, we noted the sharp decline in marriage, especially at younger ages, over the last forty years. We also noted that the decline in marriage was not uniform across subgroups, and that it was especially strong for less-educated women. Here we focus on another demographic dimension where large differences exist—race. Table 4.1 summarizes these differences. In 2002, among White women age 15 and older, more than half (53.6%) were married, spouse present, and less than one quarter (22.4%) were never married. In contrast, in the Black population, less than 30% were married, and never-married women substantially outnumbered women who were married, spouse present—42.0% versus 29.2%. This does not appear to be just a matter of differences in the timing of marriage. As shown in the second row of Table 4.1, the proportion of Black women never married does decline with age, but a very substantial proportion—just under 30%—were still never married in their early 40s, compared to just about 9% for White women.

These differences in marriage by race mean that family structure and especially the family living arrangements of children will differ as well. Among White families with children under age 18, 77% are two-parent families, and 17.7% are headed by single women. So among Whites, two-parent families

	White (%)	Black (%)
Among all women, age 15+		
Married, spouse present	53.6	29.2
Never married	22.4	42.0
Among all women, age 40–44		
Married, spouse present	71.4	41.0
Never married	8.8	29.3
Among all families with children <age 18		
% Two parent	77.0	42.8
% Female householder	17.7	51.2
Among all children		
% Residing with two parents	74.5	38.5
% Residing with mother only	17.9	48.1

Table 4.1   Race Differences in Marital and Family Status, 2002

Source: U. S. Bureau of the Census, Current Population Reports: Series P20, 547, "America's Family and Living Arrangements: March 2002."

with children outnumber mother-only families with children by more than four to one. Among Black families, however, two-parent families are a minority. About 43% of Black families with children under age 18 are two-parent families, while more than half are headed by single women. This means that White and Black children are raised in family environments that are quite different. Those figures are shown in the last row. Roughly three quarters of White children under age 18 are living in two-parent families, while just 38.5%—about half as many—of Black children are living with the same arrangements. Just under half of Black children are in mother-only families.

We can ask two broad questions about these differences. First, when did they develop? Are they long-standing and persistent, or are they of relatively recent origin? Second, and probably more importantly, why did they develop? What are the causes? Are any of the causes economic?

Let's start with the "when." Figure 4.1 shows how the martial status of Black and White women, age 15 and older, has changed since 1950.[1] Back in 1950, the proportion married was substantially higher for both groups of women, greater than 60%. The difference between the two groups of women was relatively small—about 4 percentage points. You can see that the two trends move more or less together between 1950 and 1970—the lines are roughly parallel—so there is only a small widening of the gap over these years. During the 1970s, the trends diverged sharply. The proportion married dropped a full 10 percentage points for Black women, falling below 50% by mid-decade, while for White women, the proportion married dipped just 2 percentage points. The fall in the proportion married continued in the 1980s, although at a slower pace. By 1990, a 20 percentage point difference developed, which is essentially where things stand today. The bottom line, then, is that the proportion married fell for all women—a point made in the previous chapter—but that it fell especially sharply for Black women, particularly between 1970 and 1980.

Figure 4.2 shows the sources of the decline in marriage for Black women. The proportion who are currently divorced rose from about 2% to 12%; note that the increase is sharpest in the 1970s. The corresponding change for White women isn't shown, but the change is very similar, from 2.5% to

---

[1]In Figure 4.1, we are using information on the category "married" rather than "married, spouse present" because a longer time series is available. Notice that in this figure the proportion of Black women married is substantially higher than the proportion included in Table 4.1. The difference is the result of women who are married, but are currently separated.

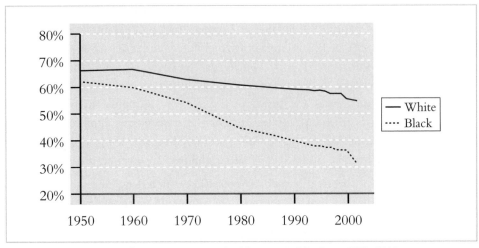

Figure 4.1   Proportion of Women Age 15 and Older, Married, by Race, 1950–2002

10.6%. So while the increase in divorce is an important part of the decline in the proportion married for both groups of women, it is not an important source of the *difference* between White and Black women in the proportion married in 2002. The more important source is the proportion of women who are never married. This fraction rose from just over 20% in 1950 to a bit over 40% in 2002—a full 20 percentage point increase. In this case, the sharp increase began in the 1960s and carried through the 1970s before slowing down a bit. For White women, the increase in the proportion never married was just 2 percentage points—from 20% in 1950 (a figure just about the same as for Black women) to 22% in 2002. Clearly, the race difference in marriage is primarily a race difference in the proportions never married, rather than in those previously married, but now divorced.

Finally, let's see how these changes affected the family life of children. Figure 4.3 shows the proportion of children under age 18 living in a two-parent family between 1960 and 2002. Back in 1960, about 90% of White children and about two thirds of Black children lived in two-parent homes. So even in 1960, there was a quite substantial difference in the proportions of children in two-parent families.

Since then, the difference has widened. For White children, the proportion in two-parent families dropped very slowly but very steadily, to 85% in 1975, then 80% in 1985, and finally falling below three quarters in 1996. Since then, the proportion has remained essentially unchanged. For Black children, the downward trend is steeper, beginning from 1960. The proportion in two-

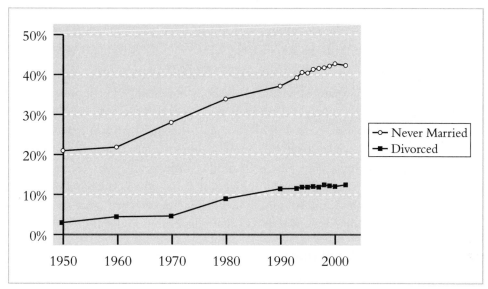

Figure 4.2   Changes in the Marital Status of Black Women, 1950–2002

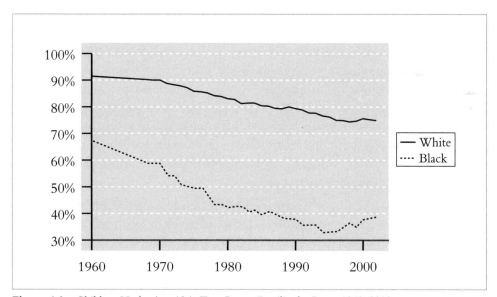

Figure 4.3   Children Under Age 18 in Two-Parent Families by Race, 1960–2002

parent families fell below 60% by 1970, below 50% by 1975, and below 40% by 1985. The sharp drop in the 1970s is particularly conspicuous—the proportion dropped 16 percentage points in that one decade alone. The downward trend continued through 1995, when the proportion bottomed out at one third. The proportion has since rebounded to 38.5%, almost exactly where it was in the late 1980s. Nearly half of all Black children reside with their mother only, as we saw in Table 4.1.

Should we care about these differences in family structure or are they just interesting but harmless patterns? A large body of research in economics, sociology, psychology, and child development suggests that there is probably a good reason to care. Family structure is strongly correlated with family income and poverty. As shown in Table 4.2, family income is more than twice as high in married-couple families as it is in mother-only families, while the poverty rate is 15 to 18 percentage points higher in the mother-only families. A great deal of research shows that family income and poverty status are strongly related to child outcomes. We discuss that relationship in detail in Chapter 15.

Economic Explanations

Let's begin by thinking like economists about the underlying message of the sharp decline in marriage among Black women. As we discussed in the last chapter, we can reasonably assume that men and women choose to marry only when they both expect to be better off married than single. Thus, it follows as a matter of economic logic that many fewer Black men and women today must expect that marriage will make them better off than in the past. And that, in turn, tells us that either the gains to marriage have fallen or the quality of single life has improved (or they both fell, but the gains to marriage fell more than the quality of single life). There is no other way to reconcile the falling marriage rates with **rational choice** behavior. Of course, men and women could be acting irrationally by making choices about marriage that leave them worse off than they might otherwise be, but that doesn't sit well with the economic way of thinking.

As simple as this logic is, it is useful in focusing our attention on forces that could have either reduced the gains to marriage or improved the quality of single life. To explain the facts fully, a potential explanation must also have affected Black men and women more strongly than White men and women and have had its biggest impact in the 1960s and especially the 1970s.

Within this framework, there are three broad kinds of economic explanations for the differences by race in family structure. One emphasizes changes in marriage markets, a second emphasizes wage rates, and the third emphasizes the role of the welfare system. The explanations are not mutually exclusive. They may all have occurred: One force may have affected some women, while another affected a different group of women.

	White	Black
Median family income		
Two-parent family	$59,953	$50,741
Mother-only family	$28,371	$20,395
As percent of two-parent family	47.3%	40.2%
Poverty rate		
Two-parent family	7.7%	20.8%
Mother-only family	22.1%	38.7%

Table 4.2   Family Income and Poverty Status of Individuals by Family Structure and Race, 2000
Source: Current Population Reports, Series P20: #613 (income) and #614 (poverty).

MARRIAGE MARKETS   A very well-known and interesting explanation for the decline in marriage among the Black population was proposed in the mid-1980s by the sociologist William Julius Wilson. Wilson has been a highly influential social scientist on contemporary matters of race and poverty. His books, *The Truly Disadvantaged*[2] and *When Work Disappears,*[3] have focused attention on the multiple problems of high-poverty, low-employment neighborhoods and on the special and severe problems of the people living in these neighborhoods, whom he called the **underclass.**

In *The Truly Disadvantaged,* Wilson suggested that the decline in marriage reflected primarily the declining marriage prospects of Black women, which were themselves the result of the declining labor market position of Black men.[4] Beginning in the mid-1970s, the labor market prospects of less-skilled and less-educated men fell both relative to more educated men and relative to their counterparts in earlier decades. That trend—the declining position of less-skilled men—continues to this day. This shift hit Black men particularly hard because a large proportion of them had less formal education. There were two important consequences: (1) Many employed Black men earned relatively little, and (2) the employment rate of Black men fell substantially.

Wilson hypothesized that the deteriorating position of Black men made them less-attractive marriage partners, or in many cases made them essentially unacceptable as marriage partners. When men are unable to support a family, he

---

[2]William Julius Wilson, *The Truly Disadvantaged,* University of Chicago Press: Chicago, 1987.
[3]William Julius Wilson, *When Work Disappears,* Vintage Books: New York, 1997.
[4]The chapter in *The Truly Disadvantaged* focusing on marriage issues was co-authored with Kathryn Neckerman.

argued, women are unwilling to take them on as husbands. To measure this concept, he constructed what he called the **Male Marriageable Pool Index** or **MMPI,** for short. The MMPI is the ratio, usually computed separately by race and age bracket, of the number of employed men to the number of women. Thus

$$\text{MMPI} = \frac{\text{number of employed men in an age by race group}}{\text{number of women in the same age by race group}}$$

In constructing the measure in this way, Wilson assumed, in effect, that women married within their own age bracket and race. Even though there are certainly exceptions, that is probably a reasonable assumption.

The MMPI ratio tells us something about the balance or imbalance in the marriage market. If this ratio equals one, then for every woman there is a potential mate with a job. As this ratio falls well below one, there is an imbalance in the marriage market, something like the difference in the number of men and women that we discussed in the supply and demand model of Chapter 3. If the ratio is quite low, many women, Wilson hypothesized, will not get married but will remain single instead.[5]

Typically, a birth cohort begins with roughly an equal number of boys and girls.[6] Nevertheless, the MMPI can fall well below one. Wilson emphasized that this ratio fell well below one in the Black population not only because of the declining employment rate of young Black men but also because of growing incarceration rates and even the higher mortality rates of young Black men. In *The Truly Disadvantaged,* Wilson computed MMPIs by age bracket and race from the mid-1950s through the mid-1980s. Summarizing his findings, he wrote: "Clearly, what our MMPI reveals is a long-term decline in the proportion of Black men, and particularly young Black men, who are in a position to support a family" (p. 83).

Representative MMPIs for 1960 through 2000 for 20–24 and 25–34 year olds are presented in Table 4.3. For convenience, we have expressed the MMPI as the number of employed men per 100 women. Two important relationships are quite evident in the data. First, the MMPIs are consistently lower for Black men and women than for White men and women. Indeed,

---

[5]The emphasis on the financial gains to marriage may be objectionable to some people, especially the notion that women (but not men) are seeking financial support in marriage. There is certainly some merit to that criticism. A long tradition in sociology, dating back to the Great Depression, documents the impact that the unemployment of the "breadwinner" has on marriage and family life.

[6]In fact, there are about 5% more boys than girls at birth.

	1960	1970	1980	1990	2000
Age 20–24					
Black	68	58	50	51	49
White	68	63	72	75	83
Age 25–34					
Black	71	73	63	65	64
White	86	87	85	93	89

Table 4.3   MMPIs by Age, Race, and Year

Figures shown are the number of employed men by age and race per 100 women of the same age and race.

Source: Data for 1960–1980 for Black from David Ellwood and Jonathan Crane, "Family Change Among Blacks: What Do We Know?" from *Journal of Economic Perspectives,* Vol. 4, No. 4, pp. 65–84, 1990). Copyright © 1990 by the American Economic Association. Reprinted with the permission of the authors and publisher. Data for 1960–1980 for White from William Julius Wilson, *The Truly Disadvantaged.* Copyright © 1987. Reprinted with permission of the University of Chicago Press. Data for 1990–2000 calculated from Employment and Earnings and Statistical Abstract.

for Blacks, the numbers are often quite low, with most figures falling between 50 and 65, and none higher than 73. While low ratios for 20–24 year olds can possibly be rationalized in terms of rising college enrollments of Black men, this is not likely to be much of a factor among 25–34 year olds. Second, there is a downward time trend in the MMPI for Blacks but not for Whites. The MMPI fell 18 percentage points between 1960 and 1980 for Black 20–24 year olds and 8 percentage points for Black 25–34 year olds. Since then, the MMPI has been stable for both age groups.

Wilson presented a fairly simple analysis of the MMPI and its impact on the percentage of families headed by women between 1960 and 1980, separately by race and region of the country, for men age 15–44. His findings are summarized in Table 4.4.

Several interesting trends are evident here. First, except for Whites in the South, the MMPI fell for each race in each region over this time period. Second, the decline is greater in every case for Blacks than Whites. It is also greater in the Northeast and North Central regions, where job loss in blue-collar employment was especially large. Third, an inverse or negative relationship clearly exists between changes in the MMPI and changes in the proportion of families headed by women. For example, the two biggest increases in this proportion are for Blacks in the Northeast and North Central regions where the MMPI decline was greatest. The increases for Blacks in the South and West are smaller, although they are still large. For Whites, the trends don't line up as well, with the biggest increase in the proportion of families headed

Region and Racial Group	Percentage Point Change in MMPI (1980 − 1960)	Percentage Point Change in Proportion of Families Headed by Women
Northeast		
Black	−11.2	24.4
White	−2.2	6.2
North Central		
Black	−12.5	26.3
White	−3.6	5.8
South		
Black	−6.1	15.6
White	2.4	3.9
West		
Black	−2.7	18.0
White	−0.9	9.4

Table 4.4   The MMPI and the Proportion of Families Headed by Women, 1960–80, by Race and Region

Source: William Julius Wilson, *The Truly Disadvantaged,* Table 4.3. Copyright © 1987. Reprinted with the permission of the University of Chicago Press.

by women coming in the West where the MMPI fell least. Finally, there is also evidence that something else is affecting family structure. The big increases in the proportion of families headed by women in the West, where the MMPI changed very little, is one obvious indication of this.

This is, however, a rather simple analysis. It does not, for example, control for the impact of other factors that were changing over time. In addition, Wilson's work does have its weaknesses. In a well-known review article, Ellwood and Crane[7] point out that marriage rates have fallen not only for Black men who are not employed (as Wilson's hypothesis suggests) but also for Black men who are employed. Indeed, between 1960 and 1990, the marriage rate for employed Black men fell from over 70% to less than 50%. Ellwood and Crane argue that employed men should be in greater demand than before, and thus their marriage rate should go up. Similarly, the proportion of Black men who were married fell both for those who were not high school graduates and

[7]David Ellwood and Jonathan Crane, "Family Change Among Blacks: What Do We Know?" *Journal of Economic Perspectives.* Vol. 4, No. 4, pp. 65–84, 1990.

those who were high school graduates. Ellwood and Crane argue that because the employment prospects of high school graduates didn't fall as much as for the dropouts, they should be marrying at rates that changed less, according to Wilson's hypothesis. This criticism is not quite as compelling because the labor market position of high school graduates also tumbled during this time period, and there are alternative forces, which we discuss later in this chapter, that may have affected the marriage behavior of more educated Black men. Finally, detailed empirical work that examines differences in MMPIs and marriage rates across geographical areas (i.e, local marriage markets) rather than over time has not always supported the relationship between the MMPI and marriage. For example, urban areas with higher MMPIs did not regularly have a higher proportion of married women than areas with lower MMPIs.

Still, despite these weaknesses, Wilson's MMPI hypothesis is important, compelling, and widely accepted. The decline in the labor market outcomes of Black men over this time period is genuine and undeniable, and the link to marriage and family formation seems quite plausible. The timing of the downward trend in the MMPI and the downward trend in marriage do correspond roughly. Furthermore, the MMPI trends differ substantially by race, and thus are consistent with a differential impact on marriage by race. Wilson's model draws an important link between what happens in the labor market and what happens in the marriage market, thereby uniting what might otherwise appear to be unrelated problem areas. It is an explanation that rings true.

WOMEN'S WAGE RATES   Women's wage rates could affect marriage in two distinct ways. First, as discussed in the first part of Chapter 3, the more alike are spouses in terms of their wages and household productivity, the smaller are the traditional productivity gains to marriage. Remember that the gains occur precisely because each person gains access to a partner whose skills are different from his/her own. This difference allows each person to specialize and "trade." The result is that any given combination of market goods and household goods can be produced at a lower cost. Equivalently, they can produce more at a given level of input. But when they are quite alike, for example, in terms of wage rates, the gains are small.

Second, as we saw in the supply and demand analysis of Chapter 3, higher wages for women make being single a more attractive alternative. In terms of our supply and demand graph, higher wages shifted the supply curve up, thereby reducing the proportion of women who are married, while increasing their share of marital output.

Both factors are almost certainly part of the explanation for the declining marriage rate of Black women. Although we discuss wages and work in more detail in later chapters, we can briefly summarize the key relevant facts here. First, both White and Black women earn, on average, considerably less than White and Black men, respectively. This has been true for as long as income statistics have been collected, and it is still true today. However, the earnings disadvantage has historically been much smaller for Black women. For example, during the 1960s and 1970s, White women who worked year-round full-time earned only about 50% of what year-round full-time White men earned.[8] In contrast, Black women who were year-round full-time workers earned about 60% or more of what otherwise similar Black men earned. When women's earnings started to increase relative to men's wages in the early 1980s, the earnings ratio for Black women stayed about 10 to 15 percentage points above the earnings ratio for White women, and in 2000 the earnings ratio is still 10 percentage points higher for Black women. Thus the gains to marriage that arise out of the differences between the partners and the specialization of labor are likely to be smaller in general for Black men and women than for White men and women.

Second, wages have risen for both White and Black women. Between 1967 and 2000, the median earnings of Black women who were year-round full-time workers increased more than 50%, even after adjusting for the impact of inflation. For White women, the corresponding increase was smaller, about one third. These increases are significant because the earnings of men (year-round full-time workers) increased just over 10%. Again, the larger earnings increase for Black women suggests that this may have affected the marriage decision of Black women more than White women. Recall from the previous chapter that an increase in women's wages is likely to decrease the proportion who are married by making nonmarried life more attractive.

Higher wages and stronger labor force attachment also operate by increasing age at first marriage. This effect probably operates most strongly for more-educated women, some of whom put off marriage while they are establishing a career for themselves. This decision could help explain why marriage has fallen among more-educated Black men, a fact that couldn't be well explained by Wilson's model. More-educated Black men are the likely marriage partners

---

[8]Year-round full-time workers are usually used in gender earnings comparisons, because this avoids the problems created by the fact that many more women now work full-time than in the past. Earnings ratios for all women and all men have risen partly because of the increase in women's hours of work, rather than in their rate of pay.

of more-educated Black women, and thus the men may find themselves having a more difficult time finding willing and acceptable marriage partners.

THE WELFARE SYSTEM

BACKGROUND   A bit of background about the U.S. welfare system is necessary to understand why the welfare system might have a role in reducing marriage and family formation. In Chapter 6, we discuss its possible impact on fertility.

The welfare system in the United States had its origins as part of the Social Security Act of 1935, the same piece of legislation that established the Social Security system. That legislation created a program called ADC (for Aid to Dependent Children), which provided cash assistance to poor families. Later, the name of the program was changed to **AFDC** (for Aid to Families with Dependent Children), although it was most often referred to as "welfare." AFDC, along with other support programs like food stamps, Medicaid, and public housing, formed the "safety net" of income-support programs. AFDC was the most well-known, the most important, and, by the 1990s, the most disliked of the safety net programs—disliked by taxpayers, recipients, and administrators alike.

When Bill Clinton ran for President in 1992, he promised to "end welfare as we know it"; shortly after his election, he began planning welfare reform. After an extremely complicated set of political events that included the Republican takeover of Congress in 1994 and a lengthy battle between President Clinton and the Republicans and between President Clinton and his own advisors, the AFDC program was abolished in 1996, and a program called **TANF** was substituted in its place. TANF stands for Temporary Assistance for Needy Families and is pronounced "TAN-EFF." TANF is quite similar in structure to AFDC in that it provides cash benefits to poor families, but it is not a legal entitlement[9] as AFDC was. It is, in fact, a much tougher version of AFDC. TANF imposes strict time limits on lifetime usage as well as such other requirements as each state may choose to impose. (We examine the details of welfare reform and its impact on women in Chapter 12.)

Let's focus on AFDC because it was the largest and most important program for poor families during most of the time period when the changes in the family structure of the Black population occurred. The most important feature of AFDC for our purposes is that benefits were largely restricted to poor,

---

[9]When a program is a legal entitlement, every person who meets the program's eligibility standards is legally entitled to receive program benefits. Because TANF is not a legal entitlement, eligible persons can be turned away if funding is insufficient.

mother-only families with children. Father-only families with children were technically eligible for benefits, but they have never accounted for more than a tiny fraction of the welfare caseload. Married couples, with or without children, and single persons without children were either ineligible for benefits or eligible for sharply reduced benefits, no matter how poor they were.

This peculiar feature of the U.S. welfare system primarily reflected the demographic and social context of the time (the 1930s) when the welfare system was established: Men and women were expected to marry and remain married, married men were breadwinners, and married women were homemakers. The notion of families "on the dole" has always been an uncomfortable one in the United States, and even President Roosevelt, who helped establish the welfare system and who was always a champion of the underprivileged, called welfare "a narcotic, a subtle destroyer of the human spirit." In the 1930s, mother-only families with children were almost exclusively widows who were deemed deserving of support while they raised their children and prior to their expected remarriage. But once they remarried, the financial support of the government was to be replaced by the support provided by their husbands.

In addition, benefits under AFDC were often quite modest and left most recipient families well under the poverty line. In 1995, the last year of AFDC, benefits in the median state for a family of two were $330 per month. We'll talk later on about the details of the benefit formula, but it suffices for now to note that in the United States, welfare could be financially attractive only to persons with very limited wage-earning opportunities. Finally, each state is allowed to choose the cash benefits it provides to families on welfare. There is substantial variation in the benefits provided. A number of mostly Southern states provide very low benefits—less than $200 per month for a family with one child. Some Northern and Midwestern states provide more than $500 a month. Admittedly, some of that reflects cost-of-living differences between the North and the South, but most of it is a genuine difference in support.

WELFARE AND MARRIAGE   How and why would the welfare system affect marriage? Many scholars, especially more conservative ones, argue this way:[10] The welfare system provides a package of benefits, including cash assistance, food stamps, health care, and/or housing to poor single women with children. It provides little or nothing to married couples, who would typically be eligible

---

[10]A well-known popular version is Charles Murray, *Losing Ground*, New York: Basic Books, 1984.

for food stamps but little else. For women with reasonable labor market skills and/or decent marriage prospects, the benefits of the welfare system are not particularly attractive. Marriage and/or work are almost always better options. But for women with fewer or less-valuable labor market skills and/or without decent marriage prospects, remaining single and receiving welfare benefits might provide a better standard of living than marriage and work. In this way, the welfare system could provide an incentive for single women to have children without marrying the father or for married women to become divorced. Similarly, it might provide a disincentive for women with children to marry or to remarry following divorce or separation. In all these ways, the incentives of the AFDC could reduce marriage and increase the number of mother-only families with children.

One might well expect this argument to apply with the most force to women with less education or with fewer labor market skills in general. Not only do they have relatively poor labor market prospects for self-support, but as mentioned previously, they may also have relatively poor marriage market prospects. It might, therefore, affect Black women more strongly than White women because educational attainment—an important factor determining labor market success—is lower among Black women.

Although the hypothesis seems quite plausible, the empirical evidence in its favor is not as strong as might be imagined. The biggest problem is that the time trends do not line up well. The various measures of marriage have all declined, especially in the 1970s. If the incentives of the welfare system were the primary cause, we would expect to find that AFDC benefits increased over that same time period, becoming attractive to increasingly more women. In fact, just the opposite happened. AFDC benefits did increase in the 1960s, but after adjusting for inflation, AFDC benefits fell throughout most of rest of this time period. Most states, which have the authority to set AFDC benefits, did not raise their AFDC benefits to keep up with inflation. Even adding in the value of Food Stamps and Medicaid, which have increased in value since 1970, total benefits have fallen about 20%.

Ellwood and Crane[11] (1990) point out that the proportion of Black children living in families receiving welfare benefits did not increase after 1970, although it did increase substantially between 1960 and 1970. At the same time,

---

[11]David Ellwood and Jonathan Crane, "Family Change Among Blacks: What Do We Know?" *Journal of Economic Perspectives,* Vol. 4, No. 4, pp. 65–84, 1990.

the proportion of Black children living in mother-only families continued to rise after 1970. This, too, suggests that something other than welfare benefits is behind the decline in marriage and in two-parent families.

The bottom line here is probably that the impact of the welfare system on family structure is substantially less than one might guess, although it is probably not zero. Robert Moffitt, an expert on this research, put it this way in his summary of the literature on the impact of the welfare system on family structure during the 1960s and 1970s, the decades where most of the marriage action was: "The studies of the 1980s show slightly stronger effects than the earlier studies, [but] the effects are still generally small in magnitude. In particular, . . . none of the studies finds effects sufficiently large to explain, for example, the increase in female headship in the late 1960s and early 1970s."[12]

Summary

If we put all these explanations together, what do we have? Quite clearly, none are perfect. Marriage is a very complex phenomenon, and more than one hypothesis could be correct, perhaps for a specific portion of the population. It would, in fact, be surprising if a single, simple hypothesis were the sole cause of an enormous change like the decline in both marriage and two-parent families among Black men and women. Women are too different from one another in their opportunities and preferences for a single explanation to hold for all of them.

Our own best guess is that all the hypotheses have some power in explaining the downward trend in marriage and the growing difference by race in that trend. The impact of rising wages for women undoubtedly has had an impact on both White and Black women, especially in delaying age at first marriage and probably in accelerating the breakup of troubled marriages. This increase may well have operated similarly for more-educated White and Black women. The smaller gender wage gap for Black women relative to Black men may be an added subtle factor contributing to the larger decline among Black women. Wilson's emphasis on the marriage market makes an important connection between the labor market status of men and the formation of two-parent families. The race difference in the MMPI is substantial, and the time trends generally support an impact. If welfare benefits affected marriage, it could only be among the least well-educated, for example, high school

---

[12]Robert A. Moffitt, "Incentive Effects of the U.S. Welfare System: A Review," *Journal of Economic Literature,* Vol. 30, No. 1, p. 31, 1992.

dropouts. Here, too, there could be a differential impact by race because a larger proportion of Black women had less than a high school education. AFDC has probably also had some impact, again especially at the lower end of the skill distribution.

Nevertheless, we must admit sometimes that we do not have a full and convincing answer for an important issue. That is probably the case here.

Marriage and the Earnings of Men

Just for a change of pace, let's talk about men, specifically about men, marriage, and earnings. Our goal is to think about the impact of marriage on men and their earnings and, in the process, to gain some insight into the model of marriage we developed in the last chapter and the way changes in family life have affected the labor market.

For about as long as statistics on individual earnings have been collected and analyzed, it has been noted that married men typically earn more than single men. This is true not only in comparisons of median or mean earnings for all single and married men but also after controlling for obvious differences between married and single men that might cause single men to earn less—such things as differences in age (the unmarried are younger and naturally earn less) or education. Even when married men are compared to single men who are otherwise quite similar in terms of age, education, race, and other standard characteristics that are known to affect earnings, married men typically earn more. This finding is so firmly entrenched that it has a name—the **male marriage premium.** Claudia Goldin[13] provides evidence that the male marriage premium has been relatively constant over much of the twentieth century in the United States, and Schoeni[14] finds that it is common and comparably sized across industrialized countries.

The obvious question to ask about the male marriage premium is *why*? Why do married men earn more than otherwise similar unmarried men? There are several possible explanations. First, it is possible that married men are no more productive workers than unmarried men, but that employers simply pay them more, perhaps because employers view married men as needing more income

---

[13]Claudia D. Goldin, *Understanding the Gender Gap,* New York: Oxford University Press, 1990.
[14]Robert F. Schoeni, "Marital Status and Earnings in Developed Countries," *Journal of Population Economics,* Vol. 8, No. 4, pp. 351–359, 1995.

to support a family. This explanation is possible but not particularly likely. In competitive labor markets, most workers are ultimately paid according to their productivity. Firms that paid married men more than equally productive single men would have higher costs than necessary and would likely get run out of business.

Two other potential explanations are more compelling. Both explanations accept the premise that married men earn more because they are somehow more productive; however, they differ in the source of that higher productivity. One explanation attributes the higher productivity to the impact of marriage itself on productivity. The now-familiar argument goes like this. The division of labor along gender lines in a traditional marriage (husband breadwinner, wife homemaker) enables married men to specialize in market activities and thereby become more proficient, more productive, and ultimately higher paid. Single men, however, cannot specialize in that way. They must divide their time between the market and the household sector. Thus the market productivity and earnings of married men rise relative to unmarried men. Let's call this the **marriage productivity effect.**

The alternative explanation for the higher productivity of married men involves what is called a **marriage selectivity effect.** Suppose that married men are different from unmarried men of the same age, education, race, and other basic observable traits in ways that enable them to have higher earnings. They could, for example, be more industrious, more responsible, more courteous, and so on. These are examples of traits that cannot be easily measured in survey data and thus cannot be included in the "control variables" typically used when researchers compare married men to otherwise similar unmarried men.

Suppose further that because of these traits, married men not only earned higher pay but were also more marriageable in the first place. Women might value these men either because of the traits themselves or because they correctly see the men as having higher earnings potential or because of other unobserved traits that are correlated with these traits. The reason doesn't matter. Then, researchers examining wages would find that married men are more productive and earn more than single men, even though marriage itself was not the source of their higher productivity. This explanation is called a selectivity effect because it is based on the selection of more productive men into marriage.

The selectivity effect is another good example of statistical bias due to omitted variables, discussed in Chapter 2. Remember the cardinal rule: The estimated impact of any variable includes its own true impact plus some of the impact of omitted variables with which it is correlated. Here the estimated impact on earnings of being married includes some of the impact of the correlated omitted traits (industriousness, responsibility, courteousness, etc.) that increase earnings.

One way to sense the potential statistical problem is to think about the corresponding controlled experiment in which some men were randomly assigned to the "marriage" treatment while others were randomly assigned to the "single" control group. In that case, simply comparing the average earnings of the two groups would provide an accurate estimate of the impact of marriage on earnings. There could be no selectivity problem precisely because of the random assignment. Of course, such a natural experiment could never be carried out, for obvious reasons. In the absence of a natural experiment, we must rely on multiple regression analysis using data on individuals who have chosen (or been chosen) to be married or single.

Sorting out these competing explanations is not simple, but there is some revealing information. Korenman and Neumark[15] compared different estimates of the marriage premium in order to assess the relative importance of the two explanations. Using standard regression techniques, they found a marriage premium of about 11% for White males who were roughly ages 25–35 in the late 1970s. This means that holding other measured traits constant, this sample of married men earned 11% more than their single counterparts. This effect could, of course, be the result of either the genuine marriage effect or the selectivity effect.

They compared this result to two other estimates. First, they estimated the impact of marriage by comparing the earnings of the same men over a number of years. Some of the single men became married over these years, while others remained unmarried or became divorced. These changes allowed Korenman and Neumark to examine the corresponding change in the men's earnings as their marital status changed. This comparison is attractive because the men themselves are the same before and after marriage. In other words, selectivity should be less of a factor; the remaining impact should be a better estimate of the genuine marriage effect on men's earnings. It's not a perfect measure because the men could change in ways that affected both their wages

[15]Sanders Korenman and David Neumark, "Does Marriage Really Make Men More Productive?" *Journal of Human Resources,* Vol. 26, No. 2, pp. 282–307, 1991.

and their marriageability. For example, a man could acquire or lose a particularly bad personality trait or behavior, such as drinking or gambling. Still, there are likely to be fewer differences in the same person over time than among different people at the same time. So selectivity should be a smaller factor.

The bigger the difference between the conventional estimate and this one, the greater is the importance of selectivity into marriage; the smaller the difference, the more important is the genuine marriage effect. When Korenman and Neumark examined this relationship, they found that the marriage premium fell from 11 to 6%. This result suggests that a bit more than half of the of the total marriage premium (6% versus 11%) was the result of a genuine marriage impact, with the rest being caused by selectivity.

The second technique examined the impact on earnings of how long a particular man had been married rather than simply whether or not he was currently married. Korenman and Neumark reasoned that a selectivity effect ought to be mostly a question of whether or not someone was married rather than how long he was married. In contrast, the productivity effect ought to increase with years of marriage. After all, if the premium reflected the labor market impact of the division of labor within marriage, those gains would accumulate over time. In that case, men who had been married longer would have a larger marriage earnings premium than newlyweds and other men who hadn't been married very long.

Using this technique, Korenman and Neumark found strong evidence for the genuine marriage interpretation in that the marriage earnings premium depended positively on years of marriage. The impact of an additional year of marriage was sizeable—roughly 1 to 2% per year—so that after ten years of marriage, the premium might be 15% or so. At the same time, after controlling for years of marriage, they found no evidence of a marital status effect per se. This, too, is evidence of a productivity impact of marriage rather than a selectivity interpretation.

In recent decades, the male marriage premium has been declining quite steadily. Blackburn and Korenman[16] examined the marriage premium using U.S. Census data from 1967 through 1988 for full-time year-round workers. In 1967, the marriage premium (after adjusting for other factors) was about

[16]McKinley Blackburn and Sanders Korenman, "The Declining Marital-Status Earnings Differential," *Journal of Population Economics*, Vol. 7, pp. 247–270, 1994.

29% for married White men relative to never-married White men and about 20% relative to divorced White men. By 1988, these two premiums had fallen to 18.5 and 10.6%, respectively (p. 251). For Black men, the absolute level of the marriage premium was smaller, but the relative decline was similar.

Again, selectivity and productivity issues are relevant. Over these years, three significant trends that might affect the male marriage premium have surfaced. One, which we discuss in detail in Chapter 7, is the steady and substantial increase in the labor force participation of married women. In 1960, approximately 30% of married women worked in the labor market; the traditional family with its division of labor on the basis of gender was very much the norm. By 1990, the proportion of married women in the labor force had doubled to 60%; it currently stands at about 62%. If the male marriage premium reflected the labor market gains to men of the division of labor within marriage, then the decline in specialization within marriage would likely reduce those gains. So, as a broad trend, the big increase in wives' labor force participation could be responsible for the decline in the marriage premium.

Grey[17] has some useful information about this effect. He examined how the marriage premium varied between men with working wives and those whose wives didn't work in the labor force. He finds a 17% wage effect for men whose wives did not work compared to a 9% effect for men whose wives worked 40 hours per week or more. This suggests that the increase over time in the proportion of men whose wives worked 40 hours per week would tend to decrease the marriage premium for men. Additionally, the 9% is a good estimate of the selectivity factor.

A second trend is in the labor market itself. The 1980s and 1990s saw a big increase in the return to skills. For example the earnings gap between more-educated men and less-educated men rose, as did the gap between more-experienced workers and younger workers; for a very thorough review of these labor market developments, see the article by Katz and Autor.[18] In a very famous paper, Juhn, Murphy, and Pierce[19] concluded that there was also an increase in the return to the kind of traits and skills that are unmeasured

[17]Jeffrey S. Grey, "The Fall in Men's Return to Marrriage," *The Journal of Human Resources,* Vol. 32, No. 3, pp. 481–504, 1997.

[18]Lawrence F. Katz and David H. Autor, "Changes in the Wage Structure and Earnings Inequality," in Orley Ashenfelter and David Card, editors, *Handbook of Labor Economcis,* Vol. 3A, 1999.

[19]Chinhui Juhn, Kevin Murphy, and Brooks Pierce, "Wage Inequality and the Rise in Returns to Skill," *Journal of Political Economy,* Vol. 101, No. 3, pp. 410–442, 1993.

but valued in the labor market. These skills are of exactly the same kind that the selectivity explanation of the marriage premium emphasizes. Thus, if selectivity marriage effects are important, this labor market trend would have caused the male marriage premium to rise. Since the marriage premium fell, not rose, some other factor (like the change in labor force participation) must have outweighed this effect.

Finally, think about what happened to marriage over this time period. We saw in Table 3.1 that the proportion of women (and, by inference, men as well) who are married has fallen steadily and substantially. The proportion of women, aged 15 and older, who were married, spouse present, fell from 63% in 1960 to 53% by 1990 and to nearly 50% now. In other words, we saw that the populations of married men and single men now are probably quite different from the same groups in the 1960s, and this could affect the male marriage premium if the selectivity effect is important. Time-series comparisons can be perilous if the groups being compared have changed over time.

It's difficult to pinpoint how the marriage premium would change under these circumstances without knowing which men who might earlier have been married are now part of the single category. Here are two extreme scenarios. Suppose, first, that men with earnings well below the median are the ones who are no longer getting and staying married. Perhaps women just don't view them as marriageable now that women's own labor market prospects have improved. This change would make the remaining population of married men more selective relative to single men—the married men are the cream of the crop. In that case, the marriage premium would increase. Now suppose instead that the men earning more than the median are no longer getting married. Then, the earnings of married men would fall relative to the earnings of single men and the marriage premium would fall. Blackburn and Korenman show that a neutral decrease in the probability of marriage at all ability levels would typically cause the marriage premium to fall.

Using national data from 1967 through 1988, Blackburn and Korenman provide some evidence on these matters. Their analysis is quite complex, so we simply summarize their conclusions. They argue that the declining rates of marriage for men have made the two groups of men—married and single— more alike in terms of their unobservable traits. This change would cause the marriage premium to fall via the selectivity effect. Similarly, the rising labor force activity of married women may, in their words, "have limited the opportunity (or motivation) for husbands to invest heavily in market-oriented human capital" (p. 268). This, too, would cause the marriage premium to fall via the productivity effect.

One of the most interesting features of this analysis of the male marriage premium is that—like Wilson's MMPI, but with a different focus—it establishes a link between the labor market and the marriage market. It also focuses attention on the genuine importance of marriage arrangements for labor market outcomes.

Finally, we can't leave this section without mentioning the companion issue—namely, the impact of marriage and children on women's earnings. We talk about that at length when women's wages are the subject in Chapter 10. Suffice it to say here that economics research shows that marriage and especially children have a negative impact on women's earnings. This impact is now often referred to as the family gap, reflecting the notion that family issues, rather than pure labor market discrimination, account for a substantial share of the gender gap in earnings.

Divorce and Its Consequences

Divorce has become a staple of modern family life, common in ways that would be unthinkable to your grandparents and great-grandparents. As we briefly noted in the last chapter, divorce was extremely uncommon until about the early 1960s. Prior to 1970, a divorce required a finding of "fault" on one party—infidelity, abandonment, and so on. It was quite difficult to obtain a divorce in many states. Because anyone could get a divorce in Reno, Nevada without a finding of fault by a court simply by residing there for a "mere" six weeks, it became known as the U.S. divorce capital. Movie star divorces were often the stuff of tabloids—pretty tame fare by contemporary standards. No-fault divorce entered the picture in 1970, and it is now available in almost every state.[20] Whether no-fault divorce caused the increase in divorce or simply made the process less costly and less acrimonious is still being debated, although most economists would probably argue against the causal role.

---

[20]According to the American Bar Association Family Law Section, 46 states and the District of Columbia have no-fault divorce either as the sole ground for divorce or in addition to traditional fault divorce. Only Hawaii, Indiana, Kansas, and Nevada lack such provisions. See http://www.abanet.org/family/familylaw for further details about state divorce and marriage laws.

Our goal here is to first review the facts, then consider possible explanations, and finally look at a controversial and important economic issue—the economic impact of divorce on women and men.

Facts and Trends

For most of the first half of the twentieth century, the U.S. divorce rate was very low, well under 1% per year. We measure the annual divorce rate relative to the number of existing marriages and often express it as the number of divorces per 1000 marriages. Thus, a divorce rate under 1% meant that fewer than 10 of every 1000 existing marriages ended in divorce in an average year. The only exception was the 1940s, especially the World War II years and just after, when the rate got as high as 1.8%. The divorce rate dropped quickly, however, and throughout the 1950s, it was down below 1% again. But, starting in the late 1950s and all through the 1960s and 1970s, the divorce rate began to rise, increasing almost every year from 1958 to 1982. In the process, the rate increased by a factor of 2.5 from 8.9 divorces per 1000 marriages in 1958 to 22.8 per 1000 in 1982. Since then, it has remained at about that same level; currently the divorce rate is about 20 per 1000 or 2.0%.

A 2% divorce rate may sound low, but because a marriage is "at risk" of a divorce year after year, even a low annual rate cumulates to a large proportion of marriages eventually ending in divorce. Demographers use life-table methods[21] to compute the expected proportion of new marriages that will end in divorce. With a divorce rate of 1% per year, about one quarter of all marriages would end in divorce after 30 years; with a divorce rate of 2% per year, the proportion ending in divorce within 30 years jumps to 45%. Using the divorce rates that prevailed in the mid-1980s along with rates computed separately for each specific year of a marriage—divorce rates are highest in the first few years and then drop—we find that the proportion of first marriages that will likely end in divorce is well over half and perhaps as high as two thirds.[22] One recent study[23] based on 1995 data estimated that 20% of marriages would be disrupted—experience either divorce or separation—within five years, one third within ten years, and 50% within twenty years. In the first

---

[21]Demographers use life-table methods to compute the proportion of the population that survives to any given age on the basis of age-specific death rates.

[22]Teresa Martin and Larry Bumpass, "Recent Trends in Marital Disruption," *Demography*, Vol. 26, No.1, pp. 37–52, 1989.

[23]M. D. Bramlett and W. D. Mosther, *First Marriage Dissolution, Divorce, and Remarriage: United States. Advance data from Vital and Health Statistics.* No. 323, Hyattsville, MD, National Center for Health Statistics, 2001.

half of the twentieth century, the corresponding proportion was between 15 and 20%.

At the same time, and not coincidentally, the proportion of women who were currently divorced rose sharply. We saw in Chapter 3 that among women age 15 and older, about one eighth (12.5%) were currently divorced in 2000 compared to less than 6% in 1970 and less than 3% in 1950.

The Economic Analysis of Divorce

THE GAINS TO DIVORCE   In at least one respect, divorce is just marriage . . . backwards. Marriage occurs so commonly because there are widespread gains to marriage; we have analyzed some of the sources. Similarly, divorce will occur when there are no longer gains to marriage or, equivalently, when both parties expect to be better off single than if they remain married.

This is actually a more subtle point than it may seem, and some arithmetic is useful to show what it really means. Let's use numbers to measure the well-being of a man and woman, both as a married couple and separately. Table 4.5 presents three hypothetical cases; for each one, we provide numbers that measure the amount of marital or single output that would be received by each individual. We are assuming that the larger the output, the better off the individual is; "output" is to be understood broadly to include all the things, material and otherwise, that a marriage produces and that are valued. The well-being of any children could certainly be an important part of the marriage output that is being valued.

In the first case, we set total marital output equal to 12, shared equally by M and F. The 12 is a totally arbitrary number and is useful only compared to the other numbers. Single output is 7 for the wife ($F = 7$) and only 3 for the husband ($M = 3$). In this situation, F is better off after divorce, but M is worse off. You might think that F will therefore break the knot, leaving M to his sorry fate. But note that the total marital output of 12 exceeds the total single output of 10. That means there is some bargaining room that can save this marriage. Suppose M altered his ways within the marriage, thereby transferring some marital output from himself to F. The change in behavior could, for example, result in his transferring 2 units of marital output to F, leaving her with 8 and him with 4. Now they are both better off remaining married. This marriage can be saved!

What exactly do we mean by "alter his ways" and "transferring output" from M to F? Economic abstraction aside, think of this as a case in which M was

	Case 1	Case 2	Case 3
Current marital output	$M = 6$ $F = 6$	$M = 6$ $F = 6$	$M = 6$ $F = 6$
Expected single output	$M = 3$ $F = 7$	$M = 7$ $F = 7$	$M = 5$ $F = 8$
Analysis	F better off single, M worse off. Total output larger if married than single (12 versus 10).	Both better off single. Total output larger if single than married (12 versus 14).	F better off single, M worse off. Total output larger if single than married (13 versus 12).
Expected result	M could give 2 units of marital output to F, leaving her with 8 and him with 4. Both are now better off married than single. This marriage can be saved!	No rearrangement of output within marriage can make one party better off than if single without making other worse off. This marriage should and probably will end.	To make F better off in marriage, M must give more than 2 units of marital output to F, leaving him with fewer than 4 units. F is now better off, but M is worse off. This marriage should and probably will end.

Table 4.5   Illustrative Analysis of "Gains to Divorce"

doing something that F disliked. The transfer of marital output from M to F could be accomplished by M agreeing to cease that irksome behavior. As long as M is still better off married than single even after giving up the behavior, he will be willing to do so. A trip to the marriage counselor is in order and may be successful.

Alas, this cannot be accomplished for the marriages depicted in Cases 2 and 3. In Case 2, both parties are better off single, so this marriage not only will end, but it should end. Case 3 is more similar to Case 1, in which one party is better off by divorce, but the other is worse off. Note that in this case, however, total output is larger if single than married (13 versus 12). In order to convince F not to divorce, M would have to give her more than 2 units of marital output, so that she would end up with more than 8 units. But in so doing, M would end up worse off than if he were single—he would have fewer than 4 units of output, whereas he would have 5 units if he were single. Thus, he wouldn't be willing to alter his ways to save this marriage. This marriage would end in divorce.

The bottom line is that the appropriate comparison is between the total benefits of the current marriage and the total benefits of the two potentially single households. If total marital output is greater, then there is always some reallocation of marital output from one party to the other that would leave both parties better off married than single. But when the combined single outputs are greater than marital output, no such reallocation is possible and the marriage will end. To an economist this is an interesting result. It means that marriage allocates individuals to each other in such a way as to maximize the overall gains that can be achieved rather than the gains to any particular individual.

ECONOMIC EXPLANATIONS   The economic analysis of the causes of the increase in divorce exactly parallels the analysis of the change in marriage that we presented earlier in this chapter. To some extent, this is testament to the power of economic thinking. Much of economic analysis is just the repeated application of basic and simple ideas to a wide variety of problems. In this case, the underlying analytical tool is rational choice, the idea the individuals usually choose the most preferred among their alternatives and act in their own interests.

Let's apply rational choice analysis to divorce by considering some particular marriage that ends in divorce. First, at some earlier point in time, the gains to this marriage were expected to be positive—both parties expected to be better off married to each other than remaining single. We can infer this from the fact that the divorcing couple was married in the first place! Second, at some later point in time, the gains to the marriage became negative so that now they are both better off single than married. Divorce is not simply concerned with the fact that the gains to marriage are negative, but rather that they were once positive and then became negative. Thus, it follows as a matter of rational choice logic that because divorce is now more common than in the past, something must be happening subsequent to marriage more often than in the past to make the gains to marriage decline enough to lead to divorce.

We can make a list of potential suspects—some familiar, some new. First, the gains to marriage that derive from specialization and trade have, on average, almost certainly become smaller as men and women have become more alike in terms of market wages and household productivity. Recall, for example, the graphs in the last chapter that we used to illustrate the gains to specialization. The gains were much larger when the underlying production possibilities curves were very different (see Figure 3.8) but much smaller when the production-possibilities curves were more similar (see Figure 3.9). In other words, there is less of a reservoir of material gains to sustain a marriage through changing emotional commitments. This deficiency is an inevitable by-product of something—the greater equality of the sexes—that is otherwise desirable. Because the gains are often smaller in the first place, marriages are more prone to negative shocks and changes. Marriages have probably become more fragile, less able to withstand bad times.

In terms of this explanation, it is not that negative things are necessarily happening after a marriage begins with greater frequency than in the past. Probably marriages have always been subject to negative shocks and changing emotional commitments. But in the past, the gains to marriage were often so large—equivalently, the alternatives to marriage were often so poor—that the marriage could withstand these changes intact. This is almost certainly less true today.

The same result may also arise because of the uncertainties that inevitably accompany a particular marriage. When we talk about the gains to marriage, we ought to recognize that there is always uncertainty about exactly how things will turn out in any particular case. A simple way to capture this idea is to think of the gains to a particular marriage as following a normal distribution with its peak at the most likely level of gains and its tails representing outcomes that are much better than or much worse than the expected gains. A result on the positive tail of the distribution is a source of great unexpected pleasure—the marriage turned out better than expected. But what would happen if gains were less than originally expected?

Figure 4.4 shows what might happen. In both panels, the bell-shaped normal curve represents the distribution of gains to marriage. The two curves are identically shaped, except that the one in Figure 4.4(A) is positioned further to the right. This means that the peak in Figure 4.4(A) represents greater gains to marriage and that more of the distribution is positive. The expected gains

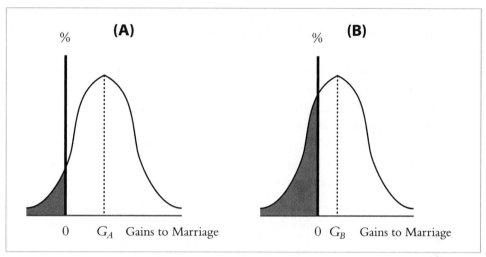

Figure 4.4   Uncertainty, the Gains to Marriage, and Divorce

for Figures 4.4(A) and 4.4(B) are G_A and G_B, respectively, where $G_A > G_B$.[24] Roughly speaking, Figure 4.4(A) represents a common situation in the past when the material gains to marriage were substantial, while Figure 4.4(B) represents a common contemporary situation where the material gains are smaller. In Figure 4.4(A), there is substantial room for worse-than-expected outcomes without divorce, which would occur only when the gains were negative (the shaded region to the left of 0). All the area under the curve between 0 and G_A are worse-than-expected outcomes in which the marriage is still better than the alternatives. In Figure 4.4(B), the wiggle room is less: A larger proportion of potential outcomes may lead to divorce. Thus the smaller gains to marriage make the marriage more vulnerable to outcomes less favorable than expected.

Figure 4.4 can also be used in conjunction with the previous analysis of negative shocks and changing emotional commitment. Now just interpret the outcomes to the left of G_A and G_B as reflecting the impact of changes subsequent to marriage. The analysis carries through: The greater are the initial gains, the smaller is the probability that a negative change causes divorce.

---

[24]The expected gains are the average of all the possible outcomes. Because the normal distribution is symmetric, the expected gain is the middle of the distribution.

One interesting piece of information about the correlates of divorce is quite consistent with these interpretations. Many studies have shown that the probability of divorce is higher when the bride and groom marry at a younger age. Why? People who marry early are typically more uncertain about themselves and their prospective spouses; consequently they have greater uncertainty about the permanent gains to marriage. In terms of our analysis, imagine that the curves in Figure 4.4 had a lower peak and fatter tails, so that there were fewer potential outcomes near the peak and more outcomes further away from it. Then it follows that a larger proportion of realized outcomes would be negative and thus lead to divorce.

Rising wages and improved labor market opportunities for women have also made being single a more attractive alternative. In terms of our analysis, these conditions would increase divorce in a straightforward way by increasing a woman's material standard of living if she is divorced. In times past, when these opportunities were far less attractive, women undoubtedly resigned themselves to unhappy marriages because their alternatives were even bleaker.

Finally, the specter of divorce undermines the benefits of specialization and itself contributes to divorce. In a world without divorce, men and women can safely specialize in market or household production, knowing that their lack of experience in the other sphere poses little risk to them. But where the possibility of divorce must be faced, specialization is often a foolhardy choice. It entails the risk of "putting all your eggs in one basket" for both parties. The risk to a woman who has specialized in the household is obvious—she may have sacrificed her labor market abilities and thus have far fewer attractive opportunities than she might have had otherwise. And the same is true for a man, who may have far fewer household skills than he might otherwise have had. (Yes, the woman's situation appears more perilous.) A man's or a woman's well-being may well fall sharply after divorce if he or she has fully specialized.

So here's the rub: The specialization that maximizes the gains to marriage and thereby reduces the probability of divorce will not occur in a world of divorce, thereby reducing the gains to marriage and making divorce more likely!

The specter of divorce also operates to undermine marriage in another way. Married couples typically make investments in what economists call **specific human capital.** Specific human capital is valuable only in the particular place in which it is acquired; **general human capital** is equally valuable in the place in which it is acquired and in all other sites. General and specific human capital are usually thought of in the context of the labor market (we talk about them later when we talk about women's earnings in Chapter 9). But they also apply to a marriage. Learning how to dance or cook might well be general human capital—current and potential future spouses might all appreciate that skill. Developing a relationship with in-laws and a spouse's old friends or learning to enjoy a spouse's particular hobbies and activities are examples of investments in spouse-specific human capital. They may be highly valuable in the current marriage, but if the marriage ends, they aren't likely to impress a future spouse. In the extreme, the value of marriage-specific human capital drops to zero if the marriage ends.

Children are often considered the prime example of marriage-specific human capital in the sense that they are almost inevitably more valued by their parents than by anyone else. Children raise the value of the current marriage but are not typically the value of another marriage. Put differently, they often bind a couple together.

In a world with little or no divorce, investments in spouse-specific human capital make a great deal of sense, and they end up raising the value of the marriage. Individuals can make those investments, secure in the knowledge that they will likely remain valuable for a very long time. In a world where divorce is more common, however, individuals may perceive that these investments have a higher probability of declining in value. As a result, individuals may quite rationally make fewer investments in spouse-specific human capital. The end result is that the marriage itself becomes less valuable than it might otherwise be. So again, the possibility of divorce may lead to behaviors that make divorce more likely.

The Economic Consequences of Divorce

In 1985, Lenore Weitzman, a well-known sociologist, reported on her study of divorced couples in California in her book, *The Divorce Revolution*. She reported that on average women's economic well-being fell by 73% in the year following a divorce and that men's economic well-being increased by 42%. (Economic well-being in this study and others that have examined this issue is usually measured by the ratio of family income to family needs. This measure, rather than just family income, is used because it builds in a sensible adjustment for the changes in family size that inevitably occur after a divorce.

Box 4.1 Did Changes in Divorce Laws in the 1970s Cause More Divorces?

During the time that divorce rates were rising, many states liberalized their divorce laws to make divorce easier and less stigmatizing. In particular, many states moved to a no-fault divorce system in which a divorce can be obtained without ascribing a fault such as adultery to a partner. Instead, "irreconcilable differences" is now given as the reason. Many states also adopted unilateral divorce laws allowing a marriage to be terminated without the explicit consent of both partners.

Casual observation suggests, and indeed there is much popular support for this supposition, that these laws actually *caused* the increase in divorce rates during this time period by making divorce easier. Religious groups and some policymakers criticized the laws for making divorce too easy and undermining the family. In fact, many states are currently considering the passage of covenant marriage laws which increase the cost of a divorce by requiring couples to receive counseling and observe a waiting period before obtaining a divorce.

The question that economists have asked is why and how these changes in the law might cause an increase in the divorce rate. If a couple wishes to divorce, does it matter whether or not fault is ascribed or whether consent is required? Economist H. Elizabeth Peters was the first to note that a famous theorem from economics called the Coase Theorem applied to this situation. The Coase Theorem states that if transaction costs are small or nonexistent, then a change in property rights does not change resource allocation but does influence wealth. What does this have to do with divorce?

If we put the Coase Theorem in the context of divorce, the "transaction costs" are costs that are incurred when obtaining the divorce, while "property rights" refer to which person in the couple gets to decide whether or not they want to divorce. Prior to the passage of unilateral divorce laws, the spouse with the property rights is the one who doesn't want the divorce. This spouse could often negotiate a large settlement at divorce—basically a payment from the spouse who did want the divorce. In the 1970s it was usually assumed that the man wanted the divorce and the wife would consent if only to get a large settlement (i.e., alimony and child support). Thus the divorce settlement is the "wealth" referred to in the theorem.

The advent of unilateral divorce simply changed the property rights in favor of the spouse who wanted the divorce. The spouse who did not want the divorce would have to try to convince the other spouse to stay or more often consent to the divorce. Under this theorem, unilateral divorce would lead to lower alimony payments and lower child support but there would be no change in the actual number of divorces as long as transaction costs were low. In other words, all the change in the law does is reassign property rights without significantly reducing transaction costs.

Peters noted that transaction costs refer to the technical constraints involved in bargaining (particularly the fact that some marital property is not easily divided) and legal costs. In her empirical research, she compared the divorce rate in states with unilateral divorce laws to the divorce rate in states without unilateral divorce laws controlling for a host of other factors expected to affect divorce. She found that during the period in which some states had unilateral no-fault and others did not (1975–1978 were the years of her sample), the variation in state laws did not cause different divorce rates across states. However, she did find that divorce settlements were lower for women in unilateral no-fault states. Both of her findings were consistent with what the Coase Theorem would predict. Peters' work generated a great deal of interest because its findings were clearly not in line with the beliefs of the general public.

Many economists have replicated and updated her findings with mixed results. One recent reexamination of this issue was undertaken by Jonathon Gruber. He used information from the decennial census for the years 1960, 1970, 1980, and 1990 to assess the impact of unilateral divorce laws on the divorce rate. One concern that Gruber addresses in his work is that underlying trends in divorce may be correlated with the passage of these laws (i.e., unilateral divorce may pass where divorce is rising so that the laws themselves are not the cause of the increase in divorce rates but are perhaps a response to the increase). In contrast to Peters, Gruber finds a fairly large and statistically significant effect of unilateral divorce laws on the divorce rate. In other words, he finds evidence that the advent of these laws did, in fact, *cause* the increase in divorce rates. He does not examine settlements at divorce.

The conflicting evidence from Peters and Gruber has yet to be reconciled. Peters notes that the passage of these laws was the work of lawyers who

 wanted the law to reflect how divorces really occurred in practice and not a public outcry against unfair divorce laws. Weitzman (1985) argues that those who passed the law were seemingly unaware that they might have a negative effect on women as they removed the property rights that mutual consent and fault-based divorce provided.

Sources: H. Elizabeth Peters, "Marriage and Divorce: Informational Constraints and Private Contracting." *American Economic Review.* Vol. 82, pp. 686–693, 1986. Jonathon Gruber, "Is Making Divorce Easier Bad for Children? The Long Run Implications of Unilateral Divorce." NBER working paper number 7968, 2000. Lenore Weitzman, *The Divorce Revolution,* New York Free Press, 1985.

Family needs are measured by the official U.S. poverty standard, a dollar figure that establishes a baseline standard of living that is adjusted for family size. Thus, family income relative to needs is a number that is a multiple of the poverty level. For example, a family that has a family income relative to needs of 3 has income three times the poverty level for its family size.)

Weitzman's book garnered a lot of press and public attention, and the 73% figure became an almost overnight sensation. It may well have been the most-cited demographic fact of the decade. It certainly suggested that divorce was an economic time bomb for women and their families.

While it was little noted at the time, Weitzman's figures were so extreme that they could hardly have been true, and, in addition, they were inconsistent with other information that she presented and that others had reported. Hoffman and Duncan were among the first to point out the serious flaws in the study.[25] They noted that since a woman's family size typically falls following a divorce—if nothing else, she no longer has a husband—a 73% fall in income relative to needs implies that income alone must have fallen by more than 73%. For example, suppose family needs fell by 20%, a figure that is close to the actual average decline in needs in Weitzman's sample. Then income would have to have fallen by nearly 80% to yield a 73% decline in well-being. If average predivorce family income was, say, $30,000, then average postdivorce income would be just $6,000, a figure that would have left almost all postdivorce families officially poor. This is inconsistent with what we know about the income of divorced women from other sources, such as the

[25]Saul D. Hoffman and Greg J. Duncan, "What Are the Economic Consequences of Divorce?" *Demography,* Vol. 25, No. 4, pp. 641–645, 1988.

Census. Weitzman's own calculations for changes in income and in income per capita were also much smaller than—and therefore inconsistent with—the 73% figure.

Other studies suggested that her figures were outliers. Using national data on a representative sample of married men and women who were divorced in the late 1970s, Duncan and Hoffman[26] calculated that women's economic well-being fell not by 73% but by 20 to 25%, depending on the nature of the calculations, and that men's well-being rose by about 10%. In another study of national data, Weiss[27] found similar figures. A 25% decline is certainly nothing to sneeze at, but it is far less frightening than a 73% decline. And a 10% increase in standard of living for men is far short of the 42% increase that Weitzman had found.

Eventually, Richard Peterson[28] reexamined Weitzman's data to see if he could replicate her results. This is an important part of the scientific process. Studies that cannot be replicated cannot be relied on, just like laboratory experiments that cannot be duplicated by others are not reliable. So what happened? Peterson found what can only be described as a simple, old-fashioned error. Using Weitzman's data and Weitzman's procedures, he computed a decline in economic status of 27% for women and an increase of 10% for men. These figures are almost identical to the figures Duncan and Hoffman had reported. How she derived her erroneous results is an unsolved mystery.

The Weitzman episode also found its way into popular accounts. Susan Faludi featured the Hoffman–Duncan criticism of Weitzman's work and the continuing use of the −73% figure despite its problems in her best-selling book, *Backlash*.[29] There is an important message here—do not believe everything you read in an uncritical fashion. Think for yourself!

At this point, the consensus estimate is that divorce reduces a woman's economic status by about 20 to 25% in the first few years and increases a man's economic status by about 10%. Remarriage is common, and with that comes a rebound to the predivorce economic status.

---

[26]Greg J. Duncan and Saul D. Hoffman, "A Reconsideration of the Economic Consequences of Divorce," *Demography,* Vol. 22, No. 4, pp. 485–497, 1985.

[27]R. S. Weiss, "The Impact of Marital Dissolution on Income and Consumption in Single-parent Households," *Journal of Marriage and the Family,* Vol. 46, pp. 115–127, 1985.

[28]Richard R. Peterson, "A Re-Evaluation of the Economic Consequences of Divorce," *American Sociological Review,* Vol. 61, No. 3, pp. 528–536, 1996.

[29]Susan Faludi, *Backlash: The Undeclared War Against American Women,* New York: Anchor Books, 1992.

Summary

This completes a two-chapter unit on marriage issues. In the first chapter, we looked at marriage through the lens of economic analysis, identified the gains to marriage, and analyzed the marriage market using a supply and demand approach. In this chapter, we used these ideas to examine three marriage-related issues. We examined race differences in marriage and family structure. The differences are substantial and important because family structure is so closely tied to economic status. We examined alternative explanations, based on wages, male incomes, and welfare income, all within a rational choice model. Then we examined the impact of marriage on earnings—male earnings, to be specific. There were two key facts: (1) Married men earn more than single men, and (2) this marriage premium has been declining. Again, we sorted through multiple alternative explanations, most of them involving the impact of the specialization within marriage that we analyzed in Chapter 3. Finally, we looked at divorce, its causes, and its consequences. Again, we adopted a rational choice model and identified economic influences. Specialization and the smaller gains to contemporary marriages were again an important part of the explanations we proposed for the increase in divorce in the past few decades. We closed this chapter by surveying what we know about the economic consequences of divorce.

Still absent from our analysis are the "bundles of joy" who are such a central feature of most marriages—children. In the next two chapters we turn to the economic analysis of fertility. Like marriage, fertility is a newcomer to economic analysis. It may appear that economics could have little to say about how married couples make decisions about such an intimate and personal matter. Economic analysis does, however, have a great deal to offer to the understanding of changing patterns of fertility in the United States and the rest of the world.

Key Terms

AFDC   113

general human capital   130

male marriage premium   117

Male Marriageable Pool Index or MMPI   108

marriage productivity effect   118

marriage selectivity effect   118

rational choice   106

specific human capital   130

TANF   113

underclass   107

CHAPTER 5

The Economics of Fertility

Introduction

In 1960, there were over four million births in the United States. Nearly one out of every eight women between the ages of 15 and 44 had a birth in that year and nearly one out of every four women between the ages of 20 and 24 had a birth. The average adult woman in 1960 had a total of 3.65 births over her lifetime.

Forty years later, there were again just about four million births in the United States, but because the population was so much larger, only one out of every sixteen women aged 15 to 44 had a birth, just about half of the 1960 figure. Now, on average, a woman has a total of just a bit more than two births over her lifetime, approximately the rate that, if maintained for a very long time, would cause the U.S. population to stop growing altogether.

These dramatic changes are not limited to the United States. Fertility has fallen throughout most of Western Europe where current fertility rates are well below those in the United States in many countries and also in much of the less-developed world.

Understanding why and how these changes occurred is the major goal of this chapter. To do that, we once again step outside the usual domain of economics, applying the tools and methods of microeconomics to a nontraditional subject. In this case, we examine the economic theory of fertility, a subject introduced into economics by Thomas Malthus in the nineteenth century and developed in its modern form by Gary Becker in the early 1960s. What can the economic theory of fertility mean? What could be more personal than decisions about how many children to have? What could an economic analysis possibly contribute? Rest assured, economic analysis has some very important insights.

In this chapter, we focus on general issues in the economic analysis of fertility. In the main part of the chapter, we examine the modern economic theory of fertility. In the appendix, we introduce the Malthusian approach. In the next chapter, we focus on some contemporary issues, especially teen and nonmarital childbearing in the United States. As always, we begin with the facts and then attempt to explain them.

Fertility Facts and Trends

Measuring Fertility

The study of population issues is called **demography.** Before we turn to the facts, we need to know something about the terms that demographers use to measure fertility.

The **birth rate** is the number of births in a year divided by the total population. In the United States in 2001 (the latest year with complete information at the time this book went to press), there were 4.03 million births, and the total population was about 285 million. Thus, the U.S. birth rate is 4.03 million divided by 285 million or about 1.41%. For ease of expression, this rate is usually expressed as the number of births per 1000 persons, so the birth rate is now 14.1 births per 1000 population. Sometimes, this is written as just 14.1 with the "per 1000 population" understood, but omitted.

This rate is useful mostly for thinking about population growth, rather than fertility per se. If, for example, you want to analyze a country's population growth, you would begin with the birth rate. The **natural rate of population growth** is simply the difference between the birth rate and the **death rate,** which is the number of deaths divided by the total population. Adding in the net immigration rate [(Number of Immigrants − Number of Emigrants)/ Total Population] gives the net rate of population increase.[1]

For our purposes in thinking about fertility, however, the birth rate isn't particularly useful because it includes in its denominator a great many people who couldn't have a birth under any circumstances. For example, it includes all men and also those women who are either too young or too old to have a birth. As a general rule for analyzing individual behavior, rates are most informative when the denominator is limited to persons capable of the event

---

[1]The population growth rate is $b - d + (i - e)$, where b is the birth rate, d is the death rate, and i and e are the immigration and emigration rates.

or behavior being measured. This group is often called the **at-risk population.**

The **fertility rate** measures fertility in this way; it is defined as the number of births to women of any age divided by the number of women, age 15 to 44.[2] As a rough rule, you can convert the birth rate to the fertility rate by first multiplying by two to eliminate from the denominator the roughly 50% of the population that are men and then multiplying by a bit more than two to eliminate the younger and older women.[3] In 2001, the U.S. fertility rate was 65.3, meaning that there were 65.3 births for every 1000 women between the ages of 15 and 44. This is almost, but not quite, the same thing as saying that 6.53% (about one in sixteen) of women aged 15 to 44 had a birth. Because some women had twins, triplets, and so on, a bit less than 6.53% of these women had a birth in 2001.

The fertility rate can be computed for different groups of women, for example, by race and ethnicity, as well as by age and marital status. Keep in mind that the denominator is always the population at risk for whatever kind of birth is measured in the numerator. When fertility rates are computed by age groups (usually five years wide), they are called **age-specific fertility rates.** The teen birth rate, which we will talk about in some detail in the next chapter, is the age-specific fertility rate for women aged 15 to 19. The **non-marital fertility rate** measures the number of births to unmarried women divided by the number of unmarried women between the ages of 15 and 44. In 2001, the nonmarital fertility rate in the United States was 43.8 births per 1000 unmarried women between the ages of 15 and 44. There have been enormous changes in this rate over time; we will talk about that further in the next chapter.

So far, we've been talking only about rates, but it is natural to think about the total number of births the average woman has over her reproductive lifetime. This could be done in two different ways. Demographers could collect information from a representative sample of women who are about 45 years old

---

[2]Note that the fertility rate includes births to women less than age 15 and older than 44, but it doesn't include the number of women in those ages in the denominator. Even though this isn't quite consistent, it doesn't affect the rate much because there aren't very many births to these women—about 9000 to girls between the ages of 10 and 14 and about 4000 to women between the ages of 45 and 54, or about 0.33% of all births.

[3]We multiply by a number greater than 2 because women aged 15 to 44 are less than half of the total female population.

and ask them about their completed fertility history—how many births they had and so on. But that means the demographers would have to wait a long time to find out what the current trend was.

Thus, instead of that, demographers compute the **total fertility rate,** which is the number of births 1000 women today would have over their lifetimes (from ages 10–14 to 45–49) if they had the age-specific fertility rates that prevail today. This isn't a perfect or foolproof measure because, for example, today's young women might well have a different fertility rate when they are older than today's older women do. Still, it is very useful and convenient. The total fertility rate is computed this way: $TFR = 5 \times (FR_{10-14} + FR_{15-19} + FR_{20-24} + \cdots + FR_{45-49})$, where TFR is the total fertility rate, FR stands for the age-specific fertility rate per thousand women (e.g., a number like 70), and the subscripts identify the age group. The age-specific fertility rates are multiplied by five in the formula because a woman spends five years in each age bracket. In 2001, the total fertility rate for U.S. women was 2034. Dividing the TFR by 1000 yields an estimate of the average number of births per woman. The current TFR of 2034 means that on average a woman would have 2.034 births over her lifetime if she followed the current age-specific fertility rates.[4]

Zero population growth (ZPG) is the total fertility rate, which, if sustained indefinitely, would cause population growth to come to a halt. Because approximately one of every two babies born is male and contributes no births, each woman born has to contribute an average of two births—and no more—to keep the population stable. But because some women die before they reach their reproductive years and others are sterile or choose not to have children, the ZPG rate is about 2.13 births per woman or a TFR of 2130. The total fertility rate in the United States is almost exactly at the ZPG mark, although it will take years and years and years of that rate for the natural rate of population increase to reach zero.[5] For much of the past few decades, the TFR in the United States was below the ZPG mark.

---

[4]The underlying age-specific fertility rates were 45.3 (age 15–19), 106.2 (age 20–24), 113.4 (age 25–29), 92.9 (age 30–34), 40.6 (age 35–39), 8.1 (age 40–44), and 0.5 (age 45–49). The TFR is $5 \times (45.3 + 106.2 + 113.4 + 92.9 + 40.6 + 8.1 + 0.5) = 2035$. This differs by one from the 2034 value in the text because of rounding error.

[5]The reason it takes a long time is because there is population momentum built into the age structure of the population. For example, if fertility rates were higher in the recent past, there will be a particularly large group of young women who are in their reproductive years, and this causes population to continue to increase. If the ZPG fertility rate is maintained long enough, however, population momentum is eliminated, and population growth ceases.

U.S. Fertility—An Overview

In the United States, fertility information is collected by the Vital Statistics System from state birth certificates. The Vital Statistics System is now part of the National Center for Health Statistics, which is itself part of the Centers for Disease Control and Prevention. An enormous amount of information about fertility in the United States and elsewhere is available. For more detailed information about U.S. fertility or more current information, check the U.S. Vital Statistics web site at http://www.cdc.gov/nchs and the Census Bureau web site at http://www.census.gov/population/www. The United Nations provides fertility information about the rest of the world at http://www.un.org/popin/. The UN web site includes links to the official population information of most member countries, so there is no end to the demographic information you can find.

Table 5.1 summarizes the terms and numbers discussed here for the United States for 2001.

By themselves these numbers don't tell us very much. Are they high or low? What can we compare them to? Figure 5.1 goes back in time and plots the annual number of births in the United States (left axis) and the fertility rate (right axis) since 1940. Some graphs of social phenomenon are straight lines, either up, down, or constant, but this one varies widely. Two abrupt changes

Term	Definition and Formula	Value
Number of births	—	4.03 million
Birth rate	Births per 1000 population = (Births/Population) × 1000	14.1
Fertility rate	Births per 1000 women, age 15–44 = (Births/Number of women, age 15–44) × 1000	65.3
Nonmarital fertility rate	Births per 1000 unmarried women, age 15 − 44 = (Births to unmarried women/Number of unmarried women, age 15 − 44) × 1000	43.8
Total fertility rate	Number of lifetime births to 1000 women if they had current age-specific fertility rates	2034

Table 5.1 Measures of U.S. Fertility, 2001

Source: National Vital Statistics Reports, Vol. 51, Numbers 2 & 4.

are prominent: the **baby boom,** that much discussed spurt of fertility that de-fined a generation as well as created problems like the looming Social Secu-rity crisis, and the somewhat less famous **baby bust** that followed it.

The exact dates of the baby boom are much debated and depend in part on whether one looks at total births or the fertility rate. The number of births jumped from about 2.8 million in 1945 to 3.4 million a year later—clearly a catch-up of births deferred by World War II. But the number of births kept increasing, finally surpassing 4 million every year from 1954 to 1964. The fer-tility rate jumped from a prewar level of about 80 births per 1000 to over 100 births per 1000 in 1946 and stayed above that figure through 1964. At the height of the baby boom, the fertility rate was about 120 for eight years in a row (1954–1961), peaking at 122.7 in 1957.[6] The total number of births peaked that year, too, at 4.3 million. It's a record that still stands, despite our much larger at-risk population of women between the ages of 15 and 44.

Just as demographers were absorbing the implications of the baby boom, things changed—and changed dramatically. The baby boom was followed by the baby bust, roughly the years from the early-1960s when the fertility rate, though still high, started to slide, to the mid-1970s, when it stabilized at about 65 births per 1000. From peak to trough, the fertility rate was nearly cut in half—in just about 15 years.

Since the mid-1970s, the fertility rate hasn't changed very much. From 1975 to 1990, the rate steadily inched up from 65 births per 1000 to 71 births per 1000, then it fell seven years in a row, before rising to its current value (65.3 births per 1000)—just about the same as the rate in the mid-1970s. The total number of births has crept up steadily despite the low fertility rate because the number of women at risk of a birth (i.e., age 15–44) is now so much larger. By the mid-1970s, the leading edge of the 4-million-plus baby boom birth cohorts reached their 20s, the prime fertility years. In 1989, the number of births passed 4 million once again, for the first time in a quarter of a cen-tury. Since then, it has bounced around in a very narrow range and is now just over 4 million.

If we look back even further, to the early part of the twentieth century, the fertility rate trend becomes clearer. In the first decades of the twentieth cen-

---

[6]At the peak of the boom, the fertility rate for 20- to 24-year-old women was greater than 250 births per 1000. In other words, approximately one in four women between the ages of 20 and 24 had a birth in a single year!

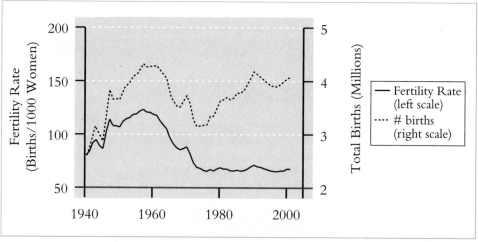

Figure 5.1 U.S. Fertility Rate and Total Births, 1940–2001

tury, the fertility rate was at baby boom levels—between 115 and 120 births per 1000 women.[7] But there is a steady slow decline; from 1910 to 1925, the rate fell almost every year. The decline was accelerated by the Great Depression of the 1930s. There is a bit of a rebound from the Depression and then the giant surge of the baby boom. When examined from this perspective, the baby boom doesn't fit. Overall, and with allowance for the complicating factors of the Depression and World War II, a pattern emerges that shows a steady overall decline in fertility, bottoming out at levels roughly consistent with two births per woman.

The total fertility rate followed the changes in the fertility rate. At the peak years of the baby boom for nine years in a row, the TFR exceeded 3500 births per 1000 women, or 3.5 births per woman. It then fell sharply, bottoming out in 1983 at 1738 births per 1000 women in 1976, less than half its baby boom level. It has since rebounded a bit to its current level of 2030.

Overall U.S. fertility does not differ very much by race and ethnicity, with perhaps one exception. Figure 5.2 summarizes this information for the major race and ethnic groups for whom the Vital Statistics System presents separate

---

[7]Looking back even further, the fertility rate was 184 per 1000 at the time of the Civil War and 278 per 1000 at the beginning of the nineteenth century. Infant mortality was much higher then so actual family size was much smaller than the fertility rates themselves imply.

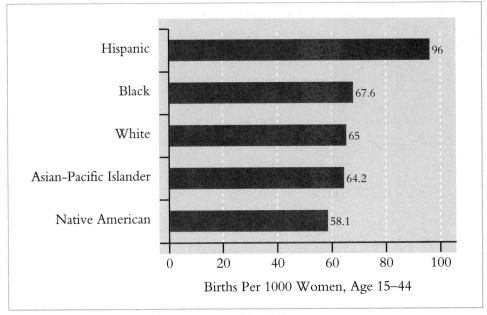

Figure 5.2   U.S. Fertility Rate by Race and Ethnicity, 2001

information. Hispanic is an ethnicity, not a race; race and ethnicity are re-ported separately on birth certificates. Hispanics are included as appropriate in each of the race categories and then also by themselves.

As you can see, the overall fertility rate is quite similar for Whites, Blacks, Native Americans, and Asian-Pacific Islanders. Hispanics have a substantially higher fertility rate. The Hispanic group is itself very diverse; the fertility rate for Cubans is quite low (50 per 1000), while the rate for Mexicans is quite high (112 per 1000).

Changing Fertility in the Rest of the World

The United States is not the only country that has experienced a dramatic fall in fertility. Indeed, fertility in the United States is actually higher than in much of Western Europe. Table 5.2 shows this information for selected coun-tries in terms of the average number of births per woman, computed from the total fertility rate. Fertility fell literally everywhere—from 2.5 to 1.7 in France, from 2.4 to an amazing 1.3 in Italy, from 2.0 to 1.3 in Germany, and from 2.0 to 1.4 in the Russian Federation. Declining fertility is clearly the norm in these countries.

	1970	1995
Austria	2.3	1.4
France	2.5	1.7
Germany	2.0	1.3
Italy	2.4	1.3
Portugal	2.8	1.4
Russian Federation	2.0	1.4
Sweden	1.9	1.7
United Kingdom	2.4	1.7

Table 5.2 Births per Woman, Selected European Countries, 1970 and 1995

Source: World Fertility Patterns 1997, United Nations Publication (ST/ESA/SER.A/165). Numbers shown are the Total Fertility Rate divided by 1000. Reprinted with the permission of the United Nations Bureau of External Relations.

Fertility remains very high in much of the less-developed world, although it is falling in most countries. For the forty-eight countries classified by the United Nations as "least developed," the average number of births per woman (computed from the total fertility rate) in the late-1990s was 5.1. Among countries with particularly high births per woman are Niger, Yemen, the Gaza Strip, Somalia, and Uganda, each of which averages more than seven births per woman. There are some famous examples of falling fertility among developing countries. In China, the number of births fell from 5.8 in 1970 to 1.9 by the mid-1990s. Taiwan is another famous case with falling fertility. In 2002, its total fertility rate was 1.76. India, too, has cut its fertility rates, with the number of births falling from 5.7 around 1970 to 3.4 in the mid-1990s.[8]

Summary

We have covered a great deal of demographic territory and introduced many terms and many numbers. A summary is in order.

- Fertility can be measured either by the fertility rate (births per 1000 women between the ages of 15 and 44) or the total fertility rate (expected

---

[8]India became a population billionaire in 2001.

lifetime number of births per 1000 women). It is also possible to compute fertility rates by age groups and by marital status.

- By any measure, fertility has fallen sharply in the United States, Western Europe, and much of the less-developed world. The current fertility rate in the United States is about half its peak during the baby boom, that period of sustained high fertility in the mid-1950s and early 1960s. The average number of births per woman is just over 2.0 in the United States and well below that in most of Western Europe. This decline is sufficiently well established that it is unlikely that we will ever see again the high fertility rates of the baby boom.

- The fertility rate remains very high in some of the poorest countries in the world. But the general trend of declining fertility applies here as well.

- In the United States, the fertility rate is relatively similar across the race and ethnic groups for which statistics are collected. Only Hispanics have higher fertility rates, and within the Hispanic group, there are substantial differences across subgroups.

The primary task of any theory of fertility is to explain the overall sustained decline in fertility. We now turn to that task by introducing the economic theory of fertility.

Fertility—The Modern Economic Approach

The modern economic approach to fertility was developed in the early-1960s, primarily by Gary Becker in an article called "An Economic Analysis of Fertility."[9] It has since been added onto by many others. In large measure, the analysis began with a puzzle: Why did fertility fall even as family incomes grew? The demand for most goods increases when income rises, but children appeared to be a conspicuous exception.

The modern economic theory of fertility set out to explain that puzzle. The approach is based on relatively simple principles and concepts in economics, but the actual analysis itself is complex and well beyond the scope of this text. The version presented here captures the basic elements, insights, and predic-

---

[9]Gary S. Becker, "An Economic Analysis of Fertility," in *Demographic and Economic Change in Developed Countries,* Princeton: Princeton University Press, 1960.

tions of the modern approach, but it makes no pretense of doing justice to the details. While to some extent that is always true in an economics text for undergraduates—and it is true in every chapter here—more is omitted here than elsewhere. With that confession, let's see what we can accomplish.

Preferences

The first basic insight is simple: *Most adults want to have their own children.* Sometimes children are useful productive assets. For example, in agricultural societies, children can provide useful labor. In a poor society without a social security system, they may provide old age support. In a family business, they can be the next generation of owners. If you were the King of England, children—male children, anyway—were once a near-necessity.[10] But even if parents never expect to get much help from their children or collect a penny, a rupee, or a Euro from them, they still seem to want them. They are, an economist would find it almost irresistible to say, a source of *utility* or satisfaction to their parents, not to mention their grandparents.

But what kind of source of utility are they? They aren't like a pizza or a good movie, which are sources of utility that are consumed and thereby used up in the process. They are a bit more like an automobile or a vacation house, a durable asset that provides many years' worth of utility. With assets like these, individuals consume and receive utility from the *services* that the asset yields, not the physical asset itself. For example, an individual doesn't literally consume his or her automobile or vacation house; instead, he or she consumes the automobile services and housing services that these goods provide. So let's say that adults get utility from the **child services** provided by their children. We will use that phrase to cover all the many things that children do and that parents gain enjoyment from.

Let's continue with the analogy. The amount of automobile services or housing services depends not only on the *quantity* of automobiles and vacation houses but also on something we might call their *quality*. A couple of Yugos is one thing, a couple of Hondas something else, and several BMWs or Ferraris is something else altogether. The same is true for a vacation house, which could range from a shack in the woods (enjoyable, to be sure) to an opulent beach house, ski chalet, or even a chateau in the south of France.

---

[10]Think about Henry VIII and his efforts to produce a male heir, which involved six wives—with no success. He was ultimately followed to the throne by his daughter, Elizabeth I.

How do we apply that concept to children? What might we mean by **child quality** or higher quality children? We're treading on treacherous linguistic ground here because we don't want to disparage any child or any parent. Still, following the same analogy, we might say that higher quality children are those children who have more child resources devoted to them, just like a BMW has more automobile resources in it than a Yugo (which hardly has any at all). We could, perhaps, call them "high-resource" children, but the standard, if unfortunate, terminology is "high quality." They are not necessarily better children or happier children, although all else equal, children with more resources available to them probably do better on average. At low resource levels, a positive relationship between the amount of resources and child well-being is reasonably clear and persuasive.[11] More resources would probably include better education, medical care, and nutrition but might also embrace piano lessons, summer camp, endless sports practices, and that special prom dress, among others.

The result of the analysis thus far is that there are inevitably two dimensions to a family's **demand for child services**—quantity and quality. Both dimensions provide utility to a parent. Ultimately, adults must make a choice about both quantity and quality. When we think about fertility per se, we are, of course, thinking about just the quantity dimension—the *number* of births a woman has. But because adults care about child services, which depend on both quantity and quality, the analysis of quantity effects is filtered through an additional layer of complexity.[12]

Adults also get utility from things that have nothing to do with children—food, clothing, entertainment, and so on. Let's lump all these things together and call them *A* for adult consumption goods. We'll let *CS* stand for child services, which, as we now know, depend on both quantity and quality. We can now write an adult's utility function as

$$U = U(CS, A) \tag{1}$$

Equation (1) simply states that adult goods and child services (*A* and *CS*, respectively) are the two broad sources of utility for an adult. Adult goods and child services are competing sources of utility. Adults can and do have very

---

[11]It is possible, of course, to spoil a child by giving him/her too many resources.

[12]Sometimes economists assume that parents provide the same quality for each child, which means that each child is essentially treated equally. That's probably roughly correct, except for extreme cases of children with special abilities or special needs. This assumption leads to an interesting interaction between quality and quantity that we will consider in the last section of the chapter.

different preferences about these kinds of things. Some adults may love a household full of children; others prefer few or none at all. All those preferences and then some are perfectly fine.

Production and Cost

The second major economic insight about children is also pretty obvious: *Children are costly.* This is true both for child quality and child quantity. In saying this, we are referring not to the amount that parents actually spend on their children but rather to something like the cost of 1 unit of child services. The *total* amount that parents spend on child services is the product of this per unit cost and the *total* amount of child services that they choose. This total amount of spending is *endogenous*—it is chosen by the family.

Before we think about the cost of child services, what determines them, and how and why they change, we need to agree on some technical details. First, whenever we talk about the cost of child services, we are talking about the cost of 1 unit of child services. Exactly how big is 1 unit of child services? The truth is that nobody knows, but it doesn't matter. Ultimately, we're not interested in exactly how many units of child services a family wants but in how that amount will change when incomes or prices change. The actual amount of child services in 1 unit doesn't make any difference in answering that question. Second, it will simplify things a bit if we assume that the cost of producing 1 unit of child services is constant, no matter how many units are produced. Essentially, this means that the cost of producing, say, 10 units of child services is ten times the cost of producing 1 unit, the cost of producing 100 units is 100 times the cost of producing 1 unit, and so on.

PRODUCTION   Needless to say, the costs of child services are quite different from the costs of most goods and services. Child services can not be purchased directly at the mall or over the Internet. Rather, they are a household-produced good, an idea we examined in the context of marriage. Many people would argue that child services are *the* single most important household-produced good, the raison d'etre of a family. So when we talk about the cost of child services, we are actually talking about the cost of *producing* child services, not the cost of *purchasing* them.

Let's think about the child services production process. To begin the production process, a woman must give birth to a child or a couple or single person may adopt a child. This is the quantity dimension of child services. Then, the child's parent(s) must nurture the child for many years. The amount of resources devoted to this nurturing is precisely what the quality dimension of child services measures. A family can produce (and consume) more child services either by increasing the number of children they have or by increasing the resources invested in or devoted to their children.[13]

The production process for child services, however complicated and varied it may be in practice, can be represented by a household production function. There are two broad classes of inputs—parental time and market goods. Thus, we can write the **child services production function** as

$$CS = F(T, Z) \tag{2}$$

where CS is the amount of child services, T is the amount of adult time spent producing child services, and Z stands for all the market goods used in the production process, such as food, clothing, shelter, and video games.

Without turning this into a class in child development, consider the nature of this production process for children of different ages. The production of child services in infants is almost certainly time-intensive, rather than goods-intensive. There are some material costs, such as a crib and toys, but day-to-day goods use is often quite moderate. For one thing, infants eat a lot less than, say, teenagers. Parental time inputs are substantial, to say the least, as any exhausted parent of a newborn or toddler can attest. As children get a bit older, parental time inputs are still required, but the ratio of goods to time almost certainly rises. Teenagers and college students involve almost exclusively goods—things like a stereo, a car, and a college education—rather than parental time, which they often seem to want almost none of.

COST   What general ideas can we deduce about the cost of producing one unit of child services?[14] The single most important point is this: *The cost of producing one unit of child services depends on the prices of parental time and on the prices of market goods because these are the inputs used to produce child services.* This is a standard conclusion of production economics: The cost of production depends on (is proportional to) the prices of the inputs used to produce a good.

---

[13]The movie, *Coal Miner's Daughter*, about the life of country music star Loretta Lynn provides a very good example of a household with high fertility and low material resources per child.

[14]It is possible to analyze quite precisely how parents might best combine market goods and parental time to produce child quality, taking account of the various costs associated with the alternative ways of combining time and goods. This is the equivalent of thinking about how firms choose between various combinations of labor and capital to produce their output at minimum cost. To actually show how to solve this quality cost-minimization problem would take us too far afield. Moreover, it is not particularly relevant to the issue of fertility, although it is important for thinking about labor force participation.

What are the costs of the inputs used to produce child quality? We can write the cost of market goods (Z) as P_Z; think of it as capturing the prices of all the market goods that children consume, everything from diapers and formula to books and toys to health care and education. What about the cost of the adult time inputs? This is tricky because parents don't literally pay each other to care for a child. Nevertheless, there is a cost. Economists would say that the cost is best measured by the wage rate, that is, by what a parent could earn if he or she were not using that time to produce child services instead. In this sense, the cost is an **opportunity cost,** the cost of something measured in terms of what is given up.

We are particularly interested in knowing what factors determine the cost of producing one unit of child services because eventually adults must decide how many units of child services they want on the basis of its cost. We can express the costs of producing child services this way:

$$C_{CS} = C(W_M, W_F, P_Z) \tag{3}$$

In words, this expression says that the cost of producing one unit of child services (C_{CS}) depends on the price of the inputs—the wage rates of the father and mother (W_M and W_F, respectively, if both are present) and the price of market goods (P_Z). We use C on the right-hand side of equation (3) to name the function because this is the cost function for child services.

As a reasonable first approximation, all families face the same price for market goods used in producing child services. The price of diapers, for example, is the same for all buyers. However, the price of parental time varies widely across households, depending on a parent's wage rate. Higher-wage parents have more costly parental time than lower-wage parents and thus they will typically have higher costs of producing child services. As an extreme example of this idea, think about the costs of home-schooling a child. Those costs are largely the foregone earnings of the parent/teacher and thus depend on what that parent could earn. The same is true whenever a parent leaves the labor market to care for a newborn: The higher the wage is, the bigger the cost is. The point is quite general; everything that involves the use of time costs more as the wage rate increases. Note that the relevant wage here is what a parent *could* earn; it is not affected by whether or not that parent is actually working. This point is very important. Every adult has a price of time, measured by the market value of their time.

CHANGES IN COSTS   An increase in the price of parental time or of market goods increases the cost of producing child services, even when families adjust to find less costly ways of producing those child services. For example, if the cost of parental time increases, families might try to reduce the amount of parental time used and substitute market goods instead. One good example is using paid daycare or sitters instead of parental care. If the cost of a parent's time is high enough, this makes economic sense. But even when this substitution is done, the cost of child services will increase if the cost of the inputs increases.[15] We can write this important idea as $\Delta P_{CS}/\Delta W_F > 0$, $\Delta P_{CS}/\Delta W_M > 0$, and $\Delta P_{CS}/\Delta P_Z > 0$. An increase in input prices always increases the cost of producing child services.

The impact of a price change on the cost of producing child services depends on how much that input is used in the production process. An increase in the price of a little-used input has a much smaller effect on the price of child services than an increase in the price of an input that is much more heavily used. The impact of an input price change on cost also depends on how easy it is to substitute another input for the one that has increased in price. If substitution is very easy, it is possible to avoid most (although not all) of the price increase. If substitution is very difficult, nearly the full impact of the price increase is felt.

PRICES   We have talked thus far exclusively about the *cost* of producing child services. Because we are actually analyzing the demand for child services and because demand usually depends on prices, it is convenient to think of this cost as if it were a price that the parent(s) face. Thus, we will often use the notation P_{CS} to stand for the price of one unit of child services. This price is exactly the same thing as the cost of one unit of child services. Let's write this idea as

$$P_{CS} \equiv C_{CS} = C(W_M, W_F, P_Z) \tag{4}$$

where P_{CS} stands for the price of child services. In words, this equation says that the *price* of one unit of child services is equivalent to (note the three bars identity symbol) the *cost* of one unit of child services, which, in turn, depends on the prices of the inputs used to produce child services. This price will be constant no matter how many units of child services are "bought" because, as we assumed earlier, the cost of producing child services is constant, no matter how many units are produced.

---

[15]This is a basic result of cost theory. Substitution away from a more costly input can never completely eliminate the impact of a price increase, although it can reduce the impact.

These ideas about the cost of child services are abstract and difficult but important. Here is a summary of the key parts of the argument:

- Child services are produced via a household production function whose inputs are market goods and adult time.

- The cost of producing a unit of child services depends on the prices of these inputs, especially on the wage rate, which is the price of adult time. Because wage rates vary widely over time and across individuals, the price of adult time will also vary.

- An increase in the price of an input always increases the cost of producing child services. The impact of an increase in input prices on cost will be greater when that input is heavily used and when it is difficult to substitute away from that input.

- It is useful to think of the cost of a unit of child services as if it were a price. This involves just a change in name and nothing more.

Choosing—The Economics of Fertility

We're almost there. With the pieces of the analysis now in place, we can solve the adult's utility-maximization problem. This is a constrained maximization problem, exactly of the form that was introduced in Chapter 2. The adults' utility function, which represents their preferences, is $U = U(CS, A)$. They chose the amount of adult consumption goods and the amount of child services in order to maximize their utility, given their preferences and the constraints they face.[16]

Let's think about the constraint a bit more carefully. Most budget constraints involve prices and income, and that's true here as well. In this case, the relevant prices are the price of adult goods and the price of child services; remember that this latter price depends on the adults' wage rates and the price of market goods. The income part of the constraint is, however, a bit unusual. In a standard consumer demand choice problem, income is usually earned income plus income from other sources. It is the income that a decision maker actually has. In this analysis, however, the relevant income is the income a family would have if all adults worked literally all possible hours. This kind of

---

[16]Perhaps you think adults don't actually think in such a rational way about how many children they will have. Many a parent has said something like "I'd love to have another child, but ..." where the "..." might be anything from giving up a burgeoning career to vowing never to change another diaper.

income is called **full income.** It is what a family *could* earn, rather than what it actually *does* earn. It is *earnable income,* rather than *earned income.*

The formula for full income for a married-couple family is

$$\text{Full Income} \equiv Y_F \equiv (W_M \times T) + (W_F \times T) + V \tag{5}$$

where Y_F stands for full income, W_M and W_F are the wage rates, T is total time available (24 hours a day or perhaps the amount left after allowing for some biologically necessary minimum hours of sleep), and V is income from other sources. In a single-parent family, the expression for full income would have only one wage term on the right-hand side. Again, note that this is an identity, not an equality: Full income is defined to be equal to the sum of the terms on the right-hand side of the equation. As you can see from the equation, full income depends on the wage rates, actual or potential, of the adults in the family and on any other income sources they may have. When the wage rate is higher, full income is higher; if the wage rate falls, full income falls as well. But note that full income is not affected by whether or not an individual is actually working and earning that income.

Now, back to the utility-maximization problem that we just summarized. It is possible to be quite specific about the solution to this problem by deriving a set of marginal rules that describe the utility-maximizing choice. However, in this case, those rules are quite complicated and don't have a convenient graphical exposition. So we'll skip the details and go straight to the demand functions, which are derived from the marginal rules. (Look back at Chapter 2, where we introduced this way of expressing the solution to an economics problem.) In this approach, the endogenous variable (fertility) is expressed as a function of all the exogenous variables, usually the variables in the constraint.

The family's utility-maximizing choice of child services will depend on the price of child services and adult goods, its full income, and its preferences. We can summarize the family's utility-maximizing choice of child services and the determinants of that choice this way:

$$CS^* = D(P_{CS}, P_A, Y_F, \text{Preferences}) \tag{6}$$

where P_A is the per unit price of adult goods (we haven't bothered to talk about them because they don't play much of a role in this analysis). The asterisk next to CS means that it represents the best possible choice of child services; it is the choice that maximizes the family's utility, given the constraints

Wage Change	Price of Child Services	Full Income
Increase	Increases, to the extent that the individual with the higher wage contributed to production of child services	Increases
Decrease	Decreases, to the extent that the individual with the lower wage contributed to production of child services	Decreases

Table 5.3   The Impact of Wages on the Price of Child Services and Full Income

and preferences. This equation is the family's demand function for child services; that's why we use D to name the function. It tells us that a family's demand for child services depends on the prices of child services and adult goods, its full income, and its preferences. For any set of values of each of these exogenous factors, there is a best choice of the amount of child services for the family.

We could write a corresponding equation for adult consumption goods, but it's not particularly important in this case, so we'll skip it.

This demand function for child services has one complicated feature that will be important. The wage rates of the adults are an important component of the price of child services; in addition, the wage rates also determine a family's full income. Each of these linkages makes perfect sense; consequently, the price of child services and a family's full income will move together if the wage changes. When the wage rate goes up, the price of producing child services increases, as does the family's full income. If the wage rate were to fall, both the price of producing child services and full income would fall. Table 5.3 summarizes these impacts.

Making New Choices—The Comparative Statics of the Demand for Child Services

As we have said repeatedly, the comparative statics are the most important part of a good microeconomic analysis. That is certainly the case here. For example, we might ask: How would a family's demand for child services change if its full income changed or if the price of child services changed? How would the number of children—its fertility—change if full income or prices changed? Then we can use those answers to try to understand how and why the fertility of women in the United States and elsewhere has fallen so sharply.

As we analyze the effect of these changes, a few complications about children are worth bearing in mind. First, a household cannot legally reduce the number of children it has, once it has acquired them, no matter how much the circumstances have changed. If the price of gasoline increases, you can sell your gas-guzzling SUV if you can find someone willing to take it. However, you can't sell your children, no matter what happens to their price. And you can't legally dispose of them in any other way, either.[17] Thus, when we analyze the comparative statics of fertility demand, it is best to think of the analysis as what a household would choose to do if it were starting from scratch, as it were, in a different environment with different constraints. Second, with the exception of adoption, children typically enter a household at age 0 and grow up, one year at a time. Thus, because you can't reduce the number of children once you have them, a decision to have a child is a decision to have a child of each age. Third, the number of children must be an integer number. You really can't have 2.3 children, although we will mostly ignore this inconvenient fact in our discussion. In contrast, the amount of spending on children—their quality—can be chosen at any value at all. Thus, the analyses should be cast in terms of finding the desired number of children; fractional amounts must be rounded up or down in practice. Finally, what we are analyzing is desired fertility. Actual fertility could be more or less than desired fertility depending on the efficacy of contraception, the availability of abortion, and/or the existence of biological fertility problems.

A Change in Full Income

The change in full income that we want to consider is one that occurs *without* changing the price of child services. Thus, let the increase in full income come from an increase in some other source of income, like a government grant or a gift; these sources were included as part of V in the equation for full income. The increase in full income could also be the result of an increase in

---

[17]Actually, it is not unheard of for children to be raised by relatives, at least temporarily, if their own parents' circumstances change for the worse. Foster care is another possibility.

the wage of a parent who contributes little or no time to the production of child services. (Guess who?)

It's almost certainly the case that child services are considered a **normal good** by most adults. A normal good is a good for which demand increases when income increases and decreases when income decreases. If child services are a normal good, then if the family's income increases and nothing else changes, including prices and preferences, the desired amount of child services increases. Exactly the opposite would occur if family income fell. There's no right or wrong answer here, but the alternative—that adults prefer fewer child services if they are richer—doesn't ring true.[18]

This kind of change is called an **income effect.** It represents the effect of a change in income on the demand for child services, all else (including prices and preferences) being held constant. We expect the income effect on child services to be positive. We can write that important relationship this way:

$$\text{Income Effect} \equiv \Delta CS^*/\Delta Y_F$$
$$(\text{with } P_{CS}, P_A, \text{ and Preferences constant}) > 0 \tag{7}$$

What about the two components of child services—quantity and quality? How would they be affected by an increase in full income? Probably, they would both increase or at least not decrease. It seems unlikely that an increase in full income would cause a family to choose to have fewer children but spend much more on each of them (so that total child services would increase) or to have many more children but to spend less on them (again, so that total child services would increase). But it is certainly possible that the income effect could be larger for one of the components than the other.

Indeed, economists believe that an increase in full income would probably affect the quantity and quality of children in much the same way that an increase in income affects the quantity and quality of such goods as housing or automobiles. Richer individuals may have more automobiles or a larger home than less well-off individuals, but they also have higher quality automobiles and homes, that is, they spend more per automobile or home. In these cases, there is often a bigger income effect on quality than on quantity. If that were true for child services, then an increase in full income, with no

---

[18]If that were the case, children would be called an inferior good. Then, parents would spend more on themselves and less on their children as family income increased. This scenario is not impossible, but it is not likely, either.

change in the price of child services, would primarily affect the quality or resources per child rather than the number of children. It would have a small effect on fertility.

A Change in the Price of Child Services

A CHANGE IN THE PRICE OF MARKET GOODS   A change in the price of child services can occur either through a change in the price of the market goods and services used to produce child services or through a change in the wage rate of the adults. Consider, first, an increase in the price of market goods—for example, education, health care, or clothing—which is easier to analyze. We already know that this will make the production of child services more expensive: $\Delta P_{CS}/\Delta P_Z > 0$. If child services were more expensive and all else, including full income and preferences, were the same, then families would typically choose to reduce their consumption of child services and substitute adult consumption goods. This is nothing more or less than the Law of Demand, the famous economics law that tells us that price and quantity demanded are negatively or inversely related. When the price of child services goes up, and if all else is constant, then the quantity demanded goes down. Technically, this is only guaranteed to be true for a normal good; however, because we suspect that child services are a normal good, we can probably assume that the Law of Demand holds.

A CHANGE IN THE WAGE RATE   Now suppose that the price of child services increases because the wage rate of an adult increases. To be specific, suppose that a woman's wage rate increases. We know that this will increase the price of child services: $\Delta P_{CS}/\Delta W_F > 0$. We might also suspect that the impact on the price of child services will be large because women's time has historically been the primary input into the production process for child services. Remember that we developed the idea that an increase in a factor of production had a bigger impact on total cost when that factor was heavily used in production and relatively difficult to substitute away from.

We might expect, then, that a family's demand for child services would fall when women's wages increase. But the analysis here is more complicated because the wage increase has two simultaneous effects—it increases the price of child services, but it also increases the family's full income. Both changes happen together, but it is easier to analyze if we examine the two changes in isolation, as if one happened before the other.

First, imagine that when the wage increases, a family's full income is somehow unchanged. In this instance, imagine that the family simultaneously loses income that was just equivalent to the increase in full income caused by the wage increase.[19] Of course, these events probably wouldn't happen this way; this is just a thought experiment, useful for analyzing the potential impact. If the price of child services were higher, but the family was no richer (its full income was the same), it would typically choose to cut back on the amount of child services it consumes and substitute the now relatively less expensive adult consumption goods for child services. This effect is called the **substitution effect.** It is always measured in a context in which there is no potentially confounding change in income; it is a pure price change effect.

We can express this idea in this way:

$$\text{Substitution Effect} \equiv \Delta CS^\star / \Delta W_F \text{ (with } Y_F \text{ constant)} < 0 \qquad (8)$$

In other words, if a woman's wage increases and if full income is somehow unchanged, the family would choose to consume fewer child services. Similarly, if the wage fell, and if full income were nevertheless unchanged, the family would choose to consume more child services because child services are now relatively less expensive. In either case, the expression in equation (8) is negative because the numerator and denominator move in different directions.

The second effect on the amount of child services demanded is a result of the increase in full income that occurs when the wage increases. Conceptually, that's exactly the same as the income effect we already analyzed, except for the source of the change. Here, the increase in full income comes from the wage increase rather than an increase in other nonwage sources of income. When full income increases, and all else remains the same, the family would typically choose to consume more child services. That's the income effect of the wage change. We can express this idea this way, repeating equation (7):

$$\text{Income Effect} \equiv \Delta CS^* / \Delta Y_F$$
$$\text{(with } P_{CS}, P_A, \text{ and Preferences constant)} > 0 \qquad (9)$$

Equation (9) states that when full income increases with all else constant, the amount of child services demanded will increase. If full income falls with all else constant, the amount of child services demanded will also fall.

---

[19]Here's an arithmetic example that may be helpful. Suppose the wage increases by $1. Then full income would increase by T. If V fell simultaneously by T, the new full income with the higher wage would just equal the old full income with the lower wage.

Because the substitution effect of a wage increase causes a decrease in the amount of child services demanded, while the income effect causes an increase, the total change in child services isn't clear. In a nutshell, the family faces a higher price but has additional full income with which to cushion the price increase. Families might not consume fewer child services in total when the price of those services increases via a change in the wage rate. If the substitution effect is greater than the income effect, then the total amount of child services demanded will fall when its price increases. But if the income effect is greater than the substitution effect, the amount of child services demanded will increase when its price increases.

We can show what is going on in Figure 5.3, which shows a pair of conventional downward-sloping demand curves for child services. The price of child services is on the vertical axis, and the amount of child services demanded is on the horizontal axis. When the demand curve is D_0 and the price is P_0, the amount of child services demanded is shown as CS_0. If the price of child services increased to P_1 and if full income was unchanged, the amount of child

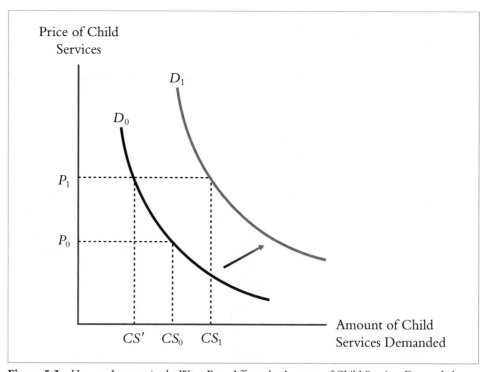

Figure 5.3   How an Increase in the Wage Rate Affects the Amount of Child Services Demanded

services demanded would fall to CS', just as the Law of Demand predicts. In fact, this is exactly the case, as discussed earlier, of an increase in the price of child services that derives from an increase in the price of market goods.

If, however, the wage rate increases, full income and the price of child services increase at the same time. If child services are a normal good, the increase in full income increases the demand for child services, causing the demand curve to shift out to D_1. The amount of child services demanded increases to CS_1. We can't be certain whether $CS_1 > CS_0$, but it might be. It is certainly possible that the family will demand more child services at the higher price P_1 than at the lower price P_0, as long as full income increases enough. This is not a violation of the Law of Demand because an extra effect that usually does not operate is at work here.

The movement along the original demand curve from P_0 to P_1 is similar to the substitution effect discussed previously, although it is not quite the same thing. The movement across the demand curves is similar to the income effect, although it, too, is not quite the same thing. For our purposes, however, they are close enough, and they are convenient ways to show what is going on.

So far, we've established that the impact of a wage increase on the total amount of child services demanded could go either way. It's very important to understand that an increase in women's wages need not necessarily lead to a reduction in child services, even though it does increase the price of child services. Now, let's turn to the likely impact of a wage increase on the quantity and quality of child services. Remember that understanding the fall in fertility (quantity) was our original objective.

Previously, we developed the idea that when the wage increases, production costs will increase more for a good that uses more of that input and less for a good that uses less of the input. Suppose that the quantity of children is highly time-intensive and that the quality of children is a bit less so. Why might this be true? An additional child necessarily involves the time-intensive early years, while additional quality can often be achieved by substituting market goods for parental time among older children. If that is true, then a wage increase might have a larger impact on the price of child quantity than on the price of child quality. It follows that the substitution effect of a wage increase would likely be more negative for quantity than quality.

In addition, we have already suggested that the income effect on quality was likely to be greater than the income effect on quantity. Taken together, this suggests that an increase in women's wages would have a relatively large negative substitution effect and a relatively small positive income effect on the quantity of children and a smaller negative substitution effect and a larger positive income effect on the quality of children. So quantity might well fall and quality might well rise when women's wages increase.

Figure 5.4 illustrates this analysis; Figure 5.4(A) focuses on child quantity (N); Figure 5.4(B) examines child quality (L). In Figure 5.4(A), an increase in the wage rate increases the price from P_0 to P_1, which would reduce quantity from N_0 to N'. The income effect on quantity is small, so the demand curve shifts out relatively little. The net effect is a decline in quantity from N_0 to N_1. In Figure 5.4(B), the increase in the price of child quality is smaller (from P_0 to P_1), and, because the income effect is larger, the demand curve shifts out further. Thus, we show a net increase in the amount of child quality from L_0 to L_1.

Putting all of this together, we get the following:

- When wages increase—especially the wages of women, whose time input into the production of child services has been substantial—the total amount of child services demanded could go up or down. The substitution effect causes families to want fewer child services, but the income effect causes them to want more.

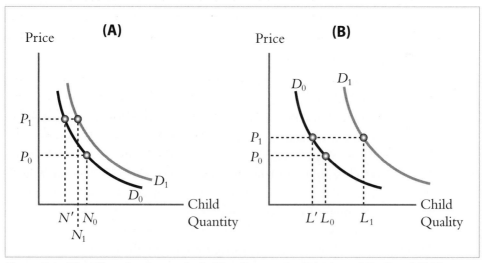

Figure 5.4   The Effect of an Increase in the Wage Rate on the Quantity and Quality of Children

- It is quite likely that child quality will increase. This occurs because the negative substitution effect is relatively small, while the positive income effect is relatively large.

- It is quite likely that child quantity—or fertility—will decrease. This occurs because the negative substitution effect is relatively large, while the positive income effect is relatively small.

That, in a nutshell, is the modern economic argument for falling fertility. When the price of time increases, families opt for fewer children, but spend more on each of them. Fertility falls, but child quality increases.

Going Further—The Interaction of Quality and Quantity[20]

Becker and Lewis[21] have argued that there is a complicated price interaction between child quality and child quantity. This interaction provides another reason why fertility has fallen. Here is an example that illustrates the logic of their argument.

Suppose you were building a brick patio. Let A stand for the square feet of area, and let Q stand for the quality of the bricks you will use. To be specific, suppose there are medium-quality bricks that cost $1 per brick and higher-quality bricks that cost $2 per brick. The bricks are identical in size but differ in some other way. To make the arithmetic easier, suppose further that a patio of A square feet requires A bricks, so a 100 square foot patio requires 100 bricks.

It follows that the cost of building a patio with A square feet is $\$A$ with the medium-quality bricks and $\$2A$ with the better bricks. The cost of improving the brick quality—upgrading from medium to high quality—is $\$A$. This is a quality-quantity interaction—the cost of improving patio brick quality depends on the patio quantity (A). If A were small, the cost of increasing quality would be small. The larger A is, the greater the cost of increasing the quality is.

---

[20]This section is optional.
[21]Gary S. Becker and H. Gregg Lewis, "On the Interaction between Quantity and Quality of Children," *Journal of Political Economy*, Vol. 82, No.2, pp. S79–88, March/April 1973.

The same thing is true for increasing the size of the patio. Suppose you were contemplating doubling the size of the patio, from A to $2A$. If you were using the medium-quality bricks, this would cost $\$2A - \$A = \$A$. But if you were using the higher-quality bricks, it would cost $\$4A - \$2A = \$2A$. Now, the cost of increasing patio quantity depends on brick quality.

The same interaction occurs between the quality and quantity of child services, as long as parents provide the same quality of child services to all their children. Here, the cost of increasing child quality is larger if family size is greater because the family must provide this improved quality to all their children. As a specific example, think about how the cost of a longer beach vacation or private school education or new bikes varies with the number of children. Do you see that the cost is greater when there are more children to feed at the beach or more tuitions to pay or more bikes to buy? So the price of quality depends on quantity.[22]

The same thing is true for an increase in quantity. Suppose parents have chosen a level of child quality, that is, the time and material resources they will provide to their children. If that level of quality is low, then the cost of having another child—who will get that same level of quality—is relatively low. But if that level of quality is high, then the cost of having another child is consequently high because it entails a substantial resource expenditure.

We can summarize these two interactions this way, where N is quantity and L is quality:

$$\Delta P_L / \Delta N > 0 \tag{10}$$

and

$$\Delta P_N / \Delta L > 0 \tag{11}$$

Equation (10) says that the price of child quality (P_L) and the amount of child quantity (N) move together. The price of quality goes up when quantity goes up and goes down when quantity goes down. Equation (11) expresses exactly the same positive relationship between the price of quantity (P_N) and the amount of quality (L).

---

[22]At a dentist's office recently, a staff member mentioned to one of the authors that she was considering a teeth-bleaching procedure for her older daughter. The problem, she said, was that she would have to do it for her other daughter as well. This is a real-world example of the quality-quantity interaction—the cost of improving (teeth) quality depends on the quantity (number of children). Imagine the cost of improving quality if she had five children.

This quality-quantity interaction adds another possible way in which a change in the wage rate could cause quality to increase and quantity to fall. We already argued that an increase in the wage might decrease quantity and increase quality. The decrease in quantity would, in turn, decrease the price of child quality, as in equation (10), which would cause a further increase in the amount of child quality. Simultaneously, the increase in child quality would increase the price of child quantity, as in equation (11). This would cause a further decline in the amount of child quantity.

What Actually Happened—Why Did Family Size Decline?

Now let's return to our original question: Why did the fertility of U.S. women and, indeed women throughout much of the world, decline so sharply in the decades since 1960? The demand function suggests several possible explanations—prices, full income, and/or preferences.

Let's start with preferences, which is, frankly, the last explanation that most economists would examine. Suppose, though, that adults now get less utility from child quantity and more from child quality than adults in the past did and thus want fewer children on whom they spend more than in the past. There's nothing inherently wrong with this analysis and it is consistent with the facts, but it's not very compelling either. First, there's no compelling empirical evidence that today's adults like children less than in the past. Second, and more importantly, it's really too easy. Changes in preferences are inherently difficult to verify, so it's an argument that is hard to refute. An argument that can't be refuted doesn't meet the standards of scientific inquiry. How are we to know if it is true or false? As economists often point out, turning to changes in preferences as the explanation for changes in behavior ought to be a last resort after seeking out changes in incomes and prices. Let's see if we can get somewhere with that approach.

Let's consider, then, possible changes in the price of child services. Historically, women's time has been the major input into the production of child services. Clearly that's true for prenatal and early postnatal time, where husband's time is not a reasonable (or often feasible) substitute. There's no rule that prevents men from contributing their time thereafter, but let's agree that women have been the primary care givers, with some occasional exceptions. It follows that changes in the value of women's time will, therefore, have a major impact of the price of child services. This is true, first, because production costs increase whenever the cost of an input increases and, second, because the increase is larger for a production process, like this one, that relies so heavily on such an input.

Consider the changes in women's wages in the twentieth century. We need to be careful here. First, we want to measure wages, not annual earnings, because we want a measure of the price of time. Second, the wage we want to measure is what a woman with, say, average education and skills could earn. This is not necessarily the same thing as the average wage that working women actually earn, if working women have different skills than nonworking women.

In the first half-century, the data are not very complete. This is the time period before the Census Bureau began its monthly labor market surveys and its annual survey of household income and individual earnings. Nevertheless, we can piece together some useful information.[23] In the very early decades of the twentieth century, most working women were employed either in education (if they were well educated) or as domestic service workers; the latter occupation was particularly common among Black women. In 1900, domestic service workers earned an average of $240 per year—about 10 cents an hour. School teachers earned an average of $470 per year; female school teachers probably earned much less. If they earned $300 a year and worked 1500 hours, that comes out to about 15 cents an hour. If we multiply these hourly wages by 20, domestic workers would have earned the equivalent of $2.00 an hour in year 2000 dollars and school teachers would have made about $3.00 an hour or perhaps a bit more. Yet another way to compute turn-of-the-century wages is to look at the average earnings for all workers, which was $418 in 1900. Women's earnings were probably no more than 50 to 60% of this— $200 to $250 a year or, once again, 10 to 15 cents per hour in year 1900 dollars, $2.00 to $3.00 per hour in year 2000 dollars.

By 1920, domestic service workers were earning an average of about $2.30 per hour, and female school teachers were earning about $3.00, both in year 2000 dollars. Women in manufacturing were earning about $3.50 an hour (year 2000 dollars), but there weren't very many of them. The average earnings of all workers was about $900 per year; translating this into likely average women's wages, and converting to a year 2000 hourly wage yields an average

---

[23]All the information in this paragraph comes from *The Historical Statistics of the United States.*

hourly wage of $3.00 to $3.50. Even by 1940, domestic service workers were still earning an average of just $3.00 an hour; teachers, as much as $6.00 to $7.00; and the average woman, probably about $5.00 per hour, all in year 2000 dollars.

Wage rates—and the price of time—began to rise in earnest in the post-World War II period. By 1960, a woman who worked full-time year-round (roughly 2000 hours) earned the equivalent of about $8.00 per hour. By 1970, she was earning about $10.00 per hour. (Of course, the increase in the amount of education was an important reason for the increase.) Wage growth slowed in the 1970s; in 1980, the median year-round full-time working woman earned the equivalent of an hourly wage of $11.40. In 1990, she earned the equivalent of $12.50 and in 1999, she earned about $12.15.[24]

The point is pretty clear—in the first half of the twentieth century, wages for U.S. women were very low by twenty-first-century standards. The flip side is that the price of time was low. Over the course of the century, and especially in the years since 1950, women's wages, and thus the price of women's time, have increased tremendously. And as the economic theory of fertility suggests, this increase in women's wages might well have caused fertility to fall and child quality to increase.

What about changes in men's wages? The average earnings for all workers rose by about one third between 1900 and 1920 and then nearly doubled by 1950. They grew by about 50% during the boom years of the 1960s. Since then, male wages have stagnated. After adjusting for inflation, median male earnings of year-round full-time workers are actually about 5% lower than in the mid-1970s, although they increased four years in a row at the end of the 1990s. Still, over the course of the twentieth century, male earnings have increased enormously. Taken by itself, the change in men's earnings would increase a family's full income and actually increase the quality and quantity of children.

The bottom line, then, is that the actual changes in women's wages over the course of the twentieth century are broadly consistent with the pattern of declining fertility. The baby boom is hard to reconcile with that pattern, but the baby boom appears, in retrospect, to be a bit of a demographic aberration.

---

[24]All the dollar figures in this paragraph are the median earnings in year 2000 dollars divided by 2000 hours and are taken from U.S. Census Bureau, Historical Income Tables, Table P-38.

Box 5.1 The Easterlin Hypothesis

The economist Richard Easterlin has offered an alternative explanation for the relationship between family income and fertility. We have already seen that because male incomes have risen over the course of the twentieth century, this change would tend to increase fertility. Easterlin proposed, however, that what mattered was not absolute income but income relative to expectations. The hypothesis is known as the "relative income" hypothesis or, in honor of its creator, the **Easterlin hypothesis.**

Easterlin reasoned this way. In childhood, individuals acquire a standard of living based on the income of their families of origin. When they are adults, they expect to have a standard of living similar to or exceeding the income they grew up with. According to Easterlin, a family's actual income matters less than its *relative income*—is it doing better or worse than it expected? Relative income, in turn, affected fertility in the expected way. Low relative income depresses fertility, while high relative income increases fertility.

Suppose we apply this hypothesis to historical U.S. data. Consider children growing up during the Great Depression of the 1930s. They grew up with low family incomes and thus formed modest expectations about their adult standard of living. They became adults, marrying and starting families in the boom years of the 1950s, just when incomes were growing rapidly. Their income far exceeded their expectations; in Easterlin's terms, their relative income was very high. The response was the baby boom.

The children of the 1950s grew up with a much higher material standard of living and, according to Easterlin, formed higher material expectations. Alas, they came of age in the turbulent economic times of the 1970s and 1980s when wages were stagnant and inflation was high. Their relative income was low. Their response was the baby bust.

While the hypothesis seems to fit the broad cohort trends, more detailed analyses of behavior at the family level are less supportive. It does not appear that the relative income hypothesis holds nearly so well for individuals. For example, individuals whose own income is far above the income of their parents ought to have higher fertility than individuals whose income is not as much higher than their parents' income. This does not appear to be the case.

Easterlin also links relative income to married women's labor force participation. In his view, married women's labor force participation responds to relative income, not absolute income. We'll talk more about that assumption when we turn to labor force participation.

For more on Easterlin's ideas, see his book, *Birth and Fortune.*[25]

Changes in men's earnings can't be an explanation for the decline in fertility, with the possible exception of the time period since the mid- to late-1970s.

Finally, let's consider a few other possible explanations. Some people explain the decline in fertility as the flip side of the rise in married women's labor force participation. It's certainly true enough that the trends are related in time. But is the relationship causal? Did rising participation *cause* the fall in fertility? That seems quite unlikely. Just as a matter of scientific logic, both fertility and participation are choice variables, what we have called *endogenous variables.* Because of that, participation could cause fertility only if women first made decisions about labor force participation and then made fertility decisions, taking as given (i.e., exogenous) the participation decision. That's not impossible, but it doesn't seem particularly sensible. It is far more likely that women jointly and simultaneously make interdependent decisions about work and children and perhaps marriage, as well, on the basis of the truly exogenous variables, such as wage rates and their preferences.

The development of modern means of contraception, especially the pill, is clearly an important factor. One way to think of its impact is that it lowered the price of controlling fertility. It made it much easier for families to adjust actual fertility to desired fertility.

Summary

Very few economists would argue that decisions about children are solely a function of incomes and prices. But we have seen that economic analysis provides an interesting window through which to view fertility decisions, especially over a long time period. The ideas that families derive utility from children, that children have both a quantity and quality dimension, and that

[25]Richard A. Easterlin, *Birth and Fortune: The Impact of Numbers on Personal Welfare,* Chicago: University of Chicago Press, 1987.

Box 5.2 "The Pill": A Tiny Tablet with a Mighty Impact

No chapter on fertility can be complete without a discussion of "the pill."

One problem women have always faced is the risk of pregnancy with intercourse. In light of this risk and the potential costs it imposed, for many hundreds if not thousands of years, single women and men in romantic relationships often either abstained from sexual intercourse or got married. This is one reason that people used to marry at younger ages and at earlier points in their relationship. The inability to control fertility even within marriage had a major impact on married women's labor force activity.

This response to fertility all started to change in 1960 when the first form of oral contraceptive—famously known as "the pill"—was approved for use by the U.S. Food and Drug Administration. Claudia Goldin and Lawrence Katz, experts on the economic history of women, have studied the impact of the pill on women's economic activity. They found that within a decade of the pill's approval and the beginnings of its widespread distribution and use, the number of women entering long-term degree programs (graduate studies and professional studies, such as PhD programs, medical school, and law school) increased. They also found that the age at which first marriages and first births occurred increased. How did the pill do all this?

Goldin and Katz explain the pill's impact like this. In the pre-pill era, women essentially had to choose between having a career and having a sexual relationship with or without marriage. (We discuss Goldin's fascinating research on this choice for college-educated women in the twentieth century in Chapter 7.) Choosing to have a career often meant deferring both sex and marriage until a later age. Goldin and Katz explain that if the career benefits outweighed her impatience for sex and marriage, a woman would defer marriage and pursue some type of career. However, if her impatience outweighed her interest in investing in a career, she would find it more beneficial to get married because this was the alternative to waiting to have sex.

After the pill entered the picture, the impatience to have sex was basically reduced to nothing—a woman could now have sex without worrying about the risk of a possible pregnancy. This allowed her to pursue a career and, if she so chose, to have sex without the need for a marriage.

Goldin and Katz argue that the pill has had both direct and indirect effects. The direct effect is that it allowed women to pursue human capital investment that would pay off only in the long run.[26] For example, it now made more economic sense to prepare for a professional career by investing in higher education. The indirect effect or "social multiplier" is also important. Those women who used the pill and waited to get married until after beginning a career increase their attractiveness to males by increasing the income they bring into a marriage. Men, too, can now wait to get married. There is no rush to marriage because the women with the higher levels of attractiveness are waiting, also, as they pursue a career. The "good ones" aren't snatched up, leaving less desirable mates for males when they are finished pursuing *their* careers. This leads to better matching for both men and women—including those women who don't even take the pill—by reducing the cost of pursuing a career (the cost being "mismatch in the marriage market" as a result of "rushing" into marriage). Now, the pill has an effect on those not even directly using it. It allows everyone to wait to get married, wait to have a first child, and pursue a career.

In Goldin and Katz's terms, the marriage market for career becomes "thicker." According to this explanation, the pill should have been associated with an increase in professional careers for women, an increase in the age of first marriage, and an increase in positive assortative. However, women with less promising labor market prospects may not find as many potential marriage partners.

Though the authors make the point that this increase in age at first marriage and first birth and the increase in enrollment in graduate and professional schools is directly correlated with the timing of the introduction of the pill into society, other factors are most probably also at work. Other various social and legal changes were occurring at the same time such as the changes to abortion laws and the passage of civil rights legislation and equal pay legislation, as well as the various factors—the pill included—that influenced the "sexual revolution." However, this tiny tablet definitely had a mighty impact!

Source: Claudia Goldin and Lawrence Katz, "The Power of the Pill: Oral Contraceptives and Women's Career and Marriage Decisions," NBER working paper 7527, 2000.

---

[26]We talk about the details of human capital investment in Chapter 9.

children are household produced goods with real costs of production are all genuine and important insights and great examples of how economic thinking can be highly creative.

The economic theory of fertility began with the puzzle of declining fertility in conjunction with rising incomes. Why, unlike most goods, did fertility fall as income rose? Could children really be "inferior goods" that adults wanted less of as their incomes rose? The answer, of course, is no. The key parts of the answer are the distinction between and quality and quantity of children and the inextricable link between rising incomes and the rising price of human time.[27] Families have gotten richer, but, at the same time, children have gotten more expensive. In response, families have reduced fertility but increased spending per child. The total demand for child services has almost certainly increased, but fertility has fallen.

In this chapter, we focused on developing a broad view of fertility, and especially the economic explanation for declining fertility. In the next chapter, we extend the discussion of fertility to focus on an important contemporary issue—teen and nonmarital fertility.

Key Terms

age-specific fertility rates   141

at-risk population   141

baby boom   144

baby bust   144

birth rate   140

child quality   150

child services   149

child services production function   152

death rate   140

demand for child services   150

demography   140

Easterlin hypothesis   170

fertility rate   141

---

[27]The interaction between the price of quality and quantity is another part of the explanation.

full income   156

income effect   159

natural rate of population growth   140

nonmarital fertility rate   141

normal good   159

opportunity cost   153

substitution effect   161

total fertility rate   142

zero population growth   5

Appendix to Chapter 5: Fertility—Malthusian-Style

Almost everyone knows something about Thomas Malthus. His is the gloomy theory that food supplies increase arithmetically, while population grows exponentially. The clash of these two growth rates spells starvation. Malthus' predictions were the source for the familiar, if unwanted, description of economics as "the dismal science."[1] He also developed the first economic approach to fertility.

It is worth seeing what Malthus had in mind both because it is interesting in and of itself but also because it is an intellectual precursor for the new approach of the 1960s. Remember that the time period about which Malthus wrote was the early 1800s, a time period in which deliberate control of fertility through contraception was not reliably accomplished.

The Not-So-Gloomy Malthusian Basics

Malthus reasoned roughly as follows. Young men and women tended to marry as soon as a young man could earn enough to support a family. Thereafter, births would follow the course of "natural fertility," which is roughly the birth rate that would ensue in the absence of contraception or abstinence.[2] Malthus argued that higher incomes would encourage earlier marriages, which, in turn, would lead to more births simply because fertility would then commence at a younger age and natural fertility would occur over a longer time period.

Malthus reasoned further that higher incomes would also reduce the mortality rate, although this is less important to his approach. Net population growth depends on the difference between the birth rate and the mortality rate. So when the wage rate is high, the birth rate increases, the mortality rate falls, and thus population begins to grow. When the wage rate is lower, cou-

---

[1] That appellation was given to economics by Thomas Carlisle, who was commenting on Malthus' ideas.
[2] This natural fertility rate reflects the underlying probabilities of reproduction, including the probability of becoming pregnant, the probability of a miscarriage, and so on. It is affected by health, the extent of breast-feeding after a birth (which inhibits pregnancy), and other factors.

ples marry later, the birth rate falls, the mortality rate increases, and thus population growth moderates or even turns negative.

In a world with rising wage rates, we can expect population to grow as the birth rate increases and the mortality rate falls. But here's the Malthusian twist, and it is not a happy one. Malthus, following the insights of his contemporary David Ricardo, argued that the wage rate depends negatively on the size of the population. This is a simple implication of supply and demand analysis. A larger population typically yields a larger supply of labor and, if the demand for labor is constant, causes the equilibrium wage to fall.

Now Malthus has created a complicated system of relationships. The wage rate affects family income, which affects fertility and mortality rates. But fertility and mortality rates affect population growth which affects labor supply which affects the wage rate. What will happen?

The Malthusian Equilibrium

These basic Malthusian relationships are shown in Figure A5.1.

Figure A5.1(A) shows the underlying population relationships, with the wage (a proxy for income) on the horizontal axis and the birth and death rate on the vertical axis. The positive relationship between wages and the birth rate is represented by the upward-sloping *BR* curve, while the negative relationship between wages and the death rate is represented by the downward-sloping

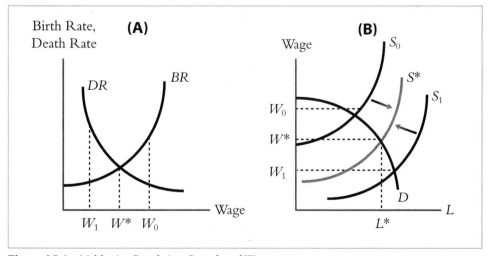

Figure A5.1 Malthusian Population Growth and Wages

DR curve. The wage W^* is the only wage rate at which the population neither grows nor declines because the two rates are equal. At a wage greater than W^*—like W_0—the birth rate exceeds the mortality rate and population grows. At a wage less than W^*—like W_1—just the opposite occurs. The mortality rate exceeds the birth rate and population grows.

In Figure A5.1(B), these effects are translated into the labor market. Here the wage rate is on the vertical axis, and the number of workers is on the horizontal axis. Note the downward-sloping relationship between wages and labor demand, represented by the D curve. Supply is upward-sloping, meaning that at higher wages, more workers are willing to work.[3] Three labor supply curves are shown for three different underlying population sizes. Labor supply curve S_0 represents the smallest population, while S_1 represents the largest population. The equilibrium wage, which is the wage likely to emerge given the supply and demand curve, is the wage at which the amount of labor demanded and the amount supplied are just equal. These wages are shown in the figure as W_0, W_1, and W^*.

Let's refer to the underlying population sizes for the three labor supply curves as P_0, P_1, and P^*, respectively. Suppose initially the population was P_0, with equilibrium wage rate W_0. As Figure A5.1(A) shows, at wage W_0, the birth rate exceeds the mortality rate, so population grows. But that population growth will eventually push out the supply curve toward S^*. The equilibrium wage will fall, and, as it does, population growth will slow. Eventually, when the supply curve has reached S^* and the equilibrium wage has reached W^*, population growth will cease. The equilibrium population will be P^*.

Now suppose that the initial population was P_1, instead of P_0, with supply curve S_1 and equilibrium wage rate W_1. Now, at this wage, in Figure A5.1(A), the mortality rate exceeds the birth rate, so population falls. That falling population will eventually push in the supply curve toward S^*. The equilibrium wage will now increase, and eventually, when the supply curve has reached S^* and the equilibrium wage has reached W^*, the population will again be steady at P^*. The wage W^* is thus a full equilibrium—in the labor market and in terms of population. Malthus' theory has thus explained wages and population and the links between them.

---

[3]Labor supply issues are discussed in detail in Chapter 7. The labor supply curve drawn here is reasonable but not important to the analysis.

The Malthusian Gloominess in Full View

To see the real gloominess of the Malthusian population model, consider what would happen if medical breakthroughs or improved nutrition caused the death rate function to shift downward, so that at each wage there were fewer deaths than before. This is shown in Figure A5.2(A) by the downward shift from DR_0 to DR_1. At the current equilibrium wage W^*, the birth rate now exceeds the mortality rate, so population grows. Population growth causes the supply curve to shift out to S^{**} in Figure A5.2(B). The eventual equilibrium wage is W^{**}, where the birth rate equals the mortality rate and the labor market is in equilibrium. The net effect of the fall in the mortality rate is a decline in living standards. This is gloomy, indeed!

Just as gloomy is the long-run effect of an increase in labor demand that might occur, for example, because of rising worker productivity. This is shown in Figure A5.3(B) as the upward shift from demand curve D_0 to demand curve D_1. The initial effect is to increase the equilibrium wage rate from W^* to W_1 in Figure A5.2(B). But that can't be the end of the story (i.e., an equilibrium) because now the birth rate exceeds the death rate in Figure A5.2(A). In the now familiar way, this will cause the population to grow, thereby shifting out the supply curve from S^* with population P^* to S^{**} with a greater population P^{**}. The new equilibrium is the original W^*. Nothing has been gained—except misery for an even larger population.

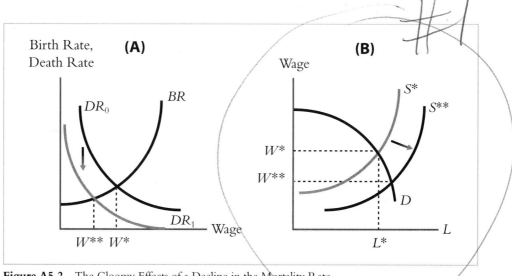

Figure A5.2   The Gloomy Effects of a Decline in the Mortality Rate

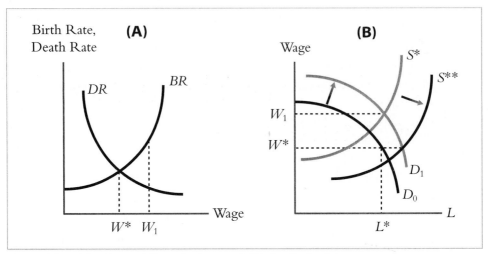

Figure A5.3   The Gloomy Effects of an Increase in Worker Productivity

In fact, things have not come to pass in exactly the Malthusian way—and we can be thankful for that. What is interesting and important about Malthus' approach is that he, for the first time, incorporated a link between an economic variable—the wage rate—and fertility. He went even further, linking it to the labor market. But the weakness, and the ultimate failure of the model, is the mechanical nature of the relationship between economic variables and fertility. In his approach, men and women make decisions about when to marry, and the wage affects that decision. But, once married, they make no explicit decisions about fertility. There is no direct effect of the wage on fertility, only an indirect effect via age at marriage. Fertility itself is not yet treated as something that married couples choose. That is what the modern economic approach to fertility does.

CHAPTER 6

Nonmarital and Teen Fertility

Introduction

In this chapter, we continue our discussion of fertility issues. In the last chapter, we focused on the economic approach to fertility and especially on the issue of the decline in fertility across the developed and developing world. Here, we focus on the other major development in fertility—the rise in nonmarital fertility—and on a closely related issue, teen childbearing.

We begin, as always, with the facts and trends. Then we turn to explanation. What are the causes of the high rate of teen and nonmarital childbearing? We focus especially on two prominent explanations that emphasize economic causes and another that emphasizes the changes in the availability of contraception and abortion. Finally, we turn to a controversial issue about the real economic consequences of teen childbearing. How does becoming a teen mother affect a woman's subsequent economic well-being? Some researchers think that teen childbearing is not necessarily a bad thing. Their conclusions are controversial, but the argument they make is interesting and important.

Nonmarital and Teen Childbearing—Facts and Trends

Nonmarital Fertility

Nonmarital fertility is measured by two related variables. The **nonmarital fertility rate** is the number of births to unmarried women divided by the number of unmarried women, age 15-44, usually expressed as the number of nonmarital births per 1000 unmarried women. Forty years ago, it was common to refer to these births as "illegitimate births." Now, these births are usually called by the more neutral descriptive terms, "nonmarital births" and "out-of-wedlock births."

The **nonmarital birth ratio** is the proportion of all births that are nonmarital. It is the ratio of nonmarital births to total births. Note that this measure is a ratio, rather than a rate. Its denominator is not the number of women at risk for a nonmarital birth, but rather the total number of births. It is easy to confuse the nonmarital *fertility rate* (where the denominator is the number of unmarried women) with the nonmarital *birth ratio* (where the denominator is the number of births). Remembering that rates almost always have the at-risk group in the denominator should help.

The link between marriage and fertility in the United States, which was once nearly universal, has weakened, to say the least. Figure 6.1 shows the pattern. In 1940, there were fewer than 10 births per 1000 unmarried women between the ages of 15 and 44 or just 1 birth for every 100 unmarried women. But the nonmarital fertility rate increased every year from 1940 through 1970, more than tripling in the process. During the mid-1970s, it dipped for a few years, before rising once again, first gradually and then quite steeply between 1984 and 1994. The peak year was 1994 with a rate of 46.9 births per 1000 single women between the ages of 15 and 44, more than six times higher than its rate in 1940. Since 1994, the nonmarital birth rate has stabilized at between 43 and 45 births per 1000 unmarried women. In 2001, the nonmarital fertility rate in the United States was 43.8 births per 1000 unmarried women.

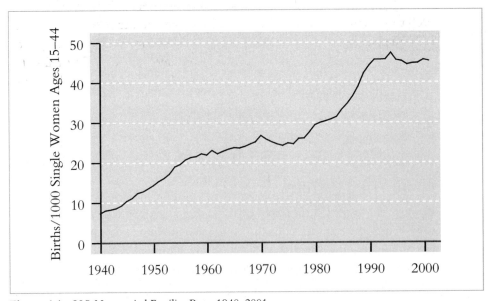

Figure 6.1   U.S. Nonmarital Fertility Rate, 1940–2001

Source: National Vital Statistics Reports, Vol. 51, No. 4 and Vol. 48, No. 16.

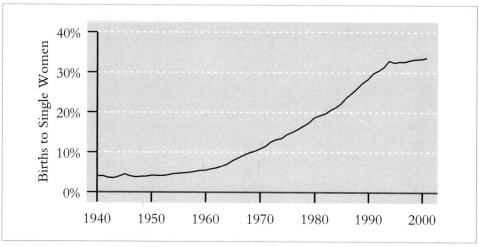

Figure 6.2   U.S. Nonmarital Birth Ratio, 1940–2001

Source: National Vital Statistics Reports, Vol. 51, No. 4 and Vol. 48, No. 16.

Figure 6.2 highlights the impact of the rise in nonmarital fertility in terms of the nonmarital birth ratio over the same time period. In 1940, only 4% of births were nonmarital and the ratio actually fell right after the war as marital fertility rose sharply. But beginning in the early 1950s, the proportion of births that are nonmarital rose year after year after year—from roughly 5% in 1960 to 10% in 1970, nearly 20% in 1980, and just under 30% in 1990. Since 1994, the rate has been stable at about one third; this reflects the recent period of decline in nonmarital fertility and the continued stability of overall fertility. In 2001, the nonmarital birth ratio for all U.S. women between the ages of 15 and 44 was 33.5%.

The nonmarital birth ratio is a tricky measure to interpret. It depends on at least three separate demographic rates: the marital fertility rate, the nonmarital fertility rate, and the proportion of women who are married.[1] Changes in any one of these factors will affect the nonmarital birth ratio. The nonmarital birth ratio could go up, even if the nonmarital birth rate fell, as long as the marital birth rate fell even more or if the proportion of women who are mar-

[1]The exact formula linking these terms is: Nonmarital Birth Ratio = (Nonmarital Fertility Rate/Fertility Rate) × (Percent of Women Who Are Unmarried). For example, in 1999, 49.5% of women aged 15–44 were unmarried; the nonmarital fertility rate was 43.9% and the fertility rate was 67.6%. Using the formula, the Nonmarital Birth Ratio = (43.9/67.6) × .495 = .33 or 33%. This formula can also be used to show the importance of changes in the three terms on the change in the overall ratio.

Race or Ethnic Group	Nonmarital Fertility Rate	Nonmarital Birth Ratio (%)
All	43.8	33.2
White	38.5	27.7
Black	68.2	68.4
American Indian	N.A.	59.7
Asian or Pacific Islander	21.2	14.9
Hispanic	87.8	42.7

Table 6.1   Fertility Measures by Race and Ethnicity, United States, 2001

Source: National Vital Statistics Reports, Vol. 51, No. 2 & 4, Various Tables.

ried fell. It is also true that some of the recent rise in nonmarital fertility represents the rise of cohabitation, marriage-like unions that lack a formal marriage certificate and thus contribute nonmarital births to the statistics. For more information about the causes of changes in the nonmarital birth ratio, see the excellent and accessible summary by Smith, Morgan, and Koropeckyj-Cox.[2]

We saw in the last chapter that differences in overall fertility were relatively small across race and ethnic groups in the United States, except for Hispanics who had a higher fertility rate. But differences in nonmarital fertility by race and ethnicity are quite large. This is shown in Table 6.1.

The nonmarital fertility rate for Black women is nearly twice as high as the rate for Whites, and the rate for Hispanic women, who may be of any race, is higher yet. This difference between White and Black women has been narrowing in recent years. Since 1990, the nonmarital fertility rate for Black women has fallen sharply from a high of over 90 births per 1000 single women in 1990, while the rate for Whites has been increasing slowly but steadily. As the last column shows, there is a large difference between the nonmarital birth ratios as well. About 28% of births to White women in 2001 were nonmarital, compared to 68.4% for Black women. The nonmarital birth

---

[2]Herbert L. Smith, S. Philip Morgan, and Tanya Koropeckyj-Cox, "A Decomposition of Trends in the Nonmarital Fertility Ratios of Blacks and Whites in the United States, 1960–1992," *Demography*, Vol. 33, pp. 141–151, 1996.

ratio has been increasing for White women and has held quite steady for Black women. The pattern for Hispanic women is similar to the pattern for Black women: The nonmarital birth rate has been falling, and the nonmarital birth ratio has been relatively steady. Asian or Pacific Island women have a conspicuously low nonmarital fertility rate and nonmarital birth ratio.

Finally, the rise in nonmarital fertility is also an international phenomenon. The United States has far from the highest proportion of nonmarital births. In Iceland, 64% of births were nonmarital in 1998; the figure was 54% in Sweden, 49% in Norway, 45% in Denmark, and 40% in France. Especially in the Scandinavian countries, cohabitation as a long-term substitute for marriage is common and accounts for the very high proportion. At the very low end were Italy (9%), Greece (4%), and Japan (1%). In virtually every country, the proportion of births that are nonmarital increased between 1980 and 1998.[3]

Teen Fertility

Teen childbearing has been a common demographic feature in the United States for many decades, but it was not until the mid-1970s that it was first identified as an important social problem. Credit for the discovery of teen childbearing as a social problem is usually given to the Alan Guttmacher Institute, a fertility research institute that published a report on it in 1976.[4] Ironically, as we will see, the rate of teen childbearing was actually falling at that time, but the number of teen births was increasing because the number of teenagers was so large—courtesy of the baby boom.

In the years since then, teen childbearing has become even more closely linked in the public eye with poverty, welfare dependency, and the problems of families and children. On the whole, teen mothers and their families fare poorly on a number of economic dimensions. President Clinton echoed this perspective in his 1995 State of the Union address when he declared, perhaps with some understandable political hyperbole, that teen pregnancy is "our most serious social problem."

The teen fertility rate in the United States in 2001 was 45.3 births per 1000 women between the ages of 15 and 19; this means that approximately 4.5% of all 15- to 19-year-old women had a birth in that year. By way of contrast, the

---

[3]For more information, see *Nonmarital Childbearing in the United States, 1940–99,* National Vital Statistics Report, Vol. 48, No. 16 (available at NCHS web site).

[4]*Eleven Million Teenagers,* New York: Alan Guttmacher Institute, 1976.

comparable fertility rate for women 15 to 44 years of age was 65.3 births per 1000. The teen pregnancy rate is approximately twice as high as the fertility rate; about one third of all teen pregnancies end in abortion and about one-sixth end in a miscarriage.

Table 6.2 summarizes the key teen fertility statistics for different population groups in the United States. Again, substantial racial and ethnic differences in teen fertility exist but they are smaller than for women as a whole. The fertility rate for Black teens is 30 percentage points higher than the rate for White teens, and the rate for Hispanics is a bit higher yet. The rate for Asian or Pacific Islanders is half the rate of Whites. The nonmarital birth ratio is uniformly high for teen births across all race and ethnic groups. Nearly four out of five births to teens are outside marriage. Fewer than 1 birth in 20 to a Black teen mother is a marital birth. It is not much of an exaggeration to note that marital births have almost disappeared among Black teens.

The U.S. teen fertility rate is very high compared to every other country at its level of economic development, where "high" means not 20 or 30% more but 200 to 600% more. Figure 6.3 shows the teen fertility rate in the United States and in selected countries in Western Europe and Japan. The numbers shown are for the mid-1990s, when the U.S. teen fertility rate was 58 per 1000, substantially above its current value. In most of the countries in Western Europe, including Sweden, Denmark, France, and the Netherlands, the teen fertility rate was less than 10 per 1000. Thus, the U.S. teen birth rate is five to six times as high as in these countries. In Japan, the rate was less than 5 per 1000, just one twelfth of the rate in the United States. Great Britain and

Race or Ethnic Group	Fertility Rate (births per 1000 women age 15–19)	Nonmarital Birth Ratio (%)
All	45.3	78.9
White	41.2	73.1
Black	71.8	95.6
Native American	56.3	81.3
Asian or Pacific Islander	19.8	66.2
Hispanic	86.4	72.1

Table 6.2   Teen Fertility in the United States by Race and Ethnicity, 2001

Source: National Vital Statistics Reports, Vol. 51, Nos. 2 & 4.

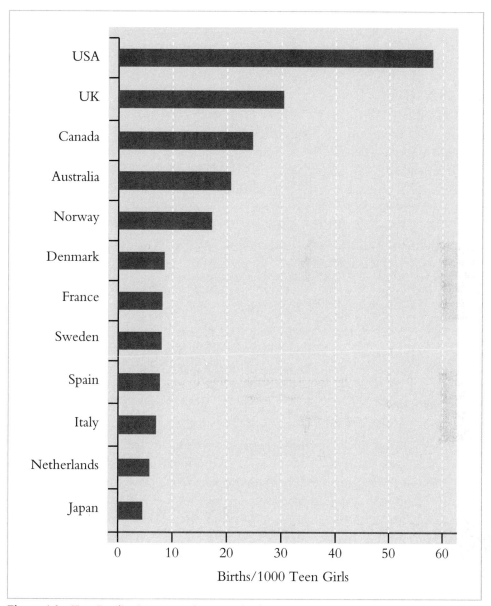

Figure 6.3   Teen Fertility Rate, United States and Selected Developed Countries, 1995–2000

Source: National Vital Statistics Reports, Vol. 51, No. 4 and Vol. 48, No. 16.

Canada come closest to the U.S. teen birth rate, with rates roughly half as large.

Though the U.S. teen fertility rate is high compared to that of other countries, it is not particularly high compared to several decades ago. Figure 6.4

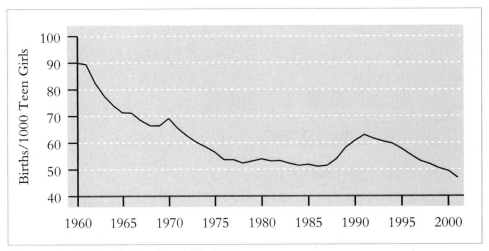

Figure 6.4   U.S. Teen Fertility Rate, 1960–2001

Source: National Vital Statistics Reports, Vol. 51, No. 4 and Vol. 48, No. 16.

shows the history of the teen fertility rate in the United States since 1960. The teen fertility rate in 1960 was nearly 90 births per 1000 and in 1970 it was just under 70 births per 1000—rates considerably higher than the current rate in the United States. As Figure 6.5 shows, teen births in the 1960s and 1970s were something quite different from teen births today—they occurred primarily within marriage. In 1960, 85% of teen births were to young married women. This makes perfect sense: The median age at first marriage for women then was 20.1 years. Pressure for so-called **shotgun marriages** among young men and their already pregnant teen girlfriends was strong.[5] Nearly 60% of all teen premarital pregnancies were resolved by marriage before delivery. Remember that this was a time period when abortion was illegal, rare, and often dangerous.

Since then, however, the link between teen marriage and teen motherhood has been steadily weakening. The proportion of teen births to unmarried mothers has risen steadily year after year after year. The proportion rose from 15% in 1960 to nearly 30% by 1970, and then to almost 50% by 1980. It has continued steadily upward since then so that currently, as shown in Table 6.2, more than three quarters of all teen births are to unmarried mothers.

[5] The colorful name derives from the image of the pregnant girl's father providing the necessary incentive for the marriage.

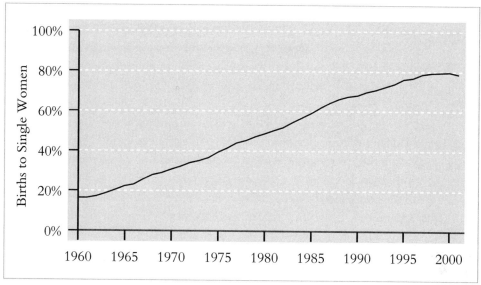

Figure 6.5   U.S. Teen Nonmarital Birth Ratio, 1960–2001

Source: National Vital Statistics Reports, Vol. 51, No. 4 and Vol. 48, No. 16.

According to Figure 6.4, the teen fertility rate shot up in the mid-1980s, after a decade of stability. The rate jumped from about 55 births per 1000 up to its recent peak of 62.3 births per 1000 in 1991. Since then, it has fallen each year, dropping more than 20% in the process. The decline has been especially dramatic for Black teens, whose rate has fallen nearly 30% since 1991.

Causes and Explanations

Now we turn to the difficult task of trying to explain the trends in nonmarital fertility. For ease of exposition, we will talk here about teen childbearing rather than nonmarital childbearing. Keep in mind that most teen childbearing is nonmarital childbearing, but that the converse is not true. Much nonmarital childbearing involves women who are not teenagers. Still, most of the arguments and explanations about teen childbearing also apply to nonmarital childbearing more generally. Where that is not true, we emphasize the differences.

We examine here a wide set of explanations. One emphasizes the role that income received via the welfare system has played in encouraging nonmarital births in general and teen births in particular. A second emphasizes the other side of the coin, namely the poor labor market and marriage opportunities of many young women. Roughly speaking, the first argument is closely associated with political conservatives; it was given public prominence in the mid-1980s by Charles Murray[6] in his book, *Losing Ground,* although economists had been researching the topic since the early 1970s. The second argument is more closely associated with liberals; its most famous advocate is the sociologist William Wilson, author of *The Truly Disadvantaged*[7] and *When Work Disappears,*[8] whose work on the decline in marriage among Black men and women we discussed in Chapter 4. Because these arguments are so well known, we examine them and the evidence for and against each in some detail. We then examine other economic influences more briefly. Finally, we look at a very different kind of argument by Akerlof, Yellen, and Katz that emphasizes the impact of changes in the availability of abortion and contraception.

The Role of Welfare and Marriage Opportunities

BACKGROUND   A bit of background about the U.S. welfare system is necessary to understand why the welfare system might have a role in teen (and nonmarital) fertility. (We already covered this ground earlier in Chapter 4.) The welfare system in the United States had its origins as part of the Social Security Act of 1935, the same piece of legislation that established the Social Security system. That legislation created a program called ADC (for Aid to Dependent Children), which provided cash assistance to poor families. Later the name of the program was changed to **AFDC** (for Aid to Families with Dependent Children), although it was most often referred to as "welfare." AFDC, along with other support programs like food stamps, Medicaid, and public housing, formed "the safety net" of income-support programs. AFDC was the most well-known, the most important, and, by the 1990s, the most disliked of the safety net programs.

When Bill Clinton ran for President in 1992, he promised to "end welfare as we know it"; shortly after his election, he began planning welfare reform. After an extremely complicated set of political events that included the Republican takeover of Congress in 1994 and a lengthy battle between President Clinton and the Republicans and between President Clinton and his own ad-

---

[6]Charles Murray, *Losing Ground,* Basic Books, New York, 1984.

[7]William Julius Wilson, *The Truly Disadvantaged,* University of Chicago Press: Chicago, 1987.

[8]William Julius Wilson, *When Work Disappears,* Vintage Books: New York, 1997.

visors, the AFDC program was abolished in 1996 and a program called **TANF** was substituted in its place. TANF stands for Temporary Assistance for Needy Families and is pronounced "TAN-EFF." TANF is quite similar in structure to AFDC in that it provides cash benefits to poor families, but it is not a legal entitlement as AFDC was. When a program is a legal entitlement, every person who meets the program's eligibility standards is legally entitled to receive program benefits. Because TANF is not a legal entitlement, however, otherwise eligible persons can nevertheless be turned away if funding is insufficient. It is, in fact, a much tougher version of AFDC. Instead, TANF imposes strict time limits on lifetime usage as well as other requirements (work, education, etc.) that each state may choose to impose. (We discuss welfare reform and its impact on women in Chapter 12).

Let's focus on AFDC because it was the largest and most important program for poor families during most of the time period when the changes in the family structure of the Black population occurred. The most important feature of AFDC for our purposes is that benefits were largely restricted to poor, mother-only families with children. Father-only families with children were eligible, but there were relatively few of them, and they have never accounted for more than a tiny fraction of the welfare caseload. Married couples, with or without children, and single persons without children were either ineligible for benefits or eligible for sharply reduced benefits, no matter how poor they were.

This peculiar feature of the U.S. welfare system primarily reflected the demographic and social context of the time (the 1930s) when the welfare system was established: Men and women were expected to marry and remain married, married men were breadwinners, and married women were homemakers. The notion of families "on the dole" has always been an uncomfortable one in the United States, and even President Roosevelt, who helped establish the welfare system and who was always a champion of the underprivileged, called welfare "a narcotic, a subtle destroyer of the human spirit." In the 1930s, mother-only families with children were almost exclusively widows who were deemed deserving of support while they raised their children prior to their expected remarriage. But once they remarried, the financial support of the government was to be replaced by the support provided by her husband.

In addition, benefits under AFDC were limited to families that were quite poor and the benefits themselves were reasonably modest. In 2001, for example, benefits in the median state for a family of two were $330 per month. We talk later about the details of the benefit formula, but it suffices for now to note that in the United States, welfare could be financially attractive only to persons with very limited wage-earning opportunities. Finally, each state is allowed to choose the cash benefits it provides to families on welfare. There is substantial variation in the benefits provided. A number of mostly Southern states provide very low benefits—less than $200 per month for a family with one child. Some Northern and Midwestern states provide more than $500 a month.

THE ECONOMIC APPROACH TO TEEN FERTILITY   Economists begin, as virtually always in the analysis of individual behavior, by trying to apply a **rational choice model.** As discussed in Chapter 2, a rational choice model means that an individual considers the available possibilities in terms of their utility, and then chooses the one that leaves him/her best off. Applying a rational choice model to teenagers may well be problematic; perhaps they don't have the foresight and planning horizon necessary to consider options fully. And in matters involving sexual behavior, rationality is not always close at hand. Let's proceed, but with some caution.

In the case of teen childbearing, a rational choice model involves comparing the utility (well-being) a young woman might have along different fertility paths—for example, one in which she has a teen birth and the other in which she delays her first birth to a later age. The utility of each path includes all that goes along with it, including the impacts of teen motherhood on education, work, income, and marriage, as well as, of course, the utility from the child. Let's write the utility of the two paths as U_{TB}^* and U_N^*, where TB and N stand for teen birth and no birth, respectively. The asterisk (*) following U means that this is the maximum utility an individual could have with that choice.

If we observe an individual having a teen birth, then, as long as the birth was chosen voluntarily[9] and the individual is choosing wisely, it must be true that for that person $U_{TB}^* > U_N^*$. By the same logic, if she doesn't have a birth (i.e., path N is chosen), then it must be true that $U_N^* > U_{TB}^*$.

Alternatively, we could reason this way. Suppose that for some particular young woman U_N^* is much greater than U_{TB}^*. In that case, we would expect that a teen birth is most unlikely. With so much to gain by avoiding a teen birth, a young woman would likely act in ways that reduced or eliminated the

---

[9]This is meant to exclude cases of rape without access to abortion or other circumstances that might make a birth seem somewhat less than fully voluntary.

risk of a birth. (There are obviously many ways to avoid a birth from abstinence to effective contraception to abortion; for this analysis, it doesn't matter what is done to prevent the birth.) Conversely, if $U_{TB}*$ is greater than
U_N*, then a teen birth is much more likely. We can summarize these ideas in
an equation as follows:

$$\text{Probability of a Teen Birth} = \text{Probability that } U_{TB}* > U_N* \qquad (1)$$

Things being what they are where matters of sexuality are involved, especially
among teenagers, nothing is certain. But the general point is that anything
that makes U_N* greater is expected to reduce the probability of a teen birth,
while anything that makes $U_{TB}*$ greater is expected to increase that probability. These statements follow from the rational choice economics perspective,
and they serve to focus our attention on the determinants of U_N* and $U_{TB}*$.

What kinds of things make U_N* large? What kinds of things make $U_{TB}*$
large? In trying to implement this approach, economists have traditionally
emphasized the income a woman would have if she has a teen birth compared to the income she would have if she delayed the birth. Because young
women who have a teen birth are quite likely to end up on welfare, their income is likely to be the income they receive from AFDC. Remember that
they will be eligible for welfare assistance if they have a birth, but not if they
marry the father of their child. Young women who delay a first birth are more
likely to continue their education; their income will come from their own
earnings and the earnings of their spouses, if they are married.

This suggests two hypotheses. The first focuses on the financial incentives
provided by the welfare system. The more generous the welfare system is, the
more likely it is that a young woman will have a birth. Because benefits vary
considerably from state to state as well as over time and across countries, it
should be possible to test whether teen births are more common where
and/or when benefits are larger.

The second hypothesis emphasizes the other side of the equation. As a young
woman's non–teen birth alternatives improve, including both the labor market and the marriage market, the less likely she is to have a birth. The worse
the alternatives, the more likely she is to have a birth. This hypothesis is called
the **opportunity cost hypothesis.** In economics, the opportunity cost of
something is what you must give up to obtain it. In this case, the opportunity
cost to a young woman of having a teen birth is abandoning the opportunities that she would otherwise have had. The sociologist Elijah Anderson put

this idea perfectly when he wrote: "The ghetto teenager sees no future to derail, no hope of a future better than today, hence little to lose by having an out-of-wedlock child."[10] Bob Dylan also put it quite clearly in "Like a Rolling Stone," although he wasn't talking about teen childbearing: "When you have nothing, you have nothing to lose." William Julius Wilson, in particular, has emphasized the impact of declining employment opportunities for young men and its impact on marriage and fertility. We've already talked about the declining marriage market opportunities as measured by the low and declining MMPI (Male Marriageable Pool Index) for young Black women.

SIMPLE EMPIRICAL TESTS   Let's look first at three simple ways to test the effect of AFDC on teen births. The first is based on a cross-sectional (i.e., single-year) comparison of teen fertility rates by state. Because some states have higher benefits than others, then, all else being equal, teen mothers will typically have a higher income and higher utility in those states than in the lower-benefit states. Thus, following the logic of equation (1), the teen fertility rate ought to be higher in the high-benefit states than in the low-benefit states. Figure 6.6 shows some basic evidence on this. It is a scattergram of teen nonmarital fertility rates and state AFDC benefits for a family of two in 1990. Each point represents a state. If the hypothesis were supported, the points ought to lie in a swarm from southwest to northeast—a positive relationship between teen fertility rates and AFDC benefits. In fact, there is absolutely no evidence of a positive relationship.

The second approach is a time-series comparison. After adjusting for inflation, a family on welfare in the mid-1990s was eligible to receive *lower* benefits than the same family would have received in 1970. The real value of median AFDC benefits—their purchasing power—fell by about 45% over this time period because most states did not raise their AFDC benefits to keep up with inflation. Even adding in the value of food stamps and Medicaid, which have increased in value since 1970, total benefits have fallen about 20%. If high AFDC benefits are an important cause of teen births, teen nonmarital fertility rates should have fallen over time. Figure 6.7 shows the evidence on this. Teen nonmarital fertility rates rose, rather than fell, through most of this time period. So this evidence certainly suggests that something besides AFDC benefits must be an important cause of teen childbearing.

---

[10]Elijah Anderson, "Sex Codes and Family Life Among Poor Inner City Youth." *Annals of the American Academy of Political and Social Science,* Vol. 501, p. 76, January, 1989.

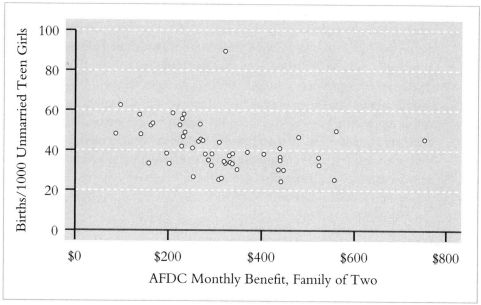

Figure 6.6 AFDC Benefits and Teen Birth Rate by State, 1990

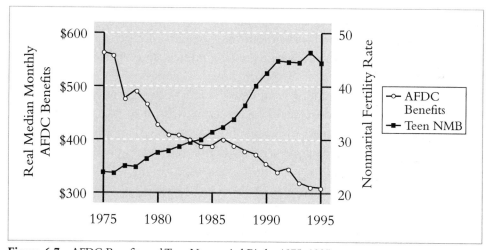

Figure 6.7 AFDC Benefits and Teen Nonmarital Births, 1975–1995

A third approach is to make international comparisons. We already know that most of the countries in Western Europe have teen fertility rates that are a fraction of those in the United States. So is it true that their welfare systems are much less generous than our own? No, it is exactly the opposite.

MORE DETAILED EMPIRICAL TESTS   None of these simple tests is perfect; none measures opportunity costs, controls for other confounding factors, or looks directly at the behavior of individuals. One of the first and still most thorough studies to test these hypotheses was by Duncan and Hoffman, who examined births among a sample of Black teens in the mid-1970s and early 1980s.[11] They wanted to test the importance of AFDC benefits as well as the opportunity cost hypothesis. To do that, they needed to know two incomes for each woman—the welfare benefits she would receive if she had a birth and what income she might have had if she had delayed a birth. Then they could examine, using statistical techniques, whether higher AFDC benefits increased the probability of a birth and whether better nonbirth alternatives decreased the probability of a birth.

They knew in which state each young woman lived, so they knew which women would be eligible for low AFDC benefits and which for higher benefits. For the women who didn't have a teen birth, they compiled information on their own income and the income of their spouses if they were married, when they were in their mid 20s. For the women who had a teen birth, there is, obviously, no way to know what their life might have been like in their mid 20s if they had avoided the birth. That outcome isn't observed—it's the fork in the road not taken. But they did know a great deal about the background of the women in both groups—things about their parents and their family income when they were growing up that are correlated with the later incomes. So Duncan and Hoffman essentially compared the teens who had a birth to otherwise similar teens who didn't have a birth, and assigned a "no-teen birth" income on that basis. In doing that, they adjusted for what is called **selectivity bias,** which in this case means that the two groups of women might differ in terms of traits and characteristics that could not be measured. Duncan and Hoffman's procedure isn't perfect, of course, but it probably gives a reasonable estimate of the income these women might have had if they hadn't had a teen birth.

Finally, they used statistical analysis to estimate the impact of these two incomes on the probability that a Black teen had a nonmarital birth. The equation they estimate looked like this:

---

[11]Greg J. Duncan and Saul D. Hoffman, "Economic Opportunities, Welfare Benefits, and Out-of-wedlock Births among Black Teenage Girls," *Demography,* Vol. 27, pp. 519–535, 1990.

$$\text{Prob (Teen Birth)} = \alpha + \beta_1 \times AFDC\$ + \qquad (2)$$
$$\beta_2 \times \text{Future Income (if no teen birth)} + \beta_3 X + \mu_i$$

where Prob (Teen Birth) is the probability that a particular young woman has a teen birth, the X's include other things (like family background) that could influence that probability, and μ captures the effect of other essentially random influences. They tested the hypotheses that $\beta_1 > 0$ and $\beta_2 < 0$.

Their findings support the opportunity cost hypothesis but are a bit less supportive of an AFDC effect. The estimate of β_1 was positive, which means that higher benefits are associated with higher rates of teen childbearing, but it was not statistically significant from zero. In other words, the estimate is not very reliable. The estimate of β_2 was negative and was statistically significant. That means that teens with better opportunities were more likely to delay their first birth to beyond their teen years. Neither impact was terribly large. For example, they found that a 25% increase in AFDC benefit levels would increase the proportion with a teen birth by about 5%, while a 25% increase in income opportunities would decrease that proportion by about 9%. As in much of the research literature in this area, the economic incentives are genuine and statistically significant, but relatively modest in size. Other influences clearly matter a great deal.

The Impact of Abortion, Contraception, and Changing Norms

A fascinating and very different explanation for the increase in nonmarital fertility has been presented by Akerlof, Yellen, and Katz (hereafter AYK).[12] They argue that the increase in nonmarital fertility is too large to be explained by either the attractiveness of the welfare system or the decline in male employment, and, as we've seen, they are probably correct about that. They focus instead on the way in which the spread of effective contraception and the legalization of abortion altered norms about the reaction of a single male to the unplanned and unwanted pregnancy of his unmarried girlfriend. The birth control pill was introduced in the mid-1960s, and at about the

---

[12]George A. Akerlof, Janet L. Yellen, and Michael I. Katz, "An Analysis of Out-of-Wedlock Childbearing in the United States," *Quarterly Journal of Economics,* Vol. CXI, No. 2, May, 1996. Akerlof won the Nobel Prize in Economics in 2001 for his work on asymmetric information in the market; a particularly famous article of his, which figured prominently in the award, is "The Market for Lemons" published in the *Quarterly Journal of Economics,* 1972.

same time it also became easier for unmarried couples to obtain contraceptives. Abortion was legalized in the *Roe v Wade* decision in 1973. For simplicity, we focus here on the abortion argument, but a parallel argument holds for contraception.

AYK note that shotgun marriages were the norm through the early 1970s but have declined sharply since then. We noted in Table 6.2 how few marital births there now are to teen mothers, and how the nonmarital birth ratio (percent of births that are nonmarital) has increased so rapidly and steadily (see Figure 6.3). Using national data on births and marriages over a long time period, AYK calculate that if the shotgun rate had remained constant at its rate in the early 1970s, the nonmarital birth ratio would have increased only one quarter as much as it actually did for Whites and about two fifths as much as it did for Blacks.

AYK present a model of the negotiations and implicit promises between a single male and his single girlfriend about sexual relations prior to marriage and their respective responsibilities in the wake of an unwanted pregnancy, both in the absence and presence of legal abortion. To analyze this situation, they use a game theory approach in which they try to describe the behavior of men and women when each has particular preferences and when the outcome depends on what each group chooses to do. Because this is a model and because the topic is, after all, sex, it is necessarily a bit abstract and stylized in order to illustrate a point.

In the AYK analysis, a woman, before engaging in premarital sexual relations, can either request a promise of marriage in the event of a pregnancy or not do so. A man can either agree to her request (i.e., make an implicit promise to have a shotgun marriage in the event of pregnancy) or decide to end the relationship and presumably try to find a less-demanding female. In deciding whether to request a promise of marriage, a woman must take into account the likely response of her partner. A man would prefer not to make a marriage promise, but will do so if it is the only way to maintain a relationship.

Suppose that there are two kinds of single women. One group has high pregnancy costs. They would terminate a pregnancy via abortion if it were available at a reasonable cost. If abortion is not available, however, they are willing to engage in premarital sexual activity only with a marriage promise. The second group has negative pregnancy costs, by which AYK mean that they want to have a baby. They would not terminate a pregnancy via abortion even if it were available at a reasonable cost. They are willing to engage in premarital sexual activity even without a marriage promise. Their preferred choice is to receive a marriage promise before engaging in premarital sex, but they prefer a baby without a husband to nothing at all.

Table 6.3 summarizes this information. Note carefully the order of preferences for the three possible outcomes for the three groups. When abortion is not available, both groups of women prefer a marriage promise to the other two outcomes, but they differ in their ranking of the other two alternatives. Men prefer no marriage promise, but they also prefer a marriage promise to no premarital sex.

In a model like this, the goal is to determine what the equilibrium situation will be. This is equivalent to asking what each group will be most likely to do when each group is doing what is best for itself, given the self-interested behavior of all the other groups. In such an equilibrium, no group can do better by changing its behavior. This kind of equilibrium is called a **Nash equilibrium,** after John Nash, a mathematician and economist who won the

Group	Pregnancy Cost	Willing to Have an Abortion?	Preferences (in rank order) if Abortion Is Not Available
Women—Type I	High	Yes	1. Premarital sex with marriage promise 2. No premarital sex 3. Premarital sex without marriage promise
Women—Type II	Low or negative	No	1. Premarital sex with marriage promise 2. Premarital sex without marriage promise 3. No premarital sex
Men	NA	NA	1. Premarital sex without marriage promise 2. Premarital sex with marriage promise 3. No premarital sex

Table 6.3   Situation of Women in AYK Premarital Sex Model

Source: George A. Akerlof, Janet L. Yellen, and Michael I. Katz, "An Analysis of Out-of-Wedlock Childbearing in the United States," Quarterly Journal of Economics, Vol. LXI, No. 2, May 1996. Copyright © 1996 by the President and Fellows of Harvard College & The Massachusetts Institute of Technology.

Nobel Prize in Economics in 1994 and whose lifelong battle with schizo-phrenia was the subject of the 2002 Oscar award–winning movie *A Beautiful Mind*.[13]

Let's begin with the situation without legal abortion. Type I women would certainly refuse to have premarital sex without a marriage promise. The costs for them are too high. Type II women are willing to have sex without a promise, so the men could refuse to give such a promise to the Type I woman, break off the relationship, and attempt to find a Type II woman. A man's prob-ability of finding such a woman depends on the ratio of Type I women to Type II women. If the ratio of Type I to Type II women is sufficiently high, then this probability will be low; for example, if 80% of women are Type I and 20% Type II, then the probability is just 25% (= 20%/80%). AYK show that if the ratio is low enough, then in the equilibrium all women will demand mar-riage promises—including the Type IIs—and all men will make such a prom-ise. The reason the men do so is that they are unlikely to do any better—there aren't enough Type II women—and in the meantime, they lose the benefits of the current relationship.

In summary, Type I women, in this no-abortion equilibrium, demand mar-riage promises because they are unwilling to proceed without them. Type II women also demand marriage promises, even though they would be willing to have premarital sex without them, because they know the men will accept them and they (the Type II women) prefer marriage and a birth to just a birth. Men provide marriage promises even though they prefer not to because they have no better alternative. Shotgun marriages will occur with some fre-quency since premarital sex is occurring and abortion is unavailable. The shotgun marriages help keep the nonmarital birth ratio relatively low.

How does the availability of abortion change the equilibrium? Type I women no longer need to insist on a marriage promise because they can now obtain an abortion rather than have a birth. In effect, their preferences have changed: A marriage promise is no longer important and consequently they now pre-fer premarital sex without a promise to no premarital sex. The men no longer have to offer a promise of marriage because there will be no birth to legit-imize in the first place. Type II women are put in a more difficult situation. They can no longer insist on a marriage promise because a man can now find

---

[13]For more on Nash's life, read *A Beautiful Mind* by Sylvia Nasar (New York: Simon & Schuster, 1998) on which the movie was loosely based.

a Type I woman who will no longer insist on such a promise (and who would not have a birth in any case). Some Type II women will continue to have unplanned pregnancies, but now, in the absence of a marriage promise, they will have nonmarital births instead of shotgun weddings. They do not take advantage of legal abortions because for them the costs of pregnancy are negative. As a result, the nonmarital birth ratio will increase.

AYK concede that "doubt will always remain about the ultimate cause for something as diffuse as a change in social custom" (p. 313). Their approach does seem to capture something very interesting and something very different from the narrow economic approaches. It is undeniable that the relationship between young single men and women is very different than it used to be and that these changes have affected marriage and fertility. This study is also a very interesting example of how modern economic analysis—here, game theory—can be used to analyze very complex behavior that is well beyond the conventional boundaries of economics.

Wage and Other Influences

Another economic cause of nonmarital (though probably not teen) childbearing is women's improving labor market opportunities. Both work and wages have increased for women, especially for more educated women. This increase makes single parenting economically viable. For some women, it is now possible to have children and a reasonable standard of living without a marriage partner. Cher, who did exactly that, is known for having concluded that "men are a luxury." We should not, however, overstate this impact. Families with a single female householder have substantially lower average income than married-couple families.

Some portion of nonmarital childbearing among nonteens reflects cohabitation. As discussed in Chapter 3, cohabitation among unmarried partners of the opposite sex is on the rise, and many of these cohabiting relationships are quite long-term and very marriage-like. Births to women in these relationships are technically nonmarital, but functionally they are more like marital births in the sense that the children have two biological parents in the family unit. There is some evidence, however, that relationships involving cohabitation are less stable than marriage.

It is also clear that the social stigma of unwed motherhood has declined substantially. In Nathaniel Hawthorne's *The Scarlet Letter,* a tale of early American New England life, Hester Prynne was made to wear the letter "A" (for adultery) permanently as punishment for her nonmarital birth. In the 1950s, the movie career of the wonderful Swedish actress, Ingrid Bergman, suffered serious harm after she had a nonmarital relationship and nonmarital birth with the Italian movie director, Roberto Rossellini. She became a pariah in America virtually overnight and was even denounced on the floor of the U.S. Senate, where she was called "Hollywood's apostle of degradation." In the 1960s, it was still common for pregnant teens to be expelled from high school; they were deemed a bad influence who ought not mix with the rest.

Clearly, things have changed. As nonmarital births became more common, they appeared to have become more accepted. Nonmarital births among movie stars and other prominent persons in the news are now common and are rarely associated with severe criticism or negative career effects. (One well-known exception was former Vice-President Dan Quayle's harsh criticism of the TV character Murphy Brown, who had a nonmarital birth. She was clearly self-supporting and appeared to be a caring parent.) In many urban communities, especially minority communities in the 1990s, nonmarital births were so common as to be the norm. Disapproval was modest to nonexistent in many cases.

Finally, the need to achieve status matters. A dependent infant and status as a mother and adult may provide important satisfaction to adolescent girls who see few other opportunities for self-esteem.

The Consequences of Teen Childbearing

What are the effects of teen childbearing on the economic status of women? For most of the past two decades, the research literature conclusively showed that "kids having kids" was a very serious problem. It compounded the already difficult situation of young women from poor families and contributed importantly to the higher incidence of poverty and welfare dependence of these women. For example, about a decade ago, an influential research panel of the National Research Council surveyed the research evidence and concluded, in a book called *Risking the Future* that "Women who become parents as teenagers are at greater risk of social and economic disadvantage throughout their lives than those who delay childbearing."[14] As we noted earlier, President Clinton called it our "most serious social problem."

---

[14]Cheryl D. Hayes, *Risking the Future,* Washington DC: National Academy Press, p. 138, 1987.

In the past decade, new research has arisen that has challenged this conventional view, arguing that the problem of teen childbearing has been exaggerated and misplaced. Some researchers argue that while teen childbearers may do poorly on average, it is not their teen childbearing that is the cause of their problems but rather other factors in their lives. Other researchers argue that a teen birth really doesn't make a young woman's own situation very much worse and that it may even have a beneficial effect on her subsequent socioeconomic status. Needless to say, these conclusions are controversial.

This research is important in and of itself. It has genuine implications for the design of effective public policy to assist teen mothers and their families. But, in addition, it's a particularly good case study of the social science research process. Thus, we discuss it here in some detail.

BACKGROUND Sociologists and economists have studied teen mothers and their families for many years and there are literally hundreds of research studies. It is well established that, on average, their family incomes are lower, they are more likely to be poor and to be receiving welfare, and they are less likely to be high school graduates, to be married, to be employed, and so on.

Figure 6.8 shows some representative information on socioeconomic outcomes for women who were teen mothers compared to all other women. The outcomes are measured as of the time the women are in their late 20s and early 30s, in the early 1990s. Teen mothers fare worse across the board in terms of education, poverty status, and receipt of welfare. Only half of the teen mothers are high school graduates, while 90% of the other women were. The rates of poverty and welfare receipt for teen mothers are at least three times as high as for the other group of women. And family incomes differ substantially, too: The average family income of the teen mothers was less than two thirds of the family income of the other women (these data are not shown in Figure 6.8).

Those findings by themselves don't establish that a teen birth is the cause of those problems in the sense that if it were possible to successfully intervene and change only a woman's age at first birth *and nothing else about her up to that point,* her life circumstances would change dramatically. Maybe something else is the cause of a teen birth and the poor outcomes. That would not be entirely surprising because teen mothers are certainly not a random sample of the population.

METHODS A social scientist could accurately measure the causal impact of teen childbearing on outcomes like educational attainment, work, and income

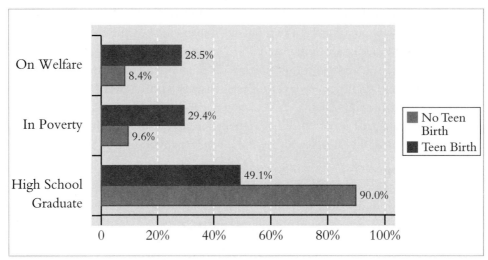

Figure 6.8   Socioeconomic Outcomes for Teen Mothers and Other Women

Source: Authors' calculations from National Longitudinal Survey of Youth

by performing a controlled scientific experiment. A researcher could randomly assign some teens to have a birth and randomly assign others not to have a teen birth. Then the researcher could study the participant for some years and examine the average difference in outcomes, knowing that because of the random assignment, only the teen birth "treatment" would be the cause of the difference. The simple difference in means between the two groups would, therefore, be an unbiased estimate of the causal impact of a teen birth. It would accurately represent what could be accomplished if a policy could delay the age of a young woman's first birth until after her teenage years. The problem is that an experiment like that can't be done for obvious reasons.

Instead, researchers have had to analyze nonexperimental data. In most of the early work on this subject—let's call them first-generation studies—researchers attempted to control statistically for the many obvious and measurable differences between young women who had a teen birth and those who did not—things like parental education and family income that affect both the likelihood that a woman has a teen birth and also her later economic status. This line of research yielded two very consistent findings: (1) Some of the apparent differences in outcomes between teen mothers and other young women are the result of factors other than their age at first birth, and (2) the remaining "causal" effects of a teen birth are substantial and negative. These findings were the source for the common knowledge about the consequences of teen childbearing.

But even the best of these first-generation studies is plagued by the inevitable inability to control for enough factors to make the remaining effect truly convincing. Since about the mid-1980s, researchers have become increasingly aware of the impact of unmeasured factors that might bias their findings. (That's why there is now so much interest in natural experiments; see Chapter 2 for a review.) For example, factors like parental attitudes, involvement, and other intangibles that defy easy measurement are likely to be important factors in determining both teen childbearing and the outcomes (like years of education or labor market earnings) that are being measured. If that's true, then the estimate that fails to control for these factors will be biased.

This general idea was discussed in the section, Empirical Methods in Economics, in Chapter 2. The main idea is repeated here: *If variables that affect the dependent variable are omitted from a statistical analysis, they bias estimates of all variables with which they are correlated.* In this case, omitted variables that influence both the probability of having a teen birth and an outcome of interest will bias the estimate of the impact of a teen birth on the outcome. In most plausible cases, it will make the impact look too big, whether positive (for bad outcomes like being poor) or negative (for good outcomes like years of education or earnings). Many researchers are skeptical about the findings of this kind of statistical research. At best, it probably provides an upper-bound estimate of the causal effect of teen childbearing.

In light of these concerns, a second generation of research studies on the consequences of teen childbearing emerged. It attempted to measure the causal effect of a teen birth by finding better "natural" comparison groups. The researchers attempted to identify a group of women who are reasonably similar to teen mothers in most meaningful ways so that one could infer that the differences between the two groups were largely the result of early childbearing.

One approach, first proposed by Geronimus and Korenman and then followed up by Hoffman, Foster, and Furstenberg, compared outcomes for sisters, one of whom had a teen birth while the other did not.[15] Because sisters share many of the same family and neighborhood characteristics, including many things that are very hard to measure, the differences in outcomes

---

[15]Arline Geronimus and Sanders Korenman, "The Socioeconomic Consequences of Teen Childbearing Reconsidered," *Quarterly Journal of Economics,* Vol. 107, pp. 1187–1214, 1992; Saul D. Hoffman, E. Michael Foster, and Frank F. Furstenberg, Jr., "Re-evaluating the Costs of Teenage Childbearing," *Demography,* Vol. 30, No. 1, pp. 1–13, 1993. There are also rejoinders by Geronimus and Korenman and Hoffman, Foster, and Furstenberg in *Demography,* Vol. 30, No. 1, 1993.

between the sisters primarily ought to represent the effect of the difference in their age at first birth. This is very much like actually measuring many of the hard-to-measure variables that bias the estimates in first-generation studies. Thus, this procedure ought to reduce the upward bias of those studies.

A second approach, implemented by Grogger and Bronars, compared teen mothers who had *twins* with teen mothers who had a *single birth*.[16] Here, the idea is that the difference between having one child and having two might be a reasonable measure of the difference between having zero and having one—that is, between having and not having a birth as a teen. Because having twins is random, there shouldn't be any systematic differences between the two sets of mothers. This is quite close to a natural experiment, courtesy of Mother Nature.

A third important and very influential study, by Hotz, McElroy, and Sanders, compared teen childbearers to teens who had a teen pregnancy but had a miscarriage instead.[17] (This study looked at births and miscarriages to teens age 17 or younger rather than age 19 or younger, as in the usual definition of a teen birth.) Because most miscarriages are random, those who had a birth and those who had a miscarriage again ought to be sufficiently similar in other ways that we can look at the subsequent differences between them to gauge the effects of a teen birth. This, too, is quite close to a natural experiment, again courtesy of Mother Nature. If teen births are costly, the women with miscarriages on average ought to be doing better than the teen mothers because the miscarriages forced them to delay the age at which they began their childbearing. The estimate of the impact of a teen birth shouldn't be biased, as long as miscarriages are random.

RESEARCH FINDINGS   The results of these studies are controversial, and it's fair to say that the dust hasn't settled yet.[18] Quite understandably, they have gotten a great deal of attention from the research and policy community. They easily meet two criteria for studies that tend to attract attention: They are genuinely innovative, and they appear to show that the "common knowledge"—in this case, that teen childbearing has substantial costs—is wrong.

---

[16]Jeff Grogger and Steven Bronars, "The Socioeconomic Consequences of Teenage Childbearing: Findings from a Natural Experiment," *Family Planning Perspectives,* Vol. 25, No. 4, pp. 156–161, 1993.

[17]V. J. Hotz, S. W. McElroy, and S. G. Sanders, "The Impacts of Teenage Childbearing on the Mothers and the Consequences of Those Impacts for Government," in *Kids Having Kids,* edited by R. Maynard, Washington, D.C.: The Urban Institute Press, 1997.

[18]For an overview of all these papers, see Saul D. Hoffman, "Teen Childbearing Isn't So Bad After All . . . Or Is It?" *Family Planning Perspectives,* Vol. 30, No. 5, pp. 236–239, 1998.

Let's begin with the sisters studies. Geronimus and Korenman looked at two different samples of sisters from national samples, and Hoffman, Foster, and Furstenberg examined yet another one. One of the samples used by Geronimus and Korenman was based on teen births that occurred primarily in the 1960s; the other data set they used and the one used by Hoffman, Foster, and Furstenberg were based on teen births primarily in the mid-1970s through the mid-1980s.[19] In their analysis of the teen sisters from the 1960s, Geronimus and Korenman found that there almost weren't any negative effects of teen childbearing at all! The sister who had a teen birth did no worse, on average, on most economic measures than her sister who had a later birth. She completed about as much education, had a standard of living that was no lower, and was no more likely to be poor. Geronimus went on to argue on the basis of these findings and other health-related findings that early childbearing might be desirable in some disadvantaged subpopulations.

In the other analysis by Geronimus and Korenman and in the work of Hoffman, Foster, and Furstenberg, the effects of a teen birth were quite consistently negative, although they were not as negative as in the earlier multivariate studies. For example, the average difference in economic well-being (measured as family income divided by the poverty line) between a teen mother and her (nonteen mother) sister was not zero but rather about one third; in the earlier studies, the impact on income was typically between 40 and 50%. There were also reasonably big differences between the sisters in the probability of being poor, receiving welfare, and attaining an educational level, all to the detriment of the sister who had the teen birth.

The question is which set of findings to accept—the earlier data showing little or no effect or the two later ones showing bigger effects. It's probably prudent to rely on the latter two analyses. First, the data used in the analysis are simply more timely. Teen births in the 1960s were far more likely to be marital births than teen births are today. Indeed, the marital/nonmarital birth proportions are nearly reversed—about 75% of teen births were marital in the mid-1960s, while about 75% are now nonmarital. So, whatever the findings, they may not have much relevance for today's teen mothers. Second, the sample of sisters

---

[19]The data sets used by Geronimus and Korenman were the National Longitudinal Survey of Young Women (NLSYW) and the National Longitudinal Survey of Youth (NLSY). Hoffman, Foster, and Furstenberg examined data from the Panel Study of Income Dynamics (PSID). The reason all three studies used births from a substantial time ago is that it is important to measure the impact of a teen birth when the teen mothers are at least in their mid 20s if not older.

from the 1960s suffered from some technical sampling problems that made it potentially unrepresentative.

Geronimus and Korenmen deserve great credit for being the first scholars to address the selectivity problem directly. The sisters approach that they proposed has been used in many studies in other contexts. Their research showed other researchers that they could not ignore unmeasured variables in analyzing the impact of teen childbearing. And their results do confirm the suspicion of social scientists that traditional methods overstated the impact of a teen birth. It is overstating, however, to read this evidence as showing that the impact of a teen birth is relatively small.

The twins versus single births approach of Grogger and Bronars yields negative but relatively small estimates of the effects of a teen birth. For example, the probability of graduating from high school is about 4 percentage points lower for the teen mothers of twins and their family income is about $1100 less per year. The mothers of twins were also more likely to be in poverty and on welfare. But none of these effects is very big. $1100 is probably about 5 to 10% of family income at most, rather than the 30 to 50% often found in other studies.

The critical question in this study is whether a comparison of teens with twins versus teens with a single birth provides a reasonable estimate of the effect of a teen birth. The authors noted, quite correctly, that it would be appropriate if and only if the impact on socioeconomic outcomes of having twins was exactly twice the impact of having one birth, that is, if the effects of a teen birth were a "linear" function of the number of children (at least up to two). Casual armchair speculation might suggest that the effects are quite nonlinear, with a decreasing marginal impact of additional children. Two kids typically don't seem to be two times as much trouble as one, and three aren't three times as much trouble. If that armchair speculation were true, then the twins versus singles comparison would underestimate the effect of a teen birth. For that reason and based on some further analyses that they performed, the authors concluded that "the twins approach provides a conservative estimate of the effect of an unplanned teenage single first birth" (p. 161). So, this study, however clever, doesn't establish that the costs of teen childbearing are low. It gives a conservative, lower-bound estimate. The true effects are undoubtedly larger.

The teen birth/miscarriage study by Hotz, McElroy, and Sanders provides the most surprising and controversial results. The researchers looked at how teen mothers and a comparison group of teens who had miscarriages fared from ages 18 to their early 30s. This allowed them to distinguish between short-run and longer-run impacts, which is an important difference not fully considered in previous research. The researchers found that by their mid to late 20s, the teen mothers actually did better over a wide range of outcomes than those who had a miscarriage! For example, the teen mothers worked more regularly and earned more than their counterparts, and their spouses had higher incomes. Differences in educational attainment (including receiving a GED) and income from welfare between the two groups were very small. The teen childbearers were worse off only on two categories—they had more births by age 30, and they spent more time as a single mother than did the teens with miscarriages.

Even though this study is careful and thoughtful, it, too, has some weaknesses that need to be considered. There are three general areas of concern. First, it is very difficult to obtain good information on teen miscarriages from survey data. Some young women might have an understandable incentive to conceal an early pregnancy that did not result in a birth. In fact, it is clear that substantial underreporting of miscarriages exists in the data they used. Compared to national data, their data have about half of the expected number of miscarriages.

Because of this underreporting, the comparison group of teens with miscarriages is very small and potentially unrepresentative. Suppose, for example, that misreporting is highest among young women who viewed their early pregnancy as an unfortunate error and who went on to do very well. Then the sample of women who reported a teen miscarriage would be more disadvantaged than the population of women who had a teen miscarriage.

Second, the teen childbearing versus miscarriage analysis is an example of a natural experiment in which having a teen birth is the treatment and having a miscarriage is the control. Just as in a controlled experiment, the women are, for the most part, randomly assigned to treatment or control group status. So far, so good. But it is necessary to maintain the distinction between the treatment and control group throughout the experiment by assuring that the control group does not have access to the treatment. Otherwise, the experiment is contaminated and the differences in outcomes between the groups cannot be attributed to the treatment.

But that is exactly what occurs in this case. More than half of the women in the teen miscarriage sample had a birth by age 20 (a conventional teen birth) and about one third had a pregnancy (in their case, a second pregnancy) by age 17 leading to a live birth, which would have been classified as a teen birth by this study's definition. That makes the control group suspect. Because the control group sample size is relatively small in the first place, this contamination of the control sample creates a serious problem.

Finally, in a natural experiment, the control group should ideally have no changes at all, as if they received a placebo. But is a miscarriage analogous to a placebo, or could it have its own independent effects on schooling or psychological well-being and on subsequent outcomes? If it does, then again the difference between the two groups is compromised and no longer provides an accurate estimate of the effect of having a teen birth. If, for example, a miscarriage has an independent negative effect, then the experiment will underestimate the true effects.

CONCLUSIONS   It is certainly fair to say that current research no longer supports the notion that teen childbearing is a devastating event. In 1968, in a famous and oft-quoted article, Donald Campbell wrote: "When a 16 year old girl has a child . . . 90 percent of her life's script is written for her." Although the nature of the script isn't indicated in the quote, it was meant to suggest the inevitability of a tough life of poverty and material deprivation. We know now that this is far too strong a statement. The new research quite appropriately recognizes and focuses attention on the important contribution of other factors, especially difficult-to-measure family and individual characteristics, to the poor average outcomes of teen mothers. Teen childbearers do often have poor outcomes, but the act of childbearing is not necessarily the exclusive or even primary cause of these outcomes. But, at the same time, there is no compelling evidence that the causal effects of teen parenting are positive, zero, or even just marginally negative.

The teen fertility rate has been falling in the past half-dozen years, and that's probably a good thing. But the research reminds us that to really help the young women who become teen mothers requires more than just convincing them to delay their first birth. Improvements in education and neighborhoods are an essential part of the policy.

Summary

This chapter completes a unit on fertility and the economic approach to fertility issues. In the previous chapter, we developed the basic ideas of how demographers measure fertility and how economists analyze it. Here we focused on teen and nonmarital fertility, two closely related issues. Teen fertility rates in the United States are conspicuously high by international standards. Marital teen fertility has all but disappeared. The good news is that teen fertility rates in the United States have fallen steadily since 1994, especially for minority teens.

In trying to explain the prevalence of teen childbearing, economists have primarily adopted a rational choice approach, applied to the likely income that a teen would have if she had a birth or managed to delay one. This approach emphasizes the roles of welfare income—a likely source of income in the case of a teen birth—and marriage and labor market opportunities—a likely source of income if a birth is delayed—as determinants of the probability that a teen girl has a birth. Much applied research has been done to examine how important these factors are. Most of this research shows that welfare benefits have a weak impact, and marriage and labor market opportunities have a larger, but still modest, impact. The commonly heard notion that the welfare system is the primary cause of the "epidemic" of teen births is almost certainly incorrect.

There are probably many causes of the increase in nonmarital and teen childbearing. The approach of Akerlof, Yellen, and Katz is particularly interesting. It emphasizes how the introduction of improved contraception and legal abortion could actually increase the nonmarital birth ratio by altering the implicit agreements between single men and women about a man's marital responsibilities in the event of an unwanted pregnancy. Increasing wages for women, the rise of cohabitation, and broad social changes are also undoubtedly part of the story.

This chapter completes the broad unit on the family, focusing first on marriage (Chapters 3 and 4) and then on fertility (Chapters 5 and 6). The next chapter, "Women at Work," is a transition from the family to the labor market. Decisions about whether or not to work in the labor market are clearly related to decisions about marriage and family. We see there how changes in the labor market transformed American family life in the twentieth century.

Key Terms

AFDC   190

Nash equilibrium   199

nonmarital birth ratio   182

nonmarital fertility rate   181

opportunity cost hypothesis   193

rational choice model   192

selectivity bias   196

shotgun marriages   188

TANF   191

CHAPTER 7

Women at Work

Introduction

The change in the labor force activity of women, especially married women, ranks among the most significant U.S. labor market phenomena of the twentieth century. Some might go further and claim that it ranks among the most important social phenomena of the century, transforming not only the labor market but family life as well, not only women's lives but also those of the men and children with whom they live. The magnitude of the change is truly staggering. In the early part of the twentieth century, fewer than one married woman in ten worked outside the home. Among all women over age 14, married or single, only about one in five women worked outside the home. Most of these working women fell into one of two categories—younger women who worked prior to marriage and women who never married. Very few women combined marriage and paid employment. But by the end of the twentieth century, all this had changed. Six in ten married women in the United States worked outside the home, and married women were just about as likely to be working as single women.

In this chapter, we examine women's labor force activity in detail in order to understand the underlying causes of the changes as well as the differences that exist today among different groups of women, for example, between more-educated and less-educated women. To do that, we first review the facts and trends and then develop an economic model that can help explain those facts. Our goal is to see how decisions about whether or not to work outside the home were affected by changes in the economic environment that women faced throughout the course of the twentieth century.

As always, we begin with the facts.

Women's Labor Force Participation

A Century of Trends and Facts

The focus of our labor supply attention will be whether or not a woman "participates" in the labor market, that is, works for pay for at least one hour per week, rather than on the number of hours per week she works. The **labor force participation rate (LFPR)** is the most common measure of work activity for different population groups. It is the proportion of women (or men), age 16 or older and who are not institutionalized, who are either working (one hour or more) or are officially unemployed. In the United States, an individual is counted as unemployed if he or she is without a job during the week of the employment survey and has made an effort to find work within the past four weeks.[1]

The officially unemployed are included because they are deemed to be actively looking for work, and thus participating in the labor market. The LFPR can be computed separately for different subgroups—for example, married women, white women, women between the ages of 25 and 34, or women with young children.

Table 7.1 presents the 2002 labor force participation rates for women and men in the United States for all workers and by age and race. On average, nearly three quarters of all men and about three fifths of all women over age 16 were in the labor force in a given month during 2002. If we focus solely on men and women in the prime working ages (25 to 54), when work is not much affected either by schooling or by retirement, about 92% of men and 76% of women were in the labor force. Thus, in either comparison, the difference in work rates by gender is about 15 percentage points. When we compare labor force participation by race, the comparisons depend on gender. Black men are less likely to be in the labor force than White men, while White women are less likely to be in the labor force than Black women. The difference is about 6 to 8 percentage points for men and 2 to 3 percentage points for women.

By far the most important things about women's labor force participation are the many ways it has changed over time. Figure 7.1 shows the LFPR for

---

[1]Statistics on employment, unemployment, and labor force participation come from a monthly survey called the Current Population Survey (CPS, for short). Workers who have not looked for work are considered to be not in the labor force. Workers who have given up looking for work are officially classified as "discouraged workers," rather than unemployed. Information on labor force statistics can be found at the BLS web site: http://stats.bls.gov.

	Men (%)	Women (%)
Age 16+	74.1	59.6
Age 25–54 (prime age workers)	92.4	75.9
White		
Age 16+	74.8	59.3
Age 25–54	93.7	76.0
Black		
Age 16+	68.4	61.8
Age 25–54	83.5	77.6
Hispanic		
Age 16+	80.2	57.6
Age 25–54	83.2	67.2

Table 7.1 Labor Force Participation Rate by Gender and Race, United States, 2002

Source: BLS Household Annual Averages, "Employment Status of the Civilian Noninstitutional Population by Age, Sex, and Race" from http://stats.bls.gov/cps/#empstat, Table 3.

women since 1900, along with the corresponding LFPR for men. At the turn of the twentieth century, more than 85% of men age 14 and older worked, compared to 20% of women. Men's labor force participation rate drifted down very slowly through 1940, jumped up by 1950, and then fell a bit more rapidly after that. The post-1950 decline primarily reflects the falling labor force participation of older workers as private pensions spread and made early retirement feasible. In contrast, women's labor force participation moved upward slowly but steadily through about 1940, and then more rapidly thereafter. The proportion of women in the labor force increased about 10 percentage points in the first half century, reaching about 30% in 1950. It then increased another 30 percentage points in the next fifty years. There is a slight flattening of the participation curve in the 1990s. Over the course of the twentieth century, the gap between men's and women's labor force participation rates narrowed by 50 percentage points, from 65 percentage points to 15.

Beneath the surface of these overall figures, the nature of women's labor force participation rates was changing in ways that would change family life permanently. At the turn of the century, participation in the paid labor market was largely an activity of single women. In 1900, when the overall participa-

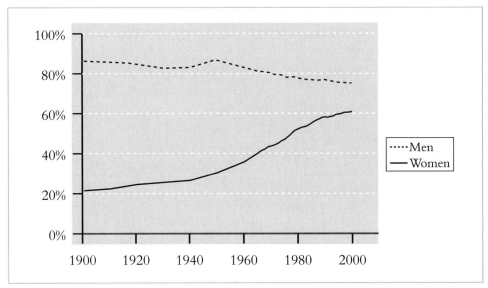

Figure 7.1   Labor Force Participation Rate, U.S. Men and Women, 1900–2000

tion rate for women was 20%, the participation rate for married women was just 5%—just one married woman in twenty worked for pay. For single women, the rate was more than eight times as high, but this was to change, as Figure 7.2 shows. From 1900 to 1940, the participation rate for married women increased slowly but steadily, about 5 percentage points every two decades. Beginning in 1940, the LFPR increased more rapidly. From 1950 to 1990, the LFPR for married women increased almost exactly 10 percentage points per decade—from 20% in 1950 to 30% in 1960, 40% in 1970, 50% in 1980, and nearly 60% in 1990. Again, there is a slight flattening in the curve beginning in the 1990s, and especially at the end of the decade. By 2000, the gap in participation rates between married and single women had shrunk to just 6 percentage points.

The jobs that women took changed as well. But we'll save that story for Chapter 8.

For most of the twentieth century, Black women were more likely to work than White women; we discuss a likely explanation for this later in this chapter. In the first decades of the century, the participation rate for Black women was two to three times greater than the rate for White women. Since then, the rate for White women has increased more rapidly, and the historical race difference has been much diminished. In the early and mid-1990s, the rates for

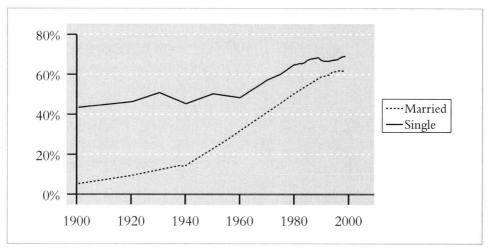

Figure 7.2   Labor Force Participation Rate, U.S. Women by Marital Status, 1900–2000

Black and White women were virtually identical, but the rate for Black women has increased more rapidly since then. For men, the exact opposite pattern has developed. Labor force participation rates for Black and White men were quite similar through the 1960s, but since then a substantial racial disparity has developed, as seen in Table 7.1.

The most telling statistics about how labor force participation has become a norm for women is the way that characteristics, especially demographic characteristics, that once predicted work status no longer do so nearly as well. In 1970, there was a noticeable decline in the labor force participation rate of women between the ages of 25 and 34, during the peak family and child-bearing years; now a difference is barely evident. In 1970, women with young children had participation rates barely half that of women with older children; now the difference is less than 10 percentage points. In 1970, marital status still made a sizable difference; now the effect is very modest. In 1970, race made a difference; now the effect is relatively small.

One characteristic that does make a difference, though, is a woman's education, a characteristic that is closely related to her potential wage. Figure 7.3 shows this for women age 25 and older in 2002. Participation is strongly and directly related to a woman's level of education. Less than one third of high school dropouts were working compared to more than half of high school graduates, more than two thirds of women with some college, and three quarters of women who were college graduates.

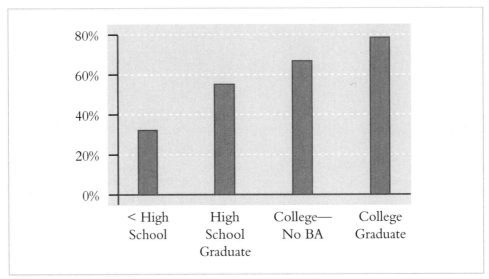

Figure 7.3   Labor Force Participation of U.S. Women, Age 25 and Older, by Level of Education, 2002

Source: Employment and Earnings, 2002, Table 7.

The increase in labor force activity by married women is by no means an American phenomenon. Indeed, as Table 7.2 shows, participation rates have increased in most countries throughout Western Europe and North America. Participation rates are highest in the United States, Canada, and Sweden, with Italy the lowest in Western Europe. In every country but Japan, the labor force participation rate rose, typically on the order of 20 percentage points. The rate barely rose in Italy and actually fell in Japan. The decline in Japan reflects the decline of the informal sector in which women worked, often in their own homes in the textile industry.

Labor Force Participation Over the Life Cycle

The trends we've examined so far show what happened over time to women of all ages. But there is another particularly interesting way to look at time in terms of women's labor force participation—that's time over a woman's own lifetime or life cycle as she ages. There have been some enormous differences in women's life cycle patterns of labor force participation over the course of the twentieth century.

Much of what we know about this topic is the result of the path-breaking research of Claudia Goldin, an economic historian. Goldin linked data on labor force participation rates by age from one census to the next in order to construct a life cycle picture of labor force activity over much of the twentieth

	1960 (%)	1975 (%)	1999 (%)
Australia	33.8	44.5	55.1
Canada	30.1	44.4	58.9
France	38.2	41.7	48.1
Germany	41.1	39.3	48.6
Italy	32.3	26.8	35.2
Japan	52.7	44.8	48.9
Netherlands	—	29.5	51.4
Sweden	46.1	55.2	58.5
UK	39.8	46.2	54.0
US	37.7	46.3	60.0

Table 7.2 Women's Labor Force Participation Rates, 1960–1999, Selected Countries

Rates are standardized to U.S. definitions. Data in 1960 column for Sweden is for 1961, for France, 1962, and for Australia, 1964.

Source: *Comparative Civilian Labor Force Statistics, Ten Countries,* BLS, Table 4.

century. For example, consider the women born in the ten-year period between 1886 and 1895. In the 1910 Census they were between the ages of 15 and 24, in the 1920 Census they were between the ages of 25 and 34, in 1930 they were between the ages of 35 and 44, and so on. By piecing the labor force participation rates together, she could see exactly what happened to them over the life cycle and could compare what happened from one cohort of women to the next.

Table 7.3 presents this life cycle information for White women.[2] The numbers in the table are the labor force participation rates by age bracket for women born in each successive ten-year period, beginning in the late nineteenth century; we will refer to a group as a **birth cohort.** The first column of figures is the labor force participation rate of never-married women between the ages of 15 and 24; the other columns are for married women by ten-year

---

[2]Census data early in the century does not separately identify Black women; instead, it combines all non-White women in a category. The data for non-White women follow a somewhat different pattern than the one discussed here for White women.

Cohort Year of Birth	Never Married	Married			
	Age 15–24	Age 15–24	Age 25–34	Age 35–44	Age 45–54
1886–1895	N.A.	N.A.	7.7	9.8	10.1
1896–1905	46.6	8.2	11.5	13.8	22.2
1906–1915	42.6	13.3	16.7	25.3	38.6
1916–1925	40.8	14.7	21.0	35.4	46.7
1926–1935	42.9	24.9	26.7	44.4	53.4
1936–1945	40.0	30.0	36.2	59.1	—

Table 7.3   Life Cycle Labor Force Participation Rates for White Women by Age and Birth Cohort

Source: Claudia D. Goldin, *Understanding the Gender Gap,* New York: Oxford University Press, 1990, Table 2.2. Copyright © 1990 by Oxford University Press, Inc. Reprinted with the permission of the publisher.

intervals from ages 15 through 54. Reading down a column traces out the experience of successive cohorts of women when they were the same age and marital status in different calendar years, ten years apart. This reveals the time-series increase in labor force participation that we've already examined. Reading across a row traces out the life cycle experience of each cohort. All the information comes from the U.S. Decennial Censuses as compiled by Goldin.

Let's see what these tables tell us about life cycle labor force participation. Consider the experience of White women born between 1896 and 1905. Between the ages of 15 and 24, nearly half (46.6%) of the never-married women worked in the labor market. At the same age, only about 8% of married women worked. What does this tell us about how many women left work more or less just at the time they married? Goldin computes a rough estimate this way. Suppose the married women between the ages of 15 and 24 had the LFPR of the never-married women in the years before the married women were married. Then their own LFPR fell with marriage from 46.6% to 8.2%, meaning that more than 80% [(46.6% − 8.2%)/46.6%] of the working women exited work simultaneously with marriage. Using the same kind of analysis, Goldin estimates that for the cohort of women born ten years earlier, more than 90% of young working women exited the labor force at marriage. (The numbers needed to compute this are not shown in the table).

Reading down the table, you can compare the participation rates for the young single women and the young married women across time. The rate for young single women is quite steady, just a few points lower, in fact; the decline probably reflects increasing school attendance at older ages. As late as the 1916–1925 cohort, the sharp divergence in labor force activity with marriage is still apparent among the young women. Using the same method as for the 1896–1905 cohort, we can see that nearly 64% of the women in the 1916–1925 cohort ceased working at about the time of their marriages. The participation rate for young married women doesn't really start to rise until the 1926–1935 birth cohort, who are between the ages of 15 and 24 in 1950. So, it is clear that through most of the first half of the twentieth century, marriage marked the withdrawal of many young working women from the labor force.

Let's return to those women born between 1896 and 1905. Not only did they leave the labor market in great numbers when they married, but their labor force participation rate also remained low as they got older. Twenty years later, when they are between the ages of 35 and 44 in 1930, only about one in seven is working. Between the ages of 45 and 54, when their children must be largely grown, still barely more than one in five is working. For this early cohort of White women—and for the cohorts who preceded them—participation in the paid labor force not only largely ceased at marriage but never really again became a particularly important factor in their lives.

That life cycle pattern of work changed dramatically over the course of the century. For the women in the 1906–1915 cohort, the participation rate is quite low through the 25–34 age bracket (1940) but then jumps up sharply in the 35–44 age bracket and then up sharply yet again at ages 45–54. Participation rates are high before marriage, drop sharply, and then return almost to their previous level. This marks a new pattern: Paid work still diminishes sharply with marriage, but eventual return to the labor market becomes far more common. Still, note that the percentages imply that perhaps well under half of married women never worked in the paid labor market.

That life cycle pattern of return to work is clearly evident in the 1916–1925 birth cohort, whose LFPR jumps more than 20 percentage points between ages 15–24 and 35–44 and reaches nearly 50% at 45–54. Finally, there's a peculiar pattern for the next cohort, those born between 1926 and 1935. Their rate as young married women is sharply higher than for the cohort that preceded them, indicating a real break with the historic pattern of work ending with marriage. Now, more often, work ended not with marriage but with pregnancy. But the fraction working barely increases as these women age from 15–24 to 25–34. What was going on? The baby boom was going on! These women turned 25 between 1951 and 1960, and they are precisely the women who had a fertility rate at that age of nearly 250 births per 1000 and a total fertility rate of 3.65 births per woman. But when their childbearing and child-rearing was over, they returned to the labor force in unprecedented numbers. Finally, the last cohort shown in Table 7.3 had a relatively modest labor force participation rate until they were in their mid 30s through mid 40s. With this group, return to the labor market became a clear norm.

Goldin emphasizes the importance of this life cycle pattern of labor force participation for understanding the gender gap in wages. As she notes, this pattern means that relatively few married women established careers in the same way that men did. Rather, she writes: "married working women who entered the labor force in their middle years had, by and large, entered a rather new world. . . . They were not bringing to the labor market recently acquired skills. Many were, instead, reentering occupations they had left many years, or possibly decades, before, and most were inadequately prepared for their new labor market roles" (p. 23). We return to this issue when we analyze the gender gap in earnings.

Goldin has also presented a fascinating history of the family and work experiences of college-educated women during the first half of the twentieth century.[3] See Box 7.1 for a summary.

An Economic Model of Women's Labor Force Participation

Labor Supply Analysis—Women and Men Are Not the Same

Economists are interested in understanding how individuals make decisions about whether or not to work in the labor market and also about how many hours they want to work. Decisions about hours of work are more often the subject of labor supply analysis in a standard intermediate-level course in microeconomics or labor economics. Two factors are probably responsible. First, often the real goal of labor supply analysis is to construct a total market labor supply curve, and, for that, hours of work are the appropriate dimension. Sec-

---

[3]Claudia Goldin, "Career and Family: College Women Look to the Past," in *Gender and Family Issues in the Workplace,* edited by Francine D. Blau and Ronald G. Ehrenberg, New York: Russell Sage Foundation, 1997.

Box 7.1 Family and Work Among College-Educated Women—A 20th Century History

At the turn of the century, a college education was an uncommon achievement for men or women. Of men and women born between 1886 and 1905, only about 5 to 10% of men and 3 to 5% of women graduated from college. We have already seen how rare labor force participation was for married women at this time. Because combining family and work was enormously difficult, these women faced some very extreme choices. They could work, or they could marry and have a family, but only rarely did they do both. What did they do? Nearly one third of them never married, compared to just 7% for women who did not attend college. (The marriage rates of men were not affected at all by a college education.) Nearly half of them never had children, including more than a quarter of those who were married. Those who never married worked virtually their entire lives. For example, when they were between the ages of 45 and 54, their labor force participation rate was nearly 90%, barely below the labor force participation rate for men. They worked primarily as elementary and secondary school teachers; a full 60% worked in just those two occupations.[4] Interestingly, marriage, not children, continued to be a major factor in determining work. Among those college-educated women who were married but had no children, less than one third worked between the ages of 45 and 54. Goldin has characterized this cohort of college-educated women as facing a "family or work" choice.

According to Goldin's research, this pattern persisted through the birth cohort of 1906–1915, who graduated college in the mid-1920s through the mid-1930s. The choices were not quite so extreme, but still 20% never married, and about 40% had no children. Thereafter, marriage rates for college-educated women rose, and the gap between them and women with less education narrowed, although it did not disappear. Like other women during the early post–World War II years, college-educated women married when they were quite young—nearly half within a year of their college graduation—and had high fertility rates. And like the others, they returned to the labor market in great numbers after an absence for family responsibilities.

---

[4] Indeed, these never-married women were the primary source of school teachers through the 1950s.

Goldin characterizes this cohort of college-educated women as following a "family, then work" pattern.

More recent cohorts of college-educated women have often deferred marriage and children while trying to establish a career. Nearly 20% are unmarried between the ages of 35 and 44, and about 25% still have no children. Differences in marriage and fertility between these women and women with less than a college education have grown again. Goldin describes them as pursuing a "career, then family" strategy.

ond, the subject of the analysis is often taken to be men (without necessarily saying so), for whom the labor force participation rate is, as we've already seen, very high. For them, choices about hours of work and how those choices are affected by economic factors such as taxes are the more interesting topic.[5]

But for women, the decision about whether or not to work in the labor market is the more interesting decision because that's where the action has been. This is true in two ways. First, as we have just seen, the proportion of women, especially married women, who are working has changed enormously over the course of the twentieth century. Second, because the fraction of women working is still lower than for men, there is more variation to explain. Why do some women work in the labor market, while others don't? To understand these changes, we need to construct a model that illuminates how individuals make decisions about work and what factors influence that decision. In doing so, we'll want to adapt the standard economics approach—constrained maximization and then comparative statics.

The traditional (male) approach to labor supply analysis involves the choice between two kinds of time—time spent at work in the labor market and time spent in leisure. A model like that isn't really a particularly good representation for the choices of men, but for women it is hopelessly inadequate. What's left out of the model is exactly what has occupied women, especially married women, for many generations—namely family and household obligations, or what we have called **household production**. Truthfully, for both men and

---

[5]Labor force participation rates of younger men, especially minority workers, and of older workers are more variable and are widely studied. The study of labor force participation rates for prime-age males is not a high priority.

women, the choice of time use is threefold—among leisure, market labor (paid), and household labor (unpaid). But for men, the two-way analysis is (or at least, was) often good enough. For women, though, it is impossible to make sense of the experience of the twentieth century without thinking about household production and building it directly into the model.

A Simple Model of Time Use and Labor Force Participation

Let's begin with an overview of the model[6] and what we hope to accomplish:

Step 1: Construct a model of a woman's choices about market work, household production, and leisure that captures some of the main elements of the real world.

Step 2: Use the model to analyze how, given her opportunities and her preferences, a woman makes her best choice about how to spend her time. Should she work in the labor market and on what does that decision depend? We will develop a very precise rule or formula that sheds light on that decision.

Step 3: Think about how a woman's best choice would change when her economic environment changed, especially when it changed in ways consistent with what actually happened in the twentieth century. This involves the comparative static analysis of labor supply choices.

ASSUMPTIONS   We begin with the following assumptions, which simplify and clarify the analysis.

1. A woman's time is spent doing one of three things—working for pay in the labor market (called M, for *market* hours of work), working in the household (H, for *household* hours), or enjoying leisure (called L for leisure). She has T total hours of time, so $M + H + L = T$. The distinction between H and L can be subtle. L stands for time spent doing something that is clearly and immediately enjoyable in and of itself. In contrast, time spent in household production is valuable because you value what it produces—a good dinner, clean clothes, a clean house, or healthy, well-adjusted children. It is not valued in and of itself. For example, do you enjoy doing laundry? Or do you do it because you enjoy wearing clean clothes?

---

[6]The model presented here is a compromise that incorporates three uses of time, rather than the two that are often used in labor supply analysis. It does not, however, use indifference curves and budget constraints. See the appendix to this chapter for an alternative analysis that does use indifference curves and budget constraints.

For most of us, the answers are "no" and "yes," so doing laundry is definitely household production. We also assume that market work is neither liked nor disliked in and of itself. For many workers, that may not be strictly true.

2. A woman has some wage rate, which we'll call w. She may also have some nonlabor income, which we'll call V. Nonlabor income is income that a woman would have even when her own market hours of work are zero. It could come from government programs, like welfare or Social Security. In a traditional old-fashioned male-breadwinner marriage, the husband's income could be regarded as nonlabor income for the wife, as long as she makes her decision about working after his.

3. A woman can choose to work as many hours in the market as she likes, from just one hour to a very large number. Assuming an unrestricted choice of hours of work may sound terribly unrealistic. But if we fix the hours she can work, we won't have anything left to analyze! And what should we fix it at? Remember, we are trying to determine desired hours of work. Do keep this simplification in mind; more complex economic models do consider limits on the choice of work hours.

4. A woman receives utility (satisfaction or pleasure) from three general kinds of commodities—consumption goods and services that are purchased in the market (C), household-produced goods (G), and leisure time (L). We write this utility function as $U = U(C, G, L)$ to represent the link between the amounts of the three goods and the amount of utility. There is a natural link between the three uses of time and the three sources of utility. Hours of market work yield the income needed to purchase consumption goods and services, hours of household production yield household goods and services via a household production function, and hours of leisure are directly enjoyable.

THE MARGINAL VALUE OF TIME   To be more concrete and to aid in the analysis to follow, let's call the value of an hour of time the **marginal value of time,** abbreviated as MVT. We have three such expressions, one for each of the three possible uses of time, which can be written as follows:

$$\text{Leisure:} \qquad MVT_L \equiv \Delta U / \Delta L \qquad (1)$$

$$\text{Household Work:} \quad MVT_H \equiv \Delta U / \Delta H \qquad (2)$$

$$\text{Market Work:} \qquad MVT_M \equiv \Delta U / \Delta M \qquad (3)$$

In these equations, U stands for utility. Utility is measured in units that are called utils, but the numbers used are arbitrary, that is, they don't have any real numerical meaning. The only important numerical property of utils is that a bigger number is better than a smaller one. The Δ in the equations is the Greek letter delta; it stands for "change in." We will often think of ΔL, ΔH, and ΔM as being an hour of time, but smaller changes are certainly possible. Notice that the two sides of all three equations are linked by a $\equiv$ symbol, rather than an equals sign. This means that the equations are identities, true for all values. They are just definitions.

Each of these three terms is related to the concept of **marginal utility,** a concept that was introduced in Chapter 2. Marginal utility is the additional utility obtained from one more unit of a good, for example, for each successive cup of coffee or piece of pizza. Typically, and quite plausibly, marginal utility falls, the more of something you already have. The first units are most highly valued, and subsequent units are less valuable. This is a very important property of consumption, and economists refer to it as **diminishing marginal utility.** Be careful, though: Don't confuse *diminishing* marginal utility with *negative* marginal utility. Negative marginal utility means that the good in question isn't a "good," but a "bad." Diminishing marginal utility means that the value of the good is falling. Marginal utility will still be positive for most goods under most reasonable circumstances.

LEISURE TIME   For leisure time, what we are calling the MVT_L is exactly the same as the marginal utility of leisure, as shown in equation (1). Thus, we can assume that the MVT_L falls as the amount of leisure (L) increases. To express this, we will often write $MVT_L(L)$, which indicates that the marginal value of leisure time is a function of L, the number of hours of leisure. Falling marginal utility of leisure makes perfect sense. Wouldn't the first hour of leisure be more valuable than the twenty-fourth? Try to imagine how much you would appreciate the first few free hours of a day relative to the last few free hours.

HOUSEHOLD PRODUCTION TIME   For household and market work, the MVT terms are related to marginal utility, but they are not quite the same thing. To see this relationship, it is useful to expand the expressions in (2) and (3) to show their components.

For household work, we need to use the idea of a **household production function.** (See Chapter 2 for a brief review.) Production functions are commonly used in analyzing the production technology of a firm, and the same idea can be applied here. In its simplest form, a production function shows the relationship between the amount of inputs that are used and the maximum amount of output that can be produced. The household production function can be written as $G = g(H; Z)$, which expresses the idea that the amount of G depends on the amounts of H and Z. Here, G stands for the amount of output produced in the household—everything from dinner to clean clothing to healthy children. H is time spent in household production, and Z stands for the available capital goods—things like washing and sewing machines and microwaves. The production function has been written with a semicolon (;) between H and Z to emphasize that H is being chosen, but Z is not, although we will think about how it has changed.[7] The production function represents the basic production relationship between G and H. Like all production functions, the amount of output (G) increases as the amount of input used (here, H) increases.

We can now expand the expression for MVT_H in equation (2) this way:

$$MVT_H \equiv \Delta U / \Delta H = [\Delta U / \Delta G \times \Delta G / \Delta H] = MU_G(G) \times MP_H(H) \quad (2')$$

Look at the two terms inside the brackets. The second term, $\Delta G / \Delta H$, is the additional household output (G) produced by an additional hour of household work (H). The first term, $\Delta U / \Delta G$, is the increase in utility from that additional household output. The effect operates from H to G and from G to U. (It is as if the two ΔGs cancel out.) Together, the product of the terms shows how and by how much an increase in household time increases utility—there is both a production effect reflecting how much is produced and a consumption effect reflecting how it is valued.

The two terms on the far right of equation ($2'$) are just notation for these terms. MU_G is the **marginal utility of household goods,** while MP_H is the **marginal product of household time.** The G in parentheses following MU_G indicates that the marginal utility of household goods depends on the amount of those goods. The H in parentheses following MP_H indicates that the marginal product of household time depends on the amount of time spent on household tasks. Just as for leisure, we assume that the marginal utility of household goods declines, the more household goods an individual already

---

[7]This is a necessary simplification. To treat household technology as something that was chosen would make the model much too complicated without really adding anything essential.

has. This means that MU_G falls as G increases. This relationship will be important later on.

The marginal product is an important idea in microeconomics, which was introduced in Chapter 2. It is the additional (or *marginal*) output produced in an additional hour of work. In virtually every production setting studied by economists, the marginal product falls as more of an input is used. This property of production is called the **Law of Diminishing Marginal Returns.**[8] The same thing is likely to be true here—the marginal product of household time falls as more time is spent working at home; fatigue might be one explanation. This means that each additional hour spent working in the household is less productive than the one preceding it.

MARKET WORK TIME   We can expand the expression for time spent in market work in equation (3) this way:

$$MVT_M \equiv \Delta U/\Delta M = [\Delta U/\Delta C \times \Delta C/\Delta M] = MU_C(C) \times w/p \qquad (3')$$

Again, look first at the two terms inside the brackets. The second term, $\Delta C/\Delta M$, is the amount of additional market goods (C) that can be purchased with an additional hour of market work. The first term, $\Delta U/\Delta C$, is the increase in utility from those additional goods. Here, the effect operates from M to C and from C to U: Additional M yields additional C, which yields additional U. Together, the product of these terms shows how and by how much an increase in market hours of work increases utility.

On the far right, we use MU_C for $\Delta U/\Delta C$; this term stands for the **marginal utility of consumption goods.** The C in parentheses following MU_C indicates that the marginal utility of consumption goods depends on the amount of those goods. Again, we assume that there is diminishing marginal utility, so that as C increases, MU_C falls. This, too, will be important.

The other term, w/p, is not just notation but measures the amount of additional goods that can be purchased with an hour of work. In one hour of work, \$$w$ are earned. If we let p stand for the price of goods and services, then w/p is the amount of additional market goods and services that can be purchased by working one more hour. For this reason, w/p is sometimes referred to as the **real wage.** It is the wage measured in terms of what you can buy. For

---

[8]When we examined specialization within marriage, we assumed that the marginal product of household time was constant. That was a useful simplifying assumption.

example, if w = \$10 and p = \$2, then an hour's work yields 5 units of market goods. Note that if w were higher, more goods could be purchased per hour of work.

THREE TIME USES AND THEIR PROPERTIES   For each possible time use, the MVT will fall as a woman spends more time at it. For leisure time, this is simply a feature of diminishing marginal utility. For household production time, MVT_H falls for two reasons: (1) additional hours yield smaller increases in household output (diminishing marginal product), and, (2) the marginal utility of that additional output is less valued (diminishing marginal utility). For market work, each additional hour provides the same additional amount of output (w/p) because the wage is constant. But the additional output is less valued, the more goods and services you already have. So the MVT of market work will fall, too.

Figure 7.4 summarizes these ideas. The horizontal axis of each graph measures the amount of time spent in that use, while the vertical axis measures the marginal value of an hour of time. The height of the curve shows the marginal value of each hour. The three MVT curves each are downward-sloping, which means that the marginal value of an hour of time in that use declines as the number of hours spent increases. The curves are drawn here as straight lines and are quite similar to one another, but that need not be the case. In addition to the negative slope, the height of the curves will be important when we try to analyze how changes over the course of the twentieth century have affected women's work choices.

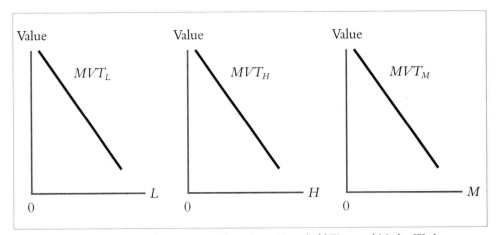

Figure 7.4   Marginal Value of Time Curves for Leisure, Household Time, and Market Work

To Work (in the Market) or Not to Work: The Economics of Making the Best Choice

We assume that a woman's objective is to spend her time working in the market, working at home, and/or taking leisure in such a way as to maximize her utility, that is, to make herself and her family as well off as possible in terms of her own preferences and opportunities. Much will depend on her particular situation—her wage rate; whether she is married and, if so, how much her husband earns; whether she has children and, if so, how many and how old they are; and many other details. Later, we will see exactly how each of those factors affect her choice. But let's start by examining the general logic behind her choice, a logic that ought to hold no matter what her particular circumstances are.

We can write out her choice situation as follows. A woman chooses values of the three uses of time—market work, household work, and leisure—to maximize utility. Utility depends on the amounts of consumption goods (C), household-produced goods (G), and leisure time (L). The amount of consumption goods depends on the amount of time spent in market work (M) and also on the amount of nonlabor income (V). The amount of household goods depends on the amount of time spent in household production. Finally, L is the time left over not spent in M or H.[9] Three separate constraints limit what she can choose:

Market goods:	$pC = wM + V$		(a)
Household goods:	$G = g(H; Z)$		(b)
Time:	$M + H + L = T$		(c)

The first of these is spending: the amount of spending on goods and services (pC) must equal the amount of income earned (wM) plus nonlabor income (V). In other words, you can't spend more than the amount of income you have. The second constraint is production: The amount of household goods that can be produced depends on the amount of time spent and on the technology and capital goods available (Z). Finally, the third constraint is time: There are only so many hours in a day (T), and the total amount of time spent in each activity can't exceed that amount.

The solution to this utility-maximization problem will be the best values for M, H, and L. Like all solutions, they will ultimately depend on the exogenous

---

[9]The utility function can be written $U = U(C(M), G(H), L)$ to reflect the links between the time inputs and the outputs they produce.

variables, here the real wage (w/p), nonlabor income (V), and household productivity (especially Z, all the other things that affect productivity). We will be particularly interested in M^* (remember, the asterisk (*) indicates that it is a best choice) and analyzing whether $M^* = 0$ (no market work) or $M^* > 0$ (some market work).

You can see in the constraints the nature of the choices that have to be made. To have more market goods requires working more hours in the labor market, which means less time is available to produce household goods and/or to enjoy leisure. To have more household production requires more household hours, which means less time is available for leisure and/or for earning the income necessary for acquiring market goods. Similarly, more leisure means fewer household goods and/or fewer consumption goods. Something has to give. Let's try to see how a best choice can be made.

NONMARKET CHOICES—LEISURE AND HOUSEHOLD PRODUCTION   It is easier to solve this problem in stages. First, consider a woman's choice between leisure and household production, ignoring work in the labor market. We'll establish a rule or condition that ought to guide her choice between those two time uses. Then we'll see if substituting work in the labor market would raise her utility. If it does, she would want to be in the labor force. If it doesn't, she wouldn't want to.

What rule should she follow for allocating her time in the household? There are three steps.

Step 1: *Think marginally, one hour at a time.*[10] A woman ought to compare the value of an hour spent in leisure with the value of that same hour spent in household production. For example, if she were currently taking twenty-four hours of leisure and zero hours of household work (an odd combination, to be sure) she ought to compare the value of the twenty-fourth hour of leisure with the value of the first hour of household work time. Next she would compare the value of the twenty-third hour of leisure with the value of the second hour of household work time, and so on and so on. Choices are made on the margin.

Step 2: *Always choose the time use with the higher marginal value of time.* If an hour spent in household production is more valuable than that same hour spent in leisure, then she ought to spend that hour in household production in order to maximize her utility. Why? If she switched the hour from

---

[10]Again, it may make sense to think of smaller time units.

leisure to household production, she would lose utility equal to the lower MVT_H and gain the utility equal to the higher MVT_L. In the preceding example, if $MVT_L(1) > MVT_H(24)$—which seems pretty likely—then she can make herself better off by switching an hour of time from household production to leisure.

Step 3: *Equalize marginal values.* The absolute best allocation of nonmarket time occurs when the marginal value of the last hour spent in leisure just equals the marginal value of the last hour spent in household production. Unless the two marginal values are equal, it is always possible to shift an hour from the use with the lower marginal value to the use with the higher marginal value and increase total utility, while spending the same number of total hours.

Here is a concrete numerical example that illustrates this logic. Suppose a woman is currently taking twelve hours of leisure (perhaps counting sleep as leisure) and spending twelve hours in household production. Suppose that the marginal value of the twelfth hour of leisure is 25 utils and the marginal value of the twelfth hour of household time is 40 utils. (Remember that these utility numbers are totally arbitrary and have meaning only in comparison with one another.) If she reduced her leisure by one hour, her utility would fall by 25 units, the marginal value of the twelfth leisure hour. But if she simultaneously increased her household time by that same one hour, utility would rise by a bit less than 40 units, the marginal value of the twelfth hour of household time.[11] She would thus be about 15 utils better off. That means that the combination of twelve hours of leisure and twelve hours of household work can't be the one that maximizes utility; thirteen hours of household production and eleven hours of leisure are clearly better. As long as the marginal values are unequal, it is always possible to increase utility by shifting an hour from the low-valued use to the high-valued use. But when the marginal values are equal, it is no longer possible to rearrange how time is spent and be better off. Shifting a small amount of time from one use to another would leave the woman no better off.

This idea is shown in Figure 7.5, which includes marginal value of time curves for leisure and household work. Hours of leisure (L) are measured in the usual way from left to right on the horizontal axis from 0 to 24. Hours of household production (H) are shown on the same axis but are measured

---

[11]Utility would increase by less than 40 utils because 40 is the marginal utility of the twelfth hour, and the marginal utility of the thirteenth hour will be slightly lower.

backward from right to left. We can do that because for the moment we are ignoring M, so that the sum of leisure and household hours must equal 24, the total amount of time available. Two MVT curves are shown, and both exhibit diminishing marginal utility. The height of the curve shows the MVT for that particular hour; both curves are downward-sloping. (Be careful to read the MVT curve for household hours from right to left.) The two curves are drawn as straight lines, but they could just as well be concave or convex, as long as they were downward-sloping.

Pick any point on the horizontal axis. That point corresponds to a particular combination of hours of leisure (measured from left to right) and hours of household work (measured from right to left). If you read vertically up to the MVT curves and then over to the vertical axis where utility is measured, you can find the MVTs corresponding to that particular combination. Look at the (12, 12) combination. Using the numbers from our example, we have $MVT_L = 25$ and $MVT_H = 40$. Since the two marginal values of time are

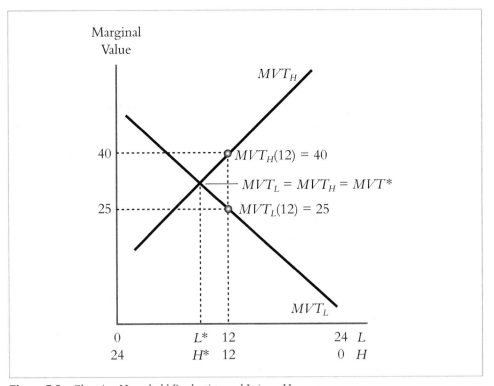

Figure 7.5   Choosing Household Production and Leisure Hours

not equal, it is possible to do better, in this case by increasing H (which will decrease its MVT) and decreasing L (which will increase its MVT).

The very best combination is always where the two marginal curves intersect. At the intersection point, the MVTs are equal; in addition, all 24 hours are accounted for.

Thus, we now know what rule a woman must follow to allocate her nonmarket time between leisure and household production in the best possible manner. She will choose L and H so that the $MVT_L(L^*) = MVT_H(H^*)$ and also $L^* + H^* = T$. Again, the asterisk (*) indicates that these are maximizing choices. If the marginal values are unequal, she can always rearrange her time use, switching time from its less-valuable use to its more-valuable use, and be better off as a result. Only when the MVTs are equal is it impossible to make a change that makes her better off.

To simplify the following discussion, let's refer to the particular value of MVT_L and MVT_H that solves this part of the problem as MVT^*. That is, MVT^* is the value of the last hour of time, when all time is spent in either leisure or household production and when that time is allocated so as to maximize utility.

LABOR FORCE PARTICIPATION—FOR BETTER OR WORSE? Now let's see whether she might be able to do better yet by working in the labor market. The analysis involves the same logic we used for the first part of this problem. If she works one hour—remember, we are assuming that she can choose any number of hours of work she likes—she will gain utility equal to the marginal value of that first hour of market time. We saw in equation (3′) that this value was equal to $MU_C \times w/p$. Because the value for the first hour of work will be particularly important, let's write it as $MVT_M(1)$, where the 1 in parentheses reminds us that the MVT in question is for that particular hour. (We could easily substitute some other minimum required amount of work time for one hour without fundamentally changing the analysis.)

If she works that first hour, she will gain utility equal to $MVT_M(1)$, and she will lose utility equal to MVT^*, which is the value of time in the nonmarket sector when market work equals zero. What should she do? Using exactly the same kind of marginal decision logic as before, she would want to compare these two marginal values. If $MVT_M(1) < MVT^*$, then she cannot increase her utility by working in the market. Her utility would fall by MVT^* and rise by the smaller amount $MVT_M(1)$. In that case, she is a *utility-maximizing nonparticipant in the labor market.*

If, however, $MVT_M(1) > MVT^*$, she will be better off by transferring an hour of time from leisure or household production to the labor market. In so doing, her utility will rise by $MVT_M(1)$ and fall by the smaller amount, MVT^*. She will end up better off, with a higher utility level.

These simple comparisons yield the utility-maximizing rules for market work. Let M^* stand for the utility-maximizing hours of work. Then, the rules for labor force participation are:

$$\text{If } MVT^* > MVT_M(1), \text{ then } M^* = 0 \tag{4}$$
This woman does not work in the labor market.

$$\text{If } MVT^* < MVT_M(1), M^* > 0 \tag{5}$$
This woman works in the labor market.

If condition (4) holds, the woman would choose 0 hours of market work. If, however, condition (5) holds, how many hours should she work? She ought to proceed hour by hour in exactly the same way, always comparing MVT_M, now evaluated at $M = 2, 3, 4$, and so on, with the corresponding MVT in the nonmarket sector. Two things will happen as hours of market work increase. First, MVT_M will fall because of diminishing marginal utility of goods: $MVT_M(3) < MVT_M(2) < MVT_M(1)$, and so on. Second, MVT_L and MVT_H will both rise because less time is now being spent in those uses, and the marginal value at fewer hours is always higher. L and H still ought to be chosen so that these two MVTs remain equal, which means that when M increases, both L and H ought to be reduced (although not necessarily equally). The best value for M occurs when its marginal value has fallen enough and the marginal value of leisure and household time have risen enough that all three are exactly equal. In symbols, this best choice, represented by an asterisk (*), is given by the following two conditions:

$$MVT_M(M^*) = MVT_L(L^*) = MVT_H(H^*) \tag{6}$$
All marginal values are equal.

$$M^* + L^* + H^* = 24 \tag{7}$$
All time is used.

Figure 7.6 shows this idea graphically. The figure on the left is the same as Figure 7.5, but now we have added on the right the MVT curve for hours of market work. Two MVT_M curves are shown, one much higher than the other. (We'll see why the position of the MVT_M curve is likely to vary across

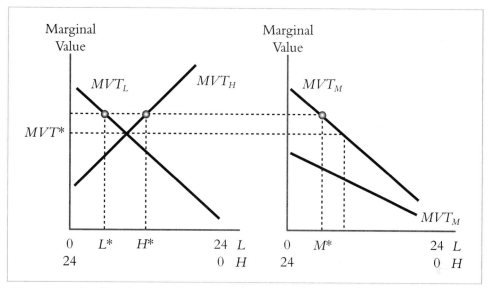

Figure 7.6 Choosing Household Production, Leisure, and Market Work

women shortly.) Both exhibit diminishing marginal value, because they slope downward. When all time is spent in leisure or household production, MVT^* is shown by the height of the curves where they intersect. Now compare that value to the value of market time at $M = 1$. For a woman represented by the lower curve, $MVT^* > MVT_M(1)$, so her best choice is to continue to spend all of her time in leisure and household production.

For a woman with the higher MVT_M curve, however, it is clear that $MVT^* < MVT_M(1)$. So her best choice is to transfer some time to the labor market. How much? Move up the two MVT curves on the left, keeping them equal at all times, and down the MVT_M curve on the right by an equivalent amount, until all three marginal values are equal. A situation like that is shown by the three points along the higher dotted line in Figure 7.6. Here, leisure (measured from left to right) equals L^*, household work (measured from right to left) equals H^* and hours of market work are M^*. M^* is also equal to the horizontal distance between L^* and H^*.

To recapitulate, we have analyzed the choice of a woman among three uses of time—leisure, household production, and market work. Each is characterized by some marginal value that depends on her preferences, her household productivity, and her wage rate, among other things. She makes a choice that maximizes the utility she obtains from leisure, household-produced goods, and market goods. That choice is determined by comparing the marginal value of time across its uses. Whether or not she is a labor force participant depends on that comparison.

We can also write out the solution to this labor force participation problem in terms of all the exogenous variables in the problem. This will be useful for analyzing the comparative statics of labor force participation decisions. The exogenous variables are found in the three constraints—the real wage (w/p), the amount of nonlabor income (V) from the spending constraint, and productivity in the household sector, which we can represent through the production function, $g(H; Z)$. Thus, we have

$$P* = P(w/p, V, g(H; Z)) \tag{8}$$

where $P*$ is the utility-maximizing choice of labor force participation. Equation (8) is a woman's labor force participation equation. In words, it says that a woman's best choice about participating in the labor market depends on her real wage rate, her nonlabor income (which may include her husband's income), and her productivity in the household sector. The next task is to see how changes in these variables affect the participation choice.

Explaining the Increase in Women's Labor Force Participation—The Effect of Changes in Wages, Income, and Household Productivity

The most important purpose of a time-use model like this one is to be able to apply it to the real-world situation of women. There are two broad ways to apply it. First, we could look over historical time—for instance, the course of the twentieth century—to examine the likely changes in the three MVT schedules and the effect of these changes on labor force participation decisions. For example, we might want to know how an increase in the wage rate for women would affect market work, household work, and leisure. Similarly, there have been enormous changes in the technology of household production and changes in the earnings of husbands, and we certainly would want to examine their likely impact. This kind of approach is called a **time-series analysis.** Second, we can look at a particular point in time and examine how differences among women in their MVT schedules affect their labor force participation. For example, we can try to explain the differences in LFPR between more-educated and less-educated women or between Black and White women. This kind of approach is called a **cross-sectional analysis.**

In analyzing these problems, we continue to focus on labor force participation decisions rather than on hours of work decisions. It is much easier to analyze participation decisions with the tools we have developed, and, as we've seen, it has changed tremendously in ways that have transformed not only women's lives, but also the lives of men and children. If we can make headway on that analysis, we'll have accomplished quite a bit.

The Effect of Husband's Income

Let's consider the effect of a husband's income on the labor force participation of a married woman in a time period in which her market work decision is clearly secondary to his. This was a time in which specialization of task on the basis of gender, as discussed in Chapter 3, was widespread. Still, some married women did work in the labor market.

We don't need to change our framework or our rule-making to analyze this. Her husband's income functions like nonlabor income (V) to her. It enables the family to purchase a certain amount of goods and services even when her own labor supply hours are zero. Let's call that amount C_H, where the subscript H indicates that it is the consumption made possible by the husband's income. If a woman's husband earns a great deal, then C_H is high; if he earns less, then C_H is lower.

Now think about the MVT_M curve that we've been working with. We saw in equation (3′) MVT_M is composed of two separate terms, one reflecting her real wage rate and the other the marginal utility of consumption goods that the family consumes based on her earnings. That equation is repeated here:

$$MVT_M \equiv MU_C(C) \times w/p \tag{3′}$$

As long as her work decision is secondary to his, then the appropriate marginal utility of consumption for the goods and services made available by her first hour of work begins at C_H, the goods and services the family *already* has from his income. If C_H is high because her husband is wealthy, then the marginal utility of the additional goods she could provide will be relatively low. Why? Because the family already has a lot of goods and the marginal utility of consumption is diminishing. If, however, C_H is much lower—her husband is poorer—then the marginal utility of the additional goods she could provide will be much higher. In this case, her income will provide more essential goods that have a higher marginal utility.

This fits in very nicely with our model of labor force participation. Look again at equations (4) and (5), which summarized the rule for labor force participation and which are repeated here:

$$\text{If } MVT^* > MVT_M(1), \text{ then } M^* = 0 \tag{4}$$
This woman does not work in the labor market.

$$\text{If } MVT^* < MVT_M(1), M^* > 0 \tag{5}$$
This woman works in the labor market.

We want to consider only the effect of having a richer or poorer husband, so imagine that everything else is unchanged. We've just shown that the higher the husband's income is, the lower the entire MU_C curve will be. This, in turn, means that the value of $MVT_M(1)$ will be lower. As a result of this, she is less likely to work in the labor market—the condition in equation (4) will be more likely to hold than the condition in equation (5). Thus, the model predicts that a wife will be less likely to work outside the home if her husband's income is high and more likely to work if her husband's income is lower.

Turn back to Figure 7.6. The two MVT_M curves there could represent two different women, with the same wage and other considerations except for the income of their respective husbands. The lower curve would be for a woman with a wealthier husband. Her MVT_M curve is lower because the value of the additional goods her earnings would provide is lower. Because the family already has a lot of consumption, she chooses no market work. The higher curve would be for a woman with a less-wealthy husband. Her MVT_M curve is higher because the value of the additional goods she could provide is higher. So for her, market work is the best choice.

In fact, this pattern is a common one. Consider, for example, the historical difference in the labor force participation of Black married women and White married women. Married Black women had substantially higher rates of work. Why? One compelling explanation involves the incomes of their husbands. On average, Black men earned much less than White men—less than 50% in the years before 1940. Thus, more Black women found themselves in the situation of the woman in Figure 7.3 with the higher MVT curve. Even today, when married women's labor force participation rates are many times higher than at the beginning of the twentieth century, differences based on the income of a woman's husband still exist.

Over the course of the twentieth century, changes in the average husband's income would have affected women's labor force participation negatively. From 1900 to about 1975, men's earnings rose steadily, doubling after adjusting for inflation just in the years between 1945 and 1971. Since then, men's average earnings have been relatively stagnant. This tells us that, in general, men's incomes were providing more consumption goods over time, which, taken by itself, would have decreased the MVT_M curve and, thus, reduced the likelihood that a married woman would work.

This is actually a very important conclusion. People often think of a married woman as being "pushed" into the labor market by the inadequacy of her husband's income. While that may be true in some cases, it really can't explain why more women are working today than in the past because, on average, men's real earnings are so much higher than in the earlier parts of the twentieth century. For an explanation of why women's work increased, we must look elsewhere.

The Effect of a Woman's Wage Rate

What about women's wages? They, too, have increased consistently and substantially over the course of the century. How would that fit into our model? Which curve would shift? Because the wage rate is part of the marginal value of market time, that curve is the natural candidate. If a woman has a higher wage rate, then, all else constant, her MVT_M curve will be higher because she can get more goods and services per hour of work. You can see that in equation (3'), repeated here once again:

$$MVT_M \equiv MU_C(C) \times w/p \qquad (3')$$

Again repeating the key equations for her decision to work in the labor market:

$$\text{If } MVT^* > MVT_M(1), \text{ then } M^* = 0 \qquad (4)$$
This woman does not work in the labor market.

$$\text{If } MVT^* < MVT_M(1), M^* > 0 \qquad (5)$$
This woman works in the labor market.

Here, a higher wage rate would increase $MVT_M(1)$, thus potentially putting a woman into the condition of equation (5) rather than the condition of equation (4′). So we would expect higher wages to increase a woman's labor force participation.[12]

Again, we can use Figure 7.6, this time interpreting the higher curve as belonging to a higher-wage woman and the lower curve as belonging to a lower-wage woman. Again, the evidence for this general effect is strong. For example, look back at Figure 7.3, which shows labor force participation rates in 1998 by level of education. There is a very strong positive relationship between level of education and labor force activity. Less than one third of women who were high school dropouts were working in 1998, compared to well over half for high school graduates, more than two thirds for women with some postsecondary schooling, and three quarters for those with a college degree. Some of this relationship could represent other factors, especially age and cohort—the high school dropouts are likely to be older and from earlier cohorts. Nevertheless, the relationship is obviously a strong one.

Over the course of the twentieth century, women's wage rates have risen enormously. In Chapter 5, we discussed changes in women's wage rates from the perspective of fertility. Here, we briefly summarize that information again. In the very early decades of the twentieth century, when most working women were employed either in education (if they were well-educated) or as domestic service workers, they earned the equivalent of about $2.00 to $3.00 per hour in year 2000 dollars. Even by 1940, the average woman probably earned no more than $5.00 per hour.

Wage rates began to rise in earnest in the postwar period. By 1960, a woman who worked full-time year-round earned the equivalent of about $8.00 per hour. By 1970, she was earning about $10.00 per hour. Wage growth slowed in the 1970s; in 1980, the median year-round full-time working woman earned the equivalent of an hourly wage of $11.40. In 1990, she earned the equivalent of $12.50 and in 1999, she earned about $12.15.

The point is pretty clear—in the first half of the twentieth century, wages for U.S. women were very low by twenty-first century standards. Over the course of the century, and especially in the years since 1950, women's wages have increased tremendously.

---

[12]If we were analyzing the effect of a wage increase on work hours for a woman already working in the labor market, the analysis would be more complicated and would involve conflicting income and substitution effects. Fortunately, those complications are not relevant here.

Children and Labor Force Participation

We all know that labor force participation is lower for women with young children, although it is remarkably high now. Where would that fit into our analysis?

Young children or a large family undoubtedly operate to increase the MVT_H curve. Young children and large families require an enormous amount of time; we would view that as an upward shift in the MVT_H curve. This would do three things. First, if all time were spent in the nonmarket sector, a woman would shift time from leisure to household production. (Ask your mothers and grandmothers.) Second, it would increase the value of MVT^*, that is, the value of time in the nonmarket sector when time is optimally divided between leisure and household work. And, third, because it raises MVT^*, it decreases the likelihood that $MVT_M(1)$ will be greater than MVT^*. Thus, it reduces the probability of labor force participation.

All of these effects are shown in Figure 7.7. It includes two MVT_H curves; the higher one is for a woman with young children or a large family or other substantial family responsibilities (perhaps an elderly parent or relative). The higher curve intersects the MVT_L curve to the left of the original intersection, so we know that leisure time falls and household work increases. It also satisfies the condition for no work in the market, since $MVT^* > MVT_M$ for the first hour of market work. A woman with that MVT_H curve wouldn't work. The woman with the lower MVT_H curve would work in the market.

Getting More Productive—At Home

Think about the vast arsenal of household technology that is now a regular part of American family life—everything from washers and dryers to dishwashers and microwave ovens. Perhaps you think they've always been there, but, of course, they haven't. In 1925, for example, about 40% of U.S. households had a telephone, 20% had a vacuum cleaner, 15% had a washing machine, and less than 10% had a refrigerator. As recently as the 1960s, dishwashers, washers, and dryers were still not a regular feature of American homes. Microwave ovens, of course, are an even newer addition to the American kitchen.

How did these changes in household technology affect work choices? In the first instance, they made individuals (usually, of course, women) much more productive. They raised the marginal product of household time in the sense

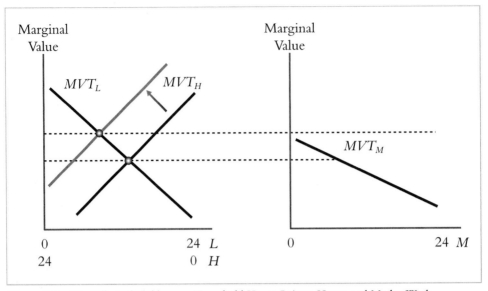

Figure 7.7   The Effect of Children on Household Hours, Leisure Hours, and Market Work

that it became possible to produce many more household goods and services per hour than in the old days. For example, producing clean clothing became a matter of an hour or two rather than a day; a dinner could similarly be produced in a fraction of the time it formerly took.

This change in marginal product affects MVT_H. Recall that the value of household time depends on two things, the marginal product and the marginal utility of household goods. The exact relationship is shown in equation (2′), which is repeated here:

$$MVT_H = MU_G(G) \times MP_H(H) \tag{2′}$$

The net change in MVT_H in this case is a bit complicated. A specific numerical example may explain. Suppose the marginal product of household time exactly doubled so that twice as much could be produced per hour as before. Because marginal utility declines the more goods a person has, the total value of an hour of household time won't double—the additional output is not as highly valued. It's not impossible to imagine that the net value of household time is much higher for the first several hours of household work, in which the most highly valued tasks—clean clothing and food on the table—are produced at a high rate. But it's also quite possible that the value of time for yet more hours could actually be lower than in the days of low productivity because the output produced in those last hours is not highly valued. In a sense, so much household output is being produced in the first few hours that the marginal value of subsequent hours is very low. In contrast, when productivity is low, the marginal value of the last hours of household production time is still highly valued. Important and needed goods and services are still being produced in those last hours.

If we drew a picture of this change, the new MVT_H curve would be twisted—well above the original curve at first, but eventually below it. This is shown in Figure 7.8. The straight line is the old MVT_H curve, showing a curve that is relatively low, declining, but not very rapidly. The other curve is much higher at first, but much steeper. It starts well above the old curve, cuts it at H_0, and then is lower for all hours beyond that.

How would this affect labor force participation? Figure 7.9 captures one possibility. Just as in Figure 7.8, the MVT_H curve twists, and the intersection with

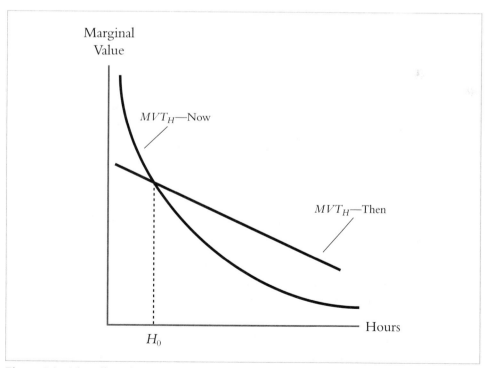

Figure 7.8   The Effect of an Increase in Household Productivity on the MVT_H Curve

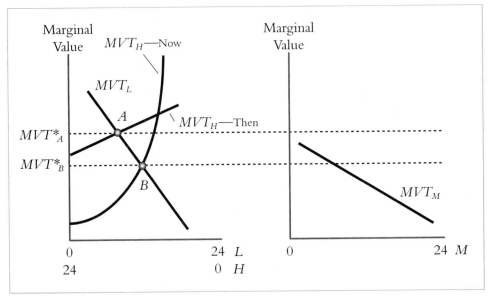

Figure 7.9   The Effect of an Increase in Household Productivity on Labor Force Participation

the MVT_L curve now occurs to the right, from point A to point B. That change involves a shift from household work to leisure and, more importantly, a fall in MVT^*, the value of the last hour of time in the household. At the situation depicted by point A, it doesn't make sense to work in the labor market because the value of time there is below MVT^*. But at the situation depicted by point B, it now makes sense to work. Thus, in this case, the sharp increase in household productivity has the effect of increasing the labor force participation rate.

Putting It All Together

Over the course of the twentieth century, there were many changes in economic constraints and opportunities so that virtually all the curves changed. Following is a summary of the most likely set of changes:

1. Women's wages increased sharply and consistently. This increased the value of work time for nonworking women, and thus increased their labor force participation.

2. Husband's wages increased sharply and consistently as well, at least through about the early 1970s. This decreased the value of work time for nonworking wives by reducing the marginal utility of the goods and services their

earnings would contribute. Taken by itself, this would have reduced women's labor force participation.

3. Household productivity increased many times over. This probably increased women's labor force participation by reducing the value of the marginal hour of household time. So much more could be accomplished in so much less time that it freed up time for market work.

Figure 7.10 shows a composite now-and-then picture of the forces behind labor force participation. Figure 7.10 (A) describes a time in the first half of the twentieth century. Figure 7.10 (B) describes a time early in the twenty-first century. The two MVT curves for leisure are identical. But the other two curves have changed in the ways described in the preceding list. The MVT_H curve in Figure 7.10 (B) is higher, but also much steeper than in Figure 7.10 (A), reflecting the much higher household productivity, but also its low marginal value. As a result, the value of MVT^* is higher in Figure 7.10 (A) than in Figure 7.10 (B). In the labor market graphs, the MVT_M curve has also shifted up in Figure 7.10 (B). This shift reflects conflicting influences. The enormous increase in women's wages pushes it up; the increase in husband's earnings pushes it down. The net effect is almost certainly a big increase. The result of all these changes is a shift from nonparticipation in Figure 7.10 (A) to participation in Figure 7.10 (B).

EVIDENCE   Costa[13] summarizes the empirical evidence about the importance of married women's wages on their participation in the paid labor force. She suggests that the twentieth century can be divided into three time periods in which the underlying influences were quite different. Through about 1930, the labor force participation of married women was influenced relatively little by their own wage rates. Rather, the primary influence was the income of their husbands. At this time period, most women worked in either domestic service, manufacturing, or agriculture, and working conditions were poor. Only a woman whose husband's income failed to support a family entered the labor market. The high labor force participation rate of Black married women, in spite of their own low wage rates, is a good example of this. In the middle part of the century, women's labor force participation was strongly influenced by her own wage rate, and the impact of the husband's income diminished. Women with better labor market prospects began to enter the labor

---

[13]Dora L. Costa, "From Mill Town to Board Room: The Rise of Women's Paid Labor," *Journal of Economic Perspectives,* Vol. 14, No. 4, Fall, 2000, pp. 101–122.

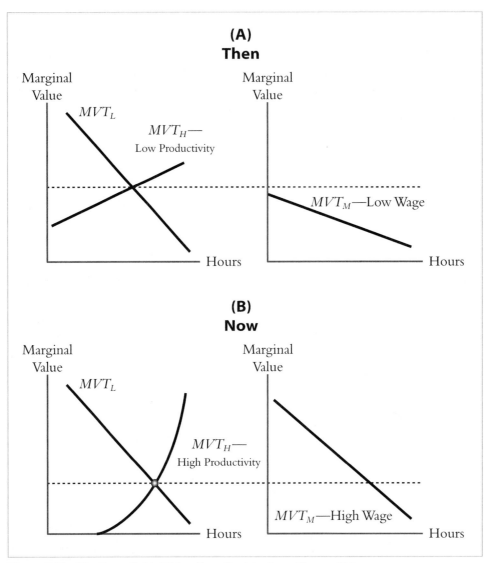

Figure 7.10   The Forces Behind Labor Force Participation—Then and Now

market, while those with poorer prospects tended not to work. By the end of the century, the impact of both her own wage and her husband's income were smaller. Participation became much more of a norm. But do recall the large, positive relationship between a woman's own education and the proportion working. This suggests that wage effects can hardly be unimportant at some wage levels.

Summary

It really is no overstatement to call the increase in the labor force participation of married women one of the most profound labor market phenomenon of the twentieth century. In the United States and throughout most of the developed world, their labor force participation rates rose from not much more than 10% in the early part of the century to 60%, 70%, or more at the end of the century. Marriage and children no longer signaled the end of regular labor force participation for women. In the United States, participation rate differences between men and women dropped from 65 percentage points in 1900 to about 15 percentage points in 2000. The demographic characteristics that previously dictated low labor force participation—such things as marriage and the presence of young children—barely make a dent in the participation rate now.

The increase in labor force participation, along with the decline in fertility, transformed family life. The traditional nuclear family—full-time working husband, full-time homemaker wife, plus children—has shrunk in numbers. In 1998, only 6.9 million families in the United States fit that traditional description out of a total of about 35 million families with children under age 18. In two thirds of married couple families with children, both the husband and wife are in the labor force.

The economic approach we took considered market work in the broader context of time-use choices among three potential uses—market work, household production, and leisure. The key concept was the marginal value of time in each of these uses. The decision rule involved choosing amounts of the three time uses so that the marginal values were everywhere equal. If they all weren't equal, a rearrangement of time from a lower-valued marginal use to a higher-valued marginal use will always make an individual better off. This is, in fact, an application of a common economic maximizing rule: To maximize the total value of something, make all marginal values equal. This kind of rule is often called an equimarginal rule.

Just as with the decline in fertility, the primary candidate for explaining the rise in women's labor force participation is the wage rate. The wage rate determines the value of market work. In the twentieth century, women's wage rates have increased many times over. The increase in wage rates is the main economic cause. Changes in household productivity are also undoubtedly important. The enormous change in household capital goods paradoxically lowered the marginal value of household production time, by making it possible to accomplish so much so quickly. The impact of changes in the earnings of men is most likely to reduce participation because men's earnings have risen over most of the twentieth century. Changes in attitudes and the development of role models are also certainly important parts of the explanation.

Wage rates have been the central explanation of virtually all of our analyses thus far. They helped explain the division of labor within households and the gains to marriage. They were an important factor in thinking about how the marriage market has changed. They played a critical role in explaining declining fertility and rising labor force participation. Now it is time to examine women's wages directly, rather than as an explanation of these other phenomenon. We do that in the next three chapters.

Chapter Terms

birth cohort   219

cross-sectional analysis   239

diminishing marginal utility   227

household production   224

household production function   227

labor force participation rate (LFPR)   214

Law of Diminishing Marginal Returns   229

marginal product of household time   228

marginal utility   227

marginal utility of consumption goods   229

marginal utility of household goods   228

marginal value of time   226

real wage   229

time-series analysis   238

Appendix: Labor Supply Analysis—An Alternative Approach

Introduction

An alternative way to present a model of labor supply behavior uses indifference curves and budget constraints. In some ways, it is a more elegant approach because it emphasizes the role and importance of prices in a way that the model in the chapter does not. It is, however, both more difficult and, at the same time, more limited. The standard model focuses almost exclusively on two time-use choices because that is the natural limit of a graphical approach. Those two choices are typically taken to be market work and leisure; thus, household production is ignored. It is possible to integrate household production into the model, but it is difficult to do so and requires some strong simplifications.

In this appendix, we first present the standard indifference curve/budget constraint approach to labor supply analysis. We assume familiarity with the basic idea of indifference curves and budget constraints and focus on applying them to the labor supply context. We continue to focus on issues of labor force participation, rather than hours of work because that is where the action has been in the twentieth century for women. We then extend the model to include household production.

The Basics of Labor Supply Analysis

Preferences

We assume that a woman derives utility from two broad categories of goods—leisure time (L) and expenditures on market goods (C). Note that C is measured in money (dollars or Euros, for example) rather than the amount of goods themselves. It is the amount spent on bananas, not the bananas themselves. This makes the following notation a bit easier without

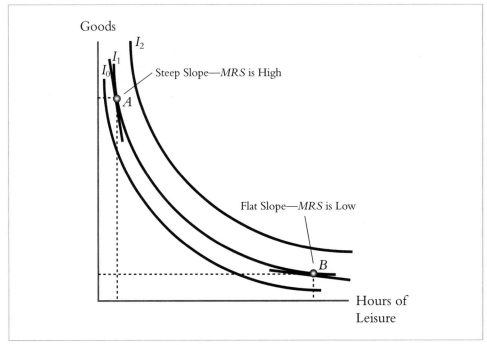

Goods

I_2

I_1

I_0

Steep Slope—*MRS* is High

A

Flat Slope—*MRS* is Low

B

Hours of
Leisure

Figure A7.1   Indifference Curves for Leisure and Consumption

changing anything important.[1] Thus, we write her utility function as
$U = U(C, L)$.

Her preferences for market goods and leisure can be represented graphically
via a set of **indifference curves.** A set of representative indifference curves is
shown in Figure A7.1. Hours of leisure are measured along the horizontal
axis, and the amount of consumption goods is measured along the vertical
axis. Any particular point represents a specific combination of leisure time and
consumption goods. By the definition of an indifference curve, all the combinations of leisure time and consumption goods along a given indifference
curve are equally desirable.

These leisure-market goods indifference curves have all the standard properties of indifference curves: They are negatively sloped and convex (bowed inward toward the origin), and the more preferred indifference curves are posi-

---

[1]An alternative way to think of this is that the price of all goods equals $1, so that expenditures and amount of
goods are equal. This is acceptable because we aren't interested in the details of consumption goods demand.

tioned toward the northeast. The slope of the indifference curve ($\Delta C/\Delta L$, holding U constant) represents the **marginal rate of substitution** (MRS). More carefully, the MRS is the negative (or absolute value) of the slope of an indifference curve: $MRS \equiv -(\Delta C/\Delta L)\,|\,U$, where $|\,U$ indicates that utility is held constant. Because this is a definition, we use the identity symbol ($\equiv$) rather than an equals sign.

The MRS is the rate at which a woman is willing to give up consumption goods to acquire an hour of leisure. The higher the MRS is, the more an hour of leisure is valued. Certainly, different individuals may value leisure differently, but more importantly, the MRS will likely also depend on the amount of goods and the amount of leisure that an individual already has. That is, the MRS isn't a constant number, but rather it varies with the amount of leisure and consumption goods one already has.

For example, suppose a woman currently has very little leisure but a lot of consumption goods, as at point A on indifference curve I_1. Then she would probably be willing to give up a great deal of consumption to acquire an hour of leisure because that hour is very valuable. Thus, her MRS at that particular combination of goods and leisure would be quite high. The high MRS at A is represented by the steep slope of the indifference curve there (see the steep tangent line at A). Conversely, if she had relatively little consumption and a great deal of leisure (point B), she would likely be willing to give up very little consumption to get yet more leisure. Her MRS would, therefore, be much lower. And there, the indifference curve has a flatter slope; see the flat tangent line at B.

In general, the more leisure one has, the less valuable yet another bit of it would be; thus the MRS is lower. This property of preferences is called a **diminishing marginal rate of substitution.** It applies not just to leisure and goods, but to almost any pair of goods. The standard shape of an indifference curve—bowed in toward the origin, steeper at the top, and flatter at the bottom—represents a diminishing MRS. In general, we will assume that the MRS falls along an indifference curve as L increases and C decreases.

Constraints

In addition to her preferences for leisure and consumption goods, a woman also faces constraints that limit her choice. There are two constraints here, a **time constraint** and a **budget constraint.** A woman's total available time (T) is assumed to be spent either working in the market (M) or enjoying leisure

(L). Thus, the time constraint is $T = L + M$. This is quite convenient because it means that hours of leisure and hours of work are perfectly negatively related. When L increases, M decreases by exactly the same amount, and conversely. Thus, we can analyze hours of work directly, or, if it is more convenient—which it is—we can analyze hours of work indirectly via hours of leisure.

It is important to note what is omitted in both the utility function and the time constraint. There are no household goods in the utility function and no household production time in the time constraint. In addition, time spent at work does not have any direct impact on utility. These are important (and limiting) simplifications.

The budget constraint limits the market goods she can purchase: She cannot spend more than her income. This constraint can be written as

$$C = wM + V$$

where w is the wage rate, M is hours worked, and V is any additional nonlabor income she may have. The left-hand side of the budget constraint is total spending on consumption goods, while the right-hand side is total income, composed of earnings (wM) plus nonlabor income (V). Nonlabor income is income that a woman receives from a source other than her own work effort. It could be income from stocks or bonds, income from a government income transfer program, or, in some cases, income from her husband.

It is useful and revealing to combine the time constraint and the budget constraint. First, let's rewrite the time constraint to isolate M: $M = T - L$. Then substitute this expression for M into the budget constraint as follows:

$$C = wM + V$$
$$= w(T - L) + V = wT - wL + V$$

Finally, move ($-wL$) from the right-hand side of the equation to the left-hand side to get

$$C + wL = wT + V$$

This is a very interesting and important equation. It is called the **full-income budget constraint.** Look first at the right-hand side of the equation. The first term, wT, is the income a woman could earn if she worked all T hours of the day. Adding V (nonlabor income) yields **full income,** which is her total maximum income (not to be confused with her total realized income, $wM + V$).

Full income is *exogenous*, which means that it does not depend on how many hours she chooses to work, while actual income is *endogenous*.

The left-hand side of the equation contains two terms. The first, C, is, again, the amount of money spent on consumption. The second term, wL, may seem a bit odd, but it can be interpreted similarly. It is the amount of full income spent on leisure, where w is the price of leisure. Again, note that *the price of an hour of leisure is the wage rate*. Of course, no one literally pays anyone $\$w$ to purchase an hour of leisure. In effect, an individual buys it from himself. It is an opportunity cost; that is, it is the income that is given up by taking an hour of leisure. It is, nevertheless, a genuine cost.

Let's draw a picture of the budget constraint. Since we will later want to combine it with the indifference curves, we again use L on the horizontal axis and C on the vertical axis. First, let's make a simplification, by setting $V = 0$. Later on, we'll add it back in.

The easiest way to draw the budget constraint is to find the two endpoints. These endpoints aren't very attractive choices, but they serve to anchor the budget constraint. If a woman were to take no leisure at all (i.e., $L = 0$), then the maximum C she could consume would be wT, her full income; remember that the full-income budget constraint is $C + wL = wT + V$ and that we are setting $V = 0$, to keep the problem simple for the moment. If, for example, $w = \$10$ and $T = 24$ hours per day, then full income = $\$240$ and that is the absolute maximum she could spend on consumption. Thus, the endpoint of the budget constraint on the vertical axis is the bundle $(L = 0, C = wT)$; in the numerical example, it is the bundle $(0, \$240)$.

If, instead, she took all T hours as leisure, then her consumption goods would equal 0 because her nonlabor income equals 0. With all T hours taken as leisure, she has no earned income with which to buy consumption goods. Thus, the endpoint on the horizontal axis is the bundle $(L = T, C = 0)$ or $(24, T)$, continuing with our example.

Finally, the slope of the full-income budget constraint is $-w$. To see why the slope has this value, start at the all-work endpoint on the vertical axis. For every hour of leisure that is taken, $\$w$ of earnings are given up and one hour of leisure is obtained. Equivalently, starting from the endpoint on the horizontal axis and moving up the constraint, every hour of leisure given up yields $\$w$ of earnings. Thus, the slope of the budget constraint is $-w/1$ or just $-w$. In the example we are using, the slope is $-\$10$.

Another way to find the slope is to use the old geometry formula, Slope = Rise/Run. In this case, we have the two points $(0, wT)$ and $(T, 0)$. Thus, the rise over run is $(wT - 0)/(0 - T)$. Simplifying, Slope = $(wT)/(-T) = -w$.

Figure A7.2 shows a typical full-income budget constraint. As explained earlier, the endpoints are $(T, 0)$ on the horizontal axis and $(0, wT)$ on the vertical axis, and the budget constraint is a straight line with Slope = $-w$. All the points on the constraint exactly satisfy the full-income budget constraint. Points toward the origin cost less than the budget constraint, while points above the constraint aren't feasible because they cost too much. Note that there are two scales along the horizontal axis, one for hours of leisure and one for hours of work. Leisure time is measured in the usual way, from left to right. But because leisure and work are the only two uses of time, we can measure hours of work backwards from right to left.

In Figure A7.2, we set nonlabor income (V) equal to zero. Adding V back in is relatively easy. The slope of the budget constraint doesn't change because

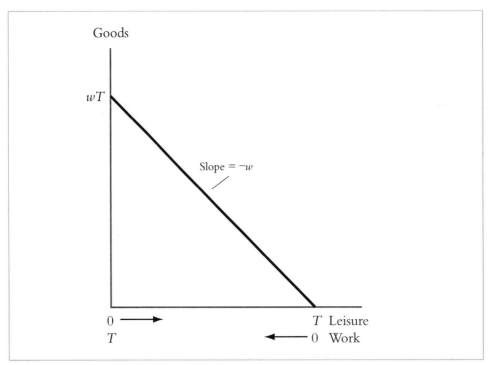

Figure A7.2   The Full-Income Budget Constraint

the wage rate isn't affected by the amount of nonlabor income. In other words, the budget line with $V > 0$ will have the same slope and be parallel to the budget line with $V = 0$. What about the endpoints of the budget line? Having nonlabor income doesn't change the maximum amount of leisure—that is still T. But it would allow an individual to have some consumption even if $L = T$. Similarly, it increases the amount of consumption possible at the other (all work) endpoint. To be specific, nonlabor income increases possible consumption at every level of L by \$V. This means that the whole budget constraint shifts up vertically by an amount equal to V.

If the wage rate changed, the slope of the budget constraint would change. If the wage were higher, the budget line would pivot around the point on the horizontal axis. The new budget line would be steeper, and the endpoint on the vertical axis would increase. This makes perfect sense: If a woman worked all hours at a higher wage rate, she would earn more and thus be able to consume more. If, instead, the wage rate were lower, the budget line would rotate inward, becoming flatter.

The impact of changes in V and w are summarized in Figure A7.3. Figure A7.3(A) illustrates the impact of a change in nonlabor income, while Figure A7.3 (B) does the same for a change in the wage rate. In Figure A7.3 (A) the

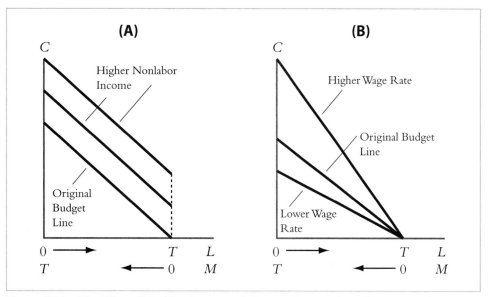

Figure A7.3   The Effect of Nonlabor Income and the Wage Rate on the Full-Income Budget Constraint

lowest curve is for $V = 0$, and the other two are for increasing amounts of nonlabor income. Note, first, that the three curves are parallel and, second, that the curves are chopped off at the lower end at the point where $L = T$. The dotted line shows that. As long as $V > 0$, it is possible to have some consumption even when all time is spent in leisure. For example, the amount a lottery winner might consume could actually be quite substantial. The chopped-off endpoints are precisely those combinations of all leisure and the consumption made possible by nonlabor income.

In Figure A7.3 (B), the middle budget line is for some initial wage rate. The steeper one represents a higher wage rate, while the flatter one is for a lower wage rate. Note that all three budget lines start at the same point on the horizontal axis (here we have set $V = 0$). The higher the wage rate is, the higher the endpoint on the vertical axis is, or, equivalently, the greater full income is.

Choosing Hours of Work

Now that we have drawn indifference curves and a budget constraint to analyze labor supply, we can solve for the best solution. The full maximization problem can be written formally this way:

An individual chooses values for C and L to maximize
U(C,L) subject to $C + wL = wT + V$

Figure A7.4 illustrates the nature of the solution. Here, we have drawn the same indifference curves as in Figure A7.1 and the same budget constraint as in Figure A7.2. We again set $V = 0$ to keep the graph a bit simpler. The individual's objective is to choose the best combination of leisure and goods along the budget constraint. That is equivalent to finding the highest attainable indifference curve, because higher indifference curves are always preferred to lower ones.

In Figure A7.4, points A and C along indifference curve I_0 are both feasible choices. But point B along indifference curve I_1 is even better, and it, too, is feasible. We know it's better because it is on a higher indifference curve, and we know it's feasible because it's on the budget constraint. Figure A7.4 illustrates two things: (1) No point on any indifference curve higher than I_1 (such as I_2) is feasible; and (2) at point B, indifference curve I_1 is tangent to the budget constraint, which tells us that the slopes are equal. Point B is the best available point; thus, it is the solution to the labor supply problem. As shown in Figure A7.4, this woman would divide her T available hours into L^*_B hours of leisure (measured in the usual way from left to right) and M^*_B hours of work, measured from right to left. As usual, we use an asterisk to indicate that this represents the best choice.

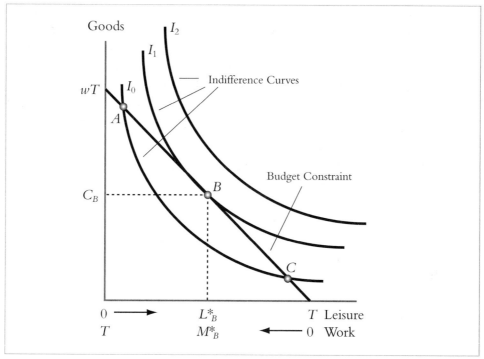

Figure A7.4 Utility-Maximization and Labor Supply

Let's focus on points A, B, and C a bit more carefully. At B, we already noted that the slope of the indifference curve just equals the slope of the budget constraint. Recall that the MRS is the negative of the slope of the indifference curve and that the slope of the budget constraint is $-w$. Using this information and the fact that the slopes are equal at B, we can write

Slope of indifference curve at B = slope of budget constraint at B

So, by substitution, $-MRS$ at $B = -w$

And after multiplying both sides by -1

MRS at $B = w$

Thus, at the best choice point, the marginal rate of substitution just equals the wage rate. This actually makes a great deal of common sense. The MRS measures how much this woman values an hour of leisure. The wage rate (w) is the price of an hour of leisure. The equality of MRS and w means that at the margin—for the last hour of leisure taken—its value is just equal to its price.

Points A and C show combinations where MRS and w are not equal. These situations will be very useful when we analyze labor force participation. At A, the indifference curve is steeper than the budget line. This means that the slope of the indifference curve is greater (in absolute value) than the slope of the budget line. So, following the same logic as before, this means that MRS at point $A > w$:

$$\text{Slope of indifference curve at } A < \text{slope of budget constraint at } A$$
$$(< \text{ means more negative})$$
$$\text{So, by substitution, } -MRS \text{ at } A < -w$$
$$\text{And after multiplying both sides by } -1$$
$$MRS \text{ at } A > w$$

Intuitively, point A can't be a utility-maximizing choice because the value of an hour of leisure (MRS) is greater than its price (w). In that situation, a woman could increase her utility by increasing the amount of leisure she takes and, in the process, working less. In doing so, she would be moving down the budget constraint from point A toward point B.

At point C, the opposite situation exists. At C, the indifference curve is flatter than the budget constraint, so MRS at $C < w$. That is also a bad choice: The last hour of leisure is valued at less than its price. Now, the way to do better is to consume less leisure and to move up the budget constraint toward point B.

Only when MRS just equals the wage is it impossible to rearrange leisure, work, and consumption and do better. Let's summarize the three arithmetic possibilities and the utility-maximizing responses:

$$MRS > w: \quad \text{increase } L, \text{reduce } M \text{ until } MRS = w$$
$$MRS < w: \quad \text{decrease } L, \text{increase } M \text{ until } MRS = w$$
$$MRS = w: \quad \text{one can't do any better}$$

Labor Force Participation

Our primary goal remains explaining labor force participation, that is, whether a particular woman is in or out of the labor force, rather than the exact number of hours she chooses to work. In this section, we draw on and extend the analysis of labor supply to focus on the decision about whether or not to participate in the labor market. We use this analysis to examine the factors that most influence labor force participation and then tie that to the increase in labor force participation of married women over the twentieth century.

Basics

The woman represented by Figure A7.4 is clearly in the labor force; for her, $M^* > 0$. The easiest way to see this is to compare the utility at her best choice point when $M > 0$ with the utility she would have with $M = 0$. This is done in Figure A7.5, which repeats the budget constraint and indifference curve I_1 from Figure A7.4 and adds in indifference curve I_0, which includes the nonparticipation (no work) point—point C in Figure A7.5. Since I_1 is higher than I_0, there is no question that it is preferred; higher indifference curves are always better. But let's look more carefully at point C. At this point, just as for point C in Figure A7.4, $MRS < w$. And, as we saw in Figure A7.4, this person will be better off reducing her leisure hours and increasing her hours of work—moving along the budget constraint toward point B.

This figure tells us something about the condition that must hold for a woman to choose to participate in the labor market. If MRS (at $L = T$) $< w$, then it is utility-maximizing to participate in the labor market. Or, put more compactly, if MRS (at $L = T$) $< w$, then $M^* > 0$. In words, if the value of

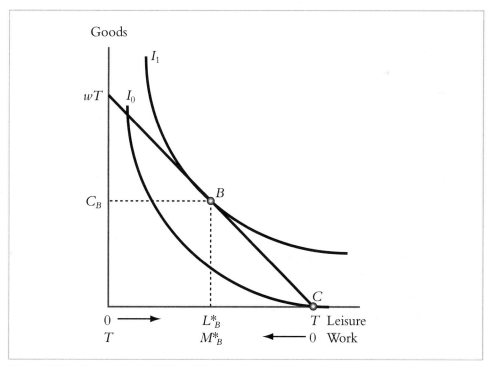

Figure A7.5 Comparing the Utility of Participation and Nonparticipation

an hour of leisure, evaluated when all time is spent in leisure, is less than the wage rate, an individual can always be better off by choosing to participate in the labor market.

Conversely, nonparticipation is the better choice if MRS (at $L = T$) $\geq w$. In that case, a woman would want to take yet more leisure and reduce her hours of work. But she is already taking the maximum hours of leisure, so her best choice is all leisure (although, as we see later, it probably wasn't and isn't leisure) and no market work.

Let's summarize these two rules for labor force participation:

$$\text{if } MRS \text{ (at } L = T) < w, \text{ then } M^* > 0,$$
and the woman participates in the labor market

$$\text{if } MRS \text{ (at } L = T) \geq w, \text{ then } M^* = 0,$$
and the woman does not participate in the labor market

In Figure A7.5, it was clear that this woman would be better off participating in the labor market. That will always be true, as long as nonlabor income (V) equals 0, because she is then in the unhappy situation of having no consumption goods at all if she doesn't work. And that is rarely the best (i.e., utility-maximizing) choice.

The Labor Force Participation of Married Women

Let's look at the more interesting situation of a married woman, and let's focus on a time period in which her market work decision is clearly secondary to that of her husband. This is a time in which specialization of task on the basis of gender, as discussed in Chapter 3, was widespread. Her husband's income functions like nonlabor income (V), at least as far as her labor supply decision is concerned. That income enables the family to purchase a positive amount of consumption goods and services, even when her own labor supply hours are zero. As we've already seen, that shifts up her budget constraint, without changing its slope.

Figure A7.6 shows how this might affect her decision about participating in the labor market. It repeats the original budget line (B_1) with $V = 0$ from Figure A7.5 plus two higher budget constraints labeled B_2 and B_3, parallel to the original budget constraint B_1. On budget constraint B_2, the best choice is point D. Hours of work are reduced, but this woman is still better off participating in the labor market. On the highest budget constraint B_3, the best choice is E, where $M^* = 0$.

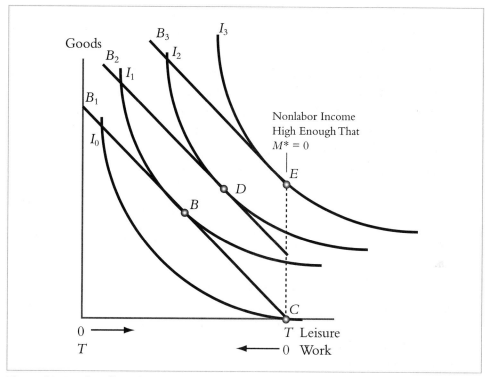

Figure A7.6   The Effect of Husband's Income on Labor Force Participation

Thus, Figure A7.6 shows that holding the wage rate constant and increasing nonlabor income causes hours of work to fall steadily, and eventually to fall to zero. This is called the **income effect.** In symbols, we can express the relationship as $\Delta M^*/\Delta V|w < 0$. As V increases, holding w constant, hours of work fall. And if V is large enough, hours of work will likely fall to zero. This is true regardless of the source of nonlabor income; it could be husband's income, but it could also be government transfer income or lottery winnings.

Finally, let's look at the effect of a woman's wage rate on labor force participation, now holding V constant. This is shown in Figure A7.7. The original situation is point A on indifference curve I_0 and on the budget constraint with the lower wage rate. With this w and V, this woman would choose not to participate in the labor market. The other budget constraint in Figure A7.7 is for the same amount of nonlabor (or husband's) income and a higher wage rate: Observe that this budget line is steeper. Now, this woman would choose

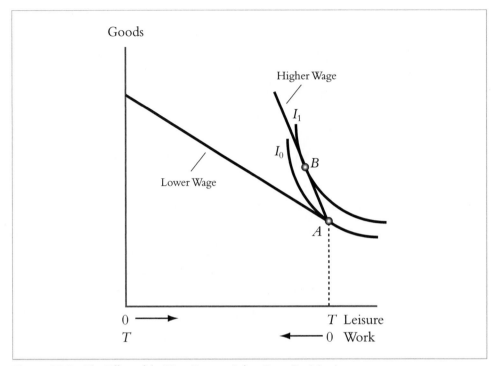

Figure A7.7   The Effect of the Wage Rate on Labor Force Participation

to participate in the labor market. Her best choice is point B on indifference curve I_1.

For a woman who is not currently a labor force participant, an increase in the wage rate can only have a positive impact on the probability that she will choose to participate in the labor market. Depending on her own particular circumstances, any particular increase in the wage rate might not be large enough to pull her into the labor market. But the impact can only be in the positive direction.[2]

Summary

Let's summarize what we have learned. In a model with just two uses of time (work and leisure), (1) a woman maximizes her utility by choosing hours of

---

[2]We make this point to distinguish this case from the case of a wage increase for a woman (or man) already in the labor force. In those cases, there are potentially conflicting *income and substitution effects*. To learn more about them, consult a standard text in labor economics, such as Ronald G. Ehrenberg and Robert S. Smith, *Modern Labor Economics*, Boston: Addison Wesley, 2003.

work where $MRS = w$; (2) a woman will choose to participate in the labor market if MRS at $L = T < w$; if MRS at $L = T > w$, then she will choose not to work in the labor market; (3) increases in V, holding w constant, increase the probability of nonparticipation; and (4) increases in w, holding V constant, increase the probability of participation.

The Analysis of Labor Force Participation with Household Production

The Household Production Function

Now we present a model that allows for both household production in the budget constraint and household goods in the utility function. The analysis was developed by Reuben Gronau in 1977.[3] It is challenging in spots; there is much more to it than we can present here.

As in Chapter 7 itself, we use H for hours of household production and G for household goods. We assume that household goods are produced by a **household production function** $G = g(H; Z)$, where Z stands for the available capital goods—things like washing machines, sewing machines, and microwaves. This function expresses the idea that the amount of G depends on the amounts of H and Z. The production function has been written with a semicolon (;) between H and Z to emphasize that H is being chosen, but Z is not, although we will think about how it has changed.[4] Like all production functions, the amount of output (G) increases as the amount of inputs (here, H) increases.

The increase in household output as the amount of time increases is the marginal product of household time; it is written $MP_H \equiv \Delta G/\Delta H \,|\, Z$ constant. (*Note*: We use the identity symbol because it is a definition.) The marginal product is an important idea in microeconomics, which was introduced in Chapter 2. It is the additional (or *marginal*) output produced in an additional hour of work. In virtually every production setting studied by economists, the

---

[3]To learn more about this analysis, see Reuben Gronau, "Leisure, Home Production, and Work—The Theory of the Allocation of Time Revisited," *Journal of Political Economy*, Vol. 85, No. 6, pp. 1099–1123, 1977. A good discussion of the model is in W. Keith Bryant, *The Economic Organization of the Household,* Cambridge: Cambridge Univ. Press, 1995, especially Chapter 5.

[4]This is a necessary simplification. To treat household technology as something that was chosen would make the model much too complicated without really adding anything essential.

marginal product falls as more of an input is used. This property of production is called the **Law of Diminishing Marginal Returns.** The same thing is likely to be true here—the marginal product of household time falls as more time is spent working at home; fatigue might be one explanation. This means that each additional hour spent working in the household is less productive than the ones preceding it. We write the marginal product as $MP_H(H)$; the H in parentheses reminds us that the marginal product depends on the number of hours.

Figure A7.8 is a picture of a household production function. We are continuing to measure leisure from left to right, so here we are measuring household production time (H) from right to left. Look at the slope of the production function; it is steep at first and then flattens out. Think about the slope: its value is $\Delta G/\Delta H$, which means that the slope of the production function is the marginal product of household time (or actually the negative of the marginal product). So the flattening slope is a representation of falling marginal product, which we noted previously is a characteristic property of production functions.

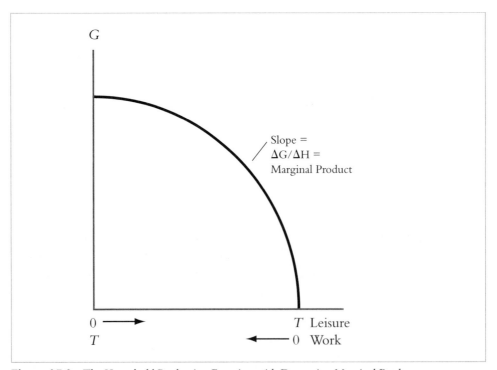

Figure A7.8   The Household Production Function with Decreasing Marginal Product

Preferences

We now have three potential ways for a woman to spend her time: leisure (L), household production (H), and market work (M). The sum must always equal T, the total time available: thus, $L + H + M = T$. We also have three goods: leisure (L), market goods (C), and household goods (G). The good we call L is the same thing as the time use L.

To represent these three goods via indifference curves, we need to make a strong assumption. It is difficult (at least for most of us) to work with curves in three dimensions. The beauty and relative simplicity of indifference curves is that they can be represented along two axes. So, to compress these three goods into two axes, it is usually assumed that C and G are **perfect substitutes.** This means that an individual cares only about the total amount of $C + G$, but not about the amounts of C or G individually: A unit of C is just as valuable as a unit of G. Then we can put L on the horizontal axis, just as before, and the sum $C + G$ on the vertical axis. With that adjustment, the indifference curves are otherwise exactly the same as before—negatively sloped, bowed toward the origin, and so on.

Constraints

There are now three constraints (the same three seen in Chapter 7).[5] We repeat them here for convenience:

$$\text{Market goods:} \qquad C = wM + V \qquad (1)$$

$$\text{Household goods:} \quad G = g(H; Z) \qquad (2)$$

$$\text{Time:} \qquad\qquad M + H + L = T \qquad (3)$$

In constructing the combined budget constraint, we build in optimization in the use of time between market work and household production. Suppose a woman has some wage w and a household production function with its associated marginal product. Let's start at the point with all time spent in leisure, and think about her options. She could work in the labor market, earn w, and get w units of consumption goods (C). Or she could work in household production and produce household goods (G) equal to $MP_H(1)$, where the 1

---

[5]There is one small difference. Here we are using C to stand for consumption expenditures; in the chapter, we used C to stand for consumption goods. Thus, the first constraint was written $pC = wM + V$, where p was the price of consumption goods.

refers to the first hour of household production time. What should she do? How should she decide?

The pretty obvious way to proceed is to compare the wage rate and the marginal product. If $MP_H(1) > w$, she would be better off spending that hour in household production rather than working in the labor market simply because she gets a larger quantity of goods that way. (Remember that we assumed that she didn't distinguish between household goods and market goods; only the total matters.) If, instead, $w > MP_H(1)$, she would be better off working in the labor market rather than spending the hour in household production.

For virtually everyone on planet Earth, it is probably true that $MP_H(1) > w$, as long as household production time is defined broadly enough to include eating, sleeping, showering, and the like. What about the second hour? Now, we compare $MP_H(2)$ and w, and again choose the larger. Probably, the result is still the same: $MP_H(2) > w$. Now, we know that MP_H is initially greater than w, and also that MP_H falls steadily. Thus, there should be some hour—call it H'—where $MP_H(H') = w$. For all hours less than H', $MP_H(H) > w$, and household production is more valuable than market work. But for all hours beyond H', $MP_H(H) < w$, and market work is more valuable than household production. At H', a woman would transfer her time from the household sector to the labor market.

Figure A7.9 shows what the budget constraint would look like with market work and household production. First note the axes. The vertical axis measures the sum $C + G$. The horizontal axis measures leisure time just as before, from left to right (from 0 to T). From right to left, it measures both H and M.

Starting at point A, where both household production time and market work equal 0, she can move either along the curved household production function (Slope $= -MP_H$) or the dotted market work line (Slope $= -w$). Clearly, she is better off using the time in household production; she gets more consumption goods—the production function lies above the market work line. The production function flattens out as more and more hours are spent in household production, representing falling household marginal product. The wage rate is constant. For each hour, she compares the wage to the marginal product and chooses the larger. Eventually, at point B, the marginal product equals the wage rate, and at that point, this woman would transfer her time from household production to the labor market. The full budget constraint is the kinked line ABD. This woman would work no more than H' hours in house-

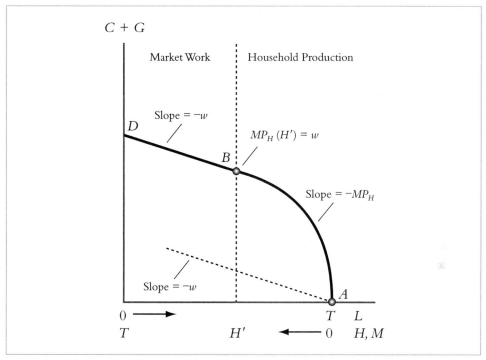

Figure A7.9   The Budget Constraint with Household Production and Market Work

hold production; any additional hours of work are in the labor market. The dotted vertical line through point B shows this; household production is to the right, and market work is to the left.

Choices

Finally, we put the indifference curves together with the budget constraint to analyze a woman's choices about household production, market work, and leisure. Figure A7.10 repeats the budget constraint from Figure A7.9 and adds in representative indifference curves for two different women, Ms. P and Ms. Q. In doing this, we are assuming that the two women face exactly the same budget constraint but have different preferences as represented by their indifference curves.[6]

The best choice is still given by the tangency between an indifference curve and the budget constraint. For Ms. P, this tangency is at point F; she works H'

---

[6]Indifference curves for the same person cannot intersect.

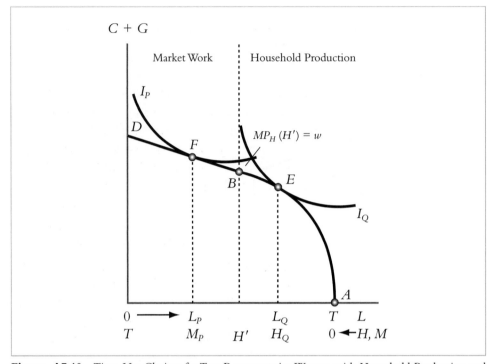

$C + G$

Market Work | Household Production

I_P

D

F

B

$MP_H (H') = w$

E

I_Q

A

| $0 \longrightarrow$ | L_P | | L_Q | T | L |
| T | M_P | H' | H_Q | $0 \longleftarrow H, M$ | |

Figure A7.10   Time-Use Choices for Two Representative Women with Household Production and Market Work

hours in household production and $H'M_P$ hours in the labor market and takes the remainder ($0L_P$, measured from left to right) in leisure. Ms. P is a labor market participant.

Ms. Q's choice is quite different. For her, the tangency point is at point E along the curved portion of the budget constraint to the right of H'. She spends H_Q hours in household production, 0 hours in market work, and all the rest ($0L_Q$, measured from left to right) in leisure. Ms. Q is not a labor market participant.

The Labor Force Participation of Married Women

Our primary interest is still in the labor force participation of married women. Husband's income operates in this model just as it did in the simpler model analyzed in Figure A7.6. It simply shifts up the budget line, as long as it is reasonable to believe that her decision about work is secondary to his. As before, if his income is high enough, her best choice may be nonparticipation. Because this is just what we have already seen, we do not spend any more time on it here. Try redrawing Figure A7.10 with enough nonlabor income to make Ms. P a nonparticipant.

What about the impact of the wage rate and, more specifically, of the rising wages of women during the twentieth century? If the wage rate were higher and nothing else changed, H'—the point where the marginal product of household time just equals the wage rate—would shift to the right, to a smaller number of hours of household production time. The point at which women would shift from household production to market work would arrive sooner, precisely because market work is now more rewarding financially.

A change like this is shown in Figure A7.11. The original budget constraint is $AEBD$, and at point B, $MP_H = w_0$, where w_0 is the initial value of the wage. When the wage increases to w_1, the constraint tilts, and the point where $MP_H = w_0$ shifts to the right to point E (which was also the choice point along the original budget constraint; this is not necessarily so, but it makes the diagram less cluttered). The new budget constraint is AED'. Faced with the higher wage rate, Ms. P does two things: She reduces her household production time from H' to H'', and she enters the labor market, choosing point E'.

Whether an increase in the wage rate causes any particular married woman to enter the labor market depends on how close she was prior to the change and how big the change is. Wage changes much smaller than the one depicted in Figure A7.11 probably wouldn't be sufficient.

As you may already sense, the key to this analysis is the point where the marginal product of household time just equals the wage rate. The further to the right this occurs (i.e., the lower the number of hours of household production at which $MP_H = w$), the more likely it is that a woman will work in the labor market. We have already seen how this works in terms of the wage rate: The higher the wage rate is, the lower H' is, and the more likely labor force participation is.

Similar impacts can be derived for the household production function. Consider the impact of very young children or very large families on the marginal product of household time. It is reasonable to suppose that, in this case, the marginal product is very high to begin with and falls relatively slowly as more time is spent. There is always something valuable to do. Clearly, this will push H' well to the left and reduce labor force participation. A somewhat different result might occur if improvements in household technology—the modern

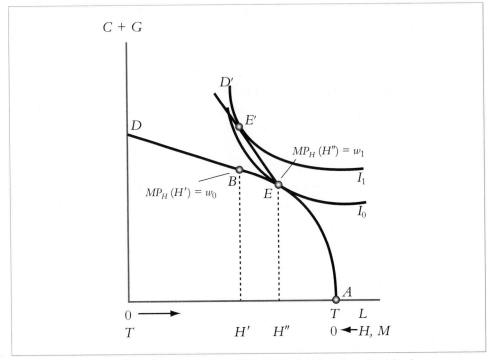

Figure A7.11   The Effect of an Increase in the Wage Rate on Labor Force Participation

kitchen!—increased the marginal product at first but caused it to fall more quickly. An explanation for this might be that there really weren't any valuable production tasks remaining after some hours. In that case, the point where the marginal product equaled the wage rate would shift right and participation would rise. Many economists think that this kind of change, along with steady increases in wage rates, is an important explanation of rising women's labor force participation.

Summary

Using the apparatus of indifference curves and budget constraints, it is possible to analyze labor force participation decisions with precision and rigor. The great advantage of this approach is making the nature of the constraints and the prices particularly clear. This insight is particularly valuable in going further, especially in thinking about the effect of taxes and government transfers on labor supply decisions. Taxes and transfers affect the budget constraint and alter the price of leisure, thereby affecting participation decisions.

In the simpler model, we examined the choice between market work and leisure; in the fuller model, we incorporated household production. The key lesson in both models is that the wage rate is the price of leisure, and that changes in the wage rate over time have clearly had a huge impact on the decisions women, especially married women, have made about becoming labor market participants.

The wage rate seems to be everywhere. In Chapter 3, it had an important role in determining the gains to marriage and the household division of labor. In Chapter 4, it had a big impact on declining marriage rates among Black men and women. In Chapter 5, it was the whole story behind the sharp decline in fertility: Higher wages made children expensive, leading men and women to substitute child quality for child quantity. And finally, in Chapter 7, we have seen the impact that wages have on labor force participation.

The reality is that all these analyses are pieces of the same cloth. The wage rate is the price of time, and time, particularly the time of married women, has been used in different ways in response to changes in the price.

Appendix Terms

budget constraint   253

diminishing marginal rate of substitution   253

full income   254

full-income budget constraint   254

household production function   265

income effect   262

indifference curves   252

law of diminishing marginal returns   265

marginal rate of substitution   252

perfect subsititutes   267

time constraint   253

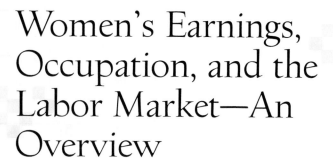

CHAPTER 8

Women's Earnings, Occupation, and the Labor Market—An Overview

Introduction

Women earn, on average, considerably less than men. That probably comes as no surprise. The earliest data for the United States for agricultural and manufacturing workers during the first half of the nineteenth century show women earning roughly 30 to 45% of what men earned.[1] One hundred fifty years later, at the beginning of the twenty-first century, the gender earnings ratio had risen substantially from that nineteenth-century level, but it was still far short of equality. In 2000, the median earnings of year-round full-time working women were 73.6% of the earnings of year-round full-time working men. In 2001, this figure increased to 76%—women's median earnings increased between 2000 and 2001, but men's earnings did not. As you will see, most of the increase in the gender earnings ratio occurred during the 1980s.

This chapter begins a four-chapter unit on women's earnings. In this chapter, we start, as always, with the facts, examining the gender gap in earnings and also the gender difference in occupations. Then we take a quick survey of how labor markets work to set wage rates via supply and demand analysis.

The basic economics question about the gender earnings gap is this: Why do women, on average, earn less than men? There are two very broad possible explanations. Women could have, on average, fewer valuable labor market skills than men. For example, if women have less education than men on average (in fact, they don't at this point in time) or have less labor market experience than men (they still do) and if education and labor market experience are valuable in the labor market, then these differences could

---

[1]Claudia Goldin, *Understanding the Gender Gap*, New York: Oxford University Press, 1990, Table 3.1.

275

be a source of "legitimate" or "deserved" differences in average earnings. Average earnings differences resulting from average differences in labor market skills would exist even if there were no labor market discrimination at all. Alternatively, the earnings differences could reflect a lower value attached to the skills that women do bring to the labor market. For example, women might be unable to obtain jobs that match their skills. Outcomes like that would reflect labor market discrimination. In practice, average earnings differences might well be caused by a combination of both factors. Thus, we might ask: What fraction of the lower average earnings of women is the result of a lower level of skills that they bring to the labor market and what fraction is caused by differences in the monetary rewards they receive for those skills? Do women deserve to earn less than men? If so, how much less?

In the next chapter, we examine these two alternative explanations of the gender gap in earnings, focusing primarily on investment in human capital and models of labor market discrimination. In Chapter 10, we examine statistical techniques that will help us sort out the quantitative importance of skills versus discrimination explanations of the gender gap in earnings; then, we look at a number of empirical studies of the gender gap. Our goal is to be able to answer the questions posed in the preceding paragraph. Finally, in Chapter 11, we look at government policy directed at the gender gap in the labor market.

The Gender Gap in Earning

In January 2000, President Clinton announced in a public address that women earned 75 cents on the dollar compared to men *doing the same work*; he proposed additional spending on labor market antidiscrimination enforcement to correct the problem. His statement was half almost correct and half quite incorrect. The 75 cents on the dollar figure was quite close to the ratio of median annual earnings for year-round full-time workers for women relative to men. But the ratio does not refer to men and women doing the same job, nor even to men and women with the same level of qualifications. It is simply the ratio of median earnings for year-round full-time workers.

Table 8.1 presents the median annual earnings in 2001 for **year-round full-time (YRFT) workers** by gender and by race and ethnicity. Year-round full-time workers are people who work at least 35 hours a week and at least 50 weeks in a year; paid vacations count as work weeks. These workers are the standard comparison group for gender earnings because they allow us to compare the earnings of men and women who work fairly similar numbers

	Women ($)	Men ($)	Women's Earnings as Percent of Men's Earnings
All	29,215	38,275	76.3
White	29,930	39,834	75.1
Black	26,595	31,351	84.8
Hispanic	21,493	25,083	85.7
Asian/Pacific Islander	30,685	41,853	73.3

Table 8.1   U.S. Median Earnings by Gender and Race/Ethnicity, Year-Round Full-Time Workers, 2001

Source: U.S. Census Bureau, Current Population Survey, Annual Demographic Supplement, "Historical Income Tables," Table P-41, P41a–d.

of hours in a year. The median is a better measure than the mean for this purpose because it is less affected by very high incomes, and thus better represents the status of a typical person.

As Table 8.1 shows, median YRFT earnings for women in 2001 were $29,215, about 76% of the $38,275 that the median YRFT man earned. There are some differences in the earnings ratio by race/ethnicity. For White women and Asian/Pacific Islanders, the earnings ratio is considerably lower than for Black and Hispanic women.[2] Both Black women and Hispanic women earn about 85% of what Black men and Hispanic men earn, compared to 75% or lower for the other two groups. You can also see in Table 8.1 the substantial differences in earnings by race and ethnicity within gender. Whites and Asians/Pacific Islanders earn far more than Blacks and Hispanics, and this is true for both men and women.

For all working men and women, the gender gap in annual earnings is larger than for YRFT workers because more women work part-time or part-year than men. In 2001, 58% of all working women worked year-round full-time, compared to 73% of all working men. The median annual earnings of all working men in 2001 were $31,364, while the median annual earnings for all

---

[2]In Census tabulations, Hispanic is an ethnic designation, not a racial classification. Hispanic individuals may be either White or Black.

working women were $20,851. Thus, the gender earnings ratio for all workers in 2001 was 66.4%. Even though this is about 10 percentage points lower than the ratio for YRFT workers, it is a record high; the ratio jumped more than 6 percentage points between 1999 and 2001. An increase in hours worked and thus annual earnings among part-time women is probably behind the substantial increase.

Figure 8.1 shows how the gender ratio of median annual earnings for year-round full-time workers has changed since 1960. For a period of at least two decades through 1980, the ratio moved in an incredibly narrow band. In 1960, the ratio was 60.7%; in 1980, it was 60.2%. In the intervening years, it stayed almost entirely between 58 and 59%. It is rare to see an economic time series that is so unchanged over such an extended time period. Indeed, the ratio was so constant that the National Organization for Women (NOW) circulated popular buttons that read "59¢ on the dollar."

The earnings ratio began to change in the early 1980s. It rose almost every year during that decade, jumping from 60% in 1980 to nearly 65% by 1985 and more than 71% in 1990. Since then, however, it has risen much more slowly and a bit less steadily. The ratio has actually fallen in a few years, including, for example, between 1997 and 1999 when it dropped 2 percentage points. But since 1999, it has risen quite a bit, and in 2001 it reached an all-time high of more than 76%.

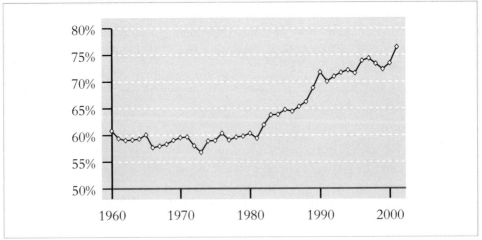

Figure 8.1   Female/Male Median Annual Earnings Ratio, U.S. Year-Round Full-Time Workers, 1960–2001.

Although the earnings gap for all workers is greater than for YRFT workers, the earnings ratio has increased even more for this group. This reflects both the narrowing in gender pay differences and the rapid increase in women's labor force activity. (An increase in labor force participation is not guaranteed to increase the earnings ratio, if the new workers are predominantly part-time or less-skilled.) In 1960, among all male and female workers, the ratio of median annual earnings was only 38.6%. The median working woman earned just $1695, the equivalent of about $8800 in today's dollars. A decade later, the ratio had actually fallen, to 38.2%, and in 1975, it was still only 40.9%. Thereafter, however, the earnings ratio moved up quite steadily, a percentage point or more almost every year, finally breaking the 60% barrier in 1992. In the 1990s, the ratio bounced around, just like the ratio for year-round full-time workers. By 1999, the ratio had dipped to 61.1%, but in 2001 it jumped up to 66.4%, its all-time record high.

As Blau and Kahn point out in a recent article,[3] the increase in the gender earnings ratio could reflect the better economic status of new cohorts of young workers entering the labor market and/or better conditions for workers already in the labor market as they move through their own careers. Table 8.2, which is based on their work, shows hourly earnings ratios (female to male) by age group in 1978, 1988, and 1998. The data come from the Current Population Survey and refer to full-time workers. Reading across the table shows how successive cohorts of the same age fared in the labor market. Reading diagonally shows what happens to the same cohort as it aged ten years. For example, the women and men who were between the ages of 25 and 34 in 1978 are aged 35 to 44 in 1988 and 45 to 54 in 1998.[4] The top panel shows the wage ratios themselves, while the bottom panels show the changes across cohorts and within cohorts.

Look first at the earnings ratios for 1998. For the youngest group of workers (ages 18–24), women earned 94% of what men earned. For 25 to 34 year olds, the ratio was 85% and then it dropped to 76 and 72%, respectively, for the 35 to 44 year olds and the 45 to 54 year olds. So, the earnings ratio clearly varies with age, perhaps because of greater differences in labor market skills

[3]Francine D. Blau and Lawrence M. Kahn, "Gender Differences in Pay," *Journal of Economic Perspectives,* Vol. 14, No. 4, pp. 75–99, 2001.

[4]They are not literally the same persons, but rather representative samples of 25 to 34 year olds in 1978, 35 to 44 year olds in 1988, and 45 to 54 year olds in 1998.

Age Range	Wage Ratio (%)		
	1978	1988	1998
18–24	82.4	93.0	94.2
25–34	70.3	82.8	85.0
35–44	58.9	68.7	76.1
45–54	58.2	64.7	71.6

Age Range	Percentage Point Change in Earnings Ratios		
		1978–1988	1988–1998
Across cohort			
18–24	—	10.6	1.2
25–34	—	12.5	2.3
35–44	—	9.8	7.4
45–54	—	6.6	6.8
Within cohort			
18–24	—	−2.4	−9.2
25–34	—	−1.6	−6.7
35–44	—	5.8	2.9
45–54	—	2.9	4.5

Table 8.2   Female/Male Hourly Wage Ratios by Age Group and Year

Source: Francine D. Blau and Lawrence M. Kahn, "Gender Differences in Pay," *Journal of Economic Perspectives,* Vol. 14, No. 4, pp. 75–99, 2001. Copyright © 2001 by the American Economic Association. Reprinted with the permission of the authors and publisher.

between the older groups of workers or because of the cumulative effects of labor market discrimination. Looking horizontally across the cohorts shows what happened over time. To see this in the top panel, subtract the entries or look directly in the second "Across cohort" section where we have already done the arithmetic. For all four age groups, the earnings ratio rose substantially between 1978 and 1988, meaning that the newer cohorts of working women did better at the same age than the cohorts that preceded them. For workers aged 18 to 24, 25 to 34, and 35 to 44, the earnings ratio rose about 10 percentage points or more, and even for the older group, it rose 6.6 points. This increase is consistent with what we already saw in Figure 8.1—the 1980s were a decade in which the gender earnings ratio rose. Here we see that it rose for all age groups. In the 1988–1998 period, the across-cohort changes were still positive, but they were quite small for the two younger groups (1–2 percentage points) and much more substantial (about 7 percentage points) for the two older groups. Again this is generally consistent with the trend in Figure 8.1.

It is also possible to use the numbers in the top portion of Table 8.1 to get an insight into how the earnings ratio changed for a particular age group as the men and women in it moved through their own career paths. For example, the 25 to 34 year olds in 1978 are between the ages of 35 and 44 in 1988 and 45 and 54 in 1998. To see what happened, read down the diagonals in the top panel, thereby following a cohort as it ages ten years. The resulting changes in the wage ratio are shown in the "Within cohort" panel. Note that the within-cohort information for the 18 to 24 year olds and the 45 and 54 year olds shown in the bottom panel doesn't come from the information in the top panel because there is no corresponding age group of 28 to 34 or 55 to 64 year olds shown there (Blau and Kahn computed these ratios separately.)

By looking at the ratios in this way, we see a mixture of positive and negative changes—consistently negative for the two younger groups and consistently positive for the two older ones. Look, for example, at the two groups of 25 to 34 year olds. The 1978 cohort saw its earnings ratio drop from 70.3% in 1978 to 68.7% in 1988, a drop of 1.6 percentage points. For the corresponding 1988 cohort, the ratio dropped from 82.8 to 76.1%, a much larger drop of 6.7 percentage points. The within-cohort declines were even larger for the 18 to 24 year olds in both 1978 and 1988, especially between 1988 and 1998. In contrast, for the two older groups of workers, the ratio rose between 3 and 6 percentage points over time in both decades.

The within-cohort changes are particularly interesting. They suggest that something is happening between roughly ages 18 and 40 that adversely affects women's earnings relative to men, and that this occurred even in an environment in which each successive group of women fared better than its predecessors. It is not clear exactly what it is, although there are two obvious candidates—responsibilities associated with marriage and family and labor market impediments that affect promotion and career paths. We will return to these issues later.

How does education affect the gender earnings ratio? Figure 8.2 shows this. The data are for 2001 and again are for median annual earnings of year-round full-time workers. Comparing the earnings of men and women with the

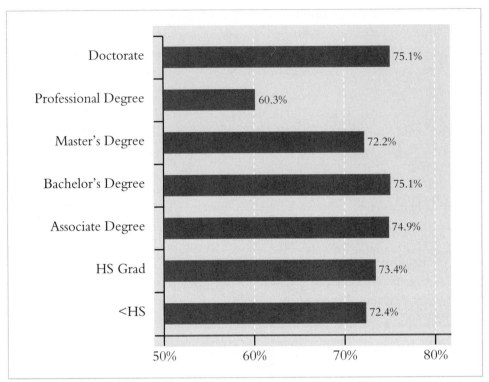

Figure 8.2   Female/Male Median Annual Earnings Ratio by Education Level, 2001

same education means that we are eliminating one possible source of skill differences and thus one possible explanation for why women earn less than men. With the exception of women and men with professional degrees, it appears that the gender earnings ratio really doesn't vary particularly much with education. All the other ratios are in a narrow range between 72% and just over 75%. For example, women with a college degree don't fare much better relative to men with a college degree than do women with a high school degree compared to their male counterparts. Women with professional degrees earn only 60% of what men with the same education earn, but without knowing the details of what professional degrees men and women have, it is hard to draw a conclusion about why the ratio is so low. It is certainly possible that this is a reflection of the so-called glass ceiling in the corporate world that allegedly prevents women from reaching the top ranks in business. Or it is possible that the kinds of professional degrees that men and women obtain are very different.

Figure 8.3 provides information about the full distribution of annual earnings by gender in 2001, still focusing on year-round full-time workers. The bars in the figure represent the proportion of men and women in each earnings bracket. What comes through clearly here are the differences in the shape of the income distribution for men and women. At the low end of the distribution, 25% of women earn less than $20,000, compared to about 15% of men. At the high end, men are nearly twice as likely to be earning between $50,000 and $75,000 and nearly three times as likely to be earning $75,000 or more. At the really high end—$250,000 and over—the disparity is even greater. In 2001, about 950,000 men and 140,000 women earned more than a quarter of a million dollars, so that men outnumber women by almost a 7 to 1 ratio. (These numbers are based on a different sample and aren't included in Figure 8.3.)

Finally, it's interesting to see how the gender earnings ratio in the United States compares to the earnings ratio in other countries. Table 8.3 provides

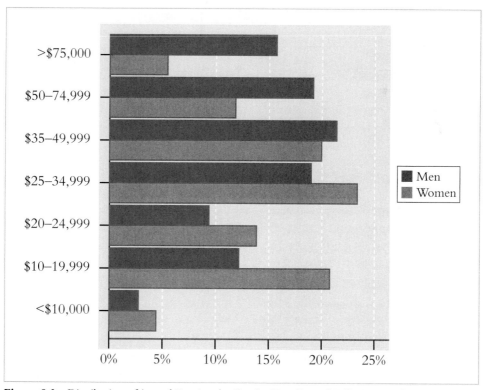

Figure 8.3   Distribution of Annual Earnings by Gender, Year-Round Full-Time Workers, U.S., 2001

Country	1979–1981	1989–1990	1994–1998	Percentage Point Change in Ratio, 1979–1981 to 1994–1998
Australia	80.0%	81.4%	86.8%	6.8
Austria	64.9%	67.4%	69.2%	4.3
Belgium	n.a.	84.0%	90.1%	6.1*
Canada	63.3%	66.3%	69.8%	6.5
Finland	73.4%	76.4%	79.9%	6.5
France	79.9%	84.7%	89.9%	10.0
Germany (West)	71.7%	73.7%	75.5%	3.8
Ireland	n.a.	n.a.	74.5%	n.a.
Italy	n.a.	80.5%	83.3%	2.8*
Japan	58.7%	59.0%	63.6%	4.9
Netherlands	n.a.	75.0%	76.9%	1.9*
New Zealand	73.4%	75.9%	81.4%	8.0
Spain	n.a.	n.a.	71.1%	–
Sweden	83.8%	78.8%	83.5%	−0.3
Switzerland	na	73.6%	75.2%	1.6*
United Kingdom	62.6%	67.7%	74.9%	12.3
United States	62.5%	70.6%	76.3%	13.8
Non-U.S. Average	71.2%	74.6%	77.8%	6.2

Table 8.3   Female/Male Earnings Ratios, Median Weekly Earnings of Full-Time Workers, Selected Developed Countries, 1979–1998

*Based on change between 1989–1990 and 1994–1998.

Source: Francine D. Blau and Lawrence M. Kahn, "Gender Differences in Pay," *Journal of Economic Perspectives,* Vol. 14, No. 4, pp. 75–99, 2001, Table 3. Copyright © 2001 by the American Economic Association. Reprinted with the permission of the authors and publisher.

some information about this for countries in Europe, as well as Australia, Canada, Japan, and New Zealand. It shows the earnings ratio for median weekly earnings of full-time workers at three points in time—approximately 1980, 1990, and the mid- to late-1990s. The last column shows the change in the ratio from 1980 to the mid-1990s or, for countries lacking 1980 data, from 1990 to the mid-1990s. In 1980, which is just before the steady increase in the earnings ratio in the United States, the ratio in the United States (62.5%) is conspicuously low. Of the eleven countries with data, only Japan had a lower ratio, with the United Kingdom, Canada, and Austria not far ahead. The average of the other ten countries was 71.2%, nearly 9 percentage points above the U.S. figure. Sweden and Australia were at the top of the list, with earnings ratios of 80% or above. As we have already seen, in the 1980s, the gender earnings ratio in the United States rose sharply and steadily to more than 70%. As a result, by 1990, the United States was no longer near the bottom of the list. It was now just 4 percentage points below the non-U.S. average, and was ahead of Austria, Canada, Japan, and the United Kingdom. By the mid- to late-1990s, the earnings ratio in the United States had nearly caught up to the other countries. The United States was still more than 10 percentage points below Australia, Belgium, and France, but it was near the middle of the pack. The gender earnings ratio rose by more in the United States than in any of the other countries; the United Kingdom and France were second and third, respectively.

It is well worth noting that no country can boast of gender equality in median earnings. The highest ratios in Table 8.3 are just about 90% (Belgium and France) with Australia, Italy, and Sweden following at 83 to 87%. Japan remained a substantial outlier among these countries at about 64%.

Occupational Segregation

It is a common observation that many of the jobs in our economy are implicitly tagged for either men or women but not usually both. Economists term this **occupational segregation** or sex segregation. Most of us have a sense of occupations that are disproportionately male or female. Table 8.4 shows the proportion female in a wide range of detailed occupations in 2002 in the United States, ranked from low to high by the proportion female.

There are no big surprises here. The first part of the table lists the highly male occupations, including automobile mechanics, carpenters, plumbers, electricians, airline pilots, and truck drivers, all with less than 5% women. Women are 10 to 12% of civil, aerospace, and chemical engineers; 16% of butchers; and less than 25% of police and detectives, correctional institution officers, and architects. Occupations with a relatively equal distribution of men and women include bus drivers, pharmacists, bartenders (exactly 50/50!), real estate and

Occupation	% Female
Automobile mechanics	1.2
Roofers	1.5
Carpenters	1.5
Plumbers, pipefitters, steamfitters, and apprentices	1.7
Electricians	1.9
Construction trades	2.1
Brickmasons and stonemasons	2.2
Firefighters	2.5
Airplane pilots and navigators	3.0
Truck drivers	4.3
Mechanical engineers	4.5
Machinists	4.8
Mechanics and repairers	4.8
Pest control	5.6
Electrical and electronic engineers	8.8
Civil engineers	9.6
Aerospace engineers	10.7
Clergy	11.2
Taxicab drivers and chauffeurs	11.7
Chemical engineers	12.2
Farming, forestry, and fishing	14.9
Butchers and meat cutters	16.4
Police and detectives	17.5
Athletes	20.0
Correctional institution officers	21.5
Architects	23.7

Occupation	% Female
Computer programmers	27.2
Mail carriers, postal service workers	28.8
Mathematical and computer scientists	29.2
Janitors and cleaners	30.3
Securities and financial services sales	32.3
Physicians	32.6
Lawyers and judges	33.7
Teachers, college and university	36.7
Bus drivers	41.3
Pharmacists	41.8
Biological and life scientists	44.5
Bakers	46.6
Bartenders	50.0
Real estate sales	51.8
Computer operators	52.9
Insurance sales	53.1
Economists	54.2
Physicians' assistant	55.6
Teachers, secondary school	56.4
Psychologists	57.6
Physical therapists	61.3
Sales counter clerks	64.5
Social workers	70.3
Waiters and waitresses	71.0
Therapists	71.1
Hotel clerks	75.0

(continued)

Occupation	% Female
Cashiers	77.7
Teachers, elementary school	81.5
Librarians	83.0
Legal assistants	84.0
Data-entry keyers	84.6
Records clerks	84.9
Dieticians	87.5
Nursing aides, orderlies, and attendants	89.0
Bank tellers	89.1
Hairdressers and cosmetologists	89.3
Financial records processing	90.6
Registered nurses	91.0
Speech therapists	94.0
Licensed practical nurses	94.4
Cleaners and servants	95.2
Dental assistants	97.7
Receptionists	97.9
Teachers, pre-kindergarten and kindergarten	98.4
Child care workers	98.5
Secretaries	98.6

Table 8.4   Proportion Female for Selected Occupations, United States, 2002

Source: Bureau of Labor Statistics, *Highlights of Women's Earnings,* 2001, Table 3.

insurance sales, economists, secondary school teachers, and psychologists. At the high end are the traditional female occupations—teachers from pre-kindergarten through elementary school, nurses, dental assistants, receptionists, child care workers, and secretaries. All these professions are more than 80% female, with secretaries topping the list at 98.6%. In 2002, there were 1.8 million women but only 25,000 men working as secretaries.

Measuring Occupational Segregation: The Duncan Index

To measure how much occupational segregation there is and to measure change in the occupational distribution, it is necessary to have some kind of summary measure of just how different the occupational distributions of men and women are. The **Duncan Index** is the most widely used measure of occupational segregation in the labor market.[5] It is calculated using the following formula:

$$S = \frac{1}{2}\Sigma_i |M_i - F_i| \tag{1}$$

In equation (1), M and F are the percentage of males and females in the labor force who work in occupation i, $|\ |$ is the absolute value indicator, and Σ is the summation indicator. Thus, the Duncan Index is computed by finding the proportion of men and women in each occupation,[6] taking the absolute value of the difference by occupation, summing across occupations, and then dividing by two. If there were no occupational segregation, M_i would equal F_i in each occupation so the Duncan Index would equal 0. If, at the other extreme, there were complete occupational segregation, then the summed term would equal 200, and after division by 2, the Duncan Index would equal 100.[7] So, the Duncan Index ranges from 0 when there is no occupational segregation to 100 when occupational segregation is absolute. The Duncan Index can also be interpreted as the proportion of men or women who would have to change occupations in order to eliminate occupational segregation.

Let's look at a simple numerical example to see how the formula works. To keep things simple, let's assume that there are 100 women and 100 men in the labor market and that there are four job categories: construction worker, lawyer, teacher, and nurse. Suppose the distribution of men and women among these occupations is as shown in Case 1 in Table 8.5, with men overrepresented in construction and as lawyers and women overrepresented as teachers and nurses.

---

[5]The Duncan Index is named after its creator, the famous sociologist Otis Dudley Duncan. It can be used to measure dissimilarity between any pair of distributions, not just occupation.

[6]Be careful—the number used in the calculation of the Duncan Index is the proportion of all men or all women who work in each occupation, not the proportion of workers in each occupation who are male or female.

[7]If there were just two occupations, one with 100% of the men and the other with 100% of the women, then $S = \frac{1}{2} \times (|100 - 0| + |0 - 100|) = 100$.

	Case 1		Case 2	
Occupation	**Male**	**Female**	**Male**	**Female**
Construction	60	0	30	10
Lawyer	25	10	25	20
Teacher	10	40	35	35
Nurse	5	50	10	35
Total	100	100	100	100
Duncan Index	75		25	

Table 8.5   Illustrative Distribution of Workers by Occupation and Gender

Conveniently, in this example, the number of individuals in an occupation is also the percentage in the occupation since there are 100 men and 100 women in the example. Now we can calculate the Duncan Index for this distribution as

$$\text{Case 1: } S = \frac{1}{2}\Sigma_i |M_i - F_i| =$$
$$\frac{1}{2} \times \{|60 - 0| + |25 - 10| + |10 - 40| + |5 - 50|\} = 75$$

This is a very high degree of segregation; 75 is obviously much closer to 100 than it is to 0. It means that 75% of the men or women need to change jobs to eliminate the sex segregation. In this case, 30 of the women teachers and 45 of the women nurses would have to change occupations, becoming, instead, lawyers or construction workers. Alternatively, all 60 construction workers and 15 of the male lawyers would have to change occupations, becoming teachers and nurses. A suitable combination of men and women totaling 75 would also work.

Now suppose that the distribution changes as shown in Case 2 of Table 8.5. On the male side, half of the construction workers have been redistributed to teaching and nursing. On the female side, some of the teachers and nurses have become lawyers and construction workers. In all, 30% of the men and 20% of the women changed jobs. Now when we calculate the Duncan Index, we have

$$\text{Case 2: } S = \frac{1}{2}\Sigma_i |M_i - F_i| =$$

$$\frac{1}{2} \times \{|30 - 10| + |25 - 20| + |35 - 35| + |10 - 35|\} = 25$$

This is a rather low estimate of occupational segregation. There is still some disparity among the occupations; in the construction field, you are still likely to find male workers and in the nursing field you are likely to find female workers. But the probability of being male or female in the teaching and law fields is close to being equalized.

The Duncan Index may mask some occupational segregation if the categories are too broad. For example, suppose we take the second set of numbers, but break out several of the categories in more detail:

	Male	Female
Construction		
Laborers	25	1
Admin. staff	5	9
Lawyers	25	20
Teachers		
Elementary	0	20
Secondary	15	15
University	20	0
Nurses	10	35

As is usually the case, the more detailed categories show far more occupational segregation. Now the Duncan Index becomes

$$S = \frac{1}{2} \times \{|25 - 1|$$

$$+ |5 - 9| + |25 - 20| + |0 - 20| + |15 - 15|$$

$$+ |20 - 1| + |10 - 35|\} = 49$$

This estimate of 49 is considerably higher than the earlier estimate of 25. We used the same occupational distribution; we just looked at it in more detail. The point is that by using categories that are too broad, it is possible to overlook the sex segregation that exists within broad occupational categories. Related to this, care must be taken to keep the number of occupational categories constant when making comparisons over time or across countries. Otherwise, any change in the index could just reflect a change in the number of categories.

Universities are a good example of this kind of within-occupation sex segregation. On the whole, there is a reasonably similar representation of both men and women, but some academic departments, like engineering and the hard sciences, are largely male, while others, like English and sociology, have more women.

History and Current Magnitude of Occupational Segregation

In a very early study on occupational segregation, two sociologists, Bielby and Barron,[8] studied data from 393 firms in California and surveyed their employment patterns between 1959 and 1979. They scored each firm using their own measure of segregation by gender. If a firm exhibited no segregation, then its score would be 0, but if no men held jobs also held by women and vice versa, the score would be 100. This score was similar to the Duncan Index in that the higher numbers mark the greater the segregation. They were astonished to find that the average score was 93.4 and that 232 of the firms they studied were perfectly segregated! Even those firms that were integrated tended to have men and women with the same job titles working in different locations.

In fact, most research on the issue of occupational segregation consistently documents that, until the 1970s, jobs were largely split along gender lines and that there was little change in the distribution. But, beginning in about 1970 and continuing since then, the degree of occupational segregation between men and women has begun to diminish.

Table 8.6 shows the proportion of females represented in broad occupational classifications and the proportion of men and women in each occupation for two years, 1972 and 2001. Remember that these years cover a time period of remarkable increase in the proportion of women who were working in the labor market. Because the occupational categories are so broad, there could be, and probably is, substantial occupational segregation within the categories. As Table 8.5 shows [see columns (1) and (2)], in 1972 women were a relatively small minority—25% or less—in executive, administrative, and managerial jobs, and also in traditional blue-collar jobs such as precision production, craft, and

---

[8]W. Bielby and J. Barron, "Men and Women at Work: Sex Segregation and Statistical Discrimination," *American Journal of Sociology,* Vol. 91, No. 4, pp. 759–799, 1986.

Occupation	Percent Female		1972—Percent of All Workers		2001—Percent of All Workers	
	(1) 1972	**(2)** 2001	**(3)** Female	**(4)** Male	**(5)** Female	**(6)** Male
Executive, administrative, and managerial	20	46	4.6	11.5	15.0	15.3
Professional specialty	44	54	12.4	9.7	18.7	13.9
Technicians and related support	38	55	2.4	2.3	3.8	2.7
Sales	41	50	11.1	10.0	12.8	11.5
Administrative support, including clerical	75	79	31.5	6.3	20.3	5.4
Service occupations	61	60	21.2	8.3	17.5	10.3
Precision production, craft, and repair	5	9	1.6	19.4	2.0	18.6
Operators, fabricators, and laborers	24	22	13.4	25.9	6.1	19
Farming, forestry, and fishing	15	22	1.9	6.4	1.0	3.3
Total	—	—	100	100	100	100
Duncan Index	—	—	41.8		32.1	

Table 8.6 Changes in the Occupational Distribution of Men and Women, 1972 and 2001

Source: Bureau of Labor Statistics, *Employment and Earnings.* Jan. 1984, Table 1 and Jan. 2002, Table A-19.

repair; operators, fabricators, and laborers; and farming, forestry, and fishing. They dominated the clerical and services occupations. By 2001, there were some significant changes, especially in executive, administrative, and managerial positions where their representation more than doubled. There were also substantial increases in professional specialty jobs, technicians and related support, and even in farming, forestry, and fishing occupations. The overall proportion of female workers increased from 38.5 to 46.5%, reflecting the increase in the labor force participation rate for women and its slight decline for men.

Columns (3)–(6) show the percentage distribution of men and women across these occupational categories for 1972 and 2001. This information allows us to calculate the Duncan Index for each year. Because the Duncan Index fell from 41.8 to 32.1 over this time period, we can see that women have made inroads into traditional male occupations. Particularly large changes occurred in the two high-end occupational categories—executive, administrative and managerial where the proportion of women increased by 10 percentage points and professional specialty where it increased more than 6 percentage points. Women's representation dropped in administrative support including clerical, as well as operators, fabricators, and laborers.

Not only are women overrepresented in low-paying occupations, but even within a particular occupation, women also earn less than men. For the detailed occupations listed in Table 8.4, women earn less than men in every single one. Occupation is not, of course, a perfect measure of job skill and job duties. It is possible that men and women are doing different tasks and have different skills even within these quite narrow occupations. But is it likely that this is true for each occupation?

Figure 8.4 documents the difference in median weekly earnings for eight professional specialty occupations. Women physicians and lawyers earn less than 70% of what men in those occupations earn. Women who are accountants and college and university teachers earn about 75% of what men earn. The highest ratios are for psychologists and counselors, who earn 83% and 85%, respectively, of what men earn.

Finally, Figure 8.5 compares the extent of occupational segregation by gender in the United States with selected other countries. The data are from 1996 to 2000, depending on the country, and come from the International Labor Organization, an arm of the United Nations. In most of the countries shown, the data are based on 100 or more occupations, which is a substantial number and which, as we know, typically leads to a higher Duncan Index indicating more occupational segregation. The figures for the Russian Federation, Pakistan, and Iran are based on thirty or fewer occupations, and thus have a downward bias relative to the other countries.

Of these countries, Thailand appears to have by far the least occupational segregation by sex. Pakistan and Russia are also low, but this is partly the result of the fewer categories used (although that doesn't seem to help in Iran). The United States is actually at the low end among this set of countries, certainly lower than Austria, France, and Germany, for example. At the high end are Poland, Iran, and Belarus, with Duncan Index scores of 60% or higher.

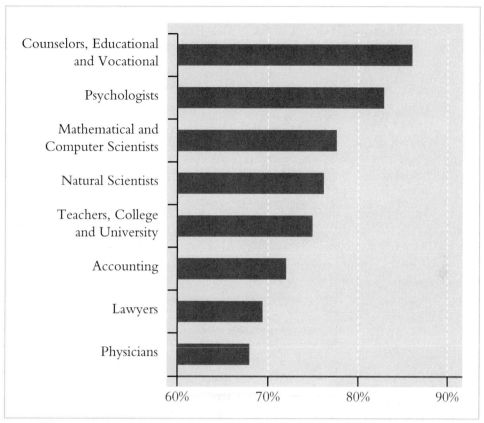

Figure 8.4   Female/Male Median Weekly Earnings Ratios for Selected Professional Occupations, 2002

The overall pattern with respect to both earnings and occupational distribution is, thus, complex, simultaneously offering both optimism and concern. The last few decades have been unparalleled for the absolute and relative improvement of women's labor market prospects. At the same time, progress has slowed a bit in the past decade, and a stubborn gap remains.

How Labor Markets Work—An Overview of Wage Determination

Because the subject of this chapter along with the next three is women's wages, it will be helpful to have a basic understanding of how wage rates are set in labor markets. The determination of wages is a complicated economic problem. Many factors determine a particular individual's wage rate—education, work

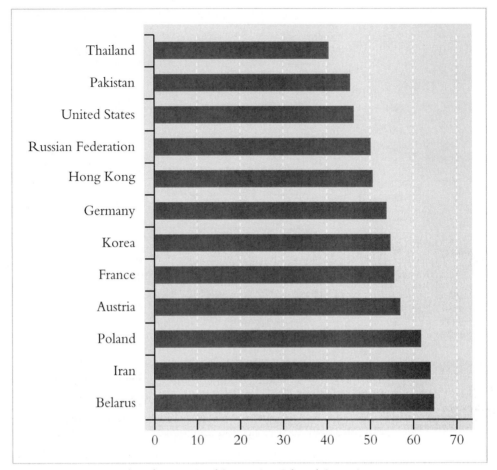

Figure 8.5 Duncan Index of Occupational Segregation, Selected Countries

experience, race and gender, whether the job is unionized, whether it is in the public or private sector, and so on. It is useful, however, to abstract from many of these factors so that we can focus on the underlying supply and demand factors and the way they interact to set the equilibrium wage rate. That approach will help us understand some issues surrounding the gender wage gap and also some of the policy solutions that have been proposed.

The Basics—Supply and Demand in Competitive Labor Markets

A **competitive labor market** is one in which there are many demanders and many suppliers and none has a significant impact on the market as a whole.

This definition follows the way a competitive output market is described. Whenever we use supply and demand analysis, there is always a price and a quantity. In the case of labor markets, the price is the wage rate, while the quantity is employment, usually measured by the number of workers. The goal of labor market analysis is to explain how the equilibrium wage rate and the corresponding equilibrium amount of employment are determined by the interaction of supply and demand forces.

The demand for labor comes from firms, where firms would include all kinds of employers such as universities and governments. Probably the most important thing to understand about labor demand is that it is an aspect of a firm's attempt to maximize its profits. You may be familiar with profit maximization viewed in terms of a firm choosing the best amount of output. For example, firms in competitive markets choose their output where the marginal cost of the last unit produced just equals the price of the product. Monopolistic firms choose their output where the marginal cost of the last unit produced just equals the marginal revenue.

In terms of employment, a similar kind of logic applies. Firms will choose their employment level where the additional cost to them of adding a worker just equals the revenues they will gain by selling the additional output they get from that worker. The additional cost of hiring another worker is, in the simplest case, just equal to the market wage rate (plus fringe benefits, which it is useful to ignore for the moment). The additional revenues are the product of two terms—the price of the product and the additional output that the worker produces. The additional output is called the **marginal product,** a concept we saw in the last chapter when we analyzed the value of time spent in household production. The additional revenue contributed by a worker is called that worker's **marginal revenue product** or MRP. In symbols, $MRP \equiv \Delta R / \Delta L =$ Price of Product $\times$ Marginal Product, where ΔR is the increase in the firm's revenues and ΔL is the change in the number of workers (usually 1). For example, if adding a worker increases output by 10 units and each unit sells for $1.00, then the worker contributes $10.00 of revenue to the firm and her $MRP = \$10.00$.

In a competitive labor market, the wage rate is exogenous, determined by the market as a whole, rather than by an individual firm. Whatever the wage ends up being, the firm must pay that wage to attract workers. This is the same idea as the price in a competitive market, which competitive firms take as given. So the firm's only decision is how many workers it wants to employ at that wage rate. The best way to see the logic of the answer is to think about what happens if a firm added another worker. It would incur costs equal to the wage rate, and it would receive revenues equal to the MRP of that worker. A profit-maximizing firm would be willing to hire that additional worker only if that worker's marginal revenue product was greater than the wage rate, that is, only if $MRP_L > w$. Why? Let's consider the opposite case. If $MRP_L < w$, the worker adds less to the firm's revenues than to its costs, and the firm's profit will, therefore, fall. If, however, $MRP_L > w$, then profits will rise when the worker is hired, paid w, and the resulting increase in output is sold at price P. Only when $MRP = w$ is it impossible for the firm either to add or to subtract workers in an effort to increase its profits. Thus, the profit-maximizing rule for employment is: hire workers up to the point where the marginal revenue product of the last worker just equals the wage rate.

Let's see what this rule implies about a firm's demand for labor. In almost all production settings, the marginal revenue product of a worker declines as more workers are employed, even if the potential employees are themselves equally productive. This generalization reflects the idea of declining marginal productivity, an idea we have seen several times already. Additional workers add less and less to a firm's output because the amount of capital is being held constant even as the number of workers is increasing. Declining marginal product means that as the number of workers increases, with the amount of capital held constant, the marginal product (the amount of additional output) decreases. This is one of the oldest economic laws of production, dating back to the economists of the early nineteenth century. (We assumed exactly the same thing when we analyzed the value of time spent in household production: The marginal product of household production time falls as more time is spent in household production.)

If the marginal revenue product falls as more workers are added and if firms are choosing employment at the level where the marginal revenue product just equals the wage rate, then the result is the usual negative relationship between price (here, the wage rate) and the quantity demanded (here, the number of workers employed). At high wage rates, a firm will hire relatively few employees. Because the cost is high, they will hire workers only up to the point where the marginal revenue product is equally high, which means limiting employment to a level where the marginal product is high. At lower wage rates, the firm will be willing to hire more workers, that is, they will be willing to expand employment until the marginal revenue product of the last worker hired is much lower. Falling marginal product, which results in falling marginal revenue product, is the root cause of the negative relationship between wages and employment.

To get the total demand for labor from all firms, we simply add up each firm's labor demand. Because each firm will hire more workers when the wage is lower, it follows that the market labor demand curve will also have a negative relationship between wages and employment.

Let's move on to the labor supply curve, which represents the behavior of workers. At relatively low wages, very few individuals may be willing to work in a particular occupation, perhaps just those who have a deep and abiding liking for it. As the wage rate rises, however, more and more persons will probably be attracted into the occupation. In other words, the labor supply curve will have a positive relationship between wages and the number of workers willing to work.

Figure 8.6 shows a typical labor demand and labor supply curve for the labor market as a whole. The wage rate is measured on the vertical axis and the

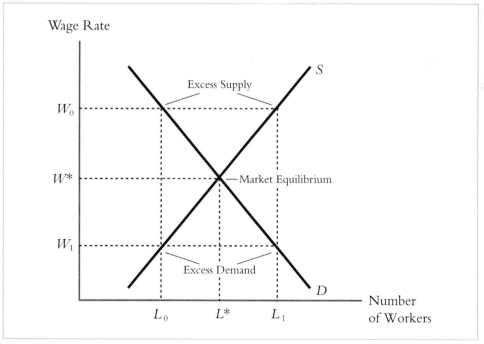

Figure 8.6   Labor Market Equilibrium

number of workers is measured along the horizontal axis. The graph in Figure 8.6 could represent the supply and demand for a particular occupation or for a particular labor market (e.g., all workers with the same underlying skills). It could, for example, be the supply and demand curves for college economics professors or nurses or secretaries. It looks like a conventional supply and demand diagram, although the basis for the shapes of the curves is very different than in the usual case. Exactly as explained earlier, the labor demand curve is downward-sloping, and the labor supply curve is upward-sloping.

Finding the Equilibrium Wage

Putting the supply and demand curves together shows how the wage rate is determined in a competitive labor market. As in every supply and demand diagram, the answer—the equilibrium wage rate and the associated amount of employment—is given where the curves intersect, that is where $S(W^*) = D(W^*)$. Here the curves intersect at a wage of W^* and total employment of L^* workers.

At every other possible wage, the amount of labor supplied and the amount of labor demanded are unequal. If the wage was higher than W^*, as at W_0, then $S(W_0) > D(W_0)$, and there is an excess supply of labor—more workers looking for work than positions available. This is shown in Figure 8.6 as the horizontal distance between the supply and demand curve at W_0. This excess supply can sometimes, although not always, be interpreted as unemployment.[9] Usually, the excess supply of labor will put downward pressure on wages, leading back to the equilibrium at W^*. As the wage falls toward W^*, the amount of labor demanded increases and the amount supplied falls, until they are equal at W^*. If, instead, the wage were lower than W^* (like W_1), then $S(W_1) < D(W_1)$, and there is excess demand or, equivalently, a labor shortage. This is shown in Figure 8.6 as the horizontal distance between the supply and demand curve at W_1. In this case, we would expect wages to rise back to market equilibrium at W^*, in the process reducing the amount of labor demanded and increasing the amount supplied. Only at a wage of W^* is there no pressure for the wage rate to change. Everything is in balance. Thus, W^* is the equilibrium wage rate, and L^* is the corresponding equilibrium amount of employment, given these particular supply and demand curves.

---

[9]To be officially counted as unemployed in the United States, a person needs not only to be jobless but also to have made a specific effort to find work. Jobless persons who are not looking for work are counted as not in the labor force. Some are counted as discouraged workers.

The Comparative Statics of Labor Markets—How Changes in Supply and Demand Affect Wages and Employment

Changes in labor supply and/or labor demand affect the equilibrium wage and employment in exactly the same way that changes in supply and demand affect prices. An increase in demand may occur either because the workers are more productive (their marginal product is higher) or because there is an increase in the demand for the product that the firm sells. In either case, the demand curve would shift up or rightward, with more workers demanded at every wage rate. This scenario is shown in Figure 8.7. At the original equilibrium, there is now a shortage, and the wage rate will rise, thereby increasing the amount of labor supplied and decreasing the amount of labor demanded. In the new market equilibrium, both wages and employment are higher than before. A decrease in labor demand, represented by a downward or inward shift of the labor demand curve, would cause wages and employment to fall. Sometimes, a legislated minimum wage or union bargaining or social convention may prevent the wage from falling back to the equilibrium. In that

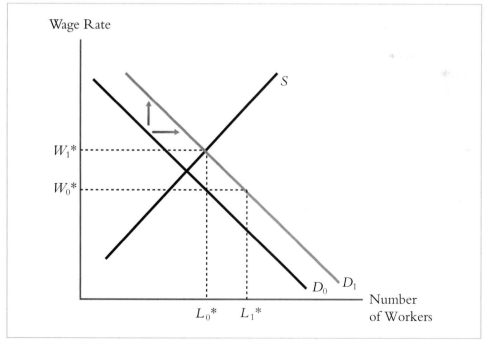

Figure 8.7   The Effect of an Increase in Demand on Wages and Employment

case, persistent excess supply will exist in the market. Some workers willing to work at the going wage will be unable to find employment.

Changes in labor supply involve a shift in the labor supply curve. An example of an increase in labor supply is shown in Figure 8.8. The supply curve shifts out or down so that there is now excess supply at the original equilibrium. This puts downward pressure on wages, yielding a new equilibrium with lower wages and larger employment, unless there are impediments to reaching equilibrium. In a sense, the wage must fall in order to accommodate the now larger number of people seeking employment in this occupation. If it doesn't, the result will likely be an increase in unemployment, as the labor market is in a situation of persistent excess supply. A decrease in labor supply would work just the opposite way. The labor supply curve would shift in or up, and the new equilibrium would feature a higher wage and smaller employment.

An Example—The Relative Wages of Young College Graduates

To fix these ideas about changes in labor supply and labor demand and their impact on wage rates, consider the situation of young college graduates over the time period from 1970 to 2000. During the 1970s, the wage premium for young college graduates relative to young high school graduates suddenly fell from 42 to 33% in the course of about six years. Many scholars thought this trend spelled the end of the golden era when a college education was a highly valuable economic asset. Then, just as suddenly, the trend reversed itself. The wage gap between young high school graduates and young college graduates started to rise, eventually exceeding 55% in the late 1990s, about where it currently stands. What happened? How can we explain these sharp changes in relative wage?

It turns out that supply and demand changes are an important part of this story. During the 1970s, there was a substantial and sudden increase in the number of young college graduates. This was due to two factors—rising college attendance rates coupled with an unusually large birth cohort, itself the "echo" of the baby boom of the 1950s. This was followed by a much smaller number of college graduates in the mid-1980s, now courtesy of the smaller birth cohorts that began in the early 1960s. Murphy and Welch[10] calculated that, on average, between 1965 and 1985, the number of college graduates in-

---

[10]Kevin Murphy and Finis Welch, "Wage Premiums for College Graduates," *Educational Researcher,* Vol. 8, No. 4, pp. 17–26, 1989.

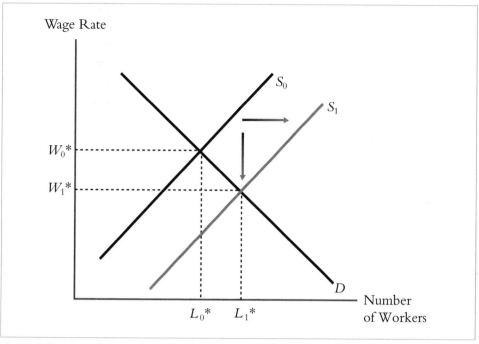

Figure 8.8   The Effect of an Increase in Labor Supply on Wages and Employment

creased annually by 2.4%. But in the mid-1970s, the average annual growth rate was well above this rate, and in the late-1970s through the mid-1980s, the growth rate was considerably below this.

These changes are easily represented in terms of shifts in the supply curve. Typically, the labor demand curve increases over time, reflecting broad increases in productivity. Taken by itself, this change would cause wages to rise. But a sharp increase in supply could outweigh this response, causing wages to fall. In this case, relative wages, not absolute wages, fell. Still, the general idea is the same: The sharp increase in supply caused the relative wages of college graduates to fall in the early 1970s.

Thereafter, two factors caused the relative wages of college graduates to skyrocket. One was the much smaller increase in the supply of college graduates. The other was almost certainly a huge increase in demand, part of what most economists think has been a widespread increase in the demand for more skilled workers. Those ingredients were necessary for the sharp increase in wages, accompanied by an increase in the number of college graduates employed, that was observed in the late-1980s and throughout the 1990s.

Thinking About Wage Rates

Finally, two more points about wage rates are important to appreciate. First, economists like to say that prices are signals that tell the participants in the economy the relative value of various goods. That, in fact, is really what prices are to an economist—highly efficient ways to communicate the value of resources. For example, when the price of a product suddenly rises, perhaps because of an increase in demand, that is a signal for consumers to cut back on their use of this product and for producers to increase their production. When utility-maximizing individuals and profit-maximizing firms act upon those signals, the result, under ideal conditions, is economic efficiency. In other words, resources in the economy are allocated where they are most valuable.

The wage rate is also a price, and in exactly the same way, the wage acts as a signal to workers and firms. Suppose, for example, that the demand for a firm's output fell. Ultimately, the price of the output would fall and that, in turn, would cause the firm's MRP curve to fall because the MRP depends on the price of the output. Following the rule for profit maximization, this firm would now hire fewer workers. While this wouldn't be a great outcome for the workers, it is absolutely essential from the standpoint of the economy as a whole. Those additional workers in that particular case are no longer as valuable to society as before because consumers don't value that output as much as before. It is necessary and proper for those workers to move to a use where they are more highly valued. Wages serve as a signal for that movement. Unless wages can adjust to reflect values, labor resources will be inefficiently allocated.

Second, there is no presumption that the equilibrium wage is a fair wage, a just wage, a living wage, or anything else of the sort. The equilibrium wage is no more and no less than the wage at which labor supply and labor demand just balance. Under the right (or perhaps wrong) circumstances, the equilibrium wage rate can be extremely low or, for that matter, extremely high. If demand is enormous and supply is small—think professional athletes, movie stars, and brain surgeons—the equilibrium wage is certain to be extremely high. If, however, demand is low and supply is large, just the opposite is likely to occur. The equilibrium wage will almost certainly be very low.

Not all labor markets are in a competitive equilibrium. In some cases, the supply of labor to an occupation may be restricted, thus keeping the wage rate above its market equilibrium level. In others, wages may be persistently above equilibrium because of legal requirements like the minimum wage, union bargaining, or social convention.[11] It is important to understand that even in these circumstances, supply and demand analysis continues to operate. If wages are held above the market equilibrium, then there will be persistent excess supply, probably resulting in unemployment. If wages are held below equilibrium, there will almost certainly be persistent labor shortages.

Summary

For as long as economic statistics have been collected, women have earned less than men. There is even a biblical reference (Leviticus 27:1–4) that refers to valuing women at thirty shekels of silver and men at fifty shekels, a ratio eerily similar to the 59% figure that held in the United States between 1960 and 1980. In the United States, the earnings ratio of median annual earnings for year-round full-time workers was well below 50% in the nineteenth century, in the 50 to 60% range for the first eighty years of the twentieth century, and above 70% since 1990. In the 1990s, the trend in the earnings ratio was erratic, but it has risen the past few years to an all-time high of more than 76%. The corresponding ratio for all workers, including part-time and part-year workers, was about 10 percentage points lower, but also at an all-time high.

When we looked more deeply at men's and women's earnings, some interesting patterns emerged. Race and ethnicity make a substantial difference in the earnings ratio. The ratio is about 10 percentage points higher for Black and Hispanic women than for White and Asian/Pacific Island women. Age also makes a difference—the earnings ratio in 2001 was highest for young women and declined steadily with age. There are also interesting within-cohort age patterns that reflect the progress of cohorts of men and women across their own careers. Even as the overall gender earnings ratio was rising, it was falling for women between the ages of 18 and 24 and 25 and 34 as they aged between 1978 and 1998 and rising for women between the ages of 35 and 44 and 45 and 54 over the same years. Education makes relatively little difference in the

---

[11]For example, it is probably true that the equilibrium wage in some academic disciplines is well below the salary that universities typically pay to new professors. One sign of this is the large number of quite-skilled new PhDs who are unable to find a job. Universities are reluctant to "take advantage" of this situation by offering a very low starting salary. Starting salaries do differ by academic department, but not by the full amount consistent with market equilibrium.

earnings ratio, with the exception of men and women with professional degrees, where the earnings ratio is quite low. And, not surprisingly, the distribution of men's and women's earnings differs as do their medians. Women are overrepresented among workers earning less than $20,000 and substantially underrepresented among workers earning more than $75,000. U.S. women are not faring particularly poorly by standards in many other similar countries, although that was conspicuously not the case twenty years ago. By the late-1990s, the earnings ratio in the United States had caught up with much of Europe, thanks to the sharp increase in the ratio during the 1980s.

Men and women still have occupational distributions that are quite different, although they are converging. The Duncan Index is the standard way to measure differences in the occupational distribution. In 2002, nearly 60% of all working men aged 16 and older and nearly three quarters of all working women aged 16 and older worked in just four occupational groups. But only two of the four groups were common to both men and women: women were overrepresented in clerical and service occupations, and men were overrepresented in precision production, craft, and repair and in sales. Since the early 1970s, women's representation in managerial and administrative positions has more than doubled. A Duncan Index computed for nine major occupation groups in 2001 is 32.1, down 9 percentage points from 1972. Compared to a selective list of other countries for which a Duncan Index is available, the United States has less occupational segregation.

In the last part of the chapter, we surveyed the basic theory of labor markets and how they operate to set equilibrium wages and employment. Labor demand curves are downward-sloping, reflecting the profit-maximizing behavior of firms in conjunction with declining marginal productivity. Labor supply curves to any occupation are typically upward-sloping, as higher wages draw in more workers. The market equilibrium occurs at a wage that just balances supply and demand. Where demand is small and supply is large, the equilibrium might well be at a very low wage. In the opposite circumstances (large demand, small supply), the equilibrium will almost certainly occur at a high wage rate. Changes in labor supply or labor demand inevitably change the equilibrium; in exactly the same way, the changes in supply or demand affect equilibrium prices. It is worth remembering that the wage rate is a price and, as such, conveys information to market participants about the value of labor in a particular kind of work. Later, as we consider policy proposals to intervene in the labor market, it will be important to keep that idea in mind.

We began this chapter by noting two very broad explanations for women's lower average earnings. Either women could have, on average, fewer valuable labor market skills or they could receive less for the skills they do have. In the former case, we might well recognize the resulting earnings differences as appropriate, reflecting the operation of a fair and impartial labor market. In the latter case, this would suggest the presence of labor market discrimination. In the next chapter, we explore these two possible explanations—and a few others—further.

Key Terms

competitive labor market   296

Duncan Index   289

marginal product   297

marginal revenue product   297

occupational segregation   285

year-round full-time (YRFT) workers   276

CHAPTER 9

The Gender Gap in Earnings: Explanations

Introduction

In this chapter, we turn to explanations of the gender gap in earnings and occupation. We noted in the last chapter that there were two very broad explanations of these gender gaps—one emphasizing possible differences in skills and the other emphasizing differences in treatment in the labor market. First, we examine skill differences, using the *theory of human capital*, one of the most widely used and influential parts of economic theory. We examine whether there are any reasons why women might, on average, have less human capital than men. The ideas developed earlier about the division of labor in families will be relevant here. Second, we examine *economic models of labor market discrimination*. We consider a variety of models, developed by Gary Becker, that analyze how discriminatory feelings or preferences about an individual's race or sex or other personal characteristic on the part of employers, employees, or customers affect market equilibrium wages and prices. Finally, we consider other approaches, including theories of occupational segregation.

Human Capital—The Supply of Skills to the Labor Market

Human Capital Basics

The phrase, **human capital,** stands for the skills that workers possess and bring to the labor market. These skills are the basis for the earnings they receive. The most important characteristic of these skills is that they don't just arise by themselves, but rather are the result of costly investments that increase an individual's productivity. Prior to the development of the human capital model,[1] economists mostly viewed workers as "raw labor," a factor of production whose productivity and skills were "givens" of the problem and were not considered further. Using the language we introduced in Chapter 2, productivity was *exogenous*, not the object of inquiry or analysis. Why some workers earned more than others was totally outside of economic analysis. Without a way of explaining why some workers were more productive than others, there was no way to explain and account for the personal distribution of income.

The other important factor of production in traditional economic analysis is capital, which represents machinery and the like and which differs from labor in that it must be produced before it can be used. Firms make investments in capital based on an analysis of the purchase cost of capital compared to the stream of benefits (higher profits) that it could provide.

From the human capital perspective, individuals are more like capital, with valuable skills that are produced via an investment process. As newborns and young children, most of us know relatively little and certainly have, with rare exceptions, few labor market skills.[2] But we typically acquire skills over time, increasing our productivity and our labor market value. Because acquiring these skills is costly in terms of time and resources, individuals can be viewed as if they were capital in human form or simply, human capital. Labor, like capital, becomes a produced factor of production. The activities that create human capital are called **investments in human capital.**

There are, of course, many important differences between human capital and physical capital.[3] For one thing, human capital is highly mobile, unlike most capital. It naturally and inevitably goes where you go, so immigrants can and do bring their human capital along with them, even if they must leave their

---

[1]Some of the central ideas in human capital theory were presented by Adam Smith in the eighteenth century in his famous book, *The Wealth of Nations*. The modern treatment was pioneered in the early 1960s by T. W. Schultz and especially by Gary Becker in his book, *Human Capital*. Both Schultz and Becker were awarded the Nobel Prize in Economics for their contributions to the theory of human capital.

[2]Shirley Temple was an exception, as were Mozart, Michael Jackson, and Haley Joel Osment, who played the kid who saw dead people in the movie *The Sixth Sense*.

[3]When the human capital model was reintroduced into economics in the early 1960s, there were heated debates about whether it was demeaning to people to analyze them as if they were capital goods. Nothing about the idea of human capital is meant to imply that people can or should be treated as if they were machinery. Many academics were particularly worried about the idea of applying investment analysis to higher education. It turned out that they had nothing to worry about—education passed the investment test with flying colors.

physical capital behind. Human capital cannot, however, be inherited as other capital goods can. Also, human capital cannot be sold or used as collateral for a loan, as physical capital can.

The two most important forms of human capital investment are education and on-the-job training. Thinking of education as an investment in human capital focuses attention on its costs and benefits. The costs of an educational investment come in two forms—direct costs and the opportunity cost of foregone earnings. For example, earning a college degree involves substantial direct costs of tuition and books plus substantial opportunity costs of the earnings that could have been obtained with full-time work. In contrast, the direct and opportunity costs of finishing fifth grade are often very close to zero, at least for students attending public school in the United States in the twenty-first century.[4] Both kinds of costs are relevant to thinking about the value of the investment. The fact that one kind of cost is out-of-pocket and the other is an opportunity cost makes no difference.

The labor market benefits of a college education are the higher earnings that an individual with more human capital receives. Currently, the earnings differential between college graduates and high school graduates is at an all-time high. Typically, individuals receive these benefits over a long time period, for example, their entire working life. There may be other nonmarket benefits as well, for example, appreciating art or music or whatever.[5]

On-the-job training or OJT for short refers to the many skills that workers learn after formal schooling that make them more productive in the labor market. They usually learn these skills at work, which accounts for the name OJT. OJT can be in the form of **general training,** which means that the skills learned will be equally valuable in the firm in which they are received *and* in other firms, or **specific training,** which means that the skills are more valuable in the firm in which they are received than in other firms. *Completely specific training* is valuable only in the firm in which it is received and usually reflects knowledge of procedures and/or people that are unique to that firm.[6]

---

[4]The private costs of attending the fifth grade—those borne by the individual or his/her family—may be close to zero. Public costs, which include the cost of all resources (teachers' salaries, supplies, buildings, etc.) are certainly not equal to zero.

[5]Investment in human capital may also provide external benefits, which are benefits that accrue to other persons.

[6]The same general versus specific distinction also applies to human capital more generally. There is general human capital—widely useful—and specific human capital—useful only in a narrow sphere.

Some jobs provide the opportunity to invest in a great deal of OJT; other jobs—dead-end jobs, we might call them—provide little or no opportunity to learn new skills.

Just like investments in education, investments in OJT carry costs and provide benefits. The benefits, again, are the higher earnings made possible by the additional human capital. The costs are entirely opportunity costs because workers almost never pay their employers directly for the opportunity to learn skills. Here the costs arise because jobs that provide extensive learning (investing) opportunities will offer lower wages than otherwise identical jobs with less of an up-side. If that weren't the case, no worker would want to take the otherwise equivalent job with less OJT. Consequently, the cost is the difference between what the worker earns in a job where he/she is investing in OJT and what the same worker could earn in an otherwise similar job without investment in OJT.

Evaluating Investments in Human Capital

Because an investment in human capital has both costs and benefits, we can investigate what the rate of return on the investment is, exactly as we might with an investment in machinery or other physical capital. Doing that correctly involves taking careful account of the fact that investment costs are incurred in the present, but the benefits are received in the future, often far in the future. For example, some of the benefits of a college education are earned at the very end of your working career, as much as forty years in the future. Why does it matter if benefits are received in the future and costs are incurred now? Benefits received in the future are worth less than their face value in today's dollars because if an individual has that same amount of money today, he/she could invest it at the market interest rate and earn interest on it until that future date, by which time it would have grown to a much larger amount. As a result, having the money sooner, rather than later, is valuable.

For any sum of money that would be received in the future, there is some smaller sum of money today that would, if it were invested at the market rate of interest, exactly accumulate to that larger sum in that future year. That smaller current sum of money is called the **present value** of the future sum. In the appendix, we review present value analysis and show exactly how it works. Here, we just summarize the key points that we need for our analysis of possible gender differences in human capital investment.

A very specific formula relates the value of sums of money available at different dates. To find the present value of a future sum, simply divide the future sum by $(1 + r)^T$, where T is the number of years in the future and r is the market interest rate expressed as a decimal.[7] For example, if the interest rate is 5%, the present value of $1000 available in ten years is $1000/1.05^{10}$ or $613.91. If the $1000 were received twenty years in the future, it would be worth even less—$1,000/1.05^{20}$ or $376.89, to be precise. Note how much smaller the present value is than its face value. It is very important to appreciate that the further in the future a sum of money is received, the lower its present value is.

An investment in human capital typically provides benefits for many years, for example, from entrance into the labor market until retirement. To calculate the present value of the full set of benefits, simply divide each year's benefits (the higher earnings) by $(1 + r)^T$. If the benefits are denoted as $B_0, B_1, \ldots B_T$, then the present value is

$$PV(B_1, \ldots, B_T) = \tag{1}$$

$$B_1/(1 + r) + B_2/(1 + r)^2 + \cdots + B_T/(1 + r)^T = \sum_{t=1}^{T} \frac{B_t}{(1 + r)^t}$$

where Σ, the Greek letter sigma, is the summation sign. Note that benefits received in the first year are divided by $(1 + r)$, benefits in the second year are divided by $(1 + r)^2$, and so on, up to year T. The term at the end involving Σ is just a compact way to express a long sum of terms; the summation starts with $t = 1$ and goes through $t = T$. The summation thereby reproduces the longer addition list on the other side of the equals sign. This is a very important expression that you should know.

To evaluate how good an investment is, economists compute its **internal rate of return.** The internal rate of return is a measure of the net value or profitability of an investment that reflects how large the benefits are relative to the costs, after properly accounting for the different timing of the costs and benefits using present value analysis. To be precise, the internal rate of return to an investment is the interest rate at which the present value of all the benefits just

---

[7] This formula applies in the simple case where interest is received once a year at the end of the year. Today, most interest is paid continuously. In that case, the formula is conceptually similar but involves that strange numerical constant, e. For our purposes, however, this formula is perfectly fine.

equals the cost of the investment. It is the interest rate r^* that solves the following expression:[8]

$$\sum_{t=1}^{T} \frac{B_t}{(1 + r^*)^t} = C \tag{2}$$

The left-hand side of this expression is the present value of the benefits, using interest rate r^*. The right-hand side of the expression is the costs, which are assumed to be entirely incurred in the current time period; that's why we don't need to compute a present value for them.[9] If the benefits are very large relative to the costs, then the internal rate of return will be large as well: It will take a high interest rate to reduce the present value of benefits to the smaller level of the costs. If the benefits are not that much larger than the costs, then the internal rate of return will be very small. An investment with a low internal rate of return is unlikely to be an attractive investment from an economic standpoint.

To determine whether any particular investment in human capital is worth making, an individual should compare the internal rate of return to the market interest rate. The market interest rate represents the rate at which an individual can borrow the funds to finance the investment or, alternatively, the rate at which he/she could invest the proceeds. The decision rule is simple: If the internal rate of return is greater than the market interest rate, then the investment makes economic sense. If the internal rate of return is smaller, however, there is no economic basis for proceeding. This means that anything that lowers the internal rate of return to an investment in human capital may cause an individual to forego the investment entirely. Could that apply to women and thereby cause them to invest in less human capital than men?

---

[8]In most equations, the variable that is being solved for (here, r^*) is all by itself on the left-hand side of the equation. Because this computation involves a long summation, that expression is impossibly complicated. Equation (2) shows the solution indirectly. As a practical matter, internal rates of return are almost always solved with a financial spreadsheet program that finds the solution by trial and error in an iterative procedure.

[9]To compute an internal rate of return with a spreadsheet program, set up a column of net benefits, treating the cost as a negative benefit. You will need to provide a starting value for the internal rate of return; the program then solves for the solution by trial and error. If the present value of benefits at the starting value is greater than the costs, the program recomputes present value using a slightly higher interest rate; if the present value of benefits at the starting value is negative, a lower interest rate is used. The program quickly solves for the internal rate of return.

Gender Differences in Human Capital

Theory—Why There Might be Gender Differences in Human Capital

Suppose a woman expects to take some time off from working in the labor market for family responsibilities. This was, as we have seen, certainly the norm in previous generations, and even today, it is certainly not uncommon. In those years, the benefits to any investment in human capital will be zero. Alternatively, if a woman works part-time to accommodate family responsibilities, her benefits will be positive, but smaller than they might otherwise be. These patterns of labor force participation lower the internal rate of return for two related reasons: First, total benefits are lower, and, second, the benefits that are lost are those with a high present value because they typically come relatively early in a woman's adult life.

Let's consider a specific example of how periods of not working in the labor market affect the internal rate of return. Figure 9.1 shows actual mean earnings in 1999 by age for women between the ages of 18 and 64 with college and high school degrees who were year-round full-time workers. The data come from the Census Bureau's annual survey of individual earnings. The earnings are by five-year age brackets, which is why the two lines have flat regions and then sudden jumps. For high-school graduates, earnings start at age 18, while they start at age 22 for college graduates.

We can use this data to compute the internal rate of return to a college degree for women under different assumptions about work. To do that, we will follow standard practice and assume that the foregone earnings during college are measured by what is *actually* earned by the high school graduates during those years (i.e., between the ages of 18 and 22). These are the opportunity costs. That is, admittedly, far from perfect, but it's probably in the ballpark. To that, we will need to add an estimate of direct costs. Similarly, the benefits can be measured by the difference in average earnings between women college graduates and women high school graduates. As you can see, the benefits are substantial. The earnings gap is about $14,000 at ages 25 to 29, nearly $20,000 at ages 30 to 34, and peaks at more than $23,000 at ages 35 to 39.[10] Thus,

---

[10]We also are assuming that current college and high school graduates will, when they are older, earn what is actually earned in 1999 by women at older ages. This assumption also is not perfect, but it is good enough for our purposes.

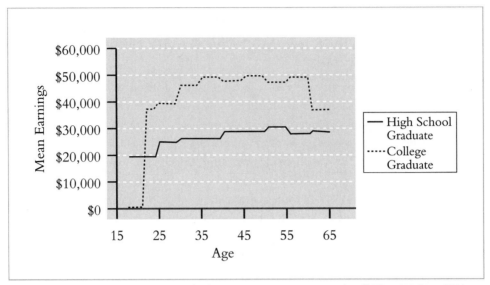

Figure 9.1   Mean Earnings by Age and Education, Women, Year-Round Full-Time Workers, 2001

Figure 9.1 shows the costs and benefits associated with full-time year-round work throughout a woman's career.[11]

Figure 9.2 shows the resulting internal rate of return for four career work paths—working all years and taking five, ten, and fifteen years off from work, beginning at age 25. Out-of-pocket expenses are assumed to be $15,000 per year for four years. If both college-educated and high-school educated women work all years from graduation until retirement, the internal rate of return for a college degree is a very respectable 11.0%. (Using comparable data for men, the internal rate of return for college is 12.4%). With rates of return like these, a college investment is a very good investment, indeed. What happens, though, if a woman takes time out of her career? If both the college graduate and the high school graduate left the labor market at age 25 and returned to year-round full-time work at age 29, the internal rate of return to the college degree falls about 2 percentage points to 8.8%. If a woman leaves the labor market for ten years (from age 25 to age 34), the internal rate of re-

---

[11]This is not quite correct because the women who are working year-round full-time at, say, age 40 or age 45, might not have worked year-round full-time in all previous years. The numbers in Figure 9.1 probably understate what could be earned with year-round full-time work in every year.

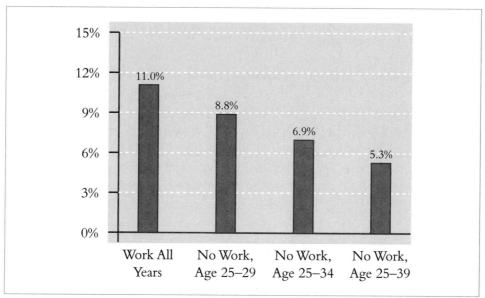

Figure 9.2   Internal Rates of Return for a Woman's College Education with Different Work Force Patterns

turn falls about another two points, all the way down to 6.9%. And with fifteen years out of the labor force, the internal rate of return is just 5.3%, less than half the value with full-time continuous work. Imagine how low the rate of return would have been for women born in the early decades of the twentieth century for whom market work often ceased with marriage. See Box 9.1 for evidence on the return to a college degree for women during the baby boom.

The impacts on the internal rate of return are so large because the years of absence from the labor market are early career years with high present value. It is easy to see that leaving the labor market can make a huge difference in the internal rate of return of the investment. If the rate of return is low enough, it may not make economic sense to make the investment in the first place. And that, in turn, would result in women having less human capital than men.

Here's another example of the internal rate of return involving investment in on-the-job training. As we discussed earlier, most jobs provide a worker with not only a wage rate but also the opportunity to acquire human capital (learn

Box 9.1   The Return for a College Degree During the Baby Boom

Claudia Goldin provides estimates of the internal rate of return for women to a college degree in the mid-1950s.[12] The median female college graduate in that time period married in the year of her graduation, worked for four years, and then exited the labor force for about eight years, returning at age 35. For high school graduates, Goldin assumed that they, too, worked four years after school, took ten years off, and then returned to work. College-educated women earned about 30% more than high-school educated women at the beginning of their careers and about 40% later on. With further allowance for out-of-pocket college costs, Goldin estimated an internal rate of return for college graduation of about 5%, certainly no goldmine and about half of the internal rate of return for men at that time. She notes that the income premium to female college graduates was about the same as for men. Their lower internal rate of return was entirely a function of their briefer employment.

College was, however, somewhat more financially lucrative for women if viewed more broadly. Goldin notes that college attendance and especially college graduation greatly increased the probability that a woman married a college graduate. For example, only 10% of high school graduate women were married to a college graduate, compared to two thirds of all college graduate women. And, of course, these more-educated men earned more than their less-educated counterparts. Goldin reports that, on average, the husband of a college graduate woman earned almost 40% more than the husband of a high school graduate woman. Taking all this into account, Goldin estimates that the "full" internal rate of return to college for women was in the 10 to 11% range rather than the 5% associated with its direct labor market impact.

skills) that will be valuable subsequently in terms of higher wages. This learning on the job is precisely what economists mean when they talk about on-the-job training. Jobs that provide OJT will typically pay lower current wages

[12]Claudia Goldin, "Career and Family: College Women Look to the Past" in *Gender and Family Issues in the Workplace*, edited by Francine Blau and Ronald Ehrenberg, New York: Russell Sage Foundation, 1997, pp. 20–58.

than jobs that offer no training but compensate for that with higher wages after the training is received. In that way, acquiring OJT is a human capital investment with costs and benefits.

In the case of general training, the skills learned are widely valuable. In that case, human capital theory shows that individuals receive *all* the benefits of training and pay *all* the costs. In the case of specific training, the skills learned have a more limited market, and in the extreme case of completely specific training, the skills are valuable only in the current firm. Completely specific training often reflects knowledge of procedures and/or people that are unique to a firm. University department coordinators are a good example of workers who have a great deal of knowledge of forms, people, and procedures that are highly university-specific. In the case of specific training, it turns out that firms and workers share the costs and the benefits of investment in training.

Precisely as in the case of education, it is possible to think about the rate of return to the investment in OJT. Suppose a job has a starting salary that is $2500 lower than another otherwise similar job but provides more on-the-job training—enough more that your earnings would increase by $500 per year thereafter for as long as you stay on the job. (Again, this is a simplified arithmetic example; in the real world, the benefits might well increase over time.) This is the typical pattern of earnings in jobs with more on-the-job training—a lower starting salary but a greater increase in earnings over time. If you use that on-the-job training for ten full years, the internal rate of return to the $5000 investment is over 15%. If, instead, you use the training for only six years and then drop out of the labor market, the return drops below 5.5%.

In the case of specific training, a firm will want to make sure that any worker that they train will stay with the firm long enough that it can recoup its costs and earn a reasonable rate of return on its investment. So here, too, women's history of intermittent labor force participation may make firms more reluctant to offer them jobs with substantial specific training.

Differences in labor force participation are not the only thing that could lead to differences in internal rates of return. Suppose that, because of labor market discrimination, women don't earn as much as men for the human capital they possess. Suppose opportunities for advancement are limited, no matter how much human capital they have. In the OJT example, suppose a woman received only $400 more per year after training, rather than $500, because she wasn't promoted. Even if she expected to have the same ten-year career as a man, her rate of return would be just over 9.5%, not the 15% that a man might receive. Again, it is easy to see that if labor market discrimination lowered rates of return sufficiently, a woman might rationally choose not to make a costly investment in human capital. "What's the point?" she might reason. I can do nearly as well without making the investment.[13]

Let's summarize the main points about the human capital approach to gender earnings differences. An investment in human capital has a financial return that can be measured by the internal rate of return. Rates of return are affected by many factors, but especially by participation in the labor market and by discrimination, both of which affect the benefits received. Individuals make decisions about investment in human capital on the basis of the rate of return it offers. If women anticipate spending some years out of the labor force for family responsibilities, this will lower the internal rate of return to human capital investment. Under these circumstances, they might well rationally choose to invest in less human capital. The ultimate source of these potential labor market human capital differences by gender is the traditional organization of households, with its characteristic division of labor on the basis of gender, that we discussed in Chapter 3. Labor market earnings depend on the amount of human capital a worker has. If women invest in less human capital than men, they will earn less than men and, in some sense, deserve to earn less.

Evidence—Are There Actually Gender Differences in Human Capital?

The actual amount of human capital that an individual has is not directly observed. For example, it is not possible to say that a certain person has 17 units of human capital or 42 units or any other number. That doesn't mean that the concept isn't useful. Human capital acquired through schooling is usually assumed to be related to the number of years of completed schooling, while human capital in the form of on-the-job training is usually assumed to be associated with the number of years of work experience.

---

[13]This kind of argument applies with great force in the case of race discrimination in the United States, South Africa, and elsewhere. Think about the human capital investment situation facing Black workers in the time period when overt discrimination was rampant and not illegal. They had very few incentives to acquire skills because they would be unlikely to reap the benefits. Note that this means that discrimination may cast a long shadow—its labor market effects are felt a long time after it may have been eliminated. An argument like this is sometimes used to support affirmative action programs.

Years of education and years of work experience are by far the two most important factors used by economists to explain differences in wages among individuals and between men and women. If human capital differences are responsible for at least some portion of the gender gap in earnings, there must be differences between men and women in these measures. Let's look at the facts.

GENDER DIFFERENCES IN EDUCATION Dating back to at least 1940, women and men have graduated from high school in nearly even proportions, with women about a percentage point or two ahead through 1970. Since then, there has been almost no difference at all. The overall high school graduation rate rose over this time period from about one in four to more than four out of five. In 2002, 83.8% of men and 84.4% of women age 25 or older were high school graduates.

In terms of college, however, the story is quite different. Figure 9.3 shows the proportion of men and women aged 25 to 34 who were college graduates, from 1940 to 2002. In 1940, just 7% of men and 5% of women between the ages of 25 and 34 were college graduates. These men and women were born between 1906 and 1915, and college graduation was a relatively rare event, no matter what the person's gender was. Not much changed during the World War II period, but after the war, the GI Bill led to a sharp increase in college graduation rates for men that is evident by the early- to mid-1950s. By 1960, men were nearly twice as likely to be college graduates as women—14.5% versus 7.5%. Over the next two decades through 1980, men's and women's college graduation rates moved up together, maintaining about a 7 percentage point difference. In 1980, about 20% of women and 27% of men, aged 25–34, were college graduates.

From that point on, however, men's and women's graduation rates followed very different trends. The men's rate drifted downward steadily throughout the 1980s, falling more than 4 percentage points, while the women's rate continued upward at a steady, if slower, rate. In 1991, women between the ages of 25 and 34 were, for the first time, more likely to be college graduates than their male counterparts. The college graduation rate for men started increasing again beginning in the mid-1990s, but the upward trend for women was even greater. As a result, we see a different kind of gender gap in college graduation rates among young men and women. In 2002, nearly a third of 25- to 34-year-old women were college graduates compared to 28.5% of young

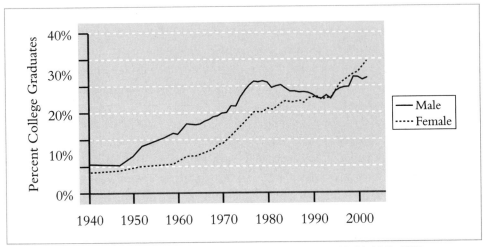

Figure 9.3   Percent College Graduates Among Men and Women, Age 25–34, 1940–2002

men. It is clear that this gap will persist or even expand in the near future. In 2001, men accounted for only 41% of new college graduates.

When we look at all age groups as of 2002, the historical pattern from Figure 9.3 shows up in a different way. Figure 9.4 shows the proportion of college graduates among men and women by age bracket. Among 25 to 34 year olds, women are more likely to be college graduates than men, exactly as just noted. For 35 to 44 year olds, the proportions are just about equal, but among the older men and women, there is a decided gender gap favoring men. For the 45 to 54 year olds, there is about a 3 percentage point difference, and for the 55 to 64 year olds, the difference is a full 10 percentage points. Among all persons age 25 and older, men are still more likely to be college graduates because of the much higher graduation rates of men in the earlier years. In 2002, 28.5% of men over age 25 were college graduates compared to 25.1% of women.

The 2002 gender difference in the proportion of college graduates—3.4 percentage points—represents the lowest differential in years. Throughout the 1970s and 1980s, the proportion of men who were college graduates was about 6 to 7 percentage points higher than the proportion of women—50 to 60% more than the figure for women. In the 1940s through 1960s, the absolute gap was smaller—about 3 to 5 percentage points—but because college graduation was much rarer then, this was a very large proportional difference. So historically men have had more education than women, although the dif-

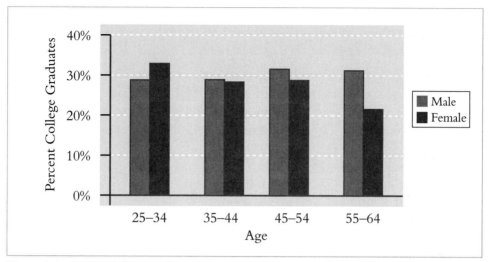

Figure 9.4   Percent College Graduates by Gender and Age, 2002

ference is narrowing, and the advantage is in the other direction entirely for younger men and women.

The specifics of higher education for women has changed as well. At the undergraduate level, women have made some inroads into the traditionally male fields. In 1970, women accounted for less than 1% of engineering degrees, 10% of business degrees, and less than 15% of degrees in the physical sciences and in computer and information sciences. By 2001, the proportion of females in engineering jumped to 18%; the proportion in business, to 50%; and the proportions in physical sciences and computer and information sciences, to about 40% and 30%, respectively.

Women are also far more likely than before to receive advanced degrees—master's degrees, doctorates, and other professional degrees. In 1962, among all persons with more than four years of college, just over a quarter were women. Forty years later, women represent almost half (46%) of all persons with an advanced degree. They are now a majority of those with master's degrees, a third of those with professional degrees, and 30% of all people with a doctorate. Among younger men and women, there is now a gender gap in favor of women, just as in college degrees. Among all 25 to 29 year olds, women earned nearly 60% of the degrees—61% of the master's degrees, 55% of the professional degrees, and 50% of the doctorates. Among 30 to 34 year olds, women are also the majority—54% of all degrees, including 56% of master's degrees, 51% of professional degrees, and 45% of doctorates. At all older ages, however, men still outnumber women among those with some kind of post-baccalaureate degree, reflecting the time trend we saw in Figure 9.3.

The increase in the proportion of women in professional schools has been particularly dramatic. As recently as 1970, women received just 1% of dental degrees, 5% of law and business degrees, and about 10% of medical degrees. In 2000, the corresponding proportions were all 40% or above, representing a five-, ten-, or, in the case of dentistry, 40-fold increase. In terms of both master's degrees and PhDs, women still lag in engineering, computer and information sciences, and physical sciences, where they make up less than one sixth of degree earners.

In terms of the overall educational human capital of men and women, it appears that men held a clear advantage for many years. Women are now catching up, including their representation in graduate and professional degree programs. On average, though, men still have more education than women in the general population. We would expect this to have an impact on wages. Women, on average, might well earn less, partly because they had, on average, less education than men especially in earlier time periods. But because the difference in educational attainment is now relatively small (and declining), the impact on wages probably wouldn't be too large. It is also possible that because women's labor force participation is strongly related to their education (see Figure 7.3 in Chapter 7), there might be a smaller difference in education between working men and women than between all men and women.

GENDER DIFFERENCES IN WORK EXPERIENCE On the human capital side, the main suspect in explaining the gender wage gap is the gender difference in years of work experience. Historically, as we discussed in Chapter 7, women have been far less likely to be in the paid workforce. In the first third of the century, participation in the paid labor market was largely confined to women before marriage and to women who did not marry. The labor force participation rate for married women was just 10% in the early part of the century and only 20% in 1950. The gender gap in participation rates didn't begin to close until the 1960s and 1970s, and even now there is a 15 percentage point gender difference in participation rates. Thus, because women's labor force participation rates were substantially lower than men's, it follows as a matter of arithmetic, that women must on average have accumulated fewer years of work experience than men. It wouldn't be surprising if this contributed to the gender gap in earnings.

In fact, the gender difference in work experience is more complex than these time trends suggest. Claudia Goldin's research on labor force participation by married women, which we discussed in Chapter 7, showed an important changing pattern involving life cycle patterns of work. Table 9.1 is an extract from Table 7.3. It shows by age bracket the labor force participation rate of White married women for three cohorts of women, each born twenty years apart from 1886 to 1926. Given the ages and birth years involved, this table covers the labor market experience of married White women from 1920 (born 1886–1895, aged 25 to 34) to 1980 (born 1926–1935, aged 45 to 54). Look carefully at the entries in the first row for women born near the end of the nineteenth century. Not only was their labor force participation rate incredibly low when they were young married women (7.7%), but it increased very little as they aged. One way to think of these numbers—imperfect, but useful—is that 7.7% of the women worked essentially steadily from age 25 to 54; 2.1% (9.8% − 7.7%) entered the labor market between the ages of 35 and 44; and another 0.3%, between the ages of 45 and 54. Thought of that way, more than three quarters (7.7%/10.1%) of the women working between the ages of 45 and 54 in 1940 had been working continuously for the previous twenty years.

The figures for the 1906–1915 birth cohort indicate that not only are the participation rates higher, but there is a substantial increase with age. This increase represents the phenomenon of labor market reentry by married women as they and, more importantly, their children aged. Thus, the participation rate increased almost 9 percentage points between those aged 25 to 34 and those aged 35 to 44 and increased another 13.3 percentage points over the next ten years. Applying the same reasoning to the 1906–1915 birth cohort that we used for the older cohort, we see that only 43% (16.7%/38.6%) of the women in the labor market at ages 45 to 54 in 1960 had been there twenty years before. This means that the average total work experience of this

Year of Birth	Age 15–24	Age 25–34	Age 35–44	Age 45–54
1886–1895	n.a.	7.7	9.8	10.1
1906–1915	13.3	16.7	25.3	38.6
1926–1935	24.9	26.7	44.4	53.4

Table 9.1 Life Cycle Labor Force Participation Rates for White Women by Age and Birth Cohort

Source: Claudia D. Goldin, *Understanding the Gender Gap,* New York: Oxford University Press, 1990.

cohort of working women at ages 45 to 54 must have been lower than for the earlier cohort because so many more of them were reentrants who had relatively little work experience. For the cohort shown in the last row of the table, exactly 50% (26.7%/53.4%) of the women in the labor market at ages 45 to 54 in 1980 had been in the labor market twenty years previously. The average total work experience of this cohort of working women at ages 45 to 54 is therefore higher than in 1960, but still substantially lower than in 1940.

Goldin emphasizes the importance of this life cycle pattern of labor force participation for understanding the trend in the gender gap in wages. In the early part of the century, relatively few women worked, but those who did, worked more or less continuously, year after year. Thus, differences in years of work experience between *working* men and *working* women were relatively small. Later in the century, more women worked, but relatively few worked continuously. As a result, a greater proportion of women working at any point in time had previously been intermittent labor force participants. Thus, differences in years of work experience between working men and women were larger than in the past. Paradoxically, the increase in women's labor force participation, which took the form of reentry into the labor market, had the initial effect of increasing the gender gap in years of work experience among working women.

Goldin notes that this pattern meant that relatively few White married women established careers in the same way that men did. Rather, she writes "married working women who entered the labor force in their middle years had, by and large, entered a rather new world. . . . They were not bringing to the labor market recently acquired skills. Many were, instead, reentering occupations they had left many years, or possibly decades, before, and most were inadequately prepared for their new labor market roles" (p. 23).

James Smith and Michael Ward have made a similar point in their research on the historical patterns of labor force participation by women.[14] They computed the average accumulated years of labor market experience from 1920 to 1986 for *all* women and for the subset of women who were *working* in those years. Table 9.2 shows the figures for working women at ages 25, 35, and 45. In 1920, average work experience among working women at age 35 was almost 12 years. One way to appreciate this number is to realize that if work began with a woman's graduation from high school at age 18, the maximum

---

[14]James P. Smith and Michael Ward, "Women in the Labor Market and in the Family," *Journal of Economic Perspectives,* Vol. 3, No. 1, pp. 9–23, 1989.

Year	Age		
	25	35	45
1920	5.6	11.8	16.4
1950	5.9	10.6	17.0
1980	6.2	11.7	18.3
1986	6.5	13.5	19.3

Table 9.2 Average Years of Work Experience for Working Women by Age and Year

Source: James P. Smith and Michael Ward, "Women in the Labor Market and in the Family," *Journal of Economic Perspectives,* Vol. 3, No. 1, 1990. Adapted from Table 2. Copyright © 1990 by the American Economic Association. Reprinted with the permission of the author and publisher.

work experience at age 35 would be 17 years. So the average working woman at age 35 had worked more than two thirds of potential years beginning at age 18. At age 45, average work experience was more than 16 years, or almost 60% of the possible work years since age 18.

By looking down the columns, we can see how average work experience changed at each age between 1920 and 1986. Remember that this is a time period in which the labor force participation rate increased by more than 30 percentage points, from 24% to 55%. Average labor force work experience among working women, however, increased very little at all. At age 35, average work experience actually fell by 0.1 years between 1920 and 1980, before rising by about two years between 1980 and 1986. Average work experience at age 45 also rose very little, not quite 3 years in more than 60 years. These figures are consistent with the information that Goldin presented on life cycle labor force participation.

When Smith and Ward computed average work experience across *all* women, whether they were currently working or not, work experience increased much more across this time period because of the large increase in labor force participation. At age 35, women's average work experience increased more than six years and at age 45, it increased nearly seven years. In 1920, the difference between the average work experience of *working* women and *all* women was very large because many women almost never worked in the paid labor market. In that time period, the average work experience of *working* women was relatively high, but the average work experience of *all* women was quite low. By 1986, however, this had changed: The averages for the two groups were much more similar because a much higher proportion of women now worked in the labor market at some time in their lives.

From our standpoint, the most important point of all this research is that women have indeed, on average, worked fewer years in the labor market than men of the same age and that, paradoxically, the gap did not narrow when the labor force participation rate of women first began to increase in the 1950s through the 1980s. The rising labor force participation rate was largely the product of reentry into the labor market by women who had been absent for many years. Their presence thus prevented the gender gap in work experience from narrowing further.

In the next chapter, we will develop a technique to determine exactly how important education and work experience differences between men and women are in explaining the gender gap in earnings.

Labor Market Discrimination and Women's Earnings

An alternative explanation for the gender gap in earnings is that women earn less because they are discriminated against in the labor market. The standard economic analysis of discrimination is based on Gary Becker's *Economics of Discrimination,* a book written in the mid-1950s. Becker's analysis was developed in the context of racial discrimination, which was by far the most widely noted form of discrimination at that time; public awareness of possible labor market discrimination against women was still at least a decade or two in the future. The application of Becker's approach to gender discrimination is relatively straightforward.

The economic approach to discrimination is often puzzling to students. First, it makes absolutely no effort to explain *why* discriminatory preferences exist. In that respect, it follows the tradition in economics of treating preferences as exogenous, that is, as a given of the situation being analyzed. For example, economists make no effort to understand why certain people like broccoli, while others prefer string beans or corn, although those preferences are certainly an important part of explaining the demand for and market prices of broccoli, string beans, and corn. The economic approach simply takes those likes and dislikes as givens, and then analyzes how, holding those preferences constant, demand is affected by incomes and prices.

Without a doubt, how people develop the preferences they have, particularly their discriminatory preferences, is an important issue. But it is not one that traditional economic analysis can shed much light on. Psychologists, anthropologists, and sociologists all have comparative advantages in analyzing that issue. The comparative advantage of economics is in analyzing how these preferences affect market outcomes.

Thus, in his work, Becker assumed that some individuals had what he called a **taste for discrimination.** This may seem like an odd choice of words, but it is part of Becker's effort to place likes and dislikes on the basis of gender, race, and other personal characteristics within the general economic framework of preferences. A taste for discrimination is not just a like or dislike but rather a like or dislike that an individual is willing to act on. In Becker's words: "If an individual has a taste for discrimination, he [sic] must act as if he were willing to pay something, either directly or in the form of a reduced income, to be associated with some persons rather than others" (p. 14).

Second, Becker's analysis of discrimination is embedded within the conventional economic analysis of utility-maximizing individuals and profit-maximizing firms, operating in markets that often constrain their behavior. Becker's approach therefore focuses on market equilibriums, and especially long-run competitive equilibrium.

Becker examined three potential sources of discrimination—employers who had tastes for discrimination regarding their employees (**employer discrimination**), employees who had tastes for discrimination regarding their co-workers (**employee discrimination**), and customers who had tastes for discrimination regarding the suppliers with whom they interacted (**customer discrimination**). We examine each in turn.

Employer Discrimination

Let there be two kinds of workers, whom we call *m* and *f* for male and female. To isolate pay differences resulting from discrimination, assume that the two groups of workers are identical in all relevant respects. Technically, they are **perfect substitutes** in production, exactly and identically productive, so no employer would have any reason to favor one group over the other in the absence of discrimination. Indeed, in the absence of discrimination, the wages for the two groups of workers would be identical because otherwise no employer would ever choose to hire the more highly paid group.

But what happens if employers have a taste for discrimination for (are prejudiced against) *f* workers. (It probably makes sense to think of the employers as members of group *m*). To give this prejudice a quantitative measure, Becker introduced what he called a **discrimination coefficient.** It operates in the following specific way. Let *d* stand for the discrimination coefficient, *w* for the money wage that an employee receives, and W for the gross (or total) wage as perceived by the employer. For an employer with discrimination coefficient d, $W = w \times (1 + d)$. The gross wage now consists of two parts—the money wage (w) and the monetary equivalent of the taste for discrimination ($w \times d$). For example, if the money wage were $5 and $d = 0.25$, the gross wage would be $5 \times 1.25 = \$6.25$. Facing a money wage of $5, this employer would act as if the wage were $6.25, composed of $5.00 in money wages and a disutility cost equal to $1.25. A more prejudiced employer would have a higher value of d and thus a higher gross wage for any given money wage.[15] An employer with no prejudice at all would have $d = 0$.

How do discriminatory preferences affect the equilibrium wages of men and women? We begin with a simple case in which all employers have the same taste for discrimination, which we denote by d'. Let w_m stand for the money wage rate for men and w_f be the money wage rate for women. To get the gross wage for women, as perceived by the employer with a taste for discrimination, we multiply that wage by $(1 + d')$, getting $w_f \times (1 + d')$. If $w_m < w_f \times (1 + d')$, then women are more expensive (inclusive of all costs) than men, so that all employers would choose to hire only men. If $w_m > w_f \times (1 + d')$, just the opposite is true—the men are too expensive and even the prejudiced employers would want to hire only women because the lower wage more than compensates for the higher psychic costs of hiring the women. These employers are prejudiced, but they are also capitalists!

The only way both groups can find employment is when their gross wages are equal. Thus, in equilibrium, the relative wages for men and women must satisfy this relationship:

$$w_m^* = w_f^* \times (1 + d') \qquad (3)$$

where the asterisk (*) means this is an equilibrium wage rate. We can rewrite this as a wage ratio:

$$w_f^*/w_m^* = 1/(1 + d') \qquad (4)$$

Equation (4) shows that the women's equilibrium wages will be less than the men's, as long as $d' > 0$. If, for example, $d' = 0.50$, then $w_f^*/w_m^* = 1/1.5 = 67\%$. If $d' = 0.25$, then $w_f^*/w_m^* = 1/1.25 = 80\%$. Equations (3)

---

[15]Note that the discrimination coefficient is multiplicative, not additive. If it were additive, so that the net wage was $w + d$, the same general results would hold.

and (4) don't establish what the actual wages for men and women will be, just the relationship between the wages. The absolute wage level will depend on general worker productivity.

Now let's make the problem a bit more realistic and also a bit more complex. Instead of assuming that all employers have the same discrimination coefficient, suppose the discrimination coefficient ranges from 0 (no taste for discrimination) for some employers to some large number which we'll call d_m; the m subscript stands for the maximum. We use d_j to stand for the discrimination coefficient for each particular employer. Just as before, each employer will compare the gross wages of men and women and hire the less expensive group. When $w_m = w_f$, employers with $d = 0$ will be the only ones willing to employ women, because for everyone else, the gross wage of women $[w_f \times (1 + d_j)]$ exceeds the gross wage for men (w_m). If w_f were just a bit lower, firms with the next lowest value of d_j would be just willing to employ women, and so on. As w_f continues to fall, more and more employers are willing to employ women, until the wage is so low that even the employer with $d = d_m$ would be willing to hire women.

Table 9.3 shows how this might work, for employers A, B, C, D, and E, arranged from lowest to highest discrimination coefficient. If $w_f = \$10.00$, the employers will view that wage as if it were \$10.00 (employer A), \$12.50 (employer B), and so on up to E, who acts as if the wage were \$100! In each case, the net wage is just $w \times (1 + d_j)$. The final column shows the wage at which they would be just willing to hire women employees, assuming that the male wage was \$10.00. This is the value of w_f, such that $w_f \times (1 + d_j) = \$10.00$; rearranging, this wage is equal to $\$10.00/(1 + d_j)$. It ranges from a high of \$10.00 (employer A who doesn't care whom he/she hires) to \$1.00 for employer E, who clearly cares an enormous amount.

Figure 9.5 illustrates this situation. Suppose, just to simplify a bit, that each of the five firms were willing to hire a maximum of ten workers and that the wage for men was \$10.00. What would the demand curve look like? If $w_f = \$10.00$, firm A is willing to hire anywhere between 0 and 10 women. (At that wage, it is indifferent between hiring men and hiring women, and ten workers is the maximum). That corresponds to the top short horizontal section of the demand curve. If the wage were \$8.00, firm A would definitely hire ten women (it would actually do so if the wage were \$9.99) and now firm B is willing to hire between one and ten women. So the demand curve is a horizontal line stretching from 10 to 20 when $w_f = \$8.00$. At a wage of

Employer	d	Net Wage [$w \times (1 + d_j)$], If $w_f = \$10.00$	Maximum Wage Willing To Pay Women, If $w_m = \$10.00$
A	0	$10.00	$10.00
B	0.25	$12.50	$8.00
C	1	$20.00	$5.00
D	3	$40.00	$2.50
E	9	$100.00	$1.00

Table 9.3   Employer Discrimination Coefficients and Willingness to Hire

$5.00, firms A and B will hire a total of twenty women, and firm C will hire anywhere from one to ten. And so on, down to firm E, whose demand for women workers kicks in when the wage for women is $1.00. The demand curve looks like a descending set of stairs.

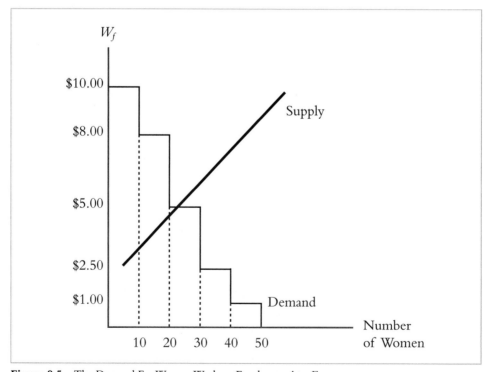

Figure 9.5   The Demand For Women Workers, Employers A to E

The actual wage in the market will depend on where the supply curve intersects this strange demand curve. For the supply curve drawn in Figure 9.5, the equilibrium wage will be $5.00. At this wage, firms A and B hire only women, firms D and E hire only men, and firm C hires both. If the supply were smaller, the wage would be higher, because then the women would need to deal with the less-prejudiced employers only.

If there are many firms instead of five, and if the value of d_j differs just slightly from one firm to the next, the demand curve will look like the smooth one in Figure 9.6, rather than the stair-step demand curve of Figure 9.5. In Figure 9.6, the vertical axis shows the relative wage of women, w_f/w_m, rather than just women's wages. The horizontal axis shows the number of women. When $w_m = w_f$, there is some demand for women workers, stemming from firms for whom $d_j = 0$. These employers are willing to hire women even when their wages are the same as men's wages. That demand is the horizontal portion of the demand curve at $w_f/w_m = 1$. Most employers, however, are still unwilling to hire women at that wage. But, as w_f falls further and further, more and more employers are willing to hire women. Each one is just willing to hire women when $w_f \times (1 + d_j) = w_m$. Thus, the number of women workers demanded increases as the relative wage of women falls. The market equilibrium will be a relative wage at which the number of women willing to work just equals the number demanded. This is shown in Figure 9.6 as $1/(1 + d^*)$, where d* is the value of d that just balances supply and demand. Women clearly continue to earn less than men. Again, it is clear that the relative wage will depend on both supply and demand; the greater the supply of women, the more prejudiced the employers they must deal with, and the lower their wages must be.

The equilibrium relative wage divides firms into two categories. For all firms with $d_j < d^*$, women are now relatively inexpensive compared to men because their own personal discrimination coefficient is low. For them, $w_f^* \times (1 + d_j) < w_m^*$, so they will employ only women and no men at all. They will pay them the market wage for women, which is lower than that for men.[16] For all firms with $d_j > d^*$, women are still too expensive relative to men because their own personal discrimination coefficient is so high. For them, $w_f^* \times (1 + d_j) > w_m^*$, so they will employ only men and no women

---

[16]This is a subtle idea. Even firms with low discrimination coefficients pay women less than men because they take wages as given. These firms are *willing* to pay women more than that, but they don't have to.

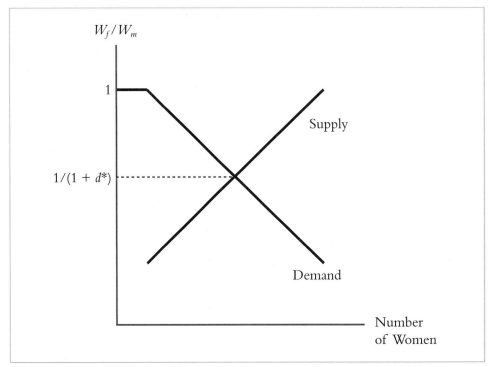

Figure 9.6   Women's Wages When Employers' Discrimination Coefficients Differ

at all. Only the marginal firm, for whom $w_f^* \times (1 + d_j) = w_m^*$, will be willing to hire both men and women.

Because of the difference in which kind of workers they hire, the profits of these two kinds of firms will differ, too. The firms hiring women have lower monetary labor costs than the firms hiring only men. Because the men and women are equally productive, the profits of the men-only firms must be lower than the profits of the women-only firms. It is easy to see why this must be true. The men-only firms could earn exactly the same revenues and have lower costs simply by replacing all their male employees with women because the women are just as productive, but cost less. That is a very powerful and important idea: *The more prejudiced firms sacrifice potential profits to indulge their prejudices. Discrimination is inconsistent with profit maximization.* It costs the firm something to indulge its discriminatory preferences.

There is one final step to the argument. Figure 9.6 might represent the state of affairs given the existing firms in the market. But the composition of the market might well change over time in a particular way. Potential firms with relatively low d_j's could enter the market to take advantage, as it were, of the lower wages of women. Precisely because they are willing to employ women, they can earn the higher profits of the women-only firms in the market. But no firms with high d_j's would want to enter the market because they would face the higher costs associated with hiring men.

Figure 9.7 shows how this entry would change the market. The entry by these firms would shift the demand curve out at higher relative wages, thereby raising the equilibrium wage for women. Eventually, the entry process might result in a demand curve composed only of firms with $d_j = 0$. In that case, the demand curve would be horizontal at $w_m = w_f$. Discriminatory wage differences have been eliminated by competitive market processes! In a famous article, the economic theorist and Nobel Prize winner Kenneth Arrow showed that this result would be attained if there was free entry, constant returns to scale,[17] and a sufficient number of potential employers with $d_j = 0$. Needless to say, this is a surprising result and an important one. As Arrow wrote: "The model predicts the absence of the phenomenon it was designed to explain."[18]

It is important to appreciate the key elements necessary for the result—the ability to enter the market, the exclusive focus on monetary profits, and the existence of a sufficient pool of potential employers with low or even zero discrimination coefficients. Many economists, perhaps especially conservative economists, take the results largely at face value and conclude that earnings differences between men and women or, for that matter, any other two groups cannot reflect labor market discrimination but must, instead, be the result of genuine differences in productivity. (Those productivity differences could, of course, be caused by discrimination, perhaps public discrimination in the provision of public education.) The market will inevitably eliminate discrimination, they argue, by virtue of the profit-seeking activities of firms. For an interesting example of this process in the world of professional sports, see Box 9.2.

---

[17]The constant returns to scale means that the market is likely to be competitive rather than dominated by a single monopolist or several oligopolists.

[18]Kenneth Arrow, "Some Mathematical Models of Race Discrimination in the Labor Market," in Anthony H. Pascal (editor), Lexington, MA: Lexington Books, 1972. Arrow was one of the first American economists to receive the Nobel Prize in Economics for his work on general equilibrium theory.

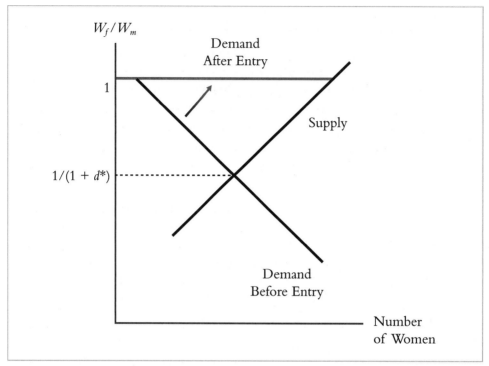

Figure 9.7   Market Equilibrium Before and After Entry

Other economists worry about the underlying conditions. Is entry sufficiently easy? Are firms sufficiently profit-oriented, or will they adhere to what may be social custom? Are there a sufficient number of unprejudiced employers? In this regard, the well-known economist and feminist, Barbara Bergmann,[19] quoted the yet more famous nineteenth-century economist, John Stuart Mill. Mill wrote that "Political economists . . . exaggerate the effect of competition. . . . They are apt to express themselves as if they thought that competition actually does, in all cases, whatever it can be shown to be the tendency of competition to do."

Customer Discrimination

The analysis of customer discrimination is quite similar to the analysis of employer discrimination. Now imagine that there are a number of firms selling an identical product in a competitive market. The firms are distinguished only

---

[19]Barbara Bergmann, "Does The Market For Women's Labor Need Fixing?" *Journal of Economic Perspectives,* Vol. 3, No. 1, pp. 43–60, 1989.

Box 9.2 Discrimination in Professional Sports

In a somewhat different context, discrimination in sports provides an interesting case exactly on point for both sides of the argument. For many years, discrimination in Major League Baseball was essentially absolute. No Black players at all were employed. There was no relative wage at which firms were willing to hire them. Instead, an alternative league, the Negro Baseball League, was formed to provide them an opportunity to play. They played there, often with great skill and always with very low wages. This situation prevailed for many years.

Why didn't the market just eliminate the unjustified earnings differences? One critical element of the "competition eliminates discrimination" argument was missing. Entry into Major League Baseball was not open. Would-be nondiscriminators could not simply set up shop and join the league, so race discrimination in baseball persisted for many years.

Eventually, however, the Brooklyn Dodgers, under the influence of a particularly broad-minded and cagey executive, Branch Rickey, signed Jackie Robinson to a contract as the first Black Major League Baseball player. He acted very much like an employer with a low value of d and recognized a great player—and a great bargain—when he saw it. The other teams acted like employers with high values of d. Within a decade, however, the color-bar had been broken on every team as a result of competitive pressures.

A similar story can be told for college athletics, where through the 1950s, most Southern schools fielded all-White football and basketball teams. Black athletes were not offered athletic scholarships. But this practice, too, eventually ended. When change finally came, it moved quickly across all universities.

The moral of this story is that discriminatory wage differences may persist for many years if the circumstances are right. But change, when it does come, can occur suddenly and thoroughly.

by the gender, race, or other personal characteristic of the seller; the firms differ in no other important respect. If customers have no taste for discrimination, then the prices charged by the firms must be identical in long-run equilibrium. No customer would ever pay more for the product from one seller if it were available at a lower price from another seller. That would eliminate price differences. The "law of one price" would hold.

Suppose, though, that m (male) customers have tastes for discrimination. Now, faced with a good sold by an f (female) firm, these customers would regard the gross price as $p_f \times (1 + d)$, where d is, once again, the discrimination coefficient. The gross price of the product is composed of two parts—the monetary cost (p_f) and the disutility of interacting with an f firm $(d \times p_f)$. If the f firm wants to sell its output to these customers, it must lower its price so that its gross price just equals the price of the good sold by m (male) firms. Thus, it must be the case that $p_f^* \times (1 + d) = p_m^*$. The discriminatory preferences result in f firms being forced to charge a lower price.

In thinking about how this might affect wage rates, imagine that the good in question is a service of some kind, where the customer interacts directly with the seller. For example, this could apply to doctors, dentists, lawyers, shop keepers, and all kinds of retail workers. Then, the price that is affected is either the worker's pay directly (as in the case of doctors, dentists, and lawyers) or the price of the good that the worker sells, which affects her pay indirectly.

If tastes for discrimination vary across customers, the analysis would follow exactly along the lines of the model of employer discrimination where the discrimination coefficient varied. The f (female) customers would presumably have $d = 0$. Each male customer would have a critical value for p_f^*/p_m^* that was just low enough to make him indifferent between the two kinds of firms by making the gross prices equal. Market equilibrium would divide customers into those with lower discrimination coefficients who buy only from the f firms and those with higher discrimination coefficients who buy only from the m firms.

As in the case of employer discrimination, the customers who are indulging their taste for discrimination pay something for exercising those preferences. They pay a higher monetary cost by buying the good from m firms rather than f firms. They are not, however, worse off in terms of their own preferences—they quite willingly pay the higher price because they prefer to do so. Unlike the case of employer discrimination where firms with high discrimination coefficients earned lower profits and could potentially be driven out of business as a result, there is no corresponding mechanism here. Nothing happens to customers who prefer to buy goods from one firm rather than another except that they are worse off than they could be if they had different (no taste for discrimination) preferences. Consequently, customer discrimination can survive in market equilibrium in the long run.

Employee Discrimination

If there is employee discrimination, then employees have tastes for discrimination concerning their co-workers. Suppose that m and f employees are again perfect substitutes. Employers have no taste for discrimination, but m employees don't like to work alongside f employees. Then, if the m money wage is w_m, their gross wage would be $w_m \times (1 - d)$ if they were working alongside women employees. Here, d enters negatively, reducing the gross wage received by m workers.

Now suppose there were two jobs that m workers could take, one with only m co-workers and one with both m and f co-workers. No m worker would take the latter job unless its money wage was sufficiently higher to offset the disutility of working with f workers. In symbols, if job 1 has only m workers and job 2 has m and f workers, then wages must be set so that $w_{1m} = w_{2m} \times (1 - d)$. The m wages in job 2 just compensate for the disutility of working alongside f workers. Women in this simple story are assumed not to care about their co-workers, so $w_{1f} = w_{2f}$. The apparent result is that men and women in job 1 will receive the same wage, but m workers in job 2 will earn more.

In fact, as Becker pointed out, an alternative result is that the workforce would be segregated by gender, thereby eliminating the need to pay higher wages to the men. Clearly, this is a lower-cost solution to the problem. So this simple model actually predicts job segregation, rather than pay differences.

In more complicated production settings, it is possible to establish wage differences on the basis of employee discrimination. For example, suppose there are m and f type 1 workers who are perfect substitutes for one another, but also m type 2 workers who are supervisors of the type 1 workers. Production requires either m or f type 1 workers and type 2 workers. If there is employee discrimination among type 1 m workers, job segregation will result, but, as above, there will be no pay differences. If type 2 m workers also have a taste for discrimination, they will receive higher pay when they supervise f workers than when they supervise m workers. In this situation, pay differences could arise from employee discrimination.

Summary of Discrimination Models

Let's review these three models of labor market discrimination. Employer discrimination can certainly affect wage rates in the short run—and the short run can last a very long time. Becker's insight that discrimination is costly to those who practice it is important, as is the prediction that market forces could operate to eliminate much of the earnings differences that are a result of discrimination. It is sensible to appreciate the insight but to be skeptical that it applies perfectly to labor markets in the twenty-first century.

Customer discrimination can certainly generate differences in prices for identical goods sold by different kinds of firms as long as there are tastes for discrimination. Unlike employer discrimination, this source of wage differentials will not be eroded by market forces. This model potentially applies, however, only to a relatively small portion of the labor market, namely services and retail. The effect probably can't be too large in the aggregate. Employee discrimination probably has the least impact of all. Firms can readily avoid paying higher wages by segregating their workforce along the dimension on which discrimination operates.

Becker's models of labor market discrimination have been very influential among economists. Many, although certainly not all, economists interpret them as indicating that labor market discrimination is not likely to be an important factor in explaining the lower wages of women. We will look at the evidence in the next chapter.

Alternative Explanations

Statistical Discrimination

Statistical discrimination is another form of discrimination that can arise in the labor market. It arises because employers have an interest in maximizing profits, which requires keeping costs as low as possible. Firms often bear the cost of hiring and training workers, and so it is in their interest to keep these costs low. Unfortunately, the firm does not always have exactly the information it needs to determine which employees are likely to be the easiest to train, the most productive, the most reliable, or the most committed to the firm. This is called **asymmetric information**—the employee has more information than the employer about his/her own skills and commitment. Because of this, the employer will often rely on a signal or a credential that the employee possesses to make a determination about whether or not to hire that person. For example, if graduates of Ivy League colleges are, in the firm's mind and experience, more productive than other college graduates, the firm may make its hiring decision based upon this criterion. The firm is using characteristics of a group (Ivy League college graduates) to make decisions about individuals and their productivity. The firm is following this course because it has imperfect information; it can't be certain about each individual's productivity, but it has found that, on average, people from this group are more productive.

From the perspective of women in the economy, this same kind of thing can happen if firms are looking to hire people into jobs where there are considerable training costs. The employer may believe that a particular woman is qualified for the job but may worry that she won't make the long-term commitment necessary to make the firm's investment in training her profitable. Perhaps in the past, the firm has had many women employees who left to raise a family. Because it is costly to investigate whether or not a particular applicant will leave the firm after a short period of time—and difficult to verify in any case—the firm may tend to offer jobs to men because they have historically had a stronger attachment to the labor force. Thus women may find it more difficult to get hired at this firm. It isn't because employers actively dislike female applicants; it is because in the past female employees have tended to leave the firm, and the firm has had to incur the costs associated with hiring and training a new employee.

Figure 9.8 makes the point quite nicely. Suppose some attribute, call it attachment to the workforce, is distributed normally throughout the population but is higher for men than for women. We can draw two bell curves (normal curves) in Figure 9.8 to illustrate this distribution. These curves are drawn under the assumption that there exists a distribution of labor force attachment across men and women and that the distribution is different for each group—in particular, men have a higher degree of labor force attachment, and the variation of men's attachment is smaller than women's attachment. Think of the situation that existed thirty or forty years ago. In Figure 9.8 the average woman has a lower average attachment to the workforce (W) than the average man (M). However, the distributions do overlap a little bit: Some women are more attached to the workforce than some men. Employers who are looking for someone more attached to the workforce will likely select a man, given

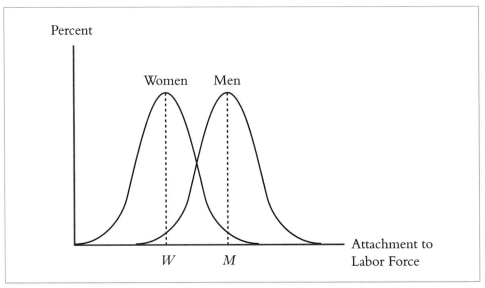

Figure 9.8   Statistical Discrimination Based on Different Distributions of Labor Force Attachment for Men and Women

that they cannot observe a given woman's attachment to the workforce and that they know that men, on average, have been more attached to the workforce.

One might think that, given the strong attachment that women have demonstrated to the labor force over the past thirty years, statistical discrimination would be less likely to occur; after all, as we have documented throughout this book, men and women are becoming more alike in their attachment to the labor force. However, statistical discrimination can occur even if men and women have a nearly equal attachment to the labor force. This may happen if employers are risk averse and fear making a costly mistake or if the indicator of attachment is a noisy signal—it doesn't predict attachment well. Then, even though they understand that women are equally committed to the labor force, they may still prefer to hire men to minimize the costs associated with hiring someone who may leave the firm after a short while. Figure 9.9 illustrates this scenario with another set of bell curves. This time the distributions overlap nearly completely, indicating the near parity in labor force attachment that we now see. Here, some risk-averse employers could end up hiring a man who is less attached to the workforce than a woman.

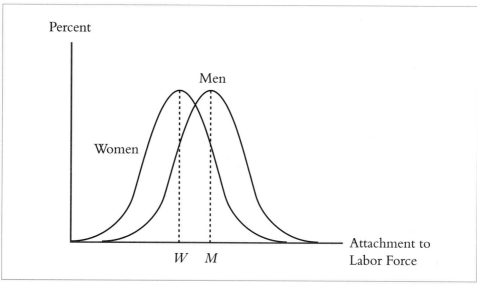

Figure 9.9   Statistical Discrimination When the Distributions by Gender are Very Similar

Explaining Occupational Segregation

As we explained in Chapter 8, **occupational segregation** by gender is still substantial, although it is on the decrease. The question is why it exists. There are several explanations for why jobs may be segregated. We discuss the major theories below.

GENDER ROLES   This explanation for occupational segregation is somewhat sociological. Gender roles refers to the belief that certain jobs are men's and others are women's. Studies done on this topic imply that many individuals have definite ideas regarding what jobs or careers are suitable for what gender. These studies also suggest that children as young as four years old show strong predilections toward occupations that are conventionally linked to a specific gender. Where these ideas of suitable occupations and roles for a specific gender came from is arguable. One idea is that jobs considered typically "masculine" demand traits considered typically masculine, such as aggression, competitive conduct, and physical strength. Jobs considered typically female entail such traits as caring, compassion, and patience. These traits are considered to be innate under this theory and each gender "self-selects" occupations because of these differences.

Still another view explains the phenomenon of occupational segregation as a direct effect from the socialization process experienced while growing up. Children are exposed to what roles are appropriate for their gender and are thus taught what occupations are "appropriate" for them as adults. An adult who chooses a job that is not within taught gender roles can endure mental stress and be ostracized, to whatever extent, by family, peers, and co-workers for his/her choice. Studies have shown that this is, in fact, the case. Women working in top management positions experience not just more mental stress than those in blue-collar jobs experience but also sexual harassment and even hostility from male co-workers. Though attitudes regarding the appropriate occupational choice for each gender have changed and bent to some degree, these traditional ideas still play an important role in selecting an occupation.

HUMAN CAPITAL THEORY   During the 1970s and early-1980s, Solomon Polachek published a series of articles developing a theory of occupational segregation by gender in a human capital theory framework.[20] He used this framework to explain occupational differences between men and women without resorting to the gender roles approach. His idea was based on the characteristics of different occupations, in particular the penalty to intermittent labor force participation. He argued that different occupations penalize intermittent participation differently. In some, the impact is substantial—a woman who leaves a job and returns to it some years later will have suffered a large wage penalty. In others, the impact is small, so that a woman could more or less pick up where she left off. The reasons for the difference in penalty could reflect the changing technological nature of a job—think of a computer programmer returning to work after a long absence. It could also reflect other peculiar institutional details of a job. For example, some jobs, such as nursing, have relatively low wage premiums to seniority, so the penalty is smaller.

Figure 9.10 shows how wage penalties might work. To make it simple, we focus on just two occupations, j and k. Assume that the skill level involved in the two occupations is relatively similar (at least well in advance) so that it makes sense to think of an individual potentially choosing at some earlier point in time between working in occupation j and working in occupation k. For

[20]Solomon Polachek, "Occupational Self-Selection: A Human Capital Approach to Sex Differences in Occupational Structure," *The Review of Economics and Statistics,* Vol. 63, No. 1, pp. 60–69, 1981.

each occupation, we've drawn two age-earnings profiles, one if the individual worked continuously and another if the individual dropped out of the labor market for a fixed interval of, say, five years. In Figures 9.10(A) and (B), the line *AB* is the likely wage path with continuous participation, and *ACDE* is the likely wage path if an individual is out of the labor force for the time period denoted by the two dashed lines. The wage penalty is shown in each figure as *DD'*.

Which job is a better choice depends on the profile selected. Occupation *k* has a higher wage, but a more substantial penalty, than occupation *j*. Clearly, for the individual who will work continuously, occupation *k* is the better choice. Technically, it has a higher present value of earnings. However, if the worker plans to leave the labor market for a number of years, occupation *j* is probably better, because he/she suffers a far smaller penalty. Thus, the two occupations offer individuals a trade-off between wage levels and the penalty they will bear if they drop out of and then reenter the labor force. Individuals who expected to work continuously would probably congregate in occupation *k* and others like it, while individuals who expected to work intermittently would congregate in occupation *j* and others like it.

It's a small step to then argue that these factors could be part of the explanation of occupational segregation by gender. Women disproportionately end up—by choice in Polachek's model—in occupations like *j*, while men disproportionately choose occupations like *k*. Polachek's key point, then, is that

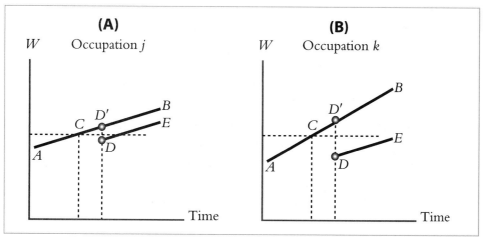

Figure 9.10   The Human Capital Explanation of Occupational Segregation by Gender—The Role of Wage Penalties to Periods of Nonwork

women, knowing they will go in and out of the labor market, pick jobs that penalize them less for doing so. For example, they would choose to be a grade school teacher rather than a college professor or a clerk rather than a technician.

Needless to say, this argument is controversial. There probably is *something* to it. Teaching and nursing, two occupations with an obvious overrepresentation of women, are also occupations where there is a relatively small promotion ladder and thus not much of a penalty to lost years of experience. The empirical evidence on this explanation is mixed. The key relationship is the link between an occupation's penalty rate and its employment of workers with intermittent labor market attachment. If Polachek is correct, there ought to be a negative relationship with workers with intermittent work patterns choosing the low-penalty occupations. Even though Polachek claimed that this was the case for wages and employment of men and women in eight occupational categories, Paula England argued that Polachek's model did not fit the facts quite as well as he claimed.[21] The details of their debate are reasonably technical, and ultimately, not particularly conclusive. Interested readers should consult the summer 1985 issue of the *Journal of Human Resources* to read the debate over this issue between England and Polachek. Perhaps the most interesting part of the debate is how angry the participants seem to be. This was a "hot-button" issue.

Summary

In this chapter, we've examined several major approaches for explaining why women earn less than men. Broadly put, earnings differences can exist either because the two groups of workers differ, on average, in their labor market skills, or because they are treated differently in the labor market, given the skills that they do have. The first of these is a human capital explanation; the second reflects labor market discrimination. We also more briefly examined statistical discrimination and theories of occupational segregation.

A human capital explanation of male-female earnings differences does have some resonance. We know that married households have often utilized a gender-based division of labor, with men specializing in labor market work and

---

[21]Paula England, "The Failure of Human Capital Theory to Explain Occupational Sex Segregation," *Journal of Human Resources,* Vol. 27, pp. 358–70, 1982.

women in household production. A natural and inevitable consequence of that division is that, on average, married women spent far fewer years in the labor market than men did. This difference was quite large in earlier cohorts in which many women exited the labor market at marriage or at first birth and did not return, if at all, for many years. Differences in actual and/or expected labor force participation rationally lead to differences in investment in human capital, because the fewer years of participation lower the internal rate of return to an investment. It certainly doesn't help that the years of nonparticipation are those in which the present value of earnings is relatively high.

Becker's model of labor market discrimination does a great job of showing how prejudices could find their way into the demand for labor and could affect the relative wages that women, or other groups that are the victims of prejudice, earn. It also yields two important counterintuitive hypotheses: (1) The practice of discrimination is costly to the firms that practice it, and (2) strong competitive pressure might eliminate discriminatory firms from the market. Although this result is certainly not guaranteed, it is not an idea to ignore either.

When the human capital argument is combined with the "competition eliminates discrimination" argument, it leaves many more conservative economists believing that all earnings differences between groups in the labor market must be legitimate. In the next chapter, we use statistical analysis to evaluate whether the earnings gap between men and women is legitimate. We then turn to studies that provide real-world evaluation and computation of the sources of the gender gap in earnings.

Key Terms

asymmetric information   340

customer discrimination   329

discrimination coefficient   329

employee discrimination   329

employer discrimination   329

general training   311

human capital   309

internal rate of return   313

investments in human capital   310

occupational segregation   343

on-the-job training   311

perfect substitutes   329

present value   312

specific training   311

statistical discrimination   340

taste for discrimination   329

Appendix: Present Value Analysis and the Return to Human Capital Investment

Present Value Analysis and Investment in Human Capital

To evaluate the value of an investment in human capital, it is necessary to account for the fact that costs are incurred now while benefits are received in the future, often far in the future. This kind of analysis is called *present value analysis*. Here we first work through an example to show exactly why benefits in the future are worth less and then show how to use present value analysis to adjust for the time pattern of benefits and cost.

Suppose that it costs a student $75,000 to get a college education in direct and opportunity costs, and, in return, average earnings are expected to increase by $5000 for each of forty working years until retirement. (Both of these numbers are low, and, in addition, the effect of education on income typically changes with age. The example is just meant to be illustrative and relatively easy to work with computationally.) The total lifetime benefits are, thus, $200,000 (40 years × $5000 per year). Has the student then made a $125,000 profit, the difference between the $200,000 return and the $75,000 costs? Absolutely not. Indeed, if we simply compare the costs to the benefits, we will have made an error of more than $100,000!

Compounding and Discounting

To see why benefits in the future are less valuable than current benefits, let's focus on the particular college investment described earlier—costs equal to $75,000 and benefits of $5000 for forty years. Suppose that the student had the $5000 benefit this year instead of one year in the future. He/she could invest that $5000 at, let's say, a 5% interest rate. At the end of the year, the student would have the $5000 invested (called the *principal*) plus interest earned of $250 (5% × $5000) for a grand total of $5250. Thus, $5000 available right now is equivalent to $5250 in one year, at an interest rate of 5%. Despite the fact that the two sums look different, they are actually identical in value, once we account for the difference in the time period in which they are received.

At the end of two years, the original $5000 would be worth $5250 + (5% × $5250) = $5,512.50, which is, again, the sum of principal plus earned interest. That means that $5000 now is equivalent to $5512.50 in two years at an interest rate of 5%. If the interest rate had been 10%, instead of 5%, the $5000 today would be worth $5500 after one year and $6050 after two years.[1] This kind of analysis—finding the future value of current sums—is called *compounding to future value.*

Let's look more closely at the calculation of the value of $5000 today in two years. Note that each year's value is equal to the previous year's value multiplied by $(1 + r)$, where r is the interest rate expressed as a decimal (e.g., 1.05 if the interest rate is 5% or 1.10 if the interest rate is 10%). Thus, $5250 (the value in year one) = $5000 × 1.05 and $5512.50 (the value in year two) = $5250 (the value in year one) × 1.05. If we substitute for $5250 from the first expression into the second one, we could rewrite the year two value as:

$$\$5512.50 = \$5250 \times 1.05 = (\$5000 \times 1.05) \times 1.05 = \$5000 \times 1.05^2$$

This is a very convenient substitution because it means that we can express the future value as a function of just the original value, the interest rate, and the number of intervening years. (This assumes that the interest rate is constant from year to year.)

Using this relationship, we can write a series of expressions for the future value of any current sum of money. Let Y_0 stand for the amount of money available now and $FV_1(Y_0)$, $FV_2(Y_0)$, and $FV_3(Y_0)$ represent its future value in years 1, 2, and 3, respectively. Then we have the following relationships:

$$FV_1(Y_0) = Y_0 \times (1 + r)$$

$$FV_2(Y_0) = FV_1(Y_0) \times (1 + r) = [Y_0 \times (1 + r)] \times (1 + r) =$$
$$Y_0 \times (1 + r)^2, \text{ where we have substituted for } FV_1(Y_0)$$
$$\text{from the first equation.}$$

$$FV_3(Y_0) = FV_2(Y_0) \times (1 + r) =$$
$$[Y_0 \times (1 + r)^2] \times (1 + r) = Y_0 \times (1 + r)^3, \text{ where we}$$
$$\text{have substituted for } FV_2(Y_0) \text{ from the second equation,}$$
$$\text{and so on.}$$

---

[1] $5000 + (0.10 × $5000) = $5500. $5500 + (0.10 × $5500) = $6050.

The general formula for finding the future value of any current sum in any year T is thus

$$FV_T(Y_0) = Y_0 \times (1 + r)^T \tag{1}$$

This equation shows that we can find the future value of a current sum by multiplying that sum by one plus the interest rate raised to a power equal to the number of years between now and then. This is exactly the equivalent of the arithmetic we did in the preceding paragraph. This is the basic formula for compounding.[2]

We can use these formulas to compute quickly and easily the future value of any sum in any future year at any possible interest rate. For example, at a 5% interest rate (0.05),

$$FV_1(\$5000; 0.05) = \$5000 \times (1.05)^1 = \$5,250.00$$
$$FV_2(\$5000; 0.05) = \$5000 \times (1.05)^2 = \$5,512.50$$
$$FV_{10}(\$5000; 0.05) = \$5000 \times (1.05)^{10} = \$8,144.47$$
$$FV_{20}(\$5000; 0.05) = \$5000 \times (1.05)^{20} = \$13,266.49, \text{ and so on.}$$

For finding the value of an investment in human capital, it is usually more convenient to reverse the problem and find the *present value* of money received in the future. That approach makes sense because the investment in human capital will yield benefits in the future; we need to compare those benefits to the costs, which are typically incurred now. Fortunately, this involves nothing more than turning the arithmetic and equations around. The present value of a future sum is the amount of money which, if it were available today, would grow (via compounding) to that sum in that year. It is the value of that future sum right now. Because we already know that $5000 grows to $5250 in one year, $5512.50 in two years, and $8144.47 in ten years (if the interest rate is 5%), it follows that the present values at a 5% interest rate of $5250 in one year, $5512.50 in two years, and $8144.47 in ten years are all exactly $5000.

The general formula for finding the present value of a current sum is exactly the opposite of equation (1). We already know that $Y_1 = Y_0 \times (1 + r)$, where we begin with Y_0 and want to find its future value Y_1. Now suppose

---

[2]This compounding formula applies in the simple case where interest is received once a year at the end of the year. Most interest today is paid continuously. In that case, the formula is conceptually similar but involves that strange numerical constant **e**. For our purposes, this formula is perfectly fine.

that we know Y_1, the amount of money available next year, and want to find its present value, Y_0, at interest rate r. By manipulating the compounding equation to solve for the present value (Y_0), we have

$$Y_0 = Y_1/(1 + r)$$

Thus, the present value in year 0 of a sum Y_1 available one year from now is that sum divided by $(1 + r)$. This makes perfect sense in terms of the definition of the present value: This is precisely the current sum that would grow via compounding to the future sum. Thus, if we multiply this present value by $(1 + r)$, we compute the future value. In this case, the future value of the present value is $(1 + r) \times [Y_1/(1 + r)] = Y_1$. This calculation confirms that Y_0 is the present value of Y_1.

Proceeding in exactly the same way, we can find the present value of some amount of money available two years from now. From the compounding formula, we have $Y_2 = Y_0 \times (1 + r)^2$. It follows immediately that the present value is $Y_0 = Y_2/(1 + r)^2$.

More generally, for any sum of money available T years in the future, the present value is

$$PV_0(Y_T) = Y_T/(1 + r)^T \tag{2}$$

where we have used $PV_0(Y_T)$ to stand for the present value in year 0 of $\$Y$ available in some year T. This equation shows that to find the present value of some future sum, we divide that sum by one plus the interest rate raised to a power equal to the number of years between then and now. This is the famous formula for discounting to present value. If we compare equations (1) and (2), we can see that discounting to present value is just compounding in reverse. Instead of multiplying the current sum by $(1 + r)^T$ to find its future value, we divide the future sum by the same factor, $(1 + r)^T$. The term $(1 + r)^T$ is often referred to as the *discount factor*.

Using this formula and applying it to the preceding numerical example, we would have

$$PV_0(\$5250_1; 0.05) = \$5250/(1.05)^1 = \$5000$$
$$PV_0(\$5512.50_2; 0.05) = \$5512.50/(1.05)^2 = \$5000$$
$$PV_0(\$8144.47_{10}; 0.05) = \$8144.47/(1.05)^{10} = \$5000$$

In these equations, the subscripts 1, 2, and 10 on the dollar amounts refer to the year in which that sum is received, and the 0.05 refers to the interest rate.

Using equation (2), it is possible to find the present value of any sum in any year at any interest rate.

Table A9.1 summarizes what we have learned about finding the present value of a future sum. The second column shows the application of the formula for discounting any sum in a given year. The third column shows the actual present values of $1000 in years 1 to 5 and 10 at an interest rate of 5%. Note how the value declines quite steeply; after ten years, $1000 is worth only about 61% of its face value. As you should be able to see from the present value formula for year T, the present value of a sum depends on the year in which it is received and on the interest rate. The further in the future we go and the larger the interest rate is, the smaller the present value of any particular sum is.

Now let's return to our original problem, with initial costs of $75,000 and benefits of $5000 per year for 40 years. Table A9.2 shows the computation of the present value of the benefits using an interest rate of 5%. Each entry in the table is the present value of $5000 received in the corresponding year and is calculated following exactly the form of Table A9.1 and equation (2). Note how quickly the present value falls. By the fourteenth year, the $5000 benefit is worth not much more than $2500; by the nineteenth year, it is worth less than $2000; and by the thirty-third year, it is worth less than $1000. The very last row shows the present value of the entire forty-year stream of benefits, and, rather than $200,000, it is just a bit under $86,000—less than half its face value. This is the $100,000 mistake referred to earlier—it is, in fact, a

Year	Present Value Now of $Y Available in Given Future Year	Present Value Now of $1000 Available in Given Future Year at an Interest Rate of 5%
1	$Y/(1 + r)^1$	$952.38
2	$Y/(1 + r)^2$	$907.03
3	$Y/(1 + r)^3$	$863.84
4	$Y/(1 + r)^4$	$822.70
5	$Y/(1 + r)^5$	$783.53
10	$Y/(1 + r)^{10}$	$613.91
T	$Y/(1 + r)^T$	$1000/1.05^T$

Table A9.1   Finding the Present Value of $Y and $1,000 in Various Years

$114,205 mistake, the difference between the $200,000 benefits received and the $85,795 present value of those benefits (at an interest rate of 5%). The mistake would be even worse at a higher interest rate because the present value of each future year's $5000 would be smaller. At a lower interest rate, the mistake would be a bit less serious.

More generally, the present value of any stream of benefits $B_0, B_1, \ldots, B_T$ at interest rate r can be written as

$$PV(B_1, \ldots B_T; r) = B_1/(1 + r) + B_2/(1 + r)^2 + \cdots + B_T/(1 + r)^T = \sum_{t=1}^{T} \frac{B_t}{(1 + r)^t} \qquad (3)$$

where Σ, the Greek letter sigma, is the summation sign. The term involving Σ is just a compact way to express a long sum of terms; the summation starts with $t = 1$ and goes through $t = T$. This is a very important expression.

Present value analysis is an integral part of wise financial planning. See Box A9.1 for examples of present value analysis in action.

Net Present Value and the Internal Rate of Return

Now we are ready to find the value of this hypothetical investment in a college education. Just how good an investment is it? There are two ways to do this. One way to proceed is to compute the *net present value* (NPV) of the investment. The NPV is the difference between the present value of benefits and the present value of costs. (Because we treat the costs as incurred all at once in the first time period, the present value of the costs just equals the costs themselves.) Expressed as an equation, the net present value is

$$NPV(B_1, \ldots, B_T; C_0; r) = \sum_{t=1}^{T} \frac{B_t}{(1 + r)^t} - C_0 \qquad (4)$$

where $B_1, \ldots, B_T$ represents the stream of benefits, C_0 is the cost, and r is the interest rate. The greater the net present value, the better the investment. As long as the net present value is positive, then the investment is a good one, as long, that is, as the interest rate (here, 5%) used in finding the present value represents the actual cost of funds. If the net present value is negative, then you'd be better off financially not making the investment. In this case, the net present value of the investment at a 5% interest rate is $10,795, which is the difference between the $85,795 present value of the benefits and the costs of $75,000. In computing the net present value, we can't use just any interest

Year	Present Value	Year	Present Value
1	$4761.90	21	$1794.71
2	$4535.15	22	$1709.25
3	$4319.19	23	$1627.86
4	$4113.51	24	$1550.34
5	$3917.63	25	$1476.51
6	$3731.08	26	$1406.20
7	$3553.41	27	$1339.24
8	$3384.20	28	$1275.47
9	$3223.04	29	$1214.73
10	$3069.57	30	$1156.89
11	$2923.40	31	$1101.80
12	$2784.19	32	$1049.33
13	$2651.61	33	$999.36
14	$2525.34	34	$951.77
15	$2405.09	35	$906.45
16	$2290.56	36	$863.29
17	$2181.48	37	$822.18
18	$2077.60	38	$783.03
19	$1978.67	39	$745.74
20	$1884.45	40	$710.23

Total Present Value @ 5% = $85,795

Table A9.2   Present Value of $5000 Per Year for Forty Years at a 5% Interest Rate

rate, but rather we must find an interest rate that really reflects either the investment opportunities or the cost of funds.

There is, however, a slightly better way to do it that is related to what we have already done. This involves finding the *internal rate of return* to this particular set of costs and benefits. The internal rate of return is the interest rate at

Box A9.1   What's It Worth?

We all know the story of how Peter Minuet purchased Manhattan Island from the Native Americans for the piddling sum of $24 of goods. Implicit in the story is the wonderful bargain that Minuet made.

Indeed, $24 sounds like a very small amount of money for Manhattan Island, but it was quite a few years ago—in 1626, to be exact. We can find the approximate current value of that $24 by using the future value formula. We want to find the value of something like $24 \times (1 + r)^{375}$. Letting $r = 3\%$, this is $1.5m$, well under the current value of Manhattan. If $r = 5\%$, the sum grows to $2.1b$, still short of the current valuation. But if $r = 7\%$, the current value exceeds $2.5 trillion.

Here's another example. Suppose you are saving for retirement. You want to know how much you must save this year to have $10,000 when you retire. Let's call that sum S (for savings). To find that sum, you need to solve for the present value of $10,000 by using the PV formula, $PV_0(Y_T) = Y_T/(1 + r)^T$, where T is the number of years until retirement. Necessary savings S just equals this present value.

Suppose retirement is forty years away, and a worker can lock in an interest rate of 5%. Then the sum the worker needs now is $S = PV_0(Y_{40}) = \$10,000/(1.05)^{40}$. Solving this, you will find that you only need to put away $1420. If retirement is only twenty years away, then $S = PV_0(Y_{20}) = \$10,000/(1.05)^{20}$ or $3769. If retirement is only ten years away, you better start saving: you'll need to save $6139 this year: $S = PV_0(Y_{10}) = \$10,000/(1.05)^{10} = \$6139$.

Here's another example, this time involving saving to finance a child's college education. Suppose the child will need $20,000 per year for each of four years of college, and the child's parents want to put aside an amount in each of the next four years that will be sufficient to cover that amount. How much will they need to save? Again, this is just the present value of $20,000, so the amount the parents need in each year of saving is $20,000/(1 + r)^T$, where T is number of years until the child will begin college. If college is eighteen years away and the parents can lock in a 5% interest rate, they must put away $8310.41: $\$20,000/(1.05)^{18} = \$8310.41$. If college is only fifteen years away, they need to save $\$20,000/(1.05)^{15} = \$9,620.34$.

In practice, the amount the parents need to save is less than these amounts, because they can save each year from now until college begins, rather than save in just the next four years. The logic behind that saving problem is similar to what we have done, but it is a bit more complicated. If the parents start saving when the child is born, then to accumulate $20,000 in eighteen years at a 5% interest rate, the parents need to save $710.92 each year. The sum of the future values will total $20,000 in eighteen years: $710.92 \times (1.05)^{18} + $710.92 \times (1.05)^{17} + $710.92 \times (1.05)^{16} + \cdots + $710.92 = $20,000$.

which the net present value of an investment equals zero. Instead of picking an interest rate and finding the net present value of the investment, here we solve for the interest rate that makes the net present value equal to zero. Expressed as an equation, the internal rate of return, denoted as r^*, is the interest rate at which $NPV(B_1, \ldots, B_T, C_0; r^*) = 0$. Substituting the expression for NPV from equation (4), the internal rate of return is the interest rate that solves the following expression:[3]

$$\sum_{t=1}^{T} \frac{B_t}{(1 + r^*)^t} - C_0 = 0 \tag{5}$$

Let's continue with the example we've been working with. We already know that at an interest rate of 5%, the net present value is $10,795. This means that the internal rate of return must be greater than 5%. Why? To reduce the present value of benefits further, we must discount using a higher interest rate. The interest rate is in the denominator of the discounting formula, so as the interest rate gets larger, the present value gets smaller.

If we recalculate the present value using an interest rate of 6.0%, the present value of the benefits falls to $75,231. That means the net present value is now $231, so the internal rate of return must be just a hair larger than 6.0%. In fact, using a spreadsheet program like Excel, it is easy to solve for the exact

---

[3]In most equations, the variable we are solving for (here, r^*) is all by itself on the left-hand side of the equation. Because this computation involves a long summation, that expression is impossibly complicated. As a practical matter, internal rates of return are almost always solved with a spreadsheet program like Excel.

internal rate of return, which in this case is equal to precisely 6.024%.[4] At this interest rate, the present value of the benefits equals $75,000 or, equivalently, the NPV equals zero. This tells us that this hypothetical investment in human capital earns a rate of return of 6.024%. The rate is not bad, but it's not great, either. Fortunately, an investment in a college education typically pays a much higher rate of return—something closer to 10 to 12%.

Equation (5) shows the factors that contribute to making the internal rate of return for an investment in human capital high or low. The internal rate of return will be greater when: (1) Costs are lower; (2) benefits in each period are greater; (3) benefits are received sooner rather than later; and/or (4) the total length of the benefit period is greater.

Investing in Human Capital

How do individuals decide whether to make a particular investment in human capital? The internal rate of return to the investment is the key piece of information, indicating how valuable or productive the investment is. (We assume that each individual has a rough enough idea of costs and benefits to compute the rate of return.) In the preceding example, if an individual could invest the $75,000 of college education costs in some other investment at an interest rate of 6.25%, he/she would be better off doing that than investing in him/herself and earning 6.024%. But if that alternative investment opportunity paid only 5% or 5.5%, the individual would be better off investing in him/herself. There might be reasons to go ahead even with a poor rate of return—maybe it's something the individual has been dying to do or the opportunity has benefits other than the increase in earnings. But from a purely monetary point of view, the decision about whether or not to invest in more human capital depends simply on a comparison of the internal rate of return with the return that can be earned investing the money elsewhere.

---

[4]To compute an internal rate of return with a spreadsheet program, set up a column of net benefits, treating the cost as a negative benefit. In this case, the first entry in the column is −$75,000, followed by forty entries of $5000. We need to provide a starting value for the internal rate of return; the program then solves for the solution by trial and error. If the present value of benefits at the starting value is greater than the costs, the program recomputes the present value using a slightly higher interest rate. If the present value of benefits at the starting value is less than the costs, a lower interest rate is used. The program quickly solves for the interest rate at which the present value of benefits just equals the costs. This rate is the internal rate of return.

How much human capital should an individual acquire? Is there some best (maximizing) amount of human capital investment? There usually is a best choice in economics problems, so let's figure out how it might work in this case. Figure A9.1 illustrates the logic. The horizontal axis measures the amount of human capital, and the vertical axis measures the internal rate of return and the cost of funds, both represented as an interest rate. Look first at the supply curve. The supply curve represents the cost of investing in human capital, measured by the interest rate available on alternative uses of the money. In Figure A9.1, the supply curve is shown as horizontal at interest rate r_m, which means that the cost of funds is constant. By drawing it as horizontal, we are assuming that an individual can always earn a rate of return equal to r_m by investing in something other than human capital. The supply curve could be upward-sloping, but that wouldn't change anything important in the analysis.

With respect to the demand curve, the return to additional human capital typically falls, the more human capital one has. One reason for this increase is

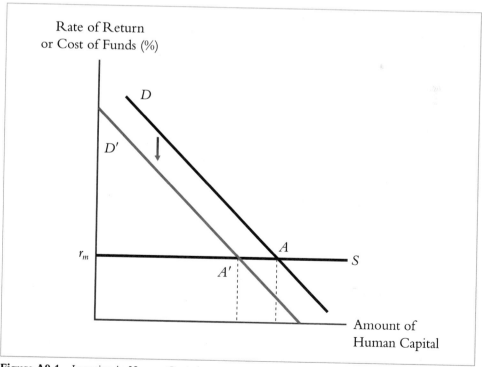

Figure A9.1   Investing in Human Capital

based on the fact that lifetimes are finite. The more time people spend acquiring human capital, the less time they have available to earn a return on it. Other things equal, that would lower the rate of return. Imagine, for example, having multiple degrees. Of course, it's nice to acquire knowledge and to have numerous degrees, but this pursuit takes time. Most people wouldn't have the opportunity to get the full potential value of the investment. Also, the more human capital people have, the higher their opportunity costs are, which would also reduce their internal rates of return. Human capital is probably also subject to diminishing marginal productivity. That would also lower the internal rate of return associated with additional human capital investment. As a result, the demand curve for human capital would likely be downward-sloping, as shown in Figure A9.1. Two demand curves are shown in Figure A9.1; D' has a lower rate of return associated with every unit of human capital investment than D. This could happen for any reason that lowers the internal rate of return—higher costs, lower benefits, later benefits, and/or a shorter benefit period.

The investment rule is simple: An individual ought to invest in human capital just up to the point where the last unit acquired (i.e., the last year or last degree) yields an internal rate of return just equal to the return that could be earned elsewhere. This rule suggests that the rate of return to human capital ought to be quite close to the rate of return to physical capital. This is shown in Figure A9.1 as point A for demand curve D and point A' for demand curve D'. Note the very important implication: Anything that lowers the internal rate of return lowers the amount of investment in human capital. An individual facing demand curve D' will invest in less human capital than an individual facing demand curve D.

CHAPTER 10

The Gender Gap in Earnings: Methods and Evidence

Introduction

We know that, on average, women still earn substantially less than men. For year-round full-time workers, the annual earnings ratio is approximately 76%, and for all workers, it is about 66%, reflecting the lower average annual work hours of many women. We also know that the gender earnings gap has risen substantially since the 1980s, after many decades of puzzling constancy at around 59%. Finally, we have already seen that earnings differences could reflect differences in human capital and/or discrimination. Historically, there have been differences in educational attainment and in accumulated years of work experience, both of which are interpreted as indicators of human capital investment. Discrimination can lead to women earning less than equally skilled men, although in a competitive market there is some reason to believe that discriminatory wage differences resulting from employer prejudice will be eliminated if entry into the market is possible and there are some nondiscriminatory employers.

The obvious next issue is to try to explain both the lower average earnings of women and the increase in their relative earnings. To accomplish that, we first need to develop quantitative methods that will be useful in assessing and measuring the relative importance of human capital differences and discrimination. In the next section, we introduce two techniques—regression analysis and a special application of regression analysis useful for explaining the difference in average earnings. Then we turn to a series of important empirical studies of the gender earnings gap. We will examine why women's average earnings are lower than men's and why the earnings ratio has risen.

The Statistical Analysis of the Gender Gap

Regression Analysis of Earnings Differences

In Chapter 2, we introduced the basic ideas of regression analysis. Here we offer a brief summary and then show how it can be used in the analysis of earnings differences by gender.

Regression analysis is a widely-used technique for measuring the relationship between a **dependent variable** and a set of **independent or explanatory variables.** We write a regression equation this way:

$$Y_i = \alpha + \beta_1 X_{i1} + \beta_2 X_{i2} + \beta_3 X_{i3} + \cdots + \mu_i \qquad (1)$$

In equation (1), Y is the dependent variable, the Xs are the independent variables—there can be and usually are many independent variables—and μ ("mew") is the **error term.** μ represents the influence of factors that affect Y but are unobserved. μ is assumed to be normally distributed, like the familiar bell curve, with a mean of zero. The i subscript on Y, X, and μ means that each observation (a person or firm, for example) has his/her/its own value of Y, all the Xs, and μ. Finally, α and β (the Greek letters alpha and beta) are the **regression coefficients.** β measures the effect on Y of a one-unit change in X, holding constant or controlling for the values of all the other X variables. It corresponds to the experiment of changing just the one variable of interest, leaving all others the same. α is the constant term of the equation.

In carrying out a regression analysis, a researcher uses the information on the values of Y and the X variables to estimate the best values of α and the βs (one estimated β for each separate X variable). The best estimates make the predicted value of Y as close as possible to the actual value of Y.

Regression analysis has been used repeatedly in the analysis of gender earnings differences. The dependent variable that we are interested in explaining is some measure of individual earnings—annual earnings or the hourly wage rate or weekly earnings. Different data sources provide different information on earnings, and sometimes one measure is available and sometimes another. So earnings are the dependent variable Y. The X variables are the factors that determine or explain earnings—certainly human capital, but usually also other traits like race, ethnicity, miscellaneous things like living in a big city versus a small town or in a particular region of the country, and, last, but certainly not least, gender. Years of education and years of work experience (and also the square of years of work experience) are the standard measures of human capital; they are imperfect but useful.[1] Thus, a typical (slightly simplified) earnings equation looks like this:

$$\text{Earnings} = \alpha + \beta_1 \times \text{Years Education} + \beta_2 \times \text{Years Work Experience} + \beta_R \times \text{Race} + \beta_G \times \text{Gender} + \mu \tag{2}$$

In equation (2), Years Education and Years Work Experience are **continuous variables,** having sensible and easily interpreted numerical values—12 or 16 or 18 years of education, for example. The corresponding estimated coefficients represent the impact on earnings of having one more year of education or one more year of work experience. Gender and race, however, do not have natural numerical values. What is the numerical value of being male or female? (That's meant to be a rhetorical question.) Variables like these are included in a regression by using a **dummy variable.** A dummy variable for gender would work this way: Let X (the dummy variable) $= 0$ if a person is male; let $X = 1$ if a person is female. For race, we might let $X = 0$ if a person is White and let $X = 1$ if a person is Black. Now, the regression coefficient for the gender dummy variable would measure the impact on earnings of being female rather than male. For example, if the estimated regression coefficient on a female dummy variable is negative, it means that women have lower earnings than men, all else being equal. The dummy variable for race is interpreted in exactly the same way. It is the impact of being Black, relative to being White, on earnings.

The first step in examining gender differences in earnings is to utilize representative data on individual earnings (Y) and on many of the X variables (years of education, years of work experience, race, gender, etc). This kind of information is available from the Census Bureau, both in the decennial Census and also in an annual survey called the Current Population Survey (or CPS[2] for short), and also in several well-known and widely used sample surveys. One of these is called the Panel Study of Income Dynamics; the National Longitudinal Survey of Youth (NLSY) is another famous survey with earnings information.

The second step is to estimate a regression like equation (2).[3] In this course, we are particularly interested in the estimate of β_G If β_G is negative and

---

[1]There are many differences in human capital among workers with the same years of education. Quality of education varies, as does innate ability and other relevant factors.
[2]The CPS is a monthly survey that is also used to measure the unemployment rate.
[3]This step is not a particularly difficult process and can be done on a PC. Carrying out a regression analysis may be a good exercise for a paper or special project. Ask for help in getting started.

statistically significant (see Chapter 2 for details), this tells us that, all else being equal, women are paid less than men; the phrase "all else being equal" refers to the skill measures included in the set of X variables in the regression equation. Sometimes, researchers will say they have "controlled for" the other independent variables in the regression equation. The estimated value of β_G is an estimate of how much less women earn than equally skilled men. If β_G is positive and statistically significant, then women earn more than otherwise similar men. Finally, if β_G is statistically insignificant, then there is no reliable difference in earnings between men and women with equal skills. In that case, gender has no effect on earnings.

The estimated value of β_G is precisely the answer to the question of whether and how much gender affects earnings. The question Do women earn less than otherwise similar men? is exactly equivalent to the question Is the estimated value of β_G negative and statistically significant? The question How much less do women earn than otherwise similar men? is exactly equivalent to the questions What is the estimated value of β_G? and Is it negative and statistically significant? And questions about changes in the gender gap are exactly equivalent to changes in the estimated value of β_G at different points in time. Is β_G becoming less negative over time? Is it no longer statistically significant? Regression analysis is the standard way to answer all these questions.

The Statistical Analysis of Gender Differences in Earnings

It is also possible to use a regression analysis like equation (2) to determine the proportion of the gender gap in earnings that is the result of differences in earnings and the proportion that is the result of discrimination. This analysis enables researchers to say something like "40% of the wage difference between men and women is explained by differences in measures of skills," which is a very useful summary statement. The technique for answering this kind of question was originally developed by the economist Ronald Oaxaca and is often called the **Oaxaca decomposition** procedure in his honor.[4] It is widely used, both in economics and other social sciences, to account for differences in group averages in a wide range of variables, not just earnings. Here's how it works.

---

[4]Oaxaca's name is pronounced something like "wah-hocka."

Suppose, to keep the explanation and the equations simple, that there is a single measure of skill, denoted as X, that determines an individual's earnings. Think of it as a measure of the total amount of human capital an individual has. (This simplification is only for purposes of exposition. In practice, the method is always applied to the case of multiple measures, such as education and years of work experience; we will consider the case with multiple Xs afterward.) The corresponding regression earnings equation is thus

$$Y_i = \beta X_i + \mu_i \tag{3}$$

This equation is essentially the same as the earnings equation in equation (2), except that there is only one X variable and there is no α (the constant term). (Again, these differences are solely to keep things simple.) Using regression analysis, we estimate the best value of β, which is written $\hat{\beta}$. It is pronounced "beta hat"; the "hat" or "carat" indicates that it is an estimated value.

Now, let $\overline{Y}$ stand for average earnings and $\overline{X}$ stand for the average level of skills for a group of workers. There is a very simple and very useful arithmetic relationship linking $\overline{Y}$, $\overline{X}$, and $\hat{\beta}$:

$$\overline{Y} = \hat{\beta}\,\overline{X} \tag{4}$$

In words, this expression says that average earnings for a group of workers equals their average level of skills multiplied by the value per unit of those skills. Suppose, for example, that education were the only factor that influenced earnings and that, on average, an additional year of education increased earnings by $2500. Then, if working women had an average of twelve years of education, their average earnings would be $30,000.

Equation (4) suggests that average earnings for two groups of workers could differ either because $\overline{X}$ differs or because $\hat{\beta}$ differs—that is, either because the average level of market skills differs or because the market value of those skills differs. The first of these is a human capital explanation; the latter sounds a lot like discrimination. After all, if women are paid less than no-more-qualified men, this should show up as a lower value for the skills that they have.

To sort out the importance of these two alternative explanations, start with regression equations for men and women, estimated separately to find $\hat{\beta}_M$ (for men) and $\hat{\beta}_F$ (for women). Then, we would have the following two equations describing the relationship between average skills and average earnings:

$$\overline{Y}_M = \hat{\beta}_M \overline{X}_M \text{ for men and } \overline{Y}_F = \hat{\beta}_F \overline{X}_F \text{ for women} \tag{5}$$

The gender difference in average earnings is $\overline{Y}_M - \overline{Y}_F$, which, substituting from (5), can be written

$$\overline{Y}_M - \overline{Y}_F = \hat{\beta}_M \overline{X}_M - \hat{\beta}_F \overline{X}_F \tag{6}$$

Now add and subtract $\hat{\beta}_M \overline{X}_F$ to the right-hand side of equation (6); since the sum of the two terms is zero, nothing changes.[5] There is no obvious reason to do that, but it turns out to be very useful. Rearranging and combining terms yields the famous Oaxaca decomposition of differences in means:[6]

$$\overline{Y}_M - \overline{Y}_F = [\hat{\beta}_M \times (\overline{X}_M - \overline{X}_F)] + [(\hat{\beta}_M - \hat{\beta}_F) \times \overline{X}_F] \tag{7}$$

The first term on the right-hand side of equation (7) is the difference in the average levels of human capital between men and women, multiplied by $\hat{\beta}_M$, the value of a unit of X for men. It represents the dollar amount of the gender wage difference that can be attributed to differences in average skills. For it to be important, there must be large skill differences, and the skill involved must be valuable. (Men and women differ in many ways, such as average height and weight, that may be of little or no labor market significance.) This portion of the gender earnings gap is usually referred to as the "explained" portion or even the "deserved" portion, because it is an earnings difference that would exist even if there were no labor market discrimination.

The second term in equation (7) is the difference in the market value of skills for men and women—the difference in the $\hat{\beta}$s—multiplied by the average skill level of women. This term measures the dollars of the gender wage gap that are the result of differences in the monetary return or reward for skills. Think of it as how much more women would earn if they had their current skills but were rewarded for those skills as men are. It is often referred to as the "unexplained" or "undeserved" portion of the earnings gap and is usually interpreted as evidence of discrimination.

Very commonly, researchers will divide equation (7) by the total wage gap $(\overline{Y}_M - \overline{Y}_F)$ to put the two terms in percentage terms. The explained portion is then $[\hat{\beta}_M \times (\overline{X}_M - \overline{X}_F)]/(\overline{Y}_M - \overline{Y}_F)$, and the unexplained portion is $[(\hat{\beta}_M - \hat{\beta}_F) \times \overline{X}_F]/(\overline{Y}_M - \overline{Y}_F)$. Together the two parts add up to 100%.

---

[5] We could, instead, add and subtract $\hat{\beta}_F \overline{X}_M$ to equation (6) and get a slightly different version of equation (7). It is more common to proceed as we are doing here.

[6] If we expand the terms on the right-hand side of equation (7), two terms cancel out. There is a $-\hat{\beta}_M \overline{X}_F$ in the first term and a $+\hat{\beta}_M \overline{X}_F$ in the second term. That leaves us with the original difference, $\hat{\beta}_M \overline{X}_M - \hat{\beta}_F \overline{X}_F$.

	Women	Men
Y	$25,000	$45,000
X	10	15
$\hat{\beta}$	2500	3000
Explained: $\hat{\beta}_M \times (\overline{X}_M - \overline{X}_F) = \$3000 \times (15 - 10) = \$15,000$		
Unexplained: $(\hat{\beta}_M - \hat{\beta}_F) \times \overline{X}_F = (3000 - 2500) \times 10 = \$5000$		

Table 10.1   A Numerical Example of a Oaxaca Decomposition

Here is a simple example of how this might work. Suppose the mean values for the two groups are as shown in Table 10.1.

Note that the basic relationship between the means holds: $\overline{Y} = \hat{\beta}\overline{X}$ for both groups. (Confirm that relationship.) The explained term is $\hat{\beta}_M \times (\overline{X}_M - \overline{X}_F) = \$3000 \times (15 - 10) = \$15,000$. The unexplained term is $(\hat{\beta}_M - \hat{\beta}_F) \times \overline{X}_F = (\$3000 - \$2500) \times 10 = \$5000$. Thus, in this example, of the original \$20,000 difference in mean earnings, \$15,000 is the result of differences in average skills, and \$5000 can be attributed to a difference in rewards. In terms of percentages, 25% of the gross or unadjusted difference is caused by the difference in treatment (\$5000/\$20,000) and 75% by the difference in mean skill levels (\$15,000/\$20,000).

In a real analysis of this sort, there are many X variables, like education, years of work experience, and marital status. It is possible to apply the same approach individually to each variable, determining how much of the difference in wages is explained by, for example, differences in education or work experience, and how much can be attributed to differences in returns to those skills. Suppose years of education is one variable affecting earnings. Let $\hat{\beta}_{ED, M}$ be the estimated value of a year of education for men, and $\overline{X}_{ED, M}$ and $\overline{X}_{ED, F}$ are the average amounts of education for men and women, respectively. Then the explained contribution of education to the gender earnings gap is $\hat{\beta}_{ED, M} \times (\overline{X}_{ED, M} - \overline{X}_{ED, F})$. The unexplained portion of the earnings difference due to education would be $(\hat{\beta}_{ED, M} - \hat{\beta}_{ED, F}) \times \overline{X}_{ED, F}$. Similar terms could be constructed for each variable of interest, thereby pinpointing which factors were most responsible for the difference in earnings.[7] Dividing the two terms by the total wage gap puts them in percentage terms. So the percentage of the earnings gap explained by differences is education is $[\hat{\beta}_{ED, M} \times (\overline{X}_{ED, M} - \overline{X}_{ED, F})]/(\overline{Y}_M - \overline{Y}_F)$, and the portion due to differences in returns to education is $[(\hat{\beta}_{ED, M} - \hat{\beta}_{ED, F}) \times \overline{X}_{ED, F}]/(\overline{Y}_M - \overline{Y}_F)$. The result of this kind of analysis is to pinpoint the sources of the gender gap in earnings.

A similar procedure can be used to examine the change in the gender wage gap over time. The formula gets much more complicated—it involves not just differences by gender but differences in differences—and we do not show it here. But the underlying idea is exactly the same. The gender gap in wages could get smaller over time either because average skill differences decrease and/or because differences in rewards decrease. By comparing mean characteristics of male and female workers and estimating the $\hat{\beta}$s for men and women at two points in time, all the necessary terms can be constructed. We show an example of this later on when we examine the time trend in the gender gap.

Going Further

The Oaxaca decomposition procedure is a very valuable tool, but it has its limitations. It is important to recognize them. The burden of proof in this analysis is on the explanatory variables, that is, on the X variables. We are not testing directly for the presence of discrimination; rather, we are looking for indirect evidence in the sense that there are wage differences unrelated to average differences in skills. This leads to two problems, both related to the X variables that are included in the model.

First, it's possible to include too many X variables, specifically to include variables that are themselves the product of discrimination. Suppose that we could somehow measure the jobs that men and women held so that we were then comparing wages for men and women doing the exact same job. We might well find that there were little or no earnings differences between men and women doing the same job and thus that skill or other individual differences explained all the earnings difference. But suppose discrimination oper-

---

[7]If you are having trouble following all of this, sit down with several sheets of scrap paper and a calculator. Write down all of the equations, and do the algebra. Then work through the numbers in the table. It is not nearly as hard as it may look.

ated to influence the jobs that men and women got, so that, for example, many women ended up in jobs that were not particularly good relative to their skills. (Think of women becoming nurses and men becoming doctors, for example.) In that case, controlling for the job controls for too much—it throws out the baby with the bath water. For example, some researchers include a measure of a worker's occupation in an analysis of the gender gap in earnings. That is inappropriate, however, if women and men end up in different occupations as a result of discrimination in the labor market. The appropriate rule is this: Don't include any variables that themselves may reflect discrimination.

At the same time, it is possible to have too few X variables, so that the skills of men and women are not being accurately and appropriately measured. Truthfully, the information available to researchers is quite limited—race, gender, age, years of education, measures of where an individual lives (region of the country and urban/rural), and sometimes a measure of actual years of work experience. Much is left out, and even the variables included, such as years of education, are often measured less than ideally.[8]

How do left-out variables affect the Oaxaca procedure? Suppose that a researcher leaves out some important variable in which men greatly outscore women and which is important in determining earnings for both men and women. Omitting that variable might cause the researcher to underestimate the portion of the wage gap that is explained by differences in skills. This is certainly a real possibility.

Many researchers seem to assume that omitted variables will lead to exactly that result. They may well be right. But Barbara Bergmann, a well-known feminist economist, reminds us about "the missing data that would show men's qualifications and behavior in a bad light relative to women's . . . [such as] men's greater tendency to alcohol abuse, drug abuse, smoking, bad driving, . . . back problems, [and] history of heart attacks."[9] Excluding information about these characteristics (which are unavailable in most data sets) might cause researchers to overestimate the skills portion.

---

[8]Certainly, the quality of education varies across individuals with the same amount of education, as do majors. Don't, however, go overboard and conclude that these studies are useless. They are imperfect, but they are helpful.

[9]Barbara Bergmann, "Does the Market for Women's Labor Need Fixing?" *Journal of Economic Perspectives,* Vol. 3, No. 1, p. 45, Winter 1989.

In the end, the Oaxaca technique must be used, like so many things, carefully and with an appreciation for what is included and excluded. The Oaxaca technique is valuable and far better than simply making guesses, but it is not perfect. Studies with more variables (but not the inappropriate endogenous ones discussed earlier) are likely to be more trustworthy than those with very few. Pay attention to details.

The Evidence—Do Women Deserve to Earn Less Than Men?

An enormous number of studies of earnings differences between men and women have been conducted, as have studies that examine, for example, just the details of women's earnings. The total number of studies is easily in the hundreds, if not thousands. In this section, we look at two different kinds of studies. One kind examines the differences in earnings at a particular point in time. These studies are called **cross-sectional studies.** The other kind of study examines differences in earnings over an extended time period, usually with the goal of determining what lies behind the time trend in the gender earnings ratio. Studies like these are called **time-series studies.**

Because there are so many studies of both kinds, we cannot possibly cover even a tiny portion of them. Instead, we focus on several representative and well-known studies, especially ones that use the research methods discussed here. We also briefly consider a number of narrower studies that examine earnings differences in specialized occupations, for example, scientists, lawyers, and orchestra members, or that focus on particular dimensions of earnings differences.

Explaining the Gender Gap in Earnings— Cross-Sectional Research

One of the first well-known studies of the gender gap in earnings is by Mary Corcoran and Greg Duncan, who examined wage differences between men and women as of the mid-1970s.[10] It is an old study, but it well captures the situation as of that time, and it has some interesting features that make it well worth studying.

---

[10]Mary Corcoran and Greg J. Duncan, "Work History, Labor Force Attachment and Earnings Differences Between the Races and Sexes," *Journal of Human Resources,* Vol. 14, No. 1, pp. 3–20, 1979.

Corcoran and Duncan analyzed wage differences from a national survey of working men and women of all ages that was part of the Panel Study of Income Dynamics. The survey was specifically designed to measure many of the important but difficult-to-measure individual traits that could affect earnings and explain the gender earnings gap. The survey asked very detailed questions about men's and women's work histories, which is an area where differences between men and women were expected, especially as of the mid-1970s. For example, the survey included information on how many times an individual had stopped working and how long he/she had stayed out of the labor force since finishing school. Previous studies usually lacked this kind of detailed information and resorted to various indirect ways to measure work history. For men, researchers usually assumed continuous work following completion of education, which might be close enough for most men. For women, there often was no decent information on work histories.

Corcoran and Duncan estimated earnings regressions separately for men and women and then used those estimates to carry out the Oaxaca decomposition. Table 10.2 summarizes their basic findings concerning wage and skill differences for White women and Black women, both compared to White men. Part A presents information on skill differences, and Part B shows the net impact of these differences on the wage gap.

Part A shows that White men earned considerably more (although note how low, by today's standards, average 1976 wages were). White women earned 65% of what White men earned and Black women earned about 57%. Differences in years of education between White men and women were minuscule, while Black women had 1.1 fewer years of education. This tells us immediately that years of education cannot be an important factor explaining earnings differences between White men and women, because there is no difference, but it could be important for explaining the lower earnings of Black women. Differences by gender do appear for measures of work history and work attachment. Both White and Black women had been out of the labor force for more years than White men, had worked fewer years with their current employer, and fewer years prior to their current job. They had also worked more years part-time, missed more hours of work as a result of illness (both their own and that of other family members), and were more likely to have placed limits on job hours or location. This tells us that these measures could be important factors explaining the gender earnings gap.

In Panel B, the net impacts on the gender wage gap are shown. Recall that for a particular variable to be an important explanation of wage differences,

A. Average Wage Rate and Skills for White Men, White Women, and Black Women

Skill or characteristic	White Men	White Women	Black Women
Hourly wage rate	$5.60	$3.61	$3.17
Years of education	12.9	12.7	11.8
Work history			
Years not in labor force	.5	5.8	4.0
Years with current employer	8.8	5.8	6.5
Years of other work experience	11.3	8.1	9.3
Proportion of years part-time	9.0%	21.0%	17.4%
Indicators of labor force attachment			
Hours of work missed because of illness	40.5	55.5	83.7
Placed limits on job hours or location	14.5%	34.2%	21.6%

B. Sources of the Wage Gap Between White and Black Women and White Men

	White Men	White Women	Black Women
Explained			
Years of education	—	2%	11%
Work history	—	39%	22%
Labor force attachment	—	3%	0%
Total explained	—	44%	33%
Unexplained	—	56%	67%

Table 10.2 Explaining the Gender Gap in Earnings, 1976

Source: Adapted from Corcoran and Duncan, "Work History, Labor Force Attachment, and Earnings Differences Between the Races and Sexes," *Journal of Human Resources*, Vol. 14, No.1, pp. 3–20, 1979, Table 1. Copyright © 1979. Reprinted with the permission of The University of Wisconsin Press.

(1) there must be a substantial average difference between the two groups, and (2) the variable itself must be valuable to the higher earning group. As we suggested earlier, education explained virtually none (2%) of the wage gap between White men and women and somewhat more (11%) of the wage gap between White men and Black women. Work history differences were far more important, accounting for 39% of the wage difference between White men and White women and 22% of the wage difference between White men and Black women. The reason for the smaller effect for Black women is that

the differences in work history between White men and Black women tended to be less than the corresponding differences between White men and White women. This is quite consistent with the historical pattern of labor force participation in which Black married women typically worked more than White married women. The indicators of labor force attachment turned out to have virtually no effect, even though we did see that there were gender differences. The reason is that the measures of labor force attachment had little or no impact on the wage rates of White men: White men with more absences or more job restrictions did not earn less than White men with fewer absences and restrictions.

The bottom line from this study is that 44% of the wage gap was explained for White women and 33% for Black women. That means that more than half of the wage gap for White women and two thirds of the wage gap for Black women was unexplained, even though the researchers used an extensive set of explanatory variables. Corcoran and Duncan concluded: "We find that the wage advantages enjoyed by white men cannot be explained solely or even primarily by superior qualifications or more attachment to the labor force. . . . Those who claim that the labor market treats workers 'fairly' in the sense that equally productive workers are paid equally, are likely to be wrong" (p. 19).

Cross-sectional analyses of the gender earnings gap have been conducted for other, more recent years with quite similar results. Blau and Kahn[11] examined the earnings gap in 1979 and 1988 using the same Oaxaca procedure. Exactly like Corcoran and Duncan, they find no difference between men and women in educational attainment in either year but a substantial gap in years of work experience (7.5 years) in 1988. This means that the lower earnings of women are partially explained by this difference in work experience. Blau and Kahn report that about 30% of the earnings gap is explained by differences in skills in 1979 and about one third is explained in 1988. These figures are very much in line with the results of Corcoran and Duncan. Almost all the explained portion comes from the difference in years of accumulated work experience.

In recent years, the analysis of the gender earnings gap has shifted in an interesting way. As we have seen, the early literature emphasized human capital issues, especially the lower average years of work experience of women, as a potential explanation for the lower earnings of women. The new literature

---

[11]Francine D. Blau and Lawrence M. Kahn, "Swimming Upstream: Trends in the Gender Wage Differential," *Journal of Labor Economics*, Vol. 15, No. 1, pp. 1–42, 1997.

focuses instead on family issues: the **gender gap** has become the **family gap.** The analysis of the family gap in pay focuses on the impact of family responsibilities—marriage and children—on women's and men's earnings. After all, we still expect that men and women will marry and, more often than not, have children. How do marriage and children affect men's and women's earnings? Are marriage and children directly responsible for the earnings gap? We can use regression analysis and the Oaxaca technique to find out.

A few facts about marriage, children, and their impact on earnings are well established. As discussed in Chapter 4, married men typically earn more than single men, even after controlling for human capital and other relevant measures. Recall that this difference is called the **male marriage premium.** Conversely, married women typically earn less than single women, again controlling for human capital and other relevant measures. As a result, the gender earnings ratio differs dramatically by marital status. In the mid-1990s, for example, single women earned 88% as much as single men, while married women earned 57% as much as married men. Further, earnings for women with no children were not only higher than for women with children, but they were increasing more rapidly.

The thrust of the family gap literature is both old and new. Certainly, in the human capital analysis of the earnings gap, family responsibilities played an important, if not central, role. They were the primary reason that women might have less human capital than their male peers and thus end up with lower wages. Differences in lifetime labor force participation led to differences in investment in human capital, which led to lower wages. But this impact is indirect, operating through its impact on human capital investment. The family gap literature focuses on the direct impact of family responsibilities, over and above any impact it may have on human capital investment. It does this by including measures of family status in an earnings regression along with the traditional measures of human capital for both men and women. As a result, researchers can examine how family status affects male and female earnings and how it contributes to the gender earnings gap.

Jane Waldfogel has analyzed the impact of marriage and family responsibilities on men's and women's earnings in a series of papers.[12] A summary of her findings is presented in Table 10.3. Using regression analysis, Waldfogel examined the wages of young men and women (average age 30) in 1980 and 1991.

---

[12]The analysis presented here is based on Jane Waldfogel, "Understanding the 'Family Gap' in Pay for Women with Children," *Journal of Economic Perspectives,* Vol. 12, No. 1, pp. 137–156, 1998.

Variable	Contribution to Wage Gap	
	Explained Portion (%)	Unexplained Portion (%)
Human capital variables		
Years work experience	10	23
Education	−6	13
Family status		
Married	−5	22
Children	−3	40
All other variables	−4	10
Total	−8	108

Table 10.3 The Impact of Human Capital and Family Status on Male and Female Earnings, 1991

Source: Jane Waldfogel, "Understanding the 'Family Gap' in Pay for Women with Children," *Journal of Economic Perspectives*, Vol. 12, No. 1, pp. 137–156, 1998, Table 6. Copyright © 1998 by the American Economic Association. Reprinted with the permission of the author and publisher.

In addition to the standard human capital variables (education and experience), she included measures of marital and family status—whether currently married, whether previously married, whether an individual has one child, and whether an individual has two or more children. These are all measured as dummy variables, so that the regression measures the impact of having that particular status (i.e., married) versus not having it.

Let's focus on her results for 1991; then we will compare them to what she found for 1980. In her sample, the young women earned 81% of what the young men earned. Human capital differences were quite small. The difference in educational attainment was slightly in favor of women, and the difference in work experience was only half a year in favor of the men; remember that these are young women of a relatively recent cohort, many of whom had a very steady pattern of labor force participation. Differences in the value of education and experience for men and women were also very tiny.

The impact of this is shown in the second row of Table 10.3, which is based on results presented by Waldfogel. The figures shown in the table are the standard Oaxaca decomposition percentages.[13] The first row shows the impact of

[13]Waldfogel presents her own Oaxaca-style results, but she uses a different and far less common form of the decomposition. We have transformed her results using the standard procedure, based on the means and co-efficient estimates she presents. The results shown here do not match exactly the Oaxaca-style results she presents in her Table 7.

human capital variables. As shown in the second column, differences in educational attainment explain −6% of the wage gap. How can −6% be correct? The negative sign is not a misprint, although it is not what is typically found in analyses like this. It does, however, make sense. In this case, the negative sign means that rather than accounting for some portion of the gender wage gap, the gender difference in education would actually, by itself, cause women to have higher wages than men.[14] So it explains a negative portion of the wage gap.[15] The small difference in work experience explains 10% of the wage gap. In the third column, differences in the value of education for men and women account for 13% of the gap, and differences in the value of work experience account for 23%.

The next row shows the impact of marriage and motherhood on earnings. Again, the explained portion is small and is actually in favor of women. Differences in the proportions married and in the number of children account for −5% and −3%, respectively. Those numbers are small, so we can essentially ignore them. The important part of the story is in the unexplained column, which summarizes differences in the impacts of marriage and children on men's and women's wages. In her regression model, Waldfogel finds that marriage increases the earnings of men by 11% and of women by 4% (these results are not shown in the table). Having children has no effect at all on men's earnings, but it decreases women's earnings by approximately 10% if she has one child and 20% if she has two or more. Those gender differences in the impact of marriage and children yield the figures in the "unexplained portion" column. Differences in the way men's and women's earnings are affected by marriage account for 22% of the gender earnings gap, and differences in the way their earnings are affected by having children account for another 40%. Voila! We have the family gap.

Putting the numbers all together, Waldfogel's analysis of wages among young men and women shows that differences by gender in human capital and in marriage and family variables actually favor women. In total, these differences

---

[14]To go further, suppose that the gender wage gap was $3.00 per hour. Then the −6% figure would mean that gender differences in years of education would cause women to have average wages that were $0.18 per hour higher ($0.18 = 0.06 × $3.00).

[15]We can be more precise about this by looking at the Oaxaca formula. The unexplained portion due to any one variable like education is $[\hat{\beta}_{M,ED} \times (\overline{X}_{ED,M} - \overline{X}_{ED,F})]/(\overline{Y}_M - \overline{Y}_F)$. Usually, we expect the higher wage group to have more of the underlying skill, so the numerator is positive. But if women have more education than men ($\overline{X}_{ED,M} < \overline{X}_{ED,F}$) and if $\hat{\beta}_{M,ED} > 0$, then the numerator will be negative.

account for -8% of the wage gap, meaning that they would cause women to have higher wages than men. But differences in the impacts of these variables more than make up for this; they explain 108% of the gap so that together the two parts exactly explain all the wage gap (as mathematically, they must). The differences in the value of these skills and characteristics more than account for the wage gap, offsetting the impact of the differences in skills.

Waldfogel argues that family factors, not human capital, are now the primary cause of the gender earnings gap. Moreover, the impact of family factors increased between 1980 and 1991. In her analysis of 1980 data, she found two important differences. First, the explained portion of the earnings gap was greater—about 27%, which is much more in line with the other studies we have examined. Virtually all of the explained portion in 1980 was related to gender differences in years of work experience. Differences in the value of human capital also played an important role, accounting for 50% of the wage gap. Second, the impact of family responsibilities was important, but much smaller than in 1991. Waldfogel found that differences in the impact of family status on male and female earnings accounted for about one third of the earnings gap in 1980, compared to more than 60% in 1991.

Some economists now argue that the family gap is the major impediment to wage equality between relatively young men and women, like the ones analyzed by Waldfogel. Human capital differences have shrunk and will continue to shrink, an inevitable consequence of the new patterns of women's labor force participation. And differences in the value of education and work experience to men and women have also shrunk and will, in all likelihood, continue to shrink. That leaves primarily marriage and children as factors that disproportionately affect women and their earnings. In Chapter 14, we focus specifically on family policy in the United States.

We began this section by asking two questions: Do women deserve to earn less? And if so, how much less? The answer to the first question is a qualified "yes." Women, on average, continue to have less attachment to the labor force than men. They accumulate fewer years of work experience, and because work experience is valuable, they would earn less even if the labor market were totally free of any discrimination. The qualification, though, is that we are treating the differences in work experience as if they were not the product of discrimination. The best answer to the second question is "not as little as they actually earn." No credible study has ever found that anything close to 100% of the earnings gap could be explained by differences in average skill levels. Thirty to fifty percent explained is a reasonable bracket, which leaves 50 to 70% unexplained. Based on that evidence, women certainly deserve to earn more than they currently do.

Explaining the Time Trend in the Gender Earnings Ratio

Between roughly 1960 and 1980 the gender earnings ratio for year-round full-time workers was remarkably steady at about 59%. Then it suddenly began to rise, reaching 70% by 1990 and rising up to 74% before dropping and then moving erratically in the late 1990s and early-2000s. In this section, we look at studies that examine and attempt to explain the trend in the gender earnings ratio.

June O'Neill, a famous economist who later served as the first woman to head the Congressional Budget Office, examined the time trend between 1955 and 1982.[16] This was, as just noted, the time period of little or no change in the gender earnings ratio—it was more or less trendless. Interestingly, however, a great deal was happening beneath the surface to keep the ratio so stable. During this time period, the labor force participation rate of women increased substantially, especially for married women (see Chapter 7 for details), whose labor force participation rate doubled from 25% in 1955 to about 50% in the early 1980s. It would be surprising if that kind of change didn't have some impact on the earnings ratio.

O'Neill found that in the early 1950s, women who were in the labor force had completed on average 12 years of education compared to just 10.4 years for men. That's an enormous difference, and it reflected primarily the more selective nature of labor force participation for women in that time period. It was not so much that women had more education than men but that *working* women had more education than *nonworking* women. (Most of these nonworking women were, of course, working, but not as part of the paid labor force; that is what we mean when we distinguish working from nonworking women.) Working women were a highly selective and unrepresentative sample of the population of adult women.

Over the next two decades, average years of education rose steadily for working men—this was a time of rising educational attainment and growing college enrollments, aided by the GI Bill—all the way up to 12.7 years in 1983.

---

[16]June O'Neill, "The Trend in the Male-Female Wage Gap in the United States," *Journal of Labor Economics*, Vol. 3, No.1, pp. S91–S116, 1985.

But for working women, there was a smaller 0.7-year increase in educational attainment, partly because labor force participation became less selective. O'Neill notes that the participation rates of older married women with less education increased particularly rapidly. By the early 1980s, the entire 1.6-year educational advantage of working women was eliminated.

Something fairly similar was also happening in terms of the average work experience of working women compared to working men. We discussed earlier the changing pattern of women's life cycle patterns of labor force participation and its implications for the average work experience of working women. As "cycling" back and forth between the labor market and household production emerged as a norm in the 1950s and early 1960s, this had a negative impact on the average work experience of working women. It is not hard to see why: Women who returned to the labor market in, for example, their mid-30s had relatively little labor force experience. They had left the labor market perhaps a decade or more ago and returned with little experience. Additionally, the experience and skills they had often were no longer as valuable. These women pulled down average years of labor force experience of working women because, up to then, the female work force had largely been composed of women with steady work patterns.

This decrease shows up in the data. Information on job tenure with current employer is available for some years, and it shows a pattern of rising gender differences during the mid-1950s and through the 1960s. For example, among men and women aged 35 to 44, there was a 1.4-year difference in job tenure in favor of men in 1951, which rose to 4.0 years in 1963, stayed at greater than 4 years throughout the 1960s, finally dropping to between 3.1 and 3.3 years in the mid-1970s. For men and women, aged 45–54, the job tenure difference increased from 3.6 years in 1951 to 6.2 years in 1968 and was still above 5 years in 1981.

These changes in education and experience by gender have direct implications for the gender earnings ratio. Suppose that there had been no changes at all in the rewards to education and work experience for men and women over this time period. Because the gap in educational attainment, which had favored women, was eliminated and the gap in work experience in favor of men expanded, women's earnings would have fallen relative to men's earnings. The average working woman in the early 1980s was less-skilled relative to her male counterparts than the average working woman in the mid-1950s was. She would have deserved to earn less.

In fact, as we know, women's earnings did not fall relative to men's but rather stayed virtually constant. This relationship tells us that the rewards for women's skills must have increased over this time period relative to the rewards for men's skills. If that had not happened, the gender gap would have increased substantially, because women's average skills had declined compared to men's. For example, in the mid-1950s, the average working woman had substantially more education than the average working man and not much less work experience. But the gender gap in earnings was large. The only explanation for the gender gap is very substantial difference in treatment and opportunity. In terms of the Oaxaca technique, virtually all the wage difference would be "unexplained," that is, unrelated to differences in labor market skills. By the early 1980s, women were no longer more educated, and now they had less work experience than men. Their lower earnings reflect both the greater skill differences by gender as well as differences in treatment and opportunity. The "explained" portion of the gender gap increased.

In another important study, Blau and Kahn analyzed the trend in the gender earnings gap between 1979 and 1988.[17] Two very important changes in the labor market occurred during the 1980s. One, which we have already noted, is the rise in the gender earnings ratio. The other is the emergence of increasing earnings inequality. This increase in earnings inequality took two forms, usually referred to as **between-group inequality** and **within-group inequality.** Between-group inequality concerns the difference in mean or median earnings between different groups of workers, especially by such measures of skill as education and years of work experience. For example, in the mid-1970s, the average earnings difference between workers with a college education and workers with a high school education was about 30 to 35%, down from 45% in the 1960s. In the 1980s, the earnings difference shot up, reaching 55% by the mid- to late-1980s, and it has stayed at that record high level since then. Average earnings differences between young workers and more senior workers started to rise in the early 1970s and has risen almost continuously since then.

Earnings inequality also increased among workers within an education or experience category. This kind of inequality, which is within-group inequality, can be difficult to understand. It means that the earnings gap between, say, the

---

[17]Francine D. Blau and Lawrence M. Kahn, "Swimming Upstream: Trends in the Gender Wage Differential in the 1980s," *Journal of Labor Economics,* Vol. 15, No. 1, pp. 1–42, 1997.

highest paid 10% of college graduates and the lowest paid 10% of college graduates or between the highest paid 10% of older workers and the lowest paid 10% of older workers increased. Within-group inequality is thought to reflect the value of workers' unobserved skills, that is, the skills that individuals bring to the labor market other than or in addition to their education and work experience. But the truth is that nobody knows exactly what it is; we know what it isn't—it isn't related to how much education you have or how long you've been working or anything else that economists typically measure and include in their analyses. One way to visualize within-group inequality is to think of the distribution of wages within a group such as college graduates. An increase in within-group inequality means that the distribution has spread out. The gap between very high and very low within the category has gotten bigger.

Many economists have interpreted the wage structure transformation of the 1980s, including both the increase in between-group inequality and within-group inequality, as a **rise in the return to skill.** Relative wages rose for more-skilled groups relative to less-skilled groups, for example, more educated versus less educated and more experienced versus less experienced. And the gap between the best paid college graduates and the worst paid college graduates and between the best paid high school graduates and the worst paid high school graduates widened as well. There is a presumption that the best paid workers within each skill group are probably the most skilled as well.

In their analysis, Blau and Kahn take account of the two conventional terms in the Oaxaca decomposition (modified slightly because this is a time-trend analysis), plus a third term that measures the impact of changing wage structure, especially the within-group inequality. Focusing first on the two conventional terms, they presume that the labor market changes in the 1980s, especially the rise in the return to work experience, would be harmful to women because, as we've seen, women, on average, still have less work experience. Taken by itself, this would tend to decrease the gender earnings ratio. Thus, Blau and Kahn wrote that women are "swimming upstream" in their quest for greater earnings equality: The underlying trend in the labor market is working against them. At the same time, however, women's skills have increased relative to men's, again especially in terms of work experience. This narrowing of average skill differences has occurred primarily because of the new, more continuous pattern of labor force participation that characterizes more recent cohorts of women. Taken by itself, this gain would tend to increase the earnings ratio.

The data Blau and Kahn analyze come from the Panel Study of Income Dynamics, the same data source used by Corcoran and Duncan, but for a more recent time period. As in that study, there is very accurate and detailed information about work histories for women. In their regression analysis, Blau and Kahn use not only the traditional variables like educational attainment and years of work experience, but also measures of occupation, industry, and collective bargaining status. Many economists would argue that these variables do not belong in the regression equation. (See the earlier discussion of limitations in the Oaxaca method.)

Their findings are summarized in Table 10.4. We have recalculated their numbers to make them easier to understand.[18] During the time period they studied, the gender earnings ratio, measured in terms of average hourly earnings, rose by 10.2 percentage points, from 62.2% to 72.4%. Interestingly, this increase derived from two changes—men's earnings fell 9.9%, and women's earnings rose 4.9%, after adjusting for inflation.[19] Let's focus on trying to explain this 10.2 percentage point increase in the earnings ratio. Why did the ratio increase? Which factors were most important in causing the increase?

As the second row of Table 10.4 shows, changes in skills would, by themselves, have increased the earnings ratio by 8.3 percentage points (0.083). These are the changes that we would describe as "explained" in terms of the Oaxaca method. Educational attainment has almost no impact because in both 1979 and 1988 there was essentially no difference in the amount of education that men and women had. We saw a similar result concerning education in the analyses of Corcoran and Duncan and also Waldfogel. The narrowing of the gender difference in years of work experience was particularly important. That gap narrowed from 7.5 years in 1979 to 4.6 years in 1988, and, taken by itself, would have caused the earnings ratio to rise by 3.5 percentage points. Changes in occupation, industry, and collective bargaining status also caused the earnings ratio to increase by a total of 4.2 percentage points. The main source was a narrowing of some of the traditional occupa-

---

[18]Blau and Kahn analyze the fall in the earnings gap of the natural logarithm of wages as well as the percentage change in the gap. For our purposes, it is more straightforward to focus on the percentage point increase in the earnings ratio or, equivalently, the percentage point decline in the earnings gap. The numbers shown in Table 10.4 are rescaled from those in Blau and Kahn, Table 3.

[19]Here is how all these numbers fit together. Women's earnings in 1988 are 1.049 times their earnings in 1979, while men's earnings in 1988 are 0.901 times their 1988 value. Thus, the earnings ratio in 1988 is $(1.049/0.901) \times$ the earnings ratio in 1979 $= (1.049/0.901) \times 0.622 = 0.724$.

Source of Change in Gender Earnings Ratio	Contribution to Absolute Change in Gender Earnings Ratio
Total change	0.102
Change in skills ("explained")	
Education	0.006
Work experience	0.035
Occupation/industry/collective bargaining	0.042
Total	0.083
Change in rewards ("unexplained")	
Education	−0.001
Work experience	−0.015
Occupation/industry/collective bargaining	−0.049
Total	−0.065
Change in wage structure	0.084

Table 10.4   Sources of Change in Gender Earnings Gap, 1979–1988, Full Time, Nonagricultural Workers, Age 18–65

Source: Adapted from Blau and Kahn, "Swimming Upstream: Trends in the Gender Wage Differential in the 1980s," *Journal of Labor Economics,* Vol. 15, No. 1, pp. 1–42, 1997, Table 2. Based on actual increase in the gender earnings ratio from 62.2% in 1979 to 72.4% in 1988. Copyright © 1997. Reprinted with the permission of The University of Chicago Press.

tional differences between men and women, especially as a result of an increase in the proportion of women in professional occupations and a decrease in the proportion in clerical occupations.

Operating against this change, however, were the changes in the value of these skills. These changes are shown in the third row. As expected, they worked to decrease the earnings ratio, as rewards increased most for characteristics in which men held an initial advantage. Of particular importance are years of work experience, which rose in value and in which men had a considerable initial advantage, and occupation, where returns fell in some areas where women were over-represented. These changes, taken by themselves, were large enough to have caused a 6.5 percentage point drop in the earnings ratio, wiping out much of the gains caused by the narrowing of skill differences. In this sense, women were "swimming upstream," trying to make progress in a difficult economic environment.

Note that in the cases of experience and occupation, there are offsetting changes, one operating through a change in differences in skills and the other through a change in rewards to skills. It is important to understand the separate impacts. In both cases, there was a substantial initial difference in skills very much in favor of men. Men had more work experience than women, on average, and ranked higher in the occupational distribution. The increase in the value of work experience and high occupational position decreased the earnings ratio (i.e., made women worse off relative to men). At the same time, women narrowed those initial differences in work experience and occupational distribution. That change increased the earnings ratio. There is nothing at all contradictory about these two factors having two effects on the trend in the gender earnings ratio that are opposite to one another, although it takes careful thinking to keep them separate.

The last row in Table 10.4 summarizes the impact of changes in wage structure, focusing on changes that are not the result of changes in observed skills like education and experience and are not caused by changes in the value of those skills. This is primarily the result of what we called within-group inequality, that is, inequality not directly related to observed skills and traits like education and work experience. The entry in Table 10.4 indicates that this source of changes contributed an 8.2 percentage point increase in the earnings ratio. To be honest, there is no easy explanation for this change. It means that, relative to men, women were doing better in terms of unmeasured skills that affect earnings. But because it deals with unobservable skills, there is no way to say exactly what it means. It did, however, contribute to increasing the gender earnings ratio.

The sum of these three effects exactly equals the change in the gender earnings ratio: $0.102 = 0.083 - 0.065 + 0.085$. The earnings ratio increased because the difference between men's and women's labor market skills narrowed and because changes in unobservable skills and the return to those skills favored women. It decreased because the market valuation of skills that men have more of increased. But the net effect is the upward trend in the earnings ratio.

Gender Discrimination in Hiring

Gender discrimination might not just occur in wages. It is also possible that hiring discrimination exists. Employers may prefer to hire men over women in some jobs. This tendency might not be entirely employer discrimination; it could also reflect customer discrimination or statistical discrimination. Hiring discrimination could help explain the occupational segregation that still exists by gender in many occupations.

Just as measuring wage discrimination is difficult, detecting hiring discrimination is not an easy task. We can take a similar approach used with wages and estimate multiple regression models of the probability of being hired. We can hold constant many observable characteristics. However, we will still have the same problems as when we used multiple regression analysis to detect wage discrimination. In addition, we have another potential problem: Women and men may apply for jobs at different rates (i.e., women may, for example, be less likely to apply for certain jobs). One way to overcome some of these problems is to conduct an **audit study.**

Audit studies represent an alternative method for assessing whether or not discrimination occurs. An audit study is particularly useful in ferreting out discrimination in hiring that might exist between men and women. In this case, testers are sent out in matched pairs—one female and one male. The testers are as alike as possible "on paper" (i.e., they have resumes indicating similar levels of education, work experience, and so on). They differ only by gender or race. These testers apply for positions (usually within a certain type of firm) within a relatively short period of time. Their different rates of job offers are calculated, and this information can be used to determine whether or not firms are systematically favoring one gender in hiring. This type of study is not as good at examining wage discrimination because the testers do not actually accept jobs at the establishments. This method overcomes the problems inherent in the multiple regression approach. First, unobservable differences between men and women are potentially eliminated by matching their characteristics. Second, because men and women apply for the jobs in equal numbers (i.e., testers are pairs of men and women), we do not need to worry that women are less likely to apply for a particular position because they believe they will be discriminated against.

A study of discrimination in restaurant hiring conducted in the spring of 1994 illustrates how an audit study works. Students in an undergraduate research seminar at the University of Pennsylvania helped conduct this study, which was motivated in part by the observation that, within the occupation of waiters/waitresses in 1993, there was a sizable wage gap: The ratio of median weekly earnings of waitresses to waiters was 0.75, before any adjustments for work experience, etc. They also found that many researchers had suggested that males are preferred in high-priced formal restaurants (where earnings are likely to be greater). To test to see if men were more likely to be hired at high-priced restaurants, they conducted an audit study. According to the authors of the study, "The principle underlying the methodology in our particular context was to try to get as close as possible to the following experiment: send pairs of men and women, who are identical in every respect except their sex, to apply for jobs at restaurants in different price categories, and observe whether there are any statistically significant differences between the sexes in the receipt of job offers" (p. 920).[20] To implement this, they identified matched pairs of students and created resumes for each student. Because they were particularly interested in seeing if discrimination existed at high-priced restaurants, each resume indicated that each tester had some type of experience that would be valued at such a restaurant. Thus, on paper, the testers were identical in education and experience.

The next step was to try to minimize other differences between testers that might influence whether or not they were offered a job and which were correlated with gender. They addressed this issue in three ways. First, two men and two women were used to search for jobs in order to mitigate the effect of any unique personality traits that each tester might possess that could influence the outcome. Second, each tester was instructed to keep the same demeanor throughout all contacts with the restaurant and to dress similarly for all the restaurants they visited. Third, they attempted to get the employer to make a decision about interviewing based solely on resumes. This was accomplished by handing the resume to the first employee they encountered, which was often a host or waitperson, rather than the manager. The host or waitperson was asked to have the manager call the tester if there were any possibility of an interview. In this way, interviews were based on resumes; the manager had usually not met the job candidate. Thus, personality traits or biases of the manager that might be correlated with sex were controlled for.

The Zagat guide for Philadelphia was used to identify restaurants in three price categories: high-price, medium-price, and low-price. During a three-week period in the spring of 1994, testers dropped off resumes at sixty-five restaurants. The results were as expected. In the high-priced restaurants males received job offers in 48% of the cases, while females received offers in only 9% of the cases! This is a difference of 0.4 in the probability of being offered

[20]David Neumark, Roy J. Bank, and Kyle D. Van Nort, "Sex Discrimination in Restaurant Hiring: An Audit Study," *The Quarterly Journal of Economics*, Vol. 111, No. 3, pp. 915–941, 1996.

a job. Furthermore, the results for interviews confirmed this. Recall offers for interviews were designed to be arranged before the manager had met the applicant; thus these results are less subject to bias attributed to personality differences or experimenter effects that are correlated with sex. Males received interviews in 61% of the cases, while females received interviews in 26% of the cases. Males were also favored in the medium-priced restaurants but outcomes for job offers and interviews at low-priced restaurants favored females—men received job offers in only 10% of the cases, while women received offers in 38% of the cases. Interview results also confirmed this outcome.

Although these findings indicate relatively strong evidence of discrimination, the authors caution that "Audit studies offer important advantages relative to other approaches to studying discrimination, and perhaps even provide the only way of drawing convincing inferences regarding discrimination. But they also suffer from the potential disadvantage that the data they use are generated by the researcher and influenced by the precise methods used, and hence are more idiosyncratic than studies using data from publicly available secondary data sources" (p. 937).

Specialized Studies of Women's Earnings

We've now seen the main structure of the gender gap in earnings, both at a point in time and over time. In this section, we focus on a series of narrower studies that examine the gender gap for particular groups. The studies we discuss are representative of the hundreds of studies of women's earnings.

Women's Employment in Symphony Orchestras: "Orchestrating Impartiality"

Prior to about 1970, very few women were employed in top symphony orchestras. The so-called top five American orchestras (Philadelphia, Boston, New York, Cleveland, and Chicago) had an average of about 4% women orchestra members. The proportion was a bit higher, but still quite low, in four other well-known American orchestras (San Francisco, Los Angeles, Detroit, and Pittsburgh). This low representation of women was the result of a number of factors, but the one that gained attention was the hiring process itself. Candidates auditioned for a position, in front of the music director and/or a committee of orchestra members. Because the candidate's identity was clearly known, it was possible that favoritism (primarily based on a candidate's music teacher) and sexism were part of the hiring process.

To remedy these problems, most orchestras eventually adopted a "blind" audition process in which a candidate performs behind a screen that completely conceals his/her identity. Elaborate procedures are used to prevent anything that might indicate a candidate's gender. For example, precautions are taken to mute the sound of shoes, which might indicate whether the candidate was wearing high heels. In this setting, the evaluators know nothing at all about the candidate—not name, race, or gender. What impact did switching to blind auditions have on gender representation among major U.S. symphony orchestras?

The effect of the blind audition process of hiring at U.S. orchestras was studied by Claudia Goldin and Ceclia Rouse in their article "Orchestrating Impartiality: The Impact of Blind Auditions on Female Musicians."[21] They collected data on auditions between 1950 and 1995 for eight major U.S. orchestras and used information on the candidates' names to determine gender. Some of the auditions were blind, some were not, because different orchestras adopted the blind audition format at different times. For each audition, Goldin and Rouse knew whether the audition was blind and how each candidate fared. Even better, the same individuals often auditioned in both a blind audition and one that was not blind. That enabled Goldin and Rouse to hold constant the musical ability of the candidates across the different kinds of auditions and essentially to see if the *same* woman or *same* man fared differently in blind and not-blind auditions. The change in the procedures provided a **natural experiment** to evaluate the impact of the selection procedure. (For more on natural experiments, see Chapter 2.)

So, did women do better in the blind auditions? Table 10.5 summarizes the basic information, arranged by audition round. Typically, there are preliminary rounds in which many candidates advance, sometimes, but not always, followed by semifinal rounds in which just a few candidates advance, and a final round in which a winner is chosen. The sample they analyzed included 588 audition rounds that involved a total of over 7000 musicians.

In nonblind preliminary rounds, men had a 3.2 percentage point advantage over women—22.5% versus 19.3%. But in blind preliminary rounds, women

---

[21]Published in the *American Economic Review*, Vol. 90, No. 4, pp. 715–741, 2000.

Percent Advanced—Preliminary Round		
	Blind	**Not Blind**
Women	28.6%	19.3%
Men	20.2%	22.5%
Difference (% women advanced − % men advanced)	8.4%	−3.2%
Difference in difference	11.6%	
Percent Advanced—Semifinal Round		
Women	38.5%	56.8%
Men	36.8%	29.5%
Difference (% women advanced − % men advanced)	1.7%	27.3%
Difference in difference	−25.6%	
Percent Advanced—Final Round		
Women	23.5%	8.7%
Men	0%	13.3%
Difference (% women advanced − % men advanced)	23.5%	−4.6%
Difference in difference	28.1%	
Percent Hired		
Women	2.7%	1.7%
Men	2.6%	2.7%
Difference (% women advanced − % men advanced)	0.1%	−1.0%
Difference in difference	1.1%	

Table 10.5 Result of Blind Auditions on Advancement to Next Audition Round

Sample is men and women who participated in both blind and nonblind auditions.

Source: Goldin and Rouse, "Orchestrating Impartiality: The Impact of Blind Auditions on Female Musicians," *American Economic Review,* Vol. 90, No. 4, pp. 715–741, 2000. Copyright © 2000 by the American Economic Association. Reprinted with the permission of the authors and publisher.

had an 8 percentage point advantage over men—28.6% versus 20.2%. The impact of the blind audition is, then, the difference in the difference in the proportions advanced. In this case it is calculated as $(W_B - M_B) - (W_{NB} - M_{NB})$, where W and M stand for the proportion of women and men advanced, and the subscripts indicate whether the audition was blind or not blind. Substituting the proportions in the paragraph, we have $(28.6 - 20.2) - (19.3 - 22.5) = 8.4 + 3.2 = 11.6$. Thus, blind auditions provided women with an 11.6 percentage point advantage in preliminary rounds.

In semifinal rounds, things worked out quite differently. Women were actually 27.3 percentage points more likely than men to advance when the audition was not blind, but only 1.7 percentage points more likely when the audition was blind. In this case, the blind audition apparently hurt women by 25.6 percentage points.

In the final rounds, however, the screen was again beneficial to women candidates. They fared 4.6 percentage points worse in nonblind semifinal auditions, but 23.5 percentage points better in blind auditions. The net effect is the sum of these two impacts, 28.1 percentage points.

Finally, what about the bottom line? Were women more likely to be hired in blind auditions, compared to nonblind auditions? The answer appears to be "yes." Of all the men who auditioned in nonblind auditions, 2.7% were hired, compared to 1.7% of women. In the blind auditions, 2.6% of the men and 2.7% of the women were hired. So the net effect of the blind audition is a 1.1 percentage point increase in the proportion of women hired $[(2.7 - 2.6) - (1.7 - 2.7)]$. Since the fraction hired is about 2%, this is a very large relative increase.

These effects were confirmed in other regression analyses by Goldin and Rouse, in which they controlled for other factors that could affect the outcomes. They conclude that the switch to blind auditions accounted for 30% of the increase in the proportion of females among the new hires and about 25% of the increase in the proportion of females among these orchestras from 1970 to 1996. The switch to blind auditions apparently eliminated subtle discrimination that impaired the ability of women musicians to gain employment in the top U.S. orchestras.

Discrimination on the Basis of Physical Appearance

Economists have explored numerous sources of labor market discrimination. Some relatively recent studies have uncovered two areas where women (and men) face discrimination—both relating to physical appearance.

In "Beauty and the Labor Market," Daniel Hamermesh and Jeff Biddle[22] examine the effects of appearance on earnings, using interviewer ratings of physical appearance in three separate data sets. The authors present evidence that standards of beauty are well established within a culture at a given point in time, and these standards evolve slowly. They also note that the interviewers' assessments of beauty are remarkably consistent. To test the hypothesis that the more beautiful receive a wage premium, they use regression analysis and include a variety of other control variables to isolate the effect of beauty on earnings. They find that individuals rated "plain" by interviewers earn 5 to 10% less than those rated "average," while those rated "beautiful" receive a premium of around 5%. Perhaps somewhat surprisingly, given our culture's emphasis on looks for women, both men and women experience the penalty and the premium, and, if anything, the authors find that men's looks may have a slightly larger impact on their earnings than those of women.

Is the premium to beauty really just a function of the type of occupation that attractive women hold? Are beautiful people more productive at work? Perhaps one can perform certain jobs better if one is more attractive. Jobs that require a considerable amount of customer contact might fall into this category. To test this hypothesis and to determine if the premium to beauty is simply a result of the type of job one holds, the authors sorted the occupations into categories based upon how much looks are likely to play a role in each occupation. They then sort the sample into the occupations and stratify based upon looks. Their results, which are only suggestive, indicate that occupations that might require attractive people may produce independent effects on earnings. In other words, some evidence suggests that the labor market sorts the attractive people into the types of occupations where their attractiveness makes them more productive. The authors conclude by noting that their results seem to provide support for the Becker model of employer discrimination, though further testing would be necessary to confirm this observation.

In another study, economists Susan Averett and Sanders Korenman[23] used data from the National Survey of Youth to examine how obesity affects earnings. They estimated wage regression models such as those discussed in the

---

[22]Daniel S. Hamermesh and Jeff E. Biddle, "Beauty and the Labor Market," *American Economic Review,* Vol. 84, No. 5, pp. 1174–1194, 1994.

[23]Susan L. Averett and Sanders Korenman, "The Economic Reality of the Beauty Myth," *Journal of Human Resources,* Vol. 31, No. 2, pp. 37–49, 1996.

text and included a variable measuring an individual's **body mass index** or BMI, for short. The BMI is a commonly used measure of obesity; it is calculated by dividing weight in kilograms by the square of height in meters.[24] An individual who was 6 feet tall and weighed 180 pounds would have a BMI equal to 24.4; someone who was 5 feet 4 inches and weighed 135 pounds would have a BMI of 23.2. A BMI value greater than 30 is considered obese.

The models were estimated separately for men and women, and an extensive set of control variables was used, including actual work experience. As discussed in the text, this is particularly important when analyzing discrimination because women have historically had lower levels of work experience. Averett and Korenman were concerned about reverse causality (i.e., the possibility that an adverse labor market outcome might have caused a woman to gain weight). This means that contemporaneous associations between obesity and earnings may be biased. To be sure that the direction of causality runs from obesity to earnings, Averett and Korenman also estimated their models with an earlier measure of the BMI, which should be less affected by reverse causality.

They found that women face an earnings penalty if they are obese. Specifically, obese women experienced wages that were 15% lower than their counterparts whose BMI's fell into the recommend range. For men, there was some evidence of lower wages for the obese, although the magnitude was almost 50% lower. Furthermore, underweight men experienced a consistent earnings penalty, but there was no corresponding penalty or premium for underweight women. In related research, Averett and Korenman found that the obesity penalty was smaller for Black rather than White women, suggesting that cultural norms about beauty may play a role.

Wage Differences Between Black and White Women

We haven't said much about the earnings of Black women versus White women. In Figure 10.1, we show the Black/White earnings ratio for women. This is the ratio of median earnings for year-round full-time workers. As you can see, Black women haven't made progress with respect to White women; in fact, up until the last few years, they have been losing ground. In the early

---

[24]In terms of pounds and inches, BMI = weight in pounds divided by height in inches squared. The result is then multiplied by 703. One kilogram = 2.2 pounds and one meter = 3.28 feet.

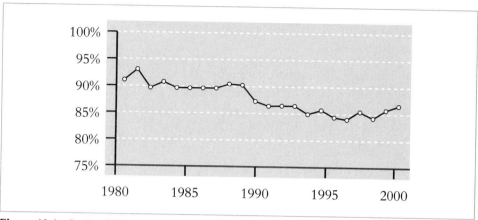

Figure 10.1   Ratio of Black to White Female Median Earnings, Year-Round Full-Time Workers, 1980–2001

1980s, Black and White women's earnings were nearly equal. Why did the ratio fall?

Anderson and Shapiro[25] investigated the causes of the changes in the Black/White female earnings gap. They used data covering the period 1968 to 1988. In 1988, according to their data set, the Black/White wage ratio was 0.849. They then asked how much of this 15% wage differential could be ascribed to differences in human capital or labor market characteristics and how much was the result of discrimination or racial differences in unmeasured characteristics or both. Estimating separate wage regressions by race and performing the Oaxaca decomposition, they determined that about 20% of the earnings difference between White and Black women is explained by observable characteristics, leaving some 80% of the difference unexplained.

They also explored the role of occupation in this differential. They calculated a Duncan Index, which is the index of occupational segregation that we discussed in Chapter 8. If the value of the Duncan Index is zero, there is no occupational segregation. If $D = 100$, there is complete occupational segregation. For their sample, the Duncan Index was 24.6 indicating that 24.6% of the women would have to change jobs for the racial structure to be equal.

---

[25]Deborah Anderson and David Shapiro, "Racial Differences in Access to High-Paying Jobs and the Wage Gap Between Black and White Women," *Industrial and Labor Relations Review*, Vol. 48, No. 2, pp. 273–286, 1996.

Could this unequal distribution across occupations explain part of the wage differential?

Including occupation in the wage regression models and recalculating the Oaxaca decomposition did indicate that the explained portion of the wage differential rose to 45%. However, it is not clear that occupation should be included in the wage regressions. Consider, for example, what happens if occupation choice is limited for some women because they are discriminated against. Specifically, what if Black women have trouble obtaining certain jobs because they are Black? As we noted earlier in the text, we usually do not want to include variables in our regression model that themselves might reflect discrimination. Thus, if Black women find themselves funneled into lower paying occupations as a result of discrimination, it is clearly inappropriate to include occupational controls in the model.

To determine whether or not occupational choice is the cause of differences in skills and how much could be attributed solely to differences in race, Anderson and Shapiro estimated a model of occupational choice. They found that between 65 and 74% of the existing occupational differential can be explained by differential access to higher paying jobs by race. In other words, most of the differences in occupation that they observed were not the result of rational choice but rather discrimination. Thus, they conclude that it is more likely that only 20% of the wage gap between Black and White women can be explained; the rest can be attributed to either unobservable differences or discrimination. As the authors themselves state: "Hence, it appears that differential access to occupations, by segregating Black women into low-paying occupations, plays a very important part in explaining the racial wage gap" (p. 285). They further note that the deteriorating economic position of Black women relative to White women in the 1980s and 1990s was the result of rising returns to skills that occurred during the 1980s as well as the decline in the enforcement of antidiscrimination laws that also occurred during this time frame.

The Compensation of Women Executives

The "glass ceiling," that invisible barrier that keeps women from top jobs, garners considerable attention from the media. A study by economists Marianne Bertrand and Kevin Hallock[26] asks how well women who do make it to the

---

[26]Marianne Bertrand and Kevin Hallock, "*The Gender Gap in Corporate Jobs*," NBER working paper 7931, 2000.

top of the corporate ladder fare compared to their male counterparts in terms of earnings and total compensation. They examine the compensation of the five most highly paid executives at about 1500 major companies that Standard and Poor's tracked from 1992 to 1997. An important advantage of their data set is that the sample of women and men is much more homogenous than other samples. Most studies of the gender wage gap, as we noted, find a sizeable unexplained portion. However, as we have already cautioned, that unexplained portion may be discrimination, but it also may reflect unobservable characteristics of both the workers and the firms that may be correlated with earnings. For example, women may not be as committed to long-term careers as men—something that is unobservable to the economist performing the analysis. Because the men and women in the Standard and Poor's data set are at the highest levels of the corporate ladder, it is safe to assume that they are probably very similar with respect to career goals, commitment to the labor force, human capital, and motivation. Thus, these data provide a unique opportunity to study the gender wage gap. Any wage differential unexplained by human capital and firm characteristics is thus more likely to represent discrimination than in other studies of the gender wage gap where the samples are not so homogenous.

The authors found that high-ranking corporate women bring home only about 67% of the earnings that top male executives command. They report that, in 1997, the average women executive earned a little less than $900,000 in compensation (1997 dollars) while the average male executive earned about $1.3 million (1997 dollars). To help ascertain whether or not these women faced pay discrimination, the authors performed the Oaxaca decomposition we outlined earlier. Their regressions included five variables to explain wages: indicators for the top three occupations, log stock market value, and stock return in the previous year. With just these five control variables, they found that 71% of the total difference in compensation between male and female executives was explained. Because this group is likely a fairly homogenous group in terms of motivation, career commitment, and human capital investment, the unexplained portion of this differential probably comes closer to reflecting discrimination toward women—an assertion that Hallock and Bertrand make themselves. It does appear that men and women holding similar functions in firms are treated fairly equally in terms of compensation.

They also documented that women tend to be concentrated in smaller corporations than men, and it has been well established in the literature that large

Title	% Female
CEO/chair	0.52
Vice chair	0.85
President	1.71
CFO	6.44
COO	1.836
Exec. VP	1.58
Other chief officer	2.66
Senior vice president	3.45
Group vice president	0.81
Vice president	4.27
Other occupations	2.88

Table 10.6   Percent Female in Various Corporate Positions

Source: Standard and Poor's ExecuComp database, 1992–1997.
Reported in Bertrand and Hallock, "The Gender Gap in Top
Corporate Jobs," NBER working paper 7931, 2000. Reprinted
with permission.

corporations pay better, all else being equal. However, there is no evidence that women are concentrated in lower-paying industries, though there is evidence that women are concentrated in the lower-paying occupational categories. Finally, women in the sample were younger than the men and had 5.6 years less seniority on average, both of which tend to lower pay.

Yet, women are also underrepresented in the top occupations. Table 10.6 demonstrates this quite clearly. Women were less than 1% of CEOs and vice-chairs in the data set and less than 2% of presidents, COOs, and executive and group vice presidents.

Thus, although women executives are compensated well, women are still underrepresented in the top corporate jobs.

Summary

In this chapter, we have sampled a bit of the extensive empirical literature in economics examining women's earning. Much of the literature attempts to sort out the relative importance of the two primary explanations for the gender gap in earnings—human capital versus discrimination. Using regression analysis and the Oaxaca decomposition technique, it is possible to determine the proportion of the wage gap due to all human capital differences or even to specific human capital measures, such as education and experience.

The research literature shows that there is certainly something to the human capital explanation. Men and women do not, on average across the entire working population, bring equal skills to the labor market. They would not, therefore, have equal earnings even if labor market discrimination could be eliminated. But despite the prediction from economic theory that market competition would eliminate discrimination due to employers, no study has found that gender differences in human capital account for all or even a substantial majority of the wage gap. In the mid-1970s, human capital differences, primarily measures of career work attachment, accounted for roughly one third to one half of the earnings gap. The remainder was the result of gender differences in the value of human capital. A later study focusing on the late 1980s found that one third of the gap was explained by human capital differences. More recent studies of gender earnings differences among younger workers have emphasized not differences in human capital but differences in the way family responsibilities affect men's and women's earnings. These analyses of the family gap have found that marriage and children have different effects on earnings for men and women and that these differences are the primary source of the difference in pay.

Even though human capital differences may not explain all the wage gap, changes in human capital differences are an important part of the time trend in the wage gap. One interesting study showed that the stability in the earnings ratio at about 60% between 1960 and 1980 was actually the result of offsetting changes in gender differences in human capital and in discrimination. During these years, women's human capital declined relative to men's as a result of the rapid influx into the labor market of women who had relatively little prior attachment to the labor market. Taken by itself, this would have led to a decline in the earnings ratio. The fact that the ratio did not decline tells us that discrimination must have eased. Many scholars are optimistic about the future narrowing of the gender gap. Women already have more education than men, and differences in labor force participation rates are narrowing. More and more women are establishing careers in the same way as men, by working more or less continuously without significant family interruptions. As gender differences in human capital narrow, the wage gap should narrow as well. The suggestion that the family gap is now the last remaining hurdle to gender equality is an important idea to bear in mind.

The gender gap in pay has led to the development of public policy measures that are intended to address that problem. We turn to these policies in the next chapter.

Key Terms

audit study   385

between-group inequality   380

body mass index   392

continuous variables   362

cross-sectional studies   370

dependent variable   362

dummy variable   362

error term   362

family gap   374

gender gap   374

independent or explanatory variables   362

male marriage premium   374

natural experiment   388

Oaxaca decomposition   364

regression coefficients   362

rise in the return to skill   381

time-series studies   370

within-group inequality   380

CHAPTER 11

Women's Employment and Earnings: Policy

Introduction

National Pay Equity Day is celebrated on a Tuesday in April because on average it takes women seven work days to earn the same amount that men earn in the previous five work days, and fifteen months to match an average man's twelve-month income. This chapter is the last in a series of four to examine this gender wage differential. In Chapter 8, we verified that there is indeed a wage differential between men and women. In particular, we compared the wages of men and women who worked full-time and all year round, and we found that the gender wage gap remained fairly steady with women earning about 60 cents for every $1 earned by a man until the 1980s when it began to narrow. Currently, women earn about 76 cents for every dollar that a man earns. Remember though that, as we discussed, this 76 cents is unadjusted for other factors such as education and work experience.

After verifying the existence of the wage differential, we noted in Chapter 9 that there are potential human capital explanations for at least some of the wage differential between women and men. In particular, women may invest less in labor market-oriented human capital. They may anticipate future family responsibilities and thus make a lower investment in education and training. Through most of the 20th century, men had more education than women, but young women are now more likely to be college graduates than young men. However, because of these anticipated family responsibilities, women may plan to cycle in and out of the labor force depending upon their children's ages. Thus, they accumulate less work experience than men, and they may have less on-the-job training than men. In addition, when women reenter the labor market after taking time off for family responsibilities, they may find that their earnings are lower than they were when they left the labor market, because some forms of human capital will deteriorate when they are not used. This human capital explanation suggests that wage differentials between men and women are the result of legitimate differences in human capital investment and are thus based upon the supply side of the labor market (e.g., differences in the workers themselves). Simply put, if women bring with them less human capital to the labor market, they will earn less money. If this decision to acquire less human capital is a choice that women willingly make, it is a legitimate reason for them to earn less money.

However, we also documented that there is still considerable occupational segregation in the workforce. Women are still more likely to be in the lower-paying occupations. One explanation for this trend concerns human capital—women choose occupations based on how much they anticipate cycling in and out of the labor force. Premarket influences and discrimination may also play a role in women's job choices. For example, social norms could lead women to prefer to be a nurse or a doctor. Additionally, there is concern that women are socialized away from math and science in school. However, occupational differences could be the result of discrimination. There is some debate as to whether this occupational segregation reflects discrimination or rational choices that women make. For example, some women may select occupations with a lower rate of skill depreciation (e.g., kindergarten teacher rather than college professor) if they anticipate cycling in and out of the labor force. However, it could also be argued that women do not have access to certain occupations or that employers are reluctant to hire women for certain jobs.

We said that sex discrimination exists when female workers with the same abilities, education, training, and experience as male workers receive different treatment with respect to wages, hiring, occupational access, or promotion. We presented several theories of discrimination. We examined Becker's personal prejudice theories of discrimination, which showed that discrimination could arise from employers, employees, or customers. Discrimination arising from employers should disappear in the long run because it is costly and will force firms to have lower profits and go out of business. However, customer discrimination can be expected to persist in the long run. We discussed the possibility of statistical discrimination. Discrimination explanations for the gender wage gap then suggest that wage differentials are the result of demand side factors (i.e., the actions of discriminatory employers not allowing women access to certain occupations, paying them less, or promoting them less often).

In Chapter 10, we examined how economists measure discrimination and the caveats that must be attached to such measures. We summarized the findings of recent empirical work that measured the gender wage differential and assessed the extent of the role of discrimination in explaining this differential. We noted that most studies attribute the wage gap's existence to both demand- and supply-side factors; these studies tend to find that somewhere between one third and one half of the gender wage differential can be explained. The unexplained portion is usually termed discrimination though researchers are quick to note that the unexplained portion can be the result of unmeasured factors, such as motivation, being left out of the model. It could also be the case that the human capital variables are the product of discrimination (i.e., women obtain less training or education because they do not believe they will be rewarded with higher earnings).

In this chapter, we examine the various government policies that exist to combat discrimination in the labor market. Because the focus of the book is on women, we naturally focus on sex discrimination. We begin by describing the laws in place and how they have evolved over time. We then assess the effectiveness of antidiscrimination legislation. We end the chapter with a look at a controversial policy that still generates some interest—comparable worth. Let's begin with a history of government programs that have been enacted to combat discrimination.

Government Programs to Combat Discrimination

Historically, women have typically experienced some sort of discrimination in the workplace. Some of the early discrimination women faced actually had its origins in being protective toward women. For example, in the early 1900s, many states adopted legislation limiting how many hours per day a woman could work—it was believed to be bad for her reproductive health if she overexerted herself. Many firms also imposed **marriage and/or pregnancy "bars."** A marriage bar often took two forms. One was a rule that stated that a woman who was single when hired and subsequently married would lose her job. Another established that a married woman could not be hired for a certain job. The same type of rules often held for women who became pregnant. Marriage bars were implemented in the late 1800s and early 1900s in the United States and were not unusual in other countries as well, such as Japan. In the United States, they largely disappeared by the 1950s.[1]

In this section of the chapter, we examine laws that are currently in place to protect women against labor market discrimination. Before we do so though,

---

[1]See Claudia Goldin, *Understanding the Gender Gap: An Economic History of American Women*, New York: Oxford University Press, 1990, pp. 160–178, for a discussion of marriage and pregnancy bars.

it is worth taking a minute to explore why we should have such laws. After all, if the labor market (as described in Chapter 8) works well, labor should be allocated to where it is most productive, and, as we saw in Chapter 9, discrimination arising from employers should disappear in the long run (although discrimination arising from other sources might not be eradicated by market forces alone and may require government intervention).

How can we justify the existence of antidiscrimination laws? From an economics perspective, there are two ways to justify these laws. The first is on the basis of *equity*. If some group—women or minorities—is being treated unfairly, we may rationalize such laws on the grounds that they force employers to treat all labor market participants equally. Why should equally qualified women or minorities be denied access to higher paying jobs or earn less money for doing equal work?

The second justification is on the basis of *efficiency*. One important task of the labor market is to allocate labor across all the possible firms in the economy in an efficient way. How many workers should be employed at this firm and how many at that one? This allocation is important because it determines how much we, as a society, can produce. When labor is allocated inefficiently, we, as a society, end up producing—and consuming—less than we otherwise could. An allocation of workers across firms is said to be efficient when it is impossible to change the current allocation and produce a set of outputs that is more highly valued.

It turns out that discrimination leads to an inefficient allocation of labor in exactly that way. We can look at discrimination, first, in a very general sense. Labor market discrimination results in economic inefficiency whenever people of one gender or race or religion are denied the opportunity to use their skills where they are best suited. Imagine, for example, a world in which talented women are employed in settings that underutilize their skills. Perhaps a woman who was a college graduate some years ago ended up as a secretary because professional jobs were not open to women. The woman in question clearly suffers financially, but society suffers, too. It loses the difference in the value of what she could have accomplished in a professional setting versus the value of what she produced as a secretary. Whenever a talented person is unable to find an appropriate job for reasons of discrimination, society loses the output that is not produced. The career of Supreme Court Justice Sandra Day O'Connor is a perfect example of this kind of inefficiency. See Box 11.1 for a discussion.

Box 11.1 Sandra Day O'Connor—Economic Inefficiency in Practice

Justice Sandra Day O'Connor graduated from Stanford Law School in 1952. She completed the degree in two years, rather than the usual three, ranked third out of the 102 students in her class, and was an editor of the *Stanford Law Review*. Soon after her own graduation, she married a fellow law student and attempted to find work with a private law firm in California while he completed his last year of law school. Despite her lofty academic credentials, she was completely unsuccessful in her job search in the private sector because of the reluctance of many firms to hire a female attorney. Apparently some firms offered her a position as a legal secretary, rather than as an attorney.

She eventually found a position as a deputy attorney for San Mateo County and worked there while her husband finished up his degree. She then followed her husband to Europe, where she worked from 1954 to 1957 as a civilian attorney for the Quartermaster Market Center in Frankfurt, Germany. When she and her husband returned to Arizona, she was again unable to find work with a local law firm; her husband had no problem. Rather than give up, she established her own law practice, later served as an Arizona assistant attorney general, a state senator, a trial judge, and a member of the Arizona court of appeals. In 1981, Sandra Day O'Connor became the first female member of the U.S. Supreme Court.

There seems little question that O'Connor suffered from a particularly harsh form of labor market discrimination solely on the basis of her gender. Despite impeccable qualifications, she was completely unable to secure the kind of legal position that her male classmates readily received. A less-determined person might well have abandoned the practice of law altogether.

Note the inefficiency here. Not only was Justice O'Connor deprived of the opportunity to utilize her skills to the fullest, but society was deprived of the value of those skills. She was underutilized. The potential output that she could have produced was squandered.

There are undoubtedly thousands of similar stories of skilled women and skilled members of other minority groups who were unable to use, in the most productive way, the many skills that they had.

We can also demonstrate this more rigorously with a numerical example. Assume that men and women are equally skilled, just as we assumed in our models of discrimination in Chapter 9. Assume further that as a result of labor market discrimination, women all work in a sector of the economy that pays them $10 per hour and that men all work in a sector of the economy in which they earn $20 per hour. For both men and women, employment is set where the **marginal revenue product** (MRP) of the last worker just equals the wage rate. Thus, given these wage rates, firms will hire men and women up to the point where the MRP of the last woman just equals $10 and the MRP of the last man equals $20. This is shown in Figure 11.1. W_m and E_m represent the equilibrium wage and employment in the men's labor market, and W_f and E_f represent the equilibrium wage and employment in the women's sector. In this example $W_m = \$20$ and $W_f = \$10$.

This employment situation is inefficient in the sense that it is possible to reallocate the men and women and end up better off. This follows directly from the fact that the MRPs of equally productive men and women are different, which in turn follows from the fact that women earn lower wages as a result of labor market discrimination. To see that this situation is inefficient, consider what would happen if one woman were moved from the women's sector to the men's sector. In the women's sector, the value of output produced would

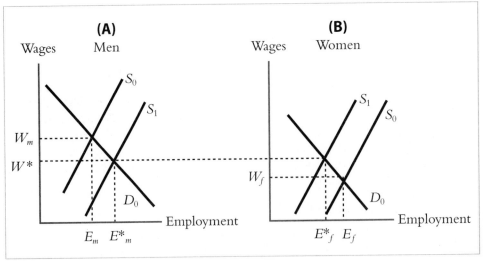

Figure 11.1   Inefficiency in the Labor Market Resulting from Discrimination

fall by $10, which was the MRP of the last worker. In the men's sector, that same woman could produce output valued at just a bit less than $20, since $20 was the MRP of the last man hired. In the process of reallocating that woman from the women's sector to the men's sector, the total value of output would increase by $10. Society would therefore end up better off, with a more highly valued bundle of goods produced.

Of course, that wouldn't be the end of the reallocation process. The next worker moved might cause the value of output to fall by, say, $10.10 in the women's sector and rise by $19.90 in the men's sector. (These numbers reflect the idea of diminishing marginal revenue product.) So the value of total output would rise by $9.80. As long as the wage differs for equally skilled men and women, then their MRPs will differ, and it will always be possible to move a worker from where her current MRP is low to where her potential MRP is higher. In the process the total value of output increases. Only when the MRPs of the last worker employed in both sectors is identical will the allocation of labor be efficient. And that requires that the wage rates be identical. In Figure 11.1, this equilibrium is illustrated by a leftward shift in the supply curve for women and a rightward shift in the supply curve for men. The final equilibrium wage is reached at W^*. Of course, now there is no longer a market exclusively for men's labor because women have joined that market.

Antidiscrimination Laws in the United States

LEGISLATIVE HISTORY   Laws expressly forbidding discrimination on the grounds of race or gender are actually relatively new in the United States. The **Equal Pay Act of 1963** was the first federal law to deal with sex discrimination. It is an amendment to the **Fair Labor Standards Act of 1938,** the same act that created the minimum wage and required overtime pay. The Equal Pay Act of 1963 makes it illegal for employers to pay different wage rates for men and women if they are doing equal work. Equal work is defined as being work that requires equal skill, effort, and responsibility and is performed under similar working conditions. This law essentially eliminated a not uncommon practice of paying women in a firm lower wages than men for doing the same jobs.

Critics charge that the weakness of the Equal Pay Act of 1963 is its narrow focus on wages—it only covers wage discrimination. Thus, a firm that segregates its employees by occupation and gender and pays the female occupations lower wages would not be violating the Equal Pay Act—even if it

Box 11.2   On the Passage of the 1964 Civil Rights Act

In the early-1960s, sex discrimination did not receive the same attention as discrimination on the basis of race and color. In fact, sex was added as an amendment to Title VII on February 8, 1964—the day it passed—by Congressman Howard W. Smith of Virginia, Chairman of the Rules Committee. He was a conservative and known to oppose all civil rights legislation. His amendment is widely believed to have been an effort to ensure that the civil rights act would not pass. In fact, as one author notes, the addition of "sex" to Title VII was "the result of a deliberate ploy of foes of the bill to scuttle it" (Whalen and Whalen, 1985, p. 238).

However, there is another interpretation of the last minute addition of "sex" to the legislation. Freeman argues that it was, in fact, the result of tireless work by women lawmakers and the National Women's Party whose strategy was to add "sex" to any legislation aimed at expanding or securing rights for any group in hopes of gaining rights for women. Because the National Women's Party had been lobbying congress for the Equal Rights Amendment (ERA) for nearly forty years, Freeman speculates that the addition of "sex" to Title VII was an attempt by some lawmakers to support the ERA.

Sources: Charles Whalen and Barbara Whalen, *The Longest Debate: A Legislative History of the 1964 Civil Rights Act*, New York: New American Library, 1985 and Jo Freeman, "How Sex Got Into Title VII: Persistent Opportunism as a Maker of Public Policy," *Law and Inequality: A Journal of Theory and Practice*, Vol. 9, No. 2, pp. 163–184, 1991.

refused to hire women into the higher-paying male jobs—or even to hire women at all!

Title VII of the **Civil Rights Act of 1964** makes it an unlawful employment practice for an employer "to refuse to hire or to discharge any individual, or otherwise to discriminate against any individual with respect to his [sic] compensation, terms, conditions, or privileges of employment, because of such individual's race, color, religion, sex or national origin." This act is widely regarded as the cornerstone of antidiscrimination legislation in the United States. Surprisingly, sex was only added to the Civil Rights Act at the last minute, as described in Box 11.2.

Over the years, Title VII has been amended by Congress several times. In 1972, it was amended to apply to all employers in interstate commerce with fifteen or more employees, to all labor unions with fifteen or more members, and to workers employed by state and local governments, federal agencies, and educational institutions. The 1972 amendment is called the Equal Opportunity Act of 1972. In 1978, the act was again amended to protect pregnant women through the Pregnancy Discrimination Act.

Title VII also addressed another type of discrimination—sexual harassment. Sexual harassment encompasses a wide range of behaviors. For example, it may take a "quid pro quo" form (i.e., an exchange of sexual favors for a promotion), or it may be unwanted sexual comments in the workplace that result in the creation of a "hostile environment." In 1986, the U.S. Supreme Court ruled that sexual harassment in the form of a hostile environment at the workplace can be the basis for a sex discrimination complaint under Title VII.[2]

ENFORCEMENT AND INTERPRETATION Enforcement of the Civil Rights Act of 1964 takes place through the **Equal Employment Opportunity Commission (EEOC)**. The EEOC is an independent, five-member agency appointed by the President with the approval of the Senate. Generally, in order to take action, the EEOC must receive a sworn complaint from an individual. If the complaint appears reasonable and well-founded, the EEOC then approaches the offending employer for conciliation. If conciliation is not achieved, the EEOC and the complainant may then go to the court system. The EEOC can also bring class action suits designed to redress discrimination among a group of workers rather than just one individual at a firm. Class action suits provide more of a threat to a firm accused of discrimination. In addition, the EEOC requires employers with at least 100 employees or government contractors with fifty employees or more than $50,000 in government contracts to fill out the EEO-1 Private Sector Report annually. This report is a snapshot of how many racial and ethnic minorities and women are working in a company; the EEOC uses it to decide which firms to investigate. Interestingly, the first year that the EEOC was in operation it did not expect to see many sex discrimination lawsuits. After all, the main purpose of Title VII was to eliminate racial discrimination—as we noted in Box 11.2, sex was added at the last minute. Yet, that first year, one third of all charges filed alleged sex discrimination.[3]

---

[2]In 1998, the Supreme Court further clarified several aspects of the law with respect to sexual harassment. See Charles J. Muhl, "Sexual Harassment," *Monthly Labor Review,* Vol. 121, pp. 61–62, July 1998, for details.
[3]For an engaging history of the EEOC and some landmark cases, see http:www.eeoc.gov/35th/milestones/1991.html.

Currently, the EEOC is in charge of enforcing the following federal laws: The Age Discrimination in Employment Act (ADEA) of 1967, as amended, prohibiting employment discrimination against individuals forty years of age and older; the Equal Pay Act (EPA) of 1963, prohibiting discrimination on the basis of gender in compensation for substantially similar work under similar conditions; Title I and Title V of the Americans with Disabilities Act (ADA) of 1990, prohibiting employment discrimination on the basis of disability in the private sector and state and local governments; Section 501 and 505 of the Rehabilitation Act of 1973, as amended, prohibiting employment discrimination against federal employees with disabilities; and the Civil Rights Act of 1991, providing monetary damages in cases of intentional discrimination and clarifying provisions regarding disparate impact actions. Although the EEOC has the power to enforce these laws, many argue that it has at many times been understaffed and underfunded, leading to large caseload backlogs. Its ability to enforce these laws depends heavily upon the political party in power and how much money it is willing to allocate to this agency. In fiscal year 2001, the EEOC filed 431 suits and resolved 354 suits. It obtained $50.6 million in monetary relief for the victims of discrimination.

Enforcing Title VII of the Civil Rights Act of 1964 is not an easy task. Since the passage of Title VII, the courts have wrestled with the question of what is and what is not discrimination. The courts use several standards when evaluating discrimination. The first is termed **disparate treatment.** It occurs if individuals are treated differently (paid different wages, offered different promotions) because of their race, sex, color, religion, or national origin, *and* if it can be shown that there was an intent to discriminate. Disparate treatment clearly seems like the obvious definition of discrimination. However, the problem with this standard is that a seemingly innocuous practice such as word-of-mouth advertising for jobs (i.e., when a job opening is announced by those already working at the firm to their friends and acquaintances) may perpetuate discrimination, even if it was not intended to be discriminatory. For example, this type of discrimination could happen when the firm is comprised only of male employees whose friends are predominately male.

Because of this tendency, the courts also rely upon the **disparate impact** standard of discrimination. Under this standard, even if a firm does not intend to discriminate, it can be held liable if its actions lead to discriminatory outcomes. Here, concern is with the result, not the motivation. A hiring policy that appears to be neutral but leads to different impacts by race, gender, and so on is prohibited unless the policy can be shown to be necessary for successful job performance. In other words, under the disparate impact standard, there does not have to be any intent to discriminate. In court cases, it is quite natural for a regression analysis of discrimination to be shown to support such claims. (See Box 11.3.)

Box 11.3 Regression Analysis in the Courtroom

Proving discrimination in a court of law appears to be a daunting task. Direct evidence of discrimination, such as a blatantly discriminating employer, is rare. Thus most cases are not prosecuted under the disparate treatment standard, but rather use the disparate impact standard. In other words, the defendant is accused of relying on employment policies that had a disparate impact on females or minorities.

In this kind of case, statistical evidence of discrimination is very helpful. However, simple percentages are not adequate to prove discrimination. Simply showing that the women in a firm are paid less than the men on average does not at all indicate discrimination. It may be that the men at the firm all have more education or work experience than the women. What is necessary is to be able to make comparisons among equally qualified men and women. This can be difficult when a number of qualifications are used to determine salary and employment-related issues such as promotion.

Fortunately, economists have the tool of regression analysis at their disposal and use this tool when they serve as expert witnesses in discrimination cases. (In fact, this can be a highly lucrative line for work for labor economists!) Beginning in 1975, the legal community recognized the usefulness of regression analysis in employment discrimination cases, and the Supreme Court formally accepted the technique in 1986. Regression analysis allows one to control for or separate out the factors that are legitimately related to wages, such as education and job tenure from those that are not legitimately related to wages, such as sex, race, or age.

A recent study examined the outcome of forty-six cases of discrimination that reached various levels within the U.S. court system. An analysis of these cases revealed that regression analysis can be a powerful tool in an employment discrimination case. Plaintiffs were more likely to win their case when

they used regression analysis, and furthermore, they were less likely to win when they did not use regression analysis but the defendant did. This study also found that it was important to present "anecdotal evidence" (i.e., testimony from an alleged victim of discrimination). The combination of regression analysis and anecdotal evidence apparently puts plaintiffs in a stronger position. These results also bode well for students of economics who may be able to secure interesting jobs as consultants on wage discrimination cases.

Source: Catherine Connolly, "The Use of Multiple Regression Analysis in Employment Discrimination Cases," *Population Research and Policy Review*, Vol. 10, pp. 117–135, 1991.

Finally, the courts also look to see if the firm engages in a **pattern or practice of discrimination.** In other words, the courts have found a pattern or practice when the evidence establishes that the discriminatory actions were the defendant's regular practice rather than an isolated incident. For a recent example of an alleged pattern or practice of discrimination, see Box 11.4.

The classic 1971 case of ***Griggs v Duke Power Company*** illustrates the disparate impact standard. Prior to the passage of Title VII, Duke Power Company was highly segregated. Blacks were generally relegated to lower-paying jobs than Whites. After the passage of Title VII, the company required all new job applicants, as well as existing employees who wished to transfer to new departments, to have high school diplomas and sufficiently high scores on two professionally-designed aptitude tests. The company argued that this requirement was nondiscriminatory because it applied equally to both Blacks and Whites. In its decision, the Supreme Court said that for an employment practice to be discriminatory, two things must be shown: First, the person charging discrimination must show that the employment practice has a disparate (unequal) impact on the members of the minority group, and second, if there is a disparate impact, the company had the burden of proof to show that the employment practice is is a matter of "business necessity" for the firm.

In the *Griggs* case, the Court found evidence of discrimination. It concluded that the company's requirements had a disparate impact on Blacks, who were far less likely to pass the aptitude test than were Whites. And the company

Box 11.4 Discrimination on Wall Street

To many readers, it may seem as if blatant gender discrimination is a thing of the past. With women now comprising more than 40% of the labor force and making inroads into many traditionally male occupations, it may be hard to believe that women still face discrimination. Yet, there is evidence that this is the case even today. Consider the cases of two well-known Wall Street firms. The first case involves Smith Barney (now known as the Salomon Smith Barney unit of Citicorp). In 1996, a group of female employees alerted authorities to the existence of a so-called "boom boom room," where women claimed they were verbally and physically harassed. That accusation led to broad charges of discrimination and harassment against the firm. In 1998, a settlement with the firm was reached, and the firm agreed to spend $15 million over a four-year period on programs aimed at improving its treatment of women with respect to hiring and promotion, among other things.

The second case involves Morgan Stanley Dean Witter, a well-known Wall Street firm, and Allison Schieffelin, a 39-year-old executive who had worked in the firm's institutional stock division since 1986. In 1998, she filed charges with the EEOC alleging that Morgan Stanley engaged in sex discrimination because the firm had not promoted her to the rank of managing director, a high-ranking position within the firm, and had paid her less than comparable men. At the time, Ms. Schieffelin earned a salary of over one million dollars per year. After filing her suit, Ms. Schieffelin was fired from the firm for allegedly vocally abusing her immediate supervisor.

On September 10, 2001, the EEOC filed a suit against Morgan Stanley on behalf of Ms. Schieffelin and about 100 other women employees, charging Morgan Stanley with having engaged in a pattern or practice of discrimination against women in the Institutional Equity Division who held positions as associate, vice president, principal, and managing director by compensating them less than their male colleagues and by limiting their opportunities for professional advancement.

Experts find this case to be particularly intriguing because the firm fired Ms. Schieffelin after she filed charges. This is an unusual step that could be viewed as retaliation for her filing of the lawsuit and could make it more difficult for Morgan Stanley to defend itself against any other charges of discrimination that might arise. At the time of this writing, the suit has yet to be resolved.

failed to convince the Court that either a high school diploma or a passing score on the aptitude tests were necessary for successful performance of the jobs, in part because many White employees had previously been hired even though they did not meet these qualifications. It is important to note that the *Griggs* case did not outlaw the use of aptitude tests as a condition of employment. The Supreme Court simply stated that "Tests must measure the person for the job; not the person in the abstract." Thus, any test that is used as part of a hiring screening must be related to the job. As a result, many firms dropped the use of ability tests over concerns that they would be sued for discrimination.[4]

The practical ramifications of *Griggs* are that job applicants can be asked about convictions but not about prior arrests (because Blacks are more likely to be arrested than Whites), and questions pertaining to marital status can be asked only if they are asked of both men and women. The *Griggs* case put the burden for proving the business necessity of such tests on the employer. Essentially, the Court reasoned that Congress directed the thrust of Title VII to consider consequences of employment practices, not simply the motivation. This decision paved the way for EEOC and charging parties to challenge employment practices that shut out groups if the employer cannot show the policy is justified by business necessity.

Under Title VII, discrimination is prohibited not only in hiring, but also in transfer, promotion, and other aspects of employment. An issue that the courts have wrestled with is the existence of **seniority systems.** Many firms, particularly unionized firms, base promotions and layoffs on seniority (i.e., length of time at the company or on the job). Such seniority systems have the potential to perpetuate discrimination. For example, consider a firm that in the past typically hired only males and bases its promotion and pay scales on seniority. If the firm decides it wants to hire more women, the women will have less seniority. If the economy falls into a recession, the women, who have the least seniority, will be laid off. Thus, seniority systems may have a disparate impact and may violate Title VII. However, Title VII permits *bona fide seniority systems,* meaning that it allowed seniority systems even if they had a disparate impact. The courts have ruled in several ways in this area and have lately allowed such systems to stand.

---

[4]For a discussion of the benefits of employment testing and the issue of the fairness of such tests, see John E. Hunter and Frank L. Schmidt, "Ability Tests: Economic Benefits versus the Issue of Fairness," *Industrial Relations,* Vol. 21, No. 3, pp. 293–308, 1982.

In 1989, several important cases came to the Supreme Court dealing with Title VII. In ***Wards Cove Packing Co. v Antonio,*** the Supreme Court issued a ruling that changed the disparate impact standard of *Griggs v Duke Power Co.* so that the employees had to show which policy used by the firm caused the disparate impact (i.e., was it the interview, the aptitude test, or the method in which the jobs were advertised?). It also put the burden of proof as to whether any testing was based on business necessity on the employee as opposed to the employer. In ***Price Waterhouse v. Hopkins*** the employee had to show that if the aptitude test in question had not been used, a different hiring decision would have been reached. Both cases made it more difficult for employees to win discrimination charges against employers.

Congress subsequently passed the **Civil Rights Act of 1991.** This act swung the pendulum back in favor of the employee in a discrimination case. For example, it reversed the *Price Waterhouse v Hopkins* ruling and again made it the responsibility of employers to demonstrate that a disparate impact was a true business necessity. Title VII was amended under this act to state that an unlawful employment practice may be established by demonstrating that race, color, religion, sex, or national origin was a motivating factor for an adverse employment decision, even though other legitimate factors also entered into the decision. Under this act, employees are now able to sue not only for back pay and court costs, as they were originally allowed under Title VII, but also for punitive damages, which can be sizable. This act substantially increases the potential liability of employers for discrimination. However, in 1999, the Supreme Court ruled that when a company has made "good faith" efforts to comply with Title VII, it cannot be required to pay punitive damages for the discriminatory actions of managers who violate company policy, thus perhaps limiting the threat of punitive damages.

Affirmative Action

The next policy to discuss is one that is currently receiving much attention in the media and is, in fact, quite controversial—**Affirmative Action.** Its official title is **Executive Order 11246**, which was signed in 1965 by President Johnson.[5] This order requires every firm with a government contract totaling $50,000 or more to develop an affirmative action plan. Usually only larger

---

[5]It was actually not until October 13, 1967, that Executive Order 11375 expanded affirmative action to include women, and this was not actually enforced until the Employment Act of 1972.

firms or those that rely heavily on federal money, such as universities and the defense industry, are legally subject to affirmative action. Many large firms also use affirmative action plans even though they are not legally required to do so.[6]

An affirmative action plan outlines the program, including numerical goals and timetables, which the firm will use to increase its employment of women and minorities. Such plans sound good but in practice, however, implementation can be difficult. The following example will illustrate some of the difficulties involved.

Suppose a firm believes that it employs too few women as managers. First, the firm must do a statistical analysis to decide whether or not it has failed to hire women in the same proportion as the labor pool. Thus, the firm must identify the potential pool of applicants from which it will hire. Defining the labor pool of available women managers is often difficult. It probably should not be based on the firm's applicant pool because if the firm has been known to be unfriendly to women, it is likely that fewer women apply to that firm. Consequently, its applicant pool will have fewer women than it otherwise might. Another choice would be to define the labor pool of women as the fraction of all managers in the area that are women. This too is problematic. Perhaps women in the area have not trained for management careers believing that they will have difficulty finding management jobs because of the firm's discrimination.

Even if the labor pool can be properly defined and the firm can set its hiring goal, the firm also faces the difficult decision about how to get its workforce to reflect that proportion defined by the goal. If the firm finds that 40% of the managers should be female and only 20% of the managers are currently female, what should the firm do? One approach is to make sure that 40% of their new management hires are female. However, if there is low turnover at this firm (i.e., managers are not likely to quit or be fired), using this hiring rule will mean that it will take quite some time for the management staff to be 40% female. Thus, the only way to quickly remedy past discrimination may be to favor females in hiring (i.e., hire disproportionately more females than

---

[6]Because our focus in this chapter is on employment discrimination, we discuss affirmative action in hiring and not with respect to admission to college, law school, or graduate school, even though affirmative action is not limited to employment discrimination. The Supreme Court recently upheld the University of Michigan's use of race as a factor in admission to its undergraduate program.

males). If the firm must turn down some better-qualified males to do so, it may be subject to charges of reverse discrimination. **Reverse discrimination** is said to occur when a less-qualified female or minority is hired in place of a more qualified White male. One of the strongest criticisms of affirmative action is that it encourages reverse discrimination. However, affirmative action does not require firms to hire less-qualified minority applicants in place of more qualified White males.

An affirmative action plan is actually only legally mandated in two cases. First, employers subjected to affirmative action must not underutilize women and/or minorities. If they are found to do so, they must file an affirmative action plan. Second, any employer who has been found liable in a discrimination case or has reached a settlement in a discrimination case must file an affirmative action plan.

To administer affirmative action, the **Office of Federal Contract Compliance Programs** (OFCCP) was established within the Department of Labor. Like the EEOC, the OFCCP's effectiveness depends partially on the political climate, and it also suffers from case backlogs and long delays. For example, it is well-documented that affirmative action did not receive much support during the 1980s.[7] However, the OFCCP has more power than the EEOC because it can initiate investigations to determine whether or not discriminatory practices exist at a particular firm. It can conduct what is called a *compliance review,* wherein the OFCCP steps in to see if the firm has complied with the affirmative action plan. Not only can it require employers to formulate affirmative action plans, but it can also impose sanctions when discrimination is discovered.[8] However, sanctions are rarely imposed, and Leonard (1984)[9] reports that the firms most likely to be targeted for review are generally large firms who already employ large numbers of women and minorities.

The affirmative action program of the OFCCP has been the center of much controversy. Critics of affirmative action charge that it amounts to a system of employment quotas, even though Title VII explicitly forbids quotas and affir-

---

[7]Jonathan S. Leonard, "Women and Affirmative Action," *Journal of Economic Perspectives,* Vol. 3, No. 1, pp. 61–75, 1989, notes that there was a lack of sanction and lack of progress with respect to affirmative action after 1980.

[8]See the OFCCP's web page at http://www.dol.gov/esa/ofcp_org.htm for more information about this organization.

[9]Jonathan S. Leonard, "Affirmative Action and Employment," *Journal of Labor Economics,* Vol. 2, No. 4, pp. 439–463, 1984.

mative action plans themselves do not include quotas. Furthermore, many critics charge that affirmative action is simply reverse discrimination. Reverse discrimination is the term used to describe the hiring of a less-qualified woman or, more generally, minority group member rather than a better-qualified White male. This is, of course, illegal under Title VII. However, some feel that reverse discrimination may be necessary to correct for a history of past discrimination. This issue is particularly thorny because Title VII prohibits firms from firing workers of one race or gender to make room for a worker of another. Another criticism of affirmative action that even some women and minorities hold is that it is stigmatizing. Co-workers may wonder if women and minorities hired under affirmative action were hired simply because they were women and not for their own qualifications. Finally, critics note that because it does not apply to all firms, affirmative action just means that qualified women and minorities will be shifted to working at firms which are federal contractors and thus, there may not be any net growth in their employment.

On the other hand, affirmative action also has many supporters.[10] They note that affirmative action forces firms to look more diligently for qualified minorities and women and thus helps remove barriers to employment. Some affirmative action supporters also argue that even if some reverse discrimination is involved, it is justified as a compensation for past discrimination against Blacks and women. Finally, even some large firms are often found to be in favor of affirmative action. It allows them to diversify their workforce, which can help sell products in an increasingly demographically diverse marketplace, and it helps provide protection from lawsuits—the company can claim that it was simply following its affirmative action plan. Furthermore, the changing demographics of the workforce, where it is predicted that White males will no longer be the majority, dictates that firms must hire a more diverse workforce to survive. Supporters argue that affirmative action can help firms to do this.[11]

---

[10]See Barbara R. Bergmann, *In Defense of Affirmative Action,* New York: Basic Books, 1996, for a compelling defense of race- and sex-based affirmative action and Barbara R. Bergmann, "The Continuing Need for Affirmative Action," *Quarterly Review of Economics and Finance,* Vol. 39, pp. 757–768, 1999.

[11]For more details on why large firms like affirmative action, see Marilyn Power, "Affirmative Action: Employers, Politics, and Labor," reprinted in *Labor Economics and Labor Relations,* edited by L. Reynolds, S. Master and C. Moser, Englewood Cliffs, New Jersey: Prentice Hall, 1991, pp. 277–283.

Effectiveness of Antidiscrimination Programs

The natural question to ask is: How successful have these laws been in terms of eliminating sex discrimination?[12] As we have documented throughout this book, women have made tremendous progress in the labor market in terms of earnings, labor force participation, and education. Yet we cannot conclude that this progress is entirely the result of antidiscrimination laws. Recall that other social changes were taking place at the same time that these laws were passed and enforced. Thus, in this section, we briefly review the literature that examines the effectiveness of these laws.

To begin with, it is unlikely that the Equal Pay Act of 1963 has had a large impact on the earnings of women. Until recently, women did not often do the same type of work at a firm as men did. However, as we saw in Chapter 8, women are increasingly moving into male-dominated occupations even though, on average, their earnings still lag behind those of men. Thus, the full impact of the Equal Pay Act may well be felt in the next few decades. As we noted earlier, critics of the Equal Pay Act say that its scope is limited; they would like to see it amended to cover jobs of comparable worth, a policy we discuss in the next section. For now, let's turn to a review of the literature that assesses the impacts of Title VII and affirmative action on women's employment, occupational status, and earnings.

Several studies have examined the effectiveness of Title VII and affirmative action on the employment and earnings of women and minorities. As Badgett and Lim (2001)[13] note, this requires detailed data collected from many firms in the United States, and the firms need to be representative of all firms in the United States in order for researchers to make generalizations about the effectiveness of these laws. We have evidence for specific firms, such as AT&T (see Box 11.5), but evidence from one firm or even several large firms is not enough for us to conclude whether it has been effective.

---

[12]It is also natural to ask how effective they have been at eradicating racial discrimination; however, our focus is on women. For a textbook review of the evidence of these laws on racial discrimination, refer to Ronald Ehrenberg and Robert Smith, *Modern Labor Economics: Theory and Policy*, Reading, MA: Addison Wesley, 2003, pp. 414–416.

[13]M.V. Lee Badgett and Jeannette Lim, "Promoting Women's Economic Progress through Affirmative Action," in *Squaring Up: Policy Strategies to Raise Women's Incomes in the United States,* edited by Mary C. King, Ann Arbor, Michigan: University of Michigan Press, 2001, pp. 188–191; "Boeing Agrees to Pay $4.5 Million at Bias Settlement," *L.A. Times,* Nov. 20, 1999.

Box 11.5 Affirmative Action in Action

One of the first affirmative action cases involved AT&T. A 1971 EEOC study of AT&T companies in large cities found that occupations within the companies were almost completely segregated by sex and that women held mostly low-paying jobs such as operator, clerk, service representative, and first-level manager. In 1973, AT&T signed a consent decree with the EEOC and agreed to distribute $15 million to 13,000 women and 2000 minority men. The company also provided approximately $30 million in immediate pay increases for 36,000 women and minorities whose advancement in the Bell system had been hampered. The consent decree involved setting up an affirmative action plan that included goals for the hiring of minorities and women in different job categories. The goals were based upon the relevant labor pools and projected job opportunities. The personnel system was centralized so that all employees knew of job openings and could compete for them. The seniority system, which had previously heavily favored White males, was modified so that women and minorities would have a greater opportunity to compete for job openings within the company. Furthermore, the company used "affirmative action overrides" to promote more minorities and women. Over the life of the consent decree (1973–1979), women at AT&T made large occupational gains.

A more recent case was settled in 1999 with Boeing Co., the nation's second largest federal contractor. Boeing agreed to pay over $4.5 million to settle OFCCP claims that they underpaid women and minorities. As part of the deal, Boeing agreed to modify its hiring and pay decisions over a four-year period and to have these modifications audited by the OFCCP. This represents the first time that a private corporation has agreed to change its pay policies in response to a government complaint. Of course, they stood to lose some $11 billion of government contracts if the case were not resolved.

Sources: M.V. Lee Badgett and Jeannette Lim, "Promoting Women's Economic Progress through Affirmative Action," in *Squaring Up: Policy Strategies to Raise Women's Incomes in the United States*, edited by Mary C. King, Ann Arbor, Michigan: University of Michigan Press, 2001, pp. 188–191; "Boeing Agrees to Pay $4.5 Million at Bias Settlement," *L.A. Times*, Nov. 20, 1999.

Fortunately for researchers, firms with at least 100 employees or government contractors with fifty employees are required to submit to the EEOC an EEO-1 Private Sector Report annually. This report is a snapshot of the demographic composition of the firm, including how many minorities and women are working in a company. Researchers who have assessed the effectiveness of affirmative action often use these data.

Because affirmative action is a program that specifically applies to firms that are federal contractors, one way to test to see if affirmative action programs are effective is to see if firms that are federal contractors increased their employment of Blacks and women more rapidly after the imposition of affirmative action than firms who were not federal contractors. Leonard examined some 68,000 firms that reported their demographic compositions to the federal government in 1974 and 1980.[14] He divided the firms into two groups based on whether they were federal contractors (and thus subject to affirmative action) or were not federal contractors (and thus not subject to affirmative action). He then analyzed the impact of OFCCP affirmative action requirements on the employment of Blacks and women in these individual companies.

According to his analysis, between 1974 and 1980 the employment of Black females grew 12.3%, while that of White females grew more modestly at 2.8%. He also examined the effectiveness of compliance reviews, which occur when the OFCCP steps in to see if the firm has complied with the affirmative action plan. Although Leonard notes that the firms most likely to be targeted for review are generally large firms that already have diverse workforces, he does find that being reviewed increased the employment of Black females by 6.1%, but surprisingly lowers the employment of White females by 3%. He attributes this latter, somewhat anomalous result to the fact that the employment of females was increasing rapidly at the same time that the reviews asked firms to do better than last year, rather than better than average. In other words, if a firm had hired a large percentage of White women last year, then hiring at least that many in the next year may prove to be difficult. Leonard's work provides evidence that affirmative action did increase

---

[14]Jonathan Leonard, "Affirmative Action and Employment," *Journal of Labor Economics*, Vol. 2, No. 4, pp. 439–463, 1984.

employment of women. However, the results for White women were gener-ally found to be small, while those for minority women were much larger.[15]

Both Title VII and affirmative action apply to larger firms, and, as we noted earlier, the larger firms have most often been subjected to OFCCP compli-ance reviews. These firms have also been found to be the most proactive in hiring women and minorities (i.e., not those most likely to discriminate).[16] In fact, many large firms undertook their own affirmative action plans even if they were not federal contractors. Thus, if these laws were effective at provid-ing opportunities for women and minorities, we should see more women and minorities working at larger firms because these larger firms were under di-rect pressure from the OFCCP. A recent study confirmed that this was indeed the case and that both minorities and women moved to larger firms after the passage of Title VII and affirmative action.[17] This study differs from Leonard's because, rather than using the EEO-1 data, it looked at variation in firm size to identify employers subject to Title VII and affirmative action. The larger firms are the ones that are subject to affirmative action. Thus, if employment of women and minorities increased at larger firms, it might well be attributed to affirmative action.

There is evidence that Title VII and affirmative action were successful in opening up to women jobs that had been traditionally male. One study found that between 1967 and 1974 both Title VII of the Civil Rights Act of 1964 and affirmative action increased a working woman's probability of being em-ployed in a male occupation relative to a man's probability, suggesting that at least some of the discrimination against women takes the form of occupa-tional segregation. Title VII and the existence of affirmative action may have induced women to train for these male-dominated jobs that were once off limits to women.[18] However, another study that focused solely on affirmative

[15]He also reaches this conclusion in his comprehensive review of his work on women and affirmative ac-tion. See Jonathan Leonard, "Women and Affirmative Action," *Journal of Economic Perspectives*, Vol. 3, No. 1, pp. 61–75, 1989. Other studies using EEO-1 data reach generally the same conclusions. See Harry Holzer and David Neumark, "Assessing Affirmative Action," *Journal of Economic Literature*, Vol. XXXVIII, pp. 483–568, 2000, for a recent review of this evidence.

[16]Harry Holzer and David Neumark, "Assessing Affirmative Action," *Journal of Economic Literature*, Vol. XXXVIII, pp. 483–568, 2000.

[17]William J. Carrington, Kristin McCue, and Brooks Pierce, "Using Establishment Size to Measure the Im-pact of Title VII and Affirmative Action," *Journal of Human Resources*, Vol. 35, No. 3, pp. 503–523, 2000.

[18]Andrea H. Beller, "Occupational Segregation By Sex: The Determinants and Changes," *Journal of Human Resources*, Vol. 17, No. 3, Summer 1982.

action found that although it helped Black women make occupational gains, there was little evidence that White women made occupational advances as a result of affirmative action. However, it was noted that during this time frame, women's labor supply increased dramatically in all sectors of the economy, making it difficult to isolate the effect of affirmative action.[19]

Other researchers have asked exactly how is it that affirmative action works to increase the employment of minorities and women? Firms can employ affirmative action in many different ways. For example, firms can engage in special recruitment efforts to elicit more female and minority job applicants. This search can include running job ads in publications widely read by these groups as well as attending job fairs aimed at women and minorities. This use of affirmative action in recruiting can help firms "cast a wider net" when searching for qualified women and minorities. It can increase the probability that female and minority applicants are qualified. Firms can also offer training and assistance programs to women and minorities after they are hired to ensure that their performance is up to the firm's usual standards. The latter can be important if there is concern that those hired are not as qualified.

A recent study surveyed large firms in four major cities about their use of affirmative action. Specifically, firms were asked whether or not they used affirmative action in recruiting and/or hiring individuals. They compared those firms that used affirmative action in recruiting to firms that used affirmative action in hiring as well as to firms that did not use affirmative action at all.[20] Firms using affirmative action in recruiting were found to screen applicants more intensely, rely more heavily on formal evaluation, and provide training to candidates they do hire. Thus, they had more minority applicants and more minority and female hires. Their hires were not found to be less qualified than other members of their workforce. Furthermore, because of the intense screening, these employers are less likely to engage in statistical discrimination.

On the other hand, firms that use affirmative action only in hiring are more likely than others to hire women or minorities with lower qualifications. This result occurs presumably because, although they use many of the same strategies

[19]Jonathan Leonard, "Employment and Occupational Advance Under Affirmative Action," *Review of Economics and Statistics,* Vol. 66, No. 3, pp. 377–385, 1984.
[20]Harry J. Holzer, and David Neumark, "What Does Affirmative Action Do?" *Industrial and Labor Relations Review,* Vol. 53, No. 2, pp. 240–271, 2000.

as firms who also use affirmative action in recruiting, they do so to a lesser extent. But, they tend to provide training to these hires with the result that job performance is not lower in these establishments compared to those who do not use affirmative action at all.[21] In a related study using the same data, Holzer and Neumark report that although there is some evidence that women and minorities hired under affirmative action have lower educational qualifications, there is no evidence that women perform less well on the job.[22]

The general conclusion with respect to women seems to be that affirmative action has had a positive and fairly large impact on the employment of Black women and a positive but very small or even negative impact on the employment of White women. It appears to have helped women obtain jobs previously open only to males. In addition, there is some evidence that wages of women are likely to be somewhat higher than they would have otherwise been without affirmative action. These higher wages may be attributed to the fact that firms subject to affirmative action are larger firms that tend to pay more and that the larger firms subject to affirmative action also have smaller sex and race differences in pay. Finally, there is some evidence that affirmative action has led to an increase in the number of government contracts awarded to female- and minority-owned businesses.[23]

Large firms are not the only ones who need or want to diversify their workforces. One large university has made some radical changes in its hiring procedures to increase the representation of women and minority faculty members. See Box 11.6 for details.

Comparable Worth: An Alternative Approach

Enforcement of the Equal Pay Act, affirmative action, and Title VII of the Civil Rights Act is not the only way to address sex discrimination. One proposed method to eradicate sex-based pay differentials that first received atten-

---

[21]Jonathan Leonard, "Women and Affirmative Action," *Journal of Economic Perspectives*, Vol. 3, No. 1, pp. 61–75, 1989, also found that there is no evidence that firms who used affirmative action were hiring less-qualified females.

[22]Harry J. Holzer and David Neumark, "Are Affirmative Action Hires Less Qualified: Evidence from Employer-Employee Data on New Hires," *Journal of Labor Economics*, Vol. 17, No. 3, pp. 534–569, 1999.

[23]Also see Jonathan Leonard, "Women and Affirmative Action," *Journal of Economic Perspectives*, Vol. 3, No. 1, pp. 61–75, 1989, for a review that focuses on the effects of affirmative action on women. His conclusion is that affirmative action has actually had very little effect on women's progress in the workplace.

Box 11.6   Efforts To Diversify the Faculty at Virginia Tech

Virginia Polytechnic Institute (commonly known as Virginia Tech) has taken a fairly radical step toward diversifying its faculty. It made the decision to centralize hiring by taking the responsibility for hiring out of the hands of faculty members and giving that power to the Dean's office. Departments themselves still do the interviewing and the screening of applicants, but the actual decision about who is hired rests with administrators, although there is some input from department heads. Administrators also lead the way in forming the hiring committees in order to ensure that females and minorities are adequately represented on these committees and sometimes bring in nonacademics from outside the university to sit on these committees. The rationale for such dramatic changes was based in part on Virginia Tech's strong military history. It has long been a place where White males were the overwhelming majority. Consequently, there was concern that if hiring were left in the hands of department members, the majority of whom are White males, they might be reluctant to hire more women and minorities.

Has this radical departure in university hiring procedures worked? In the past three years, Virginia Tech has hired twenty-five women, eight Black, and four Hispanic professors. In Spring 2002, 88% of the new hires in arts or sciences were female or minority professors compared to only 35% in the two years before the program took effect. Minority students cite the new hiring rules favorably, noting how important it is to have role models. However, there are concerns that too much power rests with the administrators and that perhaps qualified applicants will be overlooked in the name of diversity.

Source: Robin Wilson, "Diversity at What Cost?" *The Chronicle of Higher Education*, Vol. 48, No. 4, pp. A10–A12, July 12, 2002.

---

tion in the late-1970s is a policy called **comparable worth.** Critics of the Equal Pay Act of 1963 have argued that the concept of equal pay is too restrictive. Given that there is still occupational segregation, few women hold jobs identical to men's. Thus, the potential for the Equal Pay Act to reduce wage differentials is limited. To address wage differentials between men and women, comparable jobs, not identical jobs, should be considered. In other words, women should receive equal pay for jobs comparable to men's or for jobs of equal worth to the firm or organization. Therefore, advocates of comparable worth would like to see the Equal Pay Act reworded to require "equal pay for jobs of equal value."

Advocates of comparable worth argue that the gender gap in earnings is explained by two factors: One is occupational segregation, and the other is the fact that female-dominated occupations tend to pay less than male-dominated occupations both across firms and within firms.[24] Some examples from the literature will make this point clear. In Denver, nurses, whose jobs require considerable education, are paid less than tree-trimmers, whose jobs require little education. Child care workers are typically paid less than auto mechanics, yet many people would argue that the work done by child care workers is inherently more valuable to society. Proponents of comparable worth policy argue that firms should compensate workers for doing jobs of equal value to the firm—hence the name "comparable worth."

Many advocates of comparable worth argue that it is particularly necessary now given that the percentage of female headed households is increasing. They argue that comparable worth can help raise women's wages so that they will not have to rely on welfare. Some also argue that comparable worth can help married women as well. Bargaining theories of marriage and resource allocation within the family generally hold that women have more power in a marriage when they have higher earnings.[25] Comparable worth is seen by many as the fastest way to increase women's earnings.

The thorny issue with comparable worth is implementation. To pay men and women equal pay for jobs of equal worth, it is necessary to determine which jobs are of equal worth. This is typically done through a **job evaluation.** Job evaluation is actually not a new tool. It has been used by the federal government, many state governments, and many large corporations for years to help determine pay rates, though not necessarily to address sex-based pay differentials.

A job evaluation can take several forms. Here we describe what is called the **point factor system.**[26] This system is used by many pay equity studies in the

---

[24]See Paula England, "The Case for Comparable Worth," *Quarterly Review of Economics and Finance,* Vol. 39, No. 0, pp. 743–755, 1999, for a review of studies that find this result.

[25]For more information on household bargaining models see Chapter 15.

[26]This section draws heavily on Paula England, "The Case for Comparable Worth," *Quarterly Review of Economics and Finance,* Vol. 39, No. 0, pp. 743–755, 1999.

public sector. First, all the jobs in a given organization (e.g., within a firm or state government) are described fully and the actual tasks of the job are detailed. Then the job attributes or what are called the *compensable factors*—skill, effort, responsibility, the pleasantness of the working conditions, and the like—must be identified. At this point, each job is rated on each compensable factor, and a numerical value is assigned to each compensable factor. Note that each job is evaluated based upon the characteristics of the job, not those of the workers who hold the job. After the compensable factors have been determined and the jobs have been rated on each compensable factor, the evaluators assign weights to each compensable factor. The weights determine the importance of each factor.

The final step in the point factor system is to use the job evaluation to help determine pay. One way to do this is to plot the total job points against the pay of the jobs and to determine the best relationship, usually using regression analysis. This line is called the pay line. Researchers typically find that after this job evaluation has been performed, most male jobs are above the line and most female jobs are below the line, indicating that the female jobs do indeed pay less. At this point, decisions about how to adjust wages are made. In general, jobs with equal points would be compensated the same.

Figure 11.2 demonstrates a pay line that is similar to one derived for state employees in Washington in 1974.[27] A consulting firm examined the rates of pay received by men and women in state government jobs, using the procedure previously described. They then graphed the job worth points and salaries of jobs that were predominantly male as well as jobs that were predominately female. The X's show the job worth points and pay for the jobs that were primarily male, while the O's denote the job worth points and pay for the jobs that were predominantly female. The two lines (Y_m and Y_f) show the relationship between an increase in job worth points and salaries for males and females, respectively. Note that even when the job worth points were of the same value, the female-dominated jobs paid less. Furthermore, their job evaluation also demonstrated that the disparity in earnings grew as the number of job points grew (i.e., Y_m is steeper than Y_f). A diagram like this can then be used to adjust wages so that jobs of comparable worth, as measured by job worth points, pay the same.

---

[27]This figure is adapted from Donald J. Treiman and Heidi I. Hartmann, eds., *Women Work and Wages: Equal Pay for Jobs of Equal Value*, Washington, D.C.: National Academy Press, 1981.

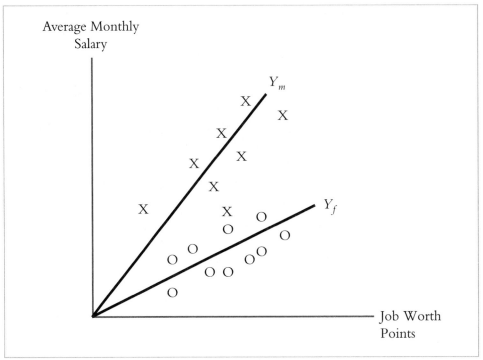

Figure 11.2   Job Evaluation

The process of assigning points and attributes and weights is quite subjective, and both sides of the comparable worth debate acknowledge that this issue needs attention.[28] The validity of the process depends critically on the reliability of the evaluations. A recent study examined the consistency of job evaluations by having three commercial job evaluation firms rate the same set of twenty-seven jobs in an actual company and found that the evaluations were not consistent.[29] Another study of job evaluations used in comparable worth found that a nurse and a social worker were ranked equally in Minnesota, a nurse was ranked more than a social worker in Iowa, and the social worker was ranked more than a nurse in Vermont.[30] This suggests that the resulting

---

[28]See Donald J. Treiman and Heidi L. Hartmann, eds., *Women Work and Wages: Equal Pay for Jobs of Equal Value.* Washington, DC: National Academy Press, 1981, for a more detailed discussion of the job evaluation process.

[29] Jane E. Arnault, Louis Gordon, Douglas H. Joines, and G. Michael Phillips, "An Experimental Study of Job Evaluation and Comparable Worth," *Industrial and Labor Relations Review,* Vol. 54, No. 4, pp. 806–815, 2001.

[30]Steven E. Rhoads, *Incomparable Worth: Pay Equity Meets the Market,* Cambridge: Cambridge University Press, 1993.

wage structure imposed by implementing comparable worth will be sensitive to the evaluator selected.

It is fair to say that there is considerable, although not universal, opposition to comparable worth among most economists.[31] A central principle of economics is that markets set prices and that distorting markets can cause unintended consequences and inefficiencies, which can be worse than the problem they are trying to rectify. Perhaps the best way to illustrate the potential pitfalls with comparable worth from a market perspective is to consider the wage decisions of a small college that hires both economics professors and philosophy professors. This example works well because the job requirements for each are very similar: teach, conduct research, and participate in college governance. They will each be expected to teach the same number of courses, probably with a similar number of students. Thus, it seems obvious that the jobs they perform are of equal worth to the college. Does it follow that they should then be paid the same?

Let's start by assuming that they do, in fact, earn the same amount as shown in Figure 11.3(A). At this initial equilibrium, both economists and philosophers are paid the same equilibrium wage of W_e. There is equilibrium employment of E_e in each market. Suppose that the demand for economics courses increases—perhaps students believe that economics is a fascinating subject. At the same time, the demand for philosophy courses falls. This means that the demand curve for economics professors shifts out and the demand curve for philosophy professors shifts in. This is shown in Figure 11.3(B). If the college continues to pay them both the same wage of W_e, there will be an excess demand for economics professors (shown by $E_d - E_e$ on the horizontal axis) and an excess supply of philosophy professors (shown by $E_e - E_d$ on the horizontal axis).

What can the college do? If it wants to continue paying the professors in the two disciplines the same wage, it can either change the hiring standards, perhaps lowering the hiring standard for economics professors by not requiring the PhD and raising it for philosophy professors by requiring some additional training beyond the PhD. This, however, means that the quality of the two groups of professors is now unequal. We could, of course, allow the market to

---

[31]See Steven E. Rhoads, *Incomparable Worth: Pay Equity Meets the Market*, Cambridge: Cambridge University Press, 1993, for an in-depth discussion of the arguments against comparable worth. Paula England, "The Case for Comparable Worth," *Quarterly Review of Economics and Finance*, pp. 743–755, 1999, presents the case for comparable worth. Mark R. Killingsworth, *The Economics of Comparable Worth*, 1990, presents a thorough economic analysis of the issues involved.

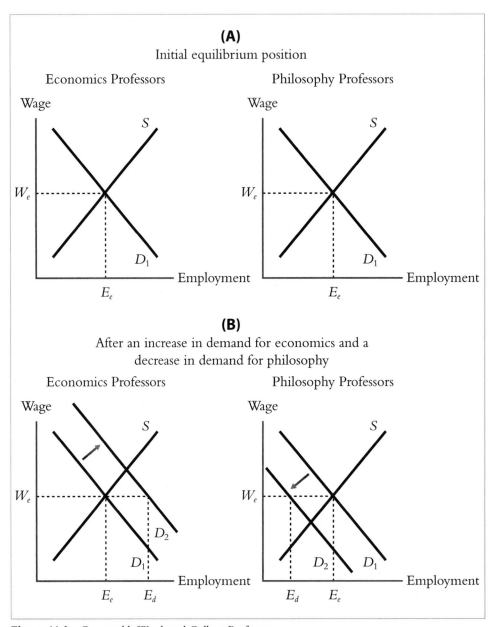

Figure 11.3   Comparable Worth and College Professors

increase the wages paid to economists to reflect the new demand for their services and decrease the wages paid to philosophy professors to reflect the decline in the demand for their services. However, this is a violation of the principle of comparable worth—the jobs are equal but the salaries are not. We could also have the economist teach larger sections of courses to accommodate the growth and keep the pay the same. However, then the jobs are no longer comparable.

You can see from this example that interfering with the market can have unintended consequences. We will end up with more philosophers and fewer economists than is socially optimal. Furthermore, if only one university engages in comparable worth, they will end up with a very good philosophy department and a relatively weak economics department.

In addition to the difficulties that the college professor example illustrates, there are other arguments against comparable worth. For example, somewhat paradoxically, women may also find themselves with lower wages after comparable worth is implemented because some sectors or groups will not be subject to the law. For example, comparable worth laws might exempt small firms from the law, perhaps because they do not have an extensive set of job titles necessary to perform a job evaluation and because job evaluation might be particularly costly to these firms. Women who lost jobs in the part of the economy covered by comparable worth (i.e. the larger firms) may now find themselves looking for jobs at the smaller, exempt firms. They may crowd into these jobs putting downward pressure on wages in the uncovered sector. Thus, some women could see their wages decline after comparable worth is implemented.

Other critics of comparable worth note that the wage gap has been narrowing precisely because the productivity characteristics of women (e.g., education and job experience) have come to resemble those of men more closely. Therefore, more women will enter into traditionally male jobs. As long as those women entering traditionally male jobs do not experience discrimination entering these jobs, the wage gap between men and women will narrow because women in these jobs will receive higher pay: At the same time, women in the traditionally female jobs will receive higher pay because these jobs will no longer be so crowded. Thus, this group argues that comparable worth is misguided. If anything, energy needs to be directed toward employing women in nontraditional jobs—not raising the pay in traditionally female jobs. In fact, these critics argue that raising wages for female-dominated jobs will ultimately hurt women because it provides women with little incentive to train for and pursue male-dominated jobs.[32]

Advocates note that comparable worth does not completely disregard the market but, in fact, needs to be undertaken with market wages clearly in mind. They note that in firms with well-developed internal labor markets, market forces typically determine wages primarily or only at the entry level, where employees are hired from the outside. As employees progress up the firm's job ladder, their earnings are less and less tied to the market, so comparable worth can help ensure that wages are set in a fair manner. Furthermore, advocates note that any job loss from comparable worth has the possibility to be beneficial. For example, women who cannot find a traditionally female job may, in fact, compete for the male-dominated jobs, and men might be attracted to the higher-paying female jobs.[33] Finally, advocates note that there are costs and benefits to any policy, and that we need to know more about how many workers might be displaced and what would happen to them before we dismiss comparable worth as unworkable.

Comparable Worth in Practice

Several U.S. states have implemented comparable worth policies at the state government level. These states have performed job evaluations and implemented comparable worth for their state government jobs. Currently, about twenty states have done so. Minnesota, Washington, Oregon, and Iowa have had their policies scrutinized extensively. Minnesota was the first state to implement comparable worth in 1986. Note that where comparable worth has been implemented in the United States, it has usually been in government sector jobs, not private industry. Governments are not profit-maximizers, and they may be able to absorb any wage increases resulting from comparable worth better than a private firm could.

We can measure the effectiveness of comparable worth by examining the male/female earnings ratio. Of course, growth in women's wage may not be entirely due to comparable worth. In the states that have implemented comparable worth, the gender earnings ratio has risen although generally not as

---

[32]Linda Levine, "The Gender Wage Gap and Pay Equity: Is Comparable Worth the Next Step?" Congressional Research Service Report for Congress, June 5, 2001.

[33]Barbara R. Bergmann, "Does the Market for Women's Labor Need Fixing?" *Journal of Economic Perspectives*, Vol. 3, No. 1, pp. 43–60, 1989.

dramatically as first hoped.[34] One study used data from public sector comparable worth laws in Iowa, Michigan, Minnesota, and Washington and estimated that comparable worth could eliminate almost half of the gender earnings gap, but that business costs would be expected to rise around 8%.[35]

Measuring employment gains is more difficult because we need to account for employment growth that would have occurred regardless of comparable worth. The effects of comparable worth on the employment of women are uncertain. There is some evidence that employment fell.[36, 37] Yet, another study found that there do not appear to be tremendously negative effects on employment.[38]

Canada has implemented an extensive system of comparable worth among its government jobs in nearly all its provinces. In addition, the Province of Ontario has implemented comparable worth in both the government sector and the private sector; this extension to the private sector is quite unusual. The policy requires employers with 100 or more employees to implement pay equity proactively whether or not there has been a complaint. Australia also has a comparable worth-like policy that applies to both the government and the private sector. In Australia, minimum wage rates are set nationally for most occupations and industries, and since 1972 it has had a policy of setting wages for "equal pay for work of equal value."

It is difficult to extrapolate from these cases to how comparable worth would fare in the United States. Despite the fact that there is a comparable worth bill in Congress (see Box 11.7), it is fair to say that it is unlikely that this policy will be enacted on a national level in the United States. In a highly decentralized market economy like that of the United States, it is unclear how costly it would be to implement such a policy. In addition to comparable worth legislation some states have introduced and/or passed legislation banning discrimination on the basis of marital status. See Box 11.8 for an example.

---

[34]Elaine Sorenson, "Implementing Comparable Worth: A Survey of Recent Job Evaluation Studies," *American Economic Review*, Vol. 76, No. 2, pp. 364–367, 1986.

[35]Elaine Sorenson, "Implementing Comparable Worth: A Survey of Recent Job Evaluation Studies," *American Economic Review*, Vol. 76, No. 2, pp. 364–367, 1986.

[36]Mark Killingsworth, *The Economics of Comparable Worth*, Kalamazoo, Mich.: W. E. UpJohn Institute for Employment Resarch, 1990, p. 135.

[37]Anita U. Hattiangadi and Amy M. Habib, *A Closer Look at Comparable Worth*, Washington D.C.: Employment Policy Foundation, 2000.

[38]See Elaine Sorensen, *Comparable Worth: Is It a Worthy Policy?* Princeton: Princeton University Press, 1994.

Box 11.7   The Status of Comparable Worth Legislation in the United States

Several states, including Washington and Minnesota, have enacted comparable worth laws that cover public sector state employees. In the last several years, comparable worth laws have gained momentum according to the Center for Policy Alternatives, a research group which tracks state efforts. In 2001, sixty-seven bills were introduced in thirty different states. There are also two bills before Congress. One is the Fair Pay Act, which would expand the Equal Pay Act of 1963 to protect against wage discrimination for workers in equivalent jobs with similar skills and responsibilities, even if the jobs are not identical. It would exempt firms with fewer than twenty-five employees. The other bill is the Paycheck Fairness Act, which would provide more resources to the EEOC, widen remedies for discrimination, and allow employees to freely discuss their salaries with their co-workers. It also would encourage employers to make voluntary efforts to narrow the gender wage gap, but it stops short of requiring comparable worth.

Source: American Association of University Women.

Summary

In this chapter, we have reviewed the various laws in place to combat sex discrimination. One notable feature of these laws is that they are, for the most part, relatively recent. We then considered how effective the Equal Pay Act, Title VII of the Civil Rights Act, and affirmative action have been in raising women's earnings. Finally, we explored the policy of comparable worth. Although not implemented at a national level, there is growing interest among state governments in adopting a pay plan that is loosely based on the principle of comparable worth. Keep in mind that whenever policies are implemented, we must be cognizant of both the benefits and the costs. Efficiency and equity are important considerations when dealing with discrimination in the labor market; however, interfering with the workings of the labor market does have costs.

The issue of comparable worth illustrates the distortions that can occur when there is interference in the marketplace. Overall, it appears that comparable worth, though it does address an important policy issue, would be compli-

Box 11.8   Do Women Face Discrimination Based Upon Their Marital Status?

The rise in single parent families, particularly single mothers raising children while working in the formal labor market, has brought to the forefront another type of discrimination. In 1994, Kiki Peppard, a single mother with two children, moved to Pennsylvania from New York. Peppard went to numerous job interviews; all but two began with two questions: "Are you married?" and "Do you have any children?" She was repeatedly told, that women with children take too much time off from work. One prospective employer told her that she would have to be paid less as a single mother because married women are covered under their husband's health insurance, but single women aren't.

Angry and frustrated, she began lobbying to rectify this situation. She joined the National Association of Working Women to help achieve her goal. Because of her efforts, two bills have been introduced in the Pennsylvania House and the Pennsylvania Senate.

Experts note that this is a particular concern in an era when many single mothers with children are searching for jobs due to welfare reform. Under the Pennsylvania bill, it would be illegal for a prospective employer to ask whether a person is single, married, widowed, separated, or divorced. According to the National Conference of State Legislatures, it is illegal in nineteen states to ask job applicants their marital status. At the federal level, such questions are legal only if they are asked of all candidates seeking a job—men and women alike.

Sources: Ovetta Wiggins, "She Fights Family Bias in Hiring," *The Philadelphia Inquirer*, Thursday, February 28, 2002, p. B1; National Conference of State Legislatures, www.ncsl.org/programs/employ/empdisc.html; and Walter Brasch, "A Case of State Sanctioned Sexism," *The American Reporter*, Vol. 8, No. 1856W, June 2, 2002.

cated to implement on a national level. In addition, most economists would probably advocate policies aimed at the sources of the discrimination rather than resorting to wage setting via comparable worth.

What we know about comparable worth in the United States is based on studies of its implementation on a very limited scale—namely state and municipal governments. A recent study examined the experience of the Canadian province of Ontario, which extended comparable worth to the private sector in the late-1980s. Results from that study indicated that the implementation was difficult particularly at smaller firms where most men and women work. (Firms with ten or fewer employees were exempted.) There were also issues with compliance. Furthermore, women's wages were found to rise only modestly if at all. The study called into question the practicality of comparable worth at a national level in a highly decentralized market economy.[39] Finally, remember that comparable worth is a policy that is designed to address pay differences between jobs within a firm. It does not address factors such as firm size or industry (such as service or manufacturing). Along these lines, segregation of women could lead to pay differentials that would not be addressed by comparable worth. Thus, even implementation of comparable worth cannot be expected to eliminate the gender wage gap completely.

Key Terms

affirmative action   413

Civil Rights Act of 1964   406

Civil Rights Act of 1991   413

comparable worth   423

disparate impact   408

disparate treatment   408

Equal Employment Opportunity Commission (EEOC)   407

Equal Pay Act of 1963   405

Executive Order 11246   413

Fair Labor Standards Act of 1938   405

Griggs v Duke Power Company   410

job evaluation   424

marginal revenue product   404

marriage and/or pregnancy "bars"   401

---

[39]Michael Baker and Nicole M. Fortin, "Does Comparable Worth Work in a Decentralized Labor Market?" NBER working paper 7937, 2000.

Office of Federal Contract Compliance Programs   415

pattern or practice of discrimination   410

point factor system   424

PriceWaterhouse v Hopkins   413

reverse discrimination   415

seniority systems   412

Wards Cove Packing Co. v Antonio   413

US current situation (stats)

2 ways to measure poverty
- absolute
- relative $\}$ +, - of each

what we use

Orshansky

measures total $ income
what does that include?

poverty thresholds
pros/ cons; changes

who is poor?
%'s; gender diff.

CHAPTER **12**

Poverty, Welfare, and Women

Introduction

One of the paradoxes of American society is that we are one of the wealthiest countries in the world, yet our income is quite unequally distributed and millions of Americans live in poverty. In the United States, the poverty problem is essentially one of income distribution. We actually have enough income to keep everyone above the poverty line, but it is not distributed equally. In fact, the United States has one of the most unequal distributions of income of any developed nation in the world, and despite our wealth, the poverty rate in the United States was 12.1% in 2002.[1] Poverty is a controversial topic. It involves questions of economic efficiency and issues of equity and justice.

In this chapter, we examine how poverty is measured and find out who is most likely to be in poverty. Then we turn to examining some of the causes of poverty and what policymakers are doing to alleviate this problem. The policy discussion will involve a look at the recent welfare reform that was instituted in the United States in 1996 and an in-depth examination of the Earned Income Tax Credit. As always, when evaluating policies, we look at both the costs and the benefits of the policies. As we shall see, designing programs to help those among us who are economically disadvantaged is not without costs.

---

[1]Poverty statistics are from U.S. Census Bureau, Current Population Reports, "Poverty in the United States: 2001," issued September 2002.

Poverty in the United States
Measuring Poverty

Poverty can be measured in two ways—in absolute terms and in relative terms. Each type of measurement has its strengths and weaknesses. An **absolute measure of poverty** defines people whose incomes fall below a certain threshold as poor. This measure is appealing because it defines poverty in terms of need. One obvious drawback is that it requires defining a poverty-level standard of living and the income needed to attain it, and there is no absolutely definitive way to do that. It is always possible to argue that the poverty threshold is too low or too high. Indeed, as critics point out, what constitutes an inadequate standard of living is often relative. For example, an amount of money that leaves someone in poverty in the United States may leave someone in Bangladesh and many other parts of the world very well off. Indeed, even within the United States, certain regions of the country are more expensive to live in than others (e.g., Honolulu, Hawaii versus Easton, Pennsylvania), and an absolute measure of poverty usually does not take this situation into account.[2]

The other approach is to use a **relative income poverty measure.** With this type of a measure, a family is poor when its income is significantly less than the average income of the population. For example, people might be defined to be in poverty if their income is 50% below the average family income. If the average income in an area is $30,000, then families with incomes below $15,000 (50% of the mean) would be defined as poor. This measure is appealing in that it takes advantage of the standard of living of the average family and puts more emphasis on inequality of incomes. Another way to conceptualize the relative income poverty measure is to define the poor as those in the bottom fifth of the income distribution. This example illustrates one of the biggest criticisms of this measure of poverty. Unless everyone makes the same amount of money, there will always be some group of people in the bottom fifth of the income distribution—thus poverty will never be eradicated even if the income of that bottom fifth is quite high.

The United States relies on an absolute income measure of poverty. The poverty measure that we use today was devised about forty years ago by a woman named Molly Orshansky (see Box 12.1 for more information about

---

[2]Of course, an absolute measure could be designed to take into account cost of living differences across states or countries.

Box 12.1 One Woman's Lasting Contribution to the Measurement of Poverty

In his State of the Union address on January 8, 1964, President Lyndon B. Johnson declared that America would fight a "War on Poverty." His **Economic Opportunity Act of 1964** was signed into law on August 20, 1964. Its objective was to prepare the poor to compete in the economy. However, to fight poverty, we first needed to measure it—we needed to know its extent so that we could know whether efforts to eradicate it were successful. This task was assigned to Ms. Molly Orshansky, who worked for the Social Security Administration. In 1963, she developed the official measure still used by the U.S. government today.

Ms. Orshansky held an A.B. in mathematics and statistics from Hunter College and did graduate work in economics and statistics at American University. Her idea was to use the cost of a "nutritionally adequate diet" as the basis for a cost-of-living estimate. She knew from a Department of Agriculture Food Consumption Survey from 1955 that families spent about one third of their income on food. She used several food budgets developed by dieticians at the Department of Agriculture. She multiplied these food budgets by three to determine the poverty thresholds for families of various sizes. Interestingly, the Department of Agriculture developed four food plans. Ms. Orshansky developed poverty thresholds for the cheapest of these plans—the economy plan. She published her thresholds and analysis of the poverty population in an article in the January 1965 issue of the *Social Security Bulletin*. The Agriculture Department, however, described this plan as being "designed for temporary or emergency use when funds are low." See "The Development and History of the U.S. Poverty Thresholds—A Brief Overview" by Gordon M. Fisher at http://aspe.os.dhhs.gov/poverty/hptgssiv.htm for more details.

how our current poverty measure was first designed), and it has been changed only slightly ever since. She was charged to develop an index of poverty during President Johnson's War on Poverty. Orshanky's measure was based on the minimum annual cost of a nutritionally adequate diet as computed by the U.S. Department of Agriculture. That cost was then multiplied by three to obtain the poverty threshold for a family of four. It is multiplied by three under the assumption that a family spends about one third of its budget on food. The resulting total income was, she reasoned, the amount necessary for a family to meet its minimum nutritional needs and its other needs at approximately the same low standard of living.[3] Thus, any family with less income than this ought to be regarded as officially poor. For smaller and larger families, the four person threshold is adjusted by recognizing the existence of economies of scale, and it also makes small adjustments for age (greater than or less than age 65) and the number of adults and children in a family.

In measuring whether a family's income is greater than its needs, the official poverty measure counts a family's total money income after all **cash transfers** (such as Social Security and welfare) and before taxes. It does not include the value of unrealized capital gains or noncash benefits such as public housing, Medicaid, and food stamps. This measure, though criticized by some, remains one of the most important measures of economic well-being in the United States.

Table 12.1 shows the official **poverty thresholds** for 2002. The poverty thresholds do not vary geographically, but they are updated annually for inflation using the Consumer Price Index. As you can see, a "traditional family" of four consisting of mother, father, and two children would find themselves in poverty if their annual income fell below $18,392 in the year 2002. The Census Bureau cautions that while the thresholds presented here in some sense represent families' needs, the official poverty measure should be viewed more as a statistical yardstick rather than a definitive statement of what people and families need to live. To get some perspective on these poverty measures, think about a family of four with one earner who has a minimum wage job. Such a family would have an annual gross income of $5.15 × 40 hours per week × 50 weeks per year = $10,300. This is well below the poverty line for a family of four.

Our measurement of poverty is not without its critics. On one hand, the measure has been criticized for being too low. Several studies have shown that families spend one quarter, not one third, of their budget on food and thus the food expenditure should be multiplied by four, not three, to construct a measure of total family needs. A related concern is that the food budget itself

---

[3] In effect, she was assuming that families spent their income in such a way that food, shelter, and other major consumption categories were all at about the same living standard. Thus, three times the amount needed for a nutritionally adequate diet would yield an overall standard of living that was just at the same level as food consumption.

2006 data

Size of Family Unit	Weighted Average Thresholds ($)
One person (unrelated individual)	9,183
Under 65 years	9,359
65 years and over	8,628
Two persons	11,756
Householder under 65 years	12,110
Householder 65 years and over	10,885
Three persons	14,348
Four persons	18,392
Five persons	21,744
Six persons	24,576
Seven persons	28,001
Eight persons	30,907
Nine persons or more	37,062

Table 12.1   Poverty Thresholds for 2002 by Size of Family and Number of Related Children Under 18 Years

Source: http://www.census.gov/hhes/poverty/threshld/thresh02.html.

is too low to adequately support a family for very long. In fact, at the time the measure was developed, the U.S. Department of Agriculture had issued guidelines for food budgets at several levels: liberal, moderate, low-cost, and economy. The low-cost and economy food budgets are what was originally used in determining the poverty thresholds. This budget provides for a minimally adequate diet but was acknowledged to be for short term use, as it was very stringent. Finally, when people are asked to define what level of income they would consider to be inadequate, they usually cite amounts well above the poverty thresholds reported in Table 12.1. For example, a poll taken in 2000 demonstrated that a majority of Americans believe it takes at least $35,000 annually to provide adequately for a family of four.[4]

---

[4]Poll taken by Lake, Snell, Perry and Associates for Jobs for the Future. See also Kathryn J. Edin, "The Myths of Dependence and Self-Sufficiency: Women, Welfare, and Low-Wage Work." *Focus*, Vol. 17, No. 2, 1995, for references to other surveys and budgets that suggest the official poverty cutoffs are too low.

However, there are also critics on the other side who claim that the government measure overstates poverty. They note that the official poverty measure only takes into account money income and neglects in-kind benefits that families receive such as food stamps, medical care available through the Medicaid program, tax credits through the Earned Income Tax Credit, and subsidized housing. Thus, critics advocate an adjustment for these in-kind transfers and tax credits.

Within the past decade, there have been renewed calls to revise the official measure of poverty. In 1995, a panel from the National Academy of Sciences issued a report that advocated making changes to our national measure of poverty, including revising the food budget to measure food consumption needs more accurately and counting transfer payments as part of income.[5] These new measures are currently experimental measures of poverty; they are being calculated along with the original poverty measures but have not yet replaced the original measures.[6] The Census Bureau has published several reports that include these experimental poverty measures. The experimental measures of poverty reveal a slightly different distribution than our traditional measure. Under the experimental poverty measures, married-couple families have higher poverty rates, while people in female-headed households have lower poverty rates compared to the traditional measures. Whether such experimental measures will be adopted as the benchmark remains to be seen. In the next section, we take a detailed look at who is poor in the United States.

Who Is Poor in the United States?

Table 12.2 presents a detailed look at poverty statistics for individuals for the year 2002 by race, ethnicity, gender, and family status. In 2002, the overall poverty rate stood at 12.1%, which means that just over 33 million Americans were poor. The poverty rate fell steadily throughout the mid- and late 1990s, as the economy boomed and the unemployment rate fell. From 1993, when the poverty rate reached 15.1% following the recession of the early 1990s, the rate fell seven years in a row, finally reaching 11.3% in 2000. This figure was just 0.2 percentage points above the all-time low U.S. poverty rate of 11.1%,

---

[5]*Measuring Poverty: A New Approach*, edited by Constance F. Citro and Robert T. Michael, Washington, D.C.: National Academy Press.
[6]Several experimental measures are calculated. For those who are interested in reading further, the Census Bureau report "Selected Experimental Poverty Measures: 1990–1999" is available at www.census.gov/hhes/poverty/povmeas/exppov/suexppov.html.

Demographic Group	Poverty Rate (%)
All people	12.1
Race/Ethnicity	
White	10.3
White, non-Hispanic	8.0
Black	23.9
Asian/Pacific Islander	10.2
Hispanic	21.8
Gender	
Male	10.9
Female	13.3
In married-couple family	
All	5.3
White	5.8
Black	9.1
Hispanic	18.4
In single-parent female-headed family	
All	28.8
White	24.1
Black	38.0
Hispanic	36.4
In single-parent male-headed family	
All	12.1
White	10.9
Black	21.8
Hispanic	16.6

Table 12.2   Poverty Status of Persons by Race, Ethnicity, Gender, and Family Structure, 2002

Source: *Current Population Reports*, "Poverty in the United States: 2002," by B. Proctor and J. Dalaker, issued September 2003. http://www.census.gov/hnes/www/poverty.html.

achieved more than thirty years ago in 1973.[7] However, in 2002 the poverty rate was up to 12.1% as a result of the recession that began in March 2001.[8]

As shown in Table 12.2, Whites—especially non-Hispanic Whites—and Asian/Pacific Islanders have lower poverty rates than Blacks and Hispanics. The poverty rate for women is about 20% higher (13.3% versus 10.9%) than the poverty rate for men. Note that this must reflect differences in poverty between men and women who do not live with a member of the opposite sex. If a family is poor, all persons in the family are classified as poor, and similarly if the family is nonpoor. Thus, men and women in married-couple families must have identical poverty rates, as do male and female children, in whatever family type they reside in. So the only source of a gender poverty rate difference can be among men and women not living with a person of the opposite sex.

The bottom rows in Table 12.2 show the impact of family structure on the poverty status of individuals. In married-couple families, less than 6% of persons are poor, much lower than the rate for persons in single-parent families. It makes a huge difference whether that single parent is male or female. The poverty rate for female-headed single-parent families is 28.8%, about twice as high as the 12.1% rate for male-headed single-parent families. What is amazing about these rates is how much marriage matters—over one quarter of all single-parent female-headed families are poor, whereas less than 6% of married-couple families are poor. Even more shocking is the realization that nearly 40% of the female-headed Black and Hispanic families live in poverty!

Figure 12.1 presents additional evidence documenting the relationship between poverty and family structure for the time period since 1973.[9] In Figure 12.1, the poverty rate is for families, not individuals; the figures shown are the proportion of families of each type that are poor. The poverty rate for married-couple families has stayed in a very narrow range between 5% and 7.5%, while the rate for female-headed, single-parent families has consistently been five or six times as high. Throughout most of this time period, the poverty

---

[7]Poverty figures are from U.S. Census Bureau, Current Population Reports, "Poverty in the United States: 2001," issued September, 2002. http://www.census.gov/hhes/www/poverty01.html.

[8]Robert Pear, "Recession Cut Incomes and Swelled Poverty Rolls, U.S. Says," *New York Times*, September 5, 2002.

[9]Poverty figures are from U.S. Census Bureau, Current Population Reports, "Poverty in the United States: 2001," issued September 2002. http://www.census.gov/hhes/www/poverty01.html.

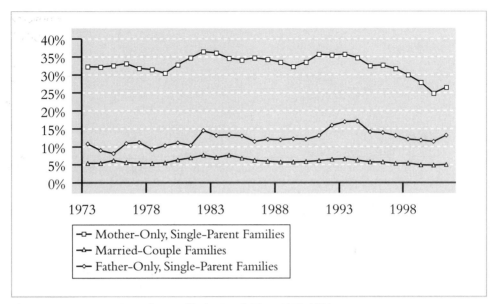

Figure 12.1   Poverty Rates for Families by Family Type, 1973–2001

rate for these families has exceeded 30%. The poverty rate has declined since the mid-1990s, and for female-headed families, it reached a historic low in 2000, dipping under 25% for the first time ever, before rising in 2001. In all, the poverty rate for female-headed families has fallen about 10 percentage points since 1992, when the rate stood at more than 36%. Single-parent families with a male householder have historically had poverty rates that are much closer to married-couple families than to single-parent female-headed families. Through the latter half of the 1990s, their poverty rate was between 10 and 15%.[10]

Not only do female-headed single-parent families have a very high poverty rate, but in addition, as we saw in Chapter 3, the proportion of all families that are female-headed has increased substantially. Because of these trends, female-headed families have come to account for an increasing proportion of all families in poverty, a phenomenon referred to in the literature as the **feminization**

[10]See Sara McLanahan and Erin Kelly, "The Feminization of Poverty: Past and Future," in *Handbook of the Sociology of Gender,* edited by Janet Saltzman Chafetz, New York: Kluwer Academic/Plenum Publishers, 1999, pp. 127–145.

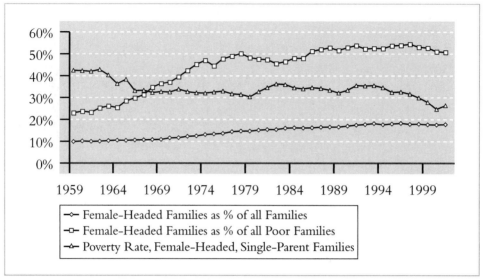

Figure 12.2   The Feminization of Poverty, 1959–2001

of poverty.[11] Figure 12.2 shows the details on these two trends—female-headed single-parent families as a proportion of all families and as a proportion of all poor families from 1959 to 2001. It also shows the poverty rate for female-headed single-parent families.

The line on the bottom shows that single-parent female-headed families increased slowly but steadily from about 10% of all families in the early 1960s to between 17 and 18% throughout the 1990s and early 2000s. Their poverty rate declined sharply in the 1960s from more than 40% to about one third and bounced around cyclically with the state of the economy throughout most of the 1970s and 1980s, before dropping in the latter half of the 1990s. As a proportion of all poor families, female-headed single-parent families grew steadily because the rise in their relative numbers outweighed the decline in their poverty rate. Back in the early 1960s, these families made up just

[11]This term was first used by Diana Pearce in 1978 as cited in McLanahan and Kelly. McLanahan and Kelly note that the feminization of poverty occurred primarily between 1950 and 1970 and then leveled off; however, when it leveled off varies somewhat by race and age. They attribute the leveling off in part to stagnating wages for men and rising wages for women. Interested readers may want to consult Sara McLanahan and Erin Kelly, "The Feminization of Poverty: Past and Future," in *Handbook of the Sociology of Gender,* edited by Janet Saltzman Chafetz, Kluwer Academic/Plenum Publishers, 1999, pp. 127–145, for a discussion of Pearce's work and a detailed discussion of the feminization of poverty.

one poor family out of four. That proportion eventually rose to more than one poor family out of two, which is right where it stood in 2001.

Because women tend to retain custody of children after divorce and because single women who have children out of wedlock generally retain custody of them, children are particularly hard hit by women's poverty. Figure 12.3 shows the poverty rate of children in female-headed families in 1980, 1990, and 1999, separately by race and Hispanic origin. Even though there are differences in the poverty rates among the groups, the most important point made by Figure 12.3 is just how high the poverty rate is for children in all female-headed families. In 1980, the poverty rate was 42% for children in White female-headed families and 65% for children in Black or Hispanic female-headed families. By 1990, the poverty rates were either the same or slightly higher, and although they have fallen since, they still remain very high. In 1999, more than one third of White children and more than half of Black and Hispanic children in these families were below the poverty line. Furthermore (not shown in Figure 12.3), 15% of Black children lived in families with incomes below 50% of the poverty line—a commonly used measure of extreme hardship. This is compared to 5% of White and 11% of Hispanic children.

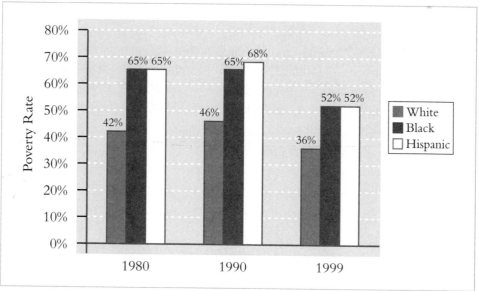

Figure 12.3 Percentage of U.S. Children Living Below the Poverty Level in Female-Headed Families, by Race and Ethnicity, 1980–1999

Source: Trends in the Well-Being of America's Children and Youth, aspe.hhs.gov.

The rise in the proportion of children living in single-parent families is an important part of the explanation for the high rate of child poverty in the United States. Thomas and Sawhill[12] compared the actual child poverty rate in the United States with a rate that they computed by assuming that there had been no change in the proportion of female-headed families since 1970. In doing that, they used the actual poverty rates for children in each type of family (married-couple and male- and female-headed single-parent families) in each year from 1970 to 2000 but kept the proportions of each family type as they were in 1970, rather than as they actually changed.[13]

Their results are shown in Figure 12.4. The top line is the actual child poverty rate in the United States, which rose from just under 15% in 1970 to over 20% for most of the period between 1980 and 1995. Like most poverty rates, it declined in the second half of the 1990s. The bottom line is their hypothetical poverty rate based on 1970 family structure and the actual poverty rates for each family type. The difference between the two lines shows the impact of the change in family structure on the overall poverty rate. By the early 1980s, family structure changes were responsible for making the child poverty rate about 3 percentage points higher than it otherwise would have been. By the 1990s, the impact was more than 4 percentage points. Another way to think about this is to compare the actual change in the child poverty rate with the change that would have occurred in the absence of changes in family structure. The actual rate rose from 14.9 to 18.3%, an increase of 3.4 percentage points. If family structure hadn't changed, the rate would have fallen a full percentage point to 13.9%. Thus, according to Thomas and Sawhill's calculations, family structure changes were responsible for boosting the poverty rate for children by 4.4 percentage points in 2000.

Some international comparisons provide some perspective on these numbers. A 2000 UNICEF report puts the child poverty rate in the United States at 22.4%, the highest rate of most industrialized nations. By comparison, Sweden's child poverty rate is less than 3%, France is just under 8%, and Germany is just over 10%.

---

[12]Adam Thomas and Isabelle V. Sawhill, "For Richer or for Poorer: Marriage as an Antipoverty Strategy," *Journal of Policy Analysis and Management*, Vol. 21, No. 4, Fall 2002, pp. 587–99.

[13]The poverty rate in any particular year can be computed as the weighted average of the poverty rates for different subgroups, where the weights are the proportion of families accounted for by that subgroup. In this case, the subgroups are family types, and Thomas and Sawhill are using 1970 population weights rather than current population weights.

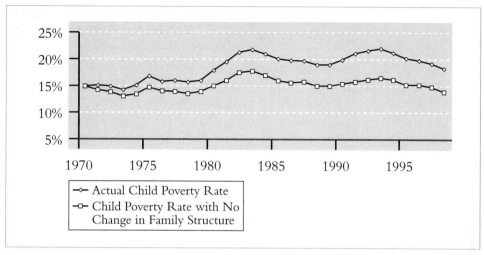

Figure 12.4   The Impact of Family Structure on Child Poverty Rates, 1970–1999

The feminization of poverty is not a phenomenon unique to the United States. In fact, as illustrated in Table 12.3, other industrialized countries also face this issue. The notable exception is Sweden, which is known for its extensive support of women's work.

Why Are Women More Likely To Be Poor?

As we have seen, in the United States one of every two families in poverty is headed by a woman. Why is it that women are particularly hard hit by poverty? In the United States, people obtain income from three possible sources: labor market earnings, transfers from their families (parents or spouses), and/or transfer payments or tax credits from the government (Social Security, TANF, and the Earned Income Tax Credit). Several explanations have been advanced for this feminization of poverty. First, as already noted, more single women live with their children than do single men. It is still true that women are more likely to retain custody of the children in a divorce, and in most nonmarital births, the children live with the mother. By definition, these female-headed families are more likely to be in poverty because poverty thresholds are adjusted for the number of children in the family. Thus when we compare two single-parent female-headed households, all else being equal, the one with more children is more likely to be poor.

Country	Families Headed by a Single Woman	Families Headed by a Single Man
Australia (1994)	38.6	27.5
Canada (1994)	40.5	17.1
France (1989)	24.7	11.1
Germany (1994)	39.1	11.1
The Netherlands (1991)	25.7	0.0
Sweden (1992)	3.4	6.9
United Kingdom (1995)	31.9	20.0
United States (1994)	47.1	22.3

Table 12.3   Percent in Poverty for Single-Parent Families in Eight Industrialized Countries

Source: Karen Christopher, Paula England, Sara McLanahan, Katherin Ross, and Tim Smeeding, "Gender Inequality in Poverty in Affluent Nations: The Role of Single Motherhood and the State," Forthcoming in *Child Well-being* in *Modern Nations*, Bristol: The Policy Press, edited by K. Vleminckx and Tim Smeeding, 2000, pp. 175–197. Copyright © 2000. Reprinted with the permission of The Policy Press. Single fathers (mothers) are men (women) living with a child under the age of 18 and without an adult female (male).

Second, women have lower earnings than men, as we established in Chapter 8. Recall that women have lower wages in part because they tend to work in lower-paying occupations. They are also more likely to work part-time or for minimum wage with few or no benefits. Furthermore, as we saw in Chapter 10, mothers tend to earn less than nonmothers. Mothers may take time out of the workforce to care for children, thus accumulating less work experience. As a result, their human capital may depreciate. In fact, poor women often have low education and few skills. Some poor women may have stopped their formal education because they had a teen pregnancy. However, even educated women may face some discrimination and may not receive pay commensurate with their level of education. Finally, more-educated people are less likely to experience an event that can plunge them into poverty such as a catastrophic illness or sudden job loss.

In the case of female-headed families, there is no spouse to rely on for income. As we know, the divorce rate, which has more than doubled since 1960, is one reason there are so many single-parent families. Potential family income is reduced by more than half with the absence of one parent. Where two parents exist in the family, one parent can potentially devote full-time to labor market activity while the other is free to combine household and labor market activity. With only one parent, the opportunity for such flexibility is lost. Although the popular media often portray divorced spouses who earn large settlements at divorce, for the vast majority of women, the reality is quite the opposite. The majority of women receive no alimony, and child support is often not collected, although states have recently stepped up their efforts to collect child support from so-called dead-beat dads (see Box 12.2 on child support). Declining wage opportunities at the low end of the earnings distribution have made it difficult for many low-skilled men to support their families, which may have also led to less collection of child support. Although child support enforcement has been increasing, many women still do not receive child support and few receive alimony. Thus, many women turn to welfare. But, as we will see in the next section, welfare benefits on their own are often not sufficient to lift most families out of poverty.

A study conducted in the 1980s confirmed that a decline in the earnings of the household head was the most common reason a family became poor. Changes in family structure also precipitated poverty—namely the transition to becoming a female-headed family. This same study also found that an earnings increase on the part of the household head was the most common route out of poverty.[14]

An additional demographic explanation for the feminization of poverty relates to women's longer life expectancy. Because women regularly outlive their husbands, they are more likely to be single at older ages and to have substantially less income than older women in married-couple families. They also tend to have smaller pensions (a topic we discuss more fully in the next chapter). Among men and women aged 65 and older, there is a substantial difference in poverty rates. For women, the rate is 12.4%, while for men it is just 7.0%.

Not all reasons for families being in poverty are gender-specific. One reason is low individual labor market productivity. Most poor people lack education. Another reason is limited labor market opportunities. Because most poor people have low education and little work experience, they usually find jobs that feature low wages, few training opportunities, few benefits, and little employment security. Other factors that cause poverty fall into the category of

---

[14]D. Ellwood and M. Bane, "Slipping Into and Out of Poverty: The Dynamics of Spells," *Journal of Human Resources*, Vol. XVI, No. 1, 1986, pp. 1–23.

Box 12.2 CHILD SUPPORT

Despite the availability of government assistance through the TANF program, poverty rates for one-parent families are quite high. In 2001, 28.7% of children living in a mother-only home fell below the poverty level, more than four times the poverty rate for children living in an intact family (5.7%). In part to improve the economic well-being of children, and in part to shift the financial burden from the state to the absent parent, the past few decades have seen the development of an elaborate system of federal and state policies aimed at increasing the collection of child support.

The collection of child support is complex; consequently, federal and state governments have become involved in many family interactions. Most of the children of divorced parents are covered by child-support awards because the paternity of a child born to married parents is legally established at the time of birth and the dissolution of a marriage is a legal process requiring financial provision for the children. For children born to unmarried parents, paternity must first be proved, often by court order but increasingly by voluntary paternity acknowledgment. After paternity is legally established, a child-support award must be decreed, and payment must be made. To achieve these outcomes, each state operates a Child Support Enforcement (CSE) office that enforces child-support policies and provides a variety of support-related services. State CSE offices assist in locating absent parents; facilitating paternity testing; working to establish, change, and enforce child-support awards; obtaining health insurance; and, in the absence of adequate parental support, securing public assistance.

Despite these efforts, only 59% of custodial parents had a child-support award or agreement in 1999, and over one quarter of those parents report receiving no child support at all. However, the picture is not entirely bleak—75% of custodial mothers owed child support report some payment during 1999, and almost half receive the full amount. These statistics have changed little since the 1980s, perhaps suggesting that the efforts by policymakers have been ineffective. However, because children whose parents never married are an increasing proportion of all children with absent parents and these are precisely the children for whom child support was not collected in the past, steady collection rates can be viewed as a sign of improvement. In fact, many studies have shown that paternity establishment and child-support award and enforcement policies have a significant influence on the probability of establishing a child-support award and subsequent payments (Freeman and Wald-fogel, 2001; Argys, Peters and Waldman, 2001).

In an effort to reduce federal and state transfer payments, policymakers see the collection of child support as being important. Because welfare reform changes such as time limits and work rules increasingly affect low-income families, private transfers such as child support grow in importance as a source of financial support. In addition, research has shown that child-support income may be more beneficial to children than other sources of income such as welfare or custodial parent earnings. This research suggests that custodial parents earmark a greater proportion of child-support income for child expenditures (Del Boca and Flinn, 1994). Other studies have shown that educational attainment is higher among child-support recipients (Graham, Beller, and Hernandez, 1994; Knox and Bane, 1994). Still others have found some evidence that test scores are higher and behavior problems lower for children whose fathers paid child support compared to children with an absent father that does not contribute financially (Argys et al., 1998; McLanahan et al., 1994). As the increased focus on the establishment and enforcement of child-support awards changes the expectations of parents and potential parents, changes in behavior may follow. If noncustodial parents view child-support awards as more equitable, voluntary compliance may increase (Lin, 2000). Furthermore, the increased cost of absent parenthood could alter divorce and out-of-wedlock fatherhood decisions.

Sources: Laura M. Argys, H. Elizabeth Peters, and Donald M. Waldman, "Can the Family Support Act Put Some Life Back Into Deadbeat Dads? An Analysis of Child Support Guidelines, Award Rates and Levels," *Journal of Human Resources*, Vol. 36, No. 2, pp. 226–252, 2001. Laura M. Argys, H. Elizabeth Peters, Jeanne Brooks-Gunn, and Judith R. Smith, "The Impact of Child Support on Cognitive Outcomes of Young Children," *Demography*, Vol. 35, No. 2, pp. 159–173, 1998. Andrea Beller and John Graham, *Small Change: The Economics of Child Support*, New Haven: Yale University Press, 1993. Daniela Del Boca and Christopher J. Flinn, "Expenditure Decisions of Divorced Mothers and Income Composition," *Journal of Human Resources*, Vol. 29, pp. 742–761, 1994. K. Freeman and J. Waldfogel, "Dunning Delinquent Dads: Child Support Enforcement Policy and Never Married Women," Institute for Research on Poverty, 2000. Richard B. Freeman and Jane Waldfogel, "Dunning Delinquent Dads: The Effects of Child Support Enforcement Policy on Child Support Receipt by Never Married Women," Vol. 36, No. 2, pp. 207–225, 2001. I. Garfinkel and P. Robins, "The Relationship Between Child Support Enforcement Tools and Child Support Outcomes," edited by I. Garfinkel, S. McLanahan, and P. Robins, Washington, D.C.: The Urban Institute Press, pp. 133–170. John W. Graham, Andrea H. Beller, and Pedro Hernandez, "The Relationship Between Child Support Payments and Offspring Educational Attainment," in *Child Support and Child Well-Being* edited by Irwin Garfinkel, Sara S. McLanahan, and Philip K. Robins, Washington D.C.: The Urban Institute Press, 1993. Virginia W. Knox and Mary Jo Bane, "Child Support and Schooling," in *Child Support and Child Well-Being* edited by Irwin Garfinkel, Sara S. McLanahan, and Philip K. Robins, Washington D.C.: The Urban Institute Press, 1994, pp. 285–310. I-Fen Lin, "Perceived Fairness and Compliance with Child Support Obligations," *Journal of Marriage and the Family,* Vol. 62, No. 2, pp. 388–398, 2000. S. S. McLanahan, J. A. Seltzer, T. L. Hanson, and E. Thompson, "Child Support and Enforcement and Child Well-Being: Greater Security or Greater Conflict?" in *Child Support and Child Well-Being* edited by Irwin Garfinkel, Sara S. McLanahan, and Philip K. Robins, Washington D.C.: The Urban Institute Press, 1994.

undesirable life events or just plain bad luck. Divorce, the death of a spouse or parent, a prolonged illness, or a job loss can all plunge a person or a family into poverty. These events reduce an individual's economic resources and/or their income-earning ability.

Another possibility is that the poor perhaps have inappropriate attitudes toward work. Researchers have often hypothesized that there is a "culture of poverty" where poverty is handed down generation to generation. Perhaps this culture fosters a sense of dependency and a lack of initiative. Poor people become "trapped" by their circumstances. Children who grow up in poor families may not have role models who successfully hold jobs. Can they escape poverty? This question was addressed in a carefully crafted piece of research that followed families for ten years.[15] The study found that there was an enormous amount of turnover in the poverty population and that only a very small percentage of people remained in poverty over a long period of time. The author concluded that because so many people cycled in and out of poverty, poor or inappropriate attitudes could not be the main causal explanation why some people remain in poverty.

It is clear that families headed by women suffer disproportionately from poverty. However, a question that arises and has been heavily debated is whether or not this shift in family structure is the cause of poverty or whether the rise in nonmarital births caused by poverty? Poor families suffer enormous stresses, and many studies show that a leading cause of divorce is financial hardship. In addition, welfare programs that often condition eligibility on the absence of a male in the house may well cause women to decide not to live with or marry the father of their children. This raises the question of whether a possible cause of poverty is the government programs that are

---

[15]Greg J. Duncan, *Years of Poverty, Years of Plenty,* Ann Arbor, Mich.: Institute for Social Research, University of Michigan. 1984.

supposed to help combat it. Paradoxically, some believe that government programs designed to help those in poverty actually foster poverty by creating little incentive for the poor to find jobs. These programs may also create *a moral hazard* effect. Moral hazard refers to the idea that welfare recipients might be motivated to engage in illegal or immoral acts to obtain more benefits. For example, a woman might have an additional child while on welfare to obtain an increase in benefits or she might choose to live apart from the father of her children to gain access to benefits.[16] We discuss this issue in more detail later in the chapter.

In the next section, we examine the government programs that are currently in place to alleviate poverty. Specifically, we explain what exactly welfare in the United States is with an emphasis on the major reform of the welfare system that occurred in 1996. We then look at a program that receives political support from both liberals and conservatives, the Earned Income Tax Credit.

Welfare Programs in the United States

Welfare in the United States is a combination of programs, some of which date back to the 1930s. For many years, the program that we think of as welfare was known as **Aid to Families with Dependent Children** or **AFDC.** In 1996, AFDC was abolished and replaced with **TANF—Temporary Assistance for Needy Families** (pronounced "TAN-EFF"), a program that we will discuss later. Welfare also consists of the **Supplemental Security Income (SSI)** program, which benefits disabled, blind, and poor elderly adults; food subsidies consisting of food stamps, the **WIC (Women, Infants, and Children)** program, and subsidized school lunches; medical care available through **Medicaid,** the government-run health care system for the poor; and housing subsidies.[17] In 2001, the **food stamp program** served 7.5 million families and provided $15.5 billion of benefits; TANF provided $25 billion to 2.1 million families; WIC provided $4.3 billion to 7.5 million persons; and Medicaid provided more than $140 billion to 40 million persons. The Medicaid total includes the low-income elderly as well as persons who are blind or permanently disabled. About $37 billion of Medicaid spending went to 25 million

---

[16]This idea was popularized by Charles Murray in his book *Losing Ground: American Social Policy 1950–1980*, New York: Basic Books, 1984.

[17]Much of this section is drawn from Robert Moffitt, "The Temporary Assistance for Needy Families Program," NBER working paper number 8749, 2002.

persons who were not elderly, blind, or disabled. Our discussion of welfare in this chapter focuses on the TANF and AFDC programs because they are (were) the main cash assistance programs. As we will discover, welfare has both costs and benefits.

How Welfare (AFDC) Works

The AFDC program was created by the Social Security Act of 1935, along with the Old-Age Social Security program and the Unemployment Insurance program. The initial program created was called Aid to Dependent Children (ADC); it was a program that served poor children, not their families. Later the name was changed to AFDC (Aid to Families with Dependent Children), and benefits were extended to adults in poor families. AFDC was what is known as an **income maintenance program.** Its main objective was to ensure a minimum level of economic support to those with little income. Because AFDC benefits were determined by financial need, it is an example of what is known as a **means-tested program.**

To be eligible for assistance, an individual not only had to fall under the assigned income and asset cutoffs, but also had to possess certain characteristics that determine eligibility. In particular, for many years, AFDC benefits were essentially limited to unmarried women with children. Married couples were typically ineligible for assistance, as were single people without children. In 1935, when the program was first started, if a woman headed a family, she was usually a widow and thus the AFDC program primarily served families who were headed by widows. This changed with rising divorce rates in the 1960s and 1970s so that during those two decades most AFDC recipients were divorced and separated women. However, in the 1980s and 1990s, most AFDC recipients were never-married single mothers.

Under the AFDC program, eligible recipients were given a dollar amount of benefits, often called the **income guarantee,** if they had no income of their own. This guarantee level was set by each state, and there was wide variation in the guarantee levels across states. Southern states typically had very low guarantees, while states in the Northeast and Midwest had much higher guarantees. As a recipient's own earnings increased, the benefits were reduced or "taxed" at the benefit reduction rate of t. Economists call this an **implicit tax rate** because it functions exactly like a tax on earned income. The benefit reduction rate was set by the federal government and varied from 67% to 100% over the life of AFDC. Sometimes, families were allowed to keep a small amount of earnings before their benefits were reduced; this amount was called

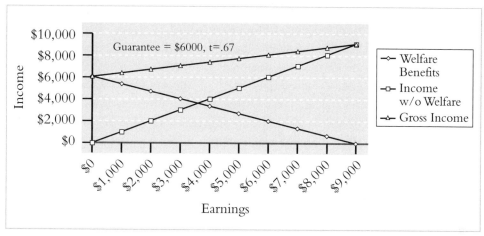

Figure 12.5   How Traditional Welfare (AFDC) Works

an **income disregard.** The purpose of the disregard was to allow recipients to cover the costs of working such as transportation and clothing. The final feature of the AFDC program was the **breakeven point.** This was the level of earnings beyond which the family no longer received any AFDC payment.

Figure 12.5 illustrates how the AFDC program worked. A family's earnings are plotted on the horizontal axis, and its gross income is plotted on the vertical axis. AFDC benefits are shown for a program with an annual guarantee (G) of $6000, a benefit reduction rate of two thirds, and no earnings disregard. As earnings increase, welfare benefits decline so that family income rises more slowly than family earnings. For example, when earnings are $0, family income is $6000, composed entirely of AFDC benefits. But if earnings increase to $3000, AFDC benefits fall by $2000 (= 2/3 × $3000) to $4000. The net increase in family income is, therefore, just $1000: the $3000 increase in earnings minus the $2000 decrease in benefits. This decrease in AFDC benefits with earnings continues until the breakeven point of earnings of $9000, above which welfare benefits are zero.

The Effect of Welfare on Work Incentives

The AFDC program created strong negative work disincentives for recipients. The income guarantee creates what economists call an **income effect**, which pulls the recipient in the direction of not working by giving her more income than she otherwise would have had. The benefit reduction rate effectively lowers the wage rate from any earnings, creating what is called a

substitution effect. The impact on the wage rate is substantial because the benefit reduction rate ranged from 67 to 100%. When the benefit reduction rate is 100%, benefits are reduced dollar for dollar with additional earnings, leaving the individual with a wage rate of $0! With a benefit reduction rate of *only* 67%, a worker's net wage rate is just one third of what she earns. This substitution effect creates an incentive to substitute away from work and toward receipt of welfare by reducing the economic value of work. In the case of AFDC, both the income effect and the substitution effect provide strong disincentives to work for those eligible for the program.

Let's use the model we developed in Chapter 7 to see how a welfare program such as AFDC would affect a woman's decision to supply labor to the labor market.[18] Recall that we developed a model where a given woman maximized her utility over leisure, market goods, and household produced goods. She was subject to three constraints. The first of these is the spending constraint. The market goods constraint in (a) simply indicates that the amount of spending on goods and services (pC) must equal the amount of income earned (wM) plus nonlabor income (V). In other words, she can't spend more than the amount of income she has. The second constraint is the production constraint: The amount of household goods that can be produced depends on the amount of time spent and on the technology and capital goods available (Z). Finally, the third constraint is the time constraint: There are only so many hours in a day (T), and the total amount of time spent in each activity can't exceed that amount. For convenience, we repeat these constraints in equation form:

(a) Market Goods: $\qquad pC = wM + V$

(b) Household Goods: $\qquad G = g(H; Z)$

(c) Time: $\qquad M + H + L = T$

We then showed how we could find her utility-maximizing choice for market work. We assumed that she began by finding MVT^*, the utility-maximizing choice between leisure and household work: MVT^* is the value of the last hour of time when all time is spent in either leisure or household production and when that time is allocated so as to maximize utility. We deter-

---

[18]See the appendix to this chapter for a graphical exposition of welfare within the context of the labor/leisure model.

mined that she would compare MVT^* to her marginal value of time in the labor market ($MVT_M(1)$) to see if she should transfer some of her time out of leisure and household work and into market work. Let M^* stand for the utility-maximizing hours of work. The rules for labor force participation we developed in Chapter 7 can be stated as

(d) If $MVT^* > MVT_M(1)$, then $M^* = 0$.
This woman does not work in the labor market.

(e) If $MVT^* < MVT_M(1)$, then $M^* > 0$.
This woman works in the labor market.

Recall that M^* is the optimal amount of time allocated to the labor market. It is relatively straightforward to use this model to determine how an AFDC program would affect the decision to participate in the labor market. To examine how an AFDC program affects this choice, let's begin by assuming that a given woman is currently working in the labor force and further that she meets the eligibility requirements for the AFDC program. Figure 12.6 shows this. The left graph shows the marginal value of time curves for leisure and household work. Recall that hours of leisure are measured from left to right, and hours of household production are measured from right to left. The right graph shows two MVT_M curves. The top one is the curve that would exist in the absence of the AFDC program. Let's start here. In the absence of the AFDC program, this woman is maximizing her utility by working some hours in the labor market. We see this because MVT^* intersects the MVT_M curve at M^*. In the language of Chapter 7, if $MVT^* < MVT_M(1)$, $M^* > 0$, then this woman works in the labor market. This is exactly what we observe before the introduction of the welfare program.

Let's incorporate the AFDC program into this model. The introduction of an AFDC program does not change the MVT_L and MVT_H curves (recall that welfare recipients often have young children so that their marginal value of time in the home is higher than it would be for women without young children). It does however shift down the MVT_M curve. A welfare program has the effect of changing two variables: It lowers the woman's wage rate because of the implicit tax, and it increases a woman's nonearned income because of the guarantee. Both act to lower the MVT_M curve. The lower wage lowers the value of her time directly (via the substitution effect), and the guarantee is simply nonearned income; it acts like husband's income did in the example in Chapter 7. More nonearned income lowers the value of the time spent in the

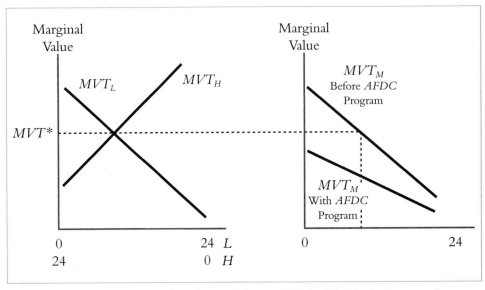

Figure 12.6   Choosing Household Production, Leisure, and Market Work in the Presence of an AFDC Program

labor market. This is the income effect. In the case of AFDC, the substitution effect and the income effect both act to shift down the MVT_M curve making it less likely that a given woman will participate in the labor market. In fact, the shift down in the MVT_M curve means that now $MVT^* > MVT_M(1)$, so her best choice is to spend all of her time in leisure and household production.

A popular perception among the general public and some policymakers is that women on welfare are inherently lazy and enjoy collecting welfare benefits and not working in the labor market. Whether or not this is an accurate depiction of any given individual we cannot say.[19] However, we can show that an alternative explanation why many low income women do not work but choose to collect welfare is that once you are eligible for a program such as AFDC, the very structure of the program creates a strong disincentive to work. Clearly, our society feels that it is important to support its most eco-

---

[19]Readers who are interested in reading about what it is like to be on welfare should consult either *Living on the Edge: The Realities of Welfare in America* by Mark Rank (New York: Columbia University Press, 1994) or *Making Ends Meet: How Single Mothers Survive Welfare and Low-Wage Work* by Kathryn Edin and Laura Lein (New York: Russell Sage Foundation, 1994).

nomically disadvantaged citizens; this is why such a program exists—this is the benefit the program provides. However, the fact that the program creates a disincentive to work is a clear cost.

Empirical studies that have examined the effect of AFDC on labor supply support the prediction that AFDC creates a work disincentive and that AFDC recipients work less in the presence of AFDC than they otherwise would.[20] Voluntary work rates (i.e., work in the absence of work requirements) have always been low in the AFDC program because, as our model of labor force participation predicts, it rarely was economically rational to work while collecting AFDC.

There was also considerable concern about the effect of AFDC on family formation. Because states individually set their AFDC guarantee levels, there was tremendous variation in AFDC levels across states at a given point in time. If we believe that AFDC caused single-parent families, we might expect to see a greater proportion of single-parent families in those states with more generous AFDC benefits. Remember that we discussed this in Chapter 6 as a possible explanation for the high rates of teen childbearing in the United States. Here, we examine it from the standpoint of all women, not just teenagers. The empirical evidence on the effect of AFDC on family structure is somewhat mixed. Robert Moffitt reviews sixty-eight separate estimates of the effect of AFDC on various aspects of marriage, fertility, and single motherhood. These studies were conducted through 1996 and generally carefully controlled for other socioeconomic factors that differ across states and individuals. Moffitt concludes that welfare is likely to have an impact on family structure, although the magnitude of the effect is somewhat uncertain.[21] Two very recent studies, published after Moffitt's review, document that welfare may in fact have a fairly large effect on the nonmarital birth rate though not for teenagers but for women in their early 20s.[22] Keep in mind, however, that changes in family structure have occurred at all socioeconomic levels, not just among poor women.

---

[20]See Robert Moffitt, "Incentive Effects of the U.S. Welfare System: A Review," *Journal of Economic Literature*, Vol. 30, March 1992, for an early review of this literature and Robert Moffitt, "The Temporary Assistance for Needy Families Program," NBER working paper #8749, 2002, for an update of this review.

[21]Robert Moffitt, "The Effect of Welfare on Marriage and Fertility," in *Welfare, the Family, and Reproductive Behavior* edited by Robert Moffitt, Washington, D.C.: National Academy Press, 1998.

[22]See Mark R. Rosenzweig, "Welfare, Marital Prospects, and Non-marital Childbearing," *Journal of Political Economy*, 1999, and Saul D. Hoffman and E. Michael Foster, "AFDC Benefits and Non-Marital Births to Young Women," *Journal of Human Resources*, Vol. 35, No. 2, pp. 375–391, 2000.

Welfare Reform

During its lifespan, the AFDC program was modified several times. For example, in 1961, Congress created the **AFDC-UP** program, which allowed families where both parents were present but the primary earner was unemployed to receive benefits. Initially, AFDC-UP was an optional program, but in 1988 the federal government required all states to offer AFDC-UP.

Perhaps the most important modifications had to do with work requirements. Various work requirements were established by the states and by the federal government with varying degrees of success. These programs generally involved some sort of job search activity that recipients were required to engage in to receive benefits. Many times there was an emphasis on training and obtaining more education. In other cases, recipients were required to work in community service jobs such as cleaning a public park. This was known as **workfare.** Several pieces of legislation preceded welfare reform and included work requirements. The most recent pieces of legislation prior to the 1996 reform were the Omnibus Reconciliation Act of 1981 and the Family Support Act of 1988.

Other modifications had to do with the receipt of Medicaid under AFDC. Until the passage of the Family Support Act of 1988, Medicaid was usually discontinued when a recipient found a job. The Family Support Act of 1988 required states to provide transitory Medicaid benefits for at least twelve months to individuals who left AFDC. Congress also expanded Medicaid to cover poor children regardless of AFDC eligibility.

During the late 1980s and early 1990s, states began to increasingly experiment with welfare reform. They experimented with various ways to encourage welfare recipients to work including increasing work requirements, imposing time limits on benefits, and imposing **family caps.** Family caps specified that AFDC recipients could not receive additional benefits if they had another child while on AFDC. States were also required to evaluate the effectiveness of these reform provisions and usually did so by assigning one group of welfare recipients to the new rules (the treatment group) and another group to the old rules (the control group). All these reform measures that took place at the state level during the 1990s ultimately led to the passage of the Personal Responsibility and Work Reconciliation Act (PRWORA) signed into law by President Clinton in August of 1996.

PRWORA represented a fundamental change in welfare programs in the United States. Prior to this time, welfare benefits were available to women with dependent children so that women who had little economic means could stay home with their children. Increasing out of wedlock births, growing welfare caseloads, and a changing political climate changed society's and ultimately policymakers' views of women on welfare. Perceptions that married women not on welfare are increasingly opting to work full-time and utilize daycare services has also contributed to the idea that poor women should not have the option of raising their children at home while collecting welfare benefits. People tend to be more sympathetic to widows and divorced mothers than to never-married mothers, which may also explain why the sentiment for PRWORA was so strong.

With the passage of PRWORA, the old Aid to Families with Dependent Children program was abolished, and, in its place, a new program named Temporary Assistance to Needy Families was established. One of the main differences between TANF and AFDC is that the federal government turned much of the authority over the program to the states. Prior to TANF, the AFDC program was financed by open-ended federal grants that matched the cash amounts provided by the states—known as matching grants. Under TANF, the previous matching grant funding model was changed to block grant funding. This means that each state is given a set amount of money to do with as it sees fit, and the amount of the block grant is determined by the projected welfare needs of the state. TANF also transferred most of the control of the program over to the states. Now, states have control not only over the level of the benefits that they can provide, but also over who is eligible, the tax rate, and even the form of the assistance. For example, states can use TANF funds for childcare support and job search support rather than for cash assistance.

Although TANF requirements vary by state, the general structure is very similar to AFDC. There is an income guarantee, an earnings disregard, and an implicit tax. But there are enormous differences from the standpoint of the recipients. First, benefits under TANF are not a legal *entitlement* as they had been under AFDC. When a program is an entitlement, there is a legal guarantee of assistance. States were legally required to assist those individuals that the federal government determined were eligible for AFDC. Second, there is a strict limit of five years on lifetime receipt of benefits under TANF. Additionally, under TANF, adult recipients must engage in some type of work-related activity within two years of welfare receipt or face loss of benefits, with few exceptions.[23] Finally, most forms of public assistance are denied to legal immigrants for five years or until they become citizens.[24]

Table 12.4 presents information on the personal characteristics of adult TANF recipients in 2001. Approximately 40% are Black, 30% are White, and 26% are Hispanic. Two thirds have never been married, with another 20% separated or divorced. This is another indication of the importance of family structure for women's economic status. Half are high school graduates, while 45% have less than a high school education. More than half have pre-school-aged children. Many of these characteristics, especially low education, the presence of young children, and the absence of a spouse, are major impediments to labor market success.

Why Reform Welfare?

Why was AFDC abolished and TANF created in its place? Perhaps the best way to address this question is to quote President Clinton at the signing of the welfare reform bill in August, 1996: "What we are trying to do today is to overcome the flaws of the welfare system for the people who are trapped on it. We all know that the typical family in welfare today is very different from the one that welfare was designed to deal with 60 years ago. We all know that there are a lot of good people on welfare who just get off of it in the ordinary course of business, but that a significant number of people are trapped on welfare for a very long time, exiling them from the entire community of work that gives structure to our lives."[25]

All welfare programs face what is sometimes called the **iron triangle of welfare.** This term refers to the fact that a welfare program has three goals that are inherently in conflict with one another. These goals are (1) lift poor people out of poverty, (2) maintain incentives to work, and (3) accomplish the first two goals at a "reasonable" cost. The problem is that these goals are often in conflict with each other. For example, one way to lift people out of

---

[23]To facilitate this work activity, the 1996 reform increased funding for childcare. The Child Care and Development Block Grant (CCDBG) was created to consolidate childcare subsidies. We discuss the CCDBG in detail in Chapter 14. Health insurance is also provided to families entering the job market.

[24]For more details regarding the differences between TANF and AFDC, see Thomas L. Gais and Richard P. Nathan, "Overview Report: Implementation of the Personal Responsibility Act of 1996," Albany, N.Y: Nelson A. Rockefeller Institute of Government, 1998.

[25]President William J. Clinton, http://www.acf.dhhs.gov/news/welfare/wr/822potus.htm, accessed 7/10/03.

Characteristic	Proportion (%)
Race/Ethnicity	
White	30.1
Black	39.0
Hispanic	26.0
Asian	2.1
Other	2.8
Marital Status	
Never Married	66.9
Married	11.7
Separated/Divorced	20.7
Widowed	0.8
Education Level	
Less Than 10 Years	15.7
10–11 Years	29.7
12 Years	49.0
More Than 12 Years	3.1
Other or Unknown	2.5
Age	
Under Age 20	7.4
20–29	42.4
30–39	31.2
Over Age 39	19.0
Age of Youngest Child	
0–1	13.8
1–2	20.2
3–5	19.4
6–8	15.2
9–11	12.4
12 and older	18.7

Table 12.4   Characteristics of Adults Receiving TANF Assistance, 2001

Source: TANF Report to Congress, 2001.

poverty is simply to give them some money each month. However, that creates an income effect—a disincentive to work—and it is very costly. Maintaining incentives to work means giving people less money, which reduces the cost of the program but does not lift as many people out of poverty. Programs that ready people to work by providing education and training are also very expensive although they may have long-term benefits.

As President Clinton alluded to, TANF was designed to deal specifically with several perceived shortcomings of the old AFDC system, and work was a main goal of the reforms. From an economic viewpoint, there were two concerns about the old welfare system. First, as we established earlier, it had clear work disincentives for recipients. Second, there was some concern as to whether or not AFDC was actually the cause of poverty by creating more families headed by single mothers. However, these costs have always been justified by a belief that there is a minimal standard of living that the government should provide for its poorest citizens. Thus, the trade-off between efficiency and equity comes into play once again.

Policymakers elected to deal with what they felt were the shortcomings of AFDC directly. For example, concerns about dependency and work incentives were addressed, and women receiving TANF are now subject to time limits and work requirements. Furthermore, two of the stated goals enacted by the PRWORA were to encourage marriage and to reduce the rate of nonmarital childbearing. To this end, there were restrictions on benefits to unwed teenage mothers. To be eligible, unwed teenage mothers must live with a parent or guardian to try to stop teens from using welfare to establish their own households. Teen mothers are also required to attend school.

Child support enforcement was also increased. As we discussed in Box 12.2 for details. To receive benefits, all unmarried welfare mothers are required to help identify the fathers of their children and establish paternity. In addition, states are now allowed to implement family caps (i.e., deny an increase in monthly welfare benefits to women who have more children while on welfare). Mandated family caps at the federal level were not instituted under TANF primarily because abortion foes raised concerns that family caps would encourage more abortions.[26] Finally, all noncitizens can be denied TANF benefits if a state so desires.[27] Childcare subsidies are also in place to

[26]Klerman, "Welfare Reform and Abortion," in *Welfare, the Family and Reproductive Behavior, Research Perspectives*, Washington, D.C.: National Academy Press, 1998, pp. 98–134.

[27]For more information on welfare reform see Alan Weil, "Ten Things Everyone Should Know About Welfare Reform," The Urban Institute, May 2002.

help low-income mothers who must now find jobs. We discuss these in Chapter 14.

There is little evidence yet as to how TANF has affected hours of work or out-of-wedlock childbearing. Part of the reason for this is that previous research on AFDC and work relied on cross-state variation in the monthly guarantee to determine the effect of AFDC on labor force participation. TANF turned over so much of the control to the states that there are now some fifty-one different TANF programs, whereas under AFDC all states essentially followed the model presented earlier with some variation in the guarantee and some variation in the implicit tax rate.[28] It is worth noting that in many states the benefit reduction rate (implicit tax rate) has dropped sharply (to 50% and below).[29] This reduction makes ascertaining the effects of the different programs much more difficult. Furthermore, TANF was introduced into all the states at the same time, making it difficult to measure its overall impact with so many factors changing at once. Finally, TANF has not been in place very long, and many studies using post-TANF data are still being conducted. Box 12.3 provides a look at how California has fared after TANF. In the next section, we examine some of the recent research that aims to determine how effective welfare reform has been.

Evaluating Welfare Reform: Has It Worked?

The 1996 welfare reform bill was designed to "end welfare as we know it," as stated by President Clinton. The time limits imposed on TANF recipients were imposed directly to address concerns that AFDC promoted dependency. Ellwood and Bane documented that most recipients of AFDC relied on it for short-term transitory assistance. However, about one quarter of new AFDC recipients would be on AFDC for more than ten years. Those individuals are primarily the ones who will find themselves subject to the lifetime benefits cutoff imposed by TANF. Furthermore, many women exited and entered welfare frequently building up a considerable amount of time on welfare.[30] Because of lifetime limits on TANF receipt, this type of behavior is no longer possible for TANF recipients.

---

[28]See http://anfdataurban.org/wrd for a look at state-specific benefit formulas.

[29]Robert Moffitt, "The Temporary Assistance for Needy Families Program," NBER working paper 8749, 2002, provides a review of the work that has thus far been done on TANF.

[30]M. J. Bane and D. Ellwood, *The Dynamics of Dependence: The Routes to Self-Sufficiency*, Cambridge, Mass.: Urban Systems Research and Engineering, Inc., 1994, and "Understanding Welfare Dynamics," in *Welfare Realities: From Rhetoric to Reform*, edited by M. J. Bane and D. Ellwood, Cambridge, Mass.: Harvard University Press, 1994.

Box 12.3 Welfare to Work: California's Success

Los Angeles (LA) County in California had one of the largest welfare case-loads in the United States in the late 1980s and early 1990s. In 1998, almost 25% of LA County's residents and nearly one third of the children living in LA County were below the poverty line. Desperate to reduce the costs of providing welfare to these families, LA County started a program called GAIN (Greater Avenues for Independence). The initial program was implemented in the late 1980s to the early 1990s. The program focused on education, but the costs were found to be much higher than the benefits mostly because so many welfare recipients needed the education services provided yet still failed to find high-paying jobs.

Between 1993 and 1995, Los Angeles County in California switched to a program known as Jobs-First GAIN. The program was designed to move welfare recipients into work. As opposed to the original GAIN program, Jobs-First GAIN emphasized job placement rather than remedial education. By regularly communicating the importance of finding a job first, aiding in identifying skills and strengths of job attainment, expecting professional behavior while using the program, and making sure recipients were educated in the benefits of finding a job, the program was able to move many welfare recipients into jobs and to increase their earnings—even among the most disadvantaged. Whether these gains will translate into long-term income growth and self-sufficiency for these women and their families remains to be seen. Advocates see this program as a model for other states who want to increase the employment and earnings of welfare recipients. Detractors note that the jobs are dead-end and that without education and training these women will not really become self-sufficient.

Source: Stephen Freedman, Marisa Mitchell, and David Navarro, "The Los Angeles Jobs-First GAIN Evaluation: Preliminary Findings on Participation Patterns and First-Year Impacts," Manpower Demonstration Research Corporation Working Paper, August 1998. Reprinted with permission of MDRC.

A recent study classified TANF recipients into three groups (as Ellwood and Bane, 1994 suggested): (1) stayers—those who first received welfare more than two years go and have remained on TANF continuously for the past two years; (2) new entrants—those who entered the welfare system for the first time in the past two years; and (3) cyclers—those who first received welfare more than two years ago but have received it only intermittently over the past

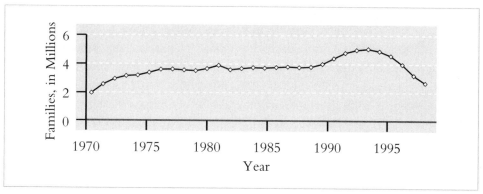

Figure 12.7   Historic Trends in AFDC/TANF Enrollments Fiscal Years 1970–1999

Source: U.S. Department of Health and Human Services.

two years. Using data from the 1999 Survey of America's Families, researchers documented that about 26% of TANF recipients were new entrants, 23% were cyclers, and 47% were stayers.[31]

The distinction is important for several reasons. First, the general public and policymakers alike are likely to be more sympathetic toward those individuals who use welfare sporadically as a temporary means of support when they have no alternative. Long-term users, who are often viewed as "milking the system," are less likely to receive public support. Second, those who are using welfare only temporarily are generally those with stronger job skills who probably have a history of employment and attachment to the labor force, whereas long-term recipients generally have lower skills to begin with and usually find that what skills they have increasingly deteriorate while they are on welfare.

We can take a look at welfare caseloads over time to see how they have changed. Figure 12.7 presents the number of families on welfare from 1970 to 1999. The increase in the AFDC caseload began in the 1970s when the number of families on welfare doubled from about 2 million to just under 4 million. The caseload remained quite steady throughout the 1980s and then rose sharply and steadily in the first half of the 1990s, finally peaking at over 5 million families (and more than 14 million recipients) in 1994. The TANF legislation was passed in August 1996 but was not implemented until July 1997. The decline in the welfare caseload began in 1995 and thus predates TANF. Since

[31]See Sheila R. Zedlewski and Donald W. Alderson, "Before and After Welfare Reform: How Have Families Changed?" The Urban Institute, Series B, No. B32, April 2001.

1994, the decline in the AFDC/TANF caseload has been unprecedented. The number of recipient families literally fell by half between 1996 and 1999—from more than 4.4 million to 2.1 million. Despite the recession in 2001, the decline continues. The latest figures from September 2002 show that the number of families receiving TANF declined from 2.102 million in September 2001 to 2.024 million in September 2002.[32] However, during the third quarter of 2002, twenty-seven states experienced a caseload increase.[33]

As Figure 12.7 illustrates, the decline post-TANF has been particularly steep, but it is not all the result of legislation. This period was also a time of rapid economic growth and very low unemployment—an ideal economic climate for welfare reform. The recent economic recession has yet to cause caseloads to increase, but that is a possibility. Under TANF, the lifetime limit of welfare receipt is five years, which means that the decline in caseloads in Figure 12.7 cannot be caused by the time limits because no one would face them until 2002. TANF work requirements may well have had something to do with the drop in caseloads since 1996 because states were required to have TANF recipients working within two years of receipt of TANF. Finally, the period from 1994 until the 2001 recession was a period of economic growth with very low unemployment rates. This created job opportunities that probably drew individuals off the welfare rolls. One estimate indicates that about one third of the observed welfare decline was the result of the 1996 reforms.[34] Another suggests that about one fifth of the decline in welfare caseloads was caused by the strong economy in the mid- to late 1990s, and the rest is related to policy changes, particularly expansion of the Earned Income Tax Credit, which we discuss in more detail later in this chapter.[35]

A recent study that evaluated the results of welfare reform used detailed data from three cities: Boston, Chicago, and San Antonio. Interestingly, this study documented that those who were most likely to leave the welfare rolls were both those who were the most ready for employment and those who were

[32]Data on caseloads from U.S. Department of Health and Human Services web page: http://www.acf.dhhs.gov/news/stats/.

[33]State data reported by CLASP at www.clas.org and collected by the U.S. Department of Health and Human Services.

[34]U.S. Council of Economic Advisors, *The Effects of Welfare Policy and the Economic Expansion on Welfare Caseloads: An Update*, Washington, D.C.: White House, August 1999.

[35]Geoffrey Wallace and Rebecca M. Blank, "What Goes Up Must Come Down? Explaining the Recent Changes in Public Assistance Caseloads," in *Economic Conditions and Welfare Reform* edited by Sheldon Danziger. Kalamazoo, Mich.: Upjohn Institute, 1999.

the least ready for unemployment. Women in the first group were able to leave welfare because they were finding jobs. Those in the latter group were leaving welfare because their benefits were reduced or discontinued as a result of noncompliance with welfare program rules.[36]

Welfare Reform and the Working Poor

The biggest objection to welfare reform among its critics is that women who move from welfare to work will not be able to support themselves and their families adequately with the low-wage jobs they will likely find. Furthermore, welfare recipients might be on welfare because they face significant barriers to employment. For example, Table 12.4 indicates that adult TANF recipients had a number of impediments to labor market success, including low education and young children. Furthermore, a recent study has shown that mental health is an important predictor of welfare receipt—particularly depression.[37] Other studies have documented that welfare recipients might not be work ready (i.e., might not understand the importance of following workplace norms such as being on time and dressing appropriately). They might have substance abuse problems, suffer from domestic violence, or lack child care or transportation to work.[38] Thus, even in a robust economy, some women on welfare may simply not be able to hold a job.

Many "welfare leavers" end up taking minimum wage jobs. A mother who works full time year round at minimum wage to support two small children will earn $10,712 a year. This is well below the 2001 poverty line for a family of three. Nationwide, 7.2 million people living in poverty are among the **working poor.** The working poor are individuals who spent at least twenty-seven weeks in the labor force (working or looking for work) but whose incomes fell below the official poverty level. Most of them (56%) live in families with children. They are the fastest-growing segment of the poverty population.[39]

---

[36]Andrew Cherlin and Robert Moffitt, "Three-City Findings Reveal Unexpected Diversity Among Welfare Leavers and Stayers," *The Forum (Research Forum on Children, Families and the New Federalism,* Vol. 4, No. 1, pp. 1–5, 2001.

[37]E. Lehrer, K. Crittendon, and K. F. Norr, "Depression and Economic Self-Sufficiency Among Inner-City Minority Mothers," *Social Science Research,* Vol. 31, pp. 285–309, 2002.

[38]See Danziger et al., "Barriers to the Employment of Welfare Recipients," in *Prosperity for All? The Economic Boom and African Americans* edited by R. Cherry and W. M. Rodgers III, New York: Russell Sage Foundation, 2000.

[39]"A Profile of the Working Poor 2001," Bureau of Labor Statistics, June 2003.

Why are the working poor poor? The primary reason that the working poor are in poverty is because they work at low-wage jobs, primarily in the service sector. Randy Albelda refers to this as one of the "fallacies of welfare-to-work policies."[40] She argues that it is not likely that women previously on welfare can just move smoothly over to the paid labor force. One point she makes is that the jobs that former welfare recipients will take are usually not "mother-ready." They are jobs that usually do not provide health care benefits, sick days, or vacation days. She notes that most studies of welfare leavers find that about 75% of those who leave welfare are employed for about 35 hours per week making an average of $7.50 per hour and do not stay employed for very long. Her main criticism is that these jobs put poor mothers, who usually have sole responsibility for their children, in a situation where they cannot possibly win. A sick child, an unexpected change in childcare, or a car that won't start can all wreak havoc on those with the least ability to deal with these situations.

President Bush wants low-income mothers to marry and is willing to support programs aimed at encouraging marriage in the welfare population.[41] West Virginia already has a program in place where 1800 welfare families are being paid a $100 monthly bonus because the children are being raised by married parents. Michigan is spending money on classes for unwed mothers of infants. The classes are mandatory for mothers of infants on welfare and include a component called "marriage exploration." President Bush's plan is to offer states funding for experiments aimed at encouraging welfare mothers to marry the fathers of their children. Many argue that two-parent families are the key to escaping poverty and are better for children (we discuss children and family structure in Chapter 15). However, new research findings are showing that welfare reform may, in fact, be reducing marriage.

Researchers who studied welfare programs in Connecticut and Iowa found that these new work requirements had an unintended consequence: reduced marriage.[42] Two possible explanations were offered. First, women who moved from welfare to work and became more self-sufficient probably were less willing to settle for the wrong man—an idea consistent with the model of

[40]Randy Albelda, "Fallacies of Welfare-to-Work Policies," *Annals of the American Academy of Political and Social Science*, Vol. 577, pp. 56–78, 2001.
[41]CNN.com: "Bush Welfare Plan Promotes Marriage, Work," 2/27/02 and Washington Post.com: "Tying Marriage Vows to Welfare Reform," 4/1/2002.
[42]See Nina Bernstein, "Strict Limits on Welfare Benefits Discourage Marriage, Studies Say," *New York Times*, Sec. A, p. 1, Col. 3, June 3, 2002.

marriage presented earlier in this text. The gains from marriage may be smaller. The second possible explanation is that these new work requirements may have sapped some of the energy from these women, leaving them less time to pursue or nurture a relationship. Women interviewed in these two states generally confirmed these explanations.

Research conducted by the sociologist Kathryn Edin confirms these findings as well.[43] She interviewed about 130 poor Black, White, and Puerto Rican mothers in nine neighborhoods across Philadelphia. Her interviews with these mothers revealed that for many of them marriage, particularly marriage to a man in their neighborhood, is a risky proposition whose reward is far from certain. The women cited four main reasons behind their decisions about marriage. The first reason was affordability—many of the eligible men simply aren't good economic prospects. This idea was proposed by William Wilson as an explanation of the low marriage rates among Black women; we discussed this idea in Chapter 4. The second reason was respectability. Marriage makes sense only if it is to a respectable man who can provide for them. The third reason was trust—there was, in fact, a lack of trust in these men when it comes to money matters and their children. Finally, many of these women reported liking the control they had over their lives and the sense that they were not dependent on a man.

In contrast to President Bush's proposals, Randy Albelda notes that single moms already have a very important job—taking care of their children—and that the work of taking care of families is sometimes inconsistent with the demands of a full-time job. She argues that this work/family dilemma appears to be overlooked in the welfare reform research and proposes that "instead of trying to reform poor mothers to become working-poor mothers, we need to take a closer look at job structures and what it will take to make work possible for mothers who support families."[44] She argues that we need universal early education programs, extended school day programs, and child allowances. Paid family and medical leave and expanded unemployment insurance would also help. Finally, pay equity is essential, given that women's earnings are typically below those of men. What is interesting to note is that many

---

[43]Kathryn Edin, "Few Good Men: Why Poor Mothers Don't Marry or Remarry," *The American Prospect*, pp. 26–31, Jan. 3, 2000.
[44]Randy Albelda, "Fallacies of Welfare-to-Work Policies," *Annals of the American Academy of Political and Social Science*, Vol. 557, pp. 66–78, 2001.

of these measures would also benefit all working mothers not just low-income mothers. According to Albelda, when these measures are in place, we can then begin to expect single mothers to work. The debate over how much work we should expect welfare recipients to engage in is heated. These policies are not without costs, and critics charge that they are unaffordable, particularly in an era where state budgets are particularly tight. Others argue that the government should not be involved in family life. As is always the case in economics, there are trade-offs.

The Earned Income Tax Credit

Technically, TANF is the replacement for AFDC as a program to assist low-income families. But with the welfare rolls shrinking in the late 1990s, a program called the Earned Income Tax Credit (EITC) has quietly become the largest transfer program for poor and moderate-income families. In 2000, the latest year with complete statistics, the EITC provided $32.5 billion to more than 19 million households; in contrast, TANF served about 2.6 million families and provided approximately $12.5 billion to them. In this section, we provide an in-depth look at what the EITC is, how it helps the poor, and the way it affects women, especially their labor force participation.[45]

How the EITC Works

How does the EITC differ from traditional welfare? The simplest and best answer is: "in almost every way." First, the EITC is actually not a welfare program but rather a refundable tax credit that is right on the 1040 tax form that taxpayers fill out each spring. After figuring out its regular income taxes, a family with earnings and with taxable income below a certain amount (discussed later) is eligible for the EITC, which it looks up in a tax table and deducts from its taxes. Unlike most tax credits, the EITC is refundable, so if the credit exceeds the taxes a family owes, it gets a check in the mail for the difference. Whether a family receives the cash or just reduces its taxes, it amounts to the same thing—an increase in a family's income.

Second, the EITC provides benefits only to families with earnings. Families without earnings receive nothing. Furthermore, the benefits from the EITC actually increase with family earnings through a portion of the income distri-

---

[45]To learn more about the EITC, see Saul D. Hoffman and Laurence S. Seidman, *The Earned Income Tax Credit: Helping Working Families*, Kalamazoo, MI: Upjohn Institute for Employment Research, 2003.

bution, before eventually phasing out at higher incomes. This is just the opposite of traditional welfare programs, like AFDC and TANF, which provided maximum benefits to households with no earnings. Take another look at Figure 12.5 where we showed the AFDC benefit schedule. Note there that AFDC benefits were largest when the family had no earnings at all and started to fall as a family's earnings increased.[46]

Third, married couples as well as single parents are eligible for the EITC under identical rules—another difference from traditional welfare. In 2001, a reform of the EITC actually made the EITC a bit more generous for married couples.

Fourth, the EITC is a transfer program that has a great deal of support across the political spectrum. Because the EITC benefit structure rewards rather than penalizes work, at least among the lower-income EITC recipients, it could be broadly seen as endorsing work. Conservative politicians, weary of the low workforce activity of AFDC recipients, have found that very appealing. Liberals have also supported it, viewing it not as a replacement for traditional welfare but as a supplement and as a potential source of cash assistance for the working poor, a group often overlooked by most poverty programs. Others have noted that it could function as a kind of substitute for a higher minimum wage and that it could do so without the concerns about higher minimum wages reducing employment opportunities and with better targeting of its benefits to low- and moderate-income households. Finally, the EITC operates without a large bureaucracy and without the welfare offices that neither clients nor administrators like.

Table 12.5 shows the details of the EITC benefit schedule for 2002. For each dollar of earnings, up to the dollar figures shown in the "Earnings Subsidy Threshold" column, the EITC provides a matching percentage credit or wage subsidy. For single persons (between the ages of 25 and 64) or households without children, the subsidy rate is 7.65%. The subsidy on earnings jumps to 34% for families with one child and 40% for families with two or more children. For families with incomes below the subsidy threshold, the EITC subsidy is exactly like receiving a wage increase of 7.65, 34, or 40%, respectively. As a family's income rises above the earnings subsidy level, the credit remains constant for a few thousand dollars and then it is steadily reduced, eventually phasing out completely at the incomes shown in the last column of the table.

---

[46]In practice, a small amount of earnings are "disregarded" in AFDC and TANF, which means that a family can earn that amount without any decrease in its benefits. But benefits never increase with earnings, as they do in the EITC program.

Number of Children in Family	Subsidy Rate	Earnings Subsidy Threshold	Maximum Credit	Phase-Out Rate	Maximum Income for EITC Eligibility
No Children (recipient must be between the ages of 25 to 64)	7.65%	$4,900	$376	7.65%	$11,060 (single) $12,060 (married)
One child	34.0%	$7,350	$2,506	15.98%	$29,201 (single) $30,201 (married)
Two or more children	40.0%	$10,350	$4,140	21.06%	$33,178 (single) $34,178 (married)

Table 12.5   EITC Benefit Schedule, 2002

The $1000 difference in the maximum income for EITC eligibility for married couples is a new feature; it was introduced in 2002 as part of the Economic Growth and Tax Relief Act of 2001 as an effort to reduce the marriage tax that some EITC recipients face.[47] (We discuss the EITC marriage tax in the next chapter as part of our discussion of the income tax and its impact on women.) In 2002, the EITC will be worth up to $4140 for a family with two children, $2500 for a family with one child, and $376 for persons without children. Just like Social Security benefits, EITC benefits are increased annually to adjust for inflation.

The unique EITC benefit schedule is illustrated in Figure 12.8 for a family with two children. Note the three "ranges" of benefits: the *phase-in range* where the credit is increasing at a 40% rate up to earnings of $10,350; the *stationary range* of about $3000 where benefits are constant; and finally the *phase-out range* where benefits are reduced, in this case at a rate of 21.06%. The benefit schedules for families with no children or with one children have the same general shape, but with the subsidy and phase-out rates shown in Table 12.5.

---

[47]By 2008, the difference between the married and single rates will be $2500.

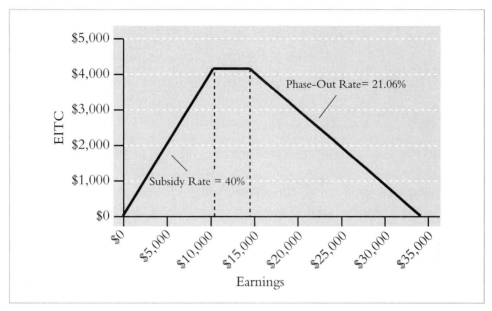

Figure 12.8   EITC Benefits by Income for Married Couple with Two or More Children, 2002

The EITC program has been around since 1975 when it was introduced as a small "work bonus" for very low-income working families, primarily to offset the payroll taxes they paid. It remained a small program during the 1980s; then, it was made a bit more generous in 1991 by the (first) Bush administration and substantially more generous during the Clinton administration. The increase in the EITC was a key part of President Clinton's initiative to "make work pay." Its current structure, including the subsidy and phase-out rates seen in Table 12.5, was put in place in 1996.

The program grew rapidly during the 1990s as a result of these increases in benefits. Between 1990 and 2000, the number of households receiving EITC benefits increased about 50% from 12 million to more than 18 million, while average benefits per recipient increased from $600 to $1650 (after adjusting for inflation) and total spending more than tripled.

The EITC and Poverty

As indicated in Table 12.5 and Figure 12.8, the EITC is not designed to be exclusively an assistance program for poor families. In 2002, the poverty threshold for a family with two children was just over $14,000 with one adult and about $18,000 with two adults (see Table 12.1—these are the poverty thresholds for three- and four-person households with two children). Because families with two children are eligible for the EITC up to an income of $34,178, many non-poor families will be eligible. The same kind of arithmetic applies to families with one child. The non-poor families will typically be on the phase-out portion of the EITC benefit schedule, where they receive reduced benefits.

At the same time, many poor families are not able to take advantage of the EITC because they have no earnings. Remember that this is an income assistance program for working families. A recent study found that just 36% of poor families were eligible to receive EITC benefits in 1996, a time when the EITC program was exactly the same as it is today.[48] Why are so many poor families ineligible for the credit? About one third of all poor households are demographically ineligible: They do not have a child, and they are either too young (less than age 25) or too old (above age 64). Most of these are elderly households. Another 30% are demographically eligible but have no earnings. These are mostly families headed by single women who were on welfare or were unable to work for other reasons.

Hoffman and Seidman estimated that about 40% of EITC recipients were in poor families and another 25% were near-poor, which meant that their incomes were less than 50% above the poverty threshold for a family of their size. Most of the EITC benefits go to these two groups: Hoffman and Seidman estimated that they received 75% of all EITC benefits.

We noted earlier that one of the main reasons for increasing the generosity of the EITC program was as part of President Clinton's goal of "making work pay." By this phrase, he meant that families that worked full-time, even at low wages, ought not to be poor. In its current form, the EITC almost accomplishes this. Consider, for example, the case of a full-time worker earning $6.00 an hour for 2000 hours a year. With earnings plus EITC, this family would have a total income of $14,506 if it has one child and $16,140 if it has two children. That's enough to push the one-child family over the poverty line whether the family has two persons (one adult and one child) or three persons (one adult and two children). The same family with two children

---

[48]Saul D. Hoffman and Laurence S. Seidman, "Helping Working Families: the Earned Income Tax Credit." Kalamazoo, Mich.: The W. E. Upjohn Institute for Employment Research, 2003.

would be non-poor if there were only one adult, but still $2000 below the poverty line for a four-person family (which is $18,392). Even so, its income is increased by more than one third by the EITC.

In spite of this, technically, the EITC has no effect at all on the official poverty rate because the poverty rate is based on a comparison of pretax, posttransfer income to family needs. Cash transfers like AFDC, TANF, or Social Security are counted as income, although in-kind benefits like food stamps and Medicaid are not. However, even though EITC benefits feel like a cash transfer, they are actually taxes—negative taxes, to be sure. Thus, EITC benefits aren't counted in the income that is used to compute the poverty rate; therefore, they don't have any impact on the official government poverty rate.

Fortunately, as we discussed earlier in this chapter, the Census Bureau also calculates a series of alternative, experimental poverty rates, based on different inclusions and exclusions of income components. One of them includes the EITC. It shows that the EITC reduced the poverty rate in 1999 by about 1.5 percentage points every year from 1996 (when the more generous EITC was fully implemented) through 1999. That means that about four million persons were lifted out of poverty as a result of the cash assistance they received from the EITC. Hoffman and Seidman found that the average poor family receiving EITC benefits received about $1500, while the near-poor families got $150 more. (The reason some poor families get less is that they don't reach the EITC maximum; the non-poor families have more earnings.) The EITC isn't enough to push deeply poor families over the poverty line, but it makes a difference for families who aren't too far below the line.

As an income-transfer policy for poor households, many economists would agree that the EITC is preferable to the minimum wage. For workers in the poorest households, the EITC operates exactly like an increase in the minimum wage, but without the potentially troubling increase in the wage rate that may reduce employment opportunities.[49] For such a worker with two children, the effective minimum wage in 2002 is not its statutory rate of $5.15, but rather $7.21, courtesy of the 40% wage subsidy provided by the EITC. For an otherwise identical low-wage worker with one child, the effective minimum wage is $6.90. Additionally, the EITC targets its benefits to

---

[49]Recall that a minimum wage acts as a price floor and creates an excess supply of labor and, hence, unemployment.

low- and moderate-income households with far more precision than the minimum wage does. Many beneficiaries of the minimum wage are teenagers in households with family income well above the poverty level.

The EITC, Women, and Work

Obviously, women benefit from the cash assistance of the EITC, just as men do. But the EITC has two interesting impacts on a woman's decision about labor force participation. The impacts arise from the subsidy of earnings on the phase-in portion of the EITC schedule and the reduction of benefits on the phase-out range.

Let's focus on women in families at the very low and very high end of the EITC schedule. Consider, first, a single woman who is not currently working and has no earned income. Suppose that she is currently on welfare, receiving benefits from TANF. She is certainly receiving a great deal of pressure to find work. For her, the EITC provides a strong positive incentive to seek work because the EITC subsidy is exactly like an increase in her wage rate. This is another example of the substitution effect and is similar to the one created by the implicit tax in the AFDC and TANF programs, except that the wage was lowered by the implicit tax in the AFDC and TANF programs. The increase in the EITC probably could not have come at a better time because it just preceded the end of AFDC and the introduction of TANF. The benefits of the EITC not only provided an incentive for women to transition from welfare to work, but it also provided them with a far better standard of living than they could have achieved on their own.

Quite a few studies have found that the EITC has increased the labor force activity of single mothers, who often face positive work incentives from the phase-in range. Interestingly, most of these studies have used a natural experiment framework, an idea we introduced in Chapter 2. It is a new research approach that is very popular in economics right now. A natural experiment is essentially identical to a traditional random assignment experiment (like a medical trial with control and treatment groups), except that a natural experiment is not designed and controlled by an experimenter, but rather is the result of some policy or some other action that affects one group but not some other otherwise similar group. In this case, the EITC is a natural experiment that changed work incentives for women with children, but had little or no impact on women without children, who were eligible either for no EITC benefits or very small ones. A comparison of work rates before and after the change in the EITC reveals the impact of the EITC.

A number of such studies have all come to the same conclusion: The EITC has had a real impact on the work decision of single mothers. Eissa and Liebman found that the 1986 EITC expansion (from a subsidy rate of just 10% to a subsidy rate of 14%) increased the labor force participation rate of single mothers by 2 to 4 percentage points.[50] Meyer and Rosenbaum found a 6 to 7 percentage point increase in employment rate of single mothers between 1990 and 1996 compared to single women without children. And they also found that the change in income taxes that single women paid (primarily the EITC) increased the LFPR of all single mothers by 1.5 to 2 percentage points between 1992 and 1996, which was approximately 35% of the total change.[51] The EITC is unique among income-transfer programs in having any evidence of a positive impact on work.

It appears that the EITC has also had an impact on women's work at the high end of the EITC range, especially among married women with family income that puts them on the phase-out range. The phase-out of EITC benefits is essential; otherwise, EITC benefits would be received by families with incomes that are clearly middle class and above. And the phase-out rate in the EITC is very low compared to AFDC and TANF. In those programs, benefits were reduced at a rate of 67%, which means that a woman lost $2.00 of her benefits for every $3.00 she earned. In the EITC, the phase-out rates are 7.65, 15.98, and 21.06% for women with no children, one child, and two children, respectively, far lower than in the other programs.

So, what's the problem? Let's consider the situation of a married woman with two children. Suppose that her husband is the primary worker and earns just enough to leave them on the EITC phase-out range.[52] She is considering whether or not to enter the job market, and she is computing what she will end up with if she works. For her, the phase-out rate operates just like a tax because, for every additional $100 she earns, the family's EITC is cut by $21.06, leaving her with take-home pay of just $78.94. That's exactly as if she faced a tax rate of 21.06%. In either case, her net earnings are $E \times (1 - t)$, where t is the tax rate or phase-out rate. In our numerical example, $E = \$100$ and $t = 0.2106$.

---

[50]Nada Eissa and Jeffrey Liebman, "Labor Supply Response to the Earned Income Tax Credit," *Quarterly Journal of Economics*, Vol. III, No. 2, pp. 605–637, 1996.

[51]Bruce D. Meyer and Dan T. Rosenbaum, "Making Single Mothers Work: Recent Changes in Policy for Single Mothers and their Effects," *National Tax Journal*, Vol. LII, No. 4, Part 2, pp. 1027–1062, 2000.

[52]The primary/secondary worker distinction is a bit old-fashioned, but it does capture a certain portion of married couples, especially, for example, couples with a preschool-aged child.

But the problem isn't just the EITC, but rather all the taxes that this woman faces. If she is married and has two children, then, starting at an income of about $19,000, the family also faces the federal income tax at a rate of 10% plus payroll taxes of 7.65%. (If she has one child or is not married, she would face the 10% rate at about $16,000.) Thus, the net tax rate for a married woman with two children and with income between $19,000 and about $30,000 is the sum of all these taxes: 21.06% + 10% + 7.65% = 38.73%. That is a pretty steep tax rate for someone with a relatively modest income. If she earned $10,000, the family would only be $6127 better off.

The problem that the EITC tax rate creates is actually a bit more complicated even than this. Not only does the EITC contribute to the high tax rate this woman faces, but it makes her a bit richer at the same time. Suppose her husband earned $20,000. Then if she didn't work, they would be eligible for EITC benefits of almost $3000. Precisely because the EITC makes the family a bit better off, there is less need for the additional income she could provide.

In effect, then, the EITC provides a strong labor supply disincentive for secondary workers in families on the phase-out range. On the one hand, the EITC reduces the benefits of working by reducing take-home pay. On the other hand, the EITC makes the family richer, and thus less in need of additional income. The first effect is a substitution effect, while the latter effect is an income effect. They both function here to reduce the incentive to work. This is the same way that the income and substitution effects work with respect to AFDC—both the income guarantee (income effect) and the implicit tax (substitution effect) worked to reduce work incentives.

There is evidence that these negative incentives have had an effect. Again, researchers have examined natural experiments, comparing the labor force participation of married women likely to face these negative incentives with the labor force participation of otherwise similar women less likely to face those incentives. For example, women with lower-income husbands, lower wage rates, or less education could be compared to women with higher-income husbands, higher wage rates, or more education. Ellwood[53] found that the 1993 EITC expansion and AFDC reform decreased the labor force participation of low-wage married mothers by 3 to 7 percentage points compared to higher-wage married mothers, Eissa and Hoynes found that the EITC decreased the labor force participation of less educated married mothers by 2 to

[53]David T. Ellwood, "The Impact of the Earned Income Tax Credit and Social Policy Reforms on Work, Marriage, and Living Arrangements," *National Tax Journal*, Vol. LIII, No. 4, Part 2, pp. 1063–1106, 2000.

4 percentage points. Interestingly, married women with incomes low enough that they faced the positive work incentives of the EITC phase-in range actually increased their labor force participation.[54] This finding reinforces the idea that these incentives really do matter for many families.

Summary

We began this chapter by defining poverty and exploring how it is measured in the United States. We then examined who was in poverty and concluded that poverty is a condition that largely affects women and children. Families headed by Black females are particularly likely to be impoverished—and over half the children in these families live in poverty. We established that changing demographics have played a large role in this feminization of poverty. We also found that this is not unique to the United States. For example, women are more likely to be in poverty in most other industrialized countries.

We then turned to a discussion of two government programs that are designed to alleviate poverty—TANF and the Earned Income Tax Credit. The TANF program imposes strict time limits on welfare receipt and gives states wide latitude to try to reduce out-of-wedlock childbearing. The EITC is a program that enjoys political support in large part because it is a tax credit for working. Policymakers are also pushing marriage as a way to alleviate poverty, and several states now have marriage initiatives.

However, how well former TANF recipients will fare when they enter the labor market is still unknown. The EITC will help supplement their earnings—in some cases by a fairly large amount. Yet, the general lack of human capital among this population makes it uncertain how well they will fare on their own.

Key Terms

absolute measure of poverty   438

AFDC-UP   462

Aid to Families with Dependent Children (AFDC)   455

---

[54]Nada Eissa and H. Hoynes, "The Earned Income Tax Credit and The Labor Supply of Married Couples," NBER working paper 6856, 2000. David T. Ellwood, "The Impact of the Earned Income Tax Credit and Social Policy Reforms on Work, Marriage, and Living Arrangements," *National Tax Journal,* Vol. LIII, No. 4, Part 2, pp. 1063–1106, 2000.

breakeven point   457

cash transfers   440

Economic Opportunity Act of 1964   439

family caps   462

feminization of poverty   445

food stamp program   455

implicit tax rate   456

income disregard   457

income effect   457

income guarantee   456

income maintenance program   456

iron triangle of welfare   464

means-tested program   456

Medicaid   455

poverty thresholds   440

relative income poverty measure   438

subsitution effect   458

Supplemental Security Income (SSI)   455

Temporary Assistance for Needy Families (TANF)   455

Women, Infants, and Children (WIC)   455

workfare   462

working poor   471

Appendix: AFDC and Labor Supply—An Indifference Curve and Budget Constraint Analysis

Labor economists have formalized the study of the effect of welfare on hours of work by making use of the standard labor/leisure model, which was presented in the appendix to Chapter 6. We can easily extend that model to discuss how welfare affects the work/leisure decision. What this discussion will illustrate is that the type of welfare programs in force in the United States create a powerful work disincentive.

Let's begin by reviewing what we know about welfare programs and their features. Although details vary greatly by state, welfare programs have four basic features:

1. The income guarantee or basic benefit (G) is the amount of assistance an individual or family would be paid if it had no earned income.

2. The benefit-reduction rate (t) refers to the rate at which a family's benefits are reduced as its earned income increases. For example, if t is 0.50, then benefits will be reduced by \$.50 for every \$1.00 earned. This means that if the market wage rate is \$5.00, the family's *net* wage rate will be just \$2.50 when the benefit-reduction provision is taken into account. The critical point is that the benefit-reduction rate reduces one's net gain from work. Economists often refer to the benefit-reduction rate as an *implicit tax rate* because t has the same impact on the net income of a person participating in a welfare program as regular income tax rates have on the earnings of individuals.

3. The earnings disregard (DR) is the amount of money an individual is allowed to earn before the benefit reduction kicks in.

4. The breakeven level of income (BE) is the level of earned income at which the actual welfare payment received by an individual or family becomes zero and the family is no longer eligible for welfare assistance. The basic benefit and the benefit-reduction rate permit the calculation of the breakeven income. As we shall see in a moment, the breakeven income depends on the sizes of the monthly guarantee, the earnings disregard, and the benefit-reduction rate.

A simple numerical illustration is helpful to relate these concepts to one another. The welfare benefits received by an individual can be determined by

$$\text{Benefits} = G - t(Y - DR)$$

Thus, if $G = \$6000$, $t = \frac{2}{3}$ (or 0.67), $Y = \$3000$, and $DR = 0$, then the actual welfare payment received will be $4000: \$4000 = \$6000 - 0.67 \times \$3000$. The breakeven income in this case (with no earnings disregard) is G/t, which can be verified by solving the benefit equation for the income (Y) at which benefits equal 0. In our numerical example, $\$G = \$6000$ and $t = 0.67$, so $G/t = \$9000$. We verify this by substituting the relevant numbers into the equation: $\$0 = \$6000 - 0.67 \times \$9000$. This means that a person is no longer eligible to receive any welfare benefits after she earns $9000 per year.

Before we examine the budget constraint, let's consider one more example where the earnings disregard is not zero but is equal to $600. In this case, the welfare payment will be $\$4400 = \$6000 - 0.67(\$3000 - \$600)$, rather than $4000. Thus, the income disregard allows families to keep their full benefits and some of their earned income. The breakeven income is now $[(G/t) + DR]$ or, in this example, $9600.

We can incorporate these ideas into the familiar labor/leisure model and see how a welfare program affects an individual's work incentives (see Figure A12.1). Recall that the labor/leisure model assumes that individuals maximize their utility and that utility is a function of income and leisure. Income is measured on the vertical axis, leisure is measured left to right on the horizontal axis, and market work is measured right to left. The line AB depicts the budget constraint confronting an individual in the absence of a welfare program. For simplicity's sake, let's assume that the wage rate is $5.00 per hour, which means that the slope of AB is -5. This is less than the federal minimum wage but it will make our calculations easier.

A welfare program, such as TANF, changes the shape of the budget constraint. Now the relevant budget constraint becomes $ACDB$ rather than the line AB. The distance from A to C represents the guarantee ($\$G$). In our example, this would be $6000. Thus, an individual who is on the TANF program and did not work at all would collect $6000 in benefits.

Line CD is the new budget constraint when the implicit tax or benefit-reduction rate becomes applicable (in this case we have assumed that the disregard is zero making it easier to illustrate our points). After the recipient begins to work, benefits are usually reduced for each additional dollar of income

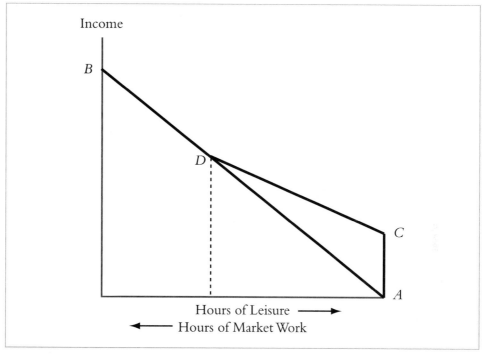

Figure A12.1   Budget Constraint

earned.[1] Thus, the slope of *CD* is flatter than that of *AB*, reflecting that some percentage of earnings, in our example 67%, is taxed away. In this case, because the wage is $5.00 per hour, the slope of *CD* is 0.67 × $5.00 or about $3.35. (What would the slope of the segment *CD* be if the benefits reduction rate were 100%? How could we modify the graph if recipients were allowed to keep $1000 in earnings before the implicit tax rate became active?) At point *D*, the breakeven point is reached; earnings are now high enough that the entire guarantee has been taxed away, and the individual is no longer eligible for the program. In this case, the breakeven point is earnings of $9000. Earning more than that means that the person is no longer eligible for welfare benefits. However, keep in mind that work may also involve childcare costs so that the actual wage taken home may be far less than $5.

---

[1] Keep in mind that under TANF, states can set the implicit tax rate and that there is considerable variation across states. We choose 67% as an example. What an actual woman faces might be higher or lower.

How does this affect an individual's decision about whether or not to work in the labor market? To answer that question we need to add indifference curves to our diagram. This is done in Figure A12.2. Imagine a woman who prior to enrollment in the welfare program is currently maximizing her utility at point E where indifference curve I_1 is just tangent to budget line AB. She is currently working some positive number of hours in the labor market. When she becomes eligible for the welfare program, we see that she now maximizes her utility at point C along the TANF budget constraint $ACDB$. In this example, she has reduced her hours of work to zero. Remember that hours of work are measured right to left in this diagram so she has reduced her hours of work because point C occurs to the right of point E.

This reduction in labor market hours is the product of two effects—the income effect and the substitution effect. We do not show these two effects, we just know that they move us from point E to point C. Usually these effects work to offset each other, but in the case of a welfare program that is not true.

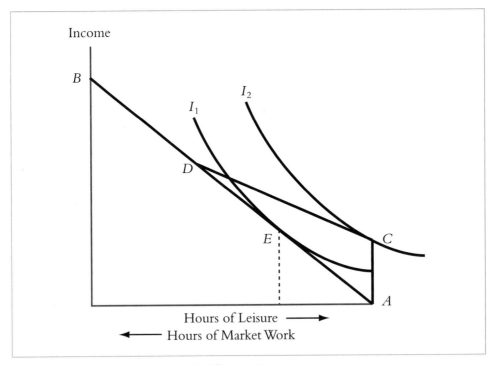

Figure A12.2   Budget Constraint and Indifference Curves

The monthly guarantee creates an income effect pulling her in the direction of working fewer hours (purchasing more leisure). The implicit tax rate creates a substitution effect: her net wage has gone down, and thus she now has the incentive to substitute toward leisure because the opportunity cost of leisure is lower now.

CHAPTER 13

Women, Taxes, and Social Security

Introduction

Many government policies affect the decisions that women make regarding family formation and time allocation. These decisions, in turn, have important consequences for a woman's economic well-being. In this chapter, we look at the features of two policies—the U.S. federal income tax and Social Security—to see how they affect decisions regarding marriage, fertility, and labor force participation.

We begin with a discussion of the effect of the income tax system on marriage and fertility decisions. Economists have long been interested in the effect of taxation on decisions concerning work and saving; only more recently have they considered the possible impact on these more personal decisions. We use economic theory to determine how and why there might be an effect and then review the empirical studies that have examined this. Following that, we look at how the tax system might effect a women's decision about work in the labor market, focusing especially on the effect of high marginal tax rates.

The federal income tax system is set up to collect revenue that the federal government then uses to finance a wide array of federal programs. However, because taxes reduce a woman's labor market earnings, they have the potential to influence any of her decisions that are based upon her earnings, including labor supply, marriage, and fertility decisions. In fact, as we will see, our tax system has consequences that are sometimes unintended (i.e., the system was not designed with these consequences in mind). We will also see that the tax system is sometimes manipulated in a direct attempt to change people's behavior. And finally, it will be clear that it is difficult to design an income tax that does not distort the behavior of those taxed in some way.

We then turn our attention to the U.S. Social Security system and its effect on both the labor market and marriage decisions that women make. Social Security was introduced in 1935 to provide financial support for the elderly. As we will see, it has lifted many elderly women (and men) out of poverty. However, there are concerns that Social Security is biased toward the "traditional family structure" (i.e., families where the husband works in the market and the wife works in the home). This has also been a criticism of the federal income tax system. Because our goal is to present the facts and the underlying economic analysis, we leave it to our readers to decide if changes in these programs are necessary and/or beneficial.

Income Taxes

The Marriage Tax: Theory and Evidence

Let's start by examining an issue that has been widely reported in the newspaper—the **marriage tax.** Generally speaking, a marriage penalty or marriage tax occurs when a married couple pays more income tax as a married couple than if they had each been single and filed separate tax returns. A **marriage subsidy** or marriage bonus occurs in the opposite situation—a married couple pays less income tax than if they were single. Before we discuss why this occurs, let's look at the U.S. federal income tax.

The U.S. income tax has been in place since 1913. Initially, the U.S. income tax was what we will call marriage neutral. This means that the individual was the unit of taxation and taxes assessed on, say, $60,000 of income were the same whether or not an individual was married. All of this changed in 1948 with the advent of income splitting. Income splitting essentially meant that the family, rather than the individual, was the unit of taxation. Couples were allowed to aggregate their income on a joint tax return; tax brackets for married couples were widened to twice those of single individuals. This was a major shift in the orientation of the federal income tax.

In Table 13.1, tax schedules similar to those that would have prevailed in 1948 are shown. This type of tax schedule prevailed from 1948 to 1969. Income brackets and marginal tax rates are shown. The **marginal tax rate** is the term that economists use to describe the percentage of income taxes paid on the last (marginal) dollar earned. You can see that the tax schedule in Table 13.1 is progressive. A **progressive tax** schedule is one where the marginal tax rate rises with income. Even today, the U.S. income tax schedule is progressive.

Single Tax Rate Schedule		Married Tax Rate Schedule	
Income	Marginal Tax Rate	Income	Marginal Tax Rate
$0–10,000	0%	$0–20,000	0%
$10,001–30,000	15%	$20,001–60,000	15%
$30,001–60,000	30%	$60,001–120,000	30%
$60,001 and up	40%	$120,001 and up	40%

Table 13.1 Tax Schedules Similar to Those That Prevailed from 1948 to 1969

Source: From Edward J. McCaffery, *Taxing Women*. Copyright © 1997. Reprinted with the permission of The University of Chicago Press.

Some examples will clarify how the tax system affects the tax burden of married and single persons. Consider Sam Single, who earns $20,000.[1] According to Table 13.1, he will pay $1500 in taxes filing as a single person (no tax on the first $10,000 he earns and 15% on the remaining $10,000). Suppose that Sam marries Samantha, who has no income. Now, the amount of tax he pays falls to zero, because the 0% tax bracket for married couples covers their (his) full $20,000 income. Sam and Samantha have received a $1500 marriage bonus. Now consider Stuart Single who earns $50,000. According to the schedule in Table 13.1, he would pay $9000 in taxes (no tax on the first $10,000 of income, 15% on the next $20,000, and 30% on the next $20,000). Let's compare Stuart to Bob and Mary Married, both of whom earn $25,000. They would pay no tax on the first $20,000 that they earn and 15% on the next $30,000, which means that they pay only $4500 in taxes—half of what Stuart pays. So they, too, have gotten a marriage bonus.

As should be clear by now, the 1948 tax change put married couples at an advantage compared to single couples; they typically received a marriage subsidy. Many couples paid lower income taxes, simply because they were married. In fact, one study found that under the type of schedule that prevailed in 1948, a single taxpayer's tax liability could be as much as 40% larger than that of a married couple with equal income.[2]

Obviously, single taxpayers were not happy with this state of affairs. The Tax Reform Act of 1969 revised the tax code to address this disparity. The

[1]These examples are adapted from Edward J. McCaffery, *Taxing Women*, Chicago: University of Chicago Press, 1997, pp. 16–17.
[2]Harvey Rosen, "Is it Time to Abandon Joint Filing?" *National Tax Journal*, Vol. 30, No. 4, pp. 423–428, 1977.

Single Rate Schedule		Married Rate Schedule	
Taxable Income	Marginal Tax Rate	Taxable Income	Marginal Tax Rate
Up to $6,000	10%	up to $12,000	10%
$6,001–27,950	15%	$12,001–46,700	15%
$27,951–67,700	27%	$46,701–112,850	27%
$67,701–141,250	30%	$112,851–171,950	30%
$141,251–307,050	35%	$171,951–307,050	35%
$307,051 and up	38.6%	$307,051 and up	38.6%

Table 13.2   Simplified Version of 2002 Income Tax Table

Source: http://taxes.yahoo.com/rates.html, 7/8/2003.

consequence was that now a single individual would only pay a maximum of 20% more than a married couple with the same combined income. With this change, the combined tax liability of two single people often increased upon marriage, creating a marriage penalty or marriage tax. After 1969, many married couples still received a marriage subsidy, but not nearly so many as did between 1948 and 1969.

Table 13.2 shows the 2002 tax schedule and can be used to help illustrate the current marriage penalty.[3] Note that Table 13.2 shows **taxable income**, whereas in Table 13.1 we showed income. Taxable income is income after deductions and exemptions; it is the income on which a family owes taxes.

Consider again, the tax consequences of marriage for some hypothetical individuals. First are Thom and Sue. Thom has taxable income of $80,000 annually, while Sue specializes in household production and does not work at all in the paid labor market. According to Table 13.2, their tax liability would be $15,396 (10% of the first $12,000 of income, 15% of the next $34,700 of income, and 27% of the remaining $33,300).

Now, consider Nancy and Jim, another married couple. They both work and each has taxable income of $40,000 per year. Their combined tax as a married

---

[3]Often people think that married people can avoid the marriage penalty simply by filing separately. This is not true. Married people can elect not to file a joint return, but they are still subject to the married person's tax schedule (i.e., they do not get to use the tax schedule used by single taxpayers). Thus, the total tax liability of a couple seldom changes and may even increase if they elect to file separately.

couple will also be $15,396 (the same as Sue and Thom), but if they were not married, each would be paying taxes of $5400 (10% of the first $12,000 and 15% on the remaining $28,000 of income). The fact that they are married means they pay $4,596 more in federal income taxes each year. In other words, after the 1969 changes, some married couples found that their tax liabilities increased simply because they were married.

In Table 13.3, we can see who actually pays a marriage tax and who receives a marriage subsidy. Here, AGI is an acronym for **Adjusted Gross Income**. Generally speaking, a taxpayer's AGI is the amount of income he/she has before itemizing or taking the standard deduction. AGI minus deductions and exemptions is taxable income.

The negative entries in the table reflect marriage subsidies—the amount that a couple's tax liability is reduced because they are married. The positive numbers reflect a marriage tax. A clear pattern emerges from examining this table. Married couples with two earners who earn roughly equal incomes are much more likely to pay a marriage penalty, while married couples with only one

AGI of One Spouse	AGI of Other Spouse							
	$0	$20,000	$40,000	$60,000	$80,000	$100,000	$150,000	$200,000
$0	$0	−$833	−$1,834	−$3,764	−$4,113	−$4,713	−$6,119	−$7,197
$20,000		$209	−$122	−$122	−$471	−$915	−$1,800	−$1,664
$40,000			$1,477	$1,477	$1,284	$1,284	$1,477	$1,866
$60,000				$1,633	$1,884	$1,884	$3,388	$3,777
$80,000					$2,135	$2,712	$4,950	$5,339
$100,000						$3,946	$6,261	$7,155
$150,000							$9,082	$10,644
$200,000								$12,075

Table 13.3   Marriage Penalties and Subsidies for Hypothetical Couples, 1998

All calculations in this table are based on the assumption that the couple has no dependents and that they use the relevant standard deduction.

Source: James Alm, Stacy Dickert-Conlin, and Leslie A. Whittington, "Policy Watch: The Marriage Penalty," *Journal of Economic Perspectives*, Vol. 13, No. 3, pp. 193–204, 1999. Copyright © 1999 by the American Economic Association. Reprinted with the permission of the author and publisher.

earner or with one high earner and one who earns relatively little are more likely to receive a marriage subsidy. For example, all the entries in the first row are negative, reflecting marriage subsidies, while the dollar figures along the diagonal where the two spouses have equal incomes are consistently positive and large. If we were to compare the marriage tax for a fixed total income, we would find that the largest marriage tax occurs when the two spouses have equal incomes. A particularly vivid example is the $1477 marriage tax when both spouses have $40,000 in AGI versus the $4113 marriage subsidy when one spouse earns $80,000 and the other has no earnings.

Furthermore, one study documents that Black couples are more likely to pay a marriage penalty than are White couples. The reason for this was made clear in Chapter 4 where we discussed some racial differences in marriage. Among Black couples, the wife is much more likely to work, and because Black men have relatively low earnings, Black couples are much more likely to be earning similar amounts of money. Among White couples, the wife is more likely to stay home, and thus they are more likely to get a subsidy.[4]

Over the years, the value of the marriage tax/subsidy has fluctuated as a result of tax law changes. For example, in 1981 a special deduction for secondary earners was introduced to reduce the marriage penalty, but this was repealed in the 1986 Tax Reform Act (TRA). The 1986 TRA also reduced marginal tax rates, causing the marriage penalty to fall. Since 1986, marginal tax rates have gradually crept up again. Alm and Whittington[5] and Feenberg and Rosen[6] provide a historical look at the value of the marriage penalty. For people who paid taxes for the year 1999, nearly half the couples filing a joint return paid a marriage penalty that averaged $1141, while 41% received a marriage subsidy that averaged $1274.[7] These averages mask a great deal of variation in marriage penalties and subsidies, as seen in Table 13.3.

We can use the tools developed in Chapter 3 to analyze the effect of the marriage tax or subsidy on the decision to marry. Recall that an individual will

---

[4]Dorothy Brown, "The Marriage Bonus/Penalty in Black and White," in *Taxing America,* NY: NY University Press, edited by K. Brown and M. L. Fellows, pp. 45–57.

[5]Alm and Whittington, "The Rise and Fall and Rise . . . of the Marriage Tax," *National Tax Journal,* Vol. 49, No. 4, pp. 571–89, 1996.

[6]Feenberg and Rosen, "Recent Developments in the Marriage Tax," *National Tax Journal,* Vol. 48, No. 1, pp. 91–100, 1995.

[7]Nicholas Bull, Janet Holtzblatt, James R. Nunns, and Robert Rebelien, "Assessing Marriage Penalties and Bonuses," *Proceedings of the National Tax Association,* 1999.

marry if the gains to marriage are expected to be greater than the gains to remaining single. Let's use the notation developed earlier to see how we can incorporate the marriage tax into our model of marriage. The output of single-person households is Z_m for men and Z_f for women. The corresponding output of a married-couple household is measured as Z_{mf}. The total marital output is divided between M and F, where S_m stands for the amount of Z_{mf} that goes to M (the husband) and S_f stands for the amount that goes to F (the wife) such that $S_m + S_f = Z_{mf}$, which means that all the marital output goes to either the husband or the wife. If Z_m is greater than S_m, the man is better off being married. Similarly, if Z_f is greater than S_f, the woman is better off being married. Thus, for a married couple, $Z_{mf} > Z_m + Z_f$.

It is straightforward to incorporate the marriage tax into this model.[8] Recall that the gains to marriage are greatest for those couples who specialize—one in labor market work and one in household work. Taxes reduce earnings, thus reducing the gains to marriage. However, as we just learned, the marriage tax is greatest for those couples who have similar earnings. These are couples who, all else equal, already have smaller gains to marriage when compared to those who specialize. If marriage increases their total taxes without changing their marginal tax rate, it can be shown that the gains from marriage will unambiguously decline. This is because the total marital output, Z_{mf}, will fall. We cannot be certain whether or not the couple will be better off not marrying because Z_{mf} will fall so much that $Z_{mf} < Z_m + Z_f$, but that is certainly a possibility.

Marriage can also change a couple's marginal tax rate. If that is the case, then the effect of the marriage tax on the decision to marry is a bit more complicated. The increase in taxes that comes with the increase in the marginal tax rate will, of course, cause Z_{mf} to fall. However, the increase in the marginal tax rate has another effect—it lowers the opportunity cost of household time, thus lowering the cost of household production. This will increase the gains to marriage. Thus, the gains from marriage depend both on the total taxes paid and on the marginal tax rates faced by both couples and singles.

The effect of a marriage subsidy on the probability of marriage is effectively the reverse of what we have already discussed. One thing to remember is that

---

[8]This discussion is adapted from James Alm and Leslie Whittington, "For Love or Money? The Impact of Income Taxes on Marriage," *Economica*, Vol. 66, pp. 297–316, 1999.

those couples who get a marriage subsidy tend to be those where one spouse specializes in market work and the other specializes in household work. Thus, these couples have relatively larger gains to marriage anyway, and the marriage subsidy reinforces this if their taxes go down when they marry and their marginal tax rate stays the same. However, if upon marriage their taxes go down and their marginal tax rate falls, the decline in the marginal tax rate increases the opportunity cost of household production and thus may decrease the gains to marriage if less specialization occurs.

Of course, other factors cause couples to wed, and we are certainly not arguing that taxes are the only reason someone would choose to marry. However, at the margin, these tax consequences can potentially make a difference. In an era where cohabitation is increasingly common and socially more acceptable, we might expect tax incentives to play a rather important role, particularly for those couples at the higher end of the income distribution where the marriage tax can be over $10,000. In other words, couples who face high marriage taxes might conclude that they are better off cohabiting rather than marrying. Because we cannot predict the exact effect of a marriage tax or subsidy on the probability of marriage, we review the available empirical evidence on this issue next.

In a series of research projects, economists Leslie Whittington and James Alm[9] used data from the Panel Study of Income Dynamics to examine how the probability of marriage, the timing of marriage, and the probability of divorce were affected by taxes.

Research in this area is complicated because it is necessary to know something about how these couples would have filed their income tax returns in order to determine what their tax liability would be if they were married versus if they were single. This involves making some assumptions about how people would file taxes, who would claim the children, how assets would be divided, and so on. Whittington and Alm employed two sets of assumptions. They first assumed that children were assigned to the higher-earning spouse who filed taxes as head of household and claimed the children as tax exemp-

---

[9]James Alm and Leslie Whittington, "Income Taxes and the Marriage Decision," *Applied Economics*, Vol. 27, pp. 25–31, 1995; "Does the Income Tax Affect Marital Decisions?" *National Tax Journal*, Vol. 48, No. 4, pp. 565–572, 1995; "The Rise and Fall and Rise of the Marriage Tax," *National Tax Journal*, Vol. 49, pp. 571–589, 1996; and "Till Death or Taxes Do Us Part," *Journal of Human Resources*, Vol. 32, pp. 388–412, 1997.

tions. Alternatively, they assumed that the wife had custody of the children, filed as the head of the household, and claimed the children as exemptions. In both cases, any nonearned income was split evenly between the couple.

They found that the marriage penalty does discourage marriage, as do the higher marginal tax rates encountered upon marriage. The effects are not large, but they are statistically significant—that is to say, they exist independently of other factors that influence marriage. They found little evidence that the marriage penalty is related to divorce. Thus, there is some evidence that taxes affect marital and divorce decisions, but the evidence is mixed. As we might expect, the effects are small. But the fact that we find an effect at all reveals that even the most personal decisions that people make can be affected by economic factors! In Box 13.1 we review a study that examines the tax consequences of legalizing same-sex marriages.

Taxes and Labor Supply: Theory and Evidence

So far, we've focused on the marriage effects of the income tax system. However, it can be argued that the more important issue to examine is the effect of taxes on labor supply. After all, for most people, the decision to work is clearly an economic decision, whereas the decision to marry involves a great many noneconomic factors. In a progressive tax system like the United States, the earnings of a working wife are often taxed at a higher level than the earnings of a primary earner. This is the inevitable result of a progressive tax system in which income is taxed at the family level.

Consider the case of a married couple with two children. Let's suppose that the husband earns $50,000 and the wife earns $25,000. Further, assume that her decision about whether or not to work follows his. He is the primary earner, and she is the secondary earner. This is not always the case, of course, but it probably characterizes some couples today. To keep the analysis simple, let's suppose that they take the standard deduction, rather than itemize their deductions. Table 13.4 reproduces the 2002 tax schedule for a married couple filing jointly that we first saw in Table 13.2.

In 2002, this family would have owed no taxes at all on the first $19,850 of its earnings, because of its four personal exemptions worth $3000 each and the standard deduction of $7,850 for married couples. To keep the arithmetic simpler, let's round the $19,850 up to $20,000. The family's total taxable income is therefore $75,000 - $20,000 = $55,000. Using the tax brackets and tax rates applicable in 2002, the family's first $12,000 of taxable income

Box 13.1 The Potential Tax Consequences of Legalizing Same-Sex Marriage

Marriage confers a host of economic benefits and responsibilities. There has been increasing pressure in many states and at the federal level for the government to allow same-sex couples to marry. The United States has yet to legalize same-sex marriages, although Canada recently did so. The *New York Times*, arguably the leading newspaper in the United States, now publishes same-sex commitment ceremony announcements in its *Sunday Styles* section alongside its heterosexual wedding announcements and the cover of the July 7, 2003 issue of *Newsweek* featured same-sex marriage.

Many controversies surround the issue of legalizing same-sex marriages, and economists are generally not equipped to comment on the moral and religious implications of such a change. However, one area where economists have something to say about same-sex marriage is the tax consequences of legalizing these marriages. Because many of these unions are likely to be between dual earners who are most likely to pay a marriage tax, there is the potential that legalizing same-sex marriages in the United States will increase tax revenues.

A recent paper by James Alm, Lee Badgett, and Leslie Whittington examined the income tax effects of allowing same-sex couples to marry. They used estimates of the number of same-sex relationships, the percentage who would marry if same-sex marriage became legal, and the average incomes of these couples to generate estimates of the tax revenue impact of allowing these couples to marry. Their figures suggest that legalizing these marriages would lead to an annual increase in government tax revenues between $0.3 billion to $1.3 billion. However, we should note that recent legislation that aims to mitigate the marriage penalty may reduce or eliminate these benefits. Although the tax consequences of legalizing same-sex marriages are not necessarily thought of by policymakers when debating whether or not same-sex marriages should be legalized, discussion surrounding the costs of such legalization often brings up issues such as increased costs of child support and of providing benefits such as medical and life insurance to same-sex couples.

Source: James Alm, M.V. Lee Badgett, and Leslie A. Whittington, "Wedding Bell Blues: The Income Tax Consequences of Legalizing Same Sex Marriages," *National Tax Journal,* Vol. LIII, No. 2, pp. 201–214, 2001.

Taxable Income Level	Tax Rate for Married Couple Filing Jointly
Up to $12,000	10%
$12,001–46,700	15%
$46,701–112,850	27%
$112,851–171,950	30%
$171,951–307,050	35%
$307,051 or more	38.6%

Table 13.4   2002 Tax Rates for Married Couple Filing Jointly

Source: http://taxes.yahoo.com/rates.html.

would be taxed at a 10% rate, the next $34,700 would be taxed at a 15% rate, and the remaining $8,300 would be taxed at a 27% rate. Thus this family's total taxes are $0.10 \times \$12,000 + 0.15 \times \$34,700 + 0.27 \times \$8300$ for a grand total of $8646. They pay 11.528% ($8646/$75,000) of their total family income in taxes.

Suppose, though, that we calculate the husband's and wife's taxes sequentially, treating her work decision as if it were secondary. Now, the allocation of taxes between the two is quite uneven. The husband is treated as the primary earner, so he takes the exemptions and standard deduction and faces the 10% and 15% tax rates on the remaining income. In this case, his taxable income (after exemptions and deductions) is $50,000 − $20,000 = $30,000. He would then pay taxes at the 10% rate on the first $12,000 and at the 15% rate on the remaining $18,000. His total tax bill would be $0.10 \times \$12,000 + 0.15 \times \$18,000$ for a total of $3900. He pays only 7.8% ($3900/$50,000) of his income in taxes.

His wife's situation is quite different. If she is the secondary earner, all her income is taxed. The first $16,700 of her $25,000 income is taxed at the 15% rate; $16,700 is the difference between $46,700 (the end of the 15% tax bracket) and her husband's taxable income of $30,000. The remaining $8300 of her earnings are taxed at the 27% rate. Thus, her total taxes are $0.15 \times \$16,700 + 0.27 \times \$8300$ for a grand total of $4746. Their total taxes are still $8646–$3900 from the husband's income and $4746 from hers. But she is paying 19.0% ($4746/$25,000) of her income in taxes—almost two and a half times the tax rate paid on her husband's income.

We could act as if the husband and the wife shared the deductions and exemptions and that each paid 11.528% of their taxable income in taxes. In that case, his taxes would be $0.11528 \times \$50,000 = \$5764$ and her taxes would be $0.11528 \times \$25,000 = \$2882$ for a total of, once again, $8646. But if she is truly the secondary earner in the family, and if the family truly wants to know how much better off they are financially if she is working, then this equal-allocation method doesn't yield the right answer. To see this, imagine that she stopped working. The equal-allocation method suggests that when the family's income falls by her $25,000, its taxes would fall by the $2882 allocated to her. But, in fact, the family would then pay taxes based only on the husband's income, so their taxes would be the $3900 we computed for him alone when he received the full value of the exemptions and deductions. Thus, family taxes would fall by $4746 from $8646 to $3900, and not by the $2882 we assigned her in the equal-allocation procedure.

As long as her labor force decision is made after his, she faces the higher taxes of the progressive tax system minus the protection of the personal exemptions and deductions. The higher effective tax rates are the result of a progressive tax system in which income is measured at the family level.

The higher effective tax rate could easily affect decisions about whether or not to work. The higher tax rate is equivalent to a lower net (after-tax, take-home) wage rate for the secondary earner. A change in a woman's wage has two conflicting effects on labor supply. If her net wage decreases due to the higher taxes, this decreases the opportunity cost of time spent in home production and thus increases the probability that she will not join the labor force or will work fewer hours. This is the substitution effect of a wage decrease. However, the decrease in the wage also means that the woman has less income and if leisure is a normal good, this will tend to increase the probability of paid work/labor force participation. Thus, we cannot predict a priori what will happen to the marginal value of time spent in market work (MVT_M) curve. It may shift up or down with a change in wages brought about by a change in the marginal tax rate.

If a woman is currently not working and if the tax rate falls, there is only a substitution effect. There is no income effect because she cannot reduce her hours in the labor market if there aren't any in the first place. Thus, reducing taxes is expected to provide a work incentive to women who are not currently participating in the labor market.

Labor economists have conducted numerous studies to try to identify whether or not our progressive income tax system reduces hours of work and/or the probability of labor force participation. What they would like to know is the **elasticity of labor supply,** which measures the responsiveness of labor supply to a change in the wage rate. Two dimensions of labor supply are important to women—first, whether or not a woman participates in the labor force and second, how many hours she works if she participates in the labor force. The labor supply elasticity captures both of these. This elasticity can either be positive or negative depending on whether or not the income effect is larger than the substitution effect. Estimating this elasticity is difficult because researchers need a change in the tax rate that does not arise from choices about labor supply. One good source of variation like this comes from a change in the tax law such that individuals face different marginal tax rates than they previously did.

A recent study by Nada Eissa[10] uses the tax rate changes created by the Tax Reform Act (TRA) of 1986 to examine the impact of taxes on labor supply. TRA 1986 essentially created a natural experiment: marginal tax rates changed for some taxpayers, but not for all. By observing the labor supply response of different groups of taxpayers who received different "treatments," she could determine how their labor supply responded to a change in tax rates. She focuses on the behavior of women in the top 1% of family income, because this group experienced the largest tax rate change. Prior to TRA 1986, women earning over $100,000 (in 1985 dollars) faced a marginal tax rate of 45%, but TRA 1986 reduced that to 33%. However, women earning $40,000 in 1985 dollars saw no change in their marginal tax rate of 28%. Thus, the treatment group is the group of women who faced large tax cuts and the control group is the group that had a small tax rate reduction.

Eissa found that the proportion of high income women who participated in the labor force increased from 46 to 55% and hours worked among those women in the treatment group who were already working increased by 13%. Her estimate of the labor supply elasticity with respect to the after-tax wage

---

[10]Nada Eissa, "Taxation and Labor Supply of Married Women: The Tax Reform Act of 1986 as a Natural Experiment," NBER working paper No. 5023, 1995.

is 0.8, which means that for every 10% increase in the after-tax wage, a woman works 8% hours more, on average. Eissa notes that about one half of the responsiveness is due to an increase in participation and the other half is due to an increase in hours of work. Feldstein and Feenberg provide other empirical evidence on this issue.[11]

Recently, a columnist writing for the *New York Times* commented on Eissa's study, noting that the impact of taxes on labor supply receives much less attention than the marriage tax. She postulated that this lack of interest is the result of the conflicting goals of policymakers. Democrats generally favor higher marginal tax rates for the rich but do not want to offend feminists by having high taxes for secondary earners who are mostly women. In contrast, conservatives like to see lower tax rates, but they do not want to admit that cutting taxes will lead more married women to get jobs.[12]

Tax Reform and the Marriage Tax

In this section, we examine the possible remedies for the marriage tax and the high marginal tax rates faced by secondary earners. We do not necessarily advocate any of these because our goal is to focus on positive economics—what is, not what should be. When thinking about how to remedy the marriage tax, it helps to first recall how it arises in the first place. Any tax system that is progressive and based on taxing the family—not the individual—will create a marriage penalty/subsidy.[13]

Economists and policymakers have long thought that the principle of **horizontal equity**—the idea of taxing equals equally—is important. A tax policy is considered horizontally inequitable if people with the same amounts of income are required to pay different amounts of tax. To understand horizontal equity, consider two couples, both earning $80,000. The first couple has one earner who earns the entire $80,000; the second couple is a dual earner couple where each spouse earns $40,000. Under current law, their marital tax liability is the same. This is what is meant by horizontal equity. However, as can be seen from Table 13.2, the dual earner couple pays more taxes than they

---

[11]See M. Feldstein and D. Feenberg, "The Taxation of Two Earner Families," in *Empirical Foundations of Household Taxation*, edited by James Poterba, Chicago: University of Chicago Press, 1996.

[12]Virginia Postrel, "The U.S. Tax System is Discouraging Married Women from Working," Economic Scene, *New York Times*, November 2, 2000.

[13]C. Eugene Steuerle, "Valuing Marital Commitment: The Radical Restructuring of Our Tax and Transfer System," *The Urban Institute*, Vol. 2, No. 9, pp. 35–45, Spring 1999, http://www.urban.org/tax/marital.htm.

would if they were single, while the single earner couple gets a marriage subsidy. Thus, our current tax policy is horizontally equitable and has a progressive rate structure. Combined, these two features of our tax system give rise to the marriage penalty/subsidy.

It is certainly possible to design a marriage neutral income tax. The reinstitution of the individual as the unit of taxation or the removal of the progressive rate structure would create an income tax in which tax liabilities did not change with marriage. Canada, Sweden, and the United Kingdom all tax the individual rather than the family. Tax provisions that mitigate the marriage tax by providing a second earner deduction (such as that in place in the U.S. between 1981 and 1986) are also possible remedies to the marriage tax. A proportional income tax would also eliminate the marriage penalty.

However, there are some arguments to be made in favor of a non-marriage-neutral tax system. For example, as noted in Chapter 3, married couples benefit from economies of scale; consequently, one could argue that marriage should be taxed because married couples have a higher standard of living than single persons with the same per-capita income. However, this implies that we also should tax cohabiting couples, adult children living with their parents, and other living arrangements that benefit from economies of scale. On the other hand, marriage may provide benefits to society. For example, one of these benefits may be that children in intact families are better off. (We discuss the effect of growing up in a single-parent family in Chapter 15.) If so, married couples with children should be subsidized via a marriage subsidy.[14]

More radical ideas for removing or mitigating the marriage tax also exist. For example, consider household production. There is no question that household production is valuable. Yet, it is neither taxed nor accounted for in GDP. This means that couples with one earner stand to gain in terms of household production. A single earner family with an $80,000 income and one spouse who produces $30,000 worth of meals and child care is better off than a two earner household with $80,000 worth of income but only $5000 worth of household production. Although it is difficult to imagine how we would value and tax household production, it is clear that families benefit from it.

---

[14]Nada Eissa and Hilary Williamson Hoynes, "Explaining the Fall and Rise in the Tax Cost of Marriage: The Effect of Tax Laws and Demographic Trends, 1984–1997," *National Tax Journal*, Vol. LII, No. 3, pp. 683–711, 2000.

Calendar Year	Standard Deduction for Joint Returns as Percentage of Standard Deduction for Single Returns	End Point of 15% Rate Bracket for Married Couple Filing Joint Return as Percentage of End Point of 15% Rate Bracket for Unmarried Individuals
2005	174%	180%
2006	184%	187%
2007	187%	193%
2008	190%	200%
2009 and later	200%	200%

Table 13.5   Phase-In of Increase of Standard Deduction for Married Couples Filing Joint Returns

Steuerle[15] argues that the United States needs to rethink the incentives present in both the tax and transfer systems to make them compatible. In many cases, the programs are separately administered, and their eligibility criteria are separately determined. In essence, he argues that a complete restructuring of the system is necessary.

The 2001 Tax Relief Act contains two provisions to mitigate the marriage tax. The first involves widening the standard deduction for married couples to twice that of singles. The standard deduction is the amount of income taxpayers can deduct from their earnings before they pay taxes. It is usually taken by low- and moderate-income families; higher-income families usually choose to itemize their deductions. The higher deduction will be phased in over a five-year period from 2005 to 2009, as illustrated in Table 13.5. The second change is an expansion of the 15% rate tax bracket for married couples filing joint returns. This increase will be phased in over a four-year period, as shown in Table 13.5.

How much these particular changes will reduce the marriage penalty is unknown because many married couples itemize their deductions separately,

[15]C. Eugene Steuerle, "Valuing Marital Commitment: The Radical Restructuring of Our Tax and Transfer System," *The Urban Institute*, Vol. 2, No. 9, pp. 35–45, Spring 1999, http://www.urban.org/tax/marital.htm.

rather than take the standard deduction. Two earner couples, who are the hardest hit by the marriage tax, are more likely to itemize and therefore less likely to benefit from this change. Furthermore, the expansion of the 15% bracket will help mostly middle- and higher-income taxpayers because some of them would have had a marginal tax rate of 28%, but will now be taxed at a 15% rate instead.

Taxes and Fertility: Theory and Evidence

As we discussed in Chapter 5, economic factors play an important role in fertility decisions. The standard economic model of fertility posits that parents receive utility from child services (CS) and adult goods (A). Child services are produced via a household production function whose inputs are market goods and adult time. The cost of a child depends upon the cost of both the parental time inputs (which are measured by the parent's wage rates) and the cost of goods and service inputs used in the production of child services. Any policy that alters the cost of child services (P_{CS}) should then increase the fertility rate.

Many European countries are now faced with below-replacement fertility. These countries have adopted extensive policies designed to encourage childbearing, including generous child allowances, paid maternity leave, and subsidized child care. Child allowances directly lower the cost of a child and thus, in theory, provide an incentive for parents to have more children. As a result, child allowances are a pronatalist policy—they are designed primarily to increase fertility by directly reducing the price of child services. They are also implemented to increase children's well-being directly by providing additional income. Virtually all developed countries offer child allowances, with the United States being a notable exception.[16]

The U.S. has no policies specifically designed to increase fertility. However, one feature of the U.S. federal income tax—the **personal exemption**—does serve as an implicit subsidy to births because it decreases the taxes that a family with children pays. The personal exemption has been part of the U.S. income tax system since 1913. The original intent of the exemption was not to

---

[16]For a comparison of child allowances and other social policies across countries, see "Social Security Programs Throughout the World—2002" available at www.sss.gov/policy/docs/progdesc/ssptw. Other information can be found in Sheila B. Kamerman, "Women, Children, and Poverty: Public Policies and Female-headed Families in Industrialized Countries," *Women in Poverty,* edited by Barbara C. Gelpi, Nancy C. M. Haretsock, Clare C. Novak, and Myra H. Strober, Chicago, Ill.: University of Chicago, 1986, p. 55.

subsidize births, but rather to provide tax relief for low-income families. This is an example of how a policy designed to do one thing can have unintended consequences. In 2003, each personal exemption reduced a taxpayer's taxable income by $3050.

A unique feature of the personal exemption is that it is an ongoing subsidy that families receive every year in which they claim a child as a dependent on their income tax form. For most families, this subsidy lasts at least 18 years. Compare this to the financial assistance provided by the welfare system through TANF, which is available only to single, poor women for no more than five years in their lifetime. In 1994, the U.S. Department of Agriculture estimated that the average out-of-pocket expenditures required to raise a child to age 18 amounted to $136,320. On the basis of this figure, Whittington, Alm, and Peters estimated that the personal exemption covered between 4 to 9% of the out-of-pocket costs of one child and up to 14% of the costs of subsequent children. Clearly, this is not an inconsequential subsidy.

The value of the personal exemption to a family depends on that family's marginal tax rate. The personal exemption is more valuable to families with higher marginal tax rates, since otherwise the exempted income would be taxed at a higher rate. For example, the $3050 exemption is worth only $305 to a family in the 10% tax bracket (.10 × $3050), but $1167.50 to someone in the 35% bracket (.35 × $3050).

The personal exemption could affect fertility by lowering the price of child services: The higher the value of the exemption, the bigger is the impact on the price. The value of the personal exemption has varied substantially over time. It is possible, therefore, that it might have affected the fertility rate.

Whittington, Alm, and Peters were among the first to examine this possibility for the U.S.[17] They used time series information for the United States over the time period 1913 to 1984 to examine if changes in the fertility rate were related to changes in the tax value of the personal exemption, taking into consideration changes in women's average wages and a variety of other control variables. Their analysis confirmed that the personal exemption did have a positive and statistically significant effect on fertility. The quantitative impact on fertility in births is modest, but not tiny—the elasticity is about .121,

---

[17]Whittington, Alm, and Peters, "Fertility and the Personal Exemption: Implicit Pronatalist Policy in the U.S.," *American Economic Review*, Vol. 80, No. 3, 1990.

which means that a 10% increase in the tax value of the personal exemption increases the birth rate by 1.21%. However, the authors noted that actual changes in the value of the personal exemption are often quite large so that, depending upon the actual increase in the personal exemption, births could increase considerably. For example, they estimated that the change in the personal exemption proposed in the 1986 Tax Reform Act had the potential to increase birth rates 11% percent.

This subsidy to fertility via the tax system has some distributional effects, since it is primarily geared to middle-income families. This occurs because low-income families often have incomes so low that they do not benefit from the personal exemption. Similarly, high-income families typically do not qualify for the personal exemption.

In contrast, most of the empirical work that has evaluated the effect of child allowances on fertility has found very little evidence that these programs increase fertility at all. For example, one study that examined twenty-two industrialized countries from 1970 to 1990 found that a 25% increase in child support benefits would increase fertility from 1.71 children per woman to 1.78 children per woman, a very modest change in fertility for a relatively generous increase in the child allowance.[18] Others have found that such programs only affect the timing of births, but not the total number of births a woman has.[19] However, there is evidence that a recent policy instituted in the Canadian province of Quebec between 1988 and 1997, called the allowance for newborn children, had a positive effect on fertility. This benefit paid up to C$8000 to families after the birth of a child.[20]

Love and Marriage at the Low End of the Income Distribution

In Chapter 12, we discussed a program called the Earned Income Tax Credit, or EITC for short, which has quietly become the largest cash assistance program for low- to moderate-income families. It currently provides more than

[18]Anne Helene Gautheir and Jan Hatzius, "Family Benefits and Fertility: An Econometric Analysis," *Population Studies*, Vol. 51, pp. 295–306, 1997.

[19]See James Walker, "The Effect of Public Policies on Recent Swedish Fertility Behavior," *Journal of Population Economics*, Vol. 8, pp. 223–251, 1995, and Anne Helene Gautheir and Jan Hatzius, "Family Benefits and Fertility: An Econometric Analysis," *Population Studies*, Vol. 51, pp. 295–306, 1997.

[20]Kevin Milligan. "Subsidizing the Stork: New Evidence on Tax Incentives and Fertility," NBER working paper no. 8845, 2002.

$30 billion of benefits to nearly 20 million households. Very briefly, the EITC program makes a refundable income tax credit available to low- to moderate-income families with at least one worker. After calculating its regular income taxes, a family with taxable income below a certain level ($12,060 for households with no children, $30,201 for families with one child, and $34,178 for families with two children in 2002) is eligible for the EITC, which it looks up in a tax table and deducts from its taxes. The credit is refundable, so if the credit exceeds the taxes a family owes, the family receives a check in the mail for the difference.

Table 13.6, repeated from Chapter 12, demonstrates how the EITC works. On earnings up to the earnings subsidy threshold, a family gets a credit shown in the second column—7.65, 34, or 40%, depending on the number of children. EITC benefits remain at that level for the next few thousand dollars of earnings and then are phased out at the rate shown in Table 13.6. In 2002, the EITC will be worth up to about $2500 for a family with one child and $4140 for a family with two children. Families without children and single persons between the ages of 25 and 64 are eligible for up to $376 if their income is below about $11,000.

In most respects, the EITC works well, and it probably enjoys more political support than any other cash transfer program for the poor. But in recent

	Subsidy Rate	Earnings Subsidy Threshold	Maximum Credit	Phase-Out Rate	Maximum Income for EITC Eligibility
No Children (recipient must be between the ages of 25 to 64)	7.65%	$4,900	$376	7.65%	$11,060 (single) $12,060 (married)
One child	34.0%	$7,350	$2,506	15.98%	$29,201 (single) $30,201 (married)
Two or more children	40.0%	$10,350	$4,140	21.06%	$33,178 (single) $34,178 (married)

Table 13.6   EITC Benefit Schedule, 2002

years, one problem has surfaced—a marriage penalty that has the potential to discourage marriage at the low end of the income distribution. Believe it or not, under just the right (or wrong) circumstances, the EITC marriage penalty can be greater than $6000. There can also be substantial bonuses, although, in practice, they are less common.

Table 13.7 presents some examples of EITC marriage penalties and bonuses, adapted from Hoffman and Seidman.[21] The three columns showing EITC benefits in Table 13.7 present the amounts the two individuals would receive if they were single and then if they were married and had the exact same incomes. The first row shows what happens in the case of a single childless full-time year-round minimum-wage earner ($5.15 per hour × 2000 hours) who marries a nonworker with two children. Given the EITC benefit structure, the worker is eligible for EITC benefits of just $59, while the nonworker receives nothing: The former lacks the children necessary for substantial benefits, while the latter lacks earnings.[22] As a married couple, however, they have both earnings and children, and they are eligible for benefits of $4120 (= 0.4 × $10,300). So, here there is a substantial EITC marriage bonus.

The next row shows what would happen if both individuals were working full-time at the minimum wage. Now, as single persons they are eligible for $59 and $4120, respectively, while as a married couple with two children, their $20,600 income places them on the phase-out range. As a married couple, by virtue of their higher income, they are eligible for only $2866, which yields a penalty of $1313.[23] In the next case, if both individuals had two children, they would each receive payments of $4120 if they were single, but only $2,866 together if married, for a total penalty of $5374—more than 25% of their earned income. With just the right incomes—equal to the point just before the phase-out begins—the EITC marriage penalty can exceed $6700.

Finally, EITC penalties can also exist among some moderately high income families, as long as one of the partners has an EITC-eligible income. The bottom row in Table 13.7 shows a case like this in which a worker with two children and earnings of $20,000 marries a worker with an income of $50,000. Individually, they receive an EITC of $2782 and $0, respectively. Together,

[21]See Saul D. Hoffman and Laurence S. Seidman, *Helping Working Families: The Earned Income Tax Credit*, Kalamazoo, MI: The W. E. Upjohn Institute for Employment Research, 2003.
[22]The EITC maximum credit of $376 for a single person without children is reduced at a rate of 7.65% for earnings above $6150. Thus, $59 = $376 − 0.0765 × ($10,300 − $6150).
[23]$2866 = $4140 − 0.2106 × ($20,600 − $14,550).

Situation	EITC Benefits		
	Person #1	Person #2	Married
Childless Minimum Wage Worker Marries Nonworker with Two Children[a]	$59	$0	$4120
Childless Minimum Wage Worker Marries Minimum Wage Worker with Two Children[a]	$59	$4120	$2866
Minimum Wage Worker with Two Children Marries Minimum Wage Worker with Two Children[a]	$4120	$4120	$2866
Worker with Two Children Earning $20,000 Marries Worker Earning $50,000	$2782	$0	$0

Table 13.7   Illustrative EITC Marriage Bonus or Penalty, 2002

[a]Minimum wage worker at $5.15 per hour $\times$ 2000 hours.

Adapted from Saul D. Hoffman and Lawrence S. Seidman, *Helping Working Families: The Earned Income Tax Credit,* Kalamazoo, MI: The W. E. Upjohn Institute for Employment Research, 2003. Reprinted with permission.

their combined income of $70,000 greatly exceeds the EITC earnings cut-off level. This kind of EITC marriage penalty is unavoidable and probably not a matter of concern.

In general, bonuses are more likely when both parties have distinct disqualifications as single persons, as in the first example. Penalties are more common and larger when both parties would be eligible for the EITC as single persons, that is, they both have earnings and children.

There have been some studies of the actual impact of EITC marriage penalties and bonuses. This is not an easy thing to study. Typically researchers take a married couple, pretend that they were divorced, and then compare their EITC as a married couple and as two single persons. The answers depend on some technical tax matters—who gets the kids, who gets the house, and so on—so there can never be a perfect answer.

Still, it seems clear that, in practice, the EITC penalizes marriage much more often than it rewards it. Ellwood[24] finds that 16% of married couples received a penalty and 11% received a bonus, with more than half of the bonuses attributable to postmarriage changes in fertility and labor supply that increased EITC benefits. Another study by Holtzblatt and Rebelein,[25] based on IRS data, found that the proportion of married couples receiving an EITC penalty ranges from 4 to 12%, and the proportion with a bonus ranges from 0.5 to 1.3%, depending on the underlying assumptions. Average penalties among married couples who are penalized certainly exceed $1000 and may be as high as $1500. Average bonuses for married couples with bonuses are also large, though probably somewhat smaller than average penalties. Total EITC marriage penalties almost certainly exceed $10 billion annually, with bonuses probably about half that amount.

In addition to the EITC, low-income individuals are often eligible for transfer payments that typically have marital disincentives. Transfer payments provide cash and in-kind benefits to families with low incomes (or no income) and are exempt from the income tax. In-kind transfers include food stamps, Medicaid, housing, and job training. Cash benefits include Temporary Assistance to Needy Families (TANF pays "welfare" payments), and Supplementary Security Income (SSI pays benefits to disabled persons). Each of these programs is "means tested" meaning that eligible individuals must fall below some income/wealth cutoff.

To fully understand the marriage incentives in the myriad of programs that low-income individuals are eligible for requires one to look at both the tax and transfer systems. Dickert-Conlin and Houser[26] used data from the 1990 Survey of Income and Program Participation to examine how a low-income couple with children would fare if they were unmarried and living apart. They document that the transfer system, with its categorical eligibility (generally single women with children are eligible for TANF) has large marital disincentives for poor women, but the income tax system often mitigates, but does not eliminate, these marriage penalties. For example, the median poor

---

[24]David T. Ellwood, "The Impact of the Earned Income Tax Credit and Social Policy Reforms on Work, Marriage, and Living Arrangements," *National Tax Journal*, Vol. LIII, No. 4, Part 2, pp. 1063–1106, 2000.
[25]Janet Holtzblatt and Robert Rebelein, "Measuring the Effect of the EITC on Marriage Penalties and Bonuses," *National Tax Journal*, Vol. LIII, No. 4, Part 2, pp. 1107–1134, 2000.
[26]Dickert-Conlin and Houser, "Taxes and Transfers: A New Look at the Marriage Penalty," *National Tax Journal*, Vol. 51, No. 2, pp. 175–217.

couple in their sample could increase its transfer payments by 26.5% of their income if they separated. Furthermore, for over 25% of the families in their sample, separation would increase their transfer payments by an amount greater than 38.8% of their income! However, the marriage subsidy for these families from the EITC partially offsets these transfer losses.

The story is a bit different for those families who have incomes between one and two times the poverty line. In this case, the marriage tax actually worsens the marriage disincentives present in the transfer system largely because of the fact that there are many dual earner couples in this income range. This research highlights the need to examine both the income tax and transfer systems together to determine marital incentives for low income families.

Social Security

As most Americans are aware, the Social Security system pays benefits to a wide array of individuals, including the elderly and the disabled. In this section we focus on retirement benefits with an emphasis on gender differences and behavioral incentives. We present just enough information about the system for you to understand our discussion, but we leave the complicated details of the system to the Social Security Administration staff.

History and Mechanics

The Social Security Act was signed into law in 1935. The purpose of the act was to ensure that the elderly and the disabled had financial security. Social Security is financed through what is known as a payroll tax. This means that, for all workers, 12.4% of their earnings are paid into the Social Security system each year up to some maximum level of earnings (in 2002 this maximum was $84,900). This 12.4% is split equally between the employee and the employer.[27] Thus, employees pay 6.2% of their earnings into Social Security each year, but only on earnings up to $84,900 per year (this maximum is adjusted annually).

To receive Social Security benefits based upon their own earnings record, individuals must have worked for forty quarters and must have reached a certain threshold level of pay. Unlike the income tax, Social Security is a **regressive tax.** With a regressive tax, the percentage of income paid in taxes

---

[27]The employee and employer each pay an additional 1.45% on all the employee's earnings for Medicare. Medicare is the health insurance system for elderly individuals in the United States.

falls as income rises. An example will make this clear. A family with an income of $15,000 per year pays 6.2% of its income to Social Security, while a family with $150,000 would have paid 6.2% of its income up to $84,900 to Social Security, but no Social Security tax on the remaining $65,100. Thus, the higher-income family pays only $5263.80 in Social Security tax ($84,900 × 0.062), which is only 3.51% of their income ($5236.80/$150,000). Therefore, the lower-income family pays a larger percentage of their income to Social Security than does the higher-income family—they pay 6.2% of their income because all their income is subject to the Social Security tax. This is in contrast to our progressive income tax system where lower-income families pay a smaller percentage of their income in taxes compared to higher-income families.

An individual is eligible to collect Social Security at age 62, though full benefits can only be collected by those aged 65 and above (since 2003, the age at which full benefits are payable has been gradually increasing and will reach age 66 in 2009 and age 67 in 2027). The monthly Social Security benefit is based upon how long an individual worked and what his/her earnings were. Those who start collecting at age 62 are subject to the Social Security *earnings test*. This currently applies to persons between the ages of 62 and 64 and reduces Social Security benefits by $1 for each $2 earned for earnings in excess of $11,280.[28]

Family Structure and Social Security Benefits

The Social Security system is structured such that individual workers pay the Social Security tax, but families receive the benefits from Social Security. This creates some inequalities where women are concerned. Let's examine some examples.[29]

When a single woman works and pays Social Security payroll taxes for ten years (ten years is generally equivalent to forty quarters), she is eligible to col-

---

[28]This amount is for 2002 and is adjusted annually to reflect the growth in the average wage in the U.S. economy. Furthermore, in the year the taxpayer reaches Normal Retirement Age (NRA) the exempt amount of income is higher.

[29]In these examples, we assume that women are the secondary earners (i.e., the spouse with the lower earnings). It is worth noting that this is increasingly not the case. Winkler (1998) finds that between 1979 and 1993 the proportion of dual earner couples increased from 39 to 61% of all married couples and that in 1996, in 23% of dual earning couples, the wife earned more than the husband. However, our analysis of the Social Security system is not changed, what holds for a widow will hold for a widower in terms of benefit receipt. Winkler, "Relative Earnings of Husbands and Wives in Dual-Earner Families," *Monthly Labor Review*, Vol. 121, No. 4, pp. 42–48, 1998.

lect benefits based on her own earnings. The amount of benefits that she collects depends on her earnings when she worked and how long she worked. When a married woman works and pays into Social Security (by paying the payroll tax described earlier) for at least ten years, she is also eligible to collect benefits based on her own earnings. However, she can also apply to receive 50% of her husband's benefit (i.e., a spouse's benefit), but she cannot collect both. Because men tend to work longer and earn more, a married woman who is currently considering retirement is likely to get a larger benefit on her husband's earnings record than on her own earnings record.[30] A woman who chooses to specialize in household production rather than market work will also be eligible for 50% of her husband's Social Security benefit upon retirement. A widow can receive 100% of her husband's Social Security benefit as long as she is age 65 or above. Finally, a divorced woman is entitled to collect benefits based on her ex-husband's Social Security if he is receiving Social Security or is deceased, as long as the marriage lasted at least ten years and the recipient is unmarried. However, a divorced woman can only collect 50% of the ex-spouse's benefits.[31]

To provide some idea of the magnitude of these benefits, Table 13.8 presents the average monthly Social Security benefit received by different groups of individuals in 1999. Note that a man collecting on his own earnings record receives the highest benefit per month. It is not surprising that a widow collecting on her husband's earnings record collects the second greatest amount. The lowest paid group are men who collect based on their wives' earnings record.

The family structure that benefits the most from the current structure of the Social Security system is the one where the husband worked in the formal labor market and the wife specialized in household production. In this case, only the husband is paying into Social Security through the payroll tax and upon his retirement the family receives 150% of his benefits—he gets his full benefits and his wife is eligible for 50% of his benefits. In the case of a two-earner family where the wife earns substantially less than the husband and/or only worked for a few years, they both pay the payroll tax and they receive 150% of his benefits, assuming her earnings were low enough that she is bet-

---

[30]The formula for Social Security benefits does provide a higher replacement rate for workers with low earnings. Thus, for the median female retiree, Social Security replaces 54 percent of average lifetime earnings compared to 41 percent for the median male.

[31]There are some other stipulations for collecting benefits from an ex-spouse, which we won't detail here.

Type of Beneficiary	Men	Women
Retired worker collecting on own earnings record	$951	$729
Spouse	$232	$419
Widows/widowers	$606	$811

Table 13.8   Average Monthly Benefit by Sex, December 1999

Source: Social Security Bulletin, Annual Statistical Supplement, 2001.

ter off collecting as his spouse. Thus, they get the same benefits they would have gotten had the wife not worked at all, even though they both paid into the system! In the case where the wife has worked continuously for relatively high earnings and the husband has as well, they will likely receive higher benefits than the family where the wife did not work at all. But, they will have both paid the payroll tax and being married does not increase their benefits at all (i.e., they each collect what they would collect if they were single). Thus, Social Security clearly provides an incentive for couples to follow a "traditional family structure." In fact, this was the most common family structure that existed when Social Security first began, which in part explains this payment system. From the standpoint of Social Security, it doesn't pay to be a secondary earner. In fact there is a clear bias against secondary earners.

In fact, as McCaffery notes,[32] wives who work in the formal labor market essentially subsidize those who do not. Table 13.9 presents the costs and benefits of the wife's work under the Social Security system under some simplifying assumptions. The first column shows the combination of husband and wife earnings, where each is classified as a low, average, or high earner. The second column shows the increase in Social Security taxes attributable to the wife's working, and the last column shows the increase in Social Security benefits resulting from the wife's working. Table 13.9 illustrates the striking differences between the increase in the Social Security tax paid and the benefits received. For a high-earning husband and an average-earning wife, her working increases their Social Security taxes by 43.3%, but only increases their benefits by 1%.

---

[32]Edward J. McCaffery, *Taxing Women*, Chicago: University of Chicago Press, 1997.

Family Earnings Pattern	Increase in Social Security Taxes Attributable to Wife's Working	Increase in Social Security Benefits Attributable to Wife's Working
Husband high/wife average	43.3%	1%
Husband average/wife low	46.6%	1.2%
Husband low/wife low	103.6%	15.2%

Table 13.9   Costs and Benefits of Wife's Work Under Social Security

Source: McCaffery, *Taxing Women*, Chicago: University of Chicago Press, Table 10, p. 97, 1997, adapted from C. Eugene Steuerle and Jon M. Bakija, "Retooling Social Security for the 21st Century: Right and Wrong Approaches to Reform," Washington, D.C.: Urban Institute Press, 1994. Reprinted with permission.

Women, Retirement, and Social Security

In this section, we examine what happens to a woman's economic situation upon retirement and how Social Security factors into women's economic well-being as they age. In general, women face greater economic challenges than men when they reach retirement age. First of all, they have a longer life expectancy—a woman who is 65 years old today can expect to live to 85, whereas a man of 65 can expect to live to 81 years. Second, as we have seen in several other places in this book, women tend to earn less than men. As you know, this occurs for several reasons. Women tend to work a shorter period on average over their life cycle. For example, of workers receiving Social Security benefits in 1998, women had worked a median twenty-nine years, while men worked a median thirty-eight years. Women also tend to work in lower paying occupations and are more likely to work part-time. Over one quarter (26%) of female workers worked part-time in 2000. Finally, women are less likely to have a pension, and if they do have a pension, it is usually smaller than a man's.[33]

Despite its bias toward traditional families, Social Security is an important component of income for older women. In 2000, women represented approximately 60% of all Social Security beneficiaries. For 26% of elderly un-

---

[33]Statistics from "Women and Retirement Security," October 1998. Prepared by the National Economic Council Interagency Working Group on Social Security, http://ftp.ssa.gov/history/reports/women.htm.

Age	All		Black		Hispanic		White	
	Women	Men	Women	Men	Women	Men	Women	Men
65 and over	12.2%	7.5%	25.8%	17.1%	19.6%	17.6%	10.8%	6.5%
75 and over	14.0%	8.2%	29.1%	22.4%	21.8%	13.1%	12.9%	6.7%

Table 13.10   Poverty Rates by Age, Race/Ethnicity and Gender

Source: Current Population Survey, 2000.

married women, Social Security was their *only* source of income. Furthermore, for unmarried women over age 65 (including widows), Social Security was 50% of their income. In contrast, Social Security benefits comprised only 37% of unmarried elderly men's retirement income and only 34% of elderly couples' income.[34]

Before Social Security was established, poverty rates for elderly individuals were quite high. It has been estimated that without Social Security the poverty rate of elderly women would be more than 50%.[35] Fortunately, this is no longer the case. Table 13.10 presents the poverty rates for older individuals by race and gender. Elderly women are much more likely to be poor than elderly men. Furthermore, elderly women who are divorced and widowed are also much more likely to be poor. Divorced elderly women face a 20.4% poverty rate, 15.9% of elderly widows are in poverty and 18.9% of elderly, never-married women are in poverty.[36] These rates compare to a rate of 4.3% for elderly married women. Among all women who are poor, 29% are over the age of 65. For all race/ethnic groups, elderly men have lower poverty rates than elderly women.

At the same time that the Social Security system helps so many women, the structure of benefit receipt helps explain why widowed and divorced women

---

[34]These figures are from www.ssa.gov, the Social Security web page.

[35]"Women and Social Security," www.ssa.gov/pressoffice/womenfact.htm, accessed 1/8/2002, and Timothy Smeeding, Carroll L. Estes, and Lou Glasse, "Social Security in the 21st Century. More than Deficits: Strengthening Security for Women," Washington, D.C.: *The Gerontological Society of America,* Issue Brief, 1999.

[36]Source: www.ssa.gov/pressoffice/womenfact.htm.

are so much more likely to be poor. As we discussed in Chapter 3, economies of scale are created by marriage. Consider the case of a widow who never worked outside the home or who found that it was more advantageous to collect the spouse's benefit rather than collect Social Security on her own earnings record. Before the death of her husband, the happy couple would have been enjoying Social Security benefits equal to 150% of the husband's Social Security benefit. Upon his death, she is now eligible to collect only 100% of his benefit—she loses her spouse's benefit. However, she still needs to heat the house, pay the mortgage/rent—expenses that do not decrease upon the death of her husband. She has lost some of the economies of scale she previously enjoyed.

Ferber[37] notes that the equivalence scale usually used in the United States assumes that a single person needs about 80% of a couple's income to maintain the same standard of living. But Social Security cuts her benefits to 67% of what she and her husband earned. In addition, when a woman is widowed, she often loses assets because they are bequeathed to someone else or used for medical or other expenses when her spouse dies. Furthermore, husbands with lower incomes do not live as long as husbands with higher incomes. Thus, many poor widows had low family incomes when they were married.

Holden and Zick[38] document that the average income of married women falls sharply when they are widowed, leaving them with a lower standard of living even though they only have to support themselves. Women who divorce before ten years of marriage lose out on any spousal Social Security benefits, and those who do collect are eligible for only 50% of their ex-spouse's income. Women who never marry tend to have lower benefits as a result of lower lifetime earnings.

Given that labor force participation rates for women have risen drastically over the past three decades, more and more women are expected to receive Social Security benefits based solely on their own earnings history, rather than on their husband's. In 1998, 37% of women received Social Security benefits on their own earnings. This is projected to rise to 60% by 2060.[39] Women are expected to continue to make earnings gains relative to men and

[37]Marianne A. Ferber, "Women's Employment and the Social Security System," *Social Security Bulletin*, Vol. 56, pp. 33–55, 1993.

[38]Holden and Zick, "An Assessment of the Wealth Holdings of Recent Widows," *Journal of Gerontology: Social Sciences*, Vol. 55B, No. 2, pp. 590–597, 2000.

[39]"Women and Retirement Security," October 1998. Prepared by the National Economic Council Interagency Working Group on Social Security. http://ftp.ssa.gov/history/reports/women.htm.

to live longer than men. However, trends in divorce rates indicate that an increasing proportion of women will be divorced when they reach retirement. If their marriages were short (less than ten years), they stand a high risk of being in poverty.[40]

Behavioral Effects of Social Security—Hours of Work and Remarriage

From an economist's point of view, it is of particular interest to examine the behavioral incentives of the Social Security system. We focus on two distinct behaviors that Social Security might affect and explore the latest economic research in these areas.

The first issue is remarriage. A woman who is widowed can collect Social Security benefits based on her deceased husband's earnings record. However, if she remarries before age 60, she must forfeit these benefits. A divorced woman whose marriage lasted ten or more years can also collect Social Security based on her ex-husband's earnings, but she too forfeits her benefits upon remarriage. As we saw in Chapter 3, economic variables are predicted to play a role in family structure decisions. Thus, we would expect that this provision in the Social Security regulations would deter some elderly women from remarrying.

To understand how this might work, recall the supply/demand model of marriage from Chapter 3. In this model, the gains from marriage were denoted as Z_{mf}, which is the output produced by a married couple household. For a couple to want to get married, the gains from marriage must be greater than $Z_m + Z_f$, where Z_m and Z_f are the output from single-person households. Losing one's Social Security benefits upon remarriage could well reduce Z_{mf} to the point where the individuals would be better off remaining single or possibly choosing to cohabit. In essence, the Social Security system seems to send the message that older people who cohabit need more money than those who choose to marry. See Box 13.2 for a look at some empirical evidence on how this provision affects remarriage among widows.

No discussion about Social Security would be complete without some discussion of the effects of the controversial **earnings test** on labor supply decisions. Although Social Security is not means tested (eligibility does not depend on need), some beneficiaries face an earnings test. The earnings test

---

[40]Barbara Butrica and Howard Iams, "Divorced Women at Retirement: Projections of Economic Well-Being in the Near Future," *Social Security Bulletin,* Vol. 63, No. 3, pp. 3–12, 2000.

Box 13.2   Widows Waiting to Wed

Brien, Dickert-Conlin, and Weaver examine the remarriage question for widows and focus on the role of the provision that widows must wait until age 60 to remarry or forfeit their widow's benefit from Social Security. Of course, remarriage does make them potentially eligible for spouse benefits on their new spouse's work record, but spouse's benefits are generally less than widow's benefits. They limit their study to widows noting that nearly all Social Security survivor benefits are paid to women; as we noted earlier, women tend to live longer than men. Their statistical analysis finds that the Social Security provision denying benefits to widows who remarry before age 60 does, in fact, discourage widows under the age of 60 from remarrying, but that marriage rates increase markedly after the age of 60. The policy is targeted so that those widows who remarry, and thus presumably do not need their Social Security survivor's benefits anymore, no longer receive them. The unintended consequence of this policy is that it may distort a widow's decision to remarry. She may delay remarriage until such a time that she does not lose her benefits or she may simply refuse to remarry. Furthermore, it is likely that not all elderly widows have full knowledge of how remarriage might affect their economic standing. For example, it may be well-known only among those wealthier recipients who may be better educated about financial matters.

There are proposals to ease this marriage penalty to reduce the distortion in marriage decisions that it creates. One proposal is to lower the age at which a widow may remarry without losing her benefits. The costs of doing this are estimated to be relatively low—there are only about 200,000 married women who are age 60 and older and who were widows and remarried in their 50s, while there are some 8.1 million persons (men and women) who collect survivors benefits from Social Security.

Source: Michael J. Brien, Stacey Dickert-Conlin and David A. Weaver, 2001, "Widows Waiting to Wed? Remarriage and Economic Incentives in Social Security Widow Benefits," ORES Working Paper Series, No. 89, 2000.

refers to the provision in the Social Security law that current recipients can earn a certain amount of money per year and still collect their full Social Security benefits. After earnings reach a certain threshold, additional earnings are "taxed" away. Earnings can be reduced such that the recipient actually earns so much she no longer qualifies to collect her Social Security benefit. In 2000, beneficiaries between the ages of 65 and 69 received $1 less in annual Social Security benefits for each $3 of earnings in excess of $17,000. For beneficiaries under age 65, the benefit reduction rate was 50% and the exempted amount was $10,080 in 2000. The limit applies only to earnings, so the retiree could have income each year from pensions, dividends, or interest without affecting the amount of the benefit.

On the one hand, it seems reasonable to ask current Social Security recipients who are working to pay into the system. On the other hand, Social Security is an entitlement—workers paid into the system and they want to collect their benefits. It is important to note that the earnings test does not significantly reduce the retiree's lifetime benefits—most of the benefits withheld under the earnings test are credited back to the retiree in later years. From an economic viewpoint, the critical issue with the earnings test is its work incentive.

Does the presence of the earnings test cause retirees subject to it to work less? After individuals reach retirement age and are eligible for Social Security benefits (and often pension benefits), they face strong incentives to retire. These benefits are a source of what economists call nonearned income and receipt of nonearned income tends to reduce the number of hours that individuals spend in the labor market. We see this trend clearly in the data—the labor force participation rates of both elderly men and women have fallen sharply over the past century, in part as a result of increases in retirement income. The earnings test presents a different sort of puzzle because an individual is subject to it only if she decides to work and collect Social Security benefits. It is widely viewed as a tax on working even though, as we noted, the benefits withheld are paid out later after the individual stops working. Prior to the year 2000, the earnings test was in effect for retirees between the ages of 62 and 70. In 2000, President Clinton signed into law the Senior Citizens Freedom to Work Act of 2000, which eliminated the earnings test for all individuals except those aged 62 to 64. Despite the fact that the bill was hailed as an important piece of legislation that would allow retired people back into the workforce, there is actually very little evidence that the earnings test affected the work decision of an elderly person.[41] Still, many see the full removal of the earnings test as important.

---

[41]Jonathan Gruber and Peter Orszag, "Does the Social Security Earnings Test Affect Labor Supply and Benefits Receipt?" NBER Working Paper 7923, 2001.

Suppose that Congress is considering removing the earnings test for the last remaining group of retirees who are subject to it, those aged 62 to 64. To understand the potential effect this will have on the hours of work of this group, it is helpful to divide workers aged 62 to 64 into three groups. The first group would be all those people who have fully retired and elected to collect their benefits early. Because they are no longer in the labor force, the removal of the earnings test will have no effect on their labor supply behavior. The second group would be those workers who are still working and work so many hours that their earnings are high enough that they are not eligible to receive any Social Security benefits—the earnings test has essentially taxed away their Social Security benefits. For this group, the removal of the earnings test will reduce their hours of work because they can continue to work and collect their full Social Security benefits. Thus, the removal of the earnings test creates an income effect inducing them to work fewer hours. The third group is the group whose behavior is the most difficult to predict. They work some number of hours in the labor market, but they also collect part of their Social Security Benefits, yet part of their labor market earnings are taxed away as a result of the earnings test.

Removal of the earnings test thus has two competing effects on their hours of work. On the one hand, removal of the earnings test increases the amount that each individual earns per hour of work. This makes working more attractive because it pays more. This is another example of a substitution effect. However, because each hour of work now pays more, the individual can cut back on hours of work and still have the same income. This is the income effect. Because the substitution effect and the income effect move in opposite directions, we cannot predict what will happen to hours of work for this group. However, the general consensus of the empirical research in this area seems to be that the removal of the earnings test will not cause a large increase in the hours worked by this group.[42]

An additional concern about removal of the earnings test for this younger group is that it may lead them to collect Social Security earlier than they otherwise might have, and collecting early means lower monthly benefits. This choice could put this group at a disadvantage during their later years. The Social Security Administration released a report in February 2000 which exam-

---

[42]Jonathan Gruber, and Peter Orszag, "Does the Social Security Earnings Test Affect Labor Supply and Benefits Receipt?" NBER Working Paper 7923, 2001.

ined what would happen to elderly poverty rates if the earnings test were repealed for those aged 62 to 64. The authors of the report assumed that removal of the earnings test for this group would cause more people to file for permanently reduced benefits and, as a result, receive a lower monthly benefit in the long run. They found that elderly poverty rates would rise by a significant amount if the retirement earnings test were deleted for those aged 62 to 64.

Women and Pensions

The majority of retirees do not rely on Social Security alone for their income. Many have access to income from a pension plan. In this section, we'll provide some background on pensions and discuss some of the issues in pension coverage for women.

Let's begin with some simple definitions. There are two types of pensions—**defined benefits plans** and **defined contribution plans.** A defined benefit plan guarantees benefits, which are determined from the number of years of service and the employee's salary. The company invests the money and guarantees the employee a certain amount at retirement. In a defined contribution plan, such as the popular 401(k) plan, benefits are determined based on contributions to the employee's account. The amount an individual has at retirement depends not only upon how much money is put into the fund but also on the return on the investment. In defined contribution plans, generally both the employee and the employer contribute to the account.

Defined contribution plans are the fastest growing type of retirement account in the United States. There are some benefits from this nationwide trend toward defined contribution plans that directly affect women. These plans have generally had shorter vesting periods. Vesting refers to the fact that pension benefits are not always owned by workers as soon as they accrue. When a worker first begins a job, his or her pension benefits may not be vested until the worker has been with the firm for several years.

Along with shorter vesting periods, defined contribution plans have greater portability. Pensions that are completely portable are plans that have values that do not change when the employer changes. This is generally the case with defined contribution plans, in part because they are often administered by a third party.

For example, the authors of this book both have defined contribution plans that are administered by TIAA-CREF. If we were to become employed at other colleges or universities, our funds would follow us. Defined contribution plans, because of their shorter vesting periods and greater portability, make it easier for a woman to accumulate money in the plan even though she may cycle in and out of the labor force. However, defined contribution plans, unlike Social Security and defined benefit plans, allow individuals to take lump sum withdrawals that may be used for other purposes (home buying, medical expenses, educational expenses), rather than retirement savings. Also, after a lump sum withdrawal is taken, certain spousal rights are lost. This could penalize those women who specialize in household production.

Current retirees are likely to be receiving pensions based on defined benefit plans. Current female retirees are less likely to receive a pension than men, and when they do receive a pension, it is likely to be smaller. This is because women are more likely to work part-time, cycle in and out of the labor force, and have lower earnings. Among women who are currently retired or approaching retirement age, they are about half as likely as men to have a pension and when they do have a pension its value is about 57% of that of a man's.[43] However, an examination of projected pension wealth for current workers is more optimistic. Richard W. Johnson demonstrates that the gender gap in pension coverage has been narrowing since the 1970s and that pension coverage for current full-time workers is about equal for men and women.[44] In fact, Shaw and Hill show that 60% of female full-time employees and 62% of male full-time employees are covered by a pension. The gender gap in pension coverage is still large for women who work part-time because they generally are not eligible for pension coverage from their employers. Extending pension coverage to part-time workers would go a long way toward closing the gender gap in pension coverage.[45]

Finally, a recent study determined that nearly all of the differences in retirement income that exist between men and women can be traced to three factors: Women earn less than men, have intermittent labor force participation, and work in lower-paying occupations than men. However, the authors of the

[43]Richard W. Johnson, "The Gender Gap in Pension Wealth: Is Women's Progress in the Labor Market Equalizing Retirement Benefits?" Urban Institute, The Retirement Project, 1999.
[44]Richard W. Johnson, "The Gender Gap in Pension Wealth: Is Women's Progress in the Labor Market Equalizing Retirement Benefits?" Urban Institute, The Retirement Project, 1999.
[45]Lois Shaw and Catherine Hill, "The Gender Gap in Pension Coverage: What Does the Future Hold?" Institute for Women's Policy Research, 2001.

study conclude that as women's work lives become more like men's in terms of earnings, occupation, and experience, the gap in retirement income between the sexes should shrink.[46]

Women and the Future of Social Security

The Social Security system clearly is an important source of income for elderly women, although there are some clear gender biases that many believe warrant attention. Changes in family structure and family life over the past few decades—including the rapid rise in the labor force participation of women, rising divorce rates, and the fact that two earner families are becoming the norm—have led to more discussion about possible ways to neutralize this gender bias. McCaffery suggests keeping the current benefit policy but exempting a wife who is a secondary earner from paying any Social Security tax until she would earn enough to qualify for Social Security benefits under her own earnings record.[47] The American Association of University Women has suggested including increasing the spouse's benefit available to divorced women from 50% to 75% and adding a family service credit that would provide a credit to the lower earner (or single parent) for the years that his/her children are under the age of six.[48] Ferber, among others, mentions *earnings sharing* as a possible reform. Earnings sharing involves assigning an equal share of family income to each spouse and dividing the earnings credits between them. This would also help women who divorce before ten years of marriage because they would then have earned some Social Security credits.[49]

What about the proposal to have some of Social Security taxes invested in individual retirement accounts? This proposal, which was very popular in the late 1990s, could leave women facing some of the same disadvantages that they already face. Because women earn less than men and on average work for fewer years than men, their contributions to these accounts would necessarily be smaller. The current Social Security system actually takes this into

---

[46]Phillip B. Levine, Olivia S. Mitchell, and John W. Phillips, "Worklife Determinants of Retirement Income Differentials Between Men and Women," NBER Working Paper no. 7243, 1999.

[47]Edward J. McCaffery, *Taxing Women*, Chicago: University of Chicago Press, 1997, pp. 16–17.

[48]More details on their proposals can be found on their web page www.aauw.org.

[49]Marianne A. Ferber, "Women's Employment and the Social Security System," *Social Security Bulletin*, Vol. 56, pp. 33–55, 1993.

account when calculating benefits, which are calculated in a progressive manner. In addition, these accounts may not offer the same protection that Social Security currently offers to women who are widowed or divorced or who collect benefits based on their spouse's working record rather than their own. Furthermore, there are concerns for all workers that tying even a portion of one's retirement income to the stock market may be too risky. In addition, these individual accounts often allow individuals to withdraw from them early, which could leave many elderly without much-needed retirement income.[50] There is also some concern that women will have lower earnings from individual retirement accounts because they are more risk-averse investors. Evidence on this issue from empirical studies is mixed.[51]

Summary

In this chapter, we have explored Social Security and the U.S. federal income tax system, to examine their impact on women's decisions about marriage, fertility, and labor force participation. We began with an in-depth examination of the marriage tax. We established that some couples pay a marriage penalty (i.e., their taxes rise upon marriage), whereas others earn a marriage premium (i.e., their taxes fall upon marriage). Like the Social Security system, the income tax system favors couples where a traditional family structure is in place. Couples where both husband and wife earn around the same amount of money are much more likely to pay a marriage penalty, while those where the wife doesn't work or earns substantially less than the husband earn a marriage premium. Empirical evidence suggests that the existence of the marriage penalty does discourage some couples from marrying. Congressional action, slated to begin in 2005, aims to mitigate this penalty, although it is unclear how much it will help.

We also examined how the structure of our tax system penalizes secondary earners. Empirical evidence clearly indicates that higher taxes do reduce the labor supply of secondary earners who are usually women. Finally, we saw

---

[50]"Women and Social Security," www.ssa.gov/pressoffice/womenfact.htm, accessed 1/8/2002, and Timothy Smeeding, Carroll L. Estes, and Lou Glasse, "Social Security in the 21st Century. More than Deficits: Strengthening Security for Women," Washington, D.C.: *The Gerontological Society of America,* Issue Brief, 1999.

[51]See Leslie Papke, "How Are Participants Investing Their Accounts in Participant Directed Individual Account Pension Plans?" *American Economic Review,* Vol. 88, No. 2, pp. 212–216, 1998.

that many industrialized countries have adopted explicit pronatalist policies to encourage women to have more children. Although the United States does not have any explicit pronatalist policies, the personal exemption in the United States federal income tax system does serve to increase births in the United States and thus acts as an implicit subsidy.

We found that Social Security, although an important source of income for elderly women, also has a bias toward traditional families (i.e., families where the wife specializes in household production and the husband works in the labor market). These families pay the lowest percentage of their income in Social Security taxes and yet receive the largest benefits. We discussed policy options that could help make the system more accurately reflect the reality of today's families. These included offering women credits for work done at home and eliminating the requirement that a marriage last at least ten years before the spouse could collect benefits. Given the dramatic changes in the labor force participation and earnings of women, it is not surprising that there is more discussion and even action being taken to reduce the bias against the traditional family in these systems.

Key Terms

adjusted gross income   495

defined benefits plans   525

defined contribution plans   525

earnings test   521

elasticity of labor supply   503

endogenous   503

exogenous   503

horizontal equity   504

marginal tax rates   492

marriage subsidy   492

marriage tax   492

personal exemption   507

progressive tax   492

regressive tax   514

taxable income   494

CHAPTER 14

Family Policy

Introduction

In this chapter, we examine the tension between work and family that many women face. We start by examining the employment status of women with children. We then reexamine the gender wage gap with a specific focus on the earnings differential between women with children and women without children. Last, we examine two policy areas that have the potential to mitigate some of this tension: parental leave and child care.

Labor Force Participation Rates of Women with Children

At the risk of being repetitive, it is important to underscore once again the striking changes that have taken place in American family life over the past five decades. As you are aware from our earlier chapters, the labor force participation rate of women has risen dramatically over the past thirty years. Table 14.1 documents the changes in labor force participation for married women by child status and by race.

Table 14.1 illustrates several patterns worth noting. First, currently, more women with infants (children under age 1) work in the labor market than do not work in the labor market. Second, Black women with children have always been more likely to participate in the labor market than not. As we saw earlier, this occurrence is partially due to the lower earnings of Black men.

	All Women (%)			White Women (%)			Black Women (%)		
	1975	1985	1999	1975	1985	1999	1975	1985	1999
No children under 18	44.4	54.2	61.6	43.6	53.3	60.7	54.1	63.8	71.6
Children under age 6	36.7	53.4	61.8	34.7	52.1	60.0	54.9	69.6	80.1
Children under age 1	30.8	49.4	59.2	29.2	48.6	57.6	50.0	63.7	83.5

Table 14.1   Labor Force Participation Rates for Wives, Spouse Present, by Age of Own Youngest Child

Source: *Statistical Abstract of the United States,* 2000, table no. 654.

Third, the rise in labor force participation rates has been greatest for those women with the youngest children. In fact, in 1999, there was near parity in the labor force participation rates of women with no children under age 18 and women with infants.

As might be expected, the labor force participation rates of single women with children are higher than those of married women with children. For these women, there is no second earner. In 1999, the labor force participation rate of single women with children under age 6 was 68.1%, an increase from its 1980 rate of 44.1%.

The increases in labor force participation for single versus married mothers occurred during different time periods. The largest increases in labor force participation rates for married mothers occurred during the 1970s and 1980s but then slowed again during the 1990s, whereas the participation rate for single women rose particularly quickly during the 1990s, especially after the enactment of the 1996 Welfare Reform Act.

As we saw in our study of the economic model of labor force participation, economists attribute some, if not most, of the rise in women's labor force participation to rising wages and rising labor market opportunities for women over this time period. Data from the Bureau of Labor Statistics show that between 1979 and 2000, women who held a bachelor's degree saw a 30% increase in their real earnings, those with a high school diploma or some college saw smaller but positive increases in real earnings, while women without a high school diploma saw a more than 10% decline in their real earnings. Men, however did not fare as well. For all but college-educated men, real earnings fell during this time period, and the increase in earnings for college men was only half that of college-educated women. Thus, there were also financial pressures on some women to enter the labor market. Certainly, changing attitudes from society about the role of women have also contributed to this rise. As more women surged into the labor force, it became the norm for a mother, even one with very young children, to work outside the home.

The rise in the number of married women who work means that there are many more **dual earner** families than before. In 2000, 64.2% of married-couple families with children under the age of 18 years were dual earners and 56.9% of married couples with children under the age of 6 years were dual earners.[1] In addition, rising divorce rates and increasing nonmarital births have also ensured that there are many more working single parents. In these families, 75.5% of the mothers worked outside the home in 2000. Furthermore, nearly half of all mothers of one-month-old infants are in the labor force.[2]

This rise in labor force participation rates of women raises several issues of interest to policymakers and families.[3] First, has the rise of women's labor force participation rates led to more parity in wages between the sexes? Despite the rapid increase in the labor force participation of women with children and the continued advancement of women into jobs that were traditionally male-oriented, there is still a persistent gender gap in earnings although it has narrowed recently. We addressed the recent evidence on this in Chapter 10 and documented that not only is there a gender gap in earnings, but there is also a family gap in earnings. We will look at possible explanations for the family gap in this chapter.

---

[1]For more information about dual earner couples, see Anne E. Winkler, "Earnings of Husbands and Wives in Dual-Earner Families," *Monthly Labor Review*, Vol. 12, No. 2, pp. 42–48, April 1998. Statistics for the year 2000 are from *Statistical Abstract of the United States*, 2001, table no. 673 and 674.

[2]J. Klerman and A. Leibowitz, "Job Continuity Among New Mothers," *Demography*, Vol. 36, No. 3, pp. 145–156, 1999.

[3]These changing patterns of labor supply, coupled with rising divorce rates, have led to tremendous changes in the American family, a topic we explore in more detail in Chapter 15.

Second, what kinds of policies, if any, should the government mandate to help parents balance the competing demands of work and family life? One issue that has received considerable attention is maternity/parental leave. We'll focus on the **Family and Medical Leave Act (FMLA)** to see what it does and how it can help women (and men) juggle family and career.

Lastly, children under age 6 whose parents both work generally are not in school and require care. Furthermore, many school-aged children also require after-school care when their parents work. Who provides that care and the quality and affordability of that care are questions that we examine closely in this chapter. We also examine the various subsidies to child care and analyze the role that the government plays in the child care market.

You may have noticed that policymakers and the media often focus on the tension that women face when trying to balance work and family. You may wonder where men fit into all of this. It turns out that the answer to this question depends critically on the man's marital status. There is mounting evidence that married men are spending more time with children and in household work, yet this increase has not fully matched the increased time that women spend in the labor force.[4] The same is not true for divorced men, who often do not see their children frequently; one estimate indicates over 50% of divorced fathers had not seen their children in the past twelve months.[5] On the other hand, despite increasing labor force participation rates, women's time with children, on average, has also remained fairly steady over this time period.[6] There is evidence that mothers have cut back on other activities such as housework, sleep, and leisure.[7] Of course, it bears remembering that even women who specialize in household production do not spend all their time with their children. They are often involved in volunteer activities, and their children may spend time in nursery school, in play groups, at lessons, or with

---

[4]See Francine D. Blau, "Trends in the Well-Being of American Women," *Journal of Economic Literature*, Vol. XXXVI, pp. 112–165, 1998.

[5]J. H. Pleck, "Balancing Work and Family," *Scientific American*, Vol. 10, pp. 38–43, 1999, presents an excellent discussion of the role of fathers in families today.

[6]For more details about this issue, see Suzanne M. Bianchi, "Maternal Employment and Time With Children: Dramatic Change or Surprising Continuity?" *Demography*, Vol. 37, No. 4, pp. 401–441, 2000, or Cordelia Reimers, "Parents' Work Time and the Family: Thirty Years of Change" in *Work and the Family*, edited by Jean Kimmel and Emily Hoffman, Kalamazoo, MI: W. E. UpJohn Institute for Employment Research, 2002.

[7]See "Families and the Labor Market, 1969–1999: Analyzing the 'Time Crunch,'" Council of Economic Advisors, May 1999, available on the web at http:clinton4.nara.gov/WH/EOP/CEA/html/whitepapers/html.

friends. However, it is still often said that women work a "second shift", as they are still primarily responsible for family life even when they work full-time in the paid labor force.

Barbara Bergmann, a noted feminist economist, argues that most of the policies aimed at helping women balance work and family life are misguided because these polices, although designed to help women balance work and family, may simply relegate women to low-paying menial jobs. This may perpetuate the stereotype that the home is the domain of women and that men's role is primarily that of breadwinner and thus reinforce traditional gender roles in the family.[8]

Others have argued for a **mommy track,** a term that stemmed from a 1989 *Harvard Business Review* article written by the late Felice Schwartz.[9] She argued that employers should put family-focused women on a slower career track and keep women who viewed their careers as coming first on the fast track. Though she didn't use the term "mommy track," it quickly became a popular buzzword. Critics of the mommy track argue that it perpetuates women's inequality relative to men by relegating them to lower-paying jobs, which carry less responsibility. Advocates of the mommy track approach note that it offers women a choice that may help them balance their responsibilities. In this chapter, we examine the costs and benefits of current and proposed policies such as parental leave and child care subsidies.

Explaining the Family Gap in Earnings

Before we get to our in-depth discussions of family leave and child care, let's revisit the family wage gap (i.e., the earnings penalty that mothers face). As we documented in Chapter 10, the gender gap in earnings is now more of a family gap than a human capital gap. When the earnings of women with and without children are compared, women with children earn substantially less than women without children, even after adjusting for differences in education and previous work experience. This difference in pay has become

[8]Barbara Bergmann, "Work-Family Policies and Equality Between Women and Men," in *Gender and Family Issues in the Workplace,* edited by F. Blau and R. Ehrenberg, New York: Russell Sage Foundation, 1997.
[9]Felice Schwartz, "Management Women and the Facts of Life," *Harvard Business Review,* January/February 1989.

known as the **family gap.** As we noted earlier, several economists have examined the family gap in pay and concluded that family responsibilities explain anywhere from 40 to 50% of the gender gap in pay observed between men and women. Most studies of the family gap find a child penalty of between 5 and 10%.

What we did not address in that chapter was *why* there is a family gap in earnings. One obvious explanation comes from human capital theory, which predicts that, all else being equal, women with intermittent labor force participation will have lower wages. However, even when researchers carefully control for previous work experience, education, and even a measure of the individuals' innate ability, generally measured with an IQ score, a sizeable family penalty still exists.[10] Thus it does not appear likely that the family gap arises solely because women take time out of the labor force to have children.

Becker[11] has suggested that mothers earn less because they exert less effort on the job. He reasoned that either they have less energy left over after working at home or they are choosing conserving their energy for household production. This has become known as Becker's **effort hypothesis.** Another explanation is that women may select mother-friendly jobs that allow them to combine career and family responsibilities more easily. These jobs may not require as much human capital and thus they pay less. A third explanation is that employers may discriminate against mothers in ways that lead them to earn lower wages. Finally, mothers may be different from nonmothers in important ways that are related to wages. Perhaps there is selection by lower productivity women into childbearing. This selection may take two forms. Women may be heterogeneous in some unobserved characteristic that is both positively correlated with the market wage and negatively correlated with the desire for children. Economists call this *unobserved heterogeneity.* For example, some women may be more career-oriented and want to focus on a career but not have children. The selection may also occur because women with lower wages are more likely to have children, all else being equal, because women's

---

[10]See, for example, Jane Waldfogel, "The Effect of Children on Women's Wages," *American Sociological Review*, Vol. 62, pp. 209–217, 1997; Sanders Korenman and David Neumark, "Marriage, Motherhood and Wages," *Journal of Human Resources*, Vol. 27, pp. 233–255, 1992; Joyce Jacobsen and Laurence Levin, "The Effects of Intermittent Labor Force Attachment on Women's Earnings," *Monthly Labor Review*, Vol. 118, pp. 14–19, 1995.

[11]Gary S. Becker, *A Treatise on the Family.* Cambridge, Mass.: Harvard University Press, 1991. See pages 54 to 79 for discussion of this "effort hypothesis."

labor market earnings represent the time cost of children. Thus, women with lower wages have lower opportunity costs of having children and therefore would be expected to have more children, all else being equal.

Many researchers have attempted to determine which of these theories explains the family pay gap for women. Korenman and Neumark[12] found some evidence suggesting that women who had lower wages in the labor market were those who were more likely to have children; in other words, the women who would be the most likely to incur a motherhood wage penalty are also the most likely to remain out of the labor force. In related research, they used data on sisters to control for **unobserved family-specific heterogeneity** (i.e., factors specific to families that cannot be measured) and found that mothers still had lower wages even after controlling for this unobserved heterogeneity.[13]

Several researchers have directly examined Becker's effort hypothesis with varying conclusions. Hersh and Stratton found that women who did more housework had lower wages, all else being equal, thus supporting Becker's effort hypothesis. However, McLennan[14] and Anderson et al.[15] find little support for the effort hypothesis.

Recent research by Budig and England[16] examines whether the motherhood penalty varies for single mothers versus married mothers. They find a child penalty of anywhere from 5 to 9%. The penalty is larger for White women and for married women. About half of the penalty is explained by human capital characteristics, mostly work experience. They also controlled for various characteristics of jobs to see if mothers took mother-friendly jobs. However, there was no evidence that controlling for occupation mitigated the motherhood wage penalty. They conclude that the motherhood penalty arises

[12]Sanders Korenman and David Neumark, "Marriage, Motherhood and Wages," *Journal of Human Resources*, Vol. 27, pp. 233–255, 1992.

[13]David Neumark and Sanders Korenman, "Sources of Bias in Women's Wage Equations: Results Using Sibling Data," *Journal of Human Resources*, Vol. 29, No. 2, pp. 379-405, 1994.

[14]Joni Hersch and Leslie Stratton, "Housework, Fixed Effects and Wages of Married Workers," *Journal of Human Resources*, Vol. 32, pp. 285–307, 1997, and Michele C. McLennan, "Does Household Labour Impact Market Wages? *Applied Economics*, Vol. 32, pp. 1541–1557, 2000.

[15]Deborah J. Anderson, Melissa Binder, and Kate Krause, "The Motherhood Wage Penalty Revisited: Experience, Heterogeneity, Work Effort and Work-Schedule Flexibility," *Industrial and Labor Relations Review*, Vol. 56, No. 2, pp. 273–294, 2003.

[16]Michelle Budig and Paula England, "The Wage Penalty for Motherhood," *American Sociological Review*, Vol. 66, pp. 204–225, 2001.

because of either discrimination or reduced effort by mothers in the labor force. However, they do not examine the issue of selection into employment.

Amuedo-Dorantes and Kimmel[17] attempt to sort out the source of the child penalty by focusing on college-educated women because they are generally more career-oriented than women with less education. Furthermore, they are more likely to delay their childbearing until their careers are established. Amuedo-Dorantes and Kimmel find that college-educated mothers do not experience a child penalty but rather have higher wages when compared to college-educated childless women. Furthermore, delaying their fertility increases the premium for having children that these women enjoy.

The motherhood pay gap is not unique to the United States. Joshi, Paci, and Waldfogel found a sizable family pay gap for women in Britain, particularly for women who took some time out of the labor force after the birth of a child.[18] Todd[19] studied the link between education and the motherhood wage gap for Canada, the United States, Germany, the Netherlands, and Sweden and found that in some countries, including the U.S., high education levels reduce the negative impact of children on women's wages. Harkness and Waldfogel[20] compared the family pay gap across Australia, Canada, the United Kingdom, the United States, Germany, Finland, and Sweden. They found considerable differences across these countries in the family pay gap. The largest motherhood penalty is faced by women in the United Kingdom, and the lowest is faced by women in Finland and Sweden.

In contrast to the child penalty faced by women, married men (many of whom have children) typically earn more than other men: See Chapter 4 for a full discussion of this. Most of the empirical evidence indicates that the male marriage premium is a result of the marriage productivity effect rather than a selection of more productive men into marriage. This is consistent with the observation that the premium is greater for men whose wives do not work

---

[17]Catalina Amuedo-Dorantes and Jean Kimmel, "The Motherhood Wage Gap for Women in the United States: The Importance of College and Fertility Delay," mimeo, 2003.

[18]Heather Joshi, Pierella Paci, and Jane Waldfogel, "The Wages of Motherhood: Better or Worse?" *Cambridge Journal of Economics,* Vol. 23, pp. 543–564, 1999.

[19]Erin L. Todd, "Educational Attainment and Family Gaps in Women's Wages: Evidence from Five Industrialized Countries," Luxembourg Income Study working paper no. 246, Jan. 2001.

[20]Susan Harkness and Jane Waldfogel, "The Family Gap in Pay: Evidence from Seven Industrialized Countries," Research in Labor Economics Worker Well-Being & Public Policy, 2003.

outside the home—they are the ones who enjoy larger productivity gains from marriage.

Perhaps surprisingly, men do not face a child penalty. Lundberg and Rose[21] have documented that the first child born is associated with a 9% increase, on average, in the father's wage rate. Interestingly the effect varies by whether or not the child is a son or a daughter. If the child is a son, men's wages rise significantly more than if the child is a daughter. The authors speculate that perhaps a son causes a father to value marriage and family more and thus work harder in the labor market to provide for the family.

The conflict between family and work has received considerable attention in the press. Several recent popular books have examined the motherhood/career nexus, including Sylvia Anne Hewlett and Ann Crittendon. We provide an overview in Box 14.1.

Family Leave Policies

Given the dramatic increase in the labor force participation rate of mothers documented earlier, there has been increased policy attention on how firms and/or government can or should accommodate the needs of women for both leave time after childbirth and stable job status. In the United States, the debate over maternity leave largely centered around the appropriate role of the government in family decisions and the costs to businesses of providing this leave. This public debate ultimately led to the adoption of the federal Family and Medical Leave Act in 1993, which was the first piece of legislation that President Clinton signed into law. It had been previously vetoed under (the first) President George Bush. The FMLA was signed on February 5, 1993, and became effective on August 5, 1993.

The provisions of the FMLA are straightforward. Employees are eligible for unpaid job-guaranteed leave of up to twelve weeks per year for family reasons or medical emergencies. During the leave time, any health insurance premiums paid by the employer for the employee must continue to be paid. To be

---

[21]See Shelly Lundberg and Elaina Rose, "The Effects of Sons and Daughters on Men's Labor Supply and Wages," University of Washington, mimeo, 1999; and Shelly Lundberg and Elaina Rose, "Parenthood and the Earnings of Married Men and Women," *Labour Economics*, Vol. 7, pp. 689–710, 2000.

Box 14.1   Family and Career: A Balancing Act for the Modern Woman

Increased women's labor force participation and more reliable contraception allow women to time their reproductive lives better than ever before. Does this fine-tuning of marriage, children, and career imply women can now combine high-powered careers with families? In *Creating a Life: Professional Women and the Quest for Children* Sylvia Anne Hewlett (PhD Economics, London University) questions whether or not women can "have it all," focusing especially on issues facing educated career women in today's labor force. She is particularly interested in how these women find a spouse and time their childbearing.

In a nationwide survey, Hewlett found that 90% of college-educated women believed that they could "easily" get pregnant in their 40s. She argues that this is a serious misconception, and the reality, according to fertility specialists, is that by the time a woman is 42 years old, there is only an 8% chance of getting pregnant at all with her own eggs. However, she argues that the general public believes that biotechnology has made such advances that issues with fertility have largely been overcome. This misconception has led many women to choose to delay their fertility until their careers are established and then they often find that they are not able to conceive. Hewlett reports that 42% of women aged 40 and above who work in corporate America are childless—but *not* by choice. She contends that women who wait to have children are finding that they cannot have them when they want to, because of their age.

Carol Hymowitz of the *Wall Street Journal* countered Hewlett's thesis by noting that most high-profile female executives are in fact wives and mothers. This list includes the CEO of Xerox, Ann Mulcahy; the president and CEO of eBay, Meg Whitman; and Betsey Holden, the co-CEO of Kraft Foods. She reports that a recent *Fortune Magazine* survey of America's most powerful women in business found that 71% were mothers with an average of 2.2 children each. No matter what your take on Hewlett's research, it is certain to give many career-minded women pause.

Ann Crittendon, an ex-*New York Times* economics reporter, recently wrote *The Price of Motherhood: Why the Most Important Job in the World Is Still the Least Valued*. She tackles a variety of issues related specifically to mothering.

She compares the social support system in place for American mothers versus what mothers in other industrialized countries receive and reports that American mothers come up far short. She argues that this forces them to make difficult choices, compared to women in other industrialized societies. For example, even if they want to be with their children, the economic reality is that many mothers have to put their young children and even infants in day care for long hours. In contrast, women in many other industrialized countries often enjoy a year's worth of paid leave after birth, along with generous child allowances and even subsidized child care.

Crittendon argues that, although women have made great strides in the labor market, their work as mothers is still unappreciated in an economic sense, even though mothers are fostering the growth of the next generation's, human capital. Raising productive citizens, the author argues, directly contributes to the overall health of the economy and wealth of the society. Today's children are tomorrow's taxpayers and will be supporting us in our old age.

In addition, Crittendon contends that there is a "tax" on mothers for this caring in the form of forgone earnings. She calculates that when a college-educated woman has one child, she loses about one million dollars in income.

Ann Crittendon, *The Price of Motherhood: Why the Most Important Job in the World Is Still the Least Valued,* New York: Henry Holt and Company, 2001. Sylvia Ann Hewlett, *Creating A Life: Professional Women and the Quest for Children,* Tall Miramax Books, 2002. Carol Hymowitz, "Women Plotting Mix of Work and Family Won't Find Perfect Plan," *Wall Street Journal,* June 11, 2002.

eligible for the FMLA, a particular employee must work at a worksite that has fifty or more employees, must have worked for at least twelve months with the employer, and must have worked for at least 1250 hours during the previous twelve months. The law does allow firms to exclude certain highly paid employees from being eligible for leave. Firms must notify workers that the leave is available and keep records regarding their compliance with the FMLA.

Under the FMLA, no firms are required by law to offer *paid* parental leave. Some firms did offer maternity leave (largely unpaid) prior to the passage of the FMLA, but in the United States, paid leave has generally been a benefit offered only to employees at large firms that pay relatively high wages or at government agencies.[22] As recently as 1995, only 2% of U.S. firms offered paid maternity leave. It is estimated that currently about half of private-sector employees are both covered and eligible for the FMLA, along with nearly all government employees. Thus, coverage under the FMLA is not universal.[23]

The FMLA provides for three distict types of leaves. The first is to care for a new son or daughter, whether the child is a biological child, an adopted child, or a foster child. The second is to allow the employee to care for his/her elderly parents; however, a wife cannot take leave to care for her husband's parents or vice versa. The third type of leave covers employees who have serious health conditions that make them unable to perform their jobs. An interesting provision of the FMLA is that the leave does not need to be taken in one large block. Employees needing part-time status or intermittent leave can arrange that with their employers. A study undertaken prior to the passage of the FMLA revealed that out of 118 countries surveyed, the United States was the only one without mandated, national maternity leave.[24]

Prior to the enactment of the FMLA, the only maternity or family leave provisions for employees were provided by state laws or through the **Pregnancy Discrimination Act of 1978,** an amendment to Title VII of the Civil Rights Act. This act requires employers to treat disabilities that result from pregnancy or childbirth as they would other disabilities. Therefore, under this act, if a firm provides disability leave or sick leave, it must allow employees to use this leave for pregnancy or childbirth-related disabilities. More generally, this act prohibits employers from discriminating against pregnant employees.

Very few women had job-protected leave prior to the passage of the FMLA. Prior to 1993, only twelve states had maternity leave legislation that was very similar in its provisions to that mandated by the FMLA. One positive aspect of the FMLA is that it is not maternity leave; it is parental leave. However, it is

[22]S. Kamerman and Alfred Kahn, "United States," in *Family Change and Family Policies in Great Britain, Canada, New Zealand and the United States,* edited by Sheila B. Kamerman and Alfred J. Kahn, Oxford: Clarendon Press, 1997, pp. 305–421.

[23]Jane Waldfogel, "Family and Medical Leave: Evidence from the 2000 Surveys," *Monthly Labor Review,* Vol. 123, No. 9, pp. 17–23, 2001.

[24]International Labor Organization (ILO), *Maternity Benefits in the 80's: An ILO Survey (1964–84),* Geneva: ILO, 1985.

still true that women are more likely to use the FMLA than men. Thus, in the discussion that follows, we assume (for ease of exposition) that it is the woman who takes the leave.

Considerable controversy and debate surrounded the passage of the FMLA. Opponents of the measure tended to focus on the cost of providing such leave. These costs include the continuation of health insurance coverage for individuals on leave, the administrative costs associated with compliance, and the cost of training replacement workers. There is no cost for replacement workers themselves because the FMLA mandates only unpaid leave. In other words, the firm incurs hiring and training costs but not salary costs because the person on leave is not paid. Additional arguments advanced by those opposed to the FMLA included the following. First, there was concern that the law would discourage small businesses from hiring younger workers who would be most likely to take the leave. Second, mandated parental leave might reduce the provision of other benefits that may be preferred by employees. Third, there was concern that women would have difficulty finding jobs, because of the increased costs of providing parental leave. Fourth, there was concern that women with access to leave might increase the number of children they have, thus making the leave more costly for employers. Finally, there was concern that job creation and entrepreneurial activity would be reduced by businesses as a result of increased costs imposed on them by having to offer parental leave. Based on these concerns, passage of the FMLA hinged critically on the exemptions for firms with 50 or fewer employees. Critics argued that the costs of the FMLA would be particularly devastating to small firms.[25]

Proponents of FMLA argued that the actual costs would be relatively low because the leave is unpaid and because the administrative costs involved in complying with the leave are low.[26] Others noted that the FMLA has the potential to reduce turnover costs, which can be quite substantial. **Turnover**

---

[25]S. Kamerman and Alfred Kahn, "United States," in *Family Change and Family Policies in Great Britain, Canada, New Zealand and the United States*, edited by Sheila B. Kamerman and Alfred Kahn, Oxford: Clarendon Press, 1997; and Eileen Trzcinski and Matia Finn-Stevenson, "A Response to Arguments Against Mandated Parental Leave: Findings from the Connecticut Survey of Parental Leave Policies," *Journal of Marriage and the Family*, Vol. 53, No. 2, pp. 445–460, 1991.

[26]A 1996 study found that the cost of compliance with the FMLA was low ("Commission on Leave," *A Workable Balance: Report to Congress on Family and Medical Leave Policies*, Washington, D.C.: U.S. Department of Labor, 1996).

costs are those costs that are incurred by a firm when an employee quits or is fired and needs to be replaced. With leave provided by the FMLA, a woman might be more likely to return to her firm after a birth thus reducing turnover. The FMLA may also bolster employee morale and increase employee loyalty and productivity. Furthermore, time off from work is arguably important for parent/child bonding and infant health. In addition, proponents argued that job-protected parental leave would help women to retain valuable human capital investments, reduce unemployment, and promote gender equality.

An Economic Analysis of Family Leave Policies

We have already discussed the controversy surrounding the passage of the FMLA. Here, we examine the economic arguments for and against parental leave. As we have already seen, there was considerable controversy surrounding the passage of the FMLA. In this section, we discuss the economic theory underlying the decision to provide benefits with a focus on parental leave.

Economic theory offers two important predictions about the provision of benefits such as parental leave and their labor market impact. First, the labor market will often provide the parental leave that employees desire. Second, workers will pay for these benefits themselves in the form of lower wages.

A simple analysis will illustrate these predictions. Begin by assuming that employees get utility or satisfaction from both wages and benefits, and that parental leave is the only benefit offered, and that it is of value to all employees at the firm (though not necessarily of the same value to all employees).[27] Employees are willing to trade off between wages and parental leave according to their preferences.[28] Employers can compensate their employees in two ways: Either they pay them cash, or they provide parental leave. From the employer's perspective, as long as the costs are the same, it doesn't matter

---

[27]Obviously this is not the case. Most firms offer a wide array of employment benefits; however, the outcome of our analysis is not changed by assuming that parental leave is the only benefit.

[28]What we are really doing is describing a set of indifference curves that exist where the employee is choosing between different combinations of wages and benefits. The indifference curves have their usual convex shape, indicating that there is a diminishing marginal rate of substitution—whatever is scarce is highly valued. Thus, when an employee has many benefits, each additional benefit is less valued.

how the employee is compensated, because the firm's profits will be the same.[29] Thus the firm is willing to provide many different combinations of wages and parental leave as long as its profits remain the same.

Employees who value parental leave will negotiate a benefits package that includes parental leave, presumably by accepting lower wages. Employees will then sort themselves into those jobs that offer the wage/leave combination that maximizes their utility.

An example illustrates how this would work.[30] Suppose that parental leave costs an employer $200 to provide, and suppose this leave is worth $300 to an employee. In this case, the employer could provide the leave and reduce the wages paid to the employee by between $200 and $300, which would leave both the employee and the employer better off. In the end, parental leave will be provided up to the point where an extra dollar spent by employers on parental leave is valued by the employee at one dollar.

As we noted, two major implications flow from this analysis. The first is that there is a tradeoff between wages and parental leave. This means that the employees who wish to have parental leave must *purchase it* by accepting lower wages. The second implication is that as long as labor markets are perfectly competitive, profit-maximizing firms will provide the leave that employees want, without government intervention. This second implication requires the assumptions of perfectly competitive labor and product markets. This means, in part, that workers must be well-informed and highly mobile (it must be easy—not very costly—for them to move from job to job). There also must be many firms and many workers, and employers and workers must have perfect information including information on wages and benefits.[31]

---

[29]In reality, some benefits may be less expensive to provide than cash. For example, large firms can often negotiate health insurance that is less costly than an extra dollar of salary because of economies of scale (i.e., they are buying so many policies). They may be able to purchase an insurance policy worth $300 for only $250, for example. Some benefits may also make employees more productive, also saving the firm money. We ignore this complication for now because incorporating this fact does not change the results of our analysis.

[30]This example is adapted from Lawrence H. Summers, "Some Simple Economics of Mandated Benefits," *American Economic Review*, Vol. 79, No. 2, pp. 177–183, 1989.

[31]For those readers who have had intermediate microeconomic theory, a more detailed exposition can be found in Bruce Kaufman and Julie Hotchkiss, "The Economics of Labor Markets and Labor Relations," 6th ed, Fort Worth, TX: The Dryden Press, 2003. See also, Lawrence H. Summers, "Some Simple Economics of Mandated Benefits," *American Economic Review*, Vol. 79, No. 2, pp. 177–183, May 1989.

This model and its corresponding implications that the market will provide leave without government intervention provided much of the support for those who argued against the passage of the FMLA. They argued that the market would provide such benefits if they are valued by employees and that, therefore, there would be no need to mandate that they be provided.

Those in favor of the FMLA acknowledge the predictions of the economic analysis, but stress that the assumption of perfect competition must be examined carefully. For example, the rapid rise in the labor force participation of mothers did not coincide with a rapid rise in the provision of family-friendly benefits, a result that may indicate that the market may be slow to respond to the needs of working families. If so, this would open the door for government intervention. Of course, the failure of the market to provide such leaves could be interpreted in an opposite manner: Given the rise in dual earner families and particularly the labor supply of mothers, if the labor market is competitive and we have not seen an increase in job-protected leaves provided by firms, perhaps it is not a benefit that employees highly desire.

Even if markets were perfectly competitive, there may be a reason for government to intervene and mandate that firms provide maternity leave. Recall from introductory economics that government intervention into perfectly competitive markets introduces inefficiency and distorts the signals sent to buyers and sellers. For example, in the case of rent control, keeping rents artificially below the market level means that there are more people who want to rent apartments than there are apartments available, creating a housing shortage.

An important exception to this argument is the case of **externalities.** An externality occurs when an activity undertaken either in production or consumption has a spillover onto a third party who is not directly involved in the transaction. In other words, an externality affects someone who is not immediately involved in the transaction. For example, a bakery, which emits a pleasant aroma, creates a **positive externality.** People who walk by the bakery are able to enjoy the smell, without compensating the baker. The key is that the aroma is not the product that the bakery produces, and the bakery cannot stop others from enjoying the aroma even if the people walking by the bakery are not buying any baked goods. When a positive externality exists, it can be shown that a competitive market will produce too little of the good with the positive externality.

An example of a **negative externality** is an oil refinery that emits toxic pollution into the air. Certainly nobody enjoys the smell of this production process, and it may be bad for our health and the environment. However, it is simply a by-product of this particular production process. In the case of a negative externality, it can be shown that a competitive market will produce too much of the product that generates the negative externality.

How does this analysis apply to parental leave? Parental leave, which enables a parent to be home with a very young child, might lead to that child receiving better health care. As we noted in the chapter on fertility (Chapter 5), children, particularly when they are young, are very time-intensive. As a result of this better care, the child might be healthier and incur fewer medical costs. To the extent that these medical care expenditures are not paid for entirely by the family (as is the case with most health insurance coverage in the United States), the parent may undervalue parental leave and thus not take enough of it. Providing parental leave would then create a positive externality. A related positive externality that might result from the provision of parental leave is that mothers on leave may be more likely to breast-feed their children. There is mounting medical evidence that breast-feeding leads to healthier and even perhaps smarter children.[32] Again, if parents do not bear the full cost of medical care, society benefits. The mother, by taking parental leave, can breast-feed the infant, and the infant will be healthier and use fewer of society's scarce resources. We discuss the empirical evidence to support this point later in the chapter.

Another argument is the problem of adverse selection under conditions of asymmetric information.[33] To understand this argument, start by noting the obvious: Employees and employers have different information about the likelihood that the employee may take a leave. The employee knows whether or not she will likely become pregnant, but the employer does not necessarily know her plans. This difference in information is called **asymmetric information** by economists, and it refers to the fact that one party (the employee)

[32] J. W. Anderson, B. M. Johnstone, and D. T. Remley, "Breast-feeding and Cognitive Development: A Meta-Analysis," *American Journal of Clinical Nutrition*, Vol. 70, No. 4, pp. 525–535, 1999.

[33] This discussion is adapted from Christopher Ruhm, "Parental Leave Policies in Europe and North America," in *Gender and Family Issues in the Workplace*, edited by Blau and Ehrenberg, New York: Russell Sage Foundation, 1997, and "The Economic Consequences of Parental Leave Mandates: Lessons from Europe," *Quarterly Journal of Economics*, Vol. 113, pp. 285–303, 1998, and Lawrence H. Summers, "Some Simple Economics of Mandated Benefits," *American Economic Review*, Vol. 79, No. 2, pp. 177–183, May 1989.

has more information about whether or not she will need parental leave than the other party (the employer).

This asymmetric information creates **adverse selection.** This refers to the fact that those individuals with a high probability of using parental leave will look for and try to obtain jobs at firms that provide leave. Adverse selection occurs if only some of the firms, but not all of them, offer parental leave. Suppose that only a few firms offered leave, and the others did not. Those individuals who do not plan to avail themselves of leave will search for higher-paying jobs at firms which do not offer leave. It is possible that some of those individuals will then have amounts of leave that are too small. They have amounts of leave that may be less than socially optimal—particularly if leave generates a positive externality as discussed previously.

Furthermore, firms offering leave will find themselves attracting workers with a higher probability of using leave than the average worker in the workforce. Thus, these firms would find their costs higher than anticipated, and this would put additional downward pressure on wages. In the end, these firms, because they will attract all the workers who want parental leave, may find it too costly to offer parental leave and cease to offer it. In this case, market forces will discourage the provision of leave. This problem can be avoided by mandating parental leave so that all firms must offer it. Adverse selection under asymmetric information would also likely result in the firms which offered leave having very few men as employees. As we noted earlier, most of the individuals who take parental leave are women. Men may not plan to use leave and thus they will look for jobs that do not offer leave, preferring instead the higher wages of those jobs. The Pregnancy Discrimination Act of 1978 made it illegal to offer a different benefits package to men versus women so firms could not avoid the loss of men by offering them a different benefits package.[34]

In the case of parental leave, the government chose to intervene by mandating that employers provide leave. However, the government could have intervened in other ways. For example, it could have taxed all employers and then used the revenue to fund a public parental leave program. Summers argues that mandated parental leave, is preferred to public provision of parental leave,

---

[34]See Chris Ruhm, "The Economic Consequences of Parental Leave Mandates: Lessons from Europe," *Quarterly Journal of Economics,* Vol. 113, pp. 285–303, 1998.

because the former is more efficient.[35] We point out other ways the government can intervene later in this chapter when we talk about the child care market.

To recap, mandating parental leave is justifiable on economic grounds in at least two cases—if such leave generates a positive externality argument or if there is adverse selection under asymmetric information. We next examine research done by economists and others to understand how the passage of the FMLA has affected the economic well-being of families.

The Economic Effects of the FMLA

Considerable research has been done on the effect of maternity and/or parental leave on women's wages. Some of this research was conducted using data collected before the passage of the FMLA. Other research was conducted to assess the probable effects of the FMLA on women's economic status by examining how women who had job-protected maternity prior to the passage of the FMLA fared compared to those who did not have such leave.

The passage of the FMLA guarantees the leave-taker the right to return to her prebirth employer in the same job or one at the same level. To the extent that a given woman is more likely to return to her prebirth employer now that she has job-protected leave, the FMLA has the potential to raise earnings, since earnings typically rise with general and firm-specific human capital. Thus, the FMLA can facilitate a woman's professional career advancement. However, the positive effect of leave-taking on women's pay may be offset if the leave is for an extended period of time and a woman's human capital depreciates. This is not likely to be an important consideration under the FMLA, because the job-protected leave is only for a maximum of twelve weeks. Furthermore, as we discussed earlier, women may have to accept lower wages in exchange for the leave.

Research shows that, before the FMLA, women who had a birth and returned to their prebirth employers, whether or not they had leave, earned higher wages than those women who did not return to the same employer.[36]

---

[35]Further development of this point is beyond the scope of this book. Interested readers should consult Lawrence H. Summers, "Some Simple Economics of Mandated Benefits," *American Economic Review,* Vol. 79, No. 2, pp. 177–183, May 1989, for a more in-depth discussion.

[36]Jane Waldfogel, "Understanding the Family Gap in Pay for Women with Children," *Journal of Economic Perspectives,* Vol. 12, No. 1, pp. 137–156, 1998.

There is also evidence that women who had employer-provided job-protected leave prior to the FMLA and returned to their jobs post-childbirth had higher wages than those who did not.[37] This supports the human capital argument that job retention allows women to continue building their firm-specific human capital. Thus, it is likely that the FMLA will increase the earnings of mothers, precisely because the FMLA will help women retain their jobs.[38]

However, as discussed earlier, there is also the concern that, to provide the leave, employers, particularly those in a competitive market environment, must lower the wages of women; thus, the wages of women overall might be lowered because of the FMLA. A recent study examined the wage effects of the FMLA and found no effect of the FMLA on wages—a finding which is most likely attributable to the fact that any negative wage effect is probably counteracted by the positive wage effect of having job-protected parental leave.[39] In contrast, data from nine European countries from the years 1969 to 1993 provides some evidence that women receive lower wages in exchange for maternity leave and that this is particularly likely when the leave is of a long duration.[40] Because the FMLA provides for unpaid leave of a relatively short duration, it is less likely to have a negative impact on women's wages.

In addition to its effects on earnings, the FMLA is also likely to affect the employment of mothers. There are two possible mechanisms through which a change in parental leave can affect employment. First, a woman who might have been expecting to drop out of the paid labor force upon giving birth might find that the leave is just long enough for her to decide to return to her job, rather than leave the labor market upon the birth of a child. Thus,

---

[37]Jane Waldfogel, "The Family Gap for Young Women in the United States and Britain: Can Maternity Leave Make a Difference?" *Journal of Labor Economics,* Vol. 16, No. 3, pp. 505–535, 1998.

[38]Budig and England, 2001, "The Wage Penalty for Motherhood," *American Sociological Review,* Vol. 66, pp. 204–225, 2001, and C. Amuedo-Dorantes and J. Kimmel, "The Motherhood Wage Gap in the U.S. The Importance of Fertility Delay," unpublished paper, 2003, also discuss various policies to mitigate the motherhood wage penalty. The latter suggests that making family leave more affordable (paid leave) and allowing for a gradual return to work might help mitigate the motherhood wage penalty. Budig and England argue that policies should be enacted because children are "public goods," an issue we take up in Chapter 15.

[39]Jane Waldfogel, "The Impact of the Family and Medical Leave Act," *Journal of Policy Analysis and Management,* Vol. 18, No. 2, pp. 281–302, 1999.

[40]Christopher J. Ruhm, "The Economic Consequences of Parental Leave Mandates: Lessons from Europe," *Quarterly Journal of Economics,* Vol. 113, No. 1, pp. 285–318, 1998.

parental leave might well increase women's commitment to the workforce and hence increase their employment.[41] This should also have a positive effect on wages, because it allows women to maintain a good "job match" and have longer job tenure. However, if the leave provision allows women to stay out of the labor force much longer than they might otherwise have done, their human capital might depreciate, and they might end up with lower wages. This is less likely to be a concern in the United States because the duration of leave provided by the FMLA is relatively short. It is also possible that firms might respond to the increased costs that mandated leave might entail by curtailing employment.

One might think that the FMLA would be expected to increase the duration of any leave a new parent might take; however, the effect of the FMLA on the duration of leaves taken is actually unclear. To understand this, consider the following analysis.[42] Let L_{FMLA} be the length of the leave allowed under the FMLA, which is up to 12 weeks. Let L_{leave} be the amount of leave that would have been taken in the absence of the FMLA. Prior to FMLA, L_{leave} would have been a function of the policies at the woman's place of employment, and the wages she would earn upon completion of the leave.

She might have an employer with a generous leave policy, including job protection, and she might work at a job where she earns high wages so that L_{leave} is greater than L_{FMLA}. She might also be at a job where any leave, if offered, is quite short and perhaps does not include job protection. If L_{FMLA} is greater than L_{leave}, then the FMLA either will have no effect on the amount of leave taken or will increase the length of the leave taken. The leave duration will be increased if the FMLA substantially reduces the costs to the worker of taking time off the job, which is particularly likely if L_{leave} does not include job protection.

---

[41]Both Jane Waldfogel, "Family Leave Policies and Women's Retention after Childbirth: Evidence from the United States, Britain, and Japan," *Journal of Population Economics,* Vol. 12, pp 523–545, 1999, and Christopher J. Ruhm, "The Economic Consequences of Parental Leave Mandates: Lessons from Europe," *Quarterly Journal of Economics,* Vol. 113, No. 1, pp. 285–318, 1998, find support for this. However, Katherin E. Ross, "Labor Pains: The Effect of the Family and Medical Leave Act on the Return to Paid Work after Childbirth," *Focus,* Vol. 20, No. 1, pp 34–36, 1999, found little evidence that the FMLA increased postnatal employment rates.

[42]This model is developed in J. Klerman and A. Leibowitz, "Labor Supply Effects of State Maternity Leave Legislation," in *Gender and Family Issues in the Workplace,* edited by F. Blau and R. Ehrenberg, New York: Russell Sage, 1997. Our exposition follows that of Christopher J. Ruhm, "The Economic Consequences of Parental Leave Mandates: Lessons from Europe." NBER working paper no. 5688, 1996.

However, if $L_{FMLA} < L_{leave}$, then the worker must decide between taking a shorter leave than she may want (i.e., reducing her leave by $L_{leave} - L_{FMLA}$) or quitting her job and perhaps returning to a new job post-childbirth. In some cases, it may become worthwhile for the employee to reduce the duration of the leave. We can state this in economic terms by noting that the employee will reduce the length of her leave if the gains from returning to the old employer exceed the costs of reducing the leave duration. The gains from returning to the old employer include job security and the higher wages that would likely result from staying with the old employer rather than taking a longer leave and then perhaps looking for a job with a new employer or perhaps returning to a lower-paying position with the old employer.

In addition to its potential effects on employment, wages, and the length, if any, of leave taken, parental leave lowers the cost of a birth whether it is paid or unpaid leave, and lowering the cost of childbirth creates a fertility incentive. In fact, as we noted in Chapter 13 when we discussed taxes and fertility, low fertility rates have prompted European countries to offer maternity and/or parental leave. To date, only two studies examine the impact of parental or maternity leave on births among U.S. women. The paucity of empirical work on this issue is surprising, given that fertility concerns are an often-cited reason for not offering such leave.

To think about how the provision of maternity leave would affect fertility, we can hypothesize that the temporal ordering of events among working women is as follows. A woman first selects her job with or without maternity leave as a benefit. Then, she either has a birth or not. Because of the waiting period often required of benefits packages, a woman may be in a position for a year or more before having access to maternity benefits. It therefore seems unlikely, though not impossible, that a woman would move to a position with maternity leave because she is already pregnant. Because maternity leave is not a benefit explicitly available with every job or firm, women may seek it out as a particular characteristic of their desired job, just as people may search for other job benefits such as flexible schedules, tuition remission, or health insurance. Determining the impact of maternity leave on fertility, therefore, requires explicit recognition of this potential sorting of women into jobs with maternity leave based on anticipated fertility. One recent study examined the effect of employer-provided maternity leave on the probability of a birth for U.S. women and found that employer-provided maternity leave can in fact have a rather large influence on births, particularly second and higher-order births. However, there was no evidence that women who expect to have children sort into jobs that offer maternity leave.[43]

As we discussed earlier, one of the main arguments for mandating parental leave is that it might have positive effects on child health, and that this generates a positive externality. It turns out that in the United States mothers who return to work after the birth of a child tend to do so much earlier than mothers in other countries.[44] The general guideline among doctors in the United States is that it generally takes a woman six weeks to recover from childbirth (perhaps longer for mothers who give birth via Caesarean section). There is concern that such short leaves could be detrimental to a child's health. For example, it takes some time to get breast-feeding established, and mothers who return to work in just six weeks may, in fact, decide not to breast-feed believing that it will conflict with their work or make the transition back to work difficult. Recent research confirms that the length of time a woman breast-feeds depends partly on the length of a leave from work she takes.[45] As we established earlier in this chapter, there is considerable evidence that breast-feeding confers many benefits to children.

A direct link between maternity leave and child health has been recently established by two studies. One study examined the relationship between parental leave and child health in sixteen European countries. The researchers established that more generous paid leave reduces the deaths of infants and young children and that such leave would perhaps be cost effective (i.e., the costs of providing the leave were lower than the benefits in terms of reduced infant mortality).[46] Another set of researchers found that family leave coverage is associated with more breast-feeding and that children whose mothers did not have family leave coverage scored lower on tests of their cognitive ability when they were ages 3 and 4. They further document that women who return to work within 6 weeks following the birth of a child are less likely to breast-feed, less likely to have taken their child to a well-baby visit,

---

[43]Susan L. Averett and Leslie A. Whittington, "Does Maternity Leave Induce Births?" *Southern Economic Journal,* Vol. 68, pp. 403–417, 2001.

[44]Lawrence Berger, Jennifer Hill, and Jane Waldfogel, "Family Leave Policies, Maternal Employment, and Child Well-Being," paper presented at the meeting of the Population Association of America, 2002.

[45]Brian Roe, Leslie A. Whittington, Sara Beck Fein, and Mario F. Teisl, "Is There Competition Between Breast-Feeding and Maternal Employment?" *Demography,* Vol. 36, No. 2, pp. 157–171, 1999.

[46]Christopher J. Ruhm, "Parental Leave and Child Health," *Journal of Health Economics,* Vol. 19, pp. 931–960, 2000.

and less likely to have had their child immunized. Thus, there is some evidence that parental leave, by providing time for parents to invest in the health of their young children, has the potential to increase child health.[47]

Family Leave Policy: The United States versus Europe

As noted earlier, even after the passage of the FMLA, the United States lags far behind other countries with respect to the provision of family leave. In particular, leave time provided in the United States is unpaid and is of a relatively short duration. Currently all European Union countries provide some income support during maternity/parental leave. Table 14.2 presents the length of maternity and parental leave coverage for several countries, including the United States. Note that the United States has one of the shortest parental and maternity leave provisions. It is also the only country listed in Table 14.2 that does not offer pay for at least some part of the leave.

Government-legislated maternity leave benefits have been a part of the European labor force experience for decades. Ruhm traces the provision of maternity leave in Germany back to 1891.[48] Most of the early leave provisions in European countries were justified on the basis of their benefits to the health of both the mother and the child and were therefore somewhat protective in nature. Following World War II, a pronatalist rationale for such policies emerged across Europe and other countries. Until the 1960s, maternity leave in most European countries was mostly a prohibition against mothers of young children working. By the late 1960s, many countries shifted their focus and began to see maternity leave as job-protected time off from work to care for a new child.

Currently, over 100 countries provide maternity/paternity leave, and such leave is often compensated. Payment is usually structured around providing a particular percentage of the woman's prior wage for a set number of weeks, including time before the expected birth as well as time after the birth. In only a few countries are maternity benefits also available to those who have not been in paid work prior to the birth and payment is via flat-rate benefits. Birth subsidies (i.e., payments to families simply for having a child) are also

---

[47]Lawrence Berger, Jennifer Hill, and Jane Waldfogel, "Family Leave Policies, Maternal Employment, and Child Well-Being," paper presented at the meeting of the Population Association of America, 2002.

[48]Christopher J. Ruhm, "The Economic Consequences of Parental Leave Mandates: Lessons from Europe, "*Quarterly Journal of Economics,* Vol. 113, No. 1, pp. 285–318, 1998.

Country	Maternity Leave	Parental Leave
Denmark	18	10–52
Finland	17.5	26–156
Norway	Falls under parental leave*	52
Sweden	Falls under parental leave*	62
Austria	16	112
Belgium	15	130
France	16	0–156
W. Germany	14	156
Switzerland	8–12	None
Japan	14	52
Australia	52	52
Canada	17	10
New Zealand	Falls under parental leave*	52
United Kingdom	14–40	None
United States	Falls under parental leave*	12

Table 14.2   Length of Maternity Leave and Paternity Leave in Weeks for Selected Industrialized Countries, 1994

*Indicates that the country has no separate maternity leave provision; maternity leave falls under parental or family leave. All the countries in the table except the United States provide for some paid leave.

Source: Adapted from Table 2 of Jane Waldfogel, "Understanding the Family Gap in Pay for Women with Children," *Journal of Economic Perspectives,* Vol. 12, No. 1, pp. 137–156, 1998. Copyright © 1999 by the American Economic Association. Reprinted with the permission of the author and publisher.

quite common. For example, Norway is a particularly generous country with respect to parental leave. It provides parental/maternity leave of forty-two weeks at 100% pay or fifty-two weeks at 80% pay. This paid leave can also be extended over a longer time in conjunction with part-time work. Both parents can use the leave, and a nontransferable father's component of four weeks has been introduced to encourage men to take leave.

In most Western European countries, paid maternity leave of up to eighteen weeks is common. These maternity leave benefits are sometimes supplemented by separate paternity benefits or offered as parental benefits, which can be accessed by either the mother or the father. Paid parental leave is also available in Austria, Belgium, Germany, France, Italy, and Canada, while fathers can access maternity leave provisions, rather than the mother, under certain conditions in Iceland, Portugal, and Sweden. In addition to parental leave, France and Germany offer tax deductions to those families who use domestic workers to provide home-based services. These services may include child care, but also can encompass other services such as home cleaning, food preparation, and gardening, which may be particularly desirable for those families where both members of a couple work and which have limited time to undertake home duties themselves. The countries of Denmark, Finland, Norway, and Sweden offered paid leave of about eighteen weeks to new mothers and, in some cases, leave over one year was offered. Some countries, such as France, make prenatal and postnatal leave compulsory.

Most of the European countries had or have a **pronatalist** rationale for their maternity/parental leave provisions. In other words, they enacted maternity leave along with generous child allowances and subsidized child care in part to help increase their birth rates. We saw in Chapter 13 that child allowances have not been very successful in raising fertility rates in these countries. Analyses of the maternity leave provisions in Sweden note that any positive fertility incentive may be dampened if there is any sort of minimum work period required in order to accrue full benefits. If workers are required to meet a minimum term of employment before becoming fully vested in maternity benefits, the existence of maternity leave might actually *increase* the time to birth, thereby decreasing the probability of a birth in early years.

Empirical evidence on this issue indicates that countries that provide paid maternity leave have lower infant mortality rates and higher female labor force participation rates and that the higher female labor force participation rates subsequently reduce fertility.[49] This underscores the importance of considering the simultaneous nature of many demographic and labor force deci-

---

[49] C. R. Winegarden and Paula M. Bracy, "Demographic Consequences of Maternal-Leave Programs in Industrial Countries: Evidence from Fixed-Effects Models," *Southern Economic Journal,* Vol. 6, No. 4, pp. 1020–1035, 1995.

sions. In other words, for many women, the decision to become attached to the paid labor force is simultaneously a decision to have fewer children. Australia is currently grappling with below-replacement fertility, and some argue that national paid maternity leave would help increase the Australian fertility rate.[50]

In the United States, supporters of expanding maternity leave coverage and of offering paid leave point to the Western European countries and Scandinavian countries as role models. However, such leaves do not come without a cost. Some countries pay for these extensive leaves through social insurance programs, while others require a contribution by employers or use general tax revenues. Spending on parental leave in Europe is substantial and is rising. Sweden and Finland spend about $900 per employed woman annually, while France spends $375 per woman annually. The higher-spending Scandinavian countries spent around 1% of their GDP on family leave in the mid-1990s, while France spent 0.35% of its Gross Domestic Product on family policies.[51] Perhaps as a result, these countries have experienced much lower employment growth than the United States.[52] Germany is currently rethinking its entire social welfare program because of a stagnating economy.[53]

When those eligible for the FMLA do not take a leave, the most frequently stated reason is that they simply cannot afford to take an unpaid leave.[54] This makes sense: Children are expensive and many families do not think that they can do without both incomes when a child is born. Others hesitate to take time off lest they lose their spot on the fast track. See Box 14.2 for a further discussion of this issue.

Recently, there has been some push toward paid maternity leave in the United States. In June 2000, the U.S. Department of Labor issued regulations that allow states to extend unemployment insurance to mothers out of work

---

[50]See the discussion on the web page http://www.eoc.sa.gov.au/public/equity23.html of the Equal Opportunity Commission of South Australia.

[51]Figures on benefit spending are from Janet C. Gornick and Marcia K. Meyers, "Support for Working Families," *The American Prospect*, Vol. 15, No. 1, January 2001.

[52]Rebecca Blank, *Does a Larger Social Safety Net Mean Less Economic Flexibility?* NBER, New York: Russell Sage Foundation, 1994.

[53]Christopher Rhoads, "In Deep Crisis, Germany Starts to Revamp Vast Welfare State," *The Wall Street Journal*, July 10, 2003, p. A1.

[54]Commission on Leave, "Executive Summary," "A Workable Balance." Report to Congress on family and medical leave policies, April 30, 1996.

Box 14.2   The Executive Woman's Maternity Leave

Women at the higher end of the earnings scale have generally had better access to maternity leave. Some of that may be because they are more likely to work at large firms that tend to have more generous maternity benefits. However, many women with substantial human capital investments are loath to take several weeks or months away, fearing that if they are gone, they will lose their edge in the competitive business world or perhaps even their livelihood. Thus, among many executive women, a new kind of maternity leave is evolving—what some call a "working maternity leave."

These women do not want to miss out on time with their newborns, but they also do not want to risk losing their status and input at the workplace. Thus, they report making a variety of arrangements to cope with the dual demands of a newborn and a career. Some arrange for colleagues to come to their house to work, others work from home via computer and cell phone, and some even bring their baby along to work. These women report that juggling job and baby is no easy task, particularly when breast-feeding is involved—having to pump breastmilk on a rigid schedule can be a tougher assignment than their actual job. Still, most feel fortunate that the positions they have attained in their careers allow them to mix career and family in a way that many women simply do not have the option or the resources to do.

Source: Melinda Ligos, "On Maternity Leave but Still on Track," *New York Times,* June 2, 2002.

owing to childbirth. In 2000 and 2001, over half the states had bills pending before their state legislatures that would allow unemployment insurance funds to cover maternity leave.

Extending leave to employees of smaller firms is also under debate. As mentioned earlier, it is estimated that only 46% of all women workers are covered by the FMLA. The recession of 2001–2002 no doubt took some of the impetus away from offering paid leave and expanding leave coverage. However, given the continued attachment of mothers to the labor force, it is likely that, as the economy turns around, such legislation will be revived.

Child Care Policy and Issues

Child care has become an increasingly important policy issue over the past two decades. As the labor force participation rate of women with preschool-age children continues to remain high, and as welfare reform pushes more single mothers into the workplace, policymakers continue to debate and enact a variety of child care subsidies and policies. However, the controversy over the extent of government subsidies and regulations in the child care industry is heated and far from over. In this section, we begin by discussing recent patterns in the use and cost of child care. We then provide an overview of the main legislation that subsidizes child care and a discussion of the debate that surrounds child care subsidies and the economic rationale for subsidizing child care expenditures. Finally, we look at the behavioral implications of subsidies to child care.

Child Care Costs and Usage

As always, let's begin with the facts. Who uses child care, how much do they pay, and what type of child care is purchased? Some of the most recent information on child care expenditures comes from the 1997 National Survey of America's Families (NSAF).[55] These data show that 48% of working families with children under age 13 incurred child care expenses in 1997. The 52% who reported no child care expenses included families with a variety of different situations. Some parents were able to juggle their work schedules so that they did not need to purchase any nonparental child care. Others reported using nonparental child care, but did not pay for it because a friend or relative or the government paid the costs. Those families with young children who paid for care paid an average of $286 per month or an average of 9% of their earnings. However, when families are divided by income level, some striking differences appear. Low-earning families (defined as those families with earnings no more than 200% of the poverty level) are spending an average of $217 per month, while higher-income families spend an average of $317 per month.

---

[55]The information in this section is from L. Giannerelli and J. Barsimantov, "Child Care Expenses of America's Families," Urban Institute occasional paper no. 40, 2000. This is a cross-section (i.e., point in time source of information). The U.S. government also tracks child care data over time since 1985 through the Survey of Income and Program Participation (SIPP). This information is available at www.census.gov/population/www/socdemo/childcare.html.

Child care expenditures can be a significant portion of a family's budget. Families generally find that child care expenditures are their third largest expense after housing and food. This is particularly true for low-income families who, according to the NSAF data, spend an average of 16% of their earnings on child care, compared to an average of only 6% by higher-income families. However, these averages mask considerable variation. For example, 27% of low-earnings families paid more than 20% of their earnings for child care while nearly half (46%) of higher-earning families spent less than 5% of their earnings on child care.[56]

What sort of arrangements do parents make for their children while they work? Information on this is available from the 1999 National Survey of America's Families. At this time, there were some 8.7 million preschool-age children (under age 5) whose parent(s) worked and used child care. This represents 73% of the children in this age group. The figures in Table 14.3 refer to the child's primary care arrangement (i.e., the arrangement in which the child spends the greatest number of hours).[57] About half of children under age 5 were cared for by a relative while their parent(s) worked (relative and parent/other categories), and this was most often a grandparent. The remaining half were cared for by nonrelatives. Overall, 28% of preschool children were at a day care center, while another 14% were in family-based day care (care by a nonrelative in someone else's home), and 4% were cared for by nannys or babysitters.

In the United States children who are 5 years old are usually entering kindergarten, which is often a part-day program. Thus, 5 year olds are shown separately in the table. We also show the care provided to school-age children who also have child care needs. Most parents believe that children under age 12 are too young to be on their own. Nevertheless, Table 14.3 documents that 10% of children between the ages of 6 and 12 are caring for themselves after school, and some feel this may be a low estimate. Researchers suspect that many parents report that they are providing the care rather than admit that their children are unsupervised for some of the time. There is generally

---

[56]For more information on the NSAF see L. Giannarelli and J. Barsimantov, "Child Care Expenses of America's Families," Urban Institute occasional paper no. 40, 2000.

[57]Many parents rely on more than one child care arrangement in a given week. The Census Bureau reports that in 1995 preschoolers of employed parents who were in child care arrangements had an average of 2.2 arrangements per week. "Who's Minding the Kids," Current Population Report, P70-70.

Type of Arrangement	Preschool Children Aged 0–4 Years (%)	Five-Year-Old Children (%)	School-Age Children Aged 6–12 years (%)
Center-based care	28	40	0
Relative care	27	19	23
Family child care	14	11	7
Nanny/babysitter	4	3	4
Parent/other care	27	19	41
Before and after school program	0	8	15
Self-care	0	0	10

Table 14.3   Primary Child Care Arrangements of Children with an Employed Parent, 1999

Source: Statistics on care are from Freya L. Sonenstein, Gary J. Gates, Stefanie Schmidt, and Natalya Bolshun, "Primary Child Care Arrangements of Employed Parents: Findings from the 1999 Survey of America's Families," The Urban Institute, 2002. Reprinted by permission. Other statistics on child care usage come from the Current Population Survey and can be found at www.census.gov/population/www/socdemo/childcare.html.

believed to be a shortage of infant care, care for school-age children, and off-hours care.[58]

Child care choices vary by the income level of the family. For example, two-parent families are less likely to use center-based care than are single-parent families according to the 1999 NSAF data, while, single-parent families are far more likely to use relative care than two-parent families. Two-parent families are sometimes able to juggle their work schedules so that one parent can be home with the child. This is not the case with single-parent families.

Data from the Survey of Income and Program Participation have tracked child care usage since 1985. Though these data are not as current as the National Survey of America's Families data, they do offer a view of how the usage of various types of child care has changed over time. From 1985 to 1994

---

[58]Rachel Connelly argues that there is no real shortage in the child care market but that the market simply clears at a price that is too high for many low-income families. See R. Connelly, "The Market for Child Care: An Application of Microeconomic Analysis for considering the Policy Issues," 1989.

the use of center-based care rose from 14 to 21.6% for all preschoolers while the percent of children cared for in a family day care home (i.e., child is cared for in the home of a nonrelative) fell from 22.3 to 15.4%. More generally, there has been a slight trend toward more center care (what one might call more formal arrangements) and away from more informal arrangements, such as family day care homes. Fathers have also been providing more care. See Box 14.3. Finally, it is worth noting that the size of the child care market, as measured by the number of children served, has grown dramatically. In 1985, there were some 8.2 million preschool-age children with employed mothers; in 1994, that number had grown to 10.3 million children. It is widely acknowledged that there are shortages of certain types of child care including care for school-age children, particularly in the summer. See Box 14.4 for a discussion of the arrangements parents make in the summer.

The Quality of Child Care

The affordability of child care and the quality of child care in the United States have received much attention in the past decade, particularly after the passage of the 1996 welfare reforms, when as we discussed at the beginning of the chapter, there was a marked increase in the labor force participation rate of single mothers. One major consequence of welfare reform is that now more women with young children will be in the labor market and hence in the child care market. Yet, these are single women who are overwhelmingly unskilled and so their earning prospects are generally not good. For these women, child care costs may be the largest barrier to work and hence to self-sufficiency. Furthermore, if they find affordable child care it may be of such low quality that it may harm the development of their children. The time limits under TANF have also meant that many grandmothers, who used to provide child care, can no longer do so because they too must find work.

Quality child care can be defined from two different but not mutually exclusive perspectives. There is **structural quality**, which refers to the characteristics of the child care environment, including the education of the provider, the size of the group, the ratio of staff to child, the immunization requirements, and the space requirements. The other quality dimension is **process quality**, which refers to the quality of the actual interaction between the caregiver and the child. The quality of care that children receive while their parents work is not a trivial issue. It affects the lives of over 10 million children today in the United States.

Box 14.3 My Daddy Takes Care of Me

Over the past decade, there has been renewed interest in the role of fathers in the family. Policymakers and the public are increasingly concerned about the role that a father plays in child development. Fathers contribute to families in a variety of ways—the traditional contribution was that of breadwinner. With the rise in labor force participation rates of mothers, some fathers are opting to stay at home to care for their kids.

Table 14.4 shows the percent of fathers who are the primary caretaker of their children. Over these years, fathers provided the primary care for between one-sixth and about one-quarter of preschool-age children and about 12–13% of school-age children. The increase in the percent of fathers providing care between 1988 and 1991 is thought to be due in part to the recession of 1990–1991. More fathers may have been unemployed or working part time during this time and thus able to provide child care. The percentages are greater when those fathers who provide some, but not all, care for their children are included.

Research shows that father care is a relatively stable form of child care; it tends to last as long as other arrangements such as center care. It is also often used in conjunction with other forms of child care. However, fathers are less likely to be the exclusive providers of child care during the first year of a child's life when mothers identify with more traditional gender roles. Hispanic fathers are also more likely to be the exclusive providers of child care during the first year of the child's life. Not surprisingly, when either parent works a nontraditional work schedule, the father is more likely to provide at least some of the child care.

Source: Lynne M. Casper, "My Daddy Takes Care of Me!" Current Population Report P70-59, 1997, and Susan Averett, Lisa Gennetian, and Elizabeth Peters, "Patterns and Determinants of Paternal Child Care During a Child's First Three Years of Life," *Marriage and Family Review,* Vol. 29, No. 2/3, pp. 115–136, 2000. Copyright © 2000. Reprinted with the permission of The Haworth Press, Inc. This article is available from The Haworth Document Delivery Service, 1-800-HAWORTH, docdelivery@haworthpress.com..

Age of Child	1988	1991	1993
Age 6–14	11.8%	13.9%	12.9%
Under age 5	16.9%	22.4%	18.5%

Table 14.4 Fathers Providing Care for Children While Mothers are Working, 1988–1993
Source: Lynne M. Casper, "My Daddy Takes Care of Me!" Current Population Report P70-59, 1997.

Box 14.4 Summer Child Care for School-Age Children

Child care for school-age children receives much less press than does child care for preschoolers. Yet, the need is no less real. Many schools and local YMCAs offer school-age programs for after-school care, but summer can be a particularly difficult time for parents to find quality care for their school-age youngsters. Some parents find great camps (often at great expense), and others beg relatives to help fill the gaps. Other parents have to settle for activities that may not be enriching, and some even leave their children unsupervised at times. Research reveals that about one third of school-age kids are cared for by relatives during the summer. Another 24% attend camps. Very few are with a nanny or a child care program in someone else's home. During the school year, one in ten school-age children report being alone or with a sibling under age 13 some of the time—that figure doubles during the summer.

There is concern about the quality of the care these kids receive during the summer. Furthermore, kids from low-income families tend to fall behind academically during the summer. Interestingly, their parents' child care expenses fall off then too, as many low-income families rely on relatives. On the other hand, higher-income families find themselves spending more for school-age child care during the summer. Do these divergent spending patterns speak to a vast difference in the quality of the summer experience for these kids? Surprisingly, no one really knows.

Source: Jeffrey Capizzano and Matthew Stagner, "When School's Out, Where Are the Kids?" *The Christian Science Monitor*, May 30, 2002.

There is disturbing evidence that much of the child care received by children in the United States is of substandard quality.[59] Since 1990, four large-scale evaluations of child care centers have been undertaken. Generally, these studies rate quality using the **Early Childhood Environment Rating Scale (ECERS),** which is a tool used to evaluate the quality of care received by preschoolers in child care centers. It is a type of checklist that trained observers can use when they observe the care in a child care center. There is a

---

[59]A summary of the findings of these studies can be found in S. Helburn and B. Bergmann, *America's Child Care Problem: The Way Out*, New York: Palgrave, 2002, Chapter 5.

corresponding scale for infant and toddler care. The scale involves rating not only the physical surroundings and types of toys available for children, but also the interactions between children and the child care providers. The results from these studies largely indicated that most of the centers provided only "good" as opposed to "excellent" care for the majority of children receiving care and that many infants were in care that was "unacceptable." One study found that care that was provided on-site by employers—a very small but growing proportion of the child care market—was of higher quality than other child care centers.[60]

There is also some evidence that what represents high-quality child care to child development experts is not what parents view as high-quality child care. Parents may be uninformed consumers of child care. They are not, after all, all child development experts. Furthermore, finding an arrangement that is affordable and convenient is likely to dominate a parent's decision making. Thus, although parents may believe they have made a high-quality choice, they may not have.

How does the quality of child care affect the well-being of the children who receive care? There is no simple answer to this question. Numerous studies have attempted to document the effects of low-quality child care on child development. This research has been conducted both by developmental psychologists and by economists. The results of this research cannot be easily summarized, because child development can be measured in many different ways and because data and methods differ across studies and sometimes across disciplines. There is some evidence that informal arrangements tend to be optimal for infants and young toddlers, but that formal arrangements are best for preschool-age children.[61]

This is an important area of research for several reasons. First, many working parents experience a great deal of stress surrounding their decision to use nonparental child care and might, in fact, alter their working schedules in response to low-quality child care. Second, there is increasing evidence that what happens during the first few years of a child's life is critically important

---

[60]For a nice discussion and examples of the checklist for the ECERS, see Suzanne Helburn and Barbara Bergmann, *America's Child Care Problem: The Way Out*, New York: Palgrave, 2002, Chapter 4. Chapter 5 of this book contains a detailed discussion of the findings of the four large-scale child care quality studies.
[61]F. Blau, A. Grossberg, and E. Lehrer, "Preschoolers with Working Mothers: An Analysis of the Determinants of Child Care Arrangements," *Journal of Population Economics*, Vol. 1, pp. 251–268, 1989.

for their development.[62] Finally, if poor-quality care harms children, we may wish to have the government subsidize child care in such a way that the quality is increased.

Although there is no clear consensus on the effect of quality of child care on child development, some patterns do seem to be emerging. In particular, higher-quality child care appears to be related to higher cognitive ability,[63] and there is some evidence that high-quality child care can be particularly beneficial to children from disadvantaged backgrounds.[64]

Given concerns about child care quality and the affordability of child care for low-income women, there has been renewed debate over the government's role in subsidizing child care. We turn to that subject next.

Government Intervention in the Child Care Market

The federal government first began subsidizing child care back in the 1930s, when the first federally funded nursery schools for poor children were opened. Currently, the federal government subsidizes child care through a myriad of policies. In 1997, the General Accounting Office (GAO) reported that there were twenty-two key sources of funding for child care and that the largest five of those accounted for more than 80% of all federal child care funding. Most of these subsidies are aimed at facilitating the employment of mothers and not at improving the quality of care received by children. In fact, these are two conflicting policy goals.

Although some people, including some economists, believe that the government should not intervene in the child care market, both the federal government and state governments are already heavily involved in the child care market. At this time, the relevant question is not whether the government should be involved, but rather how it should best be involved. We begin by reviewing the various subsidies for child care and the numerous regulations the government has imposed in this market.

---

[62]See Council of Economic Advisors, "The First Three Years: Investments that Pay," 1997, for discussion of this issue.

[63]An excellent overview and critical evaluation of the studies of child care quality on child development can be found in David Blau, *The Child Care Problem*, New York: Russell Sage Foundation, 2001, Chapter 7.

[64]The Abecedarian Project, a random assignment study of fifty-seven infants from low-income families, found that high-quality child care increased the cognitive ability of the children who received it. For a summary of the results of this study, see www.fpg.unc.edu/~abc/embargoed/executive_summary.htm.

The vast majority of subsidies to child care that exist today are intended to facilitate the employment of women in the labor market. **The Child Care and Development Block Grant (CCDBG)** is one of the largest sources of federal child care funding. The CCDBG was developed when welfare was restructured in 1996. It represented an effort to consolidate funding for child care and thus brought together many other programs under one program. It is now the primary child care subsidy program operated by the federal government and provided 4.6 billion dollars in child care assistance in 1996.

Under CCDBG states have considerable flexibility in designing their own child care assistance schemes. Funds from the CCDBG can be used to expand day care services for low-income families as well as to improve the overall quality and supply of child day care. Funds from the CCDBG are primarily directed at low-income families—nearly all recipients are below 200% of the poverty line—but it is estimated that only 12% of those families eligible for child care assistance from the federal government received it in 1999.[65] This occurs despite the fact that, over the past decade, funds for child care for low-income mothers have increased dramatically.

Other federal support for child care includes the **Head Start program,** which is an educational preschool program that serves low-income children starting as young as age one. Head Start began in 1965 as a program to ready low-income children for school. Although it was not initially meant as child care— it only provided care for a few hours a day—more Head Start programs have either become full day care providers themselves or contract with local preschools to provide full day care. Thus, Head Start is increasingly becoming a child care option for low-income families. Title XX Social Services Block grants are also another source of federal child care funding, and the federal government also supplies food to child care centers through the Child and Adult Care Food program.

Additionally, the government subsidizes child care through the federal income tax system. One such subsidy, the **Dependent Care Tax Credit (DCTC),** in place since 1976, allows employed parents to receive a tax credit worth up to 30% of their child care expenses up to a maximum of $2400 for the care of

---

[65]See U.S. Department of Health and Human Services, "New Statistics Show That Only Small Percentage of Eligible Families Receive Child Care Help," 12/6/2000, press release. www.acf.hhs.gov/news/press/2000/ccstudy.htm.

one child and $4800 for the care of two or more children, provided their adjusted gross income is below $10,000. A tax credit reduces a family's tax liability dollar for dollar. The value of the DCTC falls as income rises until it reaches 20% of actual expenses for families with adjusted gross income (AGI) in excess of $28,000. The DCTC is not refundable, however, so taxpayers who owe less in taxes than the credit do not receive the full benefit. Thus, the primary beneficiaries are middle-class individuals. In fact, in 1997, it was estimated that 48% of the benefits of the DCTC accrued to families with AGI above $50,000, while only 10% of the benefit went to families with AGI less than $10,000.[66] The DCTC would reach more low-income families if it were to become refundable. Although that option has been debated, it has not yet been enacted into law.

Another child care subsidy available through the federal income tax program is the **Child Tax Credit,** which was introduced in 1998. In 2001, it provided a $600 tax credit that is refundable to the extent of 10% of a taxpayers' income in excess of $10,000. The tax credit is reduced by $50 for every $1000 of AGI above $110,000 for married couples filing jointly and $75,000 for single filers until it eventually phases out completely. This credit differs markedly from the DCTC because the former requires child care to be purchased, whereas the Child Tax Credit can be used by families whether or not child care is purchased.

The third program that stems from the income tax system is the **Earned Income Tax Credit.** Low- and moderate-income families with labor market earnings receive a refundable tax credit that increases with the number of children they have. In 2003, the EITC could be worth up to almost $2500 for a family with one child and up to $4200 for a family with two or more children. This credit is similar to the Child Tax Credit in that it does not stipulate that child care be purchased. However, it does provide many families with the added money necessary to purchase child care.

Another tax-related program is a **flexible spending account.** Flexible spending accounts, first introduced in 1981, allow individuals to set aside some amount of their pretax earnings and to use those earnings to purchase specific items, currently only child care and medical expenses. This reduces the amount paid for child care by the amount of an employee's marginal tax rate. For example, an individual with $5000 of child care expenses can set up a

---

[66]U.S. House of Representatives 2000 Green Book, Section 13

Box 14.5 The Universal Unified Child Credit

Robert Cherry and Max Sawicky of the Economic Policy Institute have designed a policy called the **Universal Unified Child Credit (UUCC)** that aims to greatly simplify the way that the federal tax code deals with children. It builds on the Earned Income Tax Credit, which was discussed in detail in Chapters 12 and 13. The UUCC would be a credit that combines the EITC, the DCTC, and the personal exemption and would be available to all taxpayers with children whose income derives from employment. This would simplify the process for taxpayers.

The proposed credit is designed very much like the EITC. It rises for an initial range of labor market earnings, flattens out over an additional range, and then phases out. One critical difference is that it does not phase down to zero but rather is reduced to a minimum benefit of $1270 per child. It also reduces the marriage penalty in the EITC. This is because the phase-out range is more gradual, meaning that fewer benefits are lost if a couple marries and combines their two incomes. Additionally, a fixed minimum credit per child means that merged families with more than two children do not lose as many benefits as they currently do under EITC. This more gradual phase-out also reduces the work disincentive of the current credit. The annual cost of the proposal is put at $32 billion. However, given the high rates of child poverty in the United States where children 18 and under make up 39% of the poor but account for only 26% of the population, its backers hope that this reform will receive bipartisan support.

Source: Robert Cherry and Max B. Sawicky, "Giving Tax Credit Where Tax Credit Is Due. A Universal Unified Child Credit That Expands the EITC and Cuts Taxes for Working Families," Economic Policy Institute briefing paper, 2000; and Christopher Farrell, "Striking a Blow Against Child Poverty," *Business Week*, June 2, 2000.

flexible spending account for child care expenses and put $5000 in it for the year. She does not pay taxes on that money, because it is not reported as part of her taxable income. If she was in the 33% tax bracket, she would have saved $1667 in taxes and thus in child care costs ($5000 $\times$ 0.33). Because the amount of the benefit is more for those with higher marginal tax rates, flexible spending accounts, like the DCTC, benefit mostly middle- and high-income taxpayers. Furthermore, such accounts are typically available from larger employers who offer benefits—again making it more likely that middle- and high-income taxpayers will benefit. In 1999, it was estimated that about 17% of all employees have access to such accounts. Employees who work full-time at large firms are those who are most likely to have such accounts.[67]

State governments also play a role in the subsidization of child care. They disburse the funds from the CCDBG and many run their own subsidy programs targeted to low-income families. Furthermore, states are the primary regulators of child care. States regulate the maximum allowable child/staff ratio, immunization and space requirements, and maximum group sizes. They do so to protect children from the harm that might be caused if the care does not meet some minimum level of structural quality.

The many government subsidies related to child care and children can be confusing. See Box 14.5 for one proposal which aims to consolidate many of these programs. Finally, as discussed in Box 14.6, some businesses provide child care directly to their employees.

Economic Rationale for Government Intervention in the Child Care Market

In reality, the government is unlikely to stop intervening in the child care market. Yet, there is still debate over the extent to which the government should be involved in providing child care assistance to families. Furthermore, if government intervention is warranted, what form should it take?[68] In the United States, policymakers have often taken a hands-off approach when dealing with family issues, and it is still the case that most families are generally left to navigate the child care market largely on their own. However, genuine concerns over the quality of care received and the affordability of care, particularly for low-income families, are important issues. However, these are two separate issues; government subsidies that increase the quality of care will not necessarily increase the affordability of care or facilitate the employment of women.

---

[67]Bureau of Labor Statistics, "Employee Benefits in Private Industry: 1999," 2001, http://www.bls.gov/ebs/sp/ebnr0006.txt.

[68]For more information about government subsidies to child care see any of the following: David Blau, "Child Care Subsidy Programs," NBER working paper no. 7806, 2000; U.S. General Accounting Office, "Early Education and Care: Early Childhood Programs and Services for Low Income Families," Report GAO/HEHS-00-11, 1999; Washington, D.C., Council of Economic Advisors White Paper, "The Economics of Child Care," 1997; and the recently published *The Child Care Problem: An Economic Analysis* by David M. Blau, New York: Russell Sage Foundation, 2001.

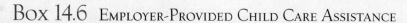

Box 14.6 Employer-Provided Child Care Assistance

A growing number of employers offer various child care assistance to their employees. This ranges from providing a resource and referral service to actually providing on-site child care for their employees. For 1999, the Bureau of Labor Statistics reports that 3% of employees reported that they have on-site child care, while 6% reported that their employer offers some type of child care assistance.

Recent changes in the federal tax code and in many state tax codes now provide tax breaks for employers who offer child care services including on-site child care. At the federal level, a new tax credit for employer-provided child care was instituted in September 2001. It provides for a tax credit worth up to $150,000 per year to employers offering care that meets the conditions outlined in the tax credit. More than twenty-five states also offer such credits.

There are many potential advantages to employers and employees of having on-site child care. From the firm's point of view, probably the most important advantage is that their employees may be more productive if their children are nearby and well cared for. In addition, on-site child care may make employees more loyal to their employer, thus reducing costly turnover. Furthermore, from the parent's perspective, the nearness of these centers to their workplace means that it is much easier for them to keep an eye on the quality of child care they are purchasing.

There is evidence that providing child care services, including on-site child care, does, in fact, increase the probability that employees are less likely to leave their employers. Lehrer et al. used data on nurses in Illinois to study whether or not employer-sponsored child care led to increased hours of work and an increased attachment to the employer. One reason for studying nurses is that hospitals have been more proactive in providing child care assistance, either by providing child care, helping with child care expenses, or providing resource and referral services. There are at least two reasons for this. First, hospitals employ a great number of young mothers as their nursing staff. Thus, many employees stand to benefit from this. Second, many of the shifts that nurses work are not compatible with the standard forty-hour daytime workweek. Therefore, providing care may be essential to having a workforce in some areas. The authors of the study found that providing some sort of child care assistance increased nurses' attachment to their employers and increased their hours of work.

There is also indirect evidence from other industries that providing child care is helpful for productivity. For example, the SAS software corporation has the following statement on its web page:

> SAS employees work in an environment that fosters and encourages the integration of the company's business objectives with their personal needs. With enviable low employee turnover that has been consistently and significantly below the industry average, SAS reaps the rewards of employee loyalty and the benefit of the most talented minds in the software business. Programs and facilities at its Cary, N.C., world headquarters include two on-site child care centers, an eldercare information and referral program, an employee health care center, wellness programs, a 77,000 square-foot recreation and fitness facility, and many other work-life programs.

SAS's work-life initiatives were recently the subject of a *60 Minutes* news story in a segment titled "The Royal Treatment." Their web page makes it very clear that they believe that providing benefits such as on-site child care will help their bottom line. The federal government and many colleges and universities also offer on-site child care. Universities with majors in early childhood education frequently have child care centers where students are able to interact with the children for research purposes.

Sources: Evelyn Lehrer, Teresa Santero, and Sumaria Mohan-Neill, "The Impact of Employer-Sponsored Child Care on Female Labor Supply Behavior: Evidence from the Nursing Profession," *Population Research and Policy Review*, Vol. 10, pp. 197–212, 1991. Bureau of Labor Statistics, "Employee Benefits in Private Industry," 1999. http://www.sas.com/corporate/worklife/index.html.

From an economic perspective, there are two reasons to subsidize care—**efficiency** and **equity.** One efficiency argument rests on the presumption that high-quality child care creates a positive externality. Recall that the possible presence of a positive externality was also a rationale for government-mandated parental leave. The case for the existence of a positive externality in the child care market is straightforward. For example, suppose that research finds that children who attend child care programs of high quality are better prepared for school and perform better in school. Students who perform better in school are less likely to commit crimes, have a teen birth, or be on welfare or use drugs. In this case, there is a clear positive spillover to society. Because individual families won't necessarily take the societal benefits into account when deciding about their child care, there is then a rationale for the government to intervene in the child care market to encourage the choice of higher quality child care.

In fact, as we noted earlier, a growing body of research indicates that what happens in the first few years of a child's life is crucially important for that child's later development. Furthermore, a considerable amount of research has examined the effects of nonmaternal and nonparental child care on child development. (This research is distinct from the research that examines the effect of the quality of care on child development.) Most of the research in this area is conducted by developmental psychologists, but economists have also conducted their own studies. Much of this research finds that nonmaternal child care is generally not harmful to child development and may well be beneficial, particularly for preschoolers.[69]

A second efficiency-related argument for government intervention is an information-based argument. If information about the quality of care is imperfect or if consumers are not fully informed about all potential suppliers, then intervention may be warranted. Consumers usually have less information than suppliers about the quality of child care that their children receive, and monitoring that quality can be costly. For example, providers may not change diapers until just before the child is to be picked up. There is some evidence that what parents believe to be high-quality child care is not what child development experts believe is high-quality child care. For example, parents may value a center that is convenient to their work place and has hours of operation that correspond with their work schedule. On the other hand, child development experts stress the importance of trained providers, small group sizes, and age-appropriate child/staff ratios as well as appropriate interactions between care providers and children (i.e., the structural and process dimensions of quality discussed earlier). Government may wish to provide resource

---

[69]See W. Steven Barnett, "Long-Term Effects of Early Childhood Programs on Cognitive and School Outcomes," *Long Term Outcomes of Early Childhood Programs, Center for the Future of Children, The David and Lucile Packard Foundation,* Vol. 5, No. 3, pp. 25–50, 1995, for more discussion of this point.

and referral services aimed at educating consumers as to which centers/programs are high quality. They also might wish to regulate directly those aspects of care related to quality such as the child/staff ratio.

Aside from efficiency concerns, another rationale for intervention in the child care market would be an equity or distributional argument. Low-income families may simply lack the means to purchase high-quality child care. If high-quality child care leads to improved outcomes for children, it seems unethical (unfair) to deprive any child of the benefits that come from such care. In addition, if a lack of affordable child care means that a low-income family cannot become self-sufficient and must rely upon government support, this may justify government support for child care.[70]

Government intervention is not without costs, of course, and sometimes the costs of intervention can outweigh the benefits. This suggests that the government should intervene in as targeted a way as possible to achieve its goal. It also indicates that if a cost-effective intervention is not found, the intervention may not be worthwhile. Several policy tools are available to policymakers who might wish to intervene in the child care market. For example, suppose government officials decide that they want to improve the quality of child care that parents use. How should it intervene to increase the quality of child care? The method often used by state governments, is to regulate various aspects of care thought to be related to the quality of care such as group sizes, child/staff ratios, and provider training. Regulation such as this allows the government to address the issue of lack of information about quality directly because now child care providers must adhere to regulations.

However, such regulation has its downfalls as well. First of all, it is impossible to regulate all providers, and some individuals may still select providers who are of a substandard quality, as defined by the regulations. For example, the government would no doubt find it too costly to regulate a neighbor who might offer to care for your child while you work and might in fact want to be paid cash to avoid taxes. Second, regulation can be costly for providers—they must comply with the regulations, and hiring additional workers to meet a prescribed child/staff ratio is costly. Thus, it may force some providers out of the market, reducing the supply of child care and driving up the price of child

---

[70]See Suzanne Helburn and Barbara Bergmann, *America's Child Care Problem: The Way Out*, New York: Palgrave, 2002, Chapter 7, for an engaging discussion of why government should intervene in the child care market.

care. Finally, to be effective, regulations need to be enforced. This can be expensive for state governments; one reporter for the *Washington Post* reported in 1997 that most child care centers in Washington, D.C., were operating with expired licenses.[71] In addition, many economists oppose regulations because they are a direct intervention in the market, and their costs and benefits are hard to measure.[72]

Another way to increase quality is to subsidize programs that train child care providers. This approach would help to ensure that the providers were having the appropriate interactions with children and were engaging the children in activities that were educational and stimulating.

Accreditation of centers is another way to increase quality. Currently, the National Association for the Education of Young Children is one organization that accredits child care centers. Their regulations are often different from those that states impose, in part because they are concerned more with quality than safety. Subsidizing accreditation would be one way to encourage centers to upgrade the quality of their care. At least one researcher advocates this avenue.[73]

An alternative way to address the quality of care is to have the government fund or perhaps even operate resource and referral services in an attempt to educate parents about what constitutes high-quality child care and which providers supply high-quality care. However, some parents may not use the referral centers or patronize the child care providers deemed to be of high quality and may still end up with low-quality child care.

The government could also target child care subsidies toward high-quality child care, perhaps by proving vouchers to centers deemed to be of high quality. Another alternative is to provide all parents with information about quality, perhaps by distributing information about quality of child care to new mothers shortly after the birth of their children.[74]

---

[71]See Katherine Boo, "Most D.C. Day Care Centers Have Expired Licenses," *The Washington Post*, October 6, 1997.

[72]See David Blau, *The Child Care Problem: An Economic Analysis*, 2001, Chapter 9, for a discussion of child care regulations and their pros and cons. Blau concludes that child care regulations most likely have very little effect on the market for child care, in part because the majority of centers in the United States voluntarily exceed the state regulations imposed for group size and child/staff ratios.

[73]See David Blau, *The Child Care Problem: An Economic Analysis*, New York: Russell Sage Foundation, 2001, for a discussion of this.

[74]David Blau, *The Child Care Problem: An Economic Analysis*, 2001, advocates this as an easy way to educate almost all mothers (families) about what constitutes high-quality child care.

Rather than increasing the quality of child care, the government might want to intervene to increase the supply of child care. Again, there are policy choices. The government could mandate that firms provide care for their employees in much the same way as it mandated that firms comply with the FMLA. This could be very costly to businesses, and it is not an avenue that policymakers in the United States have taken, although a small percentage of firms do offer on-site child care for their employees. Another way to increase the supply of child care centers would be to subsidize the centers themselves.

Despite the fact that there are strong arguments for subsidizing child care and several plausible avenues by which the government can do so, there is no widespread agreement that the government should do so. In fact, there are many arguments against subsidizing child care. One popular argument is that subsidized child care benefits those families with employed mothers at the expense of families whose mothers stay home. This reflects the popular belief that child care is the burden of the mother, although there is a small but critical mass of fathers who stay home with their children while their wives work. However, as we saw in Chapter 13, the income tax system heavily favors couples where wives stay home: they usually get a marriage subsidy, and the value of home production is not taxed.[75] Others worry that subsidies to child care will encourage more women to work outside the home and thus abandon traditional gender roles. There is some concern that subsidizing child care might lead women to have more children, because it lowers the cost of raising children. There is very little evidence on this issue, but as we noted in our discussion of maternity leave and fertility, if child care costs make it easier for women to work, this will probably lead women to have fewer children because the opportunity cost of a child increases. And, of course, many of those opposed to government intervention in the child care market believe that it is better for the child developmentally if the child is cared for by a parent.

However, as we have already seen, the government does subsidize the purchase of care. As noted earlier, a considerable amount of subsidized care in the United States goes to families who are not impoverished. Both the DCTC and the flexible spending accounts benefit the middle- to high-income segment of the population. In addition, there is concern that the current child care subsidies aimed at the low-income population are insufficient to meet

---

[75]For an excellent discussion of how the government might think about subsidizing child care that addresses some of the issues related to taxes and child subsidies see C. Eugene Steuerle, "Systematic Thinking About Subsidies for Child Care," Parts 1, 2, and 3, The Urban Institute, 1998.

demand. This is particularly important in light of the current welfare policy which encourages low-income women to work.

Child Care and Labor Force Participation

At this point, we've established why the government might want to subsidize child care, and we have examined the various subsidies that are available. Let's see if such subsidies might be useful in achieving their goals. For example, suppose that the government wants to encourage women to work and decides to subsidize their child care. Whether or not these women will join the workforce has received considerable attention lately, in part because of the 1996 welfare reform. This legislation stipulates, in part, that women who receive welfare must also work. This means that there is now a much larger segment of low-skilled women in need of child care. How will providing subsidies to child care affect the labor force participation rates of this group?

The analysis in Chapter 7 can help explain how child care costs affect the decision to allocate time to the labor market. Let's use that approach to examine how an increase in child care costs would likely decrease the probability that a woman worked in the labor market and, therefore, why subsidizing child care costs could lead to an increase in a woman's labor supply.

Recall that in Chapter 7 we developed a model where a given woman maximized her utility over leisure (L), market goods (C), and household-produced goods (G). She was subject to three constraints. The first of these is the spending constraint. The market goods constraint in equation (a) simply indicates that the amount of spending on goods and services (pC) must equal the amount of income earned (wM) plus nonlabor income (V), where p is the price of market good and w is the wage rate. In other words, you can't spend more than the amount of income you have. The second constraint is the production constraint: The amount of household goods that can be produced depends on the amount of time spent and on the technology and capital goods available (Z). Finally, the third constraint is the time constraint: There are only so many hours in a day (T), and the total amount of time spent in each activity can't exceed that amount. For convenience, we repeat these constraints in equation form:

(a) Market Goods: $\quad pC = wM + V$
(b) Household Goods: $\quad G = g(H; Z)$
(c) Time: $\qquad M + H + L = T$

M, H, and T represent the time spent in market work, household production, and leisure.

Briefly, the analysis of labor force participation depends on a comparison of the value of time in the labor market with the value of time spent either in household production or in leisure. MVT^* is the value of the last hour of time, when all time is spent in either leisure or household production (i.e., no labor market work) and when that time is allocated so as to maximize utility. The decision to be a participant in the labor market depends on a comparison of MVT^* to the marginal value of time in the labor market. Let $MVT_M(1)$ stand for the value of the first hour of time in the labor market and M^* for the best amount of time to allocate to the labor market. Then, the rules for labor force participation that maximize her utility are:

(d) If $MVT^* > MVT_M(1)$, then $M^* = 0$.
This woman does not work in the labor market.

(e) If $MVT^* < MVT_M(1)$, then $M^* > 0$.
This woman works in the labor market.

Child care costs fit nicely into this model. One approach often taken in the literature is to note that child care costs reduce the wages of a woman working in the formal labor market. Presumably she would not incur these costs if she were not working in the formal labor market. Thus, her wage is reduced directly by the amount of her child care. Each additional hour of work means that she must purchase another hour of child care.

We begin by assuming that a given woman is not participating in the labor market—perhaps because the costs of child care lower her wages so much that she has chosen not to work in the market. In Figure 14.1 we see this with the MVT_M curve labeled "Before Child Care Subsidy." At this point, MVT^* is greater than $MVT_M(1)$, and this woman has chosen not to participate in the labor market. Of course, women who need child care have small children and thus have a higher marginal value of time in the home, which already means that they are less likely to work even if they incurred very low child care costs or commanded high market wages.

However, if the government were to subsidize child care, we would see an upward shift in the MVT_M curve, and if it rose enough, she might reallocate some of her time to market work as we show her doing in Figure 14.1.[76] We

---

[76]Readers familiar with intermediate microeconomic theory will notice that there are usually two effects set in motion when wages increase—an income effect and a substitution effect. In this case there is no income effect because she is not yet working.

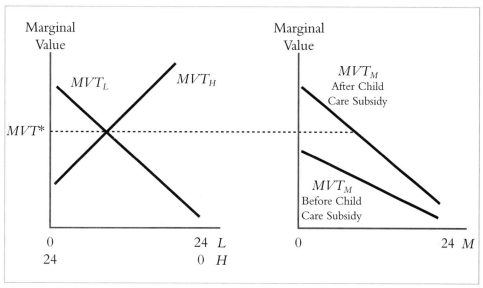

Figure 14.1 The Effect of Child Care Subsidies on a Woman's Decision to Work in the Market

see this because $MVT_M(1)$ is greater than MVT^*. In the language of Chapter 7, when $MVT^* < MVT_M(1)$, $M^* > 0$, and the woman works in the labor market.

Because a subsidy for child care lowers the cost of working, this should increase the probability of working. Welfare reform provides an extra incentive for low-income mothers to work, since they can usually collect benefits for a maximum of five years and usually must work to collect benefits. Providing them with child care subsidies may enable them to participate in the labor market and build up the human capital and work experience they need to become self-sufficient. It is important to remember though that many of the jobs that former welfare recipients will find are those that require little skill and hence pay very little. These are jobs that do not often lead to promotions or offer much opportunity for advancement. Thus, it is unclear that, by itself, working will make these women economically self-sufficient. However, it has long been believed that child care costs are a significant barrier to employment among the low-income population.

One recent study that examined the effect of child care costs on the employment and welfare participation of single mothers found that if 50% of child care expenditures were subsidized, the probability of being on welfare is reduced by a third while the probability of employment is increased by 50%.[77] Another study found that White, single women in poverty were very responsive to child care subsidies—free child care would more than double the probability that they participated in the labor force—but Black women's response to subsidized child care was much lower and not statistically significant.[78] There are other employment-related issues that plague this population, and it is not clear that simply subsidizing child care will allow them to attain financial independence. Issues such as transportation, lack of appropriate attitudes about work, difficulties of scheduling child care and work, and a general lack of skills and experience are equal and perhaps larger obstacles to employment and economic self-sufficiency for this group.[79]

Considerable research by economists has investigated the effect of the price of child care on the employment behavior of mothers in general, rather than just low-income mothers.[80] One recent study concludes that the **price elasticity of employment with respect to child care costs,** the responsiveness of employment to changes in child care costs, lies somewhere in the -0.4 to -0.9 range for married women and closer to zero for single women,[81] while another finds elasticity estimates ranging between -0.05 and -0.35.[82] An elasticity of $-.4$ indicates that if child care costs increase by 10%, employment falls by 4%. One study found that the DCTC did in fact increase the hours married women worked.[83] There is also evidence that full-time employment is more responsive to child care costs as compared to part-time employment.[84]

---

[77]See Rachel Connelly and Jean Kimmel, "The Effect of Child Care Costs on the Labor Force Participation and Welfare Recipiency of Single Mothers: Implications for Welfare Reform," *Southern Economic Journal*, Vol. 69, No. 3, 2003, earlier draft circulated as Upjohn Institute working paper no. 01-99.

[78]Jean Kimmel, "The Effectiveness of Child Care Subsidies in Encouraging the Welfare-to-Work Transition of Low-Income Single Mothers," *American Economic Review*, Vol. 85, No. 2, pp. 271–276, 1995.

[79]See Sandra Danziger, Mary Corcoran, and Sheldon Danziger, "Barriers to the Employment of Welfare Recipients," working paper, Poverty Research and Training Center, University of Michigan, 1999.

[80]David Blau, "Child Care Subsidy Programs," NBER working paper no. 7806, 2000, provides a comprehensive review of this literature.

[81]Jean Kimmel, "Child Care Costs as a Barrier to Employment for Single and Married Mothers," *Review of Economics and Statistics*, Vol. 82, No. 2, pp. 287–299, 1998.

[82]P. Anderson and P. Levine, "Child Care and Mother's Employment Decisions." NBER working paper no. 7058, 1999.

[83]Susan Averett, H. Elizabeth Peters, and Donald Waldman, "Tax Credits, Labor Supply and Child Care," *Review of Economics and Statistic,* Vol. 79, No. 1, pp. 125–35, 1997.

[84]Jean Kimmel and Rachel Connelly, "Marital Status and Full-Time/Part-Time Work Status in Child Care Choices," mimeo, July 2002.

Another research question involves the effect of subsidizing a particular kind of child care, such as center-based care, on the use of that type of care. For example, the DCTC currently subsidizes care when the provider can provide a Taxpayer Identification Number. This is essentially a subsidy for paid child care, the kind that is most often available at a child care center.[85] Some economists have argued that subsidies should be directed toward licensed care or accredited care because such care is likely to be of higher quality.[86] Other economists believe that a subsidy should not be for any specific type of care, but that parents should be able to use the subsidy to purchase the type of care that is best for their family. There is some empirical evidence that subsidizing child care will lead parents to use more formal modes of care such as day care centers because this type of care is more price elastic.[87] There is also evidence that women who work full-time are more likely to rely on center care than are women who work part-time and also that single women's choice of child care mode is more price-sensitive than that of married women.[88]

As more women on welfare move into the workplace, concerns have repeatedly been voiced about whether the supply of child care can keep up with the demand. It has been suggested that one occupation that former welfare recipients might consider is that of child care provider. This is a notoriously low-paying occupation, although we might expect to see pay rising as the demand for child care services increases. However, there is some evidence that the supply of child care workers is very wage elastic—which means that an increase in the demand for child care workers might have a relatively small positive impact on their wages.[89]

In 2000, child care workers had median weekly earnings of $264, compared to the median weekly earnings of all women in 2000, which was $491.[90] Being an assistant teacher at a day care center does not require much education,

---

[85]See Duncan D. Chaplin, P. K. Robins, S. Hofferth, D. Wissoker, and P. Fronstin, "The Price Elasticity of Child Care Demand: A Sensitivity Analysis," working paper, Washington, D.C., The Urban Institute, 1999, for a review of this literature.

[86]Suzanne Helburn and Barbara Bergmann, *America's Child Care Problem: The Way Out,* New York: Palgrave, 2002, p. 172.

[87]See Jean Kimmel and Lisa Powell, "Nonstandard Work and Child Care Choices of Married Mothers," mimeo, 2002.

[88]Jean Kimmel and Rachel Connelly, "Marital Status and Full-Time/Part-Time Work Status in Child Care Choices," mimeo, July 2002.

[89]See David Blau, *The Child Care Problem,* New York: Russell Sage Foundation, 2001, Chapter 2, pp. 29–31, for a discussion of child care workers' wages and turnover.

[90]See Bureau of Labor Statistics, "Highlights of Women's Earnings in 2000," report 952, August 2001.

although higher-quality centers prefer that their head teachers have an associate's or bachelor's degree in early childhood education. In fact, those who become child care workers are often the same people who work in fast food restaurants or in retail sales. These jobs require little education and can draw from the relatively large pool of immigrants in the United States. There is evidence that the presence of young children is a determinant in the decision to become a self-employed child care provider. Presumably, women who have young children, such as welfare mothers, may find that work as a child care provider allows them entrance into paid employment, while experiencing lower (or zero) child care costs for their own children.[91]

The relatively low earnings of child care workers means that turnover is a large problem in the child care industry. It creates costs for centers which often must run continuous job searches. Not only does it have an impact on the quality of care since children form attachments with caregivers who then leave, but it also affects the morale of the workers themselves who may feel devalued because of their low wages. During the 1990s, many child care centers experienced a shortage of workers. Many center directors reported not raising wages but hiring less-qualified people during this time.[92] One child care researcher has suggested that one way to overcome the turnover, low wages, and low levels of education among child care providers in the child care industry is to professionalize it, much as we do public education in the United States. This would then have the added benefit of paying child care providers wages that will allow them to be self-sufficient.[93] However, the fact that many women are willing to work as child care providers even when wages are low indicates that there must be some nonpecuniary benefits to the job. Perhaps they are people who love being around children and value their ability to be caregivers.

As mentioned earlier, there is a shortage of some types of child care. One particular type of care that is needed is off-hours child care. In our increasingly 24/7 economy, many mothers find themselves working nonstandard shifts,

[91]Rachel Connelly, "Self Employment and Providing Child Care: Employment Strategies for Mothers with Young Children," mimeo, 1992.

[92]Suzanne Helburn and Barbara Bergmann, *America's Child Care Problem: The Way Out,* New York: Palgrave, 2002, p. 172.

[93]E. F. Zigler and M. Finn-Stevenson, "Schools of the 21st Century—Linking Child Care and Education," Boulder, Co.: Westview Press, 1999; and Barbara Bergmann, "Decent Child Care at Decent Wages," *The American Prospect,* Vol. 12, pp. 8–12, 2001.

either at night, on weekends, or in split-shifts. Yet, there is very little child care to accommodate their needs. The group of women working these nonstandard hours are disproportionately low-income workers, and often the decision to work such hours is not a choice but a necessity of the job. Although some women can rely on their spouses to provide care during these nonstandard hours, a sizable minority cannot. There is evidence that women working nonstandard shifts tend to rely on more informal methods of care for their children.[94] If such care is of substandard quality, subsidies to higher-quality types of care could improve the choice set for these mothers.

Summary

In this chapter, we examined how women can maintain a balance between work and family, and we looked in depth at two issues—maternity leave and child care. Women, and increasingly men, face a complex set of choices when deciding how to balance career and family. Rising labor force participation rates, particularly among women with young children, have moved policy issues such as maternity leave and child care into the spotlight. This chapter explored the economic analysis behind the provision of parental leave and discussed the benefits and costs of providing such leave. One of the benefits of providing such leave is that it may help to close the family pay gap if it allows women to maintain job continuity and build their human capital. At this time, the United States lags far behind other developed countries in its provision of parental leave; for example, the United States is one of the only developed countries that does not mandate some type of paid maternity leave.

We ended the chapter with a comprehensive discussion of the child care market. We found that there is considerable heterogeneity in the type of child care chosen and the amount paid for that care. Some low-income women pay 25% or more of their income for child care while it is often less than 10% of a high-income families' expenses. There is a particular concern that much of the child care available in the United States today is of a low quality. In addition, some of the largest subsidies for child care expenditures are aimed not at poor families but at middle-class families.

---

[94]Jean Kimmel and Lisa Powell, "Nonstandard Work and Child Care Choices of Married Mothers," mimeo, July 2002.

In the end, the direction that government should take in the child care market is not clear. The government can take the approach that child care should facilitate the employment of mothers and therefore design subsidies to achieve that goal. However, policymakers may also wish to increase the quality of the care that is provided. These are not necessarily mutually exclusive, but achieving both is costly, and different types of intervention into the market would be required. Perhaps the best way to understand the dichotomy is to examine the two most recent books on child care written by three very acclaimed economists. David Blau in *The Child Care Problem: An Economic Analysis* favors subsidies aimed at increasing quality as being the appropriate policy goal. He contends that the main problem with the child care market is the low quality of much of the child care provided. However, Barbara Bergmann and Suzanne Helburn in their book, *America's Child Care Problem,* are much more concerned with equity and access to affordable child care for all families.

In both the areas of child care and family leave policies, the United States does far less than almost all other Western industrialized countries. Countries such as Sweden and France have extensive child care systems and subsidies. In the United States, parents navigate the market largely on their own. Whether this is the correct approach to take is uncertain.

Key Terms

adverse selection   548

asymmetric information   547

The Child Care and Development Block Grant (CCDBG)   567

Child Tax Credit   568

Dependent Care Tax Credit (DCTC)   567

dual earner   533

Early Childhood Environment Rating Scale (ECERS)   564

Earned Income Tax Credit   568

efficiency   572

effort hypothesis   536

equity   572

externalities   546

family gap   536

Family and Medical Leave Act (FMLA)   534

flexible spending account   568

Head Start program   567

mommy track   535

negative externality   547

positive externality   546

Pregnancy Discrimination Act of 1978   542

price elasticity of employment with respect to child care costs   580

process quality   562

pronatalist   556

structural quality   562

turnover costs   543

Universal Unified Child Credit   569

unobserved family-specific heterogeneity   537

CHAPTER 15

Family Structure and Children's Well-Being

Introduction

In this chapter, we examine the dramatic changes in family life that have taken place over the last fifty years. We carefully document these changes and ask about their implications for the well-being of children. Many view these changes in family life as lamentable. They argue that family life has suffered because of the increase in single-parent families. Others maintain that the family should not be so narrowly defined and that a family can encompass more than the traditional husband, wife, and two children definition. Whatever the definition, American family life has changed considerably. In fact, changes in family structure in the United States have been so large that many researchers refer to these changes as the family structure revolution. Let's start by documenting this revolution.

The Family Structure Revolution

Table 15.1 documents what we mean by changes in family structure. We present statistics on marriage, divorce, cohabitation, and single-parent families from 1970 to 2000. Let's begin with marriage. As we discussed in Chapter 3, the proportion of the population that is married has been steadily falling. Across nearly all age groups, the percentage of the population that has never married has been increasing, and the percentage of adults who are currently married has steadily fallen. Of the race/ethnic groups shown, Blacks are the least likely to be married. Although marriage rates are falling, the majority of Americans do marry at some point, but they marry later. Median age at first

	1970	1980	1990	*Present
Marriage rate per 1000 population	10.6	10.6	9.8	8.3 (1996)
Marriage rate per 1000 women aged 15 and over	28.4	26.1	24.1	
Median age at first marriage: women	20.8	22	23.9	25.1
Median age at first marriage: men	23.2	24.7	26.1	26.8
Never married as a percent of total population				
Men aged 20–24	54.7	68.8	79.3	83.7
Men aged 25–29	19.1	35.1	45.2	51.7
Men aged 30–34	9.4	15.9	27	30
Men aged 35–39	7.2	7.8	14.7	20.3
Men aged 40–44	5.4	4.8	8	11.8
Women aged 20–24	35.8	50.2	62.8	72.8
Women aged 25–29	10.5	20.9	31.1	28.9
Women aged 30–34	6.2	9.5	16.4	21.9
Women aged 35–39	5.4	6.2	10.4	14.3
Women aged 40–44	4.7	4.8	8	11.8
Percent of adults currently married				
All	71.7	65.5	61.9	59.5
Whites	72.6	67.2	64	62
Blacks	64.1	51.4	45.8	42.1
Hispanic origin	62.4	65.6	61.7	60.2
Divorce rate per 1000 married women age 15+	14.9	22.6	20.9	19.5 (1996)
Millions of cohabiting couples (adult, unmarried couples of the opposite sex)	0.523	1.589	2.856	4.236 (1998)
Ratio of unmarried couples per 100 married couples	1	3	5	7 (1994)

Percent of families with children under age 18 who are				
Married-couple families	89	81	76	73
Headed by a female	10	17	20	22
Headed by a male	1	2	4	5

Table 15.1   Changes in Family Structure, 1970–Present

*Present refers to the year 2000 unless otherwise noted.

Sources: *Statistical Abstract of the United States*, 2002, and U.S. Census Bureau.

marriage has increased from 20.8 years to 25.1 years for women and from 23.2 to 26.8 years for men. Increasing numbers of men and women are delaying marriage to pursue higher education and careers. At the same time, changes within marriages have had a profound impact on family life.

The rising labor force participation rates of married women has brought an entirely new dimension to families. Back in the 1950s, the typical family that was immortalized on many television shows like *Leave it to Beaver, Ozzie and Harriet*, and *Father Knows Best* consisted of two parents and two children. The father worked outside the home and the mother specialized in home production. In 1960, 44% of all households were two-parent households with children. This number dropped to 24% in 2000.[1]

The second trend documented in Table 15.1 is the rise and leveling off of the divorce rate. Divorce rates were relatively steady for most of the twentieth century and then rose markedly in the 1960s and 1970s. Since the 1980s, the rates have leveled off but remain much higher than they were earlier. The average marriage in the United States lasts just over seven years, and nearly half of all marriages will end in divorce. Many divorces occur before children are born. However, it is estimated that about one half of all children in the United States will live apart from at least one of their parents, usually the father, before reaching adulthood.[2] Likewise, in Britain, about 40% of all children will spend time apart from one parent, again usually the father.[3]

---

[1]Suzanne M. Bianchi and Lynne M. Casper, "American Families," *Population Bulletin*, Vol. 55, No. 4, 2000.
[2]Larry L. Bumpass, R. Kelly Raley, and James A. Sweet, "The Changing Character of Step-families: Implications of Cohabitation and Nonmarital Childbearing," NSFH 63, *Demography*, Vol. 32, pp. 425–436, 1995.
[3]John Ermisch and Marco Francesconi, "The Increasing Complexity of Family Relationship: Lifetime Experience of Lone Motherhood and Step-Families in Great Britain," *European Journal of Population*, Vol. 16, pp. 235–249, 2000.

Cohabitation is also on the rise. The ratio of unmarried couples per 100 married couples increased from 1 in 1970 to 7 in 1994, and it is now regularly tracked by the Census Bureau. Remember POSSLQs? Cohabitation was once very rare in the United States. However, a recent study noted that by 1995, half of all women in their 30s had cohabited outside of marriage.[4] Cohabitation is often a short-term state, and many cohabitors eventually marry. Yet, cohabitation is not necessarily a stable arrangement. Approximately one half of all cohabiting couples are together for a year or less, and only 10% will last five years or longer. This means that children of cohabitors are more likely to experience disruption in their family lives.

Less-educated individuals have had the greatest increase in cohabitation. In fact, Acs and Nelson show that between 1997 and 1999, the proportion of children under age 2 living with their unmarried biological parents increased by 1.6 percentage points. This increase is concentrated among lower-income families, leading Acs and Nelson to believe that it is, in part, driven by policy changes that were a part of the 1996 welfare reform that replaced AFDC with TANF (see Chapter 12). For example, under the TANF program, many states have relaxed their rules about the eligibility of two-parent families for benefits.[5]

We've noted in several places in this text that there has been a notable rise in nonmarital childbearing in the United States. The rise in cohabitation is part of the explanation for this, because births to cohabiting couples are counted as nonmarital. Between 1990 and 1994, 40% of all births to unmarried women were to cohabiting parents. Demographers have shown that most of the rise in nonmarital childbearing has occurred among cohabiting two-parent families. Recent estimates indicate that about 36% of cohabiting households include children under the age of 15.[6]

Overall, these changes in marriage, divorce, and cohabitation have meant enormous changes in the structure of families. Married-couple families are

---

[4]See Larry Bumpass and Hsien-Hen Lu, "Cohabitation: How the Families of the U.S. Are Changing," *Focus*, Vol. 21, No. 1, pp. 5–8, 2000. Much of the discussion of cohabitation in this section is drawn from this research.

[5]Greg Acs and Sandy Nelson, "'Honey I'm Home': Changes in Living Arrangements in the Late 1990s," Urban Institute, Series B, No. B38, The New Federalism.

[6]U.S. Bureau of the Census, 1999, http://www.census.gov/population/socdemo/ms-la/tabad-2.txt.

on the decline, while there has been a tremendous rise in the proportion of households headed by women. The rise in single-parent families is one of the defining characteristics of the new family structure. These trends are not limited exclusively to the United States but are apparent to some degree in all developed countries.[7]

Figure 15.1 documents the tremendous growth in female-headed households from 1950 to the present. In 1950, 93% of families with children under the age of 18 were two-parent families. In 2000, that number had fallen by 20 percentage points to 73%. Concurrently, the number of female-headed families has grown from just 6% to 22% of all families with children under age 18. Families headed by a male have also grown though not as dramatically. In 1950, 1% of families with children under age 18 were headed by a male, and that number increased to 5% in 2000. In 2000, some 6.3% of families with children under age 18 were headed by grandparents or a grandparent. Finally, recent estimates indicate that in 1990 about 21.7% of lesbian couples had children, while 5.2% of gay men couples had children.[8]

Single-parent families are the result of two trends that are documented in Table 15.1. Divorce is one way that single-parent families are created. Single-parent families are also created from mothers who have out-of-wedlock births (i.e., they do not marry or live with the father of their children).[9]

The rise in out-of-wedlock births has been a defining feature of American life in the past quarter century. It used to be the case that, when a teen or a young woman had an out-of-wedlock birth, considerable social stigma was attached to the event. In many cases, pregnant teens were shuttled off to special schools to finish high school and have the baby without embarrassing the family. So-called shotgun marriages were also common. Changing social norms, along with other factors have made it more acceptable for a woman to give birth without being married. In 2000, one third of all births in the

---

[7]An excellent source of statistical information on women around the world is *The World's Women 2000: Trends and Statistics*, United Nations Publishing, New York: http://unstats.un.org/unsd/demographic/ww2000/index.htm.

[8]Dan Black, Gary Gates, Seth Sanders, and Lowell Taylor, "Demographics of the Gay and Lesbian Population in the United States: Evidence from Available Systematic Data Sources," *Demography,* Vol. 37, No. 2, pp. 139–145, 2000.

[9]Single-parent families are also created when one spouse dies. This is generally regarded as a random event rather than a social trend. There have been no major changes in this area.

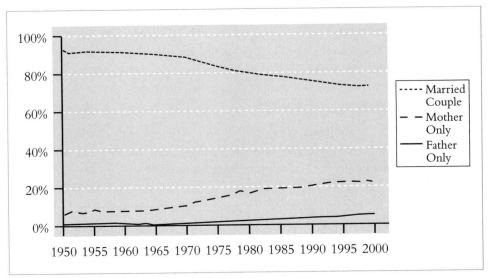

Figure 15.1   Changes in Family Type, United States, 1950–2000

Source: U.S. Bureau of the Census, Current Population Reports, March 2000.

United States were nonmarital, including nearly 70% of births to Black women and 30% of births to White women.[10]

We discussed earlier how Becker's theory of the family could be used to explain the traditional specialization of labor that we used to observe in the household (i.e., two parents, mother specializing in home production and father specializing in market work). However, that family structure depended on a maintenance of rigid gender roles and the ability of the husband to earn enough money to support his wife and children. Now, an increasing number of married-couple families are **dual earner families,** and in a number of those families, the wife earns more than her husband. With both spouses working, the family then must make a decision about child care. Although some families juggle their work schedules so that at least one parent can care for the child while the other works and vice versa, it is more often the case that some sort of nonparental child care is used when both parents work. Policymakers and the public have expressed concern over the quality of this care, and some have even questioned whether or not women should work outside the home; to our knowledge, none have questioned whether or not fathers should work outside the home.

---

[10]*Statistical Abstract of the United States,* 2001, table no. 77.

These changes in family life occurred at the same time that other related transformations were taking place in the lives of women. In the 1960s, legislation aimed at eradicating discrimination and a reemergence of the feminist movement helped women to make gains in the labor market. Women began to obtain more education and to find that there were more opportunities open to them in the labor market. Attitudes toward women working began to liberalize and traditional gender roles became more relaxed. A working woman is no longer seen as an anomaly. Society became more tolerant of a variety of living situations. Thus, many of these changes in family life are the result of women having more choice and more control over their bodies. The birth control pill, for example, freed women to control their fertility more reliably than had been possible in the past. As women became more self-sufficient, they began to expect more from their marriages and to leave those marriages if they were finding them unfulfilling. As they entered the labor force, the gains to marriage based on specialization fell. The typical American family is anything but typical. American children find themselves in myriad family relationships, and many children will live in several types of families as they grow.

The Effect of Family Structure on Child Well-Being

An enormous amount of research addresses the effect of family structure on child well-being. Researchers from many disciplines have asked how these dramatic changes in families affect the children that experience them. There are no easy answers; nevertheless, we try to synthesize the latest findings, particularly those of economists who tend to focus on establishing causality. Understanding whether or not family structure causes adverse child outcomes is critically important for policymakers. In this section, we examine the consequences of growing up in a single-parent family, and we address issues related to dual earner families in the following section.

The Impact of Family Structure—Theory and Methods

Here we start by examining the consequences for children of growing up in a family headed by only one parent. We would like to ascertain whether or not the rise in single-parent families per se has had a detrimental effect on children's well-being. However, establishing causality is difficult at best. It may be the case that the factors associated with divorce are also correlated with adverse outcomes for children. For example, families that will eventually experience divorce often go through periods of high conflict. Children growing up in this environment might find it difficult to concentrate in school; consequently, they may perform poorly in school. In this case, it is not necessarily the divorce that causes the child to perform poorly but the degree of conflict present in the home. Children in intact families may also experience conflict, but most likely it is to a much lesser degree. What we want to know is whether children now living in divorced families would be better off if their parents had not divorced. We can ask the same type of question about a child born out of wedlock. If, all else being equal, the mother had married the father of the child, how would the child's well-being be affected? Economists sometimes refer to this inquiry as the **counterfactual.** Unfortunately, we cannot observe the counterfactual. In this case, a random assignment experiment where children are randomly assigned to live in an intact family or have their parents divorced is simply not possible. Thus, it is necessary to resort to other techniques to untangle the causal effects of family structure on child well-being.

To assess child well-being, we need to have some sort of a definition of child well-being. Economists usually measure this as *children's attainment* (i.e., the level of success that a child achieves in young adulthood). In this case, success is often defined or measured as one or more of the following: schooling, occupation, earnings, whether or not the child has a teen birth, and welfare receipt. These are chosen as outcomes because all have been shown to be highly correlated with or direct indicators of adult economic success. If children reach adulthood and are able to care for themselves without receiving welfare, then the government saves money. Some researchers have also used measures of children's cognitive ability and behavior problems assessed when the child is relatively young—sometimes as young as age 3.

We also need to have a theoretical framework for assessing the mechanism by which family structure affects child well-being. As we have emphasized throughout this book, economists rely on theoretical models to guide their research. Thus, when examining family structure and child well-being, we need to determine what framework economists use to assess this relationship. The basic economic model of fertility decision making presented in Chapter 5 provides a framework for understanding how family structure affects children's well-being. Parents receive utility from child services as well as other goods. Child services are produced using a household production function.

The inputs to child services include parental time and purchased goods and services from the market. Parents make decisions about labor supply, the number of children in the family, where the family lives, and how many times the family moves or changes structure. These choices all influence children's well-being and thus can be expected to influence their economic well-being as adults. The amount of resources that the family devotes to children and the timing of the distribution of these resources also affects children's outcomes. This suggests that the characteristics of the child's parents, often referred to as family background by economists, as well as the characteristics of the child matter. Family income and time spent with children also affect attainments.[11]

The Impact of Family Structure—Evidence

Now that we have a measure of children's outcomes and a theoretical model, let's look at the research that has been conducted. Here we will focus on the biggest change to family structure—the increased likelihood that a child will spend some time living with only one parent. The best place to start is to review the work of McLanahan and Sandefur (1994)[12] whose work has been highly influential in this area. They start by asking how a father's absence is expected to lower a child's well-being (because most children still live with their mother after a divorce).

They note that there are several ways in which the absence of a father can be detrimental to a child's welfare. First, when a father leaves the family, there is a loss of economic resources. We already established in Chapter 12 that children in female-headed families are far more likely to live in poverty. Family disruption does not always need to lead to a loss of economic resources, though it is certainly common. When parents live apart, two households must be maintained—thus there is a loss of economies of scale (i.e., they can no longer benefit from sharing expenses). Remarriage would bring back some of the economies of scale, but not all divorced women remarry. When a household splits, the income is not necessarily distributed equally. Consider a family with two children and a total income of $50,000. When the parents split,

---

[11]Other disciplines, notably sociology and developmental psychology, naturally have much to say about these issues as well. Robert Haveman and Barbara Wolfe, "The Determinants of Children's Attainments: A Review of Methods and Findings," *Journal of Economic Literature,* Vol. 33, pp. 1829–1878, 1995, provide a nice summary of the various theoretical perspectives.

[12]McLanahan and Sandefur, "Growing up with a Single Parent: What Hurts, What Helps," Cambridge: Harvard University Press, 1994.

the father may get $25,000 of the income while the mother and two children must split the remainder. This is part of the reason women do not fare as well economically after a divorce when compared to men.

In addition to the loss of income experienced when a family breaks up, children lose out on other resources. A single parent has less time to supervise homework, to volunteer at a child's school, or to read to a child. Single parents may be more stressed as they try to raise their children and work without the daily support and help of a partner. Children of single parents move more often than children in intact families. This phenomenon may be attributable to a single mother taking a job or a change in family structure such as a stepfather moving into the home. Frequent moves make it less likely that a family is able to make an attachment to the community and/or to develop a network of friends and contacts.

In addition, the parental conflict that often arises before a divorce or separation may also be harmful to a child's well-being. Thus, in some cases, divorce may be good for children, although, even in the case of an amicable divorce, there is likely to be disruption to the children.

McLanahan and Sandefur examine the link between several child outcomes and growing up in a single-parent family. As measures of children's well-being, they use failing to graduate from high school, having a teenage birth, or being idle (neither employed or in school). All of these events can be expected to lower one's later economic success.

McLanahan and Sanderfur found that family structure is highly correlated with child well-being even after controlling for a wide array of factors that might affect child well-being, including race, sex of the child, parental education, number of siblings, and place of residence. Specifically, they found that children in single-parent households were more likely to drop out of high school, have a teen birth, and be idle. Their results are summarized in Figure 15.2, separately by race. The numbers in Figure 15.2 represent the probability of each outcome for each family structure group; the difference in the probabilities is a measure of the impact of family structure or child outcomes. In all cases, children raised in two-parent families do better in terms of these outcomes than children in one-parent families. Figure 15.2 clearly shows that family structure matters.

McLanahan and Sandefur then asked whether the type of single-parent family matters for example, whether children whose parents divorced or are sep-

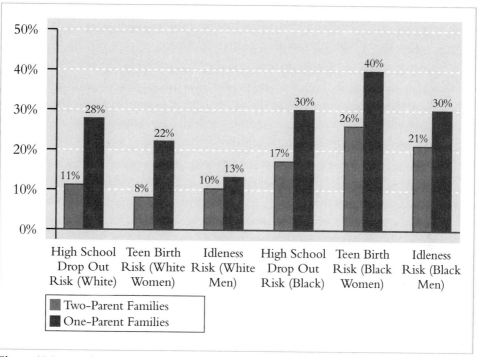

Figure 15.2   Family Structure and Child Outcomes by Race

Source: Sarah McLanahan and Gary Sandefur, *Growing Up With a Single Parent: What Hurts, What Helps* (Cambridge, Mass.: Harvard University Press, 1994.) Copyright © 1994 by the President and Fellows of Harvard College.

arated fare differently from children who lost a parent due to an untimely death or children whose mothers were not married when they were born. They expected that children of widowed moms would fare better than children who find themselves in female-headed families as a result of divorce/ separation or because their mother never married. This may be because these children are less likely to have experienced parental conflict and because their mothers are financially more stable. Widows and their children often receive life insurance and Social Security benefits upon the death of a parent.

To address these questions, McLanahan and Sandefur divided their sample of children into three groups: those whose parents were divorced or separated, those who had lost a parent through death, and those who were born to a single mother. They found that all three groups were disadvantaged compared to children in intact families but that children raised by widowed mothers do better than children raised by divorced/separated or never-married mothers. Thus, they found that being in a single-parent family, no matter what the type, has detrimental effects on child well-being, although the type of single parent family matters. These differences are worrisome for policymakers given the increasing prevalence of single-parent families. In their survey of the research on family structure and child outcomes, Haveman and Wolfe note that: "In all of the studies that included information on family structure, growing up in a one-parent family (or experiencing divorce or marital separation) is negatively related to the level of schooling attained and in most cases is statistically significant" (p.1856).[13]

It is important to stress that even McLanahan and Sandefur do not claim that their results indicate that single parenthood *causes* these adverse outcomes for children. Rather their approach is to control for a variety of factors to try to isolate the effect of family structure on children's outcomes, but they recognize that they still may not uncover the causal effect of family structure on child well-being. This is because there may be unmeasured factors that are correlated with both family structure and children's outcomes. Economists usually call this the **endogeneity problem.**

For example, single parenthood is associated with both low parental education and alcohol abuse. Although McLanahan and Sandefur were able to control for parental education, they did not have information on alcohol abuse. Thus, the results they present could be measuring the effects of alcohol abuse on children's outcomes rather than the effects of family structure. Other unmeasurable factors—such as the parent's placing a low value on education, being depressed, or lacking motivation—could be correlated with children's outcomes. Because these factors are difficult to observe and measure, we cannot be certain that we have isolated the causal effect of family structure on children's attainment unless we attempt specifically to design a study that allows us to control for these factors. In other words, what we need is **exogenous variation** in family structure (i.e., variation in family structure that is not correlated with child attainments). As we noted earlier, a **random assignment experiment** would be best. If we could take a group of intact families and randomly assign some of them to get divorced and the others to stay together, we could then measure the causal effect of divorce on children's well-being. Naturally, such an experiment is not feasible.

---

[13]Robert Haveman and Barbara Wolfe, "The Determinants of Children's Attainments: A Review of Methods and Findings," *Journal of Economic Literature,* Vol. 33, pp. 1829–1878, 1995.

From a policy perspective, determining whether family structure causes adverse outcomes for children is very important. If it is the characteristics of the parents themselves rather than not having two parents per se that matters, then policies aimed at keeping families together are not likely to be effective in improving children's well-being.

There have been recent attempts to disentangle correlation from causality in this area of research. For example, Sandefur and Wells used a study of siblings to isolate the causal effects of growing up in a single-parent family.[14] They used this information to ask how family structure affected educational attainment. Because siblings experience the same unmeasurable family characteristics, researchers are able to net out the effect of these unmeasurables thereby getting a cleaner estimate of the causal effect of family structure on educational attainment.

Consider a family with two children. When the children are 4 and 9, the parents divorce. The youngest child has spent five fewer years in the intact family than the older child. Given that both children experienced that same family environment before the divorce, a comparison of the outcomes of the oldest and youngest child provides a look at how the change in family structure affected the educational attainment of the two children. This method allows the researchers to control for unobservable family-specific factors that could be correlated with both the child's outcome and the parent's divorce/separation. Using this method, Sandefur and Wells found that, taking into account unmeasured family characteristics, the effect of family structure on educational attainment is smaller than previous estimates had indicated but still statistically significant. Specifically, each additional year of fatherlessness reduces educational attainment. However, even this approach is not perfect; divorce may have a different impact on older and younger siblings. For example, perhaps age 4 is a time of bonding with parents whereas children of age 9 are more able to withstand such events. The negative effect of divorce on the 4 year old may not really be a consequence of fewer years with the father but may instead reflect the timing of the event. This possibility makes distinguishing between the effect of the divorce per se from the effect of when the divorce occurred difficult.

---

[14]Gary Sandefur and Thomas Wells, "Using Siblings to Investigate the Effects of Family Structure on Educational Attainment," Institute for Research on Poverty, Discussion paper no. 1144-97, 1997.

Lang and Zagorsky take a different approach from Sandefur and Wells in their attempt to sort out causality versus correlation.[15] Ideally, we would like to compare children who grew up in different types of family structures (e.g., two-parent versus one-parent) but hold unobservable factors such as parenting ability constant. Thus, they examine children whose parents died, reasoning as did McLanahan and Sandefur that parental death is less likely to be correlated with the unobservable factors (such as parental ability) that might affect both the probability of living in a single-parent family and a child's outcomes.

They reason that if losing a parent from death has less of an adverse affect on a child's outcomes than losing a parent due to divorce, then some of the adverse affects of divorce are likely attributable to unobservable factors that are correlated with both the divorce and child outcomes.

They were able to control for a much larger array of family background variables than McLanahan and Sandefur, including parental alcohol abuse. They concluded that even after attempting to control more precisely for some of the unobserved factors that might cause adverse outcomes, there is still an adverse impact of divorce on child well-being but that it is much smaller than previous research would suggest. Thus, the authors note that "the social impact of this changing family structure is likely to be much less negative than simple analysis would suggest since there is little evidence that parental presence early in life affects economic well-being later".[16]

The research discussed here focused on being raised by one or two parents and examined the effect of being raised in a family where the parents were cohabiting. In fact, it is only recently that research has begun to be conducted on the well-being of children in cohabiting families. Studying the effect of cohabitation on children's well-being is complicated by the fact that not all cohabiting families are alike—some consist of the child's two biological parents who are simply not married. Others may be headed by the mother and her partner or the father and his partner. Recognizing that the dynamics and power structures in these types of families may differ from a married family is important when assessing the effects of these types of families on child well-

---

[15]Kevin Lang and Jay L. Zagorsky, "Does Growing Up with a Parent Absent Really Hurt?" *Journal of Human Resources,* Vol. 36, No. 2, pp. 253–273, 2001.

[16]Kevin Lang and Jay L. Zagorsky, "Does Growing Up with a Parent Absent Really Hurt?" *Journal of Human Resources,* Vol. 36, No. 2, pp. 253–273, 2001.

being. Questions here center around whether it is better for the child to be reared by two adults—who might be able to provide more resources including time and money to the family—or by just one parent.

Manning and Lamb[17] examined whether adolescents who live in cohabiting-parent step-families fare as well as adolescents living in married-parent step-families and whether teens in unmarried-mother-cohabiting families fare better or worse than children living with unmarried single mothers. Their results suggest that teens living in a married-parent step-family do better than teens living in a cohabiting step-family situation. However, their results only imply a correlation. Further research will be necessary to determine if the marriage of the step-parents is the cause of the advantage of teens in that family structure.

Family Structure and Income

One of the largest concerns about these changes in family structure is income. It is well known that families headed by one parent, particularly female-headed families, are more likely to be in poverty than two-parent families. In 2002, 26.5% of all female-headed families were in poverty, while only 5.3% of all married-couple families were in poverty.[18] However, many women who bear children out of wedlock will eventually marry or cohabit with a partner, and many divorced parents remarry. Thus, it is of interest to know how children's economic resources differ depending upon family structure. A large body of research establishes that family structure is related to the economic well-being of children (i.e., those in two-parent families have higher incomes than those in one-parent families). It may seem rather obvious that families with two potential breadwinners should have more economic resources than those with one, but many married women still chose not to work in the labor market when their children are small so two-parent families do not necessarily have more income than single-parent families.

In 2000, the Census Bureau reported that the median family income for a two-parent married couple family was $59,184, whereas the median family income for a female-headed family was $25,794.[19] This is a substantial differ-

[17]Wendy D. Manning and Kathleen Lamb, "Parental Cohabitation and Adolescent Wellbeing," Center for Family and Demographic Research, Bowling Green State University, Working paper series 02-04, 2002.
[18]"Poverty in the United States: 2002," *Current Population Reports,* issued Sept. 2003 by B. Proctor and J. Dalaker.
[19]http://www.census.gov/hhes/income/income00/inctab4.html.

ence. In fact, McLanahan and Sandefur (1994)[20] estimated that as much as 50% of the adverse outcome for children in single-parent families can be attributed to the lower income of single-parent families. But this does not definitively establish that the absence of one parent *causes* the lower family income. We next examine how divorce affects income.

Duncan and Hoffman (1985)[21] were among the first to consider the economic impact of divorce from a dynamic standpoint (i.e., rather than looking at divorce at a point in time, they examined it over time). They studied the impact of divorce and separation on the economic status of men and women using longitudinal data from the Panel Survey of Income Dynamics for the years 1969–1975. Using these data, they charted family income for a sample of children between the ages of 1 and 5 in the year prior to their parent's divorce, from the year before the divorce until five years after the divorce. They compared income from the divorced sample to a sample of children whose parents were continuously married during that same time frame.

They found that the average income of families with children where the parents divorced fell by 30% in the year immediately following the divorce, but five years later the average income of the families of the custodial parent was close to its pre-divorce level. This is attributed to high rates of remarriage. The incomes of those families where the mothers do not remarry remain about 30% lower. Although the family income of the children whose parents divorced does rise back to near its initial levels, those income levels are still behind those of their peers in two-parent families because the incomes in the two-parent families are also growing over this time period.

Extending the findings of Hoffman and Duncan, Page and Stevens found that the average family income of families who will eventually undergo a divorce is lower than that for those families who never experience a divorce. This suggests that at least some of the difference in income across two-parent and single-parent families is probably attributable to factors other than these differences in family structure; in other words, these families had lower incomes in the beginning. Furthermore, they showed that a woman who is single when her children are born is more likely to be Black and to have lower education

---

[20]McLanahan and Sandefur, "Growing up with a Single Parent: What Hurts, What Helps," Cambridge: Harvard University Press, 1994.

[21]Greg Duncan and Saul Hoffman, "A Reconsideration of the Economic Consequences of Marital Dissolution," *Demography,* Vol. 22, pp. 485–497, 1985.

and lower income than a woman who gives birth in wedlock. They also note that 50% of the children in single-parent families will eventually see their mothers marry. The family income of children whose parents divorce and remain divorced for six years or more falls by 40 to 45%. Children born to unwed mothers will see their family's income increase by an average of 50% if their mother marries and remains married for at least six years. However, they also find that upon divorce, the mother's behavior changes in ways that tend to mitigate the economic consequences of the martial dissolution—she may go on welfare, or start working, or other family members contribute resources to the family.[22] Finally, Page and Stevens note that their estimates of income loss associated with divorce or being born to a single mother are smaller than we previously thought because they carefully control for factors correlated with income and single parenthood.[23]

What this line of research seems to have established quite clearly is that there is a nontrivial difference in the incomes of single-parent families versus two-parent families and that some of this is simply caused by the fact that families who will eventually divorce are disadvantaged economically anyway. Remarriage, welfare receipt, cohabitation, and child support can all mitigate the income loss to some extent. What we examine next is how much these income differences matter for child well-being.

Family Income and Child Outcomes

In a recent study, economist David Blau[24] asked how much family income matters in determining the cognitive, social, and behavioral development of young children. This relationship is of paramount interest because it has clear policy implications. If, for example, it is shown that income matters with respect to child development, then the appropriate policy is to provide low-income families with more income perhaps by expanding the **Earned Income Tax Credit** (The EITC was discussed in detail in Chapters 12 and 13). However, it might be that income is not as important as providing direct interventions for children such as Head Start programs, public education, and

---

[22]Mariane Page and Ann Huff Stevens, "Will You Miss Me When I Am Gone? The Economic Consequences of Absent Parents," NBER working paper 8786, 2002.

[23]For a recent review of the literature on divorce and women's economic status see Pamela Smock, Wendy Manning, and Sanjiv Gupta, "The Effect of Marriage and Divorce on Women's Economic Well-being," *American Sociological Review,* Vol. 64, pp. 794–812, 1999.

[24]David Blau, "The Effect of Income on Child Development," *Review of Economics and Statistics,* Vol. 81, No. 2, pp. 261–276, 1999.

health insurance. In other words, what poor families might need more than income is help in raising their children—including parenting classes and other services.

Blau used data on younger children and measured their developmental outcomes. His outcomes included scores on a test of math and reading ability, a score on a picture vocabulary test, and an index of behavior problems. He documented that there are large differences between the developmental outcomes of children in different income groups. As expected, children in families with higher incomes have better developmental outcomes. He then examined the impact of income, controlling for various family background factors and child-specific factors on child outcomes. He found that income has a small effect on child outcomes and that it would take very large and lasting increases in income to increase developmental outcomes for low-income children. He noted that large changes are not likely to be politically feasible. This is a surprising finding because it indicates that government income-support programs have only a very small impact on child development. Yet, such programs are often justified on the grounds that they benefit children. If extra income does not work, what is the alternative? How else can we help raise the achievement of children from disadvantaged families?

Another option is **direct intervention.** In other words, rather than providing families with money, provide them with a service designed to increase the well-being of their children directly. One example is **Head Start,** the government-run preschool program for disadvantaged children. Head Start provides a direct intervention for poor children. Started in 1964 with President Johnson's War on Poverty, the program teaches poor children the skills that will ready them for school. Currie and Thomas[25] took a unique approach to ascertaining the effects of Head Start on a child's cognitive ability and school performance among other outcomes. They used data where there are groups of siblings in the same family. Many studies take advantage of sibling comparisons as a way to control for differences that are difficult to measure. By comparing siblings from intact families, we can be reasonably sure that they experienced the same family background and thus that we are getting a better measure of the effect of Head Start on achievement rather than confounding

---

[25]Janet Currie and Duncan Thomas, "Does Head Start Make a Difference?" *American Economic Review,* Vol. 85, No. 3, pp. 341–364, 1995.

the effect of Head Start with unobservable family background factors such as parenting practices. They compared the outcomes of siblings where one went to a Head Start program and one did not. They focused on intact families so that their findings are not confounded by the potential negative effects of being in a single-parent family.

One drawback to this approach is that when a family sends one but not all siblings to Head Start, some sort of a **child-specific selection effect** may be operating. For example, if the family has one sibling who is particularly bright (or perhaps one that is particularly slow academically), they may elect to send that sibling to Head Start believing that child will benefit from the program. In this case, the program is not benefiting the child; the apparent positive (or negative) impact of Head Start might just reflect the fact that the child is enrolled in the program because he/she is already very bright (or already behind). Because of this selection problem, Currie and Duncan supplement their analysis with a **difference-in-difference analysis.**

In Chapter 2, we discussed how a difference-in-difference analysis would work. It helps us to control for situations where there may be initial differences between groups and in some ways mimics a random assignment experiment. In this case, children enrolled in Head Start were the treatment group and children enrolled in another type of preschool were the control group. They then compared the impact of Head Start relative to no preschool as well as the impact of another type of preschool relative to no preschool. This comparison of the change in the outcome for the treatment groups with the change in the outcome for the control group is the difference-in-differences approach.

Head Start was found to have a positive and statistically significant effect on the test scores and schooling attainment of White children. However, for Black children, there is an initial increase in test scores that is quickly lost, and no positive effects on schooling attainment are recorded. Head Start does improve both White and Black children's access to health care. Specifically, both White and Black children who attend Head Start are more likely to be immunized. Overall, the authors conclude that Head Start is a success for White children, but questions remain about its cost-effectiveness for Black children.

We've shown that it is possible that children raised in two-parent families may have an edge when it comes to development and later socioeconomic status. Be careful. Correlation does *not* imply causation, and research in this area, like all others, must be critically assessed before the direction of causality can be inferred with confidence. In the next section, we turn our attention to a different kind of family structure—intact families where both parents work.

The Effects of Dual Earner Married Couple Families on Child Well-Being

In this section, we ask what the effects for children are of having both parents work in the formal labor market. Such families are called dual earner families. Table 15.2 presents some statistics on dual earner families. Our discussion here focuses on dual earner married couples. We recognize that there are many cohabitation couples who are dual earners, but data on these couples is not as readily available.

First, note that from 1970 to 2000 the proportion of dual earner families climbed from 39.3% to 62.1%. Dual earner families have incomes now that are 1.7 times larger than families with single earners, and their incomes have

	1970	1980	1990	1999 (unless noted)
Dual earners as a percent of all married couples	39.3%	50.2%	58.1%	62.1% (2000)
Median income of dual earner, married-couple family, in 1999 dollars	N.A.	$54,111	$59,625	$66,529
Median income of married-couple family, wife not in paid labor force, in 1999 dollars	N.A.	$38,405	$38,578	$38,626
Ratio of median income of dual earner married-couple families to one earner, married-couple families	N.A.	1.42	1.55	1.72

Table 15.2   Dual Earner Families and Median Income, 1970–1999.

Sources: *Statistical Abstract of the United States*, 2001, tables no. 673, 674, and U.S. Census Bureau, Historical Time Series Tables—Families, Table F-7.

grown over time, while those of single earner families have remained stagnant. This is because men's earnings have remained relatively constant over this time period while women's earnings have increased.

What kind of an impact does growing up in a family where both parents work have on the children? Although two working parents clearly leads to more economic resources for the family on average, there is concern that children are being deprived of parental time. Furthermore, when both parents work, children under the age of 12 or so require some type of care except in the case where parents work opposing work schedules so as not to place the children in nonparental child care. How does the type of care chosen affect the well-being of children? Our model of fertility, developed in Chapter 5, indicates that parents receive utility from child services (among other goods and services) and that the production of child services entails both time and money. When both parents work, child services must be, in many cases, produced with purchased market goods and services and with less of the parental time input.

Because mothers have traditionally been the primary child care providers, the sharp increase in maternal employment over the last several decades has led to substantial changes in young children's experiences and environments, which has led to concerns over the effect of the loss of maternal time on child development. We addressed the issue of the quality of child care on children's development in Chapter 14 on family policy and documented that quality child care matters—particularly for low-income children. Here we focus more specifically on the effect of the type of nonmaternal child care used on children's well-being.

First, we ask why maternal employment might be associated with child well-being. Desai, Chase-Landsdale, and Michael [26] note that there are three channels by which maternal employment might be associated with negative outcomes for children. First, particularly during a child's first year of life, separation from the mother for long periods of time may be detrimental to the mother-child attachment relationship. The child may not bond securely to the mother, and this may lead to difficulties later in life. Second, the stress that the mother may feel trying to balance work and child care may mean

---

[26]This paragraph draws from Sonalde Desai, P. Lindsay Chase-Landsdale, and Robert Michael, "Mother or Market: Effects of Maternal Employment on the Intellectual Ability of 4-Year-Old Children," *Demography*, Vol. 26, No. 4, pp. 545–561, 1989.

that the interactions she has with her children are fewer and of lower quality. Third, the quality of the nonmaternal child care she uses may affect her child's well-being.

A growing literature in economics examines the effect of nonmaternal and nonparental child care on children's well-being. Many of these studies focus on two-parent families; however, more work is being done on child care choices and outcomes for single-parent families. These studies have several features in common. They typically use data collected on thousands of children when the children were preschool aged. They have information on a child's family background (parent's age, education, race) and what kind of child care was used, and on measures of cognitive ability or behavior problems, usually assessed when the child is preschool or school age. For example, the **Peabody Picture Vocabulary test** is an often-used measure of cognitive ability, and the **Behavior Problems Index** is an often-used measure of a child's behavior. These can both be thought of as outcomes. One of the most frequently used data sets is the National Longitudinal Survey of Youth (NLSY). This data set contains extensive child care and labor force information on mothers and their children. The research discussed here is research that has used the NLSY and has mostly been conducted by economists. Developmental psychologists also conduct considerable research in this area.

The usual approach taken by economists is to use regression analysis to examine the relationships between measures of child well-being and a host of control variables including the type of child care that the child receives. The hope is that by controlling for as many family background characteristics as possible, these models can measure the effect of child care per se on the child's outcomes. The problem is that this type of analysis cannot rule out that some unobserved characteristic is driving the results. For example, mothers who work when their children are very young may differ from other mothers in ways that may affect their child's outcomes. Some researchers have been able to circumvent that problem by using comparisons of siblings. They compare siblings who had different experiences. Perhaps for one child the mother did not work, whereas for the second she did. Each child has the same family background (thus the same unobservable family characteristics) but a different child care experience.

The results of these studies are not entirely conclusive—some find that maternal work is not detrimental to the child; others find it is. It is probably fair to say that the latest research in this area has found that maternal employment during the first year of a child's life may have some detrimental effects but that the effects may disappear after the first year of the child's life.[27] Because of the potential detrimental effects of nonmaternal child care during a child's first year of life, some are calling for extended maternity and parental leave to allow parents more time home with their children.[28]

Aside from the child care concerns that dual earners face, they more generally face a time squeeze.[29] How to fit in lessons, sports, after-school activities, and other leisure activities in addition to the necessities such as sleep, food shopping, and preparation is a problem that vexes both dual earner and single-parent families.

Figure 15.3 documents the hours worked by married couples with children under age 18 from 1969 to 1999. Note that wives' hours have increased, while the husband's hours have remained relatively constant. In fact, women are working twice as many hours as they did in 1969. Clearly, time issues are important for dual earner couples, and as Box 15.1 makes clear, children's health may suffer.

As we saw in Chapter 14, the United States now provides unpaid family leave. There are also myriad child care subsidies available to families, although there is concern by some policymakers that neither of these policies goes far enough. Many firms have adopted some other family-friendly policies to help their employees cope with the increasing demands on their time. Some firms now offer **job sharing.** This is a situation where two people can share a job, giving both people more time with their families. Often benefits are not available because each person is working part-time. This may not be a problem for a married woman because she can often obtain benefits through her husband's job. Flex-time allows employees to set their own schedule, usually within some limits, as to when they will arrive at and leave work. **Telecommuting,** or virtual office, is a situation where an employee works from home

---

[27]F. D. Blau and A. J. Grossberg, "Maternal Labor Supply and Children's Cognitive Development," *The Review of Economics and Statistics,* Vol. 74, No. 3, pp. 474–481, 1992; E. Harvey, "Short-Term and Long-Term Effects of Early Parental Employment on Children of the NLSY," *Developmental Psychology,* Vol. 35, pp. 445–459, 1999; J. Waldfogel, W. Han, and J. Brooks-Gunn, "The Effects of Early Maternal Employment and Child Cognitive Development," *Demography,* Vol. 39, No. 2, pp. 369–392, 2002; and Chris Ruhm, "Parental Employment and Child Cognitive Development," *Journal of Human Resources,* forthcoming.

[28]J. Brooks-Gunn, J. Waldfogel, and W. Han, "Maternal Employment and Child Cognitive Outcomes in the First Three Years of Life," *Child Development,* Vol. 73, No. 4, pp. 1052–1072, 2002.

[29]See Council of Economic Advisors, "Families and the Labor Market, 1969–1999: Analyzing the "Time Crunch," May 1999, or Cordelia W. Reimers, "Parent's Work and the Family: Thirty Years of Change," in The *Economics of Work and Family,* edited by Jean Kimmel and Emily P. Hoffman, Upjohn: Kalamazoo, MI, pp. 71–104, 2002.

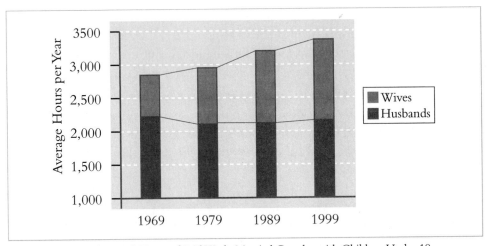

Figure 15.3   Total Annual Hours of Paid Work, Married Couples with Children Under 18

Source: Cordelia W. Reimers, "Parent's Work and the Family: Thirty Years of Change," in *The Economics of Work and Family,* edited by Jean Kimmel and Emily P. Hoffman, Upjohn: Kalamazoo, MI, pp. 71–104, 2002. Reprinted with permission from the W. E. Upjohn Institute.

and communicates with the office via e-mail and telephone. Although this is gaining in popularity, there is the possibility that employees who go this route will feel isolated and overlooked when promotion time comes.

Dual earner couples also face the choice of whose career takes precedence. For many couples, jobs where both partners are expected to meet, move, or travel on a moment's notice are not feasible when children are involved. Furthermore, when asked to move, couples often must decide who will be the spouse whose career is more important. Traditionally, many couples have given the husband's career priority, leaving the wife's career to suffer.[30] Some universities and other employers have begun to recognize this and offer programs to help spouses find jobs when a move is necessary.

The Distribution of Resources Within the Family

Thus far, we have assumed that the family is sort of a "black box." Resources come into the family and then the family distributes or allocates its resources as it best sees fit to members within the family. However, how do we know

[30]See Anne E. Winkler and David C. Rose, "Career Hierarchy in Dual-Earner Families," *Research in Labor Economics,* Vol. 19, edited by Solomon Polachek, Greenwich, Conn.: JAI Press, 2000, Chapter 6, pp. 147–172, for discussion regarding how dual earner couples make career decisions.

BOX 15.1 WOMEN'S EMPLOYMENT AND CHILDREN'S OBESITY

One final issue that is receiving some attention lately in the media is the increase in childhood obesity in the United States. Obesity is related to several health problems including diabetes. This increase has paralleled the increase in labor force participation rates of mothers. Of course, just because both have risen fairly steadily over the past several decades does not mean that one causes the other. Remember, correlation does not imply causation. However, given that dual earner families and single-parent families have less time than do families where only one parent works in the labor market, they may be more likely to rely on fast food as a way to feed their families. It is well-documented that fast food is usually much higher in calories and fat than meals that are prepared at home. Furthermore, children who are left at home while their parents work may have access to high-calorie snacks and may not make wise choices about which snacks are the healthiest. However, working parents, because they may have higher incomes, may also be more informed about nutrition. Children in after-school programs may have an opportunity to play sports and get exercise.

Recent empirical evidence suggests that there is a link between rising childhood obesity and maternal employment. Specifically, Anderson, Butcher, and Levine found that the intensity of the mother's employment (i.e., how many hours she works) is a factor in determining whether or not her child is obese. A mother increasing her hours of work from twenty to forty hours a week will likely cause a 1 to 2 percentage point increase in the probability that her child is obese.

Source: Patricia Anderson, Kristin Butcher, and Philip Levine, "Maternal Employment and Overweight Children," *Journal of Health Economics,* forthcoming.

that resources are distributed equally within the family? Why should we care? Should one family member have access to more resources than another? Recall that in Chapter 3, we developed a model of marriage where the potential gains to marriage were instrumental in the decision to marry. However, we did not discuss how these gains were distributed other than to note what would happen when the gains were distributed equally.

Until relatively recently, economists did not have much to say on this issue. The traditional approach assumed that households maximized one household utility function; the household was essentially treated as a single person. All resources were pooled and then allocated. Either an **altruistic dictator** made the allocation decision,[31] or all household members were assumed to have the same preferences—what economists call the **common preference assumption.** The altruistic dictator assumption is problematic because there is little evidence that this is how families behave. The common preference assumption is problematic because, as we have discussed so often in this book, economic theory emphasizes the importance of each individual having their own preferences. Within this framework, if the family were to experience an increase in its nonearned income, the prediction is that this additional income would be allocated in the same manner no matter which family member received the increase. In other words, if the mother receives the money, she would distribute it to family members the same way that the father would if he had received it since they are assumed to have the same preferences.

Economists are increasingly interested in the **intrafamily allocation of resources,** i.e. how resources are actually allocated within families. Researchers have taken a variety of different approaches. The key to this research is that new models of intrafamily resource allocation allow for **heterogenous preferences** among family members—a much more realistic assumption. In other words, not all family members have the same preferences, nor is there an altruistic dictator who divides resources among family members. Importantly, these models also note that rather than simply pool their income, household members often have an incentive to allocate resources that they control toward goods that they care relatively more about.

One set of models assumes a bargaining approach.[32] These **bargaining models** allow us to link our models of marriage to how the gains from marriage are distributed. As Lundberg and Pollak note: "Bargaining models place distribution within marriage in a theoretical framework that is consistent with existing analyses of marriage and of divorce: two decisionmakers with well-defined preferences choosing an action or strategy from a well-specified set of alternatives" (Lundberg and Pollak, 1996[33] (p. 156).

---

[31]See Gary S. Becker, "A Theory of Marriage: Part II," *Journal of Political Economy,* Vol. 82, No. 2, pp. 11–26, 1974, for a discussion of the altruist model that he introduced.

[32]Marjorie McElroy and Mary Jean Horney, "Nash Bargained Household Decisions," *International Economic Review,* Vol. 22, No. 2, pp. 333–350, 1981, were among the first to develop such models.

[33]S. Lundberg and R. Pollack, "Bargaining and Distribution in Marriage," *Journal of Economic Perspectives,* pp. 139–158, Fall 1996.

To understand this approach, consider a husband and wife who are making decisions about how to run their household. They must decide how to best allocate their time between market work and household production and also how to distribute what they have earned and produced. It is certainly possible that they may have different preferences about how best to spend their income; in that case, they then bargain over how income will be allocated. Each is naturally interested in allocating resources towards the goods they care the most about. The relative bargaining power of husband and wife is determined by each individual's **threat point.** The threat point is the level of well-being (utility) that each would achieve if they could not agree on an outcome within the marriage. It is a fall-back point—if their level of utility falls below the threat point the individual will exit the household

Given their preferences, there is a best allocation that makes each as well off as possible. These are called **co-operative bargaining models.** Assuming that both parties have the same information, and equilibrium reached through co-operative bargaining is always **Pareto Optimal.** Pareto optimality is an important idea in economics. When an allocation of resources is Pareto optimal, it is not possible to reallocate resources to make one party better off without making the other party worse off. In this example, when the allocation is Pareto Optimal, it is impossible to reallocate some goods or services from the husband to the wife without making the husband worse off.[34]

In a model where the threat point corresponds to divorce—economists call this a **divorce-threat model**—the threat point depends upon the amount of income that will be controlled by the husband and wife if the marriage ends. It is therefore a function of total family income and the fraction of that income that will be received by each spouse. McElroy also notes that other factors which affect the well-being of divorced men and women but do not affect marital utility also matter.[35] Such factors include the probability of remarriage, the generosity of welfare benefits, the labor market earnings each spouse could receive in the labor market, laws governing child custody and the division of marital property, and various other resources available to divorced men and women. The spouse with the most bargaining power is the

---

[34]These models have been extended to allow for asymmetric information and non cooperative bargaining. See Shelly Lundberg and Robert A. Pollak, 1996. "Bargaining and Distribution in Marriage," *Journal of Economic Perspectives,* 10(4): 139–158 for an accessible review of these models.
[35]McElroy, Majorie. 1990. "The Empirical Content of the Nash-Bargained Household Decisions" *Journal of Human Resources,* Vol. 25, No. 4, 559–583.

spouse who stands to receive the greatest share of total family income in a divorce and who has the best options outside of the marriage.

For example, consider a couple where the division of labor has been along the more traditional lines—the husband has specialized in market work and the wife has specialized in household production. The husband is likely to have the greater threat point because he has remained attached to the labor market and therefore can command higher market earnings than the wife who has been out of the labor force for some time. However, suppose that child custody laws favor women. This will lower the husband's threat point if he values the time with his children. In contrast, for a couple where both spouses have worked continuously in the labor market, the threat points may be quite similar.

The divorce-threat model indicates that the division of resources in a marriage may, in fact, depend heavily on the resources available to each spouse outside of the marriage. The spouse who can command more of the marital output will be the spouse with the higher threat point. Factors that affect the threat point will then determine who has the power within a marriage.

A growing body of empirical evidence has tested whether or not the preferences of the husband and wife differ—in other words, do husbands and wives have different preferences. One of the complicating factors in conducting such research is that a measure of the husband's and wife's relative control over resources is necessary. An obvious candidate would seem to be their labor market earnings. However, this is not a good measure because it is endogenous. As we saw in Chapter 7, labor market earnings are a major determinant of how time is allocated within the household. Thus, we need to have a measure of unearned income that is exogenous (i.e., not related to past or present household behavior). Three recent studies that have tested the common preference hypothesis and have tried to circumvent this endogeneity problem.

In one of the first empirical studies to examine the intrahousehold allocation of resources, Thomas[36] used Brazilian data to test whether or not parents had different preferences concerning nutrient intake and several measures of child health to test specifically whether or not parents wanted to allocate a differ-

---

[36]Duncan Thomas, "Intra-Household Resource Allocation: An Inferential Approach," *Journal of Human Resources,* Vol. 25, No. 4, pp. 635–664, 1990.

ent amount of resources to any of these outcomes.[37] Remember, we take it as given that the parents both care about all of these outcomes—the question is do their preferences differ. In his analysis, nonearned income is used as an indicator of power within the household. Furthermore, he tested whether either parent had a preference to allocate more resources toward sons or daughters.

Thomas found that there are distinct preferences between husbands and wives concerning how resources should be allocated, thus rejecting the common preference assumption and the altruistic dictator explanation. He also found that fathers allocated more resources to boys in terms of improving their nutritional status, while mothers did the same for girls—thus indicating that there are gender preferences.

In another important study, Lundberg, Pollak, and Wales,[38] using data from the United Kingdom, took advantage of an exogenous change in the way the welfare system changed there in the late-1970s. They were able to perform a natural experiment. In the United Kingdom, all families receive a child benefit. Before 1977, this benefit was basically paid to the father because it was a deduction from the income tax. However, after 1977, a legislative change meant that the benefit was now paid in cash to the mother. They argue that this increased women's bargaining power within the marriage.[39] With their data, Lundberg et al. determined that, this change in policy caused changes in household expenditure patterns. Specifically, expenditures on children's and women's clothing increased, evidence that the change in who received the child benefit had important implications as to how resources were allocated within the family. Simply put, when the mother received the money, more was spent on children's clothing than when the father received the money.

---

[37]He considered six outcomes: per capita intake of calories, per capita intake of protein, the number of children ever born to the mother, the survival rate of the children, the child's height for age, and the child's weight for height.

[38]Shelly Lundberg, Robert Pollak, and Terrence Wales, "Do Husbands and Wives Pool Their Resources: Evidence from the United Kingdom Child Benefit," *Journal of Human Resources,* Vol. 32, No. 3, pp. 463–480, 1997.

[39]Shelly Lundberg, Robert Pollak, and Terrence Wales, "Do Husbands and Wives Pool Their Resources: Evidence from the United Kingdom Child Benefit," *Journal of Human Resources,* Vol. 32, No. 3, pp. 436–480, 1997, include a quote from a member of Parliament made on May 13, 1975 which clearly indicates that those involved in legislating the change were well aware that this change would change the way resources were allocated in the family.

Using a related method with U.S. data, Rubalcava and Thomas[40] examined whether or not the AFDC payment level matters in a family bargaining framework. They theorized that AFDC represents a "natural fallback for a low-income woman with children who is contemplating separation from her partner" (p. 2). Thus, AFDC is their measure of power within a marriage. Low-income women with children who live in states with relatively more generous AFDC payments are theorized to have relatively more bargaining power within their marriages. They found evidence suggesting that AFDC generosity has an impact on the bargaining position of women within the household and, in particular, the share of income allocated to food and time allocated to labor market activities are affected by the maximum level of AFDC benefits in the state where the woman resides. They attribute these changes to changes in the relative bargaining power of women.

What all three of these studies (as well as many others) indicate is that the simple model of the family maximizing a common utility function with resources distributed within the family by an altruistic dictator does not seem to capture adequately the realities and the complexities of actual family life. In particular, there is evidence that income in the hands of the mother is more likely to benefit (or be spent on) children as compared to income that the father controls.

These bargaining models have been extended beyond marriage and divorce to examine issues of child custody.[41] The potential policy implications of this research are enormous. Laws that govern how marital property is split and the payment of child benefits have important implications for intrahousehold resource allocation. Policymakers looking to improve children's well-being should be cognizant of these findings.

Who Is Responsible for Children?

In all our discussions thus far, we have treated children as something produced within a family that provides benefits to that particular family in the form of child services. However, some would argue that this is a particularly narrow view of children. Some economists argue that children should be viewed as

---

[40]Luis Rubalcava and Duncan Thomas, "Family Bargaining and Welfare," mimeo, 2000.
[41]See Marco Francesconi and Abhinay Muthoo, "An Economic Model of Child Custody," mimeo, 2003, and Yoram Weiss and Robert J. Willis, "Children as Collective Goods and Divorce Settlements," *Journal of Labor Economics*, Vol. 3, No. 3, pp. 268–292, 1985.

public goods. Perhaps the best known proponent of this view is the feminist economist Nancy Folbre who has written extensively on this issue.

What is a public good? A public good is different from what we would call a **private good** in two important ways. First, it is **non-rival** in consumption— this means that one person's use of the public good does not diminish it so that others can use it as well. Public goods are also **non-exclusive**—people cannot be excluded from using them even if they do not pay for them. National defense is a frequently cited example of a public good. Public goods are inherently subject to the **free-rider problem.** This problem arises when you cannot stop someone from enjoying the public good even when he/she did not pay for it. Because these characteristics of a public good make it difficult to put a price on such a good, government often steps in to pay for the public good.

How is it that children are a public good? Folbre[42] outlines it clearly when she states: "All citizens of the United States enjoy significant claims upon the earnings of future working-age adults through Social Security and public debt. But not all citizens contribute equally to the care of these future adults. Individuals who devote relatively little time or energy to child-rearing are free-riding on parental labor" (p. 86).

In other words, all of society gains from having well-educated, productive citizens. But, not all members of society engage in child rearing. In fact, Folbre believes that many in the United States adhere to a "children as pets" view[43] (i.e., people who want children should pay for them). This is the view of many neoclassical economists. As we saw in Chapter 5 when we studied the economic model of fertility, child services are a potential source of utility to parents. If they get utility, then they will purchase child services.

Folbre argues that this might have been a reasonable view back when children conferred direct benefits to their parents such as old-age security and labor on the family farm. However, with the advent of Social Security and modernization, this view is insufficient. Today, children confer benefits to society, and yet it is mostly mothers who pay the price of children because they spend more of their time rearing them.

For example, consider two individuals who are identical with respect to their marriage and employment histories such that they will receive exactly the

---

[42]Nancy Folbre, "Children as Public Goods," *American Economic Review,* Vol. 84, No. 2, pp. 86–90, 1994.
[43]Nancy Folbre, "Who Should Pay for the Kids?" *Annals of the American Academy,* Vol. 563, p. 197, 1999.

same retirement benefits from Social Security. If one raised several children who now pay the taxes which finance the social security benefits of others, they are helping those families who did not have children. Thus, those who raise children generate a positive externality (i.e., they generate benefits that are enjoyed beyond themselves), particularly if the children raised are productive citizens who pay taxes and produce goods and services.

The cost of raising children has increased enormously over the last fifty years. These increases come, in large part, from the increased cost of a mother's time—as women's wages have risen, so have the costs of children. Education, an essential part of the development of an individual's human capital, has also become more expensive.

So who should bear the costs of children? The tradition in the United States has been to rely on parental altruism (i.e., parents rear children because they love them and privately bear the cost of doing so). Folbre argues that because children are so important to society, we need to reassess how we distribute the costs of raising children. She suggests that increased child support collection and increased public subsidies for child care would help. Furthermore, she argues that we should compensate parents for their efforts perhaps by providing them a tax credit for raising children. Or we could follow the approach taken in France and Sweden and tax the entire working-age population more highly to bear the expenses of the costs of child care. Finally, she argues that families with children should be guaranteed enough income to keep them out of poverty.

Summary

We began this chapter by documenting the tremendous changes in family structure that have occurred in the United States. Marriage rates are falling. Nonmarital births are rising as is cohabitation. Divorce rates remain high. In the majority of marriages both spouses work, even when young children are present. The traditional American family is no longer the norm, if indeed it ever was.

These changes in family structure mean that children are being raised in an environment different from that in the past. They are more likely to be with only one parent. There is considerable evidence indicating that being raised in a single-parent family is correlated with adverse outcomes for children. However, as economists, we are interested in establishing causality. In fact, some evidence indicates that being raised in a single-parent family is the cause of the adverse outcomes; however, the type of single-parent family also matters—children who lost a parent to death do not suffer as much of a penalty, for example. Disentangling correlation from causality is particularly important from the standpoint of policymakers because they have several options. If the absence of the parent is truly the cause of the adverse outcomes for children, then policymakers will want to pursue policies that aim to keep families together. If, however, there is a third factor, such as unobservable maternal ability, that perhaps causes both the adverse child outcomes and the single-parent family, policymakers might do better to focus their efforts on increasing parenting skills.

Dual earner families are quickly becoming the norm among intact families. Yet, there is little evidence to indicate that maternal employment has detrimental effects on children, and, in fact, toddler and preschool-aged children may benefit from receiving some nonmaternal child care. Both dual earner and single-parent families face an increasing time squeeze, and firms could adopt a variety of policies to help such families.

The traditional economic model of the family views the family as a little factory. Inputs of time and market-purchased goods are combined to produce the commodities, including child services that provide utility for family members. Traditionally, economists viewed families as having one utility function so that each member had the same preferences over goods and services or had an altruistic dictator who allocates resources. However, recent research on bargaining models emphasizes that husbands and wives may, in fact, have very different preferences and that the balance of power in a marriage may have important implications for child well-being. Perhaps the most provocative finding in this research is that money in the hands of the mother is more likely to benefit children than money in the hands of the father.

In the United States, we tend to view children and family decisions as private decisions. Parents who need child care contract for this largely on their own. However, this ignores the fact that today's children are tomorrow's labor force, and an educated, productive labor force benefits us all. Our pay-as-you-go Social Security system is one example. Today's workforce is currently supporting today's retirees—even those retirees who did not raise children. Some economists advocate explicit recognition of this by increasing the tax benefits available to parents for raising children.

Key Terms

altruistic dictator   612

bargaining models   612

Behavior Problems Index   608

child-specific selection effect   605

common preference assumption   612

co-operative bargaining models   613

counterfactual   594

difference-in-difference analysis   605

direct intervention   604

divorce-threat model   613

dual earner families   592

Earned Income Tax Credit   603

endogeneity problem   598

exogenous variation   598

free-rider problem   617

Head Start   604

heterogenous preferences   612

intrafamily allocation of resources   612

job sharing   609

non-exclusive   617

non-rival   617

Pareto Optimal   613

Peabody Picture Vocabulary test   608

private good   617

public goods   617

random assignment experiment   598

telecommuting   609

threat point   613

Index

A

Abortion, effect on teen child-bearing, 197–201
Absolute advantage, 69
Absolute measure of poverty, 438
Adjusted gross income (AGI), 495, 568
Advantage
    absolute, 69
    comparative, 69
Adverse selection, 547–548
AFDC. *See* Aid to Families with Dependent Children
AFDC-UP program, 462
Affirmative action, 320n13, 413–416
    effectiveness of, 417–422
After-school care, 534, 560, 561
Age
    divorce rate and marriage, 130
    at first marriage, 54, 97, 587–589
        effect of birth control pill on, 172–173
    gender earnings ratio and, 279–280
    of TANF recipients, 465
Age Discrimination in Employment Act (ADEA; 1967), 408
Agent, 75
Age-specific fertility rates, 141
AGI. *See* Adjusted gross income
Aid to Families with Dependent Children (AFDC), 113, 190–191, 455–461
    labor supply and, 485–488
    payment levels, family bargaining and, 616
    See also Welfare
Akerlof, George, 11
Alan Guttmacher Institute, 185
Albelda, Randy, 472, 473
Alimony, 451
Alm, James, 500
Alternative poverty rates, 479

Altruistic dictator, 612
American Association of University Women, 527
American Economics Association, 11n2
Americans with Disabilities Act (1990), 408
America's Child Care Problem (Bergmann & Helburn), 584
Anderson, Elijah, 193–194
Antidiscrimination laws, 402
    Age Discrimination in Employment Act (ADEA; 1967), 408
    Americans with Disabilities Act (1990), 408
    changes in family structure and, 593
    Civil Rights Act. *See* Civil Rights Act
    Equal Opportunity Act (1972), 407
    Equal Pay Act (1963), 405–406, 408, 417, 432
    Pregnancy Discrimination Act (1978), 407, 542, 548
    Rehabilitation Act (1973), Sections 501 & 505, 408
    Title VII, 405–413, 417–421
    in U.S., 405–413
Antidiscrimination programs, effectiveness of, 417–422
Arguments of the function, 27
Arrow, Kenneth, 9, 335
Asian/Pacific Islanders
    fertility rate of, 146
    teen, 186
    median earnings of, 277
    TANF recipients among, 465
    U.S. poverty rate, 443, 444
Asymmetric information, 340–341, 547–548
At-risk population, 141
AT&T, affirmative action at, 417,

418
Attainment, children's, 594, 596, 597
Audit study, 385–387
Australia
    comparable worth in, 431
    family leave policies in, 555
    gender earnings ratio in, 284, 285
    percent in poverty for single-parent families in, 450
    teen fertility rate in, 187
    women's labor force participation in, 219
Austria
    family leave policies in, 555, 556
    fertility rate in, 147
    gender earnings ratio in, 284, 285
    occupational segregation in, 294, 296
Averett, Susan, 391

B

Baby boom, 144, 170, 222, 318
Baby bust, 144, 170
Backlash (Faludi), 135
Badgett, Lee, 500
Balanced increase in supply, 90
Bargaining, 612–614
Baseball, discrimination in, 337
Becker, Gary, 10, 28, 52, 139, 148, 310n1, 328
Behavior Problems Index, 608
Belarus, 294, 296
Belgium, 284, 285, 555, 556
Benefits
    of educational investment, 311
    of general training, 319
    of on-the-job training, 312
    of specific training, 319
Bergman, Ingrid, 202
Bergmann, Barbara, 14, 336, 369, 535

Bertrand, Marianne, 394
Between-group inequality, 380
Bias
    regression analysis and, 40–41,
        205
    selection, 82
Biddle, Jeff, 391
Birth and Fortune (Easterlin), 171
Birth cohort, 219–220
Birth control pill, effect on fertil-
    ity, 171, 172–173
Birth rate, 140
    teen, 141
Birth ratio
    nonmarital, 182
    teen nonmarital, 188, 189
Birth subsidies, 554–555
Blacks
    children
        attainment among, 597
        family structure of, 104–106
        Head Start and, 605
        poverty rate of, 447
        welfare and, 115–116
    family status of, 102–103
    fertility rate of, 146
    Male Marriageable Pool Index
        and, 108–111
    marital status of, 102–103, 587,
        588
    marriage penalty and, 496
    median earnings of, 277
    nonmarital births among, 592
    sex ratio among, 89, 90
    TANF recipients among,
        463–464
    U.S. poverty rate and, 443, 444
    women
        affirmative action programs
            and, 417, 422
        decline in marriage for,
            102–104, 105
        marriage markets and,
            107–111
        welfare system and,
            113–116
        women's wage rates and,
            111–113, 116
        gender earnings gap among,
            371–373

labor force participation by,
    214, 215, 216–217, 531
    husband's income and,
        240–241, 247
    nonmarital fertility rate of,
        184–185
    response to subsidized child
        care among, 580
    teen fertility rate of, 186
    wage differences with white
        women, 392–394
    welfare and, 115
Blank, Rebecca, 11
Blau, David, 584, 603
Block grants, welfare reform and,
    463
Body mass index (BMI), 392
Boeing Co., affirmative action at,
    418
Bona fide seniority systems, 412
Breakeven point, 457
Brideprices, 84n17
Brookings Institution, The, 94
Budget constraints, 21, 225n6,
    253–258, 486–488
    full-income, 254, 256–258
Bureau of Labor Statistics, 532,
    571
Bush, George, 539
Bush, George W., 472

C

California, welfare reform in,
    468
Campbell, Donald, 210
Canada
    comparable worth in, 431, 434
    family leave policies in, 555,
        556
    gender earnings ratio in, 284,
        285
    motherhood penalty in, 538
    percent in poverty for single-
        parent families in, 450
    teen fertility rate in, 187
    unit of taxation in, 505
    women's labor force participa-
        tion in, 218, 219
Career, balancing with family,
    540–541

Career oriented, 536–537
Carlisle, Thomas, 176n1
Case for Marriage, The (Waite &
    Gallagher), 81
Cash transfers, 440. *See also* Trans-
    fer payments
Causal effects, 594
Causality
    establishing, 593
    vs. correlation, 599–600, 619
Causal variable, 38
CCDBG. *See* Child Care and De-
    velopment Block Grant
Center for Policy Alternatives,
    432
Centers for Disease Control and
    Prevention, 143
Changes, marginal, 29–30
Cherlin, Andrew, 54
Cherry, Robert, 569
Child allowances, 507, 509
Child and Adult Care Food pro-
    gram, 567
Child benefits, 615
Child care, 531, 559–583
    after-school, 534, 560, 561
    costs of, 560–563
    dual-earner families and, 592
    employer provided, 571–572
    family *vs.* non-family care, 560
    fathers providing, 563
    government intervention in,
        566–569
        economic rationale for,
            570–583
    off-hours, 582
    providers, 575, 581–582
        subsidizing training, 575
    quality of, 562–566
    subsidies, 575–581
        welfare reform and, 466
    summer, 564
    usage, 559–563
Child Care and Development
    Block Grant (CCDBG),
    463n23, 567
Child care centers, 575,
    580–581
Child Care Problem, The (Blau),
    584

Child custody, bargaining models and, 616

Child penalty, family gap and, 536–539

Child quality, 150
    effect of wage increase on, 164–165
    interaction with child quantity, 165–167

Child quantity, 150
    effect of wage increase on, 164–165
    interaction with child quality, 165–167
    See also Fertility

Children
    attainment of, 594, 596, 597
    cohabitation and, 590
    cost of, 151, 152–154
    distribution of resources within family and, 610–616, 619
    effect of family income on development of, 603–605
    effect on family gap, 376
    effect on women's earnings, 123
    effect on women's labor force participation, 243, 244, 531–535
    family structure and, 60, 61
    as marriage-specific human capital, 131
    maternal employment and health of, 609–610, 611
    maternity leave and health of, 553–554
    opportunity cost of, 153
    outcomes in married-couple families, 81–82
    parental leave and health of, 553
    parental time spent with, 534
    percent of families with, 589
    poverty rate of, 447–449
    preference for, 149–151
    as public goods, 616–618
    quality child care and development of, 564
    racial differences in family structure and, 104–106
    as time-intensive household-produced commodity, 4–5

Children's attainment, 594, 596, 597

Child services, 149–151, 594–595
    change in full income and, 158–160
    cost of, 152–153
        changes in, 153–154
    decline in family size and change in price of, 167–169
    demand for, 150
        comparative statics of, 157–165
    impact of wages on, 157
    price of, 154–155
        change in, 160–165
    production of, 151–152
    taxes and, 507–509

Child-specific selection effect, 604–605

Child support, 451, 466, 452–454, 602

Child Support Enforcement (CSE) office, 452

Child Tax Credit, 568

Child well-being
    absence of father and, 595–598
    defined, 594
    effect of dual earner married couple families on, 606–610
    effect of family structure on, 593–610

China, 147

Choices
    in analysis of labor force participation with household production, 269
    in microeconomics, 17–19

Civil Rights Act (1964), 406–413
    enforcement of, 407–409
    Equal Opportunity Act (1972), 407
    Pregnancy Discrimination Act (1978), 407, 542, 548

Civil Rights Act (1991), 408, 413

Clinton, William Jefferson (Bill), 113, 185, 190, 202, 276, 464, 523, 539

Coase Theorem, 132

Cohabitation, 53, 58, 61, 590
    effect of being raised in, 600–601
    nonmarital childbearing and, 201
    nonmarital fertility rate and, 185
    output and, 83

College athletics, discrimination in, 337

College education
    gender differences in, 321–324
    internal rate of return and, 315–317, 318
    as investment in human capital, 311
    motherhood penalty and, 538
    relative wages and, 301–303
    saving for, 356–357
    women's labor force participation and, 223–224
    See also Education

Common preference assumption, 612, 614–616

Comparable worth, 422–431
    opposition to, 427–430
    in practice, 430–431

Comparative advantage, 69

Comparative static analysis, 20–23
    of changes in supply and demand in marriage market, 88–97
    of demand for child services, 157–165
    of labor markets, 301, 302, 303
    of women's labor force participation, 224

Comparison, ordinal, 27

Compensable factors, 425

Competitive labor markets, supply and demand in, 296–299

Competitive market, defined, 33

Competitive model, 25

Completely specific training, 311

Compounding, 349–354

Congressional Budget Office, 11, 378

Constant term, 39

Constrained maximization, 18–19, 48, 155
  women's labor force participation and, 224
Constraints
  in analysis of labor force participation with household production, 267–269
  budget, 21
  on choices, 18
  on labor force participation, 231
  in labor supply analysis, 253–258
  marriage and, 52
Consumer Price Index, 440
Continuous variables, 41, 363
Contraception
  effect on fertility, 171, 172–173
  effect on teen childbearing, 197–201
  marriage market and, 93
Co-operative bargaining models, 613
Corcoran, Mary, 370
Correlation, *vs.* causality, 599–600, 619
Cost(s)
  of child care, 560–563
    effect on employment behavior, 580
  of child services, 152–153
    changes in, 153–154
  of educational investment, 311
  of Family and Medical Leave Act, 543–544
  of general training, 319
  of government intervention in child care market, 574–575
  of maternity leave, 557
  of on-the-job training, 312
  of specific training, 319
Council of Economic Advisors, 11
Counterfactual inquiry, 594
Covenant marriages, 132
CPS. *See* Current Population Survey
Crittendon, Ann, 540
Cross-sectional analysis, 238–239, 370

of gender earnings gap, 370–378
of teen fertility rates, 194, 195
Culture of poverty, 454
Current Population Survey (CPS), 214n1, 279, 363
Customer discrimination, 329, 336–339, 340, 400

D
Dally, Craig, 433
Day care centers, 575, 581–582
DCTC. *See* Dependent Care Tax Credit
Death rate, 140
Defined benefits plans, 525
Defined contribution plans, 525–526
Demand, 32–34
  analysis of change in, 35, 36
  law of, 36
Demand curve, 33, 34
  labor, 299, 300, 301
Demand for child services, 150
Demand function, 32
Demography, 140
Denmark
  family leave policies in, 555, 556
  nonmarital fertility rate in, 185
  teen fertility rate in, 186, 187
Dependent Care Tax Credit (DCTC), 567, 581
Dependent variables, 38, 41, 362
Diabetes, maternal employment and, 611
Difference-in-difference analysis, 45–47
  of Head Start, 605
Differences in sex ratios, 89
Diminishing marginal rate of substitution, 253
Diminishing marginal utility, 31, 227
Direct intervention, 604
Discount factor, 352
Discounting, 349–354
Discrimination
  based on marital status, 433
  based on physical appearance, 390–392

customer, 329, 336–339, 340, 400
employee, 329, 339, 340
employer, 329–336, 340, 384–385, 391, 400
evaluating, 408–409
gender wage differential and, 400–401
government programs to combat, 401–416
in hiring, 384–387
labor market. *See* Labor market discrimination
pattern or practice of, 410
proving via multiple regression, 409–410
reverse, 415, 416
statistical, 340–343, 400
taste for, 329
Discrimination coefficient, 329–333
Disparate impact, 408–410
Disparate impact standard, 409, 410
Disparate treatment, 408
Divorce, 53, 123–135
  changes in divorce law and, 132–134
  decline in marriage and, 103–104
  economic analysis of
    economic explanations, 127–131
    gains to divorce, 125–127
  economic consequences of, 131–135
  effect on income, 602–603
  marriage penalty and, 499
  no-fault, 123, 132–134
  rate of, 56, 124, 588, 589
    effect on marriage, 94–95
  Social Security and, 520–521
  specialization and, 76
  trends in, 124–125
Divorce Revolution, The (Weitzman), 131
Double-blind random assignment experiment, 43
Dowries, 84n17
Dual earner families, 533, 592, 619

Dual earner married couples, child well-being and, 605–610
Duesenberry, James, 18
Dummy variable, 41, 363
Duncan, Greg, 370
Duncan, Otis Dudley, 289*n*5
Duncan Index, 206, 289–292, 306, 393
Dynamic viewpoint, 602

E

Early Childhood Environment Rating Scale (ECERS), 564–565
Earned Income Tax Credit (EITC), 45, 437, 474–483, 499
    as child care subsidy, 567–568
    earnings and, 474–475, 477–480
    effect on child development, 603
    marriage and, 509–514
    mechanics of, 474–477
    poverty and, 477–480
    Universal Unified Child Credit and, 569
    women, work, and, 480–483
Earnings
    data source, 9
    Earned Income Tax Credit and, 474–475, 477–480
    effects of appearance on, 391–392
    effects of obesity on, 391–392
    inequality in, 380
    men's, 533
        marriage and, 117–123
    women's
        educational level and, 532–533
        at executive level, 394–396
        impact of marriage and children on, 123
        labor market discrimination and, 328–340
        specialized studies of, 387–396
        year-round full-time workers', 276–277, 279

See also Family gap in earnings; Gender earnings gap; Wages
Earnings disregard, 463
Earnings sharing, 527
Earnings test, 515, 521–525
Easterlin, Richard, 170
Easterlin hypothesis, 170–171
ECERS. *See* Early Childhood Environment Rating Scale
Economic analysis, 5–7
    positive, 6
    using models in, 24–25
Economic Growth and Tax Relief Act (2001), 476
Economic inefficiency, labor market discrimination and, 402–405
Economic Opportunity Act (1964), 439
Economic Policy Institute, 569
Economic problems, four-step structure of, 48
Economics
    empirical methods in, 36–38
    feminist, 6*n*1
    neoclassical, 5–6
    normative, 6–7
    positive, 6–7
    status of women in, 9–12
Economics of Discrimination (Becker), 328
Economies of scale
    loss of, after divorce, 595
    marriage and, 78–79, 82
Edin, Kathryn, 473
Education
    age at first marriage and level of, 112
    changes in women's level of, 1, 2
    child-support recipients and, 453
    earnings and level of, 315–317, 318
    gender differences in, 321–324
    gender earnings gap/ratio and, 281–282, 301–302, 371, 372, 376, 378–379
    as investment in human capital, 311

marital status and level of, 57–58, 61
    professional degrees
        gender earnings ratio and, 282, 294, 295
        women and, 323–324
    real earnings and, 532–533
    TANF and level of, 465, 466
    women's labor force participation and, 217–218, 223–224, 242
See also College education
EEOC. *See* Equal Employment Opportunity Commission
EEO-1 Private Sector Report, 419
Efficiency, 402, 572, 573
Effort hypothesis, 536–538
Eissa, Nada, 45, 503
EITC. *See* Earned Income Tax Credit
Elasticity of labor supply, 503
Empirical methods, 36–38
Employee discrimination, 329, 339, 340
Employer discrimination, 329–336, 340, 400
    hiring and, 384–385
    physical appearance and, 391
Employer-provided child care assistance, 571–572
Endogeneity problem, 598
Endogenous measures, 614
Endogenous tax rate, 503
Endogenous variables, 19, 48, 171
England, Paula, 346, 424
Equal Employment Opportunity Commission (EEOC), 407–408
Equal Opportunity Act (1972), 407
Equal Pay Act (1963), 405–406, 408, 417, 432
Equal Rights Amendment (ERA), 406
Equilibrium, 32–34
Equilibrium price, in marriage market, 86–88
Equilibrium wage, 299–300, 304
    discrimination and, 330–333
    labor supply and, 304–305

Equity, 402, 572, 574
ERA. *See* Equal Rights Amendment
Error term, 38, 362
Ethnicity
    differences in earnings ratio
        and, 277
    fertility measures and, 184
    poverty rate and, 443
    teen fertility rate and, 186
    See also Hispanics; Race
Europe
    family leave policy in, 554–558
    fertility rate in, 139, 146–147
    See also individual countries
Executive Order 11246 (1965),
    413
Exogenous measures, 614
Exogenous tax rate, 503
Exogenous variables, 19, 48
Exogenous variation, 598
Experimental measures of
    poverty, 442
Experiments
    double-blind random assign-
        ment, 43
    natural, 38, 44–47, 388, 615
    random assignment, 598
Explanatory variable, 362,
    368–369
Externalities, 546–547
    negative, 547
    positive, 546, 547

F

Fair Labor Standards (1938), 405
Fair Pay Act, 432
Faludi, Susan, 135
Family and Medical Leave Act
    (FMLA; 1993), 534, 539–544
    economic analysis of, 544–549
    economic effects of, 549–554
Family caps, 462, 466
Family gap in earnings, 123,
    374–378, 397, 533, 535–539
Family household, 59
Family(ies)
    balancing with career, 540–541
    child care choices and income
        level of, 559–561

child well-being and, 595
distribution of resources
    within, 610–616
dual-earner, 533, 592, 619
Earned Income Tax Credit and,
    474–475
as economic institution, 51
fertility and income level of,
    170–171
as miniature economy, 52–53
reasons for decline in size of,
    167–171
See also Single-parent families
Family leave policies, 539–558,
    609
    economic analysis of, 544–549
    economic effects of Family and
        Medical Leave Act,
        549–554
    maternity leave, 539, 541–543,
        549, 552–558
    paternal leave, 539–558
    in United States *vs.* Europe,
        554–558
Family policy
    child care, 559–583
    family gap in earnings,
        535–539
    family leave policies, 539–558
    labor force participation rates
        of women with children
        and, 531–535
Family structure, 59–61
    economic analysis of, 101–117
    income taxation and, 491
    poverty and, 101, 106, 107
        effect of changes in, 448,
            449, 451, 454
        effect on child well-being,
            593–610
        U.S. rate, 443, 444–447
    racial differences in, 102–103,
        104–106
    revolution in, 587–593
    Social Security system and,
        515–517
    welfare benefits and, 113–114,
        461
Family Support Act (1988), 462
Farley, Reynolds, 54

Fathers
    as caregivers, 562, 563
    child well-being and absence
        of, 595–600
Female-headed households, 591
    poverty rate, 443, 444–449, 450
    See also Single mothers; Single-
        parent families
Feminist economics, 6*n*1
Feminist Economics, 6*n*1
Feminization of poverty, 445–449
    reasons for, 449–455
Fertility, 139–140
    changes in, 1, 2
        world statistics, 146–147, 148
    data sources, 9
    economic theory of, 139,
        148–157
        Malthusian, 176–180
        preferences, 149–151
        production and cost,
            151–155
    Family and Medical Leave Act
        and, 552–553
    family income and, 170–171
    maternity leave and, 552–553,
        556
    measuring, 140–142, 147–148
    natural, 176
    nonmarital, 181–185
    reasons for decline in family
        size, 167–171
    reasons for falling, 4–5
    taxes and, 507–509
    teen, 185–189
    U.S., 139, 143–146, 148
Fertility rate, 139, 141, 143
    age-specific, 141
    nonmarital, 141, 143, 181
    personal exemption and,
        507–509
    teen, 185–186
    total, 142, 143
Finland
    family leave policies in, 555,
        556, 557
    gender earnings ratio in, 284
    motherhood penalty in, 538
Fisher, Gordon M., 439
Flexible spending account, 568

Flex-time, 609
FMLA. *See* Family and Medical Leave Act
Folbre, Nancy, 617, 618
Food stamp program, 455
Food stamps, 455
Fortune Magazine, 540
France
    child care in, 584, 618
    child poverty rate in, 448
    family leave policies in, 555, 556, 557
    fertility rate in, 146, 147
        nonmarital, 185
        teen, 186, 187
    gender earnings ratio in, 284, 285
    occupational segregation in, 294, 296
    percent in poverty for single-parent families in, 450
    women's labor force participation in, 219
Free-rider problem, 617
Friedman, Milton, 9, 10
Full income, 156–157, 254
    price of child services and change in, 158–160
Full-income budget constraint, 254, 255–256
Functions, 26–27, 48
    arguments of, 27
    demand, 32
    household production, 28–29, 48
    market supply, 33
    production, 28
    utility, 21, 27–28, 48
Future value, 350

G

GAIN (Greater Avenues for Independence), 468
Gallagher, Maggie, 81
GAO. *See* General Accounting Office
Gaza Strip, 147
Gender
    differences in human capital and evidence for, 320–328

reasons for, 315–320
    differences in work experience and, 324–328
    discrimination in hiring and, 384–387
    educational attainment and, 321–324
    life cycle pattern of labor force participation and, 222
    occupational segregation and, 343–344
Gender earnings gap, 309, 361, 399–401, 533
    comparable worth and, 424
    cross-sectional research on, 370–378
    discrimination and, 400–401
    human capital explanation for, 399–400
    regression analysis of, 362–364
    statistical analysis of, 364–370
Gender earnings ratio, 275–276, 277–285, 305–306
    changes in, 1, 2
    comparable worth and, 430–431
    education and, 281–282, 378–379
    labor force experience and, 279–280, 379, 382–384
    labor market discrimination and, 280
    marital status and, 374, 376
    occupational segregation and, 294, 295
    race/ethnicity and, 277
    time-series studies on, 378–384
    in United States, 283–285
Gender preferences, distribution of resources within the family and, 615, 619
Gender wage differential. *See* Gender earnings gap
General Accounting Office (GAO), 566
General human capital, 130–131, 311*n*6
General training, 311
    costs and benefits of, 319
Germany
    child poverty rate in, 448

family leave policies in, 555, 556, 557
    fertility rate in, 146, 147
    gender earnings ratio in, 284
    maternity leave in, 554
    motherhood penalty in, 538
    occupational segregation in, 294, 296
    percent in poverty for single-parent families in, 450
    women's labor force participation in, 219
Ginsberg, Ruth Bader, 13
Glass ceiling, 282, 394
Goldin, Claudia, 12, 117, 172, 218, 223–224, 318, 325–326
Goods
    inferior, 22*n*1, 33*n*4
    normal, 22*n*1, 33*n*4, 159
    private, 617
    public, 617–618
Government
    intervention in child care market, 566–569, 584
        economic rationale for, 570–583
    programs to combat discrimination, 401–416
        comparable worth as alternative, 422–431
        effectiveness of, 416–422
    reasons for market intervention by, 8
Greece, 185
Griggs v. Duke Power Company, 410, 412
Griswold v. Connecticut, 93*n*25
Gronau, Reuben, 265
Gruber, Jonathon, 133

H

Hallock, Kevin, 394
Hamermesh, Daniel, 391
Harvard Business Review, 535
Hawthorne, Nathaniel, 201
Head Start, 567, 604–605
Health effects
    of marriage, 81
    of maternal employment on child, 609–610, 611

Health effects *(continued)*
    of maternity leave on child,
        553–554
    of parental leave on child, 553
Heckman, James, 10
Heterogenous, 536
Heterogenous preferences, 612
Hewlett, Sylvia Anne, 540
Hiring
    affirmative action and, 421, 423
    gender discrimination in,
        384–387
Hispanics
    fathers as caregivers among,
        563
    marital status of, 588
    median earnings of, 277
    poverty rate of children, 447
    sex ratio of, 89, 90
    TANF recipients among, 465
    U.S. poverty rate, 443, 444
    women
        fertility rate of, 146, 148
        nonmarital, 184–185
        teen, 186
Hoffman, Saul, 134, 135, 196,
    205, 206, 474, 478, 511, 512
Holden, Betsey, 540
Home economics courses,
    13–14
Hong Kong, 296
Horizontal equity, 504–505
Hostile environment harassment,
    407
Household
    defined, 59
    family, 59
    non-family, 59
Household economics, 53
Householder, 59
Household production, 224–225,
    227–229, 232–235
    economies of scale and, 78–79
    taxes and value of, 505–506
Household production function,
    28–29, 48, 227–228
    women's labor force participa-
        tion and, 264–266, 272
Household productivity, gains in,
    243–246, 247

Household technology, effect on
    women's labor force partici-
    pation, 243–246, 247
Human capital, 309–312
    defined, 309
    gender differences in
        evidence for, 320–328
        reasons for, 315–320
    general, 130–131, 311*n*6
    investing in, 310–311
        evaluating, 312–314
        internal rate of return and,
            358–360
        present value analysis and,
            349–358
        occupational segregation and,
            344–346
    specific, 130–131, 311*n*6
    theory of, 309
    vs. physical capital, 310–311
Human Capital (Becker), 310*n*1
Hymowitz, Carol, 540

I
Iceland, 185, 556
Imperfect competition, theory of,
    10
Implicit tax, 463
Implicit tax rate, 456
    welfare reform and, 467
Income
    adjusted gross, 568
    child care choices and, 559–561
    effect of divorce on, 602–603
    effect on child development,
        603–605
    family structure and, 51
    fertility and, 176
    full. *See* Full income
    husband's, effects on women's
        labor force participation,
        239–241, 246
    relative, 170
    single-parent families and
        change in, 601–602
Income and substitution effects,
    263*n*2
Income disregard, 457
Income effect, 33, 159, 262, 457,
    482, 488, 524

Income guarantee, 456, 463
Income maintenance program, 456
Income splitting, 492
Income taxes, 492–514
    marriage tax, 492–499
    progressive, 499, 502, 504, 505
    proportional, 505
    See also Taxes
Independent variables, 38, 41, 362
India, 147
Indifference curve, 225*n*6,
    252–253, 486, 487–489,
    544*n*28
Indifference curve analysis, 66*n*12
Inferior goods, 22*n*1
    income effects and, 33*n*4
Information, asymmetric,
    340–341, 547–548
Internal rate of return, 313–314,
    354–358
    investing in human capital and,
        358–360
    labor force participation pat-
        terns and, 315–317
    labor market discrimination
        and, 319–320
International Labor Organization,
    294
Intrafamily allocation of
    resources, 612
Investments in human capital,
    310–311
    evaluating, 312–314
    internal rate of return and,
        358–360
    present value analysis and,
        349–358
Iran, 294, 296
Ireland, 284
Iron triangle of welfare, 464
Italy
    family leave policies in, 556
    fertility rate in, 146, 147
        nonmarital, 185
        teen, 187
    gender earnings ratio in, 284,
        285
    women's labor force participa-
        tion in, 219
It Takes a Nation (Blank), 11

J

Japan
  family leave policies in, 555
  gender earnings ratio in, 284,
    285
  marriage bars in, 401
  nonmarital fertility rate in,
    185
  teen fertility rate in, 186, 187
  women's labor force participa-
    tion in, 218, 219
Job evaluation, 424–427
Job segregation, 339
Jobs-First GAIN, 468
Job sharing, 609
John Bates Clark Prize, 11*n*2
Johnson, Lyndon B., 413, 439
Johnson, Richard W., 526
Journal of Human Resources, 346

K

Kantorovich, Leonid, 10
Katz, Lawrence, 172
Keynes, John Maynard, 10
Koopmans, Tjalling, 10
Korea, 296
Korenmark, Sanders, 391
Krueger, Anne, 11

L

Labor force attachment
  family gap and, 377
  women's, 341–342, 343
    Family and Medical Leave
      Act and, 550–552
Labor force experience, gender
    earnings ratio and, 275–276,
    279–280, 371, 372–373, 379,
    382–384
Labor force participation,
    women's, 213–222
  changes in family life and, 249
  child care subsidies and,
    576–579
  children and, 243, 244,
    531–535
  by college-educated, 223–224
  Earned Income Tax Credit and,
    480–483
  economic model of, 222–238

effect of birth control pill on,
    172–173
effect of household technology
    on, 243–246, 247
effect of husband's income on,
    239–241, 246, 262, 263
effect of wage rate on, 262–264
effect of women's wage rate on,
    241–242, 246–247
household production and,
    264–272
internal rate of return and pat-
    terns of, 315–317
labor supply analysis of,
    260–264
life cycle patterns of, 218–222,
    325–328
married women, 262–264
by married women, 219–222,
    325–326, 532, 589
of married women, 269–272
occupational segregation and,
    344–346
reasons for increase in, 238–248
relative income and, 170–171
by single mothers, 46–47, 532
Social Security earnings test
    and, 521–524
statistics on, 9
tax rate and decision to go to
    work, 502–504
Labor force participation rate
    (LFPR), 214
Labor/leisure model, 225–238,
    251–260
  welfare and, 485–488
Labor market discrimination, 8,
    309, 347
  economic analysis of, 24–25
  economic inefficiency and,
    402–405
  gender earnings ratio and, 276,
    280
  internal rate of return and,
    319–320
  unexplained portion of earn-
    ings gap and, 366
  women's earnings and,
    328–340
Labor market model, 23–24

Labor market(s)
  comparative statics of, 301, 302,
    303
  human capital and, 309–314
  male marriage premium and,
    121–122, 123
  supply and demand in compet-
    itive, 296–299
  wage determination and, 306
Labor supply
  AFDC and, 458–461, 485–488
  elasticity of, 503
  taxes and, 499–504
  utility-maximization and,
    258–260
  wage rate and, 304–305
Labor supply analysis
  basics, 251–260
    choosing hours of work,
      258–260
    constraints, 253–258
    preferences, 251–253
  of women's labor force
    participation, 222–238,
    260–264
Labor supply model, 3
Law of Demand, 21, 32, 36, 160
Law of Diminishing Marginal
    Returns, 32, 36–37, 229, 265
Leisure, 227, 230, 232–235, 251
LFPR. *See* Labor force participa-
    tion rate
Liebman, Jeffrey, 45
Life-table methods, 124*n*21
Logarithms, in regression analysis,
    41
Losing Ground (Murray), 190
Low-income families, effect of
    taxes on marriage among,
    509–514
Lucas, Robert E., 12

M

Macroeconomics, 5
Mainstream economics, 5–6
Major League Baseball, 337
Male-headed families, poverty
    rate among, 443, 444–445,
    450. *See also* Single–parent
    families

Male Marriageable Pool Index
(MMPI), 108–111, 194
Male marriage premium, 101,
117, 374
decline in, 120–121, 538–539
reasons for, 117–120
trends affecting, 121–123
Malthus, Thomas, 139, 176
Malthusian theory of fertility,
176–180
effects of decline in mortality
rate, 179–180
effects of increasing productivity, 179–180
Malthusian equilibrium,
177–178
Marginal changes, 29–30
Marginal conditions, 19–20
Marginal product, 31–32, 229,
297
Marginal product of household
time, 228
Marginal rate of substitution
(MRS), 22, 252–253,
259–260
diminishing, 253
Marginal returns, law of diminishing, 32, 36–37
Marginal revenue product
(MRP), 297–299, 404–405
Marginals, 29–32
Marginal tax rates, 492–494,
496–498
exogenous variation in,
503–504
personal exemption and, 507
remedies for secondary earners,
504–506
Marginal utility, 22, 30–31, 227
of consumption goods, 230
diminishing, 31, 227
of household goods, 228
Marginal value of time, 226–230
Marital history, 53
Marital status, 53, 54–58
discrimination based on, 433
gender earnings ratio and, 374,
376
TANF and, 465, 466
Market good expenditures, 251

Market goods, child services and
change in, 160
Market(s)
competitive, 33
reasons for government intervention, 8
Market supply function, 33
Market work time, 229–230
Marriage, 53–61
age at first, 54, 97, 172–173,
587–589
birth control pill and,
172–173
bargaining approach within,
612–614
change in rate of, 1, 2
changes in, 1, 2
changes in family structure and,
587–589
convenant, 132
current statistics on, 588
data sources, 9
decline in, 101–106
divorce and, 95, 103–104
economic explanations for,
106–116
male marriage premium and,
122
Earned Income Tax Credit and,
509–514
between economic disparates,
68–73
between economic identicals,
66–68
economics of, 52, 61–62
economies of scale and, 78–79,
82
effect of marital disincentives
and, 513–514
effect of marriage tax/subsidy
on decision to marry,
496–499
family structure and, 59–61
gains from, 81–82
health benefits of, 81
as institution, 51–53
male earnings and, 117–123
marital categories, 53
principal-agent issues in, 75–78
production and, 63–75

risk sharing and, 79–80, 82
risk-taking and, 81
shotgun, 188, 198, 200, 201,
591
single parenting and, 94–95
with small productivity differences, 73–75
social obligation and, 83
specialization and, 63–75, 82
supply and demand model of,
80–88
concepts of, 80, 83
marriage market equilib-
rium, 86–88
notation, 80, 83
supply and demand curves,
84–86
teen childbearing and opportunities for, 190–197
wealth and, 81
welfare and, 114–116
welfare reform and, 466,
472–473
women's earnings and, 123
See also Divorce
Marriage, Divorce and Remarriage
(Cherlin), 54
Marriage bars, 401
Marriage bonus, 492, 493
Marriage market, 62, 107–111,
116
changes in supply and demand
and, 88–97
sex ratio and, 89–91
effect of sexual revolution on,
93–97
equilibrium in, 86–88
race and, 102
women's wages and, 92–93
Marriage neutral tax, 492
Marriage penalty. See Marriage
tax
Marriage premium, male, 101
Marriage productivity effect,
118–120, 538–539
Marriage subsidy, 493, 495–496
Marriage tax, 492–499, 494
Earned Income Tax Credit and,
476, 511
remedies for, 504–506

Married couples
  child penalty and, 537–538
  Earned Income Tax Credit and,
      475, 476, 477
  effects on child well-being of
      dual earner, 606–610
Married women
  child penalty and, 537–538
  Earned Income Tax Credit and,
      481, 482
  labor force participation of,
      213, 217, 218–222,
      219–222, 262–264,
      269–272, 532, 589
  labor force reentry by, 325–326
Matching grants, 463
Maternity leave, 534, 539,
      541–543, 549, 552–558
  child health and, 553–554
  working, 558
Maximization, constrained,
      18–19
Means-tested program, 456
Medicaid, 455, 462
Men
  child penalty and, 539
  earnings of, 117–123, 277–278,
      378–379, 533
    changes in, 169
    effect on women's labor
        force participation,
        239–241, 246, 262, 263
    marriage and, 117–123
    median annual, 277–278
  economic consequences of di-
      vorce for, 131, 134–135
  education
    earnings and, 378–379, 533
  labor force participation rates
      of, 214, 215, 216
  U.S. poverty rate, 443, 444
Microeconomics, 5
  functions, 26–29
    household production func-
        tion, 28–29
    utility function, 27–28
  marginals, 29–32
  supply and demand analysis,
      32–36
  theory, 17–26

choices, 17–19
comparative static analysis,
    20–23
models, 23–26
solutions, 19–20
totals, 29–32
Mill, John Stuart, 336
Minimum wage, Earned Income
    Tax Credit and, 475, 477
Minuet, Peter, 356
MMPI. *See* Male Marriageable
    Pool Index
Models, 23–26
  competitive, 25
  labor market, 23–24
  purpose of, 25–26
  rational choice, 28
  use in economic analysis,
      24–25
Moffitt, Robert, 116, 461
Mommy track, 535
Monopolistic competition, 10
Moral hazard effect, 455
Morgan Stanley Dean Witter, 411
Mother-friendly jobs, 537
Motherhood
  economic worth of, 540–541,
      616–618
Motherhood penalty, 550n38
Motivating factor, 413
Moynihan, Daniel, 101
MRP. *See* Marginal revenue
    product
MRS. *See* Marginal rate of
    substitution
Mulcahy, Ann, 540
Multiple regression, 39–40
  use in discrimination cases,
      409–410
Murray, Charles, 190
$MVT^\star$, 235–237, 239–241, 243,
    246, 458–459, 578–579
MVT_H, 226, 228, 230, 233–237,
    243–246, 459–460, 580
MVT_L, 226, 227, 233–237,
    243–244, 246, 459–460, 580
MVT_M, 226, 229, 235–237,
    239–241, 243–244, 246,
    458–459, 502, 578–579
Myrdal, Gunnar, 9

N
Nash, John, 199–200
Nash equilibrium, 199–200
National Academy of Sciences, 442
National Association of Working
    Women, 433
National Campaign to Prevent
    Teen Pregnancy, 94
National Center for Health Sta-
    tistics, 143
  Vital Statistics Division, 9
National Conference of State
    Legislatures, 433
National Longitudinal Survey of
    Young Women (NLSYW),
    207n19
National Longitudinal Survey of
    Youth (NLSY), 207n19, 363,
    608
National Organization for
    Women (NOW), 278
National Pay Equity Day, 399
National Research Council, 202
National Survey of America's
    Families (NSAF), 559, 560
National Survey of Youth, 391
National Vital Statistics Reports, 9
National Women's Party, 406
Native Americans, 146, 186
Natural experiments, 38, 44–47,
    388, 615
  difference-in-difference ap-
      proach, 45–47
Natural fertility, 176
Natural log units, 41
Natural rate of population
    growth, 140
Near-poor, 478
Negative externality, 547
Negro Baseball League, 337
Nelson, Julie, 6n1
Neoclassical economics, 5–6
Netherlands
  gender earnings ratio in, 284
  motherhood penalty in, 538
  percent in poverty for single-
      parent families in, 450
  teen fertility rate in, 186, 187
  women's labor force participa-
      tion in, 219

Net present value (NPV), 354–358

New American Reality, The (Farley), 54

Newsweek, 500

New York Times, 500, 504

New Zealand, 284, 555

Niger, 147

Nixon, Richard, 12–13

NLSY. *See* National Longitudinal Survey of Youth

NLSYW. *See* National Longitudinal Survey of Young Women

Nobel Prize in Economics, 9–12

No-fault divorce, 123, 132–134

Non-exclusive, 617

Non-family household, 59

Nonmarital birth ratio, 182, 183
teen, 188, 189

Nonmarital childbearing
changes in family structure and, 590, 591–592
effect of abortion/contraception on, 197–201
effect of wages on, 201–202
poverty and, 454–455
social norms and, 197–202
welfare reform and, 466
See also Teen childbearing

Nonmarital fertility, 181–185
rate of, 141, 143, 181, 182

Non-rival, 617

Normal distribution, 38

Normal goods, 22*n1,* 159
income effects and, 33*n4*

Normal Retirement Age, 515*n28*

Normative economics, 6–7

Norway
family leave policies in, 555, 556
nonmarital fertility rate in, 185
parental leave in, 555
teen fertility rate in, 187

Notation, in regression analysis, 38–39

NOW. *See* National Organization for Women

NPV. *See* Net present value

NSAF. *See* National Survey of America's Families

O

Oaxaca, Ronald, 364

Oaxaca decomposition, 364–370, 393
of earnings gap, 371–373
formula, 376*n15*
limitations of, 368–370

Obesity
effects on earnings, 391–392
maternal employment and, 611

Occupation, housewife as, 14–15

Occupational distribution, 306

Occupational segregation, 285–295, 400
current magnitude of, 293–295
discrimination in hiring and, 385
effect of affirmative action/ Title VII on, 420–421
gender earnings differential and, 424–425
gender roles and, 343–344
history of, 292–295
human capital theory and, 344–346
measuring, 289–292
wage differences between white and black women and, 393–394

O'Connor, Sandra Day, 13, 403

Off-hours child care, 582

Office of Federal Contract Compliance Programs (OFCCP), 415

Omnibus Reconciliation Act (1981), 462

O'Neill, June, 11, 378

On-the-job training, 311–312
internal rate of return of, 317–320

Opportunity cost hypothesis, teen childbearing and, 193–194, 196–197

Opportunity costs, 4, 66, 255
children and, 153

Ordinal comparison, 27

Orie, Jane, 433

Orshansky, Molly, 438, 439

Output, 80

P

Pakistan, 294, 296

Panel Study of Income Dynamics (PSID), 51, 59*n8,* 207*n19,* 363, 371, 382, 498, 602

Parental leave, 531, 534
economic analysis of, 544–549
wages and, 545, 550

Pareto Optimal, 613

Paternal leave, 539–544

Paternity, 452

Pattern of discrimination, 410

Paycheck Fairness Act, 432

Pay line, 425, 426

Payroll tax, 514

Peabody Picture Vocabulary test, 608

Pearce, Diana, 446*n11*

Pension plans, 525
defined benefits, 525
defined contribution, 525–526

Peppard, Kiki, 433

Perfect substitutes, 266–267, 329

Personal exemption, 507–509

Personal Responsibility and Work Reconciliation Act (PRWORA), 462–463

Peters, H. Elizabeth, 132–133

Phase-in range, Earned Income Tax Credit, 476

Phase-out range, Earned Income Tax Credit, 476–477, 481, 482

Physical appearance, discrimination on basis of, 390–392

Physical capital, 310–311

Point factor system, 424–427

Polachek, Solomon, 344, 346

Poland, 294, 296

Population Association of America, 81

Population growth
natural rate of, 140
rate of, 140*n1*
zero, 142

Population momentum, 142*n5*

Population size, wage rate and, 177–178, 180

Portability, of pensions, 525–526

Portugal, 147, 556

Positive economic analysis, 6

Positive economics, 6–7
Positive externality, 546
    children and, 617
    quality child care and, 572–573
POSSLQs (persons of opposite
        sex sharing living quarters),
        58, 590
Poverty, 437
    absolute measure of, 438
    benefits of marriage and,
        79–80
    children in, 447–449
    culture of, 454
    Earned Income Tax Credit and,
        477–480
    experimental measures of, 442
    family structure and, 101, 106,
        107
    feminization of, 445–449
    measuring, 438–442
    rate of, 437
        alternative, 479
        children's, 447–449
        EITC and, 479–480
    U.S. statistics on, 442–449
    welfare reform and working
        poor, 471–474
    women in
        among elderly, 519–520,
            524–525
        reasons for, 449–455
Poverty thresholds, 79, 440, 441
Practice of discrimination, 410
Predictions
    qualitative, 37–38
    quantitative, 37–38
    testing, 48
Preference(s), 22–23
    in analysis of labor force partic-
        ipation with household
        production, 266–267
    for children, 167
    fertility and, 149–151
    in labor supply analysis,
        251–253
    revealed, 28
Pregnancy bars, 401
Pregnancy Discrimination Act
    (1978), 407, 542, 548
Premarital sex model, 198–201

Premarket influences, 400
Present value, 312–313, 351
    investment in human capital
        and, 349–358
Price elasticity of employment
    with respect to child care
    costs, 580
Price of Motherhood, The (Critten-
    don), 540
Price(s)
    of child quality *vs.* child quan-
        tity, 165–167
    of child services, 154–155
    change in, 160–165
    decline in family size and,
        167–169
    relative, 32–33
    supply and demand analysis
        and, 35
Price theory, 5
Price Waterhouse v. Hopkins, 413
Primary earner, 499, 501–502
Principal, 75, 349
Principal-agent issues, 75–78
Principal-agent problem, 75,
    77–78
Private good, 617
Process quality, 562
Product, marginal, 31–32
Production
    household, 224–225, 227–229,
        232–235
    marriage and, 63–75
Production function, 28
Production-possibilities curve,
    64–66
    marriage and, 66–73
Production-possibilities frontier,
    64–66
Productivity
    employer-provided child care
        and worker, 572
    gains in household, 243–246,
        247
    marriage and, 118–120,
        538–539
Professional degrees
    gender earnings ratio and, 282,
        294, 295
    women and, 323–324

Profit maximization
    discrimination and, 334–335
    employment, 298
Progressive tax system, 499, 502,
    505
    marriage penalty/subsidy and,
        504
Pronatalist policy, 507
Pronatalist rationale, 556
Proportional income tax, 505
PRWORA. *See* Personal Respon-
    sibility and Work Reconcilia-
    tion Act
PSID. *See* Panel Study of Income
    Dynamics
Public goods, children as, 616–618
Public policy
    defined, 2
    women's issues and, 3

Q
Qualitative prediction, 37–38
Quality, of child services, 150,
    164–167
Quality child care, 562–566
    government intervention efforts
        and, 572–576
    process quality, 562
    structural quality, 562
Quantitative prediction, 37–38
Quantity, of child services, 150,
    164–167
Quayle, Dan, 202
Quid pro quo harassment, 407

R
R^2, 42
Race
    child attainment and, 597
    earnings ratio and, 277
    economic analysis of, 101–117
    family structure and, 102–103
    fertility rates and, 145–146, 184
        teen, 186
    labor force participation rates
        and, 214, 215, 216–217
    poverty rate and, 443
    sex ratio and, 89
    See also Blacks; Ethnicity;
        Whites

Random assignment, 42–44
Random assignment experiment, 598
Rational choice, 5–6, 28, 106, 127–128
  marriage and, 62
  science of, 5
  teen fertility and, 192–194
Real wage, 230–231
Recruitment, affirmative action and, 421
Refundable income tax credit, 510. *See also* Earned Income Tax Credit
Regression analysis, 38–42
  of earnings differences, 362–364
  multiple, 39–40
  notation for, 38–39
Regression coefficients, 39, 362
Regressive tax, 514
Regulation, of child care market, 574–575
Rehabilitation Act (1973), Sections 501 & 505, 408
Reid, Margaret, 10
Relative income, 170
Relative income hypothesis, 170–171
Relative income poverty measure, 438
Relative price, 32–33
Remarriage
  effect on income, 602
  Social Security and, 521–525
Resource and referral services, 575
Resources, distribution within family and, 610–616
Retention
  employer-provided child care assistance and, 571–572
  family leave policies and, 543–544, 550–552
Retirement
  saving for, 356
  women and
    pensions and, 525–527
    Social Security and, 518–521
Return
  internal rate of, 313–314

law of diminishing marginal, 32, 36–37
Revealed preference, 28
Reverse discrimination, 415, 416
Review of Economics of the Household, The, 53
Ricardo, David, 177
Rickey, Branch, 337
Rise in return to skills, 381, 383
Risking the Future, 202
Risk sharing, marriage and, 79–80, 82
Risk-taking, marriage and, 81
Robinson, Jackie, 337
Robinson, Joan, 10
Ross, Heather, 94
Roundtable on Children, 94
Russian Federation
  fertility rate in, 146, 147
  occupational segregation in, 294, 296

S
Same-sex households, 53
  outputs of, 83
Same-sex marriage, tax consequences of, 500
Same-sex unions, 53, 58
Sampling error, 42
Samuelson, Paul, 9
SAS, work-life incentives at, 572
Savings, 356–357
Sawhill, Isabel, 11, 94–95
Sawicky, Max, 569
Scarlet Letter, The (Hawthorne), 201–202
Scattergram, 39, 40
Schieffelin, Allison, 411
Schultz, T. W., 310*n*1
Schwartz, Anna, 10
Schwartz, Felice, 535
Secondary earner bias, 517
Secondary earners, 501–502
  Earned Income Tax Credit and, 481, 482
  remedies for marginal tax rates faced by, 504–506
Selection, 536–537
  adverse, 547–548
Selection bias, 82

Selectivity bias, 196
Selectivity effect, 118–120
Senior Citizens Freedom to Work Act (2000), 523
Seniority systems, 412
Service sector jobs, 472
Sex ratios
  differences in, 89
  marriage market and, 89–91
Sex segregation, 285
Sexual harassment, 407
Sexual revolution, marriage market and, 93–97
Shotgun marriages, 188, 198, 200, 201, 591
Single mothers
  child penalty and, 537–538
  labor force participation of, 532
  Earned Income Tax Credit and, 480–481
Single-parent families
  effect of change in income on children in, 601–602
  effect on child-well-being, 595–598
  growing up in, 593–605
  poverty rate of, 443, 444–449, 450
  rise in, 591
  welfare and, 191
Single parenting, marriage and, 94–95
Single status, production and, 63–66
60 Minutes, 572
Skills, rise in return to, 381, 383
Smith, Adam, 310*n*1
Smith, Howard W., 406
Smith, James, 326
Smith Barney (Salomon Smith Barney), 411
Social multiplier, 173
Social norms
  nonmarital childbearing and, 201–202
  occupational segregation and, 400
  teen childbearing and, 197–201
Social obligation, marriage and, 83

Social Security, 491, 492, 514–528
  behavioral effects of, 521–525
  history of, 514–518
  mechanics of, 514–518
  as percent of women's income, 518–520
  reform proposals, 527–528
  women, retirement, and, 518–521
  women and future of, 527–528
  See also Pensions
Social Security Act (1935), 113, 456, 514
Social Security Bulletin, 439
Social status, teen childbearing and, 202
Solutions to choice problems, 19–20
Somalia, 147
Spain, 187, 284
Specialization
  divorce and, 76
  marriage and, 62, 63–75, 82
Specific human capital, 130–131, 311*n*6
Specific training, 311
  costs and benefits of, 319
Sports, discrimination in professional, 337
Spreadsheet program, computing internal rate of return with, 358*n*4
Standard deduction, 507
State governments, role in subsidizing child care, 568–569
Stationary range, Earned Income Tax Credit, 476
Statistical bias, omitted variables and, 40–41, 118–119
Statistical discrimination, 340–343, 400
Structural quality, 562
Substitution, marginal rate of, 22
Substitution effect, 33, 161–162, 458, 480, 482, 488, 502, 524
Summation, 354
Supplemental Security Income (SSI), 455, 513

Supply, 32–34
  analysis of change in, 35–36, 37
  balanced increase in, 90
Supply and demand analysis, 5, 32–36
  comparative statics of, 35–36
Supply and demand model of marriage, 80–88
  change in, 88–97
  concepts, 80, 83
  marriage market equilibrium and, 86–88
  notation for, 80, 83
  supply and demand curves, 84–86
Supply curve, 33
  labor, 299, 300, 301
Survey of America's Families, 469
Survey of Income and Program Participation (SIPP), 513, 559*n*55, 561
Sweden
  child care in, 584, 618
  child poverty rate in, 448
  family leave policies in, 555, 556, 557
  fertility rate in, 147
    nonmarital, 185
    teen, 186, 187
  gender earnings ratio in, 284, 285
  motherhood penalty in in, 538
  percent in poverty for single-parent families in, 450
  unit of taxation in, 505
  women's labor force participation in, 218, 219
Switzerland, 284, 555
Symphony orchestras, women's employment in, 387–390

T
Taiwan, 147
TANF. *See* Temporary Assistance for Needy Families
Taste for discrimination, 329
Taxable income, 494
Taxes
  child care subsidies and, 575–576

consequences of legalizing same sex marriage, 500
  employer-provided child care and, 571
  family structure and, 491
  fertility and, 507–509
  implicit tax rate, 456
  income, 491, 492–514
    marriage tax, 492–499
    progressive, 499, 502, 504, 505
    proportional, 505
  labor supply and, 499–504
  marginal, 492, 493
  payroll, 514
  regressive, 515
  unit of taxation, 505
  women and, 3
Taxing Women (McCaffery), 527
Tax Reform Act (1969), 493–494
Tax Reform Act (1986), 496, 503, 509
Tax Relief Act (2001), 506
Teen childbearing
  birth rate, 141
  changing social norms and, 197–201
  effect of abortion/contraception on, 197–201
  marriage opportunities and, 190–197
  pregnancy rate, 186
  role of welfare in, 190–197
  social status and, 202
  socioeconomic consequences of, 202–210
Teen fertility, 185–189
  economic approach to, 192–194
  rate of, 187
Telecommuting, 609
Temporary Assistance for Needy Families (TANF), 113, 191, 455, 463, 513
  labor supply and, 486–488
  See also Welfare
Thailand, 294, 296
Threat point, 613
Time
  cost of, 4
  leisure, 227, 230

Time *(continued)*
    marginal value of, 226–230
    market work, 229–230
    price of, 5
Time constraint, 253
Time of Transition (Sawhill &
    Ross), 94
Time-series analysis, 238, 370
    of gender earnings ratio,
        378–384
    of teen fertility rates, 194–195
Time squeeze, 609
Title I, Americans with Disabili-
    ties Act, 408
Title V, Americans with Disabili-
    ties Act, 408
Title VII, Civil Rights Act (1964),
    406–413
    effectiveness of, 417–421
    Pregnancy Discrimination Act,
        542, 548
Title XX, Social Service Block
    grants, 567
Total fertility rate, 142
Totals, 29–32
Training
    affirmative action and, 421
    completely specific, 311
    general, 311
    on-the-job, 311–312
        internal rate of return of,
            317–320
    specific, 311
Transfer payments
    cash, 440
    marital disincentives and,
        513–514
    See also Earned Income Tax
        Credit
Truly Disadvantaged, The (Wilson),
    107, 108, 190
T-statistic, 42
Turnover
    in child care industry, 582
    maternity leave and, 543–544
Tyson, Laura, 11

U
Uganda, 147
Underclass, 107

Understanding the Gender Gap
    (Goldin), 12
Unemployed, 214
Unilateral divorce laws, 132–133
Unions, 53
United Kingdom
    child benefit in, 615
    custody of children in divorced
        families in, 589
    family leave policies in, 555
    fertility rate in, 147
        teen, 186, 187
    gender earnings ratio in, 284,
        285
    motherhood penalty in, 538
    percent in poverty for single-
        parent families in, 450
    unit of taxation in, 505
    women's labor force participa-
        tion in, 219
United Nations, 143
United States
    antidiscrimination laws in,
        405–413
    birth rate in, 140, 143
    comparable worth legislation
        in, 432
    custody of children in divorced
        families in, 589
    family leave policy in, 554–558
    fertility measures by race and
        ethnicity in, 184
    fertility rate in, 139, 141,
        143–146, 148
        nonmarital, 141, 143, 182
        teen, 185–186, 186–189
        total, 142, 143
    gender earnings ratio in,
        283–285, 305, 306
    labor force participation rates
        in, 214, 215, 216
    marriage bars in, 401
    motherhood penalty in, 538
    nonmarital birth ratio in, 183
    occupational segregation in,
        286–288, 294, 296
    poverty in, 438–455
        child poverty rate, 448
        percent of single-parent fam-
            ilies in, 450

    rate of, 437
    statistics on, 442–449
    welfare programs in, 455–473
    women's labor force participa-
        tion in, 219
Universal Unified Child Credit,
    569
Unobserved characteristic, 536
Unobserved family-specific
    heterogeneity, 537
Unobserved heterogeneity, 536
Urban Institute, 94
U.S. Bureau of Labor Statistics,
    9
U.S. Census Bureau, 9, 143, 363,
    440, 442, 479
U.S. Department of Agriculture,
    439, 441, 508
U.S. Department of Health and
    Human Services, 9
U.S. Department of Labor, 557
U.S. federal income tax, 491. *See
    also* Income taxes
U.S. Office of Management and
    Budget, 94
Utility, 21, 227
    children and adult, 150–151
    marginal, 22, 30–31, 227
    marriage and, 80
Utility function, 21, 27–28, 48
Utility maximization, labor supply
    and, 258–260
Utils, 27

V
Variables
    bias and omitted, 40–41,
        118–119
    causal, 38
    continuous, 41, 363
    dependent, 38, 41, 362
    dummy, 41, 363
    endogenous, 19, 48, 171
    exogenous, 19, 48
    explanatory, 362, 368–369
    independent, 38, 41, 362
Vesting periods, 525
Virginia Tech, affirmative action
    at, 423
Vital Statistics System, 143

W

Wage determination, 295–305, 306
  comparative statics of labor
      markets, 301, 302, 303
  example, 301–303
  finding equilibrium wage,
      299–300
  supply and demand in compet-
      itive labor markets,
      296–299
  wage rates, 304–305, 306
Wages, 5, 304–305, 306
  divorce and rising, 130
  effect of education on, 324
  effect on full income, 157
  effect on price of child services,
      157, 160–165
  equilibrium, 299–300, 304
    discrimination and, 330–333
    labor supply and, 304–305
  gender gap in, 116
    women's labor force partici-
        pation and, 326
  influence on nonmarital child-
      bearing, 201–202
  marginal rate of substitution
      and, 259–260
  men's, change in, 169
  parental leave and, 545, 550
  population size and, 177–178,
      180
  real, 230–231
  women's, 242, 246, 249
    change in, 168–169
    effect on labor force partici-
        pation, 241–242,
        246–247, 262–264,
        270–271, 370
    marriage and, 111–113, 116
    marriage market and, 92–93
    racial differences in, 392–394
  See also Earnings
Waite, Linda, 81
Waldfogel, Jane, 374–375
Wall Street Journal, 540
Ward, Michael, 326
Wards Cove Packing Co. v. Antonio,
    413
War on Poverty, 439
Washington Post, 575

Wealth, marriage and, 81
Wealth of Nations, The (Smith),
    310*n*1
Web sites, economic data, 9
Weitzman, Lenore, 131, 134–135
Welfare, 455–473
  AFDC. *See* Aid to Families
      with Dependent Children
  data sources for, 9
  decline in marriage and,
      113–116
  historic trends in, 469–471
  iron triangle of, 464
  marriage and, 114–116
  poverty and, 454–455
  reform of, 113, 190–191, 437,
      462–464
    in California, 468
    child care subsidies and, 577,
        578–581
    child support and, 452–454
    cohabitation and, 590
    evaluating, 467–471
    marriage and, 472–473
    reasons for, 464–467
    TANF, 113, 191, 455, 463,
        486–488, 513
    time limits and, 467–469
    working poor and, 471–474
  role in teen childbearing,
      190–197
Welfare Reform Act (1996), 532,
    562
Welfare Reform and Beyond Ini-
    tiative, 94
When Work Disappears (Wilson),
    107, 190
Whites
  children
    attainment among, 597
    family structure of, 104–106
    Head Start and, 605
    poverty rate of, 447
  marital status of, 588
  marriage penalty and, 496
  median earnings of, 277
  men, gender earnings gap and,
      371–373
  race differences in marital and
      family status, 102–103

  sex ratio among, 89, 90
  TANF recipients among,
      463–464
  U.S. poverty rate and, 443, 444
women
  affirmative action programs
      and, 417, 420, 422
  decline in marriage for,
      102–104
  fertility rate of, 146
    nonmarital, 184–185
    teen, 186
  gender earnings gap among,
      371–373
  labor force participation by,
      214, 215, 216–217
    by birth cohort, 219–220
    over life cycle, 325–326
  nonmarital biths among, 592
  response to subsidized child
      care by, 580
  wage differences with black
      women, 392–394
  wage rate and, 112, 116
Whitman, Meg, 540
Whittington, Leslie, 500
WIC (Women, Infants, and Chil-
    dren), 455
Widows
  Social Security and, 519–521,
      522
Wilson, William Julius, 101, 107,
    190, 194, 473
Within-group inequality,
    380–381, 384
Women
  attachment to labor force,
      341–342, 343
  balancing family and career,
      540–541
  Earned Income Tax Credit and,
      480–483
  earnings
    change in, 168–169
    compensation of executives,
        394–396
    educational level of and,
        378–379
    impact of marriage and chil-
        dren on, 123

Women *(continued)*
  marriage market and, 92–93
  median annual, 278
  obesity and, 392
  economic consequences of divorce for, 131, 134–135
  educational achievement of, 321–324
  effect of maternal employment on child well-being, 606–610, 611
  employment in symphony orchestras, 387–390
  labor force participation by, 213–222
    male marriage premium and, 121, 122–123
    patterns of, 218–222, 325–328
  relative income and, 170–171
  of single women with children, 46–47
  of women with children, 531–535

poverty and, 445–455
  reasons for, 449–455
  U.S. rate of, 443, 444
reasons to study economic lives of, 2–4
retirement
  pensions and, 525–526
  Social Security and, 518–521, 527–526
status in economics, 9–12
See also Married women
Women, Infants and Children (WIC), 455
Work experience, gender differences in, 324–328
Work/family dilemma, welfare reform and, 473
Workfare, 462
Work force, gender earnings ratio and changes in, 380–381, 383
Work force attachment, women's, 341–342, 343
  Family and Medical Leave Act and, 550–552

family gap and, 377
gender earnings gap and, 371, 372–373, 379, 382–384
Working maternity leave, 558
Working poor, welfare reform and, 471–474
Work requirements, welfare reform and, 460–463

Y
Year-round full-time (YRFT) workers, 276–277
Yellen, Janet, 11
Yemen, 147
YRFT workers. *See* Year-round full-time workers

Z
Zero population growth (ZPG), 142